Western Translation Theory

from Herodotus to Nietzsche

Western Translation Theory

from Herodotus to Nietzsche

Douglas Robinson

St. Jerome Publishing
Manchester, UK & Northampton, MA

First published in 1997
Second edition 2002, reprinted 2007

Published by St. Jerome Publishing
2 Maple Road West, Brooklands, Manchester M23 9HH, UK
Fax: +44 161 905 3498. Email: stjerome@compuserve.com
www.stjerome.co.uk

ISBN 1 900650 00 2 (First edition, hardback)
ISBN 1 900650 37 1 (Second edition, paperback)

ISBN 978 1 900650 37 3 (reprint, 2007)

Printed and bound in Great Britain by
T. J. International Ltd., Cornwall, UK

Typeset by
Delta Typesetters, Cairo, Egypt
Email: delttyp@starnet.com.eg

British Library Cataloguing in Publication Data
A catalogue record of this book is available from the British Library

Library of Congress Cataloging-in-Publication Data
Western translation theory : from Herodotus to Nietzsche / [edited by]
Douglas Robinson.
p. cm.
Includes bibliographical references and index.
ISBN 1-900650-37-1 (pbk. : alk. paper) -- ISBN 1-900650-00-2 (hardback: alk. paper)
1. Translating and interpreting--History. I. Robinson, Douglas, 1954-
P306 .W46 2001
418'.02'01--dc21

2001001188

ACKNOWLEDGEMENTS

The editor and publisher wish to thank the following institutions and individuals for permission to reprint material in this volume:

The Center for Medieval and Early Renaissance Studies, Binghamton University, for Leonardo Bruni's 'On the Correct Way to Translate', from *The Humanism of Leonardo Bruni: Selected Texts*; the Paulist Press for the excerpt from Rosamund S. Allen's translation of Richard Rolle's prologue to the English Psalter, from *Richard Rolle: The English Writings*; Yale University Press for two extracts from *The Complete Works of St. Thomas More, volume 6: A Dialogue Concerning Heresies*; Cambridge University Press and Rita Copeland for extracts from C. Chirius Fortunatianus' 'Translation as *Exercitatio*', John Scotus Eriugena's 'Translator, not Expositor', Notker the German's 'Letter to Bishop Hugo von Sitten', and Jean de Meun's 'Translating for Lay People' and 'Plainly Rendering the Sense', all from *Rhetoric, Hermeneutics and Translation in the Middle Ages: Academic Traditions and Vernacular Texts*; the American Council of Learned Societies for extracts from Charles Burnett's entry on 'Translations and Translators, Western Europe' in *Dictionary of the Middle Ages* (*DMA* Volume 12), including Boethius's 'Committing the Fault of the True Interpreter' and the Anonymous 'The Three Kinds of Translating'; Suhrkamp Publishers for Ellen von Nardroff and Ernest H. von Nardoff's translation of 'On Carlyle's *German Romance*' and Robert Heitner's translation of the extract on Wieland's translations in *Poetry and Truth*, both from *Goethe's Collected Works*; W. W. Norton & Company for 'The Defense and Illustration of the French Language' by Joachim du Bellay, translated by James Harry Smith and Edd Winfield Parks, from *THE GREAT CRITICS*: *An Anthology of Literary Criticism*, third edition, revised and enlarged by James Harry Smith and Edd Winfield Parks; the University of Michigan Press for Matthew Arnold's 'The Translator's Tribunal', from *The Complete Works of Matthew Arnold* (Volume 1, *On the Classical Tradition*, edited by R.H. Super); Professor Norma Rinsler and *Modern Poetry in Translation* for James S Holmes' translation of Etienne Dolet's 'La maniere de bien traduire d'une langue en aultre'.

Contents

Editor's Preface

We are currently in the midst of an astonishing translation theory boom, one that has not only revolutionized the field (often literally – some of the new works are politically as well as methodologically radical) but has generated a spate of English-language translation theory anthologies where there were none before. When I first conceived the idea of editing an anthology of this sort, in the fall of 1987, the only anthology of translation theory in any major European language was Hans Joachim Störig's in German – a fairly brief collection from Jerome to the present that nevertheless usefully brought important translation theory readings together between the same covers. In English all we had were T. R. Steiner's anthology of English translation theory readings from 1650 to 1800 (1975) and André Lefevere's English translation of key German texts from Luther to Franz Rosenzweig (1977).

In 1989, however, the first attempt at a more comprehensive anthology appeared, albeit with so little fanfare (published by a small printing house in Finland) that many missed it. This was Andrew Chesterman's *Readings in Translation Theory*, which began with Dryden and jumped from him directly to the twentieth century; it was, in fact, more of an anthology of twentieth-century linguistic theories of translation than anything else. In the spring of 1992 Rainer Schulte and John Biguenet brought out a similar brief volume, *Theories of Translation: An Anthology of Essays from Dryden to Derrida*, also beginning with Dryden but including a few more pre-twentieth-century pieces. At Christmas, 1992, then, André Lefevere brought out the first anthology of translation theory to begin with Cicero (and proceeding more or less comprehensively up to the early twentieth century, although its brief scope again limited its comprehensivity). During the recent boom we have had three anthologies of translation theory in as many years – where before we had none.

Why then a fourth? The editors of the three previous volumes, perhaps guided by their publishers, have been rather cautious in regard to length: Chesterman's anthology contains around 80,000 words, Schulte/Biguenet's around 100,000, Lefevere's 65,000. I estimate that a truly comprehensive anthology (which, given the dearth of primary research, will be impossible to compile for many years, perhaps decades) would require upwards of a million words. Given the present state of research, and the contingencies of pricing and marketing, I felt it more prudent and practicable to shoot for a lower figure, somewhere around half that – but then this volume is only half of that half, translation theory through the end of the nineteenth century. A comprehensive twentieth-century anthology would fill out the remaining quarter of a million words, somewhere down the line. Since the existing anthologies are far stronger in the twentieth century than in the two thousand-odd years that preceded it, I decided it would be best to begin with what hasn't yet been done.

Some numbers: the anthology contains 124 texts by 90 authors. Nine of the authors are women, none of whom has ever been included in an anthology of, or discussed in a history of, translation theory, and only three of whom have even been mentioned in extant bibliographies. Sixteen texts by 14 authors appear here for the first time in English translation. Thirty-four of the authors originally wrote the texts included here in English; 21 in Latin; 12 in French; 10 in German; 5 in Greek; 2 in Italian; 2 in Anglo-Saxon; 1 in Old High German; 1 in Spanish; 1 in Portugese; and 1 in Finnish.

The obscurity and inaccessibility of translation theory readings has been a constant goad throughout this project. Bayard Quincy Morgan in 1959 and Louis Kelly in 1979 have performed Herculean labours in compiling even reasonably comprehensive bibliographies of translation theory readings from Cicero to the present, and my debt to both writers is enormous. But even their excellent lists are incomplete and increasingly outdated, lacking as they do almost everything written on translation as empire, one of the major new concerns in the field since Vicente Rafael's *Contracting Colonialism* (1988), Eric Cheyfitz's *The Poetics of Imperialism* (1991) and Tejaswini Niranjana's *Siting Translation* (1992), and almost everything written on translation by women. Both lists are largely limited to writings *overtly* concerned with translation as well, and specifically with the fairly narrow range of sense-for-sense, word-for-word, and 'free' translation – the field as it has long been defined. Cheyfitz's book made it almost impossible for me to exclude portions of Montaigne's essay 'On Cannibals' for example, which deals with cross-cultural contact in a colonial context, and only tangentially touches on translation. Frederick M. Rener's *Interpretatio* (1989) and Rita Copeland's *Rhetoric, Hermeneutics, and Translation in the Middle Ages* (1991), although in very different ways, both radically expanded my sense of what translation is by situating it in the ongoing clash between rhetoric and grammar since ancient times. George Steiner's religious and philosophical ruminations on translation in *After Babel* similarly expanded my sense of the peripheries of translation theory, leading me to anthologize St. Paul on preaching vs. speaking in tongues.

And what else might we not turn up if we looked hard enough, and with open enough minds? One of the things I was determined to include in this anthology was translation theory written by women, and in far greater numbers than the three entries in Kelly's bibliography (Philips, Dacier, and de Staël). Fortunately, the primary research in sixteenth- and seventeenth-century British literature had largely been done for me by feminists working in the field: Margaret Patterson Hannay's essay collection *Silent But for the Word: Tudor Women as Patrons, Translators, and Writers of Religious Works* and Betty Travitsky's feminist anthology *The Paradise of Women: Writings By Englishwomen of the Renaissance* in particular provided me with excellent work by early women theorists of translation in Britain. But what about other countries and other periods? My colleague at the University of Mississippi, Ellen Gardiner, steered me toward women writers of the mid-eighteenth century who were doing translations, and a few days in the library turned up Elizabeth Carter's correspondence dealing with her translation of Epictetus. But how many more women (or for that matter men) wrote about their translations and have not yet been discovered? A colleague at another university, hearing I was working on women translation theorists, called me to say that she had been asked to write on women translators in America, and could I point her in the right direction; I couldn't. The primary research has not yet been done.

In fact unearthing translation theory readings is structurally and historically very similar to unearthing women's writings. As Lori Chamberlain points out in 'Gender and the Metaphorics of Translation', in patriarchal hierarchies the translator stands to the original author as woman does to man (nurse to doctor, teacher to administrator, etc.), and this prescribed secondary and parasitic status has all too often consigned translation theory as well to oblivion. Like women, like children, translators in the West have been expected to be seen but not heard. The translator is the silent servant of the original author, 'his' 'wife'. The translator who raises his or (worse) her voice to draw attention to the work he or she has done provokes uneasiness, even open hostility. As a result few translators write prefaces to or letters about their work, let alone formal translation theory. Tens of thousands of translated books and articles have been published without mentioning the translator's name. Encyclopaedias and other biographical reference works typically list an author's original works by title and year of publication, often giving the biographical context for the writing and reception of those works, but either omit all mention of his or her translations or lump them together quickly ("X also did highly regarded translations of Homer, Virgil, Horace, and Ovid" – when? why? who regarded them highly? were they commissioned? paid for? reviewed?). Authors who achieved fame exclusively through their translations, like Nicolas Perrot d'Ablancourt in the mid-seventeenth century, often do not appear in encyclopaedias at all, even in their own countries.

Needless to say, this often made writing headnotes and footnotes to the various entries difficult, even though I decided to limit myself to the barest biographical and historical background information in both. The headnotes contain thumbnail biographical sketches of the authors, along with a very brief discussions of the significance of their remarks on translation. In addition to glossing archaic or obscure words and phrases, the footnotes provide, for important historical events, social institutions, biblical references, and the like, minimal information to facilitate understanding. Due to the inevitable repetition involved, for people mentioned in the text I have provided full names, years of birth and death, nationality, and a succinct description of their life work – but not in footnotes, rather in a biographical appendix. Where I have modernized original English texts or older English translations, I have modernized only the spellings, leaving archaic words as they are and giving their meaning in notes. The notes are marked [Au] for the author of the specific entry, [Tr] for its translator, and [Ed] for the editor of this volume; where I have borrowed a note from a previous editor, I have put that editor's last name in brackets. Suggestions for further reading have likewise been kept out of the body of the text; they appear at the end of the anthology. All bibliographical data for the anthologized texts are collected in the Works Cited.

Some of the translated entries appear here for the first time in English. Edward Capps III translated Burgundio of Pisa from Latin, Edwin Dolin Aquinas, Salutati, and Huet, also from Latin. Maria J. Cirurgõo translated Duarte from Portuguese. David G. Ross translated Dolet, Peletier, Pasquier, Chapelain, d'Ablancourt, and de Staël from French. I translated Agricola from Finnish and Leibniz from German. In addition, dissatisfied with the quality of previous translations, I retranslated (with the exception of two pieces by Goethe, for which I found adequate existing translations) everything included here by Luther, Herder, Schlegel, Novalis, Goethe, Schleiermacher, Humboldt, and Schopenhauer from German, in most cases also translating for the first time filler paragraphs and introductory passages previously omitted. Wherever I have printed an existing translation, I have provided bibliographical data for the translation alone, not the original; wherever a translation appears here for the first time, I have provided bibliographical data for the original.

I have resisted the temptation to chart pathways through the wealth of material here collected. Some readers might have found it useful to read all the selections on, say, sense-for-sense vs. word-for-word translation in one section; all the discussions of paraphrase and metaphrase in another; all the selections on Bible translation in yet another. The trouble with this sort of approach is that it tends to direct attention away from other less obvious affinities among the various entries, and thus to restrict the reader's imaginative journey in programmatic ways. As a result the march of authoritative statements of translations across the ages may seem a bit daunting, at first.

In a few cases I have attempted to communalize the site of translation theory by anthologizing various positions in an ongoing debate or discussion. Thus when Thomas More writes his *Dialogue Concerning Heresies* in 1528 and William Tyndale responds paragraph by paragraph in 1531, or when William Fulke rebuts Gregory Martin paragraph by paragraph in the 1580s, or when Matthew Arnold and Francis W. Newman argue over the translation of Homer in 1861, it seemed reasonable to cite both sides of the debate.

A rather different case is the correspondence of Elizabeth Carter with Catherine Talbot and Thomas Secker: there it seemed impossible to separate out a single voice, Carter's for example, since the three correspondents seemed to be working collectively to develop not only a theory but a practice of translation. Of the three Secker sounds the most like a traditional translation theorist, authoritarian, prescriptive; he is also a man in the company of two women, and a bishop in the company of two laypersons; but while Carter does give in to his prescriptions on the essential issue of ornamentation, the exchange as a whole is far more complex, and far more interesting, than a mere imposition of male rules on female desires. Carter is bullied (in the nicest possible way, of course) by Catherine Talbot as well, who speaks in the correspondence as the embodiment of both the patroness and the middle-class woman reader, a kind of eighteenth-century transitional figure that rarely speaks so articulately to her role in the translation process as she does here. In fact Carter's phlegmatic, almost self-effacing response to the letters from Talbot and Secker, combined with her continued perseverance with Epictetus, offers a striking paradigm of the woman translator in the period – but *only*, it seems to me, in the context of the entire three-way correspondence.

Indeed many more of the writers included here are engaged in dialogue with their precursors than just these few. Almost all of them quote from or refer to previous translation theorists, especially to Cicero, Horace, Jerome, and Augustine. Philo Judaeus revises the 'letter of Aristeas' on the creation of the Septuagint, and Epiphanius, Jerome, and Augustine either pass the story on or protest against it. In 510 Boethius alludes slyly to Horace's *fidus interpres* in terms of the *culpa* (fault) he may have committed, and in the mid-ninth century John Scotus Eriugena alludes to both Horace and Boethius. In 1662 d'Ablancourt takes issue with Huet's remarks published just the year before. In 1688 Aphra Behn writes an 'Essay on Translated Prose' to supplement the Earl of Roscommon's 'Essay on Translated Verse' four years before. In 1813 Schleiermacher argues with Goethe's autobiographical notations from *Dichtung und Wahrheit* in 1811. Wherever possible I have cross-referenced these dialogues in footnotes, though typically, for obvious reasons, mainly looking backward rather than forward: anticipating every future allusion to Cicero or Horace, for example, within the entries written by those authors, would require marathon footnoting.

One of the things editing this anthology has taught me, in fact, and I hope will teach its users, is that the history of translation theory is at once far more complex and diverse and far more dialogically intertwined than is commonly thought. Translation theory does change significantly over the centuries, at once shaped by and helping shape specific historical contingencies and local ideological needs; but translation theorists are also all reading each other, arguing with each other, misreading each other in their attempts to make sense of what they're doing and why, and of how both they and their work fit into larger social and aesthetic contexts. One of the benefits of reading widely in the history of translation theory, indeed in any intellectual history, is that it helps us do the same.

Acknowledgements

A project of this magnitude is never pursued alone. I have had lots of help. Previous work in the field, especially the books by George Steiner, Louis Kelly, Frederick Rener, Glyn Norton, Werner Schwartz, Antoine Berman, Eric Cheyfitz, Rita Copeland, and Willis Barnstone helped me enormously. Eric Cheyfitz's reader's report and several others by anonymous reviewers also helped me adjust my early thinking on key issues of inclusion and exclusion; Roger Ellis provided a detailed and thorough reading of the entire text after it was finished. Matti Suojanen, professor of Finnish at the University of Tampere, located the Agricola text for me, and checked my translation; my students in Tampere, where I taught the history of translation theory for two years at the beginning of this project, first drove me to begin compiling these texts and thinking about them in critical ways. Anthony Pym checked my translations from the German of Luther, Leibniz, Herder, Schlegel, Novalis, Goethe, Schleiermacher, Humboldt, and Schopenhauer. Mona Baker's enthusiasm for the project and willingness to invest time and money in it made it possible to get the anthology into print.

The reference librarians and interlibrary loan people at the University of Mississippi also provided invaluable assistance. A grant from the University of Mississippi Graduate School enabled me to commission translations from Latin, Portuguese, and French. Summer stipends from the National Endowment for the Humanities and the University of Mississippi English department gave me two summers to work on the project. Sara Selby, Kristen Sulser, Kathy Williams, Jennifer Cobb, Mary Leigh Murphy, Angela Langfit, Cathy Himmelwright, and Leigh S. Sorrell keyed most of the texts printed here onto the Mac, which I then attempted, with varying success, to convert into WordPerfect in DOS.

Thanks most of all, now as always, to my family: Heljä, Laura, Sara, and Anna.

Herodotus

We know little more about Herodotus (Herodotos, 484?-430/20 B.C.E.), the ancient world's first narrative historian whose works survive, than what he tells us about himself in his *Histories* (or, literally, 'Researches'). He has been called both the father of lies and the father of historiography; he was also, undoubtedly, the father of comparative anthropology.

Herodotus (whose name means 'gift of Hera') was probably born in Halicarnassus in Asia Minor (now Bodrum, Turkey), a Greek city then under Persian rule – and the focal topic of his *Histories* was the Greco-Persian war between 499 and 479 B.C.E. in the larger context of the Persian empire. Much of what he tells us about that war he based on stories told him in his childhood by men who had sailed against Greece with the Halicarnassian queen Artemisia under the Persian king Xerxes. According to Suidas in an eleventh-century-C.E. Byzantine dictionary, he came from a prominent Halicarnassian family, was exiled into Samos in young manhood, possibly around his twentieth year, by Artemisia's grandson, the despot Lygdamis, possibly for trying to overthrow the pro-Persian dynasty; and around ten years later returned to help overthrow the dynasts. We do not know how reliable this account is; it is probably more reliable than what we know today, since it precedes the destruction of Constantinople in 1204 by the Fourth Crusade. Suidas (which may be a person's name, or may be a title) also tells us that in his late thirties he found himself unpopular in Halicarnassus and departed for Thuria, an Athenian colony in southern Italy. Aristotle, in fact, called him Herodotus the Thurian; on all manuscripts his name is given as Herodotus the Halicarnassian.

This is all we have from Suidas; his extensive travels, everywhere apparent in the *Histories*, probably dated from before his move to Thuria, in his twenties, while he was living in Samos, and in his thirties, while he was living in Athens. In two or three relatively brief periods he travelled by foot and ship, possibly financing his travels by trading, across most of the Persian empire, including Egypt, Libya, Syria, Babylonia, Susa, Lydia, Phrygia, Thrace, Macedonia, and Byzantium; he went north of the Danube into what is now Russia, south to Elephantine (Aswan) in Egypt, and east to Scythia, past the Black Sea to the Don River.

He is believed to have lived in Athens both in the middle and at the end of his life, and to have known the tragic playwright Sophocles there; he probably declaimed his histories at festival gatherings as well, an ancient means of publication. He seems to have been denied Athenian citizenship; as a result of foreigners pouring into the imperial city, Athens had tightened its naturalization process in 451. Even so, his prejudices in favour of Athens, and of the Alcmeonid faction at Athens, the party of Pericles' mother, were so marked as to irritate a succession of ancient writers, culminating in Plutarch.

The years of his birth and death are both uncertain; what dates we have are conjectures from his *Histories*. The last event he mentions occurred in 430 B.C.E., at the very beginning of a four-year plague, and some modern commentators suggest that he might have died of it in Athens; another Byzantine writer, Stephanus, claims there was a tomb in the Thurian marketplace with an epitaph to Herodotus on it, so he may have returned to the colony in later life and died there.

What startles the modern reader of Herodotus is what we are pleased to call his 'modernity' – the fact that he reminds us so much of ourselves, of the best historiography, travel writing, and investigative journalism of our own day. He does a good deal of straight political, social, and military history; but he intersperses it artfully with anecdotal digressions that constantly display his own writerly persona, his tolerance for cultural difference (rare among ancient Greeks, who are known for their chauvinism and xenophobia), and his restless inquiring intelligence. Wherever he goes (and he goes everywhere) he gathers the stories people tell, tests them against each other and against his own highly complex and rather skeptical sense of plausibility, then builds them into a loose-knit but coherent narrative.

Herodotus nowhere addresses the issues of translation that we are accustomed to calling translation *theory*. He does not tell his readers how to translate; he does not even actually describe processes of translation. As a result, he has never before been associated with translation theory, which is generally thought to begin with Cicero, four centuries after Herodotus. But one of Herodotus' central concerns is with cross-cultural communication – how people speaking different languages manage to pass ideas on to each other – and he places that process in an insistently geopolitical context. Thus in the excerpts given below, we see Egyptian priestesses learning to translate their religion into Greek as a result of being abducted and sold into slavery by Phoenicians, and an Egyptian 'translator corps' being formed through the sending of Egyptian boys to live with Greeks and to learn their language: both geohermeneutical events more typical of Montaigne's account of the Brazilian kings than of Cicero translating Demosthenes or Jerome translating the Bible.

The Twittering of Birds
From *Histories*, Book Two (*Istoria*, mid-5th century B.C.E.)
Translated by Aubrey de Selincourt, revised by A. R. Burn

In ancient times, as I know from what I was told at Dodona, the Pelasgians offered sacrifices of all kinds, and prayed to the gods, but without any distinction of name or title – for they had not yet heard of any such thing.[1] They called the gods by the Greek word *theoi* – 'disposers' – because they had 'disposed' and arranged everything in due order, and assigned each thing to its proper division. Long afterwards the names of the gods were brought into Greece from Egypt and the Pelasgians learnt them – with the exception of Dionysus, about whom they knew nothing till much later; then, as time went on, they sent to the oracle at Dodona (the most ancient and, at that period, the only oracle in Greece) to ask advice about the propriety of adopting names which had come into the country from abroad. The oracle replied that they would be right to use them. From that time onward, therefore, the Pelasgians used the names of the gods in their sacrifices, and from the Pelasgians the names passed to Greece.

But it was only – if I may so put it – the day before yesterday that the Greeks came to know the origin and form of the various gods, and whether or not all of them had always existed; for Homer and Hesiod are the poets who composed our theogonies and described the gods for us, giving them all their appropriate titles, offices, and powers, and they lived, as I believe, not more than four hundred years ago. The poets who are said to have preceded them were, I think, in point of fact later.[2] This is my personal opinion, but for the former part of my statement on these matters I have the authority of the priestesses of Dodona.

About the oracles – that of Dodona in Greece and of Ammon in Libya – the Egyptians have the following legend: according to the priests of the Theban Zeus, two women connected with the service of the temple were carried off by the Phoenicians[3] and sold, one in Libya and the other in Greece, and it was these women who founded the oracles in the two countries. I asked the priests at Thebes what grounds they had for being so sure about this, and they told me that careful search had been made for the women at the time, and that though it was unsuccessful, they had afterwards learned that the facts were just as they had reported them. At Dodona, however, the priestesses who deliver the oracles have a different version of the story: two black doves, they say, flew away from Thebes in Egypt, and one of them alighted at Dodona, the other in Libya. The former, perched on an oak, and speaking with a human voice, told them that there, on that very spot, there should be an oracle of Zeus. Those who heard her understood the words to be a command from heaven, and at once obeyed. Similarly the dove which flew to Libya told the Libyans to found the oracle of Ammon – which is also an oracle of Zeus.[4] The people who gave me this information were the three priestesses at Dodona – Promeneia the eldest, Timarete the next, and Nicandra the youngest – and their account is confirmed by the other Dodonaeans connected with the temple. Personally, however, I would suggest that if the Phoenicians really carried off the women from the temple and sold them respectively in Libya and Greece, the one who was brought to Greece (or Pelasgia as it was then called) must have been sold to the Thesprotians;[5] and later, while she was working as a slave in that part of the country, she built, under an oak that happened to be growing there, a shrine to Zeus; for she would naturally remember in her exile the god whom she had served in her native Thebes. Subsequently, when she had learned to speak Greek, she established an oracle there, and mentioned, in addition, that the same Phoenicians who had sold her, also sold her sister in Libya. The story which the people of Dodona tell about the doves came, I should say, from the fact that the women were foreigners, whose language sounded to them like the twittering of birds; later on the dove spoke with a

[1] The Pelasgians were the earliest (prehistoric) inhabitants of what is now Greece. [Ed]

[2] Herodotus is not deceived by the religious poetry ascribed to 'Orpheus' and 'Musaeus' and alleged to be much older than Homer. [Tr]

[3] The Phoenicians were an Asiatic sea-going people on the Syrian coast. [Ed]

[4] Amon(-Ra) was the Egyptian equivalent of the Greek Zeus. [Ed]

[5] The Thesprotians were the ancient Pelasgian people in whose area Dodona lay. Dodona's exact location is unknown. [Ed]

human voice, because by that time the woman had stopped twittering and learned to talk intelligibly. That, at least, is how I should explain the obvious impossibility of a dove using the language of men. As to the bird being black, they merely signify by this that the woman was an Egyptian. It is certainly true that the oracles at Thebes and Dodona are similar in character. Another form of divination – by the inspection of sacrificial victims – also came from Egypt.

It was the Egyptians too who originated, and taught the Greeks to use, ceremonial meetings, processions, and liturgies: a fact which can be inferred from the obvious antiquity of such ceremonies in Egypt, compared with Greece, where they have been only recently introduced.

The Origin of the Class of Egyptian Interpreters
From *Histories*, Book Two (*Istoria*, mid-5th century B.C.E.)
Translated by Aubrey de Selincourt, revised by A. R. Burn

Now as time went on, the twelve kings, who had kept their compact not to molest one another, met to offer sacrifice in the temple of Hephaestus. It was the last day of the festival, and when the moment came for pouring the libation had come, the high priest, in going to fetch the golden cups which were always used for the purpose, made a mistake in the number and brought one too few, so that Psammetichus, who was standing last in the row, did not get one. As their custom was, all the kings were wearing their bronze helmets, and Psammetichus, finding himself without a cup, quite innocently and without any ulterior motive took his helmet off, held it out to receive the wine, and so made his libation. The other kings at once connected this action with the oracle, which had declared that whichever of them poured his libation from a bronze cup should become sole monarch of Egypt. They proceeded to question him, and when they were satisfied that he had acted with no thought of malice, they decided not to put him to death, but to strip him of the greater part of his power and banish him to the marsh-country, forbidding him to leave it or to have any communication with the rest of Egypt.

This was the second time that Psammetichus had been exiled; the first was when he fled the country to escape Sabacos, the Ethiopian, who had killed Necos his father; on that occasion he took refuge in Syria, and after the departure of Sabacos in consequence of his dream, he was brought back by the Egyptians of the province of Sais. And now it was his ill-luck to be driven again from his throne by the eleven kings, and exiled to the marshes – all because of what he did with his helmet. In bitter resentment at the treatment he had received, Psammetichus planned revenge. He sent for advice to the oracle at Buto (the most veracious in Egypt) and was told that vengeance would come from the sea, whence bronze men would appear. Psammetichus did not believe a word of this, and thought it most improbable that he would get any help from bronze men; but not long afterwards it so happened that a company of sea-raiders from Ionia and Caria were forced by bad weather to land on the Egyptian coast. They wore bronze armour, and an Egyptian, who had never seen such a thing before, hurried off to the marshes and told Psammetichus that bronze men had come from the sea and were plundering the country. Seeing in this the fulfillment of the oracle, Psammetichus made friends with the raiders, and by the promise of rich rewards persuaded them to enter his service, and by their help and the help of his supporters in Egypt defeated and deposed the eleven kings.

Having become sole master of Egypt, Psammetichus built the southern gateway of the temple of Hephaestus at Memphis, and opposite to it a court for Apis – or Epaphus, which is the Greek name.[6] Apis is kept in this court whenever he appears; it has a colonnade round it, with statues eighteen feet high instead of pillars, and is richly carved with figures.

To the Ionians and Carians who helped him to gain the throne Psammetichus granted two pieces of land, opposite one another on each side of the Nile, which came to be known as the Camps, and in addition to the grant of land kept all the other promises he had made them. He even went so far as to put some Egyptian boys into their charge, to be taught Greek; and their learning of the language was the origin of the class of Egyptian interpreters. The tracts of land where the Ionians and Carians settled, and where they lived for many years, lie a little distance seaward from Bubastis, on the Pelusian mouth of the Nile. Amasis subsequently turned them out and brought them to Memphis, to protect him from his own people. They were the first foreigners to live in Egypt, and after their original settlement there, the Greeks began regular intercourse with the Egyptians, so that we have accurate knowledge of Egyptian history from the time of Psammetichus onward. The docks and ruined houses of their first home, where they lived

[6] Hephaestus, a smith, was the Greek god of fire. Apis/Epaphus, son of Zeus and Io, married Memphis, daughter of the Nile, and had a daughter by the name of Libya. He was commonly used to explain the source of place names. [Ed]

before Amasis moved them to Memphis, were still to be seen in my day. This, then, is the story of how Psammetichus won the throne of Egypt.

Aristeas

We do not know who wrote the famous 'letter of Aristeas' about the creation of the Septuagint translation in early-third-century Alexandria; lively and full of topical detail as it is as an eyewitness account, internal and external evidence both strongly suggest that it was in fact written pseudonymously a century and a half later, by a Hellenized but devout Alexandrian Jew of the late second century.

The 'legend of the Septuagint', as the several versions of this story are often called, was picked up by several other influential ancient authors, most notably Josephus, who recapitulates *Aristeas* very closely, almost line by line, and Philo Judaeus, whose somewhat embellished account is printed below; Philo was the first to suggest that the seventy-two translators produced identical versions in total isolation from each other, proof positive that the translation was divinely inspired. *Aristeas* explicitly says that the translators consulted with each other until they reached a scholarly consensus on the best translation of each passage; but a long succession of ancient authors repeated Philo's invention with great enthusiasm, including Irenaeus in *Against the Heresies* (175 CE), Clement of Alexandria in his *Stromateis* ('Streams' or 'Miscellanies', late second or early third century), Epiphanius in *On Weights and Measures* (excerpted below), and Augustine in *On Christian Doctrine* (excerpted below) and *City of God* (413-426). Despite jeering from Jerome, and his long and careful analysis of the many 'errors' made by the Seventy (also printed below), the legend of the divinely inspired translators at Alexandria survived well into the Renaissance, when it was finally discredited by Juan Luis Vives, Julius Scaliger, and Humphrey Hody.

The 'letter of Aristeas' is also significant for the light it sheds on the widespread anxiety felt in the ancient world about the translation of sacred texts – an anxiety that may partially explain the need to present this particular translation as divinely inspired. The translators at Alexandria ritually wash their hands before beginning to translate each day; upon hearing the translation read aloud the populace insists that not a word of it ever be changed; and, most strikingly, Demetrius tells two stories of Greek writers who were struck with debilitating physical disorders when they were about to include in their writing passages from the Hebrew Scripture in Greek translation, and only recovered when they desisted from their intentions of making God's Word known to non-Hebrew speakers.

The Work of the Seventy-Two
From *Aristeas to Philocrates* (around 130 B.C.E)
Translated by Moses Hadas

"King Ptolemy to Eleazar the High Priest, greeting and good health. Whereas it is come about that many Jews have been settled in our country, some forcibly removed from Jerusalem by the Persians during their period of power and others who came into Egypt as captives in the train of our father – of these he enrolled many in the armed forces at higher than ordinary pay, and likewise when he judged their chief men to be loyal he gave them fortresses which he built, so that the native Egyptians might be in awe of them; and we too, since we have assumed the realm, meet all men in a very humane manner but your countrymen to a special degree – we, then, have given liberty to above a hundred thousand captives, paying their owners proper market prices and making good whatever injury may have been inflicted through the impulses of the mob. Our resolve in this matter was to do a pious deed and to dedicate a thank-offering to God the Most High, who has preserved our kingdom in tranquillity and in the mightiest esteem throughout the inhabited world. Those in the flower of their age, moreover, we have enrolled in our forces, and to those capable of being about our person and worthy of the trust of the royal court we have assigned offices of state. Now since we desire to show favour to these and to all the Jews in the world and to their posterity we have resolved that your Law should be translated into Greek writing from the Hebrew tongue in use among you, so that these writings should find place in our library along with other royal books. It will be a courteous act, therefore, and one worthy of our own zeal if you will choose elders of exemplary life who possess skill in the law and ability to translate, six from each tribe, so that it may be discovered wherein the majority agree, for the investigation concerns a matter of great weight. We think that we shall bear off great renown by the accomplishment of this task. We have sent upon this business Andreas, of the keepers of the bodyguard, and Aristeas, men whom we hold in honour, to converse with you. They bring with them dedicatory offerings for the Temple, and for sacrifices and other purposes a hundred talents of silver. And if you should write us concerning any desires of yours, you would gratify us and act as friendship requires; be assured that your wishes shall be fulfilled most speedily. Farewell."

To this letter Eleazar replied as well as might be in the terms following: "Eleazar the High Priest to his true friend King Ptolemy [II Philadelphus], greeting. Yourself fare well, and Queen Arsinoe your sister, and the children: so will it be well and as we wish; we too are in good health. When we received your letter we rejoiced greatly because of your resolution and your goodly plan, and we assembled our entire people and read it out to them, in order that they might know the piety you cherish for our God. We displayed also the flagons which you sent, twenty of gold and thirty of silver, the five bowls, the table for dedication, and for the offering of sacrifices and whatever repairs the Temple might require a hundred talents of silver. These gifts were brought by Andreas, who holds a place of honour with you, and by Aristeas, true gentlemen both, outstanding in culture, and in every respect worthy of your own conduct and righteousness. They have also communicated your message to us, and from our lips have heard a reply in accordance with your letter. Whatever is to your advantage, even if it be contrary to nature,[1] we shall hearken; for to do so is a mark of friendship and affection. You too have vouchsafed our countrymen great and unforgettable benefits in many ways. We have therefore straightway offered sacrifices on your behalf and on behalf of your sister and children and friends, and the entire multitude prayed that your affairs might always turn out as you desire, and that God Lord of all might preserve your kingdom in peace wth honour, and that the transcription of the holy Law might come about to your advantage and with security. And in the presence of all we selected elders good and true, six from each tribe, with whom we have sent the book of the Law. We shall be obliged to you, righteous king, if you enjoin that when the transcription of the books is completed the men may be restored to us again in safety. Farewell."

"Their names are, of the first tribe, Joseph, Hezekiah, Zechariah, Johanan, Hezekiah, Elisha; of the second, Judah, Simeon, Samuel, Adaiah, Mattathias, Eschlemias; of the third, Nehemiah, Joseph, Theodosius, Besai, Araunah, Dakis; of the fourth, Jonathan, Heber, Elisha, Hananiah, Zechariah, Hilkiah; of the fifth, Isaac, Jacob, Joshua, Sabbatai, Simeon, Levi; of the sixth, Juhah, Joseph, Simeon, Zechariah, Samuel, Selemiah; of the seventh, Sabbatai, Zedekiah, Jacob, Isaac, Jesse, Nattai; of the eighth, Theodosius, Jason, Joshua, Theodotus, Johanan, Jonathan; of the ninth, Theophilus, Abraham, Arsamus, Jason, Endemias, Daniel; of the tenth, Jeremiah, Eliezer, Zechariah, Baneas, Elisha, Dathaius; of the eleventh, Samuel, Joseph, Judah, Jonathan, Caleb, Dositheus; of the twelfth, Isael, Johanan, Theodosius, Arsamus, Abietes, Ezekiel. In all, seventy-two." Such, then, was the reply to the king's letter given by Eleazar and his colleagues ...

And so Eleazar, after he had offered sacrifice and had chosen the men and prepared many gifts for the king, sent us on our way in great security. When we reached Alexandria word of our arrival was brought to the king. Upon our admission to the court Andreas and I gave friendly greeting to the king and delivered the letters from Eleazar. Being very eager to receive the delegates, the king gave orders that all the other officials be dismissed, and that the men be summoned. This procedure struck everyone as strange, for it was the custom that those who came on official business gained access to the royal presence on the fifth day, while visitors from kings and prominent cities were barely admitted to the court in thirty days. But he thought that these men who had come were worthy of higher honour and rightly judged the eminence of him who had sent them, and so, dismissing all persons he considered superfluous, he waited, walking to and fro, to greet them on their arrival ...

After three days Demetrius took the men with him and crossed the breakwater,[2] seven stades long, to the island; then he crossed over the bridge and proceeded to the northerly parts. There he called a meeting in a mansion built by the seashore, magnificently appointed and in a secluded situation, and called upon the men to carry out the business of translation, all necessary appliances having been well provided. And so they proceeded to carry it out, making all details harmonize by mutual comparisons. The appropriate result of the harmonization was reduced to writing under the direction of Demetrius. The sessions would last until the ninth hour [3 pm], and afterwards they would break up to take care of their bodily needs, all their requirements being lavishly supplied. In addition, everything that was prepared for the king Dorotheus arranged for them also, for he had been so instructed by the king. Every day they would come to the court early in the morning, and when they had made their salutation to the king they departed to their own place. When they had washed their hands

[1] This may refer simply to odd or unusual requests; some scholars speculate that it refers to Eleazar's religious anxiety about translating the Word of God out of the sacred Hebrew. [Ed]

[2] Connecting Alexandria with the island of Pharos, where the translation work was performed. [Ed]

in the sea, as is the custom of all Jews, and had offered prayer to God, they addressed themselves to the interpretation and clarification of each passage. I questioned them on this point too, why it was that they washed their hands before praying. And they explained that it was in witness that they had done no wrong, since the hands are the organs of all activity; in such beautiful and holy spirit do they make all things symbols of righteousness and truth. Thus, as we have said before, they foregathered every day to this spot, so delightful for its seclusion and its clear light, and carried out their appointed task. And so it came about that the work of transcription was completed in seventy-two days, as if this coincidence had been the result of some design.

When the work was concluded Demetrius assembled the community of the Jews at the place where the translation was executed, and read it out to the entire gathering, the translators too being present; these received a great ovation from the community also, in recognition of the great service for which they were responsible. And they accorded Demetrius a similar reception, and requested him to have a transcription of the entire Law made and to present it to their rulers. When the rolls had been read the priests and the elders of the translators and some of the corporate body and the leaders of the people rose up and said, "Inasmuch as the translation has been well and piously made and is in every respect accurate, it is right that it should remain in its present form and that no revision of any sort take place". When all had assented to what had been said, they bade that an imprecation be pronounced, according to their custom, upon any who should revise the text by adding or transposing anything whatever in what had been written down, or by making any excision; and in this they did well, so that the work might be preserved imperishable and unchanged always.

When these proceedings were reported to the king he rejoiced greatly, for he thought that the purpose he cherished had been securely carried out. The whole work was read out to him also, and he marvelled exceedingly at the intellect of the lawgiver. To Demetrius he said, "How has it not occurred to any of the historians or poets to make mention of such enormous achievements?". And he said, "Because the Law is holy and has come into being through God; some of those to whom the thought did occur were smitten by God and desisted from the attempt". Indeed, he said, he had heard Theopompus say that when he was on the point of introducing into his history certain matter which had previously been translated from the Law, too rashly, he suffered a derangement of the mind for more than thirty days; upon the abatement of the disorder he implored God that the cause of what had befallen be made plain to him, and when it was signified to him in a dream that it was his meddlesome desire to disclose divine matters to common men, he desisted, and was thereupon restored to health. And of Theodectes also, the tragic poet, "I have heard", he added, "that when he was on the point of introducing into one of his plays something recorded in The Book,[3] his vision was afflicted with a cataract. Conceiving the suspicion that this was the reason for his calamity, he implored God and after many days recovered".

Marcus Tullius Cicero

Cicero (106-43 B.C.E.), also called Tully in English, was probably the most famous Roman rhetor and rhetorician: a powerful speaker whose greatest orations have been assigned countless schoolchildren to imitate, and a cogent theorist whose formulation of what has come to be known as 'Ciceronian rhetoric' has dominated Western thinking on the subject. Widely considered the originator of the 'periodic' style, Cicero was less an original thinker than a highly gifted transmitter of Greek thought. He might be thought of as a Roman encyclopedist who synthesized in Latin the important work of the Stoic, Academic, Peripatetic, and Epicurean traditions, with particular debts to Aristotle and Heracleides Ponticus.

Cicero's life was rocky, largely due to the fervent dogmatism with which he threw himself into the turbulent Roman politics of the day. A 'new man' – from a wealthy but not noble family – he had to fight his way into the ruling circles with his tongue rather than with connections, and those circles never fully accepted him. His oratorial talents, especially when applied to the projects and proteges of powerful men, won him a succession of increasingly important posts (quaestor, praetor, consul, governor of Cilicia); but they also provoked attempts on his life, exile, and finally execution at the hands of Octavian.

Cicero's encyclopedic interests are evident in such works as *De legibus* (52), *De republica* (51), and a group of books written in 45-44: *De finibus, De natura deorum, De divitatione, De amicitia, De officiis*, and others. His writings on rhetoric include *De inventione* (84), *Oratoriae*

[3] The Book, Greek *ton Biblion*: the first recorded reference to the Hebrew scriptures as the 'Bible'. [Ed]

partitiones (54?), *Orator* (46), and the three works represented here, the three-volume *De oratore*, the short essay *De optimo genere oratorum*, given in its entirety, and *De finibus bonorum et malorum*.

Cicero is often considered the founder of Western translation theory; certainly he is the first to comment on the processes of translation and offer advice on how best to undertake them. His remarks on the pedagogical use of translation from Greek to Latin in the training of an orator were expanded by Horace, Pliny the Younger, Quintilian, and Aulus Gellius in Rome, adapted for medieval Christian theology by Jerome, and cited repeatedly by Catholics and Reformers and Humanists in support of their translatorial and pedagogical principles from the fourteenth to the seventeenth centuries.

De Oratore is a dialogue modelled on the works of Plato; the speaker here is Lucius Crassus, born in 140 B.C.E. and thus 49 years old when the conversation takes place, in September, 91 B.C.E. (a few days before Crassus' death). As Sutton and Rackham, Cicero's translators, note: "He was the most illustrious Roman orator before Cicero, and when Cicero was a boy he acted as his tutor in rhetoric. In the present dialogue he is the mouthpiece of Cicero's own opinions".

Translating Greek Orations into Latin
From *On the Orator* (*De oratore*, 55 B.C.E.)
Translated by E. W. Sutton and H. Rackham

For my part, in the daily exercises of youth, I used chiefly to set myself that task which I knew Gaius Carbo, my old enemy, was wont to practice: this was to set myself some poetry, the most impressive to be found, or to read as much of some speech as I could keep in my memory, and then to declaim upon the actual subject-matter of my reading, choosing as far as possible different words. But later I noticed this defect in my method, that those words which best befitted each subject, were the most elegant and in fact the best, had been already seized upon by Ennius, if it was on his poetry that I was practising, or by Gracchus, if I chanced to have set myself a speech of his. Thus I saw that to employ the same expressions profited me nothing, while to employ others was a positive hindrance, in that I was forming the habit of using the less appropriate. Afterwards I resolved, and this practice I followed when somewhat older, to translate freely Greek speeches of the most eminent orators. The result of reading these was that, in rendering into Latin what I had read in Greek, I not only found myself using the best words, and yet quite familiar ones, but also coining by analogy certain words such as would be new to our people, provided only they were appropriate.

The Best Kind of Orator (*De optimo genere oratorum*, 46 B.C.E)
Translated by H. M. Hubbell

I. It is said that there are various kinds of orators as there are of poets. But the fact is otherwise, for poetry takes many forms. That is to say, every composition in verse, tragedy, comedy, epic, and also melic and dithyrambic[1] (a form more extensively cultivated by Greeks than by Romans) has its own individuality, distinct from the others. So in tragedy a comic style is a blemish, and in comedy the tragic style is unseemly; and so with the other genres, each has its own tone and a way of speaking which the scholars recognize. But in the case of orators if one in the same way enumerates several kinds, regarding some as grand, stately or opulent, others as plain, restrained or concise, and others in an intermediate position, forming as it were a mean between the other two, he gives some information about the men but does not tell us enough about the art of oratory. For in an art we ask what is ideal perfection; in a man we describe what actually is. Therefore, one may call Ennius supreme in epic, if he thinks that is true, and Pacuvius in tragedy and Caecilius, perhaps, in comedy. The orator I do not divide into types, for I am looking for the perfect example. There is only one kind of perfect orator: those who do not belong to this group do not differ in genre as Terence differs from Accius, but though classified with him do not equal him in attainments. The supreme orator, then, is the one whose speech instructs, delights and moves the minds of his audience. The orator is in duty bound to instruct; giving pleasure is a free gift to the audience, to move them is indispensable. We must grant that one does it better than another, but the difference is in degree, not in kind. There is one best, and the next best is that which resembles it most. It is plain from this that what is most unlike the best is the worst.

II. For as eloquence consists of language and thought,[2] we must manage while keeping our diction

---

[1] *Melic*, Greek lyric poetry (as opposed to iambic or elegiac poetry); *dithyrambic*, Greek choral song with an impassioned theme. [Ed]

[2] The Latin *sententia* means a thought, and also the expression of it, a sentence, or if the expression is pointed, a maxim or apophthegm. All these meanings hover over this paragraph and can hardly be brought out in English. [Tr]

faultless and pure – that is in good Latin – to achieve a choice of words both 'proper' and figurative. Of 'proper' words we should choose the most elegant, and in the case of figurative language we should be modest in our use of metaphors and careful to avoid far-fetched comparisons. On the other hand, there are as many kinds of thoughts as I said above there are of styles of oratory. For exposition and explanation they should be pointed, for entertainment, bright and witty, for rousing the emotions, weighty and impressive. In addition to this, there is a way of putting words together – a structure as it were – to produce the two effects of rhythm and smoothness, and a way of arranging the ideas and an order which is best suited to proving one's case. But all these are but parts of a building as it were; the foundation is memory; that which gives it light is delivery.

The man who is supreme in all these departments will be the most perfect orator; one who attains moderate success will be mediocre; he who has the least success will be the worst speaker. Still they will all be called orators, as painters are called painters, though they may be inferior, and will differ in ability, not in kind. Therefore, there is no orator who is unwilling to resemble Demosthenes, but Menander did not wish to write like Homer, for he was working in a different genre. But the same is not true of orators, or, even if one in pursuit of weight and dignity avoids simplicity, and on the other hand, another prefers to be plain and to the point rather than ornate, though he is tolerable as an orator, he is not the best if it is true that the best style is that which includes all virtues.

III. I have made this introduction briefer than the subject deserved, but for our present purpose there was no need of a fuller statement. Since there is but one kind of oratory, we are searching for what its nature is. It is the kind that flourished at Athens. The distinction of the Attic orators in their style is well known, but their essential characteristics are unknown. Many see one side – that there was nothing in them with which to find fault – but few see the other side that there was much to praise. For it is a fault in an idea if it is absurd, or irrelevant, or pointless, or flat; a word is faulty if it is impure, mean, inappropriate, harsh, or far-fetched. These errors have been avoided by well nigh all who are accounted Attics or who speak the Attic tongue. But those who have attained only to this may be considered sound and spare as far as that goes, but may be compared to athletes who are fit to promenade in the gymnasium, but not to seek the prize at Olympia. The prize-winners, though free from all diseases, are not content with merely good health, but seek strength, muscles, blood, and even as it were an attractive tan. Let us imitate them if we can; if not, let us imitate those whose purity is untainted – which is characteristic of the Attic writers – rather than those whose opulent style is full of faults; Asia produced this latter sort in abundance. In doing this – if indeed we can accomplish even this much, for it is a very great achievement – let us imitate Lysias, if possible, and his simplicity above all. He does indeed rise toward a loftier style in many passages, but because he wrote private speeches almost exclusively, and even these were for other people and concerned with trifling affairs, he seems excessively meagre, since he purposely filed down his style to match the nature of the petty suits.

IV. If anyone speaks in this manner without being able to use a fuller style if he wishes, he should be regarded as an orator, but as a minor one. The great orator must often speak in that way in dealing with cases of such a kind. In other words, Demosthenes could certainly speak calmly, but Lysias perhaps not with passion. But if they think that at the trial of Milo,[3] when the army was stationed in the Forum and in all the temples round about, it was fitting to defend him in the same style that we would use in pleading a private case before a single referee, they measure the power of eloquence by their own limited ability, not by the nature of the art.[4]

Therefore we must make an answer to the claims of certain people which have now gained some currency: one group say that they themselves speak in the Attic manner, the others that no Roman does. The second group we may neglect, for they are sufficiently answered by the facts, since they are not invited to conduct trials, or if invited, they are laughed out of court; for if it was their wit which caused the jury to laugh, this would be prime evidence that they were 'Attic'. But those who deny that we speak in the Attic manner, but confess that they themselves are not orators, if they have cultivated ears and an intelligent judgement, we consult them as a painter consults people invited to view a painting, who have no ability to paint, but a certain skill in criticism. If, on the other hand, they make intelligence consist in fastidiousness of taste in oratory and take no pleasure in

---

[3] Titus Annius Milo, accused of the murder of Clodius in 52 B.C.E. Cicero attempted his defence, but was unnerved by the unusual situation described in the text. The extant oration *In Defence of Milo* was written and published after the trial. [Tr]

[4] 'They' in this sentence refers to the self-styled 'Attic' orators at Rome, who are not formally introduced until the next paragraph. [Tr]

anything lofty and magnificent, let them say that they prefer a plain and refined style and despise the grand and ornate. But let them cease to claim that the plain orators are the only ones who speak in the Attic manner, that is, as they say, sparely and without fault. A grand, ornate, and copious style that is equally faultless is the mark of Attic orators. Is there any doubt whether we desire our eloquence to be merely tolerable, or to arouse admiration as well? For we are not inquiring what speaking in the Attic manner is, but what is the best manner. It can be inferred from this that since the most outstanding Greek orators were those who lived at Athens, and of these Demosthenes was easily the chief, one who imitates him will speak in the Attic manner and in the best manner, so that, since they set up Attic orators as models for our imitation, speaking in the Attic fashion means speaking well.

V. But since there was a complete misapprehension as to the nature of their style of oratory, I thought it my duty to undertake a task which will be useful to students, though not necessary for myself. That is to say I translated the most famous orations of the two most eloquent Attic orators, Aeschines and Demosthenes, orations which they delivered against each other.[5] And I did not translate them as an interpreter, but as an orator,[6] keeping the same ideas and the forms, or as one might say, the 'figures' of thought, but in language which conforms to our usage. And in so doing, I did not hold it necessary to render word for word, but I preserved the general style and force of the language. For I did not think I ought to count them out to the reader like coins, but to pay them by weight, as it were. The result of my labour will be that our Romans will know what to demand from those who claim to be Atticists and to what rule of speech, as it were, they are to be held.

"But Thucydides will rise up against you; for some admire his eloquence." Right they are; but that has no bearing on the orator whom we are seeking. For it is one thing to set forth events in an historical narrative, and another to present arguments to clinch a case against an opponent, or to refute a charge. It is one thing to hold an auditor while telling a story, and another to arouse him. "But his style is beautiful." Is it better than Plato's? For the orator whom we are seeking must treat cases in court in a style suitable to instruct, to delight, and to move.

VI. Therefore, if there shall ever be a man who professes to plead cases in court in the style of Thucydides, he will prove that he has not the faintest notion of what goes on in political and legal life. But if he is content to praise Thucydides, let him enter my vote beside his.

Even Isocrates, whom the divine Plato, practically his contemporary, represents as receiving high praise from Socrates in the *Phaedrus* [278E-279b], and whom all scholars have cited as a consummate orator, even him I do not include in the class of perfection. For his oratory does not take part in the battle nor use steel, but plays with a wooden sword, as I may say.[7] But, to compare the magnificent with the insignificant, what I am now doing is rather introducing a famous pair of gladiators. Aeschines like Aeserninus, not a nasty fellow as Lucilius says, but bold and clever; he is matched with Pacideianus, by far the best fighter since the creation of man, for I think nothing can be imagined more inspired than the orator Demosthenes.[8]

Two sorts of objections can be raised to this undertaking of mine.

The first is: "It is better in the original Greek". One

---

[5] The Oration against Ctesiphon of Aeschines and The Oration on the Crown (or In Defence of Ctesiphon) by Demosthenes. [Tr]

[6] This famous, oft-quoted, and frequently misunderstood phrase in Latin is: *non converti ut interpres sed ut orator*, or, literally, 'I did not convert/turn [them] as a translator, but as an orator'. The *interpres* for Cicero was a literal translator, whose main concern was rendering the source text as exactly as possible; the *orator* was more concerned with the impact of his words on the target audience than on literal accuracy. Cicero does not specifically speak of 'sense-for-sense' translation here (that phrase was coined by Jerome, by analogy with Cicero's 'word-for-word', below), but he is usually taken to mean something like it. In fact, his famous pronouncement might be translated more loosely (as an orator), using Eugene Nida's terminology, as "I sought in my translations not formal but dynamic equivalence", or, using Peter Newmark's, "My aim was not semantic but communicative equivalence". [Ed]

[7] A wooden sword was used by gladiators and soldiers for practice. Isocrates, lacking nerve and a good voice, refrained from public appearances; almost all of his 'speeches' were written to be read. [Tr]

[8] Cicero is quoting freely from the second satire of Lucilius. The passage in full is (text and translation by E. H. Warmington, *Remains of Old Latin* iii, pp. 56, 57 (LCL)):

Aeserninus fuit Flaccorum munere quidam
Samnis, spurcus homo, vita illa dignus locoque.
Cum Pacideiano componitur, optimus multo
post homines natos gladiator qui fuit unus.

"In the public show given by the Flacci was a certain Aeserninus, a Samnite, a nasty fellow, worthy of that life and station. He was matched with Pacideianus, who was by far the best of all the gladiators since the creation of man". [Tr]

might ask this critic whether they themselves can produce anything better in Latin. The second is: "Why should I read this translation of yours, rather than the Greek original?". But at the same time they accept the *Andria*, the *Synephebi* and likewise the *Andromache* or the *Antiope* or the *Epigoni* in Latin.[9] Why their aversion to speeches translated from the Greek when they have none to translations of poetry?

VII. But let us now turn to our task, after an introductory explanation of the case which was brought before the court. There was a fundamental law at Athens that no one should propose a bill to crown a citizen while he was a magistrate before he had rendered an account of his office; and another law providing that those who were rewarded by the Council should receive it in the Council chamber. Demosthenes was superintendent in charge of repairing the city walls, and repaired them at his own expense. For this service, then, Ctesiphon proposed in a bill, though Demosthenes had not rendered an account of his office, that he should receive a crown of gold, and that the presentation should be made in the theatre before the assembled people, though this was not the place for a legal assembly; and that proclamation should be made that he received the crown for his virtue and the benevolence which he had shown to the people of Athens. Aeschines then summoned this Ctesiphon to court charging him with proposing a bill contrary to the fundamental law in that the crown was to be presented before Demosthenes had rendered his account, and in that the presentation was to be made in the theatre, and because the statement about virtue and benevolence was untrue, since Demosthenes neither was a good man nor had deserved well of the city.[10]

This case in its very nature is far removed from the customary procedure of our courts; still it is important. For it involves a very nice interpretation of the law on both sides, and a comparison of the public services of the two orators which is extremely impressive. Furthermore, as Aeschines had been accused by Demosthenes on the capital charge of malfeasance on an embassy,[11] he had reason to seek vengeance on his enemy by subjecting the career and reputation of Demosthenes to a judicial review under the guise of an attack on Ctesiphon. Therefore, he did not make so much of the charge that Demosthenes had not rendered his account as he did of his having been praised as the best of citizens when he was a villain. Aeschines instituted this prosecution against Ctesiphon four years before the death of Philip of Macedon, but the trial was held several years later when Alexander was now master of Asia.[12] The trial was attended by a crowd from every part of Greece. For what was so worth going to see or hear as two consummate orators engaged in a desperate struggle for which they had prepared with great effort and in which they were influenced by personal animosity? If I shall succeed in rendering their speeches, as I hope, by retaining all their virtues, that is, the thoughts, the figures of thought and the order of topics, and following the language only so far as it does not depart from our idiom – if all the words are not literal translations of the Greek, we have at least tried to keep them within the same class or type – there will be a norm by which to measure the speeches of those who may wish to speak in the Attic manner. But enough of myself. Now at last let us listen to Aeschines himself speaking in the Latin tongue.

Translating Greek Philosophy into Latin
From *De finibus bonorum et malorum* (45-44 B.C.E.)
Translated by Harris Rackham

1. My dear Brutus, – The following essay, I am well aware, attempting as it does to present in a Latin dress subjects that philosophers of consummate ability and profound learning have already handled in Greek, is sure to encounter criticism from different quarters. Certain persons, and those not without some pretension to letters, disapprove of the study of philosophy altogether. Others do not so greatly object to it provided it be followed in dilettante fashion; but they do not think it ought to engage so large an amount of one's interest and attention. A third class, learned in Greek literature and contemptuous of Latin, will say that they prefer to spend their time in reading Greek. Lastly, I suspect there will be some who will wish to divert me to other fields of authorship, asserting that this kind

[9] The *Andria* of Terence; Caecilius' *Synephebi* (Companions in Youth), fragments in Warmington, ROL i, pp. 536-540; the *Andromacha* of Ennius, ROL i, pp. 244-254; the *Antiopa* of Pacuvius, ROL ii, pp. 158-170; the *Epigoni* of Accius, ROL ii, pp. 420-428. [Tr]

[10] According to the spurious indictment inserted in Demosthenes, *On the Crown* (55), this last charge involved violation of a fundamental law forbidding false statements in bills; Cicero does not mention this law above. [Tr]

[11] In 343 B.C.E. Both orations are extant. [Tr]

[12] The complaint was lodged in 336 and the trial took place in 330. As a matter of fact, Philip was murdered in 336 shortly after Aeschines' complaint against Ctesiphon. The error arises from a confusion of the event here mentioned with an earlier crowning of Demosthenes in 340. [Tr]

of composition, though a graceful recreation, is beneath the dignity of my character and position. To all of these objections I suppose I ought to make some brief reply. The indiscriminate censure of philosophy has indeed been sufficiently answered already in the book[13] which I wrote in praise of that study, in order to defend it against a bitter attack that had been made upon it by Hortensius. The favourable reception which that volume appeared to obtain from yourself and from others whom I considered competent to sit in judgment encouraged me to embark upon further undertakings; for I did not wish to be thought incapable of sustaining the interest that I had aroused. The second class of critics, who, however much they approve of philosophy, nevertheless would rather have it less eagerly prosecuted, are asking for a restraint that it is not easy to practise. The study is one that when once taken up admits of no restriction or control. In fact, the attitude of the former class, who attempt to dissuade us from philosophy altogether, seems almost less unreasonable than that of those who would set limits to what is essentially unlimited, and expect us to stop half-way in a study that increases in value the further it proceeds. If Wisdom be attainable, let us not only win but enjoy it; or if attainment be difficult, still there is no end to the search for truth, other than its discovery. It were base to flag in the pursuit, when the object pursued is so supremely lovely. Indeed if we like writing, who would be so churlish as to debar us from it? Or if we find it a labour, who is to set limits to another man's exertions? No doubt it is kind of Chremes in Terence's play to wish his new neighbour not

> To dig or plough or any burden bear:[14]

for it is not industry in general, but toil of a menial kind, from which he would deter him; but only a busybody would take exception to an occupation which, like mine, is a labour of love.

II. A more difficult task therefore is to deal with the objection of those who profess a contempt for Latin writings as such. What astonishes me first of all about them is this, – why should they dislike their native language for serious and important subjects, when they are quite willing to read Latin plays translated word for word from the Greek? Who has such a hatred, one might almost say, for the very name of Roman, as to despise and reject the *Medea* of Ennius of the *Antiope* of Pacuvius, and give as his reason that though he enjoys the corresponding plays of Euripides he cannot endure books written in Latin? What, he cries, am I to read *The Young Comrades* of Caecilius, or Terence's *Maid of Andros*, when I might be reading the same two comedies of Menander? With this sort of person I disagree so strongly that, admitting the *Electra* of Sophocles to be a masterpiece, I yet think Atilius' poor translation of it worth my while to read. 'An iron writer', Licinius called him; still, in my opinion, a writer all the same, and therefore deserving to be read. For to be entirely unversed in our own poets argues either the extreme of mental inactivity or else a refinement of taste carried to the point of caprice. To my mind no one can be styled a well-read man who does not know our native literature. If we read

> Would that in forest glades –[15]

just as readily as the same passage in the Greek, shall we object to having Plato's discourses on morality and happiness set before the reader in Latin? And supposing that for our part we do not fill the office of a mere translator, but, while preserving the doctrines of our chosen authorities, add thereto our own criticism and our own arrangement: what ground have these objectors for ranking the writings of Greece above compositions that are at once brilliant in style and not mere translations from Greek originals? Perhaps they will rejoin that the subject has been dealt with by the Greeks already. But then what reason have they for reading the multitude of Greek authors either that one has to read? Take Stoicism: what aspect of it has Chrysippus left untouched? Yet we read Diogenes, Antipater, Mnesarchus, Panaetius, and many others, not least our friend Posidonius. Again, Theophrastus handles topics previously treated by Aristotle, yet he gives us no small pleasure all the same. Nor do the Epicureans cease from writing as the spirit moves them on the same questions on which Epicurus and the ancients wrote. If Greek writers find Greek readers when presenting the same subjects in a different setting, why should not Romans be read by Romans?

III. Yet even supposing I gave a direct translation of Plato or Aristotle, exactly as our poets have done with the plays, would it not, pray, be a patriotic service to introduce those transcendent intellects to the acquaintance of my fellow-countrymen? As a matter

[13] This book was called *Hortensius*, and formed an introduction to Cicero's philosophical writings. Fragments only are extant. [Tr]

[14] Terence, *Heauton timorumenos* ['The Self-Tormentor'], I. 1. 17. [Tr]

[15] The opening of Ennius's *Medea Exsul*, cp. Euripides, *Medea* 3f. [Tr]

of fact, however, this has not been my procedure hitherto, though I do not feel I am debarred from adopting it. Indeed I expressly reserve the right of borrowing certain passages, if I think fit, and particularly from the philosophers just mentioned, when an appropriate occasion offers for so doing; just as Ennius regularly borrows from Homer, and Afranius from Menander. Nor yet shall I object, like our Lucilius,[16] to all the world's reading what I write. I only wish his Persius were alive today! and still more Scipio and Rutilius, in fear of whose criticism Lucilius protests that he writes for the public of Tarentum, Consentia, and Sicily. This no doubt is neat enough, like the rest of Lucilius; but there were not such learned critics in his day, to tax his best efforts; and also his writings are in a lighter vein: they show consummate wit, but no great erudition. I, however, need not be afraid of any reader, if I am so bold as to dedicate my book to you, who rival even the Greeks as a philosopher. Still, you yourself challenged me to the venture, by dedicating to me your delightful essay *On Virtue*. But I have no doubt that the reason why some people take a dislike to Latin literature is that they have happened to meet with certain illiterate and uncouth productions which are bad Greek books in worse Latin versions. I have no quarrel with those persons, provided that they also refuse to read the Greek writers on the same subjects. But given a noble theme, and a refined, dignified and graceful style, who would not read a Latin book? Unless it be someone ambitious to be styled a Greek out-and-out, as Albucius was greeted by Scaevola when the latter was praetor at Athens. I am again referring to Lucilius, who relates the anecdote with much neatness and point; he puts the following excellent lines into the mouth of Scaevola:

> You vow'd, Albucius, that to suit ye
> 'Twas as a Greek we must repute ye;
> 'Roman' and 'Sabine' being names
> Your man of *ton* and taste disclaims!
> You scorn'd to own your native town,
> Which bore such captains of renown
> As Pontius and Tritannus bold,
> Who in the van Rome's ensigns hold.
> And so, at Athens when I lay,
> And your respects you came to pay,
> My worship, humouring your freak,
> Gave you good-morrow straight in Greek,
> With '*Chaire*, Titus!' '*Chaire*', bawl
> Guards, aides-de-camp, javelin-men and all!
> – Hence comes it that Albucius hates me,
> Hence as his bitterest foe he rates me.

Mucius [Scaevola]'s sarcasm was however deserved. But for my part I can never cease wondering what can be the origin of the exaggerated contempt for home products that is not fashionable. It would of course be out of place to attempt to prove it here, but in my opinion, as I have often argued, the Latin language, so far from having a poor vocabulary, as is commonly supposed, is actually richer than the Greek. When have we, that is to say when have our competent orators or poets, at all events since they have had models to copy, ever lacked any of the resources either of the florid or the chaste style?

Philo Judaeus

Also called Philo of Alexandria, Philo Judaeus (15/10 B.C.E.- 45/50 C.E.) was a Greek-speaking Jewish philosopher who constructed the first influential synthesis of Judaic theology and Greek philosophy – 'faith' and 'reason'. Hellenistic thought had been flowing into Judaism for several centuries when he wrote; indeed the Jewish community in Alexandria had been Hellenized since at least the third century B.C.E., when the Hebrew Scriptures were translated into Greek by seventy-two translators (the Septuagint, the text whose genesis Philo relates in the excerpt given below). Philo's particular synthesis of Plato and Judaism was foundational for Christian theology; Paul's Platonic/Judaic thought in the New Testament shows Philonian influences, and many of the later Church Fathers quoted the aphorism, "Either Plato philonizes or Philo platonizes". His description of the Platonic Logos as the first-begotten Son of God and the secondary image of God reappears centrally in Christian theology, beginning in the first verses of John's Gospel.

Little is known of Philo's life. According to Josephus, the first-century Jewish historian, he came from a wealthy family of high noble lineage. His father moved the family from Palestine to Alexandria, where Philo probably attended Greek schools and received a broad liberal education. He seems to have received little instruction in Judaism; yet his commentaries on the Pentateuch,

[16] Lucilius, the satirist, 148-103 B.C.E., avowed that he wrote for the moderately learned like Laelius, not for great scholars like Persius: 'Persium non curo legere, Laelium Decimum volo' (Cic. *de Or* 2.25). In the next sentence here Cicero seems to refer to some other passage of Lucilius, in which he put his claims still lower and professed to write for illiterate provincials, not for cultured noblemen like Scipio Africanus Minor and P. Rutilius Rufus. [Tr]

Allegories of the Laws and *On the Special Laws*, were the fullest sources on Jewish law (after the Talmud) until the Middle Ages.

Philo follows the anonymous letter of Aristeas in depicting the Greek translation of the Scriptures as divinely inspired – an account that Augustine will invoke in *On Christian Doctrine* as a basis for his notion that the translator can and should be guided by the Holy Spirit to the 'perfect' version. The most important addition Philo brings to the story is the isolation of each translator from all the others, a crucial point for the claim of divine inspiration: in the letter of Aristeas the translators consulted and collaborated with each other to produce a single document.

The Creation of the Septuagint
From *The Life of Moses* (*De vita Mosis*, 20 B.C.E.?)
Translated by F. H. Colson

V. That the sanctity of our legislation has been a source of wonder not only to the Jews but also to all other nations is clear both from the facts already mentioned and those which I proceed to state. In ancient times the laws were written in the Chaldean tongue,[1] and remained in that form for many years, without any change of language, so long as they had not yet revealed their beauty to the rest of mankind. But, in course of time, the daily, unbroken regularity of practice exercised by those who observed them brought them to the knowledge of others, and their fame began to spread on every side. For things excellent, even if they are beclouded for a short time through envy, shine out again under the benign operation of nature when their time comes. Then it was that some people, thinking it a shame that the laws should be found in one half only of the human race, the barbarians, and denied altogether to the Greeks, took steps to have them translated. In view of the importance and public utility of the task, it was referred not to private persons or magistrates, who were very numerous, but to kings, and amongst them to the king of highest repute. Ptolemy, surnamed Philadelphus, was the third in succession to Alexander, the conqueror of Egypt. In all the qualities which make a good ruler, he excelled not only his contemporaries, but all who have arisen in the past; and even till today, after so many generations, his praises are sung for the many evidences and monuments of his greatness of mind which he left behind him in different cities and countries, so that, even now, acts of more than ordinary munificence or buildings on a specially great scale are proverbially called Philadelphian after him. To put it shortly, as the house of the Ptolemies was highly distinguished, compared with other dynasties, so was Philadelphus among the Ptolemies. The creditable achievements of this one man almost outnumbered those of all the others put together, and, as the head takes the highest place in the living body, so he may be said to head the kings.

VI. This great man, having conceived an ardent affection for our laws, determined to have the Chaldean translated into Greek, and at once dispatched envoys to the high priest and king of Judaea, both offices being held by the same person, explaining his wishes and urging him to choose by merit persons to make a full rendering of the Law into Greek. The high priest was naturally pleased, and, thinking that God's guiding care must have led the king to busy himself in such an undertaking, sought out such Hebrews as he had of the highest reputation, who had received an education in Greek as well as in their native lore, and joyfully sent them to Ptolemy. When they arrived, they were offered hospitality, and, having been sumptuously entertained, requited their entertainer with a feast of words full of wit and weight. For he tested the wisdom of each by propounding for discussion new instead of the ordinary questions, which problems they solved with happy and well-pointed answers in the form of apophthegms, as the occasion did not allow of lengthy speaking.

After standing this test, they at once began to fulfil the duties of their high errand. Reflecting how great an undertaking it was to make a full version of the laws given by the Voice of God, where they could not add or take away or transfer anything, but must keep the original form and shape, they proceeded to look for the most open and unoccupied spot in the neighbourhood outside the city. For, within the walls, it was full of every kind of living creatures, and consequently the prevalence of diseases and deaths, and the impure conduct of the healthy inhabitants, made them suspicious of it. In front of Alexandria lies the island of Pharos, stretching with its narrow strip of land towards the city, and enclosed by a sea not deep but mostly consisting of shoals, so that the loud din and booming of the surging waves grows faint through the long distance before it reaches the land. Judging this to be the most suitable place in the district, where they might find peace and tranquility and the soul could commune with the laws with none to disturb its privacy, they fixed their abode there; and, taking the sacred books, stretched them out towards heaven with the hands that held them, asking of God that they might not fail in their purpose. And He assented to their prayers,

[1] A Semitic language spoken in Babylonia. [Ed]

to the end that the greater part, or even the whole, of the human race might be profited and led to a better life by continuing to observe such wise and truly admirable ordinances.

VII. Sitting here in seclusion with none present save the elements of nature, earth, water, air, heaven, the genesis of which was to be the first theme of their sacred revelation, for the laws begin with the story of the world's creation, they became as it were possessed, and, under inspiration, wrote, not each several scribe something different, but the same word for word, as though dictated to each by an invisible prompter. Yet who does not know that every language, and Greek especially, abounds in terms, and that the same thought can be put in many shapes by changing single words and whole phrases[2] and suiting the expression to the occasion? This was not the case, we are told, with this law of ours, but the Greek words used corresponded literally with the Chaldean, exactly suited to the things they indicated. For, just as in geometry and logic, so it seems to me, the sense indicated does not admit of variety in the expression which remains unchanged in its original form, so these writers, as it clearly appears, arrived at a wording which corresponded with the matter, and alone, or better than any other, would bring out clearly what was meant. The clearest proof of this is that, if Chaldeans have learned Greek, or Greeks Chaldean, and read both versions, the Chaldean and the translation, they regard them with awe and reverence as sisters, or rather one and the same, both in matter and words, and speak of the authors not as translators but as prophets and priests of the mysteries, whose sincerity and singleness of thought has enabled them to go hand in hand with the purest of spirits, the spirit of Moses.

Therefore, even to the present day, there is held every year a feast and general assembly in the island of Pharos, whither not only Jews but multitudes of others cross the water, both to do honour to the place in which the light of that version first shone out, and also to thank God for the good gift so old yet ever young. But, after the prayers and thanksgivings, some fixing tents on the seaside and others reclining on the sandy beach in the open air feast with their relations and friends, counting that shore for the time a more magnificent lodging than the fine mansions in the royal precincts. Thus the laws are shown to be desirable and precious in the eyes of all, ordinary citizens and rulers alike, and that too though our nation has not prospered for many a year. It is but natural that when people are not flourishing their belongings to some degree are under a cloud. But, if a fresh start should be made to brighter prospects, how great a change for the better might we expect to see! I believe that each nation would abandon its peculiar ways, and, throwing overboard their ancestral customs, turn to honouring our laws alone. For, when the brightness of their shining is accompanied by national prosperity, it will darken the light of the others as the risen sun darkens the stars.

[2] The Greek for 'changing single words and whole phrases' is *metaphrazonta kai paraphrazonta,* or 'metaphrasing and paraphrasing' – the first use in Western writing on translation of these terms that Quintilian will pick up in his *Institutes of Oratory* (see below, 20) and Renaissance and neoclassical writers will build into their translational pedagogies and taxonomies (see Roger Ascham, 109, and John Dryden, 172-75, below). [Ed]

Horace

Born of a freed slave in the Sabellian hills in central Italy, Horace (Quintus Horatius Flaccus, 65-8 B.C.E.) became one of the greatest of all Roman lyric poets and satirists. He attended lectures at the Academy in Athens, and when Julius Caesar was murdered in 44 B.C.E. and Athens came under the control of Caesar's assassins Brutus and Cassius, he fought in Brutus' army against Antony and Octavian, rising to the rank of military tribune, an unusual honour for one so lowly born. Upon Octavian's victory, Horace fled back to Rome, partook of the general amnesty, and was introduced into Octavian's (later called Augustus) circle of writers by Gaius Maecenas. For the remaining two decades of his life, Horace was a virtual poet laureate, given a house and farm and other lavish gifts in return for poetic odes to Augustus and Augustan Rome.

Horace has played a role in the history of translation theory that is somewhat disproportionate to the passing dismissive remarks he made on the translator in the *Art of Poetry*: frequently cited in the same breath as Cicero, his disparagement of the 'faithful translator' is often turned on its head to support translational fidelity to the original. His specific concern is with the poet who works with received materials, and who might thus be thought of as 'translating' a story from another writer's Greek into Latin. His call for the original imitation of these materials extends to the poet Cicero's admonitions to the orator-in-training. His impulse, like Cicero's, Pliny's, and Quintilian's, is toward originality: toward a *personal* revitalization of a public text that has become well-worn with use.

Imitating in Your Own Words
From *Art of Poetry* (*Ars Poetica*, 20 B.C.E?)
Translated by E. C. Wickham

It is a hard task to treat what is common in a way of your own; and you are doing more rightly in breaking the tale of Troy into acts than in giving the world a new story of your own telling. You may acquire private rights in common ground, provided you will neither linger in the one hackneyed and easy round; nor trouble to render word for word with the faithfulness of a translator; nor by your mode of imitating take the "leap into the pit"[1] out of which very shame, if not the law of your work, will forbid you to stir hand or foot to escape; nor so begin as the old cyclic writer: "Of Priam's fate and glorious war I'll sing". What will this high promise give us that will not put to shame such mouthing? Mountains will be in labor, the birth will be a single laughable little mouse. How much more wisely the poet who begins with no foolish effort: "Of him, my Muse, who, when Troy's ramparts fell, / Saw many cities and men's manners, tell".[2] His thought is not to give flame first and then smoke, but from smoke to let light break out. He means by and by to bring from his store things striking and marvelous, Antiphates and Scylla, the Cyclops and Charybdis. He does not begin a "Return of Diomede" from the death of Meleager, nor the war of Troy from the twin eggs.[3] He ever hastens to the issue, and hurries his hearers into the midst of the story, just as if they knew it before; and what he thinks his touch will never turn to gold, that he lets alone; and while he gives his imagination free play, he so mingles false with true, that the middle never strikes a different note from the beginning, nor the end from the middle.

Paul of Tarsus

Most of what we know of the Apostle Paul (d. c. 67) is from the New Testament: born in Tarsus a Roman citizen (the town is now in Turkey but was then part of the Roman province of Cilicia) and possibly educated at the university there, which was known for its school of Greek philosophy; a member of the Hebrew tribe of Benjamin and a zealous Pharisee famous for his persecutions of Christians; a convert to Christianity on the road to Damascus (34 or 35 C.E.) and subsequently an indefatigable proselytizer for the new sect throughout the Middle East and author of the letters to various churches that began to theologize the life of Jesus (40s and 50s); imprisoned in Jerusalem (59 C.E.?), transferred to Rome (61?), released (63?), rearrested and executed (67?).

Paul's role in the formation of Christian theology cannot be underestimated; indeed one influential theologian has called him less a disciple of Jesus than the second founder of Christianity. He is known as a proponent of the freedom of the believer, of the doctrine that Jesus freed his believers from sin and thus from the dictates of the law; he opposed incorporating the Hebrew Scriptures into Christian reading and worship, because the Old Testament (as it came to be known long after Paul's day) was the repository of the law from which Jesus had freed Christians.

Paul was apparently well read in both Hellenistic and Hebraic literatures; scholars have traced the Stoic and Gnostic influences on his letters, and the impact of Plato is clear, if perhaps mediated by Philo Judaeus, himself an eclectic blender of Hebraic and Hellenistic thought. Paul is patently more 'Greek' than Jesus in his eschatology (especially his dualistic conception of body and spirit, men and women, heaven and earth); but he is also arguably more 'Jewish' than Jesus in his fervent expectation of a future *parousia* or messianic 'coming' of Christ.

The famous fourteenth chapter of Paul's first letter to the Corinthians is a signal attempt to place a cap on the mysticism of the early church: to replace (or at least supplement) the 'closedness' of the esoteric speaking in tongues with the 'openness' of translation and translatability, an exoteric principle that it would take the medieval church a thousand years to instil in European believers.

Rather Five Words With the Mind Than Ten Thousand in a Tongue
1 Corinthians 14 (55 C.E.?)
Revised Standard Translation

1. Make love your aim, and earnestly desire the

[1] Aesop told the story of the goat who happened upon a fox trapped in a well: told by the crafty fox that there was going to be a drought, the goat leaped into the well to guard against thirst, whereupon the fox climbed on the goat's back and escaped. Horace is warning the poet working with 'received' materials, such as the Homeric tales, against believing whatever the original author (the crafty fox) tells him. [Ed]

[2] A rendering of the first lines of the *Odyssey*. [Tr]

[3] The legendary Greek warrior Diomedes was born after the death of his uncle Meleager; Leda was raped by Zeus in the form of a swan and gave birth to two eggs, one containing Helen (the woman over whom the Trojan War was fought), the other the twins Castor and Pollux. [Ed]

spiritual gifts, especially that you may prophesy. For one who speaks in a tongue speaks not to men but to God; for no one understands him, but he utters mysteries in the Spirit. On the other hand, he who prophesies speaks to men for their up-building and encouragement and consolation. He who speaks in a tongue edifies himself, but he who prophesies edifies the church. Now I want you all to speak in tongues, but even more to prophesy. He who prophesies is greater than he who speaks in tongues, unless someone interprets, so that the church may be edified.

6. Now, brethren, if I come to you speaking in tongues, how shall I benefit you unless I bring you some revelation or knowledge or prophecy or teaching? If even lifeless instruments, such as the flute or the harp, do not give distinct notes, how will anyone know what is played? And if the bugle gives an indistinct sound, who will get ready for battle? So with yourselves; if you in a tongue utter speech that is not intelligible, how will anyone know what is said? For you will be speaking into the air. There are doubtless many different languages in the world, and none without meaning; but if I do not know the meaning of the language, I shall be a foreigner to the speaker and the speaker a foreigner to me. So with yourselves; since you are eager for manifestations of the Spirit, strive to excel in building up the church.

13. Therefore, he who speaks in a tongue should pray for the power to interpret. For if I pray in a tongue, my spirit prays but my mind is unfruitful. What am I to do? I will pray with the spirit and I will pray with the mind also. I will sing with the spirit and I will sing with the mind also. Otherwise, if you bless[1] with the spirit, how can any one in the position of an outsider[2] say the "Amen" to your thanksgiving when he does not know what you are saying? For you may give thanks well enough, but the other man is not edified. I thank God that I speak in tongues more than you all; nevertheless, in church I would rather speak five words with my mind, in order to instruct others, than ten thousand words in a tongue.

20. Brethren, do not be children in your thinking; be babes in evil, but in thinking be mature. In the law it is written, "By men of strange tongues and by the lips of foreigners will I speak to this people, and even then they will not listen to me, says the Lord" [Isaiah 28:11-12]. Thus, tongues are a sign not for believers but for unbelievers, while prophecy is not for unbelievers but for believers. If, therefore, the whole church assembles and all speak in tongues, and outsiders or unbelievers enter, will they not say that you are mad? But if all prophesy, and an unbeliever or outsider enters, he is convicted by all, he is called to account by all, the secrets of his heart are disclosed; and so, falling on his face, he will worship God and declare that God is really among you.

26. What then, brethren? When you come together, each one has a hymn, a lesson, a revelation, a tongue, or an interpretation. Let all things be done for edification. If any speak in a tongue, let there be only two or at most three, and each in turn; and let one interpret. But if there is no one to interpret, let each of them keep silence in church and speak to himself and to God. Let two or three prophets speak, and let the others weigh what is said. If a revelation is made to another sitting by, let the first be silent. For you can prophesy one by one, so that all may learn and all be encouraged; and the spirits of prophets are subject to prophets. For God is not a God of confusion but of peace.

As in all the churches of the saints, the women should keep silence in the churches. For they are not permitted to speak, but should be subordinate, as even the law says. If there is anything they desire to know, let them ask their husbands at home. For it is shameful for a woman to speak in church. What! Did the word of God originate with you, or are you the only ones it has reached?

37. If any one thinks that he is a prophet, or spiritual, he should acknowledge that what I am writing to you is a command of the Lord. If any one does not recognize this, he is not recognized. So, my brethren, earnestly desire to prophesy, and do not forbid speaking in tongues; but all things should be done decently and in order.

Lucius Annaeus Seneca

Lucius Annaeus Seneca (c. 4 B.C.E.-65 C.E.) and a close circle of his friends dominated the Roman world in the mid-first century of the Christian era, during the reign of the Emperor Nero: philosopher, orator, tragic poet, and statesman, Seneca had his hands on enormous power until his political enemies forced him to commit suicide in 65 C.E.

Seneca was born to a wealthy Roman family in Spain, second son of Lucius Annaeus Seneca the Elder, who had won fame as a rhetoric teacher; his younger brother was father to the poet Lucan. Taken to Rome as a boy by an aunt, he was trained there in philosophy at the school of

[1]That is, *give thanks to God.* [Tr]

[2]Or *him that is without gifts.* [Tr]

the Sextii, a Stoic/ascetic group descended from the Pythagoreans. Ill health drove him to Egypt to recuperate; upon his return to Rome in 31, in his late 20s, he began to establish himself in politics and the law, only to fall afoul of the Emperor Caligula, who was convinced not to have him killed because his ill health would surely cut his life short.

In 41 he became involved romantically with the Princess Julia Livilla, niece to the Emperor Claudius, who banished him to Corsica for adultery; after eight years of reading and writing on that island, he was recalled to Rome through the influence of Claudius' wife Agrippina, mother of the future Emperor Nero, whose tutor he soon became. In 50 he married a wealthy woman named Pompeia Paulina and made powerful friends, including Sextus Afranius Burrus, the prefect of the guard; Seneca himself was made praetor. Four years later Claudius was murdered, and Seneca and Burrus, Agrippina's protégés, became the most powerful men in Rome – the men controlled by Agrippina in order to control her 17-year-old emperor son. Seneca, Nero's tutor, wrote speeches for the tyrant, drafted legislation and fiscal and judicial reforms, managed distant wars through other well-placed friends – and, in 59, was forced into collusion with the murder of Agrippina, either by arranging it or by looking through his fingers at whoever arranged it.

Burrus died in 62, and Seneca lost interest in politics; granted permission to retire, he wrote most of his finest philosophical works in the last three years of his life, including the 124 letters to Lucilius excerpted below. His tragedies were probably meant to be recited rather than acted, and they are often more dialogized Stoicism than drama; but they had an immense influence on Renaissance drama, including Shakespeare's *Titus Andronicus* and John Webster's *The Duchess of Malfi*. His Stoic philosophy remained popular throughout late antiquity and the Middle Ages, inspiring Jerome and Augustine and Boethius, Dante and Chaucer and Petrarch, Calvin and Montaigne and Rousseau.

His passing remarks on translation in the 58th letter to Lucilius deal more with philosophy, and the transmission of philosophy from the Greeks to the Romans, than with translation; in this they hark back to Cicero's comments on translation in *De finibus*, and ahead to Martin Heidegger's comments in *Der Satz vom Grund* (1957).

What Is

From *Moral Letters to Lucilius* (*Epistulae morales ad Lucilium*, letter 58, 63-65 C.E.)
Translated by E. Phillips Barker

Seneca to his friend Lucilius, greeting

Today I realized more clearly than ever our native poverty – destitution rather – in the matter of vocabulary. We were talking about Plato, as it happened, and any number of things cropped up which needed names and had none, and some on the other hand which had lost the names they once had because we're so finical. Beggars who must be choosers would vex a saint! What the Greeks call οἶστρος, the gadfly that chases the cattle and scatters them all over the ranges, Romans once called *asilus*. You may take Virgil's word for that.

> Nigh Silarus' grove and Alburn's holm-woods green
> Swarmeth a fluttering fiend which Roman tongue
> *Asilus* nameth, Greece to *oestrus* turns –
> Fell fly whose furious trumpet drives amaz'd
> Through forest wilds the herd.
> [*Georgics* 3.144ff]

This means, I imagine, that the word's obsolete. Not to detain you very long, there were some uncompounded forms in use: for example, their phrase for decision by the sword was *cernere ferro inter se*. Virgil again shall prove you that.

> *Ingentiis genitos diversis partibus orbis*
> *Inter se coiisse viros et cernere ferro –*
> [*Aeneid* 12.708-9]

> 'Those mighty twain in climes far sundered born
> Here met to seek the sword's arbitrement – '

cernere for our *decernere*. The use of the uncompounded verb is lost. That earlier age said *si iusso*, that is, *iussero*. Take Virgil's word for it again, not mine, please.

> *Cetera, qua iusso, mecum manus inferat arma.*
> [*Aeneid* 11.467]

> 'The rest with me, where I ordain, shall charge.'

This precision isn't designed to show how much time I've wasted at the philologists' feet, but to make you understand how many words in Ennius and Accius lie in the lumber-room, when even in Virgil, whose pages are ransacked daily, there are some which have been stolen from us. 'What's the meaning of these preliminaries?' you ask. 'Where are they leading?' I'll be open with you: I want, if I can, to win your ears' good will for the word *essentia* – 'essence': if I can't, I shall use it even with their ill will. I have Cicero as my sponsor for it – a sound one, I think. If you want someone more modern, there's Fabianus, who has power of expression, taste, and a style that sparkles even to our jaded appreciation. Indeed, Lucilius my friend, what's to be done? How is οὐσία – that necessary thing which by nature comprehends the basis of all things – to be expressed? That's why I ask you to let me use the word. Nevertheless, I'll do my best to exercise the right you give me as sparingly as possible: perhaps I shall be satisfied with the bare permission. But what good will your charity do me, when, if you please, I can't render in Latin by any means the very idea over which I raised my outcry against this language of ours? Less quarter will you give to the national unpreparedness when you learn that the word I can't translate's a monosyllable. You want to know what it is? τὸ ὄυ. You think me a dunce? The word's obvious? I can translate it 'what is'? Ah, but I see a considerable difference: I'm forced to put a verb for a noun. Still, if it must be, I'll let it pass as 'what is'. A learned friend of mine was saying today that it's used by Plato in six senses. I'll expound you them all, first calling your attention to the distinction of genus and species ...

Pliny the Younger

The adopted son of his natural historian uncle, Pliny the Elder, Pliny the Younger (Gaius Plinius Caecilius Secundus, 61/62-113 C.E.) is largely known for the ten books of private letters he published on a wide variety of subjects, including the emperors under whom he served as praetor and consul, his contemporary Tacitus' composition of the *Histories*, the literary *demimonde* of the day, and various social and moral issues. Writing letters of this sort was fashionable among the Roman upper classes, to which Pliny belonged; he elevated the fashion into an artistic genre whose progeny in our day probably includes contemporary collections of work by syndicated columnists.

Pliny the Younger's political success was based partly on his family connections, but partly also on his skill as an orator. He began to practice law at the age of eighteen, and at the peak of his career effected the conviction of several officials for corruption. It was apparently while investigating corruption in Bithynia, a district in what is now northwestern Turkey, that he died in 113.

Pliny's letter to Fuscus Salinator (85 C.E.?), written almost a century and a half after Cicero's books on the orator, adds two new ingredients to Cicero's theory. The first is the heuristic value of translating in both directions, an exercise Cicero never imagined; the second is open competition with the original writer, a kind of one-upmanship whose ultimate aim (apart from the self-aggrandizing joy of winning, of course) is the amassing of expressive capital.

Imitation of the Best Models
Letter to Fuscus Salinator (85 C.E.?)
Translated by Betty Radice

You ask me what course of study I think you should follow during your present prolonged holiday. The most useful thing, which is always being suggested, is to translate Greek into Latin and Latin into Greek. This kind of exercise develops in one a precision and richness of vocabulary, a wide range of metaphor, and power of exposition, and, moreover, imitation of the best models leads to a like aptitude for original composition. At the same time, any point which might have been overlooked by a reader cannot escape the eye of a translator. All this cultivates perception and critical sense.

When you have read a passage sufficiently to remember the subject-matter and line of thought, there is no harm in your trying to compete with it; then compare your efforts with the original and consider carefully where your version is better or worse. You may well congratulate yourself if yours is sometimes better and feel much ashamed if the other is always superior to yours. You may also sometimes choose a passage you know well and try to improve on it. This is a daring attempt, but does not presume too far when it is made in private; and yet we see many people entering this type of contest with great credit to themselves and, by not lacking confidence, outstripping the authors whom they only intended to follow. You can also revise the speeches you have put aside, retaining much of the original, but leaving out still more and making other additions and alterations. This I know you will think a tedious labour, but its very difficulty makes it profitable to rekindle your fire and recover your enthusiasm when once its force is spent; to graft new limbs, in fact, on to a finished trunk without disturbing the balance of the original.

I know that your chief interest at the present time is forensic oratory, but that is not a reason for advising you to limit yourself to this provocative and somewhat pugnacious style. The soil is refreshed when sown with successive changes of seed, and so are our minds if cultivated by different subjects. I should like you sometimes to take a passage of historical narrative or turn your attention to letter-writing, for often even in a speech the subject calls for a narrative or a poetic style of description; and letters develop brevity and simplicity of style. It is permissible, too, to seek relaxation in writing poetry, by which I mean not a long continuous poem (which can only be finished if one has plenty of leisure), but one of those short, polished sets of verses which make a break in your duties and responsibilities, however pressing. This is called light verse, but it sometimes brings its authors as much fame as serious work. In fact (for why shouldn't I versify to encourage you to take to verse?)

The beauty of wax is its power to yield
    To the fingers' skilful touch;
Thus taught, it can shape the god of War,
    Chaste Wisdom or Love or her son.
The secret springs can quench a flame,
    Or gladden the flowers and fields;
So the mind of man, through the gentle arts
    Is taught the wisdom of change.

The greatest orators, and the greatest men, too, used to train or amuse themselves in this way – or rather, combine their training with amusement, for it is remarkable how the mind is both stimulated and relaxed by these trifles. They comprise our loves and hatreds, our indignation, compassion and wit, in fact every phase of life and every detail of our public and professional activities. They also offer the same advantages as other forms of poetry; when we have been bound by the restrictions of metre, we delight in the freedom of prose and gladly return to what comparison has shown to be the easier style.

Perhaps this is more than you wanted, but there is one more thing. I have said nothing about what I think you should read, though this was implied when I was telling you what to write. Remember to make a careful selection from representative authors in each subject, for the saying is that a man should be deeply, not widely, read. These authors are too well known and approved to need further indication; and, besides, I have let this letter run on so far that I am robbing you of time for work with all my advice on planning it. Back then to your books and writing – either something on the lines I suggest, or what you have already started.

Quintilian

Like Cicero and Pliny the Younger, Quintilian (Marcus Fabius Quintilianus, 35-after 96 C.E.) was trained as an orator for the law courts; unlike them, who only *wrote* about oratorical training, he was actually employed as a teacher of rhetoric under the emperors Vespasian, Titus, and Domitian – indeed he was the first teacher of rhetoric to receive a state salary. After retiring from that job, he was employed as the private tutor of Domitian's two grandnephews and heirs; he probably died soon after Domitian's assassination in 96.

His major work, the *Institutio oratoria*, was written at the end of his life. In it he distilled not only a lifetime of practical pedagogical experience but his wide reading in theories of rhetoric and pedagogy, and the work is considered a founding document of Western rhetoric, pedagogy, and literary criticism. His remarks on translation are very much in the Ciceronian tradition; his main contribution is a rigorous systematization of Cicero's rather unstructured thoughts on the subject into a pedagogical regimen that would prove enormously influential for later uses of translation in foreign language teaching. The distinction he takes from Philo Judaeus between *metaphrasis* or replacing a single word with a single word and *paraphrasis* or replacing a phrase with a phrase later became a mainstay of translation theory, culminating in John Dryden's famous three-way classification of translations as metaphrases, paraphrases, and imitations.

On What We Should Employ Ourselves When We Write
From *Institutes of Oratory; or, Education of an Orator* (*Institutio oratoria*, 96 C.E.?)
Translated by John Selby Watson

1. The next point is, to *decide on what we should employ ourselves when we write*. It would be a superfluous labour, indeed, to detail what subjects there are for writing, and what should be studied first, or second, and so on in succession; for this has been done in my first book [C 9], in which I prescribed the order for the studies of boys, and in my second [C 4, 10], where I specified those of the more advanced; and what is now to be considered is whence copiousness and facility of expression may be derived.

2. To translate Greek into Latin our old orators thought to be a very excellent exercise. Lucius Crassus, in the well-known books of Cicero *De Oratore*, says that he often practised it; and Cicero himself, speaking in his own person, very frequently recommends it, and has even published books of Plato and Xenophon translated in that kind of exercise.[1] It was also approved by Messalla; and there are extant several versions of speeches made by him, so that he even rivalled the oration of Hyperides for

[1] The *Timaeus* and *Protagoras* of Plato, and the *Œconomicus* of Zenophon. [Tr] For Cicero's pronouncements, see 7-12, above. [Ed]

Phryne in delicacy of style, a quality most difficult of attainment to Romans.[2]

3. The object of such exercise is evident; for the Greek authors excel in copiousness of matter, and have introduced a vast deal of art into the study of eloquence; and, in translating them, we may use the very best words, for all that we use may be our own. As to [verbal] figures, by which language is principally ornamented, we may be under the necessity of inventing a great number and variety of them, because the Roman tongue differs greatly from that of the Greeks.

4. But the conversion of Latin writing into other words will also be of great service to us. About the utility of turning poetry into prose, I suppose that no one has any doubt; and this is the only kind of exercise that Sulpicius[3] is said to have used; for its sublimity may elevate our style, and the boldness of the expressions adopted by poetic license does not preclude the orator's efforts to express the same thoughts in the exactness of prose. He may even add to those thoughts oratorical vigour, supply what has been omitted, and give compactness to that which is diffuse, since I would not have our paraphrase to be a mere interpretation, but an effort to vie with and rival our original in the expression of the same thoughts.

5. I therefore differ in opinion from those who disapprove of paraphrasing Latin orations, on the pretext that, as the best words and phrases have been already used, whatever we express in another form, must of necessity be expressed worse. But for this allegation there is no sufficient ground; for we must not despair of the possibility of finding something better than what has been said; nor has nature made language so meagre and poor that we cannot speak well on any subject except in one way; unless we suppose, indeed, that the gestures of the actor can give a variety of turns to the same words, but that the power of eloquence is so much inferior that when a thing has been once said, nothing can be said after it to the same purpose.

6. But let it be granted that what we conceive is neither better than our original nor equal to it; yet it must be allowed, at the same time, that there is a possibility of coming near to it.

7. Do not we ourselves at times speak twice or oftener, and sometimes a succession of sentences, on the same subject, and are we to suppose that though we can contend with ourselves we cannot contend with others? If a thought could be expressed well only in one way, it would be but right to suppose that the path of excellence has been shut against us by some of our predecessors; but in reality there are still innumerable modes of saying a thing, and many roads leading to the same point.

8. Conciseness has its charms, and so has copiousness; there is one kind of beauty in metaphorical, another in simple expressions; direct expressions become one subject, and such as are varied by figures another. In addition, the difficulty of the exercise is most serviceable. Are not our greatest authors by this means studied more carefully? For, in this way, we do not run over what we have written in a careless mode of reading, but consider every individual portion, and look, from necessity, thoroughly into their matter, and learn how much merit they possess from the very fact that we cannot succeed in imitating them.

Aulus Gellius

Little is known of Aulus Gellius (1st-2nd century C.E.), who was also known to the Middle Ages (mistakenly) as Agellius. The *Attic Nights* is a miscellany written in Athens about his many distinguished friends and teachers and other topical subjects; his remarks on translation are notable largely because they differ so strikingly in tone and tenor from the Ciceronian tradition mined by Horace and Pliny.

There is continuity here also. Where Horace guided the poet or translator past slavish imitation to original creativity, Aulus Gellius guides the literary or translation critic to an appreciation of that creativity. Taking Horace's contemporary Virgil as a 'translator' or poet working with received materials, Gellius defends his 'free' translations from Homer, Theocritus, and others, arguing that, since what the Greek writers did in Greek cannot be rendered exactly into Latin without suffering a loss of charm and grace, Virgil did quite rightly in leaving out what was un-translatable and adding his own "almost more charming and graceful" effects.

On the Importance of Avoiding Strict Literalness
From *Attic Nights* (*Noctes Atticae*, 100 C.E.?)
Translated by John C. Rolfe

Whenever striking expressions from the Greek poets

[2] Hyperides, defending the famous courtesan Phryne in court, is said to have won the jury's sympathy for her by tearing her clothes and displaying her bosom – no doubt the "delicacy of style" to which Quintilian refers. [Ed]

[3] Quintilian's reference is not clear; he may mean Publius Sulpicius Rufus or Servius Sulpicius Rufus. [Ed]

are to be translated and imitated, they say that we should not always strive to render every single word with exact literalness. For many things lose their charm if they are transplanted too forcibly – unwillingly, as it were, and reluctantly. Virgil therefore showed skill and good judgment in omitting some things and rendering others, when he was dealing with passages of Homer or Hesiod or Apollonius or Parthenius or Callimachus or Theocritus, or some other poet.

For example, when very recently the *Bucolics* of Theocritus and Virgil were being read together at table, we perceived that Virgil had omitted something that in the Greek is, to be sure, wonderfully pleasing, but neither could nor ought to have been translated. But what he has substituted for that omission is almost more charming and graceful. Theocritus writes:

> But when her goatherd boy goes by you should
> see my Cleärist
> Fling apples, and her pretty lips call pouting to
> be kissed.
> [*Idyls* v. 88f; translation by L.C.L. Edmonds]

Virgil has:

> My Phyllis me with pelted apples plies,
> Then tripping to the woods the wanton hies,
> And wishes to be seen before she flies.
> [*Eclogues* 3.64 ff., translation by John Dryden]

Also in another place I notice that what was very sweet in the Greek was prudently omitted. Theocritus writes:

> O Tityrus, well-beloved, feed my goats,
> And lead them to the fount, good Tityrus;
> But 'ware yon buck-goat yellow, lest he butt.
> [*Idyls* 3.3 ff.]

But how could Virgil reproduce τό καλόν πεφιλημένε ('well-beloved'), words that, by Heaven! defy translation, but have a certain native charm? He therefore omitted that expression and translated the rest very cleverly, except in using caper for Theocritus' ἐνόρχας; for, according to Marcus Varro, a goat is called *caper* in Latin only after he has been castrated. Virgil's version is:

> Till I return – not long – feed thou my goats;
> Then, Tityrus, give them drink, but as you go,
> Avoid the buck-goat's horn – the fellow butts!
> [*Eclogues* 11.23]

And since I am speaking on the subject of translation, I recall hearing from pupils of Valerius Probus, a learned man and well trained in reading and estimating the ancient writings, that he used to say that Virgil had never translated Homer less successfully than in these delightful lines which Homer wrote about Nausicaa:

> As when o'er Erymanth Diana roves,
> Or wide Taygetus' resounding groves,
> A silver train the huntress queen surrounds,
> Her rattling quiver from her shoulder sounds;
> Fierce in the sport, along the mountain's brow
> They bay the boar or chase the bounding roe;
> High o'er the lawn, with more majestic pace,
> Above the nymphs she treads with stately grace;
> Distinguished excellence the goddess proves,
> Exults Latona as the virgin moves:
> With equal grace Nausicaa trod the plain,
> And shone transcendent o'er the beauteous train.
> [*Odyssey* 6.102ff., translation by John Dryden]

This passage Virgil renders thus:

> As on Eurotas' banks or Cynthus' heights
> Diana guides her dancing bands, whose train
> A thousand Oreads follow, right and left;
> A quiver bears she on her shoulder fair,
> And as she treads, the goddesses o'ertops;
> Joys thrill Latona's silent breast.
> [*Aeneid* i. 498 ff.]

First of all, they said that Probus thought that in Homer the maiden Nausicaa, playing among her girl companions in solitary places, was consistently and properly compared with Diana hunting on the mountain heights among the rural goddesses; but that Virgil had made a comparison that was by no means suitable, since Dido, walking with dignified dress and gait in the midst of a city, and surrounded by the Tyrian chiefs, "pressing on the work of her rising kingdom", as he himself says [*Aeneid* 1.504], can have no points of similarity corresponding with the sports and hunts of Diana. Then secondly, that Homer mentions plainly and directly Diana's interest and pleasure in the chase, while Virgil, not having said a word about the goddess' hunting, merely pictures her as carrying a quiver on her shoulder, as if it were a burden or a pack. And they said that Probus was particularly surprised at this feature of Virgil's version, that while Homer's Leto rejoices with a joy that is unaffected, deep, and springing from the very depths of her heart and soul – for the words γέγηθε δέ τε φρένα Λητώ, or "Leto rejoiced in heart", means nothing else – Virgil, on the other hand, in his attempt to imitate this, has depicted a joy that is passive, mild, slow, and as it were floating on the surface of the heart; for Probus said that he did not know what else the word *pertemptant* could mean.[1] Besides all this, Virgil seemed to have left out the flower of the whole passage, by giving only a faint shadow of this verse of Homer's:

> And shone transcendent o'er the
> beauteous train.[2]

For no greater or more complete praise of beauty can be expressed than that she alone excelled where all were beautiful, that she alone was easily distinguished from all the rest.

Epiphanius of Constantia (Salamis)

Epiphanius (315-403) is best remembered today as a fanatical opponent of Origenism who unflaggingly and somewhat uncritically sought and finally (in 400) gained the official condemnation of Origen, the third-century Christian theologian whose work was enormously influential for the early Church.

Born in Palestine, a native speaker of Syrian, Epiphanius studied classics in Egypt, where he learned Coptic and Hebrew and lived for a time with monks. Powerfully drawn to asceticism, upon his return to Palestine he founded and governed for thirty years a monastery near his home city of Eleutheropolis. In 367 he was appointed bishop of Constantia (Salamis), and he threw himself into the controversies of the day with a fervour, opposing the Arians and Origenists and seeking to force other powerful bishops (notably, and unsuccessfully, John of Jerusalem) to do the same. When Origen was condemned in 400, the 85-year-old Epiphanius travelled to Constantinople to agitate against John Chrysostom, who had succored four Origenist monks known as the Tall Brothers. When he discovered that Theophilus of Alexandria was already forcefully denouncing John (who was later deposed), he left for home but died en route at sea.

As a theologian Epiphanius was rigidly anti-intellectual; his religious views were uncritically and uncomplicatedly polarized, the good being perfectly pure and the bad being thoroughly wicked. His insistence in his Bible study guide *On Weights and Measures* that the Septuagint was divinely inspired, and that the best proof of this is the legend that they did their translations in isolation from each other but the results were nevertheless identical, was a commonly held belief in his day (Augustine, for example, shared it); only the hotheaded Jerome, Epiphanius' sometime ally in the battle against Origen, scoffed at it.

Producing an Unadulterated Translation
From *On Weights and Measures* (392 C.E.)
Translated by Moses Hadas

They were seventy-two in number and were shut up from morn till eve in the Pharian island ... over against Alexandria, in six and thirty cells, one pair to each cell. At even[ing] they would cross over in thirty-six skiffs to the palace of Ptolemy Philadelphus and feast with him. They slept in pairs in thirty-six bed-chambers. Such was the life they led, to the end that they should have no collusion with each other and should produce an unadulterated translation. The thirty-six cells which I mentioned were erected by the aforesaid Ptolemy in the island across the water. He made them in two compartments and shut in the men two and two, as I said; and he shut in with them two ministering attendants to cook and to wait upon them, and they had shorthand writers in addition. He did not so much as make windows in the walls of those cells, but had what are called "skylights" opened in the roofs above their heads. So they lived from morn to eve under lock and key and so they translated. To each pair one book was delivered, that is to say, the book of the Genesis of the world to one pair, the *Exodus* of the children of Israel to a second pair, Leviticus to a third, and so on. Thus were translated the scriptural and canonical books, twenty-seven in all, or twenty-two if the reckoning is made to correspond to the number of letters in the Hebrew alphabet ... The method was as already described: the books were distributed periodically to each pair of translators, passing from the first pair to the second, and again from the second to the third in rotation. Thus each book was translated thirty-six times; such is the story which is told. There were also twenty-two of the apocryphal books. When the work was completed, the king took his seat on a lofty throne, and thirty-six readers sat at his feet having the thirty-six reproductions of each book, while one held a copy of the Hebrew volume. Then one reader recited and the rest diligently attended; and there was found no discrepancy ... Where they added a word they all added it in common, and where they omitted the omission was made by all alike.

Jerome

Jerome (Eusebius Hieronymus, c. 347-419/420), who also used the pseudonym Sophronius,

---

[1] *Pertempto* means 'try thoroughly', hence 'affect deeply'. Probus must have taken *per* in the sense of 'over', 'on the surface', thus giving *pertempto* a meaning of which no example exists. [Tr]

[2] Literally, 'And is readily recognized, though all are fair'. [Tr]

was revered throughout the Middle Ages and (by Catholics) well into the modern era as the 'official' translator of the Bible, the author of the Vulgate Latin translation that in matters of doctrinal dispute took precedence over all Hebrew and Greek texts until the sixteenth century and beyond. His letter to Pammachius on the best kind of translator, written in Bethlehem in 395, is the founding document of Christian translation theory; along with Cicero, Luther, and Goethe, Jerome is one of the most influential translation theorists in the Western tradition.

Jerome was born to a wealthy Christian family in Dalmatia, or what was more recently Yugoslavia, and was sent to Rome (which had converted to Christianity in 313) at the age of twelve to continue his education. His twenties and thirties were spent in travel and further learning, in the course of which he became associated with an ascetic circle of writers and scholars that included Rufinus, the translator of Origen who would later become his bitter enemy and the butt of his letter to Pammachius. In a famous dream from 375, one that was to shape the first major shift in Western translation theory, he was called before the Lord and accused of being a Ciceronian rather than a Christian; twenty years later he would formulate the first truly post-Ciceronian translation theory, incorporating Ciceronian elements into a new ascetic regimen that stressed the accurate transmission of the meaning of the text rather than the budding orator's freely ranging imitation.

Jerome's attraction to asceticism appeared early, but it was not until the dream in 375 that he acted upon it, becoming a hermit in the desert of Chalcis. His eremitical sojourn only lasted two years, during which time he also learned Hebrew from a Jewish convert and maintained a lively correspondence with other scholars around the world. When he left the desert he was ordained and continued his theological studies in Antioch, where he also translated and updated the *Chronicle* of the church historian Eusebius that he discusses in the letter to Pammachius. In 382 he returned to Rome as secretary to Pope Damasus; here he took his first steps as a Bible translator, revising existing Latin translations of the Gospels (384) and other Scriptural texts based on the best Greek manuscripts. Here he also laid the groundwork for the rest of his life: his polemics for the monastic life and virulent attacks on lax clergy won him the favour of the wealthy Roman virgin Paula and the enmity of the clerical community, and when, upon Damasus' death in 384, the latter drove him out, the former followed him to Palestine. There, in Bethlehem, she financed a monastery for men under Jerome's direction and a cloister for women under her own direction, and it was in this monastery that Jerome was to spend the remaining 34 years of his life.

During this period Jerome wrote antiheretical polemics (most notably *Dialogi contra Pelagianos* ['Dialogues Against the Pelagians'], 415), books on Hebrew names and Biblical places in Palestine, and exegeses of various books of the Bible. His most famous work from this period, however, is the Vulgate translation of the Bible (391-406). This included his revisions of earlier New Testament translations, which he extended to cover the entire Testament, and a new translation of the Old Testament based on Origen's *Hexapla* (before 235), a parallel edition in six columns: the Hebrew text in both Hebrew and Greek characters, and four different Greek translations.

The letter to Pammachius reflects Jerome's fiery, irascible nature, which strained all of his friendships (including that with Augustine) and led to permanent breaks in several. In this he strongly resembles Martin Luther, who, eleven and a half centuries later, was to engineer a break with monasticism but not, finally, with Jerome's translation theory.

The Best Kind of Translator
Letter to Pammachius, #57 (395 C.E.)
Translated by Paul Carroll

Bethlehem, 395 C.E.

My dear Pammachius,

When the Apostle Paul appeared before King Agrippa to answer the criminal accusation brought against him, desiring to be articulate and understood by his audience, and confident of a victory for his cause, he began his defense, almost as if rejoicing, with these words: "I consider myself fortunate today, O King Agrippa, because I am to defend myself in your presence against these charges of the Jews. No man is more familiar than you with Hebrew customs and controversies" [Acts 26:2-3]. Obviously Paul had profited from that aphorism in Ecclesiasticus which calls a man fortunate if he addresses ears that listen [Ecclesiasticus 25:9]; and he had realized that an orator only succeeds in proportion to the impression he creates. So it is that on this occasion I consider myself fortunate that your educated ears will hear my defense against the accusation of ignorance and falsehood charged to me by an inexperienced, bumptious tongue.[1]

[1] Rufinus and Jerome were good friends until both were accused of Origenism in 393; Jerome promptly recanted but Rufinus did not, and the enmity between the two former friends grew steadily. Rufinus's attack on Jerome in 395, which occasioned the letter to Pammachius,

This tongue, it seems, claims that I have made mistakes through misinterpretation or carelessness when I translated into Latin a letter written by another in Greek. Of error, or of a downright crime, it would convict me.

Now, lest it should happen that my accuser, facilitated by a loquacity which stops at nothing and an impunity which grants itself all possible license, should actually convict me – he has already charged "criminal" action against our Pope Epiphanius – I am writing this letter to you, and hope that it will also reach others who consider me dignified enough for their affection. I feel compelled to inform my friends of the true facts of this situation. About two years ago Pope Epiphanius sent a letter to John, Bishop of Jerusalem,[2] in which he exposed some of John's opinions, and then, in a mild way, called him to penitence. So great was the reputation of the author, or else the elegance of the letter, that all Palestine fought for copies of it. Now there was in our monastery a man of considerable distinction in his own country, one Eusebius of Cremona; when he discovered that this letter was on everyone's tongue, and that the cultured and uneducated alike admired it for its doctrine and the purity of its style, Eusebius began to entreat me to translate it for him into Latin, and, at the same time, to arrange and simplify the content so that he could more easily understand it, for he had no knowledge of Greek. This I agreed to do. Calling a secretary, I quickly dictated a translation, briefly paraphrasing on the margin the argument in each main section. The point is that Eusebius asked me to translate a copy only for himself; and in return I requested that he keep the copy private and not circulate it publicly.

Eighteen months passed; then, by a novel stratagem, the translation "migrated" from his desk to Jerusalem. It was the work of a wolf in monk's clothing. Either he was bribed to steal it – as there is good reason to believe – or he was prompted by his own malice, as his corruptor[3] vainly attempts to convince us. In any case, he showed himself another Judas by pilfering Eusebius' property, and his theft afforded the adversary an occasion to brawl against me. So now my enemies tell the uneducated Christian crowd that Jerome falsified the original letter, that Jerome has not translated word for word, that Jerome has written "beloved friend" in place of "honorable Sir," and that – more disgraceful still! – Jerome has maliciously condensed by omitting the epithet "most reverend."[4] These, and similar trifles, constitute my criminal acts.

At the very beginning, before I defend my translation, I wish to interrogate those men who call cunning and malice prudence. Where did you obtain your copy of my translation? Who gave it to you? How dare you display something obtained by your fraud? What place will be safe when a man cannot keep his secrets even behind his own walls and in his private desk?

If I were to bring such charges against you before a civil court, I could subjugate you to the laws which, even in financial cases, appoint penalties against informers and condemn a traitor even while they accept his treacherous information. Civil courts clearly welcome the advantage supplied by traitors and informers; what they disapprove is the motive behind betrayal. Not too long ago a consul named Hesychius, against whom the patriarch Gamaliel waged an important war, was condemned to death by Emperor Theodosius simply because he had obtained possession of some official papers by bribing a secretary. And in the ancient histories[5] we also read that the tutor who betrayed the Faliscan children was sent back to his boys and delivered to them in chains because the Romans refused to accept a victory through the dishonorable means he offered; and when Pyrrhus, King of Epirus, was lying wounded in his camp, his doctor went to the enemy and offered to poison him, but the enemy general Fabricius, thinking it a disgrace that the king should perish by such treachery, sent the traitor back in chains to his master, for he would not approve of a crime even when the victim happened to be his enemy. This principle, then, preserved by public laws, held sacred even during a state of warfare, had been unquestioned also among monks and priests of Christ. Can any one

was in fact mild compared with Jerome's counterattack; and two years later, in 397, Rufinus published his translation of Origen's *De principiis* ('On First Principles') with a preface calling Jerome an admirer of Origen, and Jerome responded with a vituperative assault next to which the letter to Pammachius pales. Like most exegetes of the day, Jerome was heavily indebted to Origen's Bible scholarship. [Ed]

[2] John of Jerusalem, attacked by Bishop Epiphanius and Jerome in 393 for his Origenism, retaliated against Palestinian anti-Origenists by blocking their access to the holy places in Jerusalem and refusing them the sacraments of baptism and holy burial. Jerome's vicious denunciation of John in the fall of 396 became a *cause célèbre* throughout the Greek and Western churches; the two were reconciled the next year. [Ed]

[3] It is likely that Rufinus is meant here. And one may suppose that he is the 'heretic' addressed from time to time in the letter. Rufinus was in Jerusalem at the time, and had sided with Bishop John in the Origenistic controversy. [Tr]

[4] *Aidesimotate Pappa* or 'most reverend Pope', a title that had long been granted to all bishops but was in Jerome's day increasingly becoming restricted to metropolitans and patriarchs. Jerome's use of the epithet seems to have been rather partisan: he refers to Bishop Epiphanius (his ally) as Pope but omits the phrase in referring to Bishop John (Epiphanius' opponent). [Ed]

[5] See Livy's history of Rome, 5:27. [Ed]

of them presume now, knitting his eyebrows and snapping his fingers, to belch and say, "What if a monk did bribe, or employ other inducements? He only did what suited his purpose." An astonishing way to defend fraud! As if bandits, thieves, and pirates did not do the same! It could be as truly said that when Annas and Caiaphas seduced miserable Judas they merely did what they thought expedient.

If I happen to write in my notebook this or that absurd remark, or to comment on Scripture, to bite back at my calumniator, to chew at my irritation, to exercise my style in the use of idiomatic phrases, or to store up sharp arrows for a future battle: so long as I do not publish my thoughts, they are hardly malicious or criminal; it is never a question of libel if the public ear does not hear the thought. O my enemy, you may corrupt my servants and solicit my supporters, and, as the fable reads, you may penetrate into Dana's brazen tower,[6] and then concealing what you have done, call me a liar. But, doing so, will you not have to plead guilty yourself to a more serious accusation than any you are able to bring against me? One man blames you for being a heretic, another for being a perverter of orthodox dogma. How silent you remain. Not daring to answer, you lacerate the translator of the letter, concocting false charges against mere syllables, and imagining your defense complete if the one you detracted remains silent. Suppose that I have committed some mistake or omission in my translation: your entire case hinges on this trifling point. What a defense! If I happen to be a poor translator, does that absolve you from being a heretic? Now I do not say you are heretical – such indictment I leave to Epiphanius who wrote the original. All I do say is this: it is most foolish on your part when you are accused by one man to turn and attack another, and when your body is covered with wounds to find comfort by stabbing one who is still peacefully sleeping and unconcerned.

In the above remarks, Pammachius, I have assumed that I did make some alterations in my translation, and that a simple version like mine may contain errors but not mistakes of criminal proportion. On the other hand, since the translation shows that no changes have been made in the sense, and that no extraneous doctrine has been fabricated into it, obviously, as Terence says, "Their purpose in understanding is to understand nothing"; and while my enemies desire to demonstrate another's ineptitude, they really exhibit their own. Now I not only admit but freely announce that in translating from the Greek – except of course in the case of Holy Scripture, where even the syntax contains a mystery – I render, not word for word, but sense for sense.

[6] Danae was locked in a bronze tower (or dungeon with bronze doors) by her father Acrisius for sleeping with his twin brother Proetus, but was raped by Zeus (and bore Perseus) in the form of a shower of gold. [Ed]

For this practice I have behind me the authority of Cicero himself; he employed it in his versions of Plato's *Pythagoras*, the *Oeconomicus* of Xenophon, and those two noble and beautiful orations of Aeschines and Demosthenes delivered against each other. What additions, omissions and alterations Cicero made, substituting the idiom and peculiarity of his own language for the original Greek – this is not the place to say. As far as I am concerned, it will be sufficient merely to quote his own justification for translating as he did. "I have considered it right," Cicero remarks in the prologue to the Latin version of the above orations:

> I have considered it right for me to undertake a labor which, though not necessary for myself, should prove useful to other students. Here I have translated the noblest speeches of two of the most eloquent Attic orators, the debate between Aeschines and Demosthenes; but I have not interpreted and rendered them as a mere translator but as an orator, maintaining the sense but altering the form by adapting both Greek metaphors and diction to suit our own manner of speaking. Not thinking it necessary to render word for word, I have reproduced the general style; but I have not imagined myself obligated to pay out each and every word to the reader; instead, I have paid out an equivalent in value.[7]

This justification is repeated at the prologue's conclusion:

> If my orations are found, as I hope they will be, true to this principle, I shall be satisfied. In translating this debate I have employed all the virtues of the original, that is, the sentiments and metaphors and order of the different parts. On the other hand, the literal wording has been followed only as far as I could without offending our notions of taste. If all that I have written is not to be found in the Greek, I have at least attempted to make the translation correspond with the original.

Similar advice is given by Horace, an acute and learned man, in *The Art Of Poetry* when he tells the intelligent translator:

> Try not to render words literally
> Like some faithful translator.[8]

[7] See 9, above. [Ed]

[8] See 15, above. [Ed]

Menander has been translated by Terence, the ancient comic poets by Plautus and Caecilius. But do they ever stick to the literal words? or instead, do they attempt to preserve the beauty and elegance of their originals? What is called fidelity in "interpretation" the learned designate as pestilent minuteness. Twenty years ago, my teachers favored such minuteness; and even then I remember being the victim of a mistaken notion of translation similar to the one which attacks me today, though I must say I never imagined that even you would look askance at my way of translating. When I put into Latin the *Chronicle* written by Eusebius of Caesarea,[9] among other remarks in the preface I said: "In the following sentence composed by another man, it is difficult not to diverge somewhere; and in translating it is hard to preserve the beauty of idiom which in the original is most distinguished. Each particular word has a significance of its own. Possibly I have no equivalent by which to express some word, and if I then must go out of my way to reach the goal, miles are spent to cover what in reality is a short city block. To this difficulty must be added the windings of word transpositions, the dissimilarities in the use of cases, the varieties in figures of speech, and, most difficult of all, the peculiar vernacular marrow of the language itself. If one translates each and every word literally, the passage will sound absurd; and if by necessity I change anything in the order and wording, it will seem that I have abused the function of translator." Then, after a lengthy discussion, which would be a bit boring to follow here, I added the following: "If anyone does not see how translation adulterates the charm of the original, let him squeeze Homer word for word into Latin – I will even go further and ask him to render Homer into Latin prose: the result will be that the order of the words will seem ridiculous, and that the most eloquent of poets will be hardly articulate."

Now if my own opinion seems to lack authority – in quoting the above my only object was to establish that from my adolescence I have always attempted to translate the substance, not the literal words – read and consider this short preface from a biography of St. Anthony of Egypt:[10]

> A literal translation from one language into another conceals, as with a coat, the original sense, just as an exuberance of grass strangles the crops. Diction is subject to grammatical cases and figures of speech; and when used for translation must explain by weary circumlocution what a few words would otherwise make evident. This blemish I have attempted to avoid in translating, at your request, the life of blessed Antony. Although my version is hardly literal, I have preserved the sense. Others may chase after syllables and exact duplicate words, I have only regarded the substance.

Time would run out if I were to mention all those who have translated according to this principle. Here it is sufficient to notice Hilary the Confessor as an example for the rest. When he turned some homilies on Job and several Psalms from Greek into Latin, he did not bind himself to the drowsiness of literal translation, or allow himself to be chained to the literalism of an inadequate culture, but, like some conqueror, he marched the original text, a captive, into his native language.

That secular and ecclesiastical writers should have adopted this attitude when translating need not astonish us when one considers that the Seventy Translators of Alexandria, the Evangelists and the Apostles have done the same with the Sacred Books. One reads, in Mark for example, of the Lord saying, *Talitha cumi,* and the text immediately adds: "this is interpreted: 'Young woman, I say to you, Arise'" [Mark 5:41]. Now the Evangelist could be accused here of deceit for having added the words, "I say to you," to the original Hebrew sentence. To emphasize this command in the original, "Young woman, Arise," and to convey the impression of one calling, Mark amplified "I say to you." Again, in Matthew, when the thirty silver pieces are returned to Judas, and the potter's field is purchased with them, it is written, "And so the word was fulfilled which was spoken by Jeremiah the Prophet: "And they took the thirty pieces of silver, the price of him who was appraised, for the men of Israel valued him, and spent them to buy the potter's field, as the Lord had appointed me" [Matthew 27:9-10]. But this sentence is not found in Jeremiah at all; it is in Zechariah [11:12-13], and even then in quite different words and a completely different order. In fact the Vulgate edition[11] has it, "And I will say to them, If it seems good, pay me my wages; or if not, then refuse

[9] Jerome not only translated but revised and continued the *Chronicle*, in 381-82. [Ed]

[10] Written by Athanasius in Greek; Jerome is quoting from the preface to Evagrius' Latin translation. [Ed]

[11] Jerome does not mean his own Vulgate translation, as Carroll's translation of "vulgata quippe editio ita se habet" seems to suggest. He simply means the currently available 'vernacular' or 'common' translation (into the 'vulgar' or common people's language, Latin). At the time of this writing, with Jerome's Vulgate still ten years in the future, the 'common' Latin translation was what is now generally referred to as the Itala or 'Old Latin'; in fact Jerome's translation did not officially displace the Itala and become the 'common' or Vulgate translation until the 16th-century Council of Trent. [Ed]

them. So they paid me for wages thirty pieces of silver. And the Lord commanded me: Put the silver into the furnace, and test if it has been tried as I have been tried by them. And I gathered the thirty pieces and cast them into the Lord's house." It must be apparent how radically the Septuagint translation differs here from the quotation given by the Evangelist; and in the original Hebrew, though the sense is identical with that in the Septuagint, the words are dissimilar, and are quite differently arranged. The original reads: "And I said to them, If it seems good in your eyes, give me my wages; and if not, withhold them. So they weighed for my thirty pieces of silver. And the Lord said to me, Cast the pieces to the potter, a good price I was priced at by them. And I took the thirty pieces of silver and cast them to the potter in the house of the Lord." Should one accuse the Apostle Matthew of adulterating his translation? It agrees neither with the Hebrew original, nor with the Greek Septuagint, and, worse than that, one could claim that Matthew has mistaken even the author's name, attributing the passage to Jeremiah instead of Zechariah.

Far be it from Jerome, however, to speak like this about a follower of the Christ. The truth is that Matthew made it his business to formulate dogmas rather than scurry after words and syllables.

To illustrate this, here is another example from Zechariah quoted from the Hebrew by John the Evangelist: "They shall gaze on him whom they pierced" [John 29:37; Zechariah 12:10]. This phrase the Septuagint renders, "And they shall look upon me because they have mocked me"; and in our translation,[12] "And they shall look upon me for those things they have mocked or insulted." Here are three discrepant versions, yet the variety in the phrasing is brought into concord by a oneness in the spirit.

Another place in Matthew one reads of the Lord preaching flight to His Apostles, confirming His counsel with a sentence from Zechariah. "It is written," He tells them, "I will strike the shepherd, and the sheep shall be scattered" [Matthew 26:31; Zechariah 13:7]. This read differently in both Septuagint and Hebrew, for it is not God Who speaks in person, as the Evangelist has it, but the prophet who petitions God the Father, "Strike the shepherd, and the flock shall be scattered." According to my opinion – and I have prudent commentators with me – here the Evangelist is guilty of a fault in presuming to attribute a phrase to God which the prophet utters. Again, the same Evangelist, Matthew, writes that, at the warning of an angel, Joseph took the Infant and His mother, traveled into Egypt and remained there until Herod died; these events occurred, according to Matthew, so that the Lord's words, spoken through the mouth of the prophet Hosea, might be fulfilled, "Out of Egypt I have summoned my son" [Matthew 2:15, quoting Hosea 11:1]. The Latin manuscripts do not give the quotation in this way, for the authoritative Hebrew text has the following from the Book of Hosea, "When Israel was a child I loved him then, and called my son out of Egypt." This the Septuagint translates, "When Israel was a child I loved him then, and called his sons out of Egypt." Now, are these translations to be repudiated because they have altered a passage referring primarily to the mystery of Christ? Or would it be better to forgive the translators on the ground of human frailty, using as justification that saying of James, "In many things we offend everybody. If any man does not offend by what he says, then he is a perfect man and able also to restrain the whole body" [James 3:2].

One further example should clarify this point. "And He came and resided in a city called Nazareth," Matthew writes, "so that the prophets' saying might be accomplished: 'He shall be called a Nazarene'" [Matthew 2:23]. Let those men affecting to use only the most felicitous phrase, those fastidious critics of everything that is published, tell us where they first read the above quotation in Matthew. They cannot? Then let me inform them that the source is from Isaiah, for in the passage which reads and translates, "There shall come forth a bough out of the stem of Jesse, a bough should grow from its roots," in the Hebrew idiom this reads, "There shall come forth a bough out of the stem of Jesse, and a Nazarene shall grow from his roots" [Isaiah 11:1]. How can the Septuagint omit the word Nazarene? Why, is it not forbidden to substitute one word for another? It is sacrilegious to conceal or disregard a mystery of God.

But we should move on to other examples. The brevity of a letter forbids one to linger over a single point.

The same Matthew says elsewhere, "Now all this was accomplished to fulfill the word spoken by the prophet, Behold, a virgin shall conceive and bear a son, and *she* shall call him Emmanuel" [Matthew 1:22-23; Isaiah 7:14]. Now Ahaz shall not call Him this, for he was convicted of a lack of true belief; nor shall the Jews, for they eventually denied the Lord; but it is the virgin herself, who is to conceive and bear Him, who shall name Him.

Even greater discrepancies may be discovered in another passage from Matthew – the one in which we read how Herod was disturbed at the Magi's arrival, and how, gathering the scribes and priests, he demanded

[12] Translation modified from Carroll's "in the Vulgate", for *nostraque translatio* 'our translation'. A few lines below Carroll has "are the Vulgate and the Septuagint to be repudiated" for *repudiandi sunt* '[they] are repudiated'; this has been modified to "are these translations to be repudiated". Later "in the Vulgate" for *in vulgata editione* has been changed to "in the Greek translation". [Ed]

that they inform him where the Christ was supposed to be born. They replied, according to Matthew, "In Bethlehem of Judaea: for thus it is written by the prophet, And you, O Bethlehem in the land of Judah, for out of you shall emerge a leader who shall rule my people Israel" [Matthew 2:5-6]. In the Greek translation this passage stands, "And you, O Bethlehem, house of Ephratah, are a small part among the thousands of Judah, yet one shall emerge from you for me to be a prince in Israel." You will be even more astonished, Pammachius, at the discordancy in words and order between Matthew and the Greek Septuagint if you refer to the Hebrew, which reads, "And you, O Bethlehem Ephratah, though you be little among the thousands of Judah, yet out of you he shall emerge to me who is to rule in Israel." Consider the Evangelist's phrase word by word. For his "the land of Judah," the Hebrew has "Ephratah" while the Greek gives "the house of Ephratah." Again, Matthew's "are not the least among the leaders of Judah," becomes in the Seventy Translators "are a small part among the thousands of Judah," while in the original it is "though you be little among the thousands of Judah" [Micah 5:2]. Here is a contradiction – and not merely a verbal one – between the Evangelist and the original prophet and the Greek version which agrees, here at least, with the Hebrew. Notice that the Evangelist says he is not small among the rulers of Judah, while the original passage says exactly the contrary: "you are indeed small and insignificant; but small and insignificant as you are out of you shall emerge a leader in Israel," – an opinion, by the way, similar to that of the Apostle when he remarks, "God has chosen the infirm things of the world to confound the powerful things" [1 Corinthians 1:27]. And finally, the last clause in Matthew, "who shall rule" or "who shall feed my people Israel" clearly runs differently in the original prophet.

Now I have not referred to these passages in order to convict the Evangelists of falsification – an indictment applicable only to impious men like Celsus, Porphyry and Julian Apostate. To bring home to my critics their own paucity of information, and to obtain from them such consideration in the matter of a mere letter which, whether they like it or not, they must concede to the Apostles in the Gospel: this was my only intention. One or two more illustrations might help to establish my case. Mark, the disciple of Peter, begins his Gospel, "This is the beginning of the Gospel of Jesus Christ, as it is written in Isaiah the prophet: Behold, I send my angel before your face who shall prepare your way. The voice of one crying in the wilderness, Prepare the way of the Lord, straighten his paths" [Mark 1:1-3]. Two different prophets, however, were called on here to make this one quotation: the first half, "Behold, I send my angel," comes from Malachi, the second, describing the voice in the wilderness, from Isaiah [Malachi 3:1; Isaiah 40:3]. On what grounds, then, has Mark attributed the entire prophecy to Isaiah, when it is really a compound of two prophets? Ignorant presumption may solve this trifling question – that is, if it is able – and I will in turn beg pardon for the way in which I translated Epiphanius' letter.

The same Mark, however, brings in front of us the Savior addressing the Pharisees, "Have you never read what David did when he and his followers were hard pressed and hungry? David entered the House of God in the days when Abiathar was high priest, and ate the bread of proposition which only the priests could lawfully eat" [Mark 2:25-26]. If we confirm the source of this incident in Samuel (commonly called *The Book of Kings*), we discover that the high priest's name was not Abiathar but Ahimelech, the same who later was executed with the other priests of Doeg at Saul's command [1 Samuel 21:1, 22:16-18].

Similar trifling mistakes occur in the Apostle Paul. To the Corinthians he writes, "If they had known it, they would not have crucified the Lord of glory. But, as it is written, eye has not seen nor ear heard, nor has it entered into the heart of man, the things God has prepared for those who love him" [1 Corinthians 2:8-9]. Some Biblical commentators trace the source of Paul's quotation to the ravings of the apocryphal books, maintaining that the phrase comes from the Revelation of Elijah.[13] The fact, however, is that Isaiah is the real source, for, according to the Hebrew text, "Since the very beginning the ear has not heard, nor has the eye perceived those things which, O God, besides Yourself You have prepared for those who wait for You" [Isaiah 64:4]. This passage the Septuagint alters considerably, "Since the beginning we have heard not, neither have our eyes seen any God besides You and Your true operations, and You will show mercy to them who wait for You." Understanding, then, the actual source of the quotation, one notices that Paul has not translated literally word for word, but, using a paraphrase, has given the sense though in different phrasing. One more example from St. Paul could in his letter to the Romans, where he quotes the following selection from Isaiah, "Behold, I place in Sion a stone to stumble on, an offensive rock" [Romans 9:33; Isaiah 8:14, cf. also 28:16]. Strangely enough, here Paul's quotation disagrees with the Greek version, yet agrees with the original Hebrew. A completely opposite meaning is given by the Septuagint, "that you should not fall on an offensive rock or a disastrous stone." And when Peter employs the same passage he agrees with both Paul and the Hebrew, "For men who do not have faith, a stone to stumble on and an offensive rock" [1 Peter 2:8].

[13] A lost apocalyptic text. [Ed]

For all these examples it should be apparent that the Apostles and the Evangelists in quoting from Old Testament sources have tried to communicate the meaning rather than the literal words, and that they have not cared greatly to preserve exact phrases and sentence constructions, so long as they could clearly present the substance of their subject to men's understanding.

One of the most striking misquotations is made by Stephen, Christ's first martyr, in the story he narrates to the Jewish Assembly, according to St. Luke's Gospel:

> With seventy five souls (Stephen recalls) Jacob traveled down into Egypt, and died there himself; and our fathers were removed to Sichem, and laid there in the graveyard purchased by Abraham for a sum of money from the sons of Hamor. [Acts 7:15-16]

One discovers that in Genesis this story is quite another matter. There, Abraham actually purchases a double cave and its neighboring field from Ephron the Hittite, son of Zohar, and eventually buries his wife Sarah in this new graveyard. As far as Jacob is concerned, after he returned with his wives and sons from Mesopotamia he pitched his tents near Salem, a city of Shechem in Canaan, and there he remained, purchasing "a piece of land where he encamped from Hamor, father of Sichem, for the sum of a hundred lambs. After constructing an altar on this land, Jacob invoked the God of Israel" [Genesis 33:18-20]. Obviously then, Stephen the Martyr is wrong: Abraham bought the field from Ephron, not Hamor; he was not buried in Sichem but in Hebron, corruptly called Arboch; and the twelve patriarchs, "our fathers," were not laid in Arboch but in Sichem, in the graveyard purchased by Abraham, not Jacob.

I am going to postpone any solution to this delicate problem of misquotation and paraphrase, so that my critics may have time to compare texts and sources, and realize that in dealing with the Bible one must consider the substance and not the literal words.

One more example of this, however, might be edifying. In Hebrew the twenty-second Psalm opens with the exact words Our Lord later utters from the cross "*Eli, Eli, lama sabachthani*? – my God, my God, why have you abandoned me?" [Psalm 22:1; Matthew 27:46; Mark 15:34]. Perhaps my learned critics can enlighten me why the Greek translation here inserts the imperative, "look down on me," right after the invocation, "My God, my God." They will answer, I have little doubt, that no harm is done to the meaning by adding a few additional words. Then let them also realize that, if in the rush of dictating my translation to Epiphanius' letter, I have omitted a word here and there, I have not jeopardized the position of the churches.

To enumerate what noticeable additions and omissions the Septuagint has made, and catalogue all the passages in church copies marked by asterisks and daggers, would, I am sure, be tedious indeed. But there is another problem that should be mentioned here. The Jews usually ridicule our Greek version [the Septuagint] of this sentence from Isaiah, "Blessed is the man who has seed in Sion and servants in Jerusalem" [Isaiah 31:9], and also the phrase in Amos following the description of luxurious living, "They have thought of these things to be halting and not likely to fly" [Amos 6:4-6] – a very rhetorical sentence, by the way, worthy of Cicero himself. But the question is: how shall Christians deal with the authentic Hebrew text when these two sentences above and others like them are omitted in the Septuagint, passages so numerous that it would take an infinity of books to reproduce them? In the older translations used by Christians, omissions are indicated by an asterisk, and could also be discovered by a careful comparison between our interpretation and the older ones.[14] Nevertheless, the Septuagint has rightly kept its place in Christian churches, either because it is the original translation made before Christ's coming, or else because the Apostles used it – only, however, in those sections where it does not contradict the Hebrew original.

On the other hand, Christians are right in rejecting the version made by Aquila, proselyte and controversial translator, who attempted to translate not only words but their etymologies as well. Who could accept, for instance, his version of "corn, wine and oil" which runs: χεῦμα, ὀπωρισμόν, στιλπνότητα or, as we might say, "pouring, fruitgathering, and shining" [Deuteronomy 7:13]. And, because Hebrew has other prefixes in addition to the article, Aquila must with his unfortunate pedantry translate syllable by syllable, letter by letter, like this: οὖν τόν οὐρανόν καί οὖν τήν γήν, a grammatical construction allowed by neither Greek nor Latin.[15] How many phrases there are which, though beautiful in Greek, if translated literally sound

[14] Translation again modified from Carroll's "my Vulgate version", for *nostra interpretatio* 'our interpretation/translation'. It is unclear here whether Jerome is referring to (a) the Itala, (b) the ongoing but still unpublished work he had at this writing been doing for four years (since 391) on the translation that would be called 'Jerome's Vulgate', or (c) the interpretation or exposition he has been presenting in this letter. It is most likely the first; even if it is the second, however, it should not be described as 'the Vulgate', because it became the 'Vulgate' or *vulgata* by being accepted into common usage. [Ed]

[15] Genesis 1:1. Since the Hebrew sign for the accusative is identical to that for the preposition 'with', Aquila translated '[God created] the heaven and the earth' as "with the heaven and with the earth". [Ed]

awkward in Latin; and how many are pleasing in Latin but, if the word order remains unaltered, sound discordant in Greek.

But to move on from this infinite field of discussion and to show you, O most Christian of noblemen, O most noble of Christians, the kind of so-called falsehood which has been reprehended in my translation of Epiphanius' letter, here are the opening words in the original, and then my rendition:'Ἔδει ἡμᾶς, ἀγαπητέ, μὴ τῇ οἰήσει τῶν κλήρων φέρεσθαι, which I recall having rendered as: "Dearly beloved, we should not abuse our position as clergymen to gratify our own pride." Look, look! they howl, how many lies in one single sentence! In the first place, they point out, ἀγαπητός means "loved one," not "dearly beloved." Next οἴησις means "estimation," not "pride," for this and not οἴδημα is the word used. Οἴδημα means "a swelling" but οἴδημα signifies judgment.

Now I do not ridicule any Christian because he happens to lack ability to express himself. Would that all Christians could say with Socrates: "I know that I know nothing,"[16] and fulfill the command of another wise man: "Know yourself".[17] Holy simplicity I have always admired, but not rude verbosity, for whoever claims he imitates the Apostles' literary style should first emulate their lives. That plainness in their speech and style came from their profound sanctity; and by raising men from death they were able to confute the syllogisms of Aristotle and the contorted ingenuities of Chrysippus.

On the other hand, it would be ridiculous if one of us – living as we do among the wealth of Croesus and the luxuries of Sardanapalus – were to brag about mere simplicity and ignorance. It would be rather like saying that all thieves and criminals would be cultivated gentlemen if they were to hide their bloodstained swords in philosophy books instead of the usual hiding place, hollow tree trunks.

This has certainly exceeded the proper length of a letter, my dear Pammachius, but I have hardly exceeded the length of my indignation. Although I am called a liar, and am torn to pieces among the sewing-rooms of women, I am content to repudiate the accusations against me without stooping to retaliate in kind. I leave everything to your good judgment. If you wish, you can read Epiphanius' letter in the original and in my translation; and, if you do, you will immediately see the true value of my accusers' melancholy dirges and complaints. Above all, I am satisfied if I have taught something to one of my dearest friends, and am content simply to remain concealed in my cell here in Bethlehem and wait for Judgment Day. If it is possible, and my enemies permit, I hope soon to write for you – not philippics[18] like Demosthenes and Cicero – but useful commentaries on the Bible.

Who Was The First Lying Author?
From *Preface to the Pentateuch* (*Praefatio in Pentateuchem*, 401)
Translated by Moses Hadas

I know not who was the first lying author to construct the seventy cells at Alexandria, in which they were separated and yet all wrote the same words, whereas Aristeas, one of the bodyguard of the said Ptolemy, and long after him Josephus have said nothing of the sort, but write that they were assembled in a single hall and conferred together, not that they prophesied. For it is one thing to be a prophet, another to be an interpreter.

Augustine

Augustine (Aurelius Augustinus, 354-430) is one of the pivotal thinkers in the Western tradition: the man who not only formulated but instituted, politically, a synthesis of Plato and the New Testament that informs most of our deepest 'intuitions' about ourselves and our world today. As the chief architect of medieval theology, which defined intellectual orthodoxy for over a thousand years, he has presided over philosophical and scientific 'correctness' well into our era – though often not in name. *On Christian Doctrine* in particular has been foundational for modern science, including the mathematical sciences (see 2.31.48-2.32.50) and especially linguistics and semiotics; due to the Renaissance myth according to which 'science' rejected and displaced 'theology', however, Descartes and Galileo and Saussure and others are given credit for methodological innovations that are spelled out clearly by Augustine.

Augustine was born to a pagan father and Christian mother in what is now Algeria, and was sent to Carthage to get the best education his parents' slender financial resources could buy. Originally intending to go into government service, he happened to read Cicero's *Hortensius* (now lost) and dedicated himself to philosophy; immersed himself in Manichean Christianity, then in Neoplatonism, then in Plato's own works, and finally in the New Testament. Having agreed to Christianity intellectually, he was converted spiritually in 386 through a vision of Continence calling him to celibacy. His story of his intellectual, emotional, sexual, and spiritual development

[16] Plato, *Apology* 21d. [Ed]

[17] Often attributed to the Spartan magistrate Chilon. [Ed]

[18] Philippic: one of the orations Demosthenes delivered against Philip II of Macedonia, or, by extension, any oratorical denunciation. [Ed]

in the *Confessions* (397-98) is a classic of world literature.

Now began Augustine's political life as a spiritual leader in the Christian church of Northern Africa, in Hippo. Ordained in 391 and installed as bishop of Hippo in 396, he fought tenaciously and highly successfully for the exclusion of groups he considered heretics (notably the Pelagians and Donatists) from the 'true' church, and wrote prolifically. His major works included exegeses of Genesis, the Psalms, and the sermon on the mount; polemics against the various heretical groups he was attempting to expunge; his monastic *Rule*, which was adopted by his own monastic order and over a hundred others throughout the Middle Ages; and, most important for Western civilization, the *Confessions*, *On Christian Doctrine*, and *The City of God* (413-426), the last of which was the founding document of the medieval church as theocratic utopia.

Augustine's role in the history of translation theory cannot be overestimated. He conceived translation specifically as a systematic undoing of the scattering of tongues at the Tower of Babel, by identifying the *translatum* or tranferred message with the unitary Word of God and then policing the transfer. Translation may seem to be a mere ineffectual crossing of linguistic barriers carried out by imperfect, fallible humans; it may seem to partake of the marketplace (the bartering of meanings, this for that) or of the nomadic life (the constant reinscription of culture on a shifting geography, flux the nomad's only stability). But for Augustine these are mere appearances, mere surface; in the depths lies true translation, perfect translation, ideal translation, the perfect transfer of a stable meaning from one language to another by the ideal interpreter.

The Use of Translations
From *On Christian Doctrine* (*De doctrina Christiana*, 428)
Translated by D. W. Robertson, Jr.

I

1. Just as I began, when I was writing about things, by warning that no one should consider them except as they are, without reference to what they signify beyond themselves, now when I am discussing signs I wish it understood that no one should consider them for what they are but rather for their value as signs which signify something else. A sign is a thing which causes us to think of something beyond the impression the thing itself makes upon the senses. Thus if we see a track, we think of the animal that made the track; if we see smoke, we know that there is a fire which causes it; if we hear the voice of a living being, we attend to the emotion it expresses; and when a trumpet sounds, a soldier should know whether it is necessary to advance or to retreat, or whether the battle demands some other response.

2. Among signs, some are natural and others are conventional. Those are natural which, without any desire or intention of signifying, make us aware of something beyond themselves, like smoke which signifies fire. It does this without any will to signify, for even when smoke appears alone, observation and memory of experience with things bring a recognition of an underlying fire. The track of a passing animal belongs to this class, and the face of one who is wrathful or sad signifies his emotion even when he does not wish to show that he is wrathful or sad, just as other emotions are signified by the expression even when we do not deliberately set out to show them. But it is not proposed here to discuss signs of this type. Since the class formed a division of my subject, I could not disregard it completely, and this notice of it will suffice.

II

3. Conventional signs are those which living creatures show to one another for the purpose of conveying, in so far as they are able, the motion of their spirits or something which they have sensed or understood. Nor is there any other reason for signifying, or for giving signs, except for bringing forth and transferring to another mind the action of the mind in the person who makes the sign. We propose to consider and to discuss this class of signs in so far as men are concerned with it, for even signs given by God and contained in the Holy Scriptures are of this type also, since they were presented to us by the men who wrote them. Animals also have signs which they use among themselves, by means of which they indicate their appetites. For a cock who finds food makes a sign with his voice to the hen so that she runs to him. And the dove calls his mate with a cry or is called by her in turn, and there are many similar examples which may be adduced. Whether these signs, or the expression or cry of a man in pain, express the motion of the spirit without intention of signifying or are truly shown as signs is not in question here and does not pertain to our discussion, and we remove this division of the subject from this work as superfluous.

III

4. Among the signs by means of which men express their meanings to one another, some pertain to the sense of sight, more to the sense of hearing, and very few to the other senses. For when we nod, we give a sign only to the sight of the person whom we wish by that sign to make a participant in our will. Some signify many things through the motions of their hands, and actors give signs to those who understand with the motions of all their members as if narrating

things to their eyes. And banners and military standards visibly indicate the will of the captains. And all of these things are like so many visible words. More signs, as I have said, pertain to the ears, and most of these consist of words. But the trumpet, the flute, and the harp make sounds which are not only pleasing but also significant, although as compared with the number of verbal signs the number of signs of this kind are few. For words have come to be predominant among men for signifying whatever the mind conceives if they wish to communicate it to anyone. However, Our Lord gave a sign with the odor of the ointment with which His feet were anointed [John 12:3-8]; and the taste of the sacrament of His body and blood signified what He wished [Matthew 26:28; Luke 22:19-20]; and when the woman was healed by touching the hem of His garment [Matthew 9:20-22], something was signified. Nevertheless, a multitude of innumerable signs by means of which men express their thoughts is made up of words. And I could express the meaning of all signs of the type here touched upon in words, but I would not be able at all to make the meanings of words clear by these signs.

IV

5. But because vibrations in the air soon pass away and remain no longer than they sound, signs of words have been constructed by means of letters. Thus words are shown to the eyes, not in themselves but through certain signs which stand for them. These signs could not be common to all peoples because of the sin of human dissension which arises when one people seizes the leadership for itself. A sign of this pride is that tower erected in the heavens where impious men deserved that not only their minds but also their voices should be dissonant [Genesis 11:1-9].

V

6. Thus it happened that even the Sacred Scripture, by which so many maladies of the human will are cured, was set forth in one language, but so that it could be spread conveniently through all the world it was scattered far and wide in the various languages of translators that it might be known for the salvation of peoples who desired to find in it nothing more than the thoughts and desires of those who wrote it and through these the will of God, according to which we believe those writers spoke ...

X

15. There are two reasons why things written are not understood: they are obscured either by unknown or by ambiguous signs. For signs are either literal or figurative. They are called literal when they are used to designate those things on account of which they were instituted; thus we say *bos* [ox] when we mean an animal of a herd because all men using the Latin language call it by that name just as we do. Figurative signs occur when that thing which we designate by a literal sign is used to signify something else; thus we say 'ox' and by that syllable understand the animal which is ordinarily designated by that word, but again by that animal we understand an evangelist, as is signified in the Scripture, according to the interpretation of the Apostle, when it says, "Thou shalt not muzzle the ox that treadeth out the corn" [Deuteronomy 25:4].

XI

16. Against unknown literal signs the sovereign remedy is a knowledge of languages. And Latin-speaking men, whom we have here undertaken to instruct, need two others for a knowledge of the Divine Scriptures, Hebrew and Greek, so that they may turn back to earlier exemplars if the infinite variety of Latin translations gives rise to any doubts. Again, in these books we frequently find untranslated Hebrew words, like *amen*, *alleluia*, *racha*, *hosanna*, and so on, of which some, although they could be translated, have been preserved from antiquity on account of their holier authority, like *amen* and *alleluia*; others, like the other two mentioned above, are said not to be translatable into another language. For there are some words in some languages which cannot be translated into other languages. And this is especially true of interjections which signify the motion of the spirit rather than any part of a rational concept. And these two belong to this class: *racha* is said to be an expression of indignation and *hosanna* an expression of delight. But a knowledge of these two languages is not necessary for these few things, which are easy to know and to discover, but, as we have said, it is necessary on account of the variety of translations. We can enumerate those who have translated the Scriptures from Hebrew into Greek, but those who have translated them into Latin are innumerable. In the early times of the faith when anyone found a Greek codex, and he thought that he had some facility in both languages, he attempted to translate it.

XII

17. This situation would rather help than impede understanding if readers would only avoid negligence. For an inspection of various translations frequently makes obscure passages clear. For example, one translator renders a passage in the prophet Isaiah: "Despise not the family of thy seed"; but another says: "Despise not thy own flesh" [Isaiah 58:7]. Either confirms the other, for one may be explained by means of the other. Thus the "flesh" may be taken literally, so that one may find himself admonished that no one should despise his own body, and the "family of the seed" may be taken figuratively so that it is understood to mean 'Christians' born spiritually from the seed of the Word which produced us. But a collation of the translations makes it probable that the meaning is a literal precept that we should not despise those of our own blood, since when we compare "family of the seed" with

"flesh", blood relations come especially to mind. Whence, I think, comes the statement of the Apostle, who said, "If, by any means, I may provoke to emulation them who are my flesh, and may save some of them" [Romans 11:14], that is, so that, emulating those who had believed, they also might believe. He calls the Jews his "flesh" because of blood relationship. Again, a text of the prophet Isaiah reads: "If you will not believe, you shall not understand", and in another translation: "If you will not believe, you shall not continue" [Isaiah 7:9]. Which of these is to be followed is uncertain unless the text is read in the original language. But both of them nevertheless contain something of great value for the discerning reader. It is difficult for translators to become so disparate that they do not show a similarity in one area of meaning. Thus, although understanding lies in the sight of the Eternal, faith nourishes as children are nourished with milk in the cradles of temporal things. Now "we walk by faith and not by sight" [2 Corinthians 5:7]. Unless we walk by faith, we shall not be able to come to that sight which does not fail but continues through a cleansed understanding uniting us with Truth. On account of this principle one said, "If you will not believe, you shall not continue", and the other said, "If you will not believe, you shall not understand".

18. Many translators are deceived by ambiguity in the original language which they do not understand, so that they transfer the meaning to something completely alien to the writer's intention. Thus some codices have "their feet are sharp to shed blood", for the word *oxús* in Greek means both 'sharp' and 'swift'. But he sees the meaning who translates "their feet swift to shed blood" [Romans 3:15, from Proverbs 1:16]; the other, drawn in another direction by an ambiguous sign, erred. And such translations are not obscure; they are false, and when this is the situation the codices are to be emended rather than interpreted. The same situation arises when some, because *móschos* in Greek means 'calf', do not know that *moscheúmata* means 'transplantings', and have translated it 'calves'. This error appears in so many texts that one hardly finds anything else written, although the sense is very clear and is supported by the succeeding words. For the expression "bastard slips shall not take deep root" [Wisdom of Jesus Son of Sirach 4:3] makes better sense than to speak of 'calves', which walk on the earth and do not take root in it. The rest of the context, moreover, supports this translation.

XIII

19. Since the meaning which many interpreters, according to their ability and judgment, seek to convey is not apparent unless we consult the language being translated, and since many translators err from the sense of the original authors unless they are very learned, we must either seek a knowledge of those languages from which Scripture is translated into Latin or we must consult the translations of those who translate word for word, not because they suffice but because by means of them we may test the truth or falsity of those who have sought to translate meanings as well as words. For often not only single words but whole locutions are translated because they cannot be expressed in Latin if one wishes to adhere to the ancient and customary idiom of the Latin language. These unidiomatic expressions do not impede the understanding, but they offend those who take more delight in things when the signs for them are governed by a certain correctness. For what is called a solecism is nothing else than an arrangement of words which does not conform to the law followed by those who have spoken before us with some authority. Whether one says 'among men' by saying *inter homines* or by saying *inter hominibus* does not affect the person considering things rather than signs. In the same way, what else is a barbarism except a word pronounced with letters or sounds different from those which those who spoke Latin before us were accustomed to use? Whether *ignoscere* [to forgive] is spoken with a long or short third syllable makes little difference to a man asking God to forgive his sins, in whatever way he can pronounce the word. What then is integrity of expression except the preservation of the customs of others, confirmed by the authority of ancient speakers?

20. The more men are offended by these things, the weaker they are. And they are weaker in that they wish to seem learned, not in the knowledge of things, by which we are truly instructed, but in the knowledge of signs, in which it is very difficult not to be proud. For even the knowledge of things frequently raises the neck unless it is disciplined by the yoke of the Lord. It does not impede the understanding of the reader to find written: "What is the land in which these dwell upon it, whether it is good or evil, and what are the cities in which these dwell in them?" [Numbers 13:20]. I consider this to be the idiom of an alien tongue rather than the expression of a more profound meaning. There is also the expression that we cannot now take away from the chant of the people: "but upon him shall my sanctification flourish" [Psalm 131:18, 132:18]. Nothing is detracted from the meaning, although the more learned hearer may wish to correct it so that *florebit* is spoken instead of *floriet*, and nothing impedes the correction but the custom of the chanters. These things may easily be disregarded if one does not wish to pay attention to that which does not detract from a sound understanding. Then there is the expression of the Apostle: "The foolishness of God is wiser than men; and the weakness of God is stronger than men" [1 Corinthians 1:25]. If anyone wished to keep the Greek idiom and say "The foolishness of God is wiser of men, and the weakness of God is stronger of men",

the labor of the vigilant reader would lead him to the true meaning, but a somewhat slower reader might either not understand it or misunderstand it. For not only is such a phrase incorrect in the Latin language, it also obscures the truth in ambiguity. Thus the foolishness of men or the weakness of men might seem wiser or stronger than God's. And even *sapientius est hominibus* [wiser than men] does not lack ambiguity, although it contains no solecism. Without the illumination of the idea being conveyed it is not clear whether *hominibus* is ablative or dative. It would be better to say *sapientius est quam homines* and *fortius est quam homines*, which express the ideas 'wiser than men' and 'stronger than men' without any possible ambiguity.

XIV

21. We shall speak later of ambiguous signs; now we are discussing unknown signs, of which there are two forms, in so far as they apply to words. For either an unknown word or an unknown expression may impede the reader. If these come from foreign languages we must consult one who speaks those languages, or learn them ourselves if we have leisure and ability, or make a comparison of various translations. If we do not know certain words or expressions in our own language, we become familiar with them by reading and hearing them. Nothing is better commended to the memory than those types of words and expressions which we do not know, so that when one more learned appears who may be questioned, or when a passage appears in reading where the preceding or following context makes their meaning clear, we may easily with the aid of the memory refer to them and learn them. Such is the force of habit even in learning that those who are nourished and educated in the Holy Scriptures wonder more at other expressions and think them poorer Latin than those used in the Scriptures, even though these do not appear in the writings of the Latin authors. In this matter of learning a comparison and weighing of various translations is also useful. But falsity should be rejected. For those who desire to know the Sacred Scriptures should exercise their ingenuity principally that texts not emended should give way to those emended, at least among those which come from one source of translation.

XV

22. Among these translations the *Itala* is to be preferred, for it adheres to the words and is at the same time perspicacious regarding meaning.[1] And in emending Latin translations, Greek translations are to be consulted, of which the Septuagint carries most authority in so far as the Old Testament is concerned. In all the more learned churches it is now said that this translation was so inspired by the Holy Spirit that many men spoke as if with the mouth of one. It is said and attested by many of not unworthy faith that, although the translators were separated in various cells while they worked, nothing was to be found in any version that was not found in the same words and with the same order of words in all of the others. Who would compare any other authority with this, or, much less, prefer another? But even if they conferred and arrived at a single opinion on the basis of common judgment and consent, it is not right or proper for any man, no matter how learned, to seek to emend the consensus of so many older and more learned men. Therefore, even though something is found in Hebrew versions different from what they have set down, I think we should cede to the divine dispensation by which they worked to the end that the books which the Jewish nation refused to transmit to other peoples, either out of envy or for religious reasons, might be revealed so early, by the authority and power of King Ptolemy, to the nations which in the future were to believe in Our Lord. It may be that the Holy Spirit judged that they should translate in a manner befitting the people whom they addressed and that they should speak as if with one voice. Yet, as I have said before, a comparison with those translators who adhered most closely to the words of the original is not without use in explaining their meaning. Latin translations of the Old Testament, as I set out to say, are to be emended on the authority of the Greeks, and especially on the authority of those who, although there were seventy, are said to have spoken as if with one voice. Moreover, if the books of the New Testament were confusing in the variety of their Latin translations, they should certainly give place to the Greek versions, especially to those which are found among more learned and diligent Churches.

C. Chirius Fortunatianus

Little is known about C. Chirius or Curius Fortunatianus (late fourth to mid-fifth century C.E.), except that he was a Roman lawyer who drew up a compendium of technical rhetoric in three books, all in the same question-and-answer format. All we know about when he lived is that Cassiodorus,

[1] The 'Itala' or 'Vetus Itala', as it was also often called, is nowadays referred to as the 'Old Latin' version – actually more a fragmentary collection of translations of individual books than an entire Bible translation (when it was done the Biblical canon had not yet been formalized; that happened in 387 C.E.). No one knows who the translators were or when they wrote, but internal evidence (the prevalence of Hebraisms) suggests that they may have been Jews; scholars date the translation work in the second century C.E. Jerome's Vulgate was partly a revision of the Old Latin. [Ed]

whose life spanned most of the 6th century, quotes from him.

Translation as 'Exercitatio'
From the *Artis rhetoricae scholicae* (5th century)
Translated by Rita Copeland

In what ways are words coined? First we carry over Greek words, so that from them we can invent new Latin words ... What is the chief point of exercise, that is, what does it consist of? Four things. What are they? That you translate Greek into Latin, write challenging compositions, practice paraphrasing,[1] and diligently practice speaking *ex tempore*.

Anicius Manlius Severinus Boethius

Boethius (470/475-524) was a Roman philosopher and statesman who was best known through the Middle Ages as the author of *The Consolation of Philosophy*, a work that he wrote in prison in the years before his execution for treason in 524. Called by Roger Bacon "the first translator", he set himself the task of translating into Latin the complete works of Aristotle, and possibly afterwards Plato; he fell far short of his goal, but did complete the *Categories* and the six volumes of the *Organon*, along with sundry Greek commentaries on Aristotle (including Porphyry's) that became basic texts for the scholastics. It is often said that Boethius gave the Middle Ages as much of Aristotle as they would have until the conquest of Islamic Spain in the eleventh and twelfth centuries – and that at his death translation from Greek into Latin ground to a near-complete halt for 600 years.

Boethius came of the ancient Roman Anicius family, which had counted among its ancestors the Emperor Olybrius. The family had been Christian for a century when Boethius was born, and he was read by the Middle Ages as a Christian scholar, though in fact the *Consolation* is explicitly a Neoplatonic credo and shows no signs of Christian faith. His father was consul in 487, and Boethius himself became consul under the Ostrogothic king Theodoric in 510; in 520 he was elevated to the position of *magister officiorum*, a kind of White House Chief of Staff, and his two sons shared the consulship in 522. Around the same time he became embroiled in the ongoing battle between Rome and Constantinople: apparently accused of conspiring with the Byzantine emperor Justin I, who was an orthodox Christian, against Theodoric, an Arian Christian, he was jailed for treason and various other crimes (including magic) and eventually executed.

Boethius was one of the most widely read writers of the Middle Ages. His *Consolation* was second only to Jerome's Vulgate Bible in popularity; it charmed with its alternating prose and verse style the medieval readers to whom it introduced the thought of Plato, and it sparked several philosophical controversies, most notably that between nominalism and realism. His translations of and commentaries on Aristotle helped lay the groundwork for scholasticism; and his remarks on word-for-word translation joined catchphrases from Cicero, Horace, and Jerome as the theoretical commonplaces of the era.

Porphyry's *Eisagoge* was a third-century introduction to Aristotle's logic; Boethius wrote a Latin commentary on Victorinus' translation of it, then later, some time before his appointment as consul in 510, retranslated it himself and added a second volume to his commentary. His famous remarks on translation, printed below, are the opening lines of that second volume.

Boethius' remarks are most famous for their sly twisting of Horace on the faithful translator, which set the stage for many a later quasi-Horatian defense of literalism as well.

Committing the Fault of the True Interpreter
From 'Commentary on Porphyry's *Eisagoge*' (*In Isagoge Porphyrii Commenta*, 510 C.E.?)
Translated by Charles S. F. Burnett

I fear that I shall commit the fault of the faithful interpreter when I render each word by a word corresponding to it.[1] The reason for this approach is that, in the writings in which knowledge of the subject matter is sought, it is not the charm of limpid speech but the unsullied truth that has to be expressed. Therefore I feel I have been most useful if, in composing books of philosophy in the Latin language, not a single letter of the Greek is to be found missing.

Gregory the Great

Pope Gregory I (c. 540-604), also known as St. Gregory the Great, was the first pope to transform the papacy into the imperial power we associate it with today. Best known to the Middle

[1] From verse into prose and prose into verse. [Tr] For 'paraphrase' in his Latin original Fortunatianus has the Greek word *metaphrasis*, Quintilian's term for intralingual paraphrasing. [Ed]

[1] The 'faithful interpreter' or *fidus interpres* is Horace's derogatory term for the slavish word-for-word renderer (see above, pp. 15). [Ed]

Ages as the author of *The Book of Pastoral Care* (591), a spiritual and practical guide for bishops, he is best known today as the founder of the Papal States and thus of the pope's political authority.

The great-grandson of Pope Felix III (reigned 483-492), Gregory was born in Rome to patrician parents – like Boethius a century or so earlier, his mother Silvia may have come from the powerful Anicius family. In his young manhood he was apparently drawn into Roman politics by social strife (the Lombards threatened and finally attacked Italy in Gregory's 29th year), and he became administrative president of Rome at 32; but social strife seems also to have driven him out of politics after only two years in that post. Shortly thereafter he converted his entire considerable estate into funding for seven monasteries, one in the family's palace in Rome, six others on family holdings in Sicily. After several years as a diaconate in Rome, he was appointed papal nuncio to Constantinople by Pope Pelagius II (reigned 579-590), where he served until he was elected – against his own strenuous opposition – Pelagius' successor.

Known for his social concerns, Gregory devoted much of his papal rule to the alleviation of suffering among the poor; but in order to do so he also centralized the papal administration and consolidated the extensive papal land holdings, and thus contributed to the establishment of the imperial papacy. Drawing heavily on Augustine's *City of God*, he formulated the first overarching transcendental justification for the church's political power; he is remembered for his letters advocating a 'holy war' against heathens to convert them to Christianity, the military conversion of whole populations that Charlemagne and Pope Gregory VII were later to put into notoriously successful practice.

Gregory's passing remarks on translation are notable for their dogmatically 'correct' insistence on sense-for-sense rather than word-for-word translation – following the new Christian asceticism of Jerome and Augustine rather than, like Boethius earlier in the century, the ancient tradition of strict literalism.

Giving the Sense
From Letter to Aristobulus, Ex-Prefect and *Antigraphus* [secretary] (590/91)
Translated by James Barmby

Furthermore, if you should by any chance receive for interpretation a lengthy letter of mine, translate it, I pray you, not word for word, but so as to give the sense; since usually, when close rendering of the words is attended to, the force of the ideas is lost.

Mangling the Sense
From Letter to Narses, the Religious[1] (597/98)
Translated by James Barmby

But with respect to your saying in your letter that I ought to write to my most excellent daughter the lady Gurdia, and her most holy daughter the lady Theocrista, and their magnificent husbands, the lord Marinus and the lord Christidorus, and to give them some admonition about their souls, your most sweet Greatness well knows that there are none at present in the city of Constantinople who can translate well into Greek what has been dictated in Latin. For keeping to the words, but attending little to the sense, they both fail to make the words understood and also mangle the sense. On this account I have written shortly to my aforesaid daughter the lady Gurdia; but have not addressed the others.

John Scotus Eriugena

John Scotus Eriugena (or Erigena, 810-c. 877) was a theologian, scholar, and translator who is best known for his work in integrating Greek and Neoplatonist thought with Christian doctrine.

Born in Ireland, called the Scot, John spent the last three or so decades of his life at the court of the West Frankish king Charles II the Bald, who commissioned his many translations from Greek patristic writings – by St. Maximus the Confessor, St. Gregory of Nyssa, St. Epiphanius, and Pseudo-Dionysius the Areopagite. He also wrote original scholarly works on predestination (851) and "the divisions of nature" (862-66); the latter, his massive attempt to reconcile Neoplatonist theories of emanation with Christianity and his major work, was later condemned by the church for pantheism.

Like many medieval translators, John made only passing remarks on his work in prefaces; the remarks printed below are interesting, however, for the important distinction they draw between the translator, who simply (and literally) transfers the original text into Latin, and the expositor, who reframes it interpretively. The famous last line alludes to Horace via Boethius.

---

[1] The Narses here addressed as 'Religiosus' was probably the same as the 'Narses Comes' of I.6, and VI.14, and the 'Narses Patricius' of IV.32. For it is evident from the letters that he was of high rank at Constantinople, and greetings are sent through him to the same persons as in the other letters. He had now, we may suppose, devoted himself to the service of the Church in some capacity. [Tr]

Translator, Not Expositor
From prologue to translation of *De caelesti hierarchia* by Pseudo-Dionysius the Areopagite (mid-9th century)
Translated by Rita Copeland

If someone should find the language [of this translation] too cumbersome or unfamiliar let him bear in mind that neither he nor I can have a greater capacity for understanding than what God, who doles out each person's given powers (as He wishes), has provided. If someone should find the text of the aforesaid translation obscure or impenetrable, let him consider me the *translator* of this work, not its *expositor*. Indeed I fear that I have incurred the blame of the faithful translator.

King Alfred

King Alfred the Great (Aelfred, 849-899), king of Wessex from 871 to his death, has come down to us famous for promoting learning and preventing England from falling to the Danes.

Alfred always said he never wanted to be king (a scholar's life would probably have satisfied him), and as the fifth son in his family it might have seemed he had nothing to fear. All four of his older brothers died, however – the last, King Aethelred I, in battle against the Danes – and Alfred was crowned. As king he continued to fight the Danes until 878, when a massive victory compelled King Guthrum to surrender and to convert to Christianity. Seven years later the Danes who had conquered East Anglia attacked Wessex, and Alfred's army not only defeated them but captured London, causing all England not under Danish rule to declare him their king (and setting the stage for his son to reconquer the rest of England from the Danes).

Alfred was convinced, like many in his day, that the Viking raids were divine retribution for the decline of learning in England, and he worked throughout his reign to redress that problem. He ordered all wealthy young men to learn to read and write English. He convened learned men from Mercia, Wales, and the Continent. He commissioned the writing of the Anglo-Saxon Chronicle, which continued to be written for several centuries. He studied ancient and recent principles of legislation and instituted a significant new legal code. He attempted, largely unsuccessfully, to revive monasticism in England.

Above all, he learned Latin and began to translate "certain books which are most necessary for all men to know", including Augustine's *Soliloquies*, Boethius' *Consolation of Philosophy*, and St. Gregory the Great's *Pastoral Care* – and to commission other translations, such as Bishop Waerferth's Anglo-Saxon rendering of Gregory's *Dialogues*.

The letter to Bishop Waerferth was a kind of cover-letter enclosed with the manuscript of Alfred's Anglo-Saxon translation of St. Gregory's *Liber Regulae Pastoralis* or *Pastoral Care* (591); as he says in the letter, Alfred's idea was to send a manuscript of his translation to every one of his bishops, and the copy sent to Bishop Waerferth was apparently one of the first to be made and delivered. St. Gregory was especially beloved by the Anglo-Saxon clergy because he had been instrumental in their conversion, through the missionary he had sent to England, St. Augustine, three centuries earlier; and since St. Gregory's book was particularly concerned with Christian education, it was the perfect channel for Alfred's own educational program.

Translating Plainly and Clearly
Preface to Translation of Boethius' *Consolation of Philosophy* (887?)
Translated by Samuel Fox

King Alfred was translator of this book, and turned it from book Latin into English, as it is now done. Sometimes he set word by word, sometimes meaning of meaning,[1] as he the most plainly and most clearly could explain it, for the various and manifold worldly occupations which often busied him both in mind and in body. The occupations are to us very difficult to be numbered, which in his days came upon the kingdoms which he had undertaken, and yet when he had learned this book, and turned it from Latin into the English language, he afterwards composed it in verse, as it is now done. And he now prays, and for God's name implores every one of those who lists to read this book, that he would pray for him, and not blame him, if he more rightly understood it than he could. For every man must, according to his leisure, speak that *which* he speaketh, and do that which he doeth.[2]

Translating Books Which Are Most Necessary For All Men to Know
Letter to Bishop Waerferth, Preface to St. Gregory's *Pastoral Care* (890/97)
Translated by Michael Swanton

---

[1] Modern commentators note that there is actually very little word-for-word translating in the text. [Ed]

[2] Fox italicizes the *which* in that last sentence for the same reason King James's literalists did: to make a literal translation more or less comprehensible (a literal rendition would be "and by his leisure speak that he speaks"). [Ed]

This book is to go to Worcester
King Alfred sends greetings to Bishop Waerferth with his loving and friendly words, and would declare to you that it has very often come to my mind what wise men there were formerly throughout the English people, both in sacred and in secular orders; and how there were happy times then throughout England; and how the kings who had rule over the people in those days were obedient to God and his messengers, and both maintained their peace and their morality and their authority at home, and also enlarged their territory abroad; and how they prospered both in warfare and in wisdom; and also how zealous the sacred orders were both about teaching and about learning and all the services which they had to perform for God; and how men from abroad came here to this land in search of knowledge and instruction, and how we should now have to get them from abroad, if we were to have them. So complete was its decay among the English people that there were very few this side of Humber who could comprehend their services in English, or even translate a letter from Latin into English; and I imagine that there were not many beyond the Humber. There were so few of them that I cannot even remember a single one south of the Thames when I succeeded to the kingdom. Thanks be to Almighty God that now we have any supply of teachers. And therefore I command you to do, as I believe you wish, that you disengage yourself as often as you can from the affairs of this world, so that you can apply the wisdom which God has given you wherever you are able to apply it. Think what punishments then came upon us in this world when we neither loved it ourselves nor allowed it to other men – we loved only to be called Christians, and very few loved the virtues.

When I remembered all this, then I also remembered how, before it was all ravaged and burnt, I had seen how the churches throughout all England stood filled with treasures and books, and there was also a great multitude of God's servants – they had very little benefit from those books, because they could not understand anything of them, since they were not written in their own language. As if they had said: "Our forefathers who formerly held these places loved knowledge, and through it they acquired wealth and left it to us. One can see their footprints here still, but we cannot follow after them and therefore we have now lost both the wealth and the knowledge because we would not bend our mind to that course". When I remembered all this, then I wondered greatly at those good wise men who formerly existed throughout the English people and had fully studied all those books, that they did not wish to translate any part of them into their own language. But then I immediately answered myself and said: "They did not imagine that men should ever become so careless and learning so decayed; they refrained from it by intention and hoped that there would be the greater knowledge in this land the more languages we knew".

Then I remembered how the law was first found in the Hebrew language, and afterwards, when the Greeks learned it, they translated it into their own language, and all the other books as well. And afterwards in the same way the Romans, when they had learned them, they translated them all into their own language through learned interpreters. And all other Christian nations also translated some part of them into their own language. Therefore it seems better to me, if it seems so to you, that we also should translate certain books which are most necessary for all men to know, into the language that we can all understand, and also arrange it, as with God's help we very easily can if we have peace, so that all the youth of free men now among the English people, who have the means to be able to devote themselves to it, may be set to study for as long as they are of no other use, until the time they are able to read English writing well; afterwards one may teach further in the Latin language those whom one wishes to teach further and wishes to promote to holy orders.

Then when I remembered how the knowledge of Latin had previously decayed throughout the English people, and yet many could read English writing, I began amidst other various and manifold cares of this kingdom to translate into English the book which is called *Pastoralis* in Latin and 'Shepherd's Book' in English, sometimes word for word, sometimes in a paraphrase, as I learned it from my archbishop Plegmund, and my bishop Asser, and my priest Grimbold and my priest John. When I had learned it, I translated it into English as I understood it and as I could interpret it most intelligibly; and I will send one to every bishopric in my kingdom; and in each there will be a book-marker worth fifty mancuses. And in the name of God I command that no one remove the book-marker from the book, nor the book from the minster; it is uncertain how long there may be such learned bishops, as now, thanks be to God, there are almost everywhere; therefore I desire that they should always lie at that place, unless the bishop want to have it with him, or it be anywhere on loan, or anyone be copying it.

Aelfric

Aelfric (c. 955-c. 1010) was an English abbot, writer, and translator whose efforts to instruct monks and spread medieval learning have become emblems of tenth-century England.

He was probably born into a middle-class family in Wessex, where he seems to have lived all his life; scholars have speculated that his father was a court official or a merchant. All we know of his childhood is that he had a Latin tutor whose

Latin was weak, and that he entered Aethelwold's monastic school in Winchester in the early 970s. This school was the hub of the intellectual reform movement of the late tenth century. He was sent to the newly-founded monastery of Cernel in 987, where spent eighteen years as a simple priest. In 1005, at the age of 50, he was appointed abbot at yet another newly-founded monastery at Eynsham.

Aelfric was brought to Cernel to teach the monks, and his writings grew organically out of that pedagogical program. Like King Alfred a century earlier, he was concerned about the decline of learning in England (a decline now attributed to the Danish invasions), and concocted a plan similar to Alfred's of providing in English, specifically for monastic students and monks ignorant of Latin, a compendium of the knowledge essential to faith.

The first of these works to be written was the *Catholic Homilies* (989, 992), a collection of eighty sermons geared to the liturgical year that took the priest from Creation to the Last Judgment. In the next thirteen years, before his removal to Eynsham, he wrote treatises on cosmography and Latin grammar, a Latin-English glossary, a Latin textbook in dialogical form, the *Lives of Saints*, and various theological works; and translated several books of the Bible into Anglo-Saxon, including Genesis, Joshua, Numbers, and Judges.

Striking in Aelfric's prefatory remarks on translation is not only his insistence on easily accessible, idiomatic translations, but his overwhelming sense of the taboos surrounding the act and the products of translation. This is particularly clear in his preface to Genesis, where he expresses, in terms that anticipate the counter-reformation, his fear that easy access to the Bible in the vernacular will make people think they can live as the Old Testament patriarchs did.

Translating Into Our Ordinary Speech
From Preface to Book I of *Catholic Homilies* (989)
Translated by Benjamin Thorpe

I, Aelfric, scholar of Aethelwold, the benevolent and venerable Superior, send greeting of good wishes to his Lordship Archbishop Sigeric in the Lord. However rashly or presumptuously undertaken, I have nevertheless formed this book out of Latin writers and from Holy Scripture, translating into our ordinary speech, for the edification of the simple, who know only this language both for reading and for hearing; and for that reason I have used no difficult words, but only plain English; so that our message might the more readily reach the hearts of those who read or hear, to the profit of the souls of those who cannot be taught in any other tongue than that to which they were born.

Pure and Plain Words
Preface to Book II of *Catholic Homilies* (992)
Translated by Benjamin Thorpe

I have hastened to form this following book, according as the grace of God has guided me. I have tried to do this avoiding garrulous verbosity and strange expressions, and seeking rather with pure and plain words in the language of their nation, to be of use to my hearers, by simple speech, than to be praised for the composition of skillful discourse, which my simplicity has never acquired.

Translating into Idiomatic English
Preface to Genesis (997?)
Translated by Albert S. Cook

Aelfric the monk sends greeting in all humility to Aethelweard the earl.

When you desired me, honoured friend, to translate the Book of Genesis from Latin into English, I was loth to grant your request; upon which you assured me that I should need to translate only so far as the account of Isaac, Abraham's son, seeing that some other person had rendered it for you from that point to the end. Now, I am concerned lest the work should be dangerous for me or any one else to undertake, because I fear that, if some foolish man should read this book or hear it read, he would imagine that he could live now, under the new dispensation, just as the patriarchs lived before the old law was established, or as men lived under the law of Moses. At one time I was aware that a certain priest, who was then my master, and who had some knowledge of Latin, had in his possession the Book of Genesis; he did not scruple to say that the patriarch Jacob had four wives – two sisters and their two handmaids. What he said was true enough, but neither did he realize, nor did I as yet, what a difference there is between the old dispensation and the new. In the early ages the brother took his sister to wife; sometimes the father had children by his own daughter; many had several wives for the increase of the people; and one could only marry among his kindred. Any one who now, since the coming of Christ, lives as men lived before or under the Mosaic law, that man is no Christian; in fact, he is not worthy to have a Christian eat with him. If ignorant priests have some inkling of the sense of their Latin books, they immediately think that they can set up for great teachers; but they do not recognize the spiritual signification, and how the Old Testament was a prefiguration of things to come, and how the New Testament, after the incarnation of Christ, was the fulfillment of all those things which the Old Testament foreshadowed concerning Christ and his elect. Referring to Paul, they often wish to know why they may not have wives as well as the apostle Peter; but they will neither hear nor know that the blessed Peter lived according to Moses' law until Christ came to men and began to preach his holy gospel, Peter being the first companion that he chose; and that Peter forthwith forsook both wives and goods, and followed Christ's teaching to that new law and purity which he himself set up ... We say in advance that this book has a very profound spiritual signification, and we undertake to do nothing more than relate the naked facts. The uneducated will think that all the meaning is included in the simple narrative, while such is by no means the case ... We dare write no more in English than the Latin has, nor change the order except so far as English idiom demands. Whoever translates or teaches from Latin into English must always arrange it so that the English is idiomatic, else it is very misleading to one who does not know the Latin idiom ... Now I protest that I neither dare nor will translate any book hereafter from Latin into English; and I beseech you, dear earl, not to urge me any longer, lest I should be disobedient to you, or break my word if I should promise. God be gracious to you for evermore. Now in God's name I implore, if any one should transcribe this book, that he will strictly follow the copy, since I cannot help it if an inaccurate scribe introduces corruptions. In such case he does it at his own risk, not mine; and the careless copyist does much harm, unless he corrects his mistake.

Notker the German

Notker the German, also called Notker III or Notker Labeo (mid-tenth century – 1022), was a monk of St. Gall who did a good deal of translating from Latin into Old High German. His letter to Bishop Hugo von Sitten is an interesting document for the insight it gives us not only into the anxieties attendant upon translating (especially scriptural texts, like the psalter) into the vernacular, which was evident in Aelfric as well several decades earlier, and into the pedagogical applications of those vernacular translations; but also into the political and financial realities of translating in the period. The letter is basically an advertisement for his translations, an attempt to 'sell' them to the Bishop for the cost of his labour and materials, the work of his scribes and the expensive parchment.

Letter to Bishop Hugo von Sitten (1015)
Translated by Rita Copeland

There are Christian books – and principally those read in the schools – which cannot possibly be fully comprehended without introductory study. Since I wanted my students to have an introduction to these texts, I presumed to do something almost unprecedented: I ventured to translate them from Latin into our language, and to elucidate syllogistic, stylistic, and rhetorical precepts according to the teachings of Aristotle, Cicero, or other arts authors.

Because of what I had done with two books by Boethius – the *Consolation of Philosophy* and a good deal of *On the Trinity* – I was asked to translate some metrical texts into the same language: Cato's *Distichs*, Virgil's *Bucolics*, and Terence's *Andrias*. Soon they wanted me to try prose and arts texts, and I translated the *Marriage of Mercury and Philology* [of Capella], the *Categories* of Aristotle, the *Peri hermeneias*, and the *Principles of Arithmetic*. From this, turning to divine matters, I completed the whole Psalter, translating it and providing an exposition based on Augustine. I also began the Book of Job, although I scarcely completed the exposition of more than one third. Not only did I do these translations, but I also wrote a new rhetoric, a new computus,[1] and certain other Latin works.

I don't know whether any of these things are worthy of your attention. But if you want to see them – they are costly to produce – send several skins of parchment and expenses for the scribes, and you will receive copies of them. When they have been delivered to you, think of me as present. I know that while at first you will recoil from them as if from things unfamiliar, nevertheless they will, by degrees, begin to commend themselves to you forcefully, and you will be able to read and construe them. Things which are understood only partially and with difficulty in a language that is not one's own are quickly grasped in one's native language.

Burgundio of Pisa

One of the best-known translators of the twelfth century, Burgundio of Pisa (d. 1193) produced Latin translations of St. John of Damascus (the 'Thomas Aquinas of the East'), St. John Chrysostom, Galen, and many other Greek writers that remained in common use among scholars for three centuries.

Trained as an advocate, he was appointed to a judgeship in Pisa, and served Frederick Barbarossa as envoy to Ragusa in 1169 and Constantinople in 1172. Our earliest knowledge of him is as a conferee, along with other Western translator-theologians like Anselm of Havelberg, Moses of Bergamo, and James of

[1] A medieval set of tables used to calculate astronomical occurrences and thus moveable calendar feasts; in practice, a calendar. [Ed]

Venice, in the famous 1136 debate in Constantinople between members of the Eastern and Western churches, organized by the Archbishop of Nicomedia; the date suggests that he must have been in his eighties at least at his death in 1193. He was also an eminent authority in medicine, and his Latin translations of ten books by Galen were still read avidly by the early Renaissance.

His preface to St. John Chrysostom's commentary on St. John, here appearing for the first time in English translation, was a famous twelfth-century defence of strict literalism.

The Risk of Altering So Great an Original
Preface to Latin Translation of St. John Chrysostom, *Homilies on the Gospel of John* (early 1170s)
Translated by Edward Capps III

Judge Burgundio's prologue to John Chrysostom's commentary on St. John.

Burgundio, a civil judge of Pisa, sends greetings in the name of the Lord to all the faithful in Christ. After my fellow citizens had sent me to Constantinople as an ambassador to the Emperor Manuel in public negotiations of my state, I lost Hugolinus, the one of my sons that I had brought with me, to a sudden illness; I then decided to translate from Greek into Latin the commentary on the Gospel of St. John by the blessed patriarch of Constantinople John Chrysostom, both because I had already translated his entire commentary on Matthew for the late Pope Eugenius III and because there was a great deficiency of Latin interpretations of St. John. Indeed I found no other continuous exposition besides St. Augustine's. As long as official negotiations were imminent, I could accomplish little on this task there, nor could I buy the book to bring back with me to be translated at Pisa – for due to the acumen of its propositions[1] as much as its thoughtful moral instruction, a great many people, monks in particular, most avidly desired it. I therefore borrowed two copies from different monasteries and assigned a book each to two scribes, one to transcribe from the beginning, the other from the middle, and, obtaining it quickly in this way, I checked it diligently and emended it faithfully one night and the next day during my spare time. When I had completed my state's business and received permission from the Emperor to return, I began to translate the book on the journey home, writing myself without a scribe, first during a stopover at Messina and then throughout the trip, in Naples and Gaeta and wherever I spent the night, using every spare moment. Finally, after two long years, with God's help and against every expectation, I completed the entire book, translating from Greek into Latin word for word ...

Therefore, I, Burgundio, in fear that, if I wrote in my own idiom when translating this holy father's commentary, I would be changing the true meaning of one or more propositions of these two very wise men,[2] and would be incurring the risk of altering so great an original (for these are words of faith) through my own error, I resolved to take a more difficult journey and preserve in my translation not only words with the same meaning as in the original Greek but also the same style and order of words. Indeed it is well known that the ancient translators of both Greek and Latin texts always translated like this. For the seventy-two Jewish translators, six from each tribe, whom the head priest chose and sent from Jerusalem to Alexandria, and who were equally knowledgeable in Hebrew and Greek, did a word-for-word translation of the entire Old Testament from Hebrew into Latin for King Ptolemy of Egypt. Because Aquila, Theodotion, and Symmachus shared with many other Greek Christians the suspicion that those seventy-two – who were, after all, translating for an idolatrous king – had substituted one word for another, they undertook to correct that translation. After a long and most diligent investigation of the Septuagint translation, however, they at last discovered that the seventy-two had scarcely erred in any respect. Still, asserting that the seventy-two had added certain superfluous words without quite daring to change the text in any way, these Christian translators signified what should be struck out by an obelus[3] located in the book's outside margin. In regard to the univocal translation of certain equivocal expressions in the seventy-two's translation, these modern correctors, presuming to alter nothing concerning the solemn sequence of the Septuagint, also noted a different sense under an asterisk, which they themselves then translated from the Hebrew into Greek word for word.

Therefore our ancient fathers translated this entire corrected edition of the Septuagint which these modern translators had prepared word for word from Greek into Latin. Nevertheless, St. Jerome did not follow the Septuagint in making his new translation of Isaiah, which we still use; in his commentary on this new translation he mentions a flawed older Latin translation made directly from the Septuagint. Because in his own commentary on Isaiah St. Basil follows the Septuagint translation with astonishing exactitude, however, when I did my word-for-word translation of that commentary for the late Pope Eugenius III, I, Judge Burgundio, followed the older Latin translation made

[1] The Latin *sentencia* (classical *sententia*) refers to the content more than the external form of a sentence. [Tr]

[2] I.e., John the Evangelist and John Chrysostom. [Tr]

[3] The Greek word for 'a spit', usually the symbol †. The 'dagger', once called an obelisk ('a little spit'), was originally a variant of this mark. [Tr]

from the Septuagint, since St. Basil's explication corresponded so little to St. Jerome's new translation that I found could not follow the latter in my commentary at all.

The Psalms too were translated word for word from Greek into Latin, and we still see new copies being made of two different Latin translations, namely the 'Roman' and the 'Frankish',[4] the difference between them arising I think from the ambiguity of Greek expressions, with different translators assigning different meanings to them. In truth, the entire New Testament, even including Paul's Epistle to the Romans and the exceedingly suspect Gospel of St. Mark, has been translated word for word from Greek to Latin.[5]

Indeed many other ancient texts have also been translated literally in this way. The Roman decemviri did word-for-word translations of the laws of the most famous philosopher Solon and the most beloved Plato at Athens and, bringing them to Rome, produced from them the ancient law of the Twelve Tables.[6] The Emperor Justinian, a very famous man and most knowledgeable in all matters, rendering the Digest and Codex word for word, translated from Latin back into Greek so that, however they may disagree in the formulation of laws, the eloquence of Diocletian and other emperors as well as Papinian and other jurists might be clearly evident to both Latin and Greek speakers, in both their elevated sentences and their style. His *Institutes*, too, has not even a single word more or less in the Greek than it does in Latin. Justinian also directed that the *Novels*, which he afterwards continued composing assiduously in Greek for the new cases emerging daily, be translated from Greek into Latin word for word for the whole world to obey.

A certain patriarch of Constantinople[7] translated a dialogue of Pope Gregory the Great word for word from Latin into Greek, which is the reason they call the dialogue the 'Greek Gregory's'. Chalcidius translated Plato's *Timaeus* word for word from Greek into Latin and explained it in a commentary. Priscian, a very learned man, translates everything that he can from Greek into Latin, and draws everything from that spring – in no way following the example of Donatus when writing about the eight parts of speech, the kinds of proper and common nouns, atticisms, and accents. The famous philosopher Boethius rendered Porphyry, Aristotle's *Categories*, *On Interpretation*, *Topics*, and *Elenchi*, and also Nicomachus' *Introduction to Arithmetic*, from Greek into Latin by translating word for word.

The *Aphorisms* of Hippocrates, the wisest of physicians, and Galen's *Techne* were miraculously translated word for word from Greek into Latin. When the Gaelic John [Eriugena] translated the work of the great Dionysius the Areopagite[8] along with the marginal notes the blessed Greek Maximus[9] had added to it – a work that is as profound in the acumen of its propositions as it is eloquent in the weighty structure of the composition of new phrases – at King Charles' request he did not presume to attempt anything but a word-for-word translation, although he knew it could be turned into admirable Latin, for the same compositional complexion could have been preserved in Latin. Finally, Theophilus' *Concerning Various Urines* became known to Latin readers after being rendered faithfully word for word.

Indeed it is desirable that the author of a book derive authority as much from the ornament of his style and the grace of his words as from his propositions. After all, a building will impress the viewer with the architect's talent as much by its stones as by the excellence of its structure. If a painter seeks to portray every type of figure, intelligent critics will praise him as readily for an ugly shape as for a beautiful one, as long as it is as a prototype, that is, an exemplar. Likewise, all admire the high and sublime style of Paul's epistles by comparison with that of Aristotle and other humble and rough instructional writings. Therefore, so long as the phrases and idioms of the other language do not become an impediment, and one does not wish to establish one's own glory and pretend that others' words are one's own, a word-for-word translation should by no means be rejected by the diligent and faithful translator.

For if you wish another's material to be regarded as yours, "you will", as Horace says, "take pains not to render word for word like a faithful translator",[10] but rather, taking up a sentence of that material, you will cast it into the structure of your own diction; thus you will appear not to have translated but to have composed the text out of your own head, which both Cicero and Terence admit that they did. For imbued as they

[4] The 'Gallic' edition, as it is usually called, is Jerome's later edition of his earlier rougher 'Roman' one. [Tr]

[5] These two New Testament books' authenticity was doubted by some early Christians because of references to 'Romans'. [Tr]

[6] Dated c. 450 B.C.E. [Tr]

[7] Burgundio is in error here. Pope Zacharias was the actual translator. [Tr]

[8] Now, of course, called Pseudo-Dionysius and dated c. 500 A.D. although traditionally attributed to the Dionysius of Acts xvii 34. [Tr]

[9] The purpose of Maximus' commentary, however, was to attack the Areopagite's monophysitism! [Tr]

[10] *Ars Poetica* 133-4, *nec verbo verbum curabis reddere fidus / interpres*, also used by Salutati in his letter without the ametrical *ut* that has been inserted into this text before *fidus*. Burgundio also substitutes *non* for *nec*. [Tr] See Horace above, 15, and Salutati, below, 52-53. [Ed]

were with the highest wisdom, and disdaining to be slaves to the cases and figures of the Greeks, they did not adhere to the Greek words but rather by their own eloquence preserved the beauty and elegance of the original sentences in their translations. On the contrary, if they had rendered word for word, others' adoption of their native style could not have been easily detected. St. Jerome himself, devoted as he is to word-for-word translation, says that when translating from Greek apart from the sacred scriptures, where even the order of the words is a mystery, he renders not word for word but sense for sense. And even Horace says, "If they fall from a Greek spring, only sparingly changed".[11]

Since, therefore, this translation of mine is sacred scripture, and since I am seeking through this labor of mine not glory but the Lord's forgiveness of my sins and those of my son, by preserving in Latin the glory of his work in honor of this holy father of ours, John Chrysostom, I decided to translate word for word, only filling in an occasional deficiency of diction by adding two or three words, and reshaping an idiom that is a barbarism or metaplasm or schema or trope into a right and proper discourse.

Anonymous

This anonymous twelfth-century commentator on Boethius' *De arithmetica* develops a tripartite taxonomy of translation models, the first such in the history of Western translation theory, in order to synthesize the polarized camps of sense-for-sense and word-for-word translation into a single hierarchically integrated ideal for *all* translation.

The Three Kinds of Translating
From Commentary on Boethius' *De arithmetica* (12th century)
Translated by Charles S. F. Burnett

There are three kinds of translating. The first is when only the substance is transmitted; the second is when the substance is transmitted and the sense of the words is preserved; the third gives the substance and the sense and is a word-for-word translation.

Thomas Aquinas

St. Thomas Aquinas (San Tommaso D'Aquino, 1224/25-1274) was the foremost scholastic theologian of the Middle Ages: his two *Summas*, of theology and against the Gentiles, literally summed up or systematized medieval Roman Catholic theology.

Thomas was born near Aquino in what is now Italy to minor feudal aristocrats, and placed in the monastery of Monte Cassino at around six years of age as an oblate or prospective monk; but after Thomas had spent nine years there, Emperor Frederick II banished the monks from the monastery for their too strict obedience to the pope, and the fifteen-year-old Thomas was sent home to his parents. He was then enrolled in the University of Naples, where he joined the modern (recently founded), progressive, democratic Dominican order of mendicant friars. His parents, disapproving of this step, had him abducted on the road to Paris, but he held firm to his intentions and after a year of captivity his parents freed him and he went to Paris to study under the great scholar Albertus Magnus.

This break with his feudalistic parents and the paternalistic rules of the older monastic orders was indicative of the direction Thomas would take in his intellectual life, and reflective of the social changes going on all around him, as the old feudal, agrarian social order began to be displaced by a modern urban society and a market economy. He studied and taught at various European universities, served as theological adviser to the Papal Curia, was pulled into various earthshaking controversies that occasionally discredited him and could well have led to his condemnation and execution as a heretic – indeed in 1277, three years after his death, twelve of his theses were among the 219 condemned by the masters of Paris. That he survived these controversies as well as he did, and in so doing opened a window within scholastic theology to Aristotelianism, scientific rationalism, cultural and anthropological realism, and emergent humanism, was largely due to his placid, almost bovine manner of argumentation in public disputations and to the overwhelming intellectual authority of his writings.

Translation is one of the few areas of pressing concern for medieval theologians on which Thomas did not write extensively; as a result it would be the late sixteenth or early seventeenth century before anyone would undertake a systematization of translation theory. His brief introductory remarks on translation in his 'little work' against the errors of the Greeks are strictly orthodox in promoting sense-for-sense translation, as Jerome, Augustine,

[11] *Ars Poetica* 52-3, *si / Graeco fonte cadent parce detorta*, the end of a sentence beginning *et nova fictaque nuper habebunt verba fidem* "and newly coined words will be accepted ...". Horace is believed to be describing Latin words made by analogy with Greek derivatives; Burgundio, however, is probably using it out of context as a truism about how to translate from Greek! [Tr]

and Gregory the Great had done before him.

Proem
From *Against the Errors of the Greeks* (*Contra errores Graecorum*, 1263?)
Translated by Edwin Dolin

Most holy father Pope Urban, I have very carefully read the little book presented to me by your Excellency. I have found in it many things that are clearly stated and useful for the enunciation of our faith. On the other hand, it has occurred to me that profit from the book could be hindered for many persons because of certain things contained in the opinions of the holy fathers that seem obscure and from which these persons could produce material for errors and provide opportunity for dispute and falsehood. And so in order that, after all ambiguity has been removed, the purest profit for the true faith might be obtained from the opinions contained in the said book, I have decided, first, to explain those things that seem obscure and afterwards to show how from them the truth of the Catholic faith might be taught and defended.

As to the fact that certain things are found in the writings of the Greek saints that seem obscure to moderns, I believe this situation exists for two reasons. First of all, errors that arose concerning the faith gave occasion to the sainted doctors of the church to write with greater precision concerning matters of faith in order to eliminate these errors. As an example, consider that the sainted doctors who lived before the error of Arius did not speak as clearly about the unity of the divine essence as did the doctors who follow them. And the same sort of thing occurred with respect to other errors, as appears clearly not only in various doctors but in one who is outstanding among the doctors, Augustine. In books that he published after the occurrence of the heresy of the Pelagians he spoke more carefully about the power of free will than in the books which he published before the occurrence of said heresy. In those earlier books, while defending freedom of the will against the Manicheans, he published some things that the Pelagians took up in defense of their error, as they carried on their opposition to divine grace. On this account it is not surprising if modern doctors of the faith, after the occurence of various errors, speak more carefully and, as it were, more precisely about the teachings of the faith in order to avoid all heresy. So, if some things that are found in the writings of the ancient doctors that are not written with as much care as is practiced by the moderns, these things should not be despised or rejected; neither should they be prolonged but explained reverently.

Second, many things that are well expressed in the Greek language are not, perhaps, well expressed in Latin, because the Latins proclaim the same truth of faith in different words. For example, among the Greeks it is said correctly and according to Catholicism that the Father, Son, and Holy Spirit are three hypostases. Among the Latins, on the other hand, if someone should say that they are three substances, the statement is not well expressed, even though hypostasis is the same thing among the Greeks that substance is among the Latins according to the specific nature of the word.[1] For among Latins substance is quite commonly and normally used for essence, which we as much as the Greeks assert is one in the divine persons. For this reason, just as the Greeks say three hypostases we say three persons, as Augustine, in fact, recommends in the seventh chapter of the book *On the Trinity*. Nor is there any doubt that the situation is similar in many other cases.

Consequently, an obligation of a good translator is, when translating matters of the Catholic faith, to keep the meaning, while changing the manner of expression according to the specific character of the language into which he is translating. It is obvious, certainly, that if what is said in Latin in a literal way is expressed in a popular way, the expression will be improper if the translation is word for word. All the more, therefore, when something said in one language is translated into another language so that the translation is word for word: there's nothing remarkable if some uncertainty remains.

Roger Bacon

Known as Doctor Mirabilis or 'Wonderful Teacher', Roger Bacon (1220-1292) was an English philosopher, educational reformer, and renowned proponent of empirical science whose methodological ruminations preceded the actual blossoming of scientific method by three centuries. While himself less of an actual experimenter than his reputation would suggest, he 'introduced' to European science, primarily by describing them, a wide range of inventions from gunpowder to spectacles, and speculated on the possibility of hot-air balloons, airplanes that flap their wings, and mechanically propelled ships and cars.

Bacon was born into a wealthy family and given a classical education, and began his career lecturing on Aristotle in Paris. At 27 he returned to England to study at Oxford, where he came under

[1] *Substance* is an etymologically correct translation of *hypostasis*, since *sub* is Latin for Greek *hypo* and *stance* is Latin for Greek *stasis*. *Substance*, however, as Aquinas explains, had come to be used in Latin for *essence*, which translates Greek *ousia*. So the Greeks used *ousia* for God and *hypostasis* for members of the Trinity; the Latins used *substance* for God and *person* for members of the Trinity. [Tr]

the influence of Robert Grosseteste; and for the next ten years he trained himself in languages, optics, and alchemy. At 37 he joined the Fransiscan Order of Friars Minor, where his frantic work pace and abrasive treatment of anyone who disagreed with him caused him to be censured and closely restricted. In his mid-forties, hoping to escape the rigid discipline of the order, he wrote a letter to Pope Clement IV suggesting that more accurate scientific knowledge of nature would help confirm Christian doctrine; the pope requested Bacon's 'treatise', which was not yet written, and in response Bacon wrote (secretly, lest his superiors discover him) a kind of three-volume encyclopaedia of medieval learning, the *Opus Maius* ('Great Work'), the *Opus Minus* ('Lesser Work'), and the *Opus Tertius* ('Third Work'). Unfortunately, Pope Clement died shortly after receiving these volumes, and Bacon had to give up his hope of introducing the new learning into the university curriculum.

Bacon was imprisoned in his late fifties for 'suspected novelties' in his teaching – for how long, and for what specific irregularities, is not known. Any one of his heterodox hobby horses – his empiricism, his alchemical and astrological researches, his adherence to the millenarian cult of Joachim da Fiore – might have sufficed, as indeed might the fierce, antagonistic style in which he rode those horses over the cherished dogmas of his theological peers.

Bacon's pronouncements on translation in the *Opus Maius* are by way of making a systematic case for the study of grammar, which he understands in the restricted sense of *foreign-language* grammar – specifically the grammar of Hebrew, Greek, and Arabic, the languages of scripture and philosophy. Less a translation theory than an anti-translation theory, this call for the institutionalization (or at least systematization) of foreign-language training rests on the back of Bacon's disparagements of translation. His attack on translation is three-pronged: (1) the differences between languages make translations unreliable; (2) the lack of adequate target-language (in this case, Latin) terminology makes translations difficult to understand; and (3) the lack of translators qualified in both the source and the target languages and in scholarship (philosophy and science) makes translations mutually contradictory and virtually impossible to read.

On the Usefulness of Grammar
From *Great Work* (*Opus Maius*, 1268?)
Translated by Robert Belle Burke

After making the statement, therefore, that there is one perfect wisdom, which is contained in the Scriptures and must be expounded by canon law and philosophy, by which the world must be directed, nor is there needed any other science for the advantage of the human race, for it contains in itself the whole power of law and philosophy; I now wish to take up those parts of philosophy which are especially valuable for the exposition of this splendid wisdom. These are five, without which neither divine nor human things can be known, while a sure knowledge of them makes it easy for us to know all things. First, there is grammar, developed in the foreign tongues from which the wisdom of the Latins has sprung.[1] For it is impossible for the Latins to reach what is necessary in matters divine and human except through the knowledge of other languages, nor will wisdom be perfected for them absolutely, nor relatively to the Church of God and to the remaining three matters noted above. This I now wish to state, and first with respect to absolute knowledge. For the whole sacred text has been drawn from the Greek and Hebrew, and philosophy has been derived from these sources and from Arabic: but it is impossible that the peculiar quality of one language should be preserved in another. For even dialects of the same tongue vary among different sections, as is clear from the Gallic language, which is divided into many dialects among the Gauls, Picards, Normans, Burgundians, and others. A fitting and intelligible expression in the dialect of the Picards is out of place among the Burgundians, nay, among their nearer Gallic neighbours; how much more then will this be true as between different languages? Therefore an excellent piece of work in one language cannot be transferred into another as regards the peculiar quality that it possessed in the former. Hence Jerome in his epistle on the best kind of interpretation speaks thus,

> If I translate literally, the result is absurd in sound. But if any one does not think that the grace of a language is changed by translation let him translate Homer literally into Latin. I shall make a further statement; let him translate this same author in his own tongue in the words of prose, he will see a ridiculous order and a very eloquent poet speaking with difficulty.[2]

[1] The remaining four, dealt with in books four through seven of the *Opus*, are mathematics, optics, experimental science, and moral philosophy. These make up what might be described as Bacon's 'quinquivium', a pointed condensation of the seven medieval liberal arts, which in Bacon's day were divided into the 'lower' or 'literary' arts or the trivium – grammar, rhetoric, and logic – and the 'higher' or 'mathematical' arts or quadrivium – arithmetic, geometry, astronomy, and music. [Ed]

[2] See above, 26. [Ed]

For let any one with an excellent knowledge of some science like logic or any other subject at all strive to turn this into his mother tongue, he will see that he is lacking not only in thoughts, but words, so that no one will be able to understand the science so translated as regards its potency. Therefore no Latin will be able to understand as he should the wisdom of the sacred Scripture and of philosophy, unless he understands the languages from which they were translated.

Secondly, we must consider the fact that translators did not have the words in Latin for translating specific works, because they were not first composed in the Latin tongue. For this reason they employed very many words from other languages. Just as these words are not understood by those ignorant of those languages, so are they neither pronounced correctly nor are they written as they should be. And, what is bad, owing to their ignorance of Latin they have used Spanish, and other native tongues, to an almost endless extent in place of Latin. For let one example suffice for many from the book on Plants of Aristotle where he says, "*Belenum* which is very harmful in Persia when transplanted to Jerusalem becomes edible". This word is not the scientific one but colloquial Spanish. For *jusquiamus* [henbane] or the seed of the cassilago, is its name in Latin. After being laughed at by my Spanish students, familiar as they were with the words of their own language, when I did not understand what I was reading, I at length learned from them the meaning of this word and of many more besides.

Thirdly, although the translator ought to be perfectly acquainted with the subject which he wishes to translate and the two languages from which and into which he is translating, Boethius alone, the first translator, had full mastery of the languages; and Master Robert, called Grosse-Teste, lately bishop of Lincoln, alone knew the sciences. Certain other ordinary translators, like Girardus Cremonensis, Michael Scotus, Aluredus Anglicus, Hermannus Alemannus, whom we saw in Paris, have failed greatly as well in the languages as in the sciences; even as this same Hermannus has confessed concerning himself and others, as their translation shows.[3] For so great is the perverseness, crudity, and terrible difficulty in the translated works of Aristotle that no one can understand them, but each one contradicts another, and false statements are found again and again, as is clear from a comparison of the different translators and of the texts of the different languages. Likewise in the sacred text false statements are found and many bad translations. For Jerome proves that the translation of the Seventy Interpreters and of Theodotion and of Aquila had many errors; and since these errors were published throughout the whole Church, and all men stood for the translation of the Seventy as for their own life, Jerome was considered a falsifier and a corrupter of the Scriptures, until little by little the truth of the Hebrew became clear when turned into Latin by the sainted Jerome. Lest, however, he should hinder the Latins by too much alteration, for this reason, as he himself writes, he sometimes adapted himself to the Seventy Interpreters, sometimes to Theodotion, sometimes to Aquila; and therefore has left much as it was translated by others, and for this reason many false statements have remained. For, as Augustine proves in the second book on Christian Doctrine, the translation given in the book of Wisdom is a bad one, "Spurious vines will not produce deep roots". For it should be, Spurious plantings, or adulterous plantings, as Augustine proves by the Greek.[4] And yet Jerome let this pass like many other places for the peace of the Church and of the doctors. And it is clearly known that Jerome, subject to human frailty, sometimes erred in his own translation, as he himself frequently confesses. For since he had made a bad translation of the nineteenth chapter of Isaiah, he takes it up again in the original in the fifth book saying, "In this place also which we translated *curving* and *bridling* we can say *curving* and *frisking*. But while hastily translating what was written, deceived by the ambiguity we translated the Hebrew word *acmon* as *bridling*". He also again considered another place which he had translated badly in the same chapter saying,

> I think it better to censure my error rather than while blushing to confess my ignorance to persist in the error. In the passage which I translated, "and the land of Judah shall be a festivity to Egypt", the reading in Hebrew is *agga* which can be translated both as *festivity*, whence *aggeus* is translated as festive, and as *fear*, which Aquila has more significantly translated by *girosin*, since any one fearful and afraid turns about his eyes and fears a coming foe. Therefore if we wish to take it in a good sense that the recollection of Judah is a joy to Egypt, festivity is the right word: but if, as I judge, the idea is one of fear instead of joy we translate it terror or fear.

Jean de Meun

Jean Clopinel (or Chopinel) de Meun (or de Meung, c. 1240 – before 1305) was a French poet and translator best remembered for his work completing the *Roman de la Rose* (begun by Guillaume de Lorris around 1240), an encyclopaedic work in verse that interwove translated

[3] Modern scholars regard Bacon's attack on the quality of these translations as unwarranted. [Ed]

[4] See above, 33. [Ed]

passages from Ovid's *Art of Love* with classical and medieval Ovidian commentaries, passages translated from Boethius' *Consolation of Philosophy*, and a wealth of contemporary materials. He also later translated the *Consolation* as *Livres de Confort de Philosophie*, probably as a classroom crib to help students with the Latin.

Little is known of Jean's life. The title de Meun(g) refers to Meung-sur-Loire, his birthplace; he may at some point have been archdeacon of the Beauce, between Paris and Orléans.

His work on the *Roman* and the French Boethius proved enormously influential for vernacular culture in fourteenth-century France and England, partly because Jean divagated so sharply and originally from the Ovidian theme established by Guillaume in order to take forceful stances on issues of contemporary interest, partly also because his stances were so insistently bourgeois, as opposed to the aristocratic sensibilities of Guillaume. Geoffrey Chaucer translated nearly 5000 lines of it (including 3000 of Jean's) into English, and the *Roman* is generally considered the strongest literary influence on Chaucer's work.

His prefatory matter in both works, the verse prologue to his section of the *Roman* and his dedicatory preface to the *Livres de Confort*, are of interest for translation theory in their contextualization of medieval French translation – their overt sense of the complexly dual audience they were addressed to, the aristocracy and commoners, clergy and the laity.

Translating for Lay People
From prologue to *Roman de la Rose* (c. 1280)
Translated by Rita Copeland

Your country is not on earth. One can readily learn this from clerks who study Boethius' *Consolatio* and the meanings that lie within it. Whoever would properly translate this for lay people would do something of great benefit for them.

Plainly Rendering the Sense
From dedication to translation of Boethius' *Li Livres de Confort de Philosophie* (between 1285 and 1305)
Translated by Rita Copeland

To Your Royal Majesty, most noble prince, by grace of God King of the French, Philippe IV, I, Jean de Meun, who previously, in the *Romance of the Rose*, after the point where Jealousy put Fair Welcome in prison, showed how to capture the castle and pluck the rose, and who translated from Latin into French Vegetius' *On Warfare*, the *Marvels of Ireland*, the life of Peter Abelard and the letters of Abelard and his wife Heloise, and Aelred's book *On Spiritual Friendship*, now present Boethius' *Consolation of Philosophy*, which I have translated from Latin into French. Although you understand Latin very well, it is nevertheless much easier to understand French than Latin. Since you told me – and I take your word as a commandment – that I should plainly render the sense of the author without following the words of the Latin too closely, I have done this, as much as my meager skills permit, just as your graciousness has commanded. Now I beg all those who will see this book to pardon me if it seems to them that in any passages I have strayed too far from the words of the author, or if sometimes I have used more or fewer words than the author. For if I had sought to render the Latin word for word in French, the book would be too obscure for lay readers, and the clerks, who are no less lettered, would be unable to get a clear reading of the Latin from the French.

Dante Alighieri

Dante Alighieri (1265-1321), author of the *Divine Comedy*, was one of the greatest poets in world literature, the father of literary Italian and progenitor of the literary vernacular throughout late-medieval Europe, and a well-read intellectual whose theoretical writings anticipated Renaissance humanism.

Dante was born into a Florence torn by strife between the Ghibellines (from German 'Waiblingen'), partisans of the German emperors, notably Frederik I and II, and the Guelfs (from German 'Welf'), who fought for the papacy. Dante's father was a Guelf, but apparently not important enough to be exiled or killed, since it was not until Dante was a year old that his father's party seized permanent control of Florence from the ruling Ghibellines. Dante was later to fight as a cavalryman against the Ghibellines in their attempt to recapture the city, and at 35 became a prior or chief magistrate in Guelf-controlled Florence. Two years later, in 1302, internecine strife among the 'Black' and 'White' Guelfs led to a death sentence for Dante, a White; fleeing execution, Dante spent the rest of his life in exile.

Dante's three great poetic works, *La vita nuova* ('The New Life', 1293), *Il convivio* ('The Banquet', 1304-1307), and *La divina commedia* ('The Divine Comedy', 1308-1321), were all written in Italian rather than Latin; their brilliance and spectacular popularity in late-medieval Europe not only cleared the way for the artistic and intellectual use of Italian in Italy but made Italian all Europe's cultural *lingua franca* for the next several centuries. The first book of *Il convivio* in particular, in which Dante's famous discussion of translation appears, is a spirited defence of the vernacular, and by implication of an emergent lay urban literate class that communicated in the vernacular rather than Latin – the class that in the next two centuries would build the Renaissance.

Translation Destroys the Sweetness of the Original
From *The Banquet* (*Il convivio*, 1304-1307)
Translated by Katherine Hillard

1. Having proved that the Latin commentary would not have been an intelligent servant, I will show why it would not have been an obedient one. He is obedient who has that good disposition which we call obedience. True obedience should have three things, without which it is none: it must be sweet, and not bitter; entirely under command, and not spontaneous; and it must be limited, and not unbounded. These three things it was impossible for the Latin commentary to possess; and therefore it was impossible for it to be obedient.

2. That this would have been impossible to the Latin, as has been said, is shown thus: Everything that proceeds by inverse order is wearisome, and therefore is bitter, and not sweet; such as waking by night and sleeping by day, or going backwards instead of forwards. For the subject to command the sovereign is a reversal of order, because the right order is for the sovereign to command the subject; and thus it is bitter, and not sweet. And because it is impossible to yield sweet obedience to a bitter command, when the subject commands, it is impossible that the obedience of the sovereign should be sweet. Therefore, if Latin be the sovereign of the vulgar tongue, as has been already shown by other reasons, and the canzoni, which take the place of command, are in the vulgar tongue, it is impossible that its exposition could be sweet.

3. And obedience is entirely under command, and not spontaneous, when the person obeying would not have done the thing, either wholly or in part, of his own will. And therefore, if I were ordered to wear two gowns, and, without being told, should wear one, then I say my obedience would not be entirely under command, but partly spontaneous. And such would have been that of the Latin commentary; and therefore it would have been an obedience not entirely under command. That it would have been such appears by this – that the Latin without the command of this master [the canzoni in Italian] would have explained much of their meaning (for that it explains itself is known to those who study Latin writings carefully) which the vulgar tongue never does.

4. Again, obedience is limited, and not unbounded, when it executes the command to the letter, but does not go beyond it; as individual Nature is obedient to universal Nature when she gives man thirty-two teeth, neither more or less, and gives the hand five fingers, neither more nor less; and man is obedient to justice when he does what the law commands, and neither more nor less. Now, the Latin would not have done this, nor would it have sinned only in failure or in excess, but in both; and thus its obedience would not have been limited, but unbounded, and therefore it would not have been obedient. That the Latin would not have fulfilled the command of its master, but would have exceeded it, can be easily shown. This master (that is, these canzoni, to whom this commentary is assigned as servant) desires and commands that they shall be explained to all those to whom their meaning can be so conveyed that when they speak they shall be understood. And no one can doubt that had they the voice to speak, such would be their orders. But the Latin could only have explained them to scholars; for the rest would not have understood it. Therefore, as among those who desire to understand these [canzoni] there are many more illiterate than learned, it follows that it [the Latin] would not have fulfilled this behest as well as the vulgar tongue, which is understood both by the learned and the unlearned. Also the Latin would have explained them to people of other nations, such as Germans, English, and others; in doing which it would have exceeded their order. For it would have been against their will, I say, speaking generally, to have explained their meaning where their beauty could not go with it. And, moreover, let all observe that nothing harmonized by the laws of the Muses[1] can be changed from its own tongue to another one without destroying all its sweetness and harmony. And this is the reason why Homer is not turned from Greek into Latin like the other writings we have of theirs [the Greeks]; and this is why the verses of the Psalter lack musical sweetness and harmony; for they have been translated from Hebrew to Greek, and from Greek to Latin, and in the first translation all this sweetness perished. And thus is concluded what was promised in the beginning of the chapter immediately before this one.

Anonymous

Nothing is known of the author/translator of the *Ovide moralisé*. Written in Middle French in the first quarter of the 14th century, it was a kind of integrated compendium of Ovid's *Metamorphoses*, classical and medieval (and the author/translator's own) commentaries, and other, more recent materials of a similar nature, such as a Norman version of Pyramus and Thisbe and a twelfth-century French translation of the Philomela legend attributed to Chrétien de Troyes.

Interestingly, the author/translator integrates the

[1] That is, any poetical work. [Tr]

'spiritual' or 'allegorical' hermeneutic that had been developed since the fifth century of the Christian era for the fourfold reading of scripture (according to which every passage had a literal, allegorical, moral, and anagogical meaning) with the vernacular translation of overtly pagan texts like Ovid, so that literal 'interpretation' (meaning both 'translation' and 'exposition') is rejected as superficial and misleading not only on translational grounds, because languages differ syntactically, but on moral or doctrinal grounds as well, because the literal meaning of a pagan text is 'obviously' a lie. It is also interesting that s/he does so *in* the text, in four-footed iambs that are structurally indistinguishable from the 'translated' material.

Another Meaning
From *Ovide moralisé*, early 14th century
Translated by Rita Copeland

Book 1, lines 1-30
If Scripture doesn't lie to me, all that is written in books, whether good or evil, is for our instruction. For anyone who really wants to pay attention, evil is presented there so that one may guard against it, and good so that one may imitate it. Anyone to whom God gives good fortune and grace to attain wisdom and knowledge ought not to refrain from speaking and expounding what is proper, for one ought not to hide wisdom, since wisdom kept under wraps is worth no more than riches buried underground. Thus I am pleased to commence my translation of the ancient stories from Latin into the vulgar tongue, just as Ovid presents them – and I will relate what I understand about them. Many others have made valid attempts to do what I propose without accomplishing their whole purpose; and although I am not endowed with more wisdom and knowledge than those others who believed they could do this, in undertaking this task I put faith in God, who hides and conceals his secrets from wise and knowing men, but reveals them to beginners who diligently seek Him.

Book 6, lines 2211-16
But I will not recount the story other than as Chrétien told it, for he has translated the letter of the text very well.[1] I do not wish to supersede his version. I will relate his whole poem to you, and then I will extract his allegory.

Book 15, lines 2525-57
Certainly, whoever would take Ovid's texts at the literal level and not understand another sense, another meaning than what the author crudely presents in recounting the story, to this person everything would be a lie, of little profit and great obscurity, ... and would clearly be a heretic. But beneath the fable, the most profitable meaning lies hidden. Thus whoever fixes on the fable alone doesn't care what it is really about; and he who believes that in the fable there is another meaning, another sense, ought not blame or condemn the fable rashly just because he cannot understand it or the good meaning that it can have. Whoever knows how to expound the letter can derive from the fable a meaning that is good and consistent with truth. Indeed, even sacred Scripture is difficult and obscure in many places and seems to be mere fable. He who cannot derive another meaning which Scripture does not seem to have at its literal level, and who would believe, through ignorance, that there is no other meaning there, would certainly deceive himself and place his own soul in damnation.

[1] The author/translator is speaking of a translation of the Philomela legend attributed (probably falsely) to Chrétien. [Ed]

Richard Rolle

Richard Rolle de Hampole (c. 1300-1349) was a Yorkshire hermit and mystic whose Middle English translation of the Psalter played an important role in the later history of English Bible translation.

Rolle took classes at Oxford University for a while, but hated the academic regimen (especially the disputatiousness), and quit school to become a hermit, first on the estate of John Dalton of Pickering, later here and there across the English countryside, wherever his wanderings took him. He was associated with the convent at Hampole for a while (thus 'de Hampole' after his name), and may have served as spiritual advisor to the nuns; and it was in Hampole that he died.

His mystical writings were highly regarded until the Reformation; his painfully literal translation of the Psalter was read to non-Latin-speaking church-goers from the pulpit for at least a century, and – anticipated, perhaps, by his own fears that his work would fall into the wrong hands – formed the backbone for Lollard translations later in the century. The preface is fairly conventional; its most obvious model is King Alfred's preface to his translation of Gregory the Great's *Pastoral Care.*

Following the Letter
Prologue to English Translation of the Psalter (1330s)
Translated by Rosamund S. Allen

In this work I shall not be using learned expression but the easiest and commonest words in English which approximate most closely to the Latin, so that those who do not know Latin can acquire many Latin words from the English. In the translation I follow the letter as much as I am able to, and where I cannot find an exactly equivalent English word, I follow the sense, so that those who are going to read it need have no fear of not understanding. In the explanation I follow the holy doctors of the church since it could be that it will come into the hands of someone malicious who has no idea how he ought to interpret the work, and who will declare that I did not know what I was saying, and in this way will cause grave harm to himself and to others by despising a work which is beneficial both for himself and for others.

John of Trevisa

Little more is known of the fourteenth-century writer John of Trevisa than that he undertook the massive labour of translating the *Polychronicon* of Ralph Higden or Ranulph(us) Higdon (1280-1364) and the *De Proprietatibus Rerum* of Bartholomew into English. According to William Caxton in a fifteenth-century prologue to the *Polychronicon*, Trevisa was vicar of Berkeley, and translated the work at the behest of Sir Thomas, Lord Berkeley. He was also an Oxford scholar who may have been involved in the Wycliffite project of translating the Bible into English.

Higden was an English monk and historian who wrote in the *Polychronicon* a universal history of the world from creation to the 1340s, in seven parts for the seven days of creation. The work recorded a good deal of fourteenth-century scientific, geographical, and historical knowledge, along with various miracles and other supernatural events. After Higden's death, the *Polychronicon* was continued during the reign of Richard II (1377-1399).

Dialogue Between a Lord and a Clerk upon Translation (1387)

THE LORD. Since the time that the great and high tower of Babel was built, men have spoken with diverse tongues, so that diverse men are strange to each other and do not understand others' speech. Speech is only known when it is learned; common learning of speech is by hearing, and so he that is deaf is always dumb, for he may not hear speech so as to learn. So men of far [various] countries and lands that speak diverse languages, if neither of them has learned the other's language, neither of them wot [knows] what the other means. Though they meet and have great need of information and of lore of talking and of speech, no matter how great the need, neither of them understands the other's speech, any more than the gaggling of geese. For jangle that one never so fast, that other is never the wiser, though he shrew him instead of "good-morrow"![1] This is a great mischief that now follows mankind; but God of His mercy and grace has ordained a double remedy. One is that someone learns and knows many diverse languages, and so between strange men, neither of whom understands the other's speech, such a man may be mean [in the middle] and tell either what the other means. The other remedy is that one language is learned, used, and known in many nations and lands. And so Latin is learned, known, and used, especially on this half [side of] Greece, in all the nations and lands of Europe. Therefore clerks [learned people], out of their goodness and courtesy, make and write their books in Latin, in order that their writing and books should be understood in various nations and lands. And so Ranulphus, monk of Chester (Ralph Higden), wrote in Latin his books of Chronicles, that describe the world about in length and in breadth, and make mention and mind of doings and deeds of marvels and wonders, and count the years to his last days from the first making of heaven and of earth. And so therein is great and noble information and lore to them that can therein read and understand. Therefore I would have these books of Chronicles translated out of Latin into English, so that more men should understand them and have cunning [knowledge], information and lore thereof.

THE CLERK. These books of Chronicles are written in Latin, and Latin is used and understood on this half [side of] Greece in all the nations and lands of Europe. And commonly English is not so widely understood, nor known; and the English translation would be understood by none but English men alone; then how should the more men understand the Chronicles, though they were translated out of Latin, that is so widely used and known, into English, that is not used and known but of English men alone?

THE LORD. This question and doubt is easy to assoil [absolve]. For if these Chronicles were translated out of Latin into English, then they should be understood by so many the more men as understand English, and no Latin.

THE CLERK. You can speak, read, and understand Latin; then there is no need to have such an English translation.

THE LORD. I deny this argument; for though I can speak, read, and understand Latin, there is much Latin in these books of Chronicles that I cannot understand, nor can you, without studying, advisement, and looking in other books. Also, though it were not needful for me, it is needful for other

[1] I.e., no matter how fast one person jabbers, the other will not understand him, even if he is cursing him instead of saying hello. [Ed]

men that understand no Latin.

THE CLERK. Men that understand no Latin may learn and understand.

THE LORD. Not all; some may not due to other manner of business, some due to age, some for default of wit, some for default of chattel [wealth, possessions], or of friends to find them to [provision them for] school, and some for other diverse defaults and lets [obstacles].

THE CLERK. It needs not [is not necessary] for all such to know the Chronicles.

THE LORD. Speak not too straitly [strictly] of thing that needs; for straitly to speak of thing that needs, only what is, and may not fail, needs to be. And so it needs that God be, for God is, and may not fail. And, so for to speak [in that sense], no one needs to know the Chronicles, for it might and may be that no one know them. Otherwise to speak of thing that needs, something needs for to sustain or to have other things thereby, and so meat and drink need for keeping and sustenance of life. And, so for to speak, no man needs to know the Chronicles. But in the third manner to speak of thing that needs, all that is profitable needs, and, so for to speak, all men need to know the Chronicles.

THE CLERK. Then they that understand no Latin may ask and be informed and taught of [by] them that understand Latin.

THE LORD. You speak wonderly [strangely], for the lewd [uneducated] man wots not what he should ask, and namely of [especially about] lore of deeds that come never in his mind; nor wots of whom commonly he should ask. Also, not all men that understand Latin have such books to inform lewd men; also some can not, and some may not, have while [time], and so it is necessary to have an English translation.

THE CLERK. The Latin is both good and fair, therefore no English translation is needed.

THE LORD. The reason [argument] is worthy to be plunged in a puddle and laid in powder of lewdness and of shame. It might well be that you make it only in mirth and in game [jest].

THE CLERK. The reason must stand but [unless] it be assoiled [absolved].

THE LORD. A blear-eyed man, but [unless] he were all blind of wit, might see the solution of this reason; and though he were blind he might grope the solution, but if his feeling him failed. For if this reason were worth anything, by such manner of arguing men might prove that the three score and ten [Septuagint] interpreters, and Aquila, Symmachus, Theodotion, and he that made the first translation, and Origenes were lewdly occupied when they translated holy writ out of Hebrew into Greek; and also that Saint Jerome was lewdly occupied when he translated holy writ out of Hebrew into Latin, for the Hebrew is both good and fair and written by inspiration of the Holy Ghost; and all these for their translations be highly praised of all Holy Church. Then the foresaid lewd reason is worthy to be powdered, laid in water and soused. Also holy writ in Latin is both good and fair, and yet to make a sermon of holy writ all in Latin to men that can English and no Latin, it were a lewd deed, for they be never the wiser for the Latin, unless it is told them in English what it is to mean; and it may not be told in English what the Latin is to mean without translation out of Latin into English. Then it is necessary to have an English translation, and to keep it in mind so that it will not be forgotten, it is better that such a translation be made and written than said and not written. And so this foresaid lewd reason should move no man that has any wit to leave [desist from] the making of English translation.

THE CLERK. A great deal of these books stand much by holy writ, by holy doctors, and by philosophy; then these books should not be translated into English.

THE LORD. It is wonder that you make such feeble arguments, and have gone so long to school. Aristotle's books and other books also of logic and of philosophy were translated out of Greek into Latin. Also at praying [the request] of King Charles, John Scot [Eriugena] translated Denys' [Pseudo-Dionysus the Areopagite's] books out of Greek into Latin, also holy writ was translated out of Hebrew into Greek and out of Greek into Latin, and then out of Latin into French; then what has English trespassed that it might not be translated into English? Also King Alfred, that founded the University of Oxford, translated the best laws into the English tongue, and a great deal of the Psalter out of Latin into English, and caused Wyrefrith [Waerferth], Bishop of Worcester, to translate Saint Gregory's books, the dialogues, out of Latin into Saxon. Also Caedmon of Whitby was inspired of the Holy Ghost, and made wonder poesies in English nigh of all the stories of holy writ.[2] Also the holy man Beda translated St. John's gospel out of Latin into English. Also you wot where the Apocalypse[3] is written in the walls and roof of a chapel, both in Latin and in French. Also the gospel, and prophecy, and the right faith of holy church must be taught and preached to English men that can no Latin. Then the gospel, and prophecy, and the right faith of holy church must be told them in English, and that is not done but by English translation, for such English preaching is very translation, and such English preaching is good and needful; then English translation is good and needful.

THE CLERK. If a translation were made that might be amended in any point, some men would blame it.

[2] I.e., made wonderful verse renditions of nearly all the stories in the Bible. [Ed]

[3] The Book of Revelation. [Ed]

THE LORD. If men blame that [which] is not worthy to be blamed, then they be to blame. Clerks know well enough that no sinful man does so well that he might not do better, nor make so good a translation that he might not be better. Therefore Origenes made two translations, and Jerome translated thrice the Psalter. I desire not translation of these [books] the best that might be, for that were an idle desire for any man that is now here alive, but I would have a skilful translation, that might be known and understood.

THE CLERK. Whether is you liefer [Which would you rather] have, a translation of these chronicles in rhyme or in prose?

THE LORD. In prose, for commonly prose is more clear than rhyme, more easy and more plain to know and understand.

THE CLERK. Then God grant us grace grathly [readily] to [be]gin, wit and wisdom wisely to work, might and mind of right meaning to make translation trusty and true, pleasing to the Trinity, three persons and one God, in majesty, that ever was and ever shall be, and made heaven and earth, and light for to shine, and departed light and darkness, and called light, day, and darkness, night; and so was made eventide and morrowtide one day, that had no morrowtide. The second day He made the firmament between waters, and departed waters that were under the firmament from the waters that were above the firmament, and called the firmament heaven. The third day He gathered waters that be under the firmament into one place and made the earth unheled [unconcealed], and named the gathering of waters, seas, and dry earth, land; and made trees and grass. The fourth day he made sun and moon and stars, and set them in the firmament of heaven there for to shine, and to be tokens and signs to depart times and years, night and day. The fifth day He made fowls and birds in the air, and fishes in the water. The sixth day He made beasts of the land, and man of the earth, and put him in Paradise, for he should work and wone [dwell] therein. But man broke God's [be]hest and fell into sin, and was put out of Paradise into woe and sorrow worthy to be damned to the pain of hell without any end. But the Holy Trinity had mercy of man, and the Father sent the Son, and the Holy Ghost alighted on a maid, and the Son took flesh and blood of that blissful maid, and died on the Rood [Cross] to save mankind, and arose the third day, glorious and blissful, and taught his disciples, and ascended into heaven when it was time; and shall come at the day of Doom and deem [judge the] quick [living] and dead. Then all they that be written in the Book of Life shall wend [go] with Him into the bliss of heaven, and be there in body and soul, and see and know His Godhead and Manhood in joy without any end.

Thus ends the Dialogue.

Coluccio Salutati

Lino Coluccio di Piero Salutati (1331-1406) was an Italian humanist and chancellor of Florence whose Latin letters were renowned for their power and influence; one of his targets, the autocratic Duke of Milan, said he would rather face a thousand Florentine horsemen than a single letter from Salutati.

Born in Stignano and raised in Bologna, he set off on a law career, but broke off his studies before he had progressed very far, professing himself unsuited to the field. The death of his father left him an orphan while still underage, and, without any great inclination for this field either, he apprenticed himself to a notary. At twenty he returned to Stignano and began an administrative career that would take him up the ladder from chancellor of Todi (1367), or Lucca (1371), of the Papal Curia at Viterbo (early 1370s), and finally, of Florence (1375). This last post, which he was to hold for 31 years (until his death), was a difficult one, given the volatile state of Florentine (and generally Italian) politics; but Salutati was able to find time in between his administrative duties for an active philosophical and literary life as well. His library was substantial, containing numerous 'lost' manuscripts, and his correspondence with both younger and more established humanist scholars was voluminous. Among his many disciples and protégés was the young Greek scholar and future successor to Salutati as chancellor of Florence, Leonardo Bruni, whose essay on right translation appears below.

Salutati's letter to Antonio Loschi is significant not only for its specific exploration of 'correct' translation as conceived in late-fourteenth-century Florence, a generation ahead of Bruni, but also for the light it sheds on literary patronage in the period.

Letter to Antonio Loschi (1392)
Translated by Edwin Dolin

To the most eloquent Antonio Loschi, citizen of Vicenza, I am delighted, very dear son, that, after finding yourself in possesion of a translation of the Homeric *Iliad*,[1] although it's a repulsive and crude translation, you have thought of its improvement and desire to give to Latium this divine work in the form of an epic poem. Since only by their title do we know such works as

> the *Iliad* of Attius
> Intoxicated with hellebore ...
> [Persius *Satires* I 50-51]

[1] A prose translation by Leonzio Pilato. [Ed]

as it is described by our satirist; or the like-named work by Gnaeus Matius, who wrote the mediocre versicule "most swift Hector rushes forward ..."; also, the poem of Ennius, which, as Macrobius testifies, had the following lines about Troy:

> those things which could not perish in the Dardanian fields and could not, while they were captured, be captured nor, while burned, be burned ...

as well as certain other poems, fragments of which turn up as we read; since, as I said, we know these works only by their titles, may there rise up now in our time a young Ligurian who will take out of Homer not merely one short verse or several, something that is a source of glory for Virgil even amid the outcry of the hostile and envious, but who will claim for himself the whole of the *Iliad* and will transform it from a Greek into a Latin work of most glorious poetry or, rather, transform it from a bloodless, charmless translation into a highly refined and beautiful poem.

I urge you to undertake this work with total devotion, since you had already conceived of it by yourself, while I was suggesting it to you at a time when I knew nothing of your intention. In fact, in my view, this Pierian enthusiasm has come to you not without some divine act, since no one was urging you to it, while I, ignorant of your intention, urged you to do what you had already decided to do by yourself.

Believe me, if your translation had been known to me when I was young, it would have taken me away from you and from others as well, since I would have thought it a most beautiful action to set out along the path and in the footsteps of so great a poet.

Do not be frightened by the ugliness of that translation and by the fact that nothing in it is pleasing, so far as the words are concerned. I hope you will concentrate on the subject matter, not the words. You should embellish the subject matter and beautify it and adorn it, now with the proper words, now with novel words, and you need to add such brilliance of diction that you present and express that Homeric quality which all of us have in mind, not merely in plot formulation and thought but also in words.

You will do all this easily, if you will not be complacent, if you will make an effort to write again in a different way what you have already written with different words and embellishments and, finally, if you will select what you judge to be the better or best or in fact gather from all possibilities what has the more divine or more artistic sound. If you write something only once, you will never be a good judge of your own work, because everything that we ourselves do pleases us. But if you go over the same thing more than once and in different ways, you will be a very good judge of, and selector among, your writings, especially if you also arrange for a delay and refuse to make instantaneous judgments. Do not, as Horace warns, "render word for word, a faithful translator"[2] and do not make your poem exactly equal to its model in length. Finally, you will be giving due grandeur to everything, if you connect whatever is not connected through the use of different or added conjunctions; if you enkindle things that are rather cold with exclamations or with questions, as if lighting them with little fires; if, finally, transforming what you encounter either through omitting something or adding something, you are able to make the logical sequence more pleasing; and certainly if at first you try to make more use at one time of proper words and at another time of splendid or sonorous words than the other translator did and try to use these same words in prose, not in verse, for the same idea.

Now, contrary to my intention, I am writing again to Pasquino, asking that he reply some day. Not satisfied with that, I have given him the formula for a two-word letter. It's enough if he will write, *valeo, vale* ("I am well, you be well"). Wherefore, since in these two words there could be neither risk with respect to speech nor work with respect to writing, urge him, I beg you, to humor me in so little a favor, so that I do not seem completely neglected and scorned, not simply abandoned but despised.

For the rest, I look forward to those letters of Cicero, as if to some divine gift. From them I would like to ask you to gather copies in sets of four and, if there be ways and means, be an organizer and busybody so that they are sent to me through our learned men who are there, so that my desire may be satisfied. It's actually impossible to say with what anxiety I am possessed while waiting.

I am surprised, and not just a little bit, that you have done no investigation of Varro and have written me back nothing. Not that I will transfer this task away from you and confide it to him, since he is preoccupied with greater matters, but because perhaps you will be able to get through him more easily than by yourself or through Pasquino what is expedient. I ask you not to neglect this. Farewell, fortunate and very dear son. You will achieve the highest honors of our age, if life will be a comrade to you and if you do not abandon what you have begun.

Anonymous (John Purvey?)

This preface to the second Wycliffite Bible (and indeed the translation of that edition) was first attributed to John Purvey by Daniel Waterton in 1729; in 1903 Alfred W. Pollard argued that it may in fact have been written by John of Trevisa, but

[2] See above, 15. [Ed]

later scholars like Margaret Deansley in 1920 and F. F. Bruce in 1970 have adduced still more persuasive evidence that Purvey was in fact the author.

John Purvey was John Wycliffe's secretary and a member of the Wycliffite group engaged at Oxford in translating the Bible into English. It is not known to what extent Wycliffe actually participated in the (probably collective) effort of translation, or to what extent the various editions can be attributed to specific hands. Linguistic similarities between the second edition and this preface suggest that both were written by the same author(s) – but who that author or those authors might have been is a matter of conjecture. The best conjecture at present is that Nicholas of Hereford was largely responsible for the first (strictly literal) version, done between 1382 and 1387, and that John Purvey did an extensive sense-for-sense revision some time before 1397.

The second edition was extremely popular until printed copies of Tyndale's new translation (from the original languages, not like the Wycliffite versions from Latin) began to circulate in the 1520s. Copied without prologues and marginal glosses (where all evidence of Wycliffite 'heresy' was to be found), it could even pass muster as an 'orthodox' translation; F. F. Bruce suggests that this may in fact be the English Bible Thomas More refers to in laudatory terms, below.

On Translating the Bible
Chapter 15 of the Preface to the Second Version of the Wycliffite Translation of the Bible into English (1395/97)

Since Christ says that the gospel shall be preached in all the world [Matthew 24:14], and David says of the apostles and their preaching, "the sound of them went out into each land, and the words of them went out into the ends of the world" [Psalms 19:4], and after that David says, "the Lord shall tell in the scriptures of the peoples, and of these princes that were in it" [Psalms 87:6], that is, in the holy church, and as Jerome says on that verse, "holy writ is the scripture of peoples, for it is made that all peoples should know it" – so the princes of the church that David mentions are the apostles, who had authority to write holy writ, for since the apostles wrote their scriptures by the authority and the confirmation of the Holy Ghost, it is holy scripture, and faith of Christian men, and this dignity has no man after [in comparison with] them, no matter how holy, no matter how cunning [learned], as Jerome witnesses on that verse. Also, Christ says of the Jews that cried "Hosanna" to him in the temple, that if they were silent, stones would cry out [Luke 19:40]; and by stones he means heathen men who worshipped stones for their gods. And since we English men come of heathen men, we too can be signified by these stones that would cry holy writ; and as Jews, interpreted 'with knowledge', signify clerks who should [ac]knowledge to God by the repentance of sins and by the voice of God's praising, so our lewd [uneducated] men, following Christ the cornerstone, may be signified by stones that are hard and abiding in the foundation. For though covetous clerks be mad by simony, heresy and many other sins, and despise and stop holy writ as much as they may, yet the unlearned people cry after holy writ, to learn it, and keep it, with great cost and peril of their life.

For these reasons and other, with common charity to save all men in our realm, whom God would have saved, a simple creature has translated the Bible out of Latin into English.[1] This simple creature had much travail, first with various fellows and helpers, to gather many old Bibles, and other doctors [scholastic authorities], and common glosses, and to make one Latin Bible in some part true; and then to study it of the new, the text with the gloss, and other authorities he might get, especially [Nicholas of] Lyra on the Old Testament, which helped very much in this work; and third to counsel with old grammarians and old divines, of hard words, and hard sentences, how they might best be understood and translated; the fourth time to translate as clearly as he could to the sentence [sense for sense], and to have many good fellows and cunning at the correcting of the translation. First, it is to know that the best translating out of Latin into English is to translate after the sentence, and not only after the words, so that the sentence be as open or opener in English as in Latin, and not go far from the letter; and if no appeal may be made to the letter in the translating, let the sentence ever be whole and open, for the words owe to serve to the intent and sentence, and else the words be either superfluous or false. In translating into English, many resolutions may make the sentence open, as an ablative case absolute may be resolved into these three words, with convenable verb, *the while*, *and*, *if*, as grammarians say; as thus, *the master reading, I stand*, may be resolved thus, *while the master reads, I stand*, or *if the master reads*, etc., or *for the master*, etc.; and sometimes it will accord well with the sentence to be resolved into *when*, or into *afterward*, thus *when the master read, I stood*, or *after the master read, I stood*; and sometimes it may well be resolved into a verb of the same tense, as other be in the same reason [sentence], and into this word *et*, that is, *and* in English, as thus, *arescentibus hominibus prae timore*,

[1] The self-description "simple creature" is one of the indications that John Purvey was indeed the author of this preface; Purvey uses it of himself elsewhere. [Ed]

that is, *and men shall wax dry for dread*. Also a participle of a present tense, or preterite, of active voice, or passive, may be resolved into a verb of the same tense, and a conjunction copulative, as thus, *dicens*, that is, *saying*, may be resolved thus, *and says*, or *that says*; and this will, in many places, make the sentence [sense] open, where to English it [translate it into English] after the word [word for word] would be dark and doubtful. Also a relative, *which*, may be resolved into its antecedent with a conjunction copulative, as thus, *which runneth, and he runneth*. Also when a word is once set in a reason [sentence], it may be set forth as often as it is understood, or as often as reason and need ask; and this word *autem* or *vero*, may stand for *forsooth*, or for *but*, and thus I use commonly; and sometimes it may stand for *and*, as old grammarians say. Also when rightful construction is letted by relation, I resolve it openly, thus, where this reason [sentence], *Dominum formidabunt adversarii ejus*, should be Englished thus by the letter, *the Lord his adversaries shall dread*, I English it thus by resolution, *the adversaries of the Lord shall dread him*; and so of other reasons [sentences] that be like. At the beginning I purposed, with God's help, to make the sentence as true and open in English as it is in Latin, or more true and more open that it is in Latin; and I pray, for charity and for common profit of Christian souls, that if any wise man find any default of the truth of translation, let him set in the true sentence and open of holy writ, but look that he examine truly his Latin bible, for no doubt he shall find full many bibles in Latin full false, if he look at many, namely [especially] new; and the common Latin bibles have more need to be corrected, as many as I have seen in my life, than hath the English bible late translated; and where the Hebrew, by witness of Jerome, of Lyra, and other expositors discords [diverges] from our Latin bibles, I have set in the margin, by manner of a gloss, what the Hebrew has, and how it is understood in some place; and I did this most in the Psalter, that of all our books discords most from Hebrew; for the church does not read the Psalter by the last translation of Jerome out of Hebrew into Latin, but another translation of other men, that had much less cunning [knowledge] and holiness than Jerome had; and in full [very] few books the church reads the translation of Jerome, as it may be proved by the proper originals of Jerome, which he glossed. And whether I have translated as openly or more openly in English than in Latin, let wise men deem [decide], that know well both languages, and know well the sentence [meaning] of holy scripture. And whether I have done this, or nay, no doubt, they that con [know] well the sentence [meaning] of holy writ and English together, and will travail, with God's grace, thereabout, may make the bible as true and as open, yea, and more open in English than it is in Latin. And no doubt to a simple man, with God's grace and great travail, men might expound much more openly and shortly the bible in English than the old great doctors have expounded it in Latin, and much more sharply and groundly [fundamentally] than many late postillators, or expositors, have done. But may God, of his great mercy, give us the grace to live well, and to say the truth in convenable manner, and acceptable to God and his people, and to spill [waste] not our time, be it short, be it long, at God's ordinance. But some, that seem wise and holy, say thus, if men now were as holy as Jerome was, they might translate out of Latin into English, as he did out of Hebrew and out of Greek into Latin, and else [if not] they should not translate now, as they think, for default of holiness and of cunning. Though this replication seem colourable [well-founded], it has no good ground, nor reason, nor charity, because this replication is more against saint Jerome, and against the first seventy translators, and against holy church, than against simple men that translate now into English; for saint Jerome was not so holy as the apostles and evangelists, whose books he translated into Latin, nor had he so high gifts of the Holy Ghost as they had; and much more the seventy translators were not so holy as Moses and the prophets, and especially David, nor had they so great gifts of God, as Moses and the prophets had. Furthermore holy church approves, not only the true translation of mean Christian men, steadfast in Christian faith, but also of open heretics, that did away many mysteries of Jesus Christ by guileful translation, as Jerome witnesses in a prologue on Job, and in the prologue of Daniel. Much more let the Church of England approve the true and whole translation of simple men, that would for no good in earth, by their witting and power, put away the least truth, yea, the least letter or tittle, of holy writ, that bears substance or charge.[2] And dispute they not of the holiness of men now living in this deadly life, for they con not thereon, and it is reserved only to God's doom.[3] If they know any notable default by the translators or helpers of them, let them blame the default by charity and mercy, and let them never damn a thing that may be done lawfully by God's law, as wearing of a good cloth for a time, or riding on a horse for a great journey, when they wit not wherefore it is done; for such things may be done of [by] simple men with as great charity and virtue as some that hold them[selves] great and wise can ride in a gilt saddle, or use cushions and beds and cloths of gold

[2] I.e., men who would not sell out ("for no good in earth") and knowingly alter anything substantial in the Bible. [Ed]

[3] I.e., judgment. The gist is that, since the church cannot know who in this life is holy and who is not, that being a matter for God to decide on judgment day, priests should not decide who is fit to translate the Bible. [Ed]

and of silk, with other vanities of the world.[4] God grant pity, mercy, and charity, and love of common profit, and put away such foolish domes [criticisms], that be against reason and charity. Yet worldly clerks ask greatly what spirit makes idiots hardy [bold] to translate now the bible into English, since the four great doctors [Ambrose, Jerome, Augustine, and Gregory the Great] dared never do this? This replication is so lewd, that it needs no answer, nothing but stillness or courteous scorn; for the great doctors were not English men, nor in any case could they the language of English, but they ceased never till they had holy writ in their mother tongue, of their own people. For Jerome, that was a Latin man of birth, translated the Bible, both out of Hebrew and out of Greek, into Latin, and expounded full much thereto; and Austin [Augustine], and many more Latins expounded the bible, for many parts, in Latin, to Latin men, among which they dwelt, and Latin was a common language to their people about Rome, and beyond, and on this half [side], as English is common language to our people, and yet this day the common people in Italy speak Latin corrupt, as true men say, that have been in Italy; and the number of translators out of Greek into Latin passes man's knowing, as Austin witnesses in the 2nd book of Christian Teaching [*On Christian Doctrine* 2.11.16], and says thus,

> the translators out of Hebrew into Greek may be numbered, but Latin translators, either [or] they that translated into Latin, may not be numbered in any manner. For in the first times of faith, each man, as a Greek book came to him, and he seemed to himself to have some cunning of Greek and of Latin, was hardy to translate; and this thing helped more than letted [hindered] understanding, if readers be not negligent, because the beholding of many books has often showed or declared some darker sentences.[5]

This says Austin there. Therefore Grosted [Grosseteste] says that it was God's will that diverse men translated, and that diverse translations be in the church, for where one said darkly, one either [or] more said openly. Lord God! since at the beginning of faith so many men translated into Latin, and to great profit of Latin men, let one simple creature of God translate into English, for profit of English men; for if worldly clerks look well their chronicles and books, they should find that Bede translated the bible, and expounded much in Saxon, that was English, or common language of this land, in his time; and not only Bede, but also King Alfred, that founded Oxford, translated in his last days the beginning of the Psalter into Saxon and would more, if he had lived longer.[6] Also French men, Beemers [Bohemians] and Bretons have the bible, and other books of devotion and of exposition, translated in their mother language; why should not English men have the same in their mother language, I can not wit, no but for falseness and negligence of clerks, or for our people is not worthy to have so great grace and gift of God, in pain of their old sins.[7] God for his mercy amend these evil causes, and make our people to have, and con [know], and keep truly holy writ, to life and death!

But in translating of words equivocal, that is, that hath many significations under one letter, may lightly be peril, for Austin says in the 2nd book of Christian Teaching, that if equivocal words be not translated into the sense, or understanding, of the author, it is error; as in that place of the Psalm, *the feet of them be swift to shed out blood*, the Greek word is equivocal to *sharp* and *swift*, and he that translated *sharp feet*, erred, and a book that has *sharp feet*, is false, and must be amended; as that sentence *unkind young trees shall not give deep roots*, owes to be thus, *plantings of auoutrie [adultery] shall not give deep roots*.[8] Austin says this there. Therefore a translator has great need to study well the sentence [meaning], both before and after, and look that such equivocal words accord with the sentence, and he has need to live a clean life, and be full devout in prayers, and have not his wit occupied about worldly things, that the Holy Spirit, author of wisdom, and cunning, and truth, might dress him in his

[4] I.e., a simple man can arrive as safely and surely at his destination on horseback as a rich man in his fancy carriage; so also can a 'simple' man translate the Bible as well as a learned divine. [Ed]

[5] See above, 32. [Ed]

[6] King Alfred did not found Oxford University, but did translate St. Gregory I's *Pastoral Care*. See above, 37-38. [Ed]

[7] I.e., the only two possible explanations for the lack of an English Bible are that priests have been false and negligent or (a largely rhetorical alternative) the English people are being punished for their sins. [Ed]

[8] Augustine, *On Christian Doctrine* 2.12.18. The author seems to be a bit confused as to the specific terminological point Augustine is making. Augustine chides Latin translators for not knowing what the Greek word *moscheumata* 'transplantings' means and so deriving a new Latin word from *moschos* 'calf' – *uitulamina* 'calvings?' from *uitulus* 'calf'. The author's "*unkind young trees shall not give deep roots*" and "*plantings of auoutrie shall not give deep roots*" seem both to be versions of the Latin phrase Augustine takes to be correct, "*Adulterinae plantationes non dabunt radices altas*" (lit. "adulterated plantings [do] not give roots deep", or as Robertson translates it, "Bastard slips shall not take deep root"; see above, p. 33). [Ed]

work, and suffer him not for to err. Also this word *ex* signifies sometimes *of*, and sometimes it signifies *by*, as Jerome says; and this word *enim* signifies commonly *forsooth*, and, as Jerome says, it signifies *cause, thus, because*; and this word *secundum* is taken for *after* [according to], as many men say, and commonly, but it signifies well *by*, or *up*, thus *by your word*, or *up your word*. Many such adverbs, conjunctions, and prepositions be set often one for another, and at free choice of authors sometimes; and now they shall be taken as it accords best to the sentence. By this manner, with good living and great travail, men may come to true and and clear translating, and true understanding of holy writ, seem it never so hard[9] at the beginning. God grant to us all grace to con well, and keep well holy writ, and suffer joyfully some pain for it at the last! Amen.

[9] I.e., no matter how hard it seems. [Ed]

Leonardo Bruni

Usually referred to in his own day as Leonardo Aretino ('Leonardo of Arezzo'), Leonardo Bruni (1369-1444) was an Italian humanist, statesman, and man of letters whose most lasting accom plishments included translations of Plato, Aristotle, Petrarch, and other Greek writers into Latin and Italian biographies of Dante, Petrarch, and Boccaccio.

Born and raised in the provincial town of Arezzo, the son of a grain merchant, Bruni was regarded as something of an upstart and an outsider in the Florence to which he moved in his early twenties to continue his education. Despite his lack of family ties in Florence, he was adopted 'like a son' by the city chancellor Coluccio Salutati. Having learned Greek in his late twenties, he began translating classic Greek texts into Latin, and soon found himself in the middle of a controversy that was raging over whether schoolboys should be allowed to read prechristian classics. From age 35 to 45 he served as 'apostolic' or papal secretary to four Roman popes, for whom he drafted papal bulls to a variety of correspondents. His work placed him in the middle of controversies between the Roman and the Avignonese popes and between the pope and the Roman people for signorial control of the city; Bruni's sympathies were entirely with the Roman pope, and his efforts helped consolidate papal power.

Bruni's most productive scholarly period was from 1415 to his appointment in 1427 as chancellor of Florence; it was during this period that he wrote most of his biographies and histories, though he did not complete the lives of Dante and Petrarch until early in his term as chancellor, which continued until his death in 1444. During his lifetime and for about a century after his death, Bruni was an internationally renowned Florentine scholar and statesman and a best-selling author (Bruni manuscripts number in the thousands, more than any other Renaissance author); his most popular works were his Latin translations of Aristotle.

On the Correct Way to Translate (*De interpretatione recta*, 1424/26)
Translated by James Hankins

Some time ago I translated from Greek into Latin Aristotle's *Nicomachean Ethics*, and added to it a preface in which I discussed and refuted a great many mistakes made by the old translator.[1] There are some persons, as I now hear, who are critical of my refutation as having been too ungentle. They say that, whatever his errors, the old translator brought his work before the public in good faith, to the extent of his understanding, and deserves therefor not blame, but praise. The well-regulated disputant (they say) does not as a rule expose obvious slips in such detail, but prefers concrete refutation to verbal harassment.

Now I admit that I was rather more heated in my criticism than I ought to have been, but the reason was my sense of indignation. It gave me real pain, anguish even, to see books that in Greek were filled with elegance, delight, and a certain fathomless beauty, defiled and disfigured in Latin by the worst sort of translationese. Suppose I were enjoying a delightful and well-executed painting of Protagenes, say, or Apelles or Aglaophontes, and it should be vandalized. Surely that would be unbearable, and grounds for anger – grounds, indeed, for verbal and physical retaliation against the vandal. In the same way it was for me a source of mental suffering and violent agitation to see thus defiled the works of Aristotle, more brilliant and well-executed than any picture. So if I have seemed to anyone too heated, let him know that that was the cause, a cause surely of such a kind as ought to deserve some excuse, even though it exceeded the mean.

Not that, in my opinion, I *did* exceed the mean. I was angry, to be sure, but I observed discretion and humanity throughout. For consider: did I say anything

[1] The 'old translator' was William of Moerbeke, who was until Bruni the most renowned Latin translator of Aristotle. At the urging of his colleague Thomas Aquinas, usually a proponent of sense-for-sense translation, Moerbeke made his translations literal cribs for the use of scholastics. Bruni's refutation is "Preface to the Appearance of a New Translation of Aristotle's *Ethics*". [Ed]

against his behavior? His life? Did I accuse him of perfidy, or wickedness, or lust? Surely not. What then did I allege against him? Only his ignorance of literature. And what, by God Immortal, does that amount to? Surely a man can be morally good, and yet be wanting in that extensive knowledge I require of him; he might, for that matter, lack any knowledge of letters at all. I did not say he was a bad man, only a bad translator. I might as easily say the same of Plato if he wanted to be the navigator of a ship, but had no knowledge of navigation. I should be detracting nothing from his philosophy, I should only be criticizing the circumstance that he would be ignorant and incapable as a navigator.

In order that the whole subject may be understood from a broader perspective, I shall first of all explain to you my opinion of the correct way to translate. I shall then explain why my criticisms were justified. Thirdly, I shall show that, in criticizing his errors, I have followed the practice of the most learned men.

In my view, then, the whole essence of translation is to transfer correctly what is written in one language into another language. But no one can do this correctly who has not a wide and extensive knowledge of both languages. Nor is even that enough. There are many men who have the capacity to understand an activity, though they cannot themselves exercise it. Many persons, for instance, appreciate painting who cannot themselves paint, and many understand the art of music without themselves being able to sing.

Correct translation is therefore an extremely difficult task. One must have, first of all, a knowledge of the language to be translated, and no small or common knowledge at that, but one that is wide, idiomatic, accurate, and detailed, acquired from a long reading of the philosophers and orators and poets and all other writers. No one who has not read, comprehended, thoroughly considered and retained all these can possibly grasp the force and significance of the words, especially since Aristotle himself and Plato were, I may say, the very greatest masters of literature, and practiced a most elegant kind of writing filled with the sayings and maxims of the old poets and orators and historians, and frequently employed tropes and figures of speech that have acquired idiomatic meanings far different from their literal meanings. We in our language, for instance, employ such expressions as 'I humor you', 'soldiers lost in battle', 'take in good part', 'it would be worthwhile', 'to take pains', and a thousand others like them. The rawest schoolboy knows what 'pains' are, and what 'to take' means, but the whole phrase means something else. To say 'a hundred soldiers were lost in battle', means, literally, that 'a hundred soldiers cannot be found'. It is the same with the other examples: the words mean one thing, the sense is another. 'Deprecor hoc' (lit. 'I pray for') has a negative sense ('I ward off'). The raw and inexperienced schoolboy will understand something as being desired, instead of deprecated, and if required to translate, will give me a meaning the opposite of the one in the original language. The words 'youth' and 'youths' have different meanings: the first means a time of life, the other, a number of young men. "If that youth should be mine", says Vergil, and elsewhere, "In their first flower the youths exercise their horses", and Livy says, "when the youths were armed, they made an incursion into Roman territory". The expression 'to be free from' has a positive sense, while 'to lack' is pejorative. We say 'something is lacking' when we mean something good is lacking, as for example when we say that an orator lacks good diction, or an actor lacks effective gestures. We use the expression 'to be free from' when we mean 'free from something bad', as for instance, when a doctor is free from ignorance, or a lawyer from corruption. 'Penalty' and 'evil' seem closely related, but in fact are far different. 'To pay a penalty' means to suffer or undergo it; 'to pay evil for evil' means to bring an evil on someone else. On the other hand, what words could ever appear more dissimilar than the words 'accept' and 'grant'? Yet they are sometimes synonymous. For when we say 'I grant you that', it means the same as 'I accept it'. I could mention practically unlimited idioms of this kind which the ill-educated person might easily misunderstand. He who fails to take them into account will mistake one thing for another.

Again, we frequently make use of brief allusions to suggest complete thoughts, as when Juvenal, quoting Vergil's phrase "the spoil of Auruncan Actor", speaks in jest about a mirror. "Would that never in Pelion's wood" is a phrase that alludes to the origin and primitive cause of an evil. Such allusions are very common in Greek authors. Even Plato in many instances employs them, and Aristotle, too, commonly uses them. He applies the Homeric phrase "when two go together" to the power and strength of friendship. In his *Politics* he describes a dishonored exile by quoting the oration Achilles made to the ambassadors of Ajax. He uses the words spoken by the Trojan elders about Helen's beauty and grace as a figure for the nature of pleasure. Much could be said on this score. The Greek language covers a broad field, and there are innumerable examples in Aristotle and Plato of illustrations drawn from Homer, Hesiod, Pindar, Euripides, and other ancient poets and writers. Then, too, there is a frequent use of figures of speech, so that a man not familiar with a wide variety of every kind of author is likely to be misled and to mistake the sense of what he is to translate.

Agreed, then, that the first concern of the translator is to acquire a thorough knowledge of the language out of which he translates, and that this knowledge can only be achieved by a repeated, varied and close reading of all kinds of writers. Next he must have such a grasp of the language into which he translates, that he will have a thorough command of it, have it completely within his power, so when he must render word for word, he will not beg or borrow or leave the word in Greek out of ignorance of Latin; he will know subtly the nature and the force of words, so he will not say 'middling' when he means 'small', 'adolescent' when he means 'adolescence', 'courage' when he means 'strength', 'war' when he means 'battle', 'city' when he means 'city-state'. He will moreover observe the distinctions between 'to be fond of' and 'to love', between 'to choose out' and 'to seek out', between 'to desire' and 'to wish', 'to perorate' and 'to persuade', 'to accept' and 'to grant', 'to expostulate with' and 'to complain of', and a thousand similar cases. He will be familiar with the idioms and figures of speech used by the best authors, and will imitate them when he translates, and he will avoid verbal and grammatical novelties, especially those that are imprecise and barbarous.

The foregoing qualities are all necessary. In addition, he must possess a sound ear so that his translation does not disturb and destroy the fullness and rhythmical qualities of the original. For since in every good writer – and most especially in Plato and Aristotle – there is both learning and literary style, he and he only will be a satisfactory translator who is able to preserve both.

In short, these are the vices of a translator: to understand badly what is to be translated, or to turn it badly; and to translate in such fashion that the beauty and precision of the original author is rendered clumsy, confused, and ugly. The man whose ignorance of learning and literature is such that he cannot avoid all those vices, is rightfully criticized and condemned when he tries to translate. By mistaking one thing for another, he leads men into diverse errors, and by making him seem ridiculous and absurd he threatens the majesty of his original author.

So it is by no means correct to say that, in the case of those arts which demand knowledge, the man who makes public his efforts deserves not blame, but praise. A poet who made bad verses would not deserve praise, even if he tried to make them good: we would criticize and condemn him for attempting a thing he knew nothing about. We would blame a sculptor who spoilt a statue even though it were the result of ignorance rather than of bad faith. Just as men who copy a painting borrow the shape, attitude, stance and general appearance therefrom, not thinking what they themselves would do, but what another has done; so in translation the best translator will turn his whole mind, heart, and will to his original author, and in a sense transform him, considering how he may express the shape, attitude and stance of his speech, and all his lines and colors.

By this means, marvellous success is obtained. For every writer has his proper style: Cicero his sonority and richness, Sallust his dry and succinct expression, Livy his rough grandeur. So the good translator in translating each will conform himself to them in such a way that he follows the style of each one. Hence, if he is translating Cicero, with a variety and richness of expression matching his, the translator must fill up the entire period with large, copious, and full phrasings, now rushing them along, now building them up. If he translates Sallust, he must needs decide in the case of nearly every word to observe propriety and great restraint, and to this end must retrench and cut down. If he translates Livy, he must imitate the latter's forms of expression. The translator should be carried away by the power of the original's style. He cannot possibly preserve the sense to advantage unless he insinuates and twists himself into the original's word order and periodic structure with verbal propriety and stylistic faithfulness. This then is the best way to translate: to preserve the style of the original as well as possible, so that polish and elegance be not lacking in the words, and the words be not lacking in meaning.

Correct translation, because of the many and varied talents it requires, which we have mentioned above, is difficult enough, but it is surpassingly difficult to translate correctly when the original author has written with a sense of prose rhythm and literary polish. For in rhythmic prose, one must carefully observe and follow the cola [clauses or clause-groups], commata [smaller groups of words], and periods to precisely and squarely mark out the word order. And in preserving other figures of speech and of thought, great care must likewise be employed. Unless the translator preserves them all, he will crack and spoil completely the majesty of his original. But such preservation is impossible without great diligence and literary knowledge. The translator must understand the virtues, as it were, of the original composition and reproduce them correspondingly in his own tongue. There are two varieties of figures, figures of speech ('schemes') and figures of thought ('tropes'), both of which present difficulties to the translator. Those of speech, however, are more difficult than those of thought because they frequently consist in rhythmical effects, as when two phrases employ the same number of syllables, or when they are inverted or opposed in meaning, a figure the Greeks call 'antithesis'. For the corresponding Latin words often have either more or fewer syllables than the Greek, which makes it difficult to attain the same effect. Again, the darts which sometimes the orator throws strike with force only when they are discharged rhythmically; if they are feeble, lame or confused, they do little damage. The translator must study all these effects carefully and reproduce the rhythm to a nicety. And what of figures of thought, which light up one's style and give it distinction? The best writers employ these as much as the other figures. Can a translator without disgrace be ignorant of them, omit them, or fail to give them in his translation their full majesty?

In order that what I have said about all these matters may be better understood, I should like to set out several examples to make it clear that it is not only the orators, but also the philosophers who employ these sorts of figures, and that, unless they are preserved in the translation, the majesty of their style is completely destroyed ...

The works of Plato and Aristotle are full of beauties and elegancies of this kind which would require a great deal of time to explicate in detail. To be sure, the reader will easily ascertain this for himself, if he possesses the erudition. By these examples it is abundantly clear that no one can preserve the majesty of the original unless he preserve its figures of speech and its rhythmical character. A loose and clumsy translation spoils immediately the whole reputation and influence of the original author. For this reason, it should be thought an inexcusable act of wickedness for a man who is not really learned or literary to attempt a translation.

Duarte (Edward, King of Portugal)

Duarte (1391-1438, reigned 1433-1438) was known as the philosopher-king; author of a famous legal treatise on 'The Loyal Counselor', he was a legal scholar whose land-grant reforms strengthened the Portugese monarchy.

Duarte (called King Edward in English) ascended to the throne upon the death of his father John I, at the age of 42. His interest in geographical exploration led him to back his brother Henry the Navigator in his expeditions to the West Coast of Africa; later, in 1437, he supported Henry in the disastrous invasion of Tangier, part of a plan to conquer Morocco. Duarte died shortly afterward of the plague.

Duarte's instructions on proper translation methods are closely related to those offered by Leonardo Bruni a few years earlier and by Etienne Dolet a century later; the 'job description' for the good translator has become by our time a classical genre of translation theory.

The Art of Translating From Latin
From *The Loyal Counselor* (*O Leal Conselheiro*, 1430s)
Translated by Maria J. Cirurgião

Whereas many who are lettered do not know how to translate well from Latin into our mother tongue, I thought of writing these words of advice applicable towards that purpose.

First, to be well-acquainted with the meaning of the sentence to be translated and to render it entirely, neither changing, nor augmenting, nor diminishing in any way that which is written. Second, not to use latinized words, nor words from other tongues, but the whole to be written in our own vernacular, as near to the good usage of our speech as possible. Third, always to use words that are direct language, faithful to the Latin [text], and not to substitute one word for another; therefore, where the Latin states 'to glide' not to use 'to distance' and so on in other similar cases, deeming one [word] to be as good as another; for it is of great importance, for a good understanding, that these words be appropriately selected. Fourth, not to use words that, according to our habits of speech, are considered offensive. Fifth, that the same precepts be maintained which need be maintained when writing any other matter, namely, that the writing be wholesome, that it be clear and easily understandable, that it be as captivating as possible and concise to the extent possible. And, towards this end, the use of proper paragraphs and good punctuation is very advantageous. As to one person doing the mental work of rendering from Latin into the vernacular, and another person doing the writing, I am of the opinion that the whole is best done by one person.

William Caxton

As a translator and the first English printer, William Caxton (c. 1422-1491) exerted an enormous influence over later English literature.

Caxton was apprenticed to a mercer around the age of 16; when his master died three years later he moved to Bruges, where he was to live for the next 30 years, growing wealthy and powerful as a member of the English trading community in Holland and Flanders – of which community he was appointed 'governor' in 1463. In 1470 he stepped down from this post to enter the service of Margaret, duchess of Burgundy, most likely as her financial advisor.

It was in this period that Caxton increasingly became interested in literature, first as a translator, then as a printer. He began translating Raoul Le Fèvre's *Recueil des histoires de Troye* in 1469, but, finding that copying the book tired his hand and eye, he learned printing, and printed his finished translation of Le Fèvre, under the title *The Recuyell of the Historyes of Troye*, in 1475 – the first printed English book. The next year he published three other books before returning to England, where he continued to translate, write, and print books for kings, nobles, and rich merchants. His encyclopedia *The Myrrour of the worlde* (1481) was the first illustrated book printed in English. He also printed English literature, including Geoffrey Chaucer, John Gower, Sir Thomas Malory, and John Lydgate. By his death in 1491 he had published around 100 books, 24 of which were his own translations.

Caxton's prologue to his translation of the *Aeneid*, reprinted below, is especially interesting for its discussion of the problems of dialect, a problem that the Finnish Bible translator Mikael Agricola too will discuss a few decades later.

Prologue to *Aeneid* (1490)

After diverse works made, translated and achieved, having no work in hand, I sitting in my study where as lay many diverse pamphlets and books, [it] happened that to my hand came a little book in French, which late was translated out of Latin by some noble clerk of France, which book is named *Aeneid*, made in Latin by that noble poet and great clerk [learned man] Virgil.

Which book I saw over and read therein how after the general destruction of the great Troy, Aeneas departed bearing his old father Anchises upon his shoulders, his little son Iulus on his hand, his wife with much other people following, and how he shipped and departed, with all the history of his adventures that he had ere he came to the achievement of his conquest of Italy as all along shall be showed in this present book.

In which book I had great pleasure, by cause of the fair and honest terms and words in French, which I never saw before like, nor none so pleasant nor so well-ordered. Which book as meseemed should be much requisite to noble men to see as well for the eloquence as the histories, how well that many hundred years passed was the said book of *Aeneid* with other works made and learned daily in schools, specially in Italy and other places.

Which history the said Virgil made in metre, and when I had advised me in this said book, I deliber[at]ed and concluded to translate it into English, and forthwith took a pen and ink and wrote a leaf or twain, which I oversaw again to correct it. And when I saw the fair and strange terms therein, I doubted that it should not please some gentlemen which late blamed me, saying that in my translations I had overcurious terms which could not be understood of [by] common people, and desired me to use old and homely terms in my translations.

And fain would I satisfy every man, and so to do took an old book and read therein, and certainly the English was so rude and brood that I could not well understand it. And also my lord Abbot of Westminster [John Estney] did do show to me late certain evidences written in Old English for to reduce it into our English now used. And certainly it was written in such wise that it was more like to Dutch [German] than English. I could not reduce nor bring it to be understood.

And certainly our language now used varies far from that which was used and spoken when I was born. For we English men are born under the domination of the moon, which is never steadfast, but ever wavering, waxing one season and wanes and decreases another season. And that common English that is spoken in one shire varies from another. In so much that in my days happened that certain merchants were in a ship in Thames for to have sailed over the sea into Zeeland, and for lack of wind they tarried at Foreland and went to land for to refresh them. And one of them, named Sheffield, a mercer, came into a house and asked for meat, and specially he asked after eggs. And the goodwife answered that she could speak no French. And the merchant was angry, for he also could speak no French, but would have had eggs, and she understood him not. And then at last another said that he would have eyren; then the goodwife said that she understood him well.[1]

Lo what should a man in these days now write, eggs or eyren? Certainly it is hard to please every man, by cause of diversity and change of language. For in these days every man that is of any reputation in his country will utter his communication and matters in such manners and terms that few men shall understand them.

And some honest and great clerks have been with me and desired me to write the most curious terms that I could find. And thus between plain rude and curious I stand abashed. But in my judgment the common terms that be daily used are lighter [easier] to be understood than the old and ancient English. And for as much as this present book is not for a rude [uncultured] uplandish man to labour therein, nor read it, but only for a clerk and a noble gentleman that feels and understands in feats of arms in love and noble chivalry, therefore in a mean [middle] between both I have reduced and translated this said book into our English not overrude nor curious but in such terms as shall be understood by God's grace according to my copy. And if any man will intermit [engage] in reading of it and finds such terms that he can not understand, let him go read and learn Virgil, or the epistles of Ovid, and there he shall see and understand lightly all, if he have a good reader and informer. For this book is not for every rude and unconning [ignorant] man to see, but to clerks and very gentlemen that understand gentleness [gentility] and science.

Then I pray all them that shall read in this little treatise to hold me for excused for the translating of it.

[1] In the fifteenth century, northerners said 'eggs', southerners 'eyren'. [Ed]

For I acknowledge myself ignorant of conning [knowledge] to enprise [undertake] on me so high and noble a work. But I pray master John Skelton, late created Poet Laureate in the University of Oxford, to oversee and correct this said book. And to address and expound where as shall be found fault to them that shall require it. For him I know for sufficient to expound and English every difficulty that is therein. For he has late translated the epistles of Tully [Cicero] and the book of Diodorus Siculus, and diverse other works out of Latin into English, not in rude and old language, but in polished and ornate terms craftily [expertly], as he that has read Virgil, Ovid, Tully, and all the other noble poets and orators to me unknown; and also he has read the IX muses and understood their musical [muse-related or artistic] sciences, and to whom of them each science is appropred [attributed]. I suppose he has drunk of Alcyon's Well.[2] Then I pray him and such other to correct, add, or [di]minish where he or they shall find fault; for I have but followed my copy in French as nigh as me is possible, and if any word be said therein well, I am glad, and if otherwise I submit my said book to their correction. Which book I present unto the high-born, my to-coming [future] natural and sovereign Lord Arthur by the grace of God Prince of Wales, Duke of Cornwall, and Earl of Chester, first-begotten son and heir unto our most dread [revered] natural and sovereign Lord and most Christian King Henry the VII by the grace of God King of England and of France and Lord of Ireland, beseeching his noble grace to receive it in thanks of me his most humble subject and servant. And I shall pray unto Almighty God for his prosperous increasing in virtue, wisdom, and humanity, that he may be equal with the most renowned of all his noble progenitors.

And so to live in this present life, that after this transitory life he and we all may come to everlasting life in heaven. Amen.

Desiderius Erasmus

Desiderius Erasmus of Rotterdam (1469-1536), the foremost scholar in sixteenth-century Europe, steered a precarious middle course through the stormy religious controversies of his day, rejecting the doctrine of papal infallibility and encouraging the spirit of reform that generated Protestantism, but rejecting Luther's doctrine of predestination and working to preserve the unity of the church. His pioneering philological studies of the Greek New Testament and the church fathers, drawing on methods developed by the Italian humanists, laid the foundation for what would later be called historical-critical theology; and his Latin translation of the New Testament was the first new translation accepted by the church since the Vulgate over a thousand years before.

Erasmus was born in Rotterdam, the second illegitimate son of a priest, Roger Gerard, and a physician's daughter named Margaret. Classically educated, Erasmus entered an Augustinian monastery at 16 and stayed there until he was ordained into the priesthood at 23; calling his monastic superiors 'barbarians' for discouraging his classical studies, he then set off on a journey through a variety of posts, as secretary to the bishop of Cambrai, as tutor to University of Paris students, and professor of divinity at the University of Louvain. He spent many years in England at the house of Sir Thomas More, where he wrote his famous *Praise of Folly* (*Moriae encomium*, 1511), dedicated to More, and where John Colet encouraged him to cultivate the 'primitive theology' of the early Church Fathers – as opposed to the arid and litigious scholasticism of the academic theologians of his day.

Erasmus fought throughout his life to maintain a unified church, and while he engaged in a celebrated controversy with Luther, he strenuously avoided attacking Luther or the other Reformers with the virulence desired by what he called the 'pharisaic' ecclesiastical and secular authorities. He loathed all religious persecution, and while clinging to his own radical definition of Catholic orthodoxy, he argued fervently for tolerance toward religious dissenters. In his *Handbook of a Christian Knight* (*Enchiridion militis Christiani*, 1503/04) he defended lay piety against monasticism; and in his popular proverb collection *Adagia* (1515) he forthrightly attacked Christian society for its self-righteous defenses of its refusal to imitate Christ.

Erasmus wrote the first three letters reprinted below in his thirties, and describes the classical translations he had done (from Greek to Latin) as apprentice-work; it is interesting to watch him move, as he gains practice in translating, from a severe literalist position in the first two letters to a more expansive paraphrast position in the third.

The 1518 letter to Maarten Lips is a defense of his new Latin translation of the New Testament from the best Greek sources, which he had published two years earlier. The year after his letter, in 1519, the second edition of the translation supplanted the Vulgate New Testament that carried Jerome's name; three more editions were published in Erasmus' lifetime.

Conservative theologians all across Europe,

[2] Helicon's Well in Boeotia, a classical image for the bursting forth of the poetic imagination. [Ed]

most of them ignorant of Greek, rose up in arms at the 'impudence', as they called it, of questioning the authority of Jerome, who, as Erasmus here points out, did not even translate the New Testament, but merely revised an existing translation. His friend Maarten Lips, an Augustinian canon in Louvain, showed him an attack on his translation made by an English scholar named Edward Lee who was then at the University of Louvain, and Erasmus wrote his response while travelling on the Rhine to Basel. The letter may never have actually been sent to Lips; it was written for quick publication (hence Erasmus' coy hinting at Lee's identity in paragraph 5). The controversy between the two men continued to rage through several more rebuttals and counterrebuttals.

Following Jerome's letter to Pammachius by eleven centuries and preceding Luther's circular letter on translation by twelve years, Erasmus' letter is in the grandest (and quirkiest) tradition of Western translation theory: the indignant epistolary response to an ill-informed conservative attack on a new translation.

Letter to Nicholas Ruistre (1503)
Translated by R. A. B. Mynori and D. E. S. Thomson

Louvain, 17 November 1503

TO THE REVEREND FATHER IN CHRIST, NICHOLAS RUISTRE, BISHOP OF ARRAS, CHANCELLOR OF THE RENOWNED AND MOST FLOURISHING UNIVERSITY OF LOUVAIN, COUNCILLOR OF HIS HIGHNESS THE ARCHDUKE PHILIP OF AUSTRIA, FROM ERASMUS DESIDERIUS OF ROTTERDAM, GREETINGS

I have recently come into possession of certain Greek declamations, illustrious prelate, and have resolved to translate these into Latin with the object of determining how far I have made any considerable progress in the knowledge of both these tongues. Accordingly, when I looked about for the person to whom I might most fitly dedicate this my aprentice work, yours was the first and indeed the only name that came to mind. For, all else apart, to whom could I better pay tribute with the fruits of my studies than the chancellor of this flourishing university, who is the governor of all its scholarly pursuits, and its permanent head? Coming to Louvain as I have by choice, I received much encouragement and inspiration, not only from the universal report of your good qualities "current on the lips of humankind",[1] but also in a pronounced degree from the almost daily eulogies he has endowed the king with the attributes of supreme magnanimity, combined however with enormous self-control and good humour: for Menelaus goes so far as to praise Priam, while he diverts all the odium attaching to the crime from the Trojans at large to Paris alone; and even against him he does not say a word that is ill-natured or vindictive. Also he speaks against the war in such a way that he appears to be personally confident of victory and only have the interests of the others at heart. Lastly the author has even represented his brevity of utterance in express terms: which not only is, as it were, the heritage of all Spartans, but, as the evidence of Cicero and Quintilian and Gellius shows, in Menelaus was specially associated with subtlety, elegance, and gaiety; but all of them follow a single source, namely Homer, whose words, in the passage I have quoted, are the following:

> ᾿Αλλ᾿ ὃτε δήμύθους καὶ μήδεα πᾶσιν ὕφαινον
> ῎Ητοι μέν Μενέλαος ἐπιτροχάδην άγόρευε
> Λαῦρα μέν, ἀλλά μάλα λιγέως, ἐπεί οὐ πολύμυθος
> Οὐδ᾿ ἀφαμαρτοεπής, εἰ καί γένει ὕστερος ἦεν.
> [Iliad 3.312-15]

This I have roughly translated as follows:

> But when they speech and counsel 'gan to weave
> In all men's sight and Menelaus spoke,
> Few were his words, and quick, but clear withal;
> For much to say inclined he not, not yet
> Wandered in talk, though of more youthful age.

The second declamation is taken from a tragedy; the third from the last book of the *Iliad*, where Andromache utters almost the same kind of lamentation in bewailing Hector. Both of these are of uncertain authorship and of much inferior quality as well. Of course the whole exercise is somewhat trivial; yet I thought it might be suitable for attempting my first ventures in this kind of work, in order, of course, to avoid "learning the potter's art on a great jar", as the Greek proverb has it, but rather to "to take risk with a Carian". I have followed Cicero's old rule: in translating I thought it my duty to weigh the meaning, not count the words. However, as an apprentice-translator I have preferred to err on the side of accuracy rather than of boldness. But others must judge how far my efforts have been successful. I can testify to one fact which I have learned by trying: nothing is harder than to turn good Greek into good Latin. If, however, I find that these my preliminary essays and first fruits, so to call them, have not displeased you, then I shall go on with confidence to greater tasks, relying upon your verdict and the support of your authority; and I shall take the liberty of sending you, not mere flowerets, but harvests gathered from the fields of learning.

Farewell, illustrious prelate and father in God; I beg

[1] A fragment of Ennius, cited by Cicero *Tusculanae disputationes* 1.15.34. [Tr]

that you may vouchsafe to enrol me, and my studies likewise, in the ranks of your devoted humble servants.

Louvain, 17 November 1503.

Letter to William Warham (1506)
Translated by R. A. B. Mynori and D. E. S. Thomson

London, 24 January [1506]

TO THE MOST REVEREND FATHER IN CHRIST, WILLIAM [WARHAM], ARCHBISHOP OF CANTERBURY, PRIMATE OF ENGLAND, FROM ERASMUS OF ROTTERDAM, A CANON OF THE ORDER OF ST. AUGUSTINE, GREETINGS

Having resolved, most illustrious prelate, to translate Greek authorities in order to restore or promote, as far as I could, the science of theology which had fallen into a most shameful condition through scholastic trifling, but wishing to avoid risking my potter's skill all at once on a great jar, as the Greek adage has it, or rushing into such a large enterprise with feet as yet unwashed, as the saying goes, I determined first to test whether the labour I had spent on Greek and Latin had been wasted by experimenting on a subject which, though very taxing, was secular in nature; one that was hard enough to afford me good practice, while any mistake I made would be at the cost of my intellectual reputation alone, causing no harm to Holy Writ. Accordingly I took in hand the translation of two tragedies by Euripides[2] – perchance blow from Heaven to forward so bold an endeavour. Presently I observed that a sample of my proposed work did not displease certain persons well versed in both tongues – and England of course now contains several who, if one may speak the truth without giving offence, deserve everyone's admiration, even throughout Italy, in all branches of scholarship. Thus with the muses' favour I finished it in a very few months. How much sweat this cost me, only those who have stepped into the same wrestling-ring can understand. For, considering that the very task of turning good Greek into good Latin is one that demands exceptional skill, and not only the richest and readiest vocabulary in both languages but also an extremely sharp and alert intelligence, so that for several generations past nobody who has undertaken it has earned approval by the votes of the learned world – you may quite easily guess how painful a task it was to render verse metrically, especially when its metres are so various and so unfamiliar, the work of an author who is not only of great antiquity, and a tragedian at that, but remarkably succinct, delicate, and exquisite in his style; in whom there is not a spare word or anything one could subtract or alter without doing him great violence; who, moreover, is so fond of, and clever at, handling rhetorical themes that he seems to be for ever making declamatory speeches. Besides this there are the choruses, which are so obscure, because of some sort of deliberate artifice, that they need an Oedipus, or Delian prophet,[3] rather than a commentator. These difficulties are increased by poor texts, shortage of manuscripts, and a lack of commentators to whom we may have recourse; so that I am not really surprised if even in the present fortunate age no Italian has ventured to embark on the task of translating any tragedy or any comedy, whereas several have attempted Homer (and, among those, Poliziano himself was dissatisfied with his own work); and a certain translator has tried Hesiod, though here too with unhappy results; while another has attacked Theocritus, still more unsuccessfully; and Francesco Filelfo in one of his funeral orations translated (I discovered after I had begun my own version) the first scene of *Hecuba*, but did so in such a fashion that I, usually bashful to a fault, was considerably encouraged by this great scholar's performance.

For my part, then, I was not deterred, either by these distinguished examples or by the work's many difficulties, but rather attracted by the more than honeyed sweetness of this poet's style (a sweetness conceded to him even by hostile critics). Accordingly I did not hesitate to embark on a task unattempted hitherto, in the hope that, even if I produced little in the way of a result, yet kindly readers might still deem that this attempt of mine deserved some praise, while those of a less friendly disposition should at least be indulgent to a novice's version of a work so hard, especially since I had deliberately added considerably to the other difficulties by my scrupulous accuracy in translation, attempting as far as possible to reproduce the shape and, as it were, the contours of the Greek poems, striving to render verse for verse and almost word for word, and everywhere trying zealously to adapt the force and effect of the meaning to Latin ears, with all fidelity. This I did, perhaps because I do not fully share the freedom in translating authors that Cicero both allows others and (I should almost say excessively) practises himself, or perhaps because as a novice in translation I preferred to err in seeming to keep too close rather than to be too free, or in other words to run aground occasionally through hugging the shore, rather than to suffer shipwreck and be left swimming in the ocean; and I thought it better that scholars should perhaps find me wanting in grace, let us say,

[2] The *Hecuba*, to which this letter is Erasmus' dedication, and the *Iphigenia*, to which the following letter to Warham is his dedication. [Ed]

[3] Oedipus, legendary king of Thebes who killed his father Laius and married his mother Jocasta; here invoked as the solver of the riddle of the Sphinx. Delian prophets were oracles of Apollo on the island of Delos, birthplace of Apollo. [Ed]

and elegance of poetic style than in accuracy. Lastly, I did not wish to announce that I was but paraphrasing, and so provide myself with the refuge wherein many translators excuse their ignorance and, like the cuttle-fish, spread an inky obscurity round themselves to escape detection. And if my critics fail to find in my work the elevated language of Latin tragedy, the bombast and words of giant size that Horace speaks of, they should not reckon it a fault in me that, as a translator, I have chosen to reproduce the concise clarity and neatness of my original rather than a pomposity that does not belong to it and in which I take little pleasure in any case.

I am accordingly prompted to be full of confidence that my present efforts may be both immune to unfair disparagement and likely to earn the good will of fair-minded and friendly readers, if, most worshipful Father, they have also gained the seal of your approval. It was indeed easy for me to choose you, out of a multitude of eminent princes, to receive the dedication of these fruits of my nightly labours, for besides the supreme eminence of your position I perceived you to be so endowed, adorned, and abundantly furnished with learning, eloquence, prudence, piety, humility, uprightness, and, lastly, unparalleled benevolence towards all who cultivate good letters, that the name of primate suits none better than yourself; for you take the primacy not only in rank and office but much more still in every kind of virtue, and are at one and the same time the chief adornment of the court and the pinnacle of eminence in the church. And if it should be my fortune to win for my work the esteem of one who is so highly esteemed, certainly I shall neither regret that I endured my labours so far, not be reluctant in future to assist theology by some greater undertaking.

Farewell: and pray regard your humble servant as one of those who are most sincerely devoted to your fatherhood.

London, 24 January

Letter to William Warham (1507)
Translated by R. A. B. Mynori and D. E. S. Thomson

[Bologna, November 1507]

TO WILLIAM, ARCHBISHOP OF CANTERBURY, FROM ERASMUS, GREETINGS

My Lord Archbishop, after I had begun to labour at this tragedy [Euripides' *Iphigenia*] it seemed to me that I detected a different flavour in the language, and another style of poetry; for, if I am not mistaken, it has somewhat more naturalness and its style is more flowing. For which reason it might seem to be by Sophocles: but again it rather suggests Euripidean paternity by its close-packed themes and a sort of rhetorical ability in marshalling arguments on one side or the other of a question. However it is not my province to determine to which of the two it should be ascribed, nor do I think it matters much. All the same, I have decided to relax my former strictness somewhat in order to avoid failure to do justice to the theme in this respect as well. Accordingly I have translated the *Iphigenia* a little more freely and also a little more expansively, but again in such a way as in no degree to fall short of a translator's duty to convey the meaning. In one respect I have dared in both plays to depart from my author's practice: I have to some extent reduced that metrical diversity and licence of the choric parts, hoping that scholars would take my difficulties into account and pardon me for this; after all, Horace did not strive to reproduce the great freedom in prosody and variety in metres shown by the lyric poets, nor Seneca those of the tragedians, although each of them was merely imitating the Greeks, not translating them as well. But even if I had time among my more important studies to translate a number of other tragedies, not only should I not repent of this boldness, but I should not be reluctant to alter the style and topics of the choruses; and I should prefer either to treat of some commonplace or to deviate into some agreeable digression, rather than to waste effort upon what Horace calls "melodious trifles" [*Ars Poetica* 322]. For it seems to me that nowhere did the ancients write more foolishly than in choruses of this sort, where, through excessive striving for novelty of utterance, they destroyed clarity of expression, and in the hunt for marvellous verbal effects their sense of reality suffered. Farewell, my honoured patron.

Letter to Maarten Lips (1518)
Translated by R. A. B. Mynori and D. E. S. Thomson

ERASMUS OF ROTTERDAM TO MAARTEN LIPS, GREETING

Do you not think me exceptionally fortunate? There comes to me unasked a blessing which other men scarcely obtain by great effort and expense: everyone offers to instruct Erasmus. And so of necessity, unless I am a mere blockhead, I must some day make progress. In one point, however, I may be thought somewhat unlucky: most of my would-be teachers play the part of hostile critics rather than instructors. Some of them have as their object not to make me a better scholar or a better man, but by joining battle with me to earn, they hope, some pittance of reputation for themselves. All are furious, none more so than those who can teach me absolutely nothing. They are like some schoolmasters, always shouting and clouting and flogging the boys' skin off their backs, and can teach nothing for all that except bad grammar, which they will soon have to unlearn. The man whose pamphlet you have sent me is one of these; it is so illiterate that I could hardly endure to read it, so comical that I could not fail to, though I kept it for a journey by boat.[4] I should be as mad as he is if I tried to answer such malicious falsehoods. But I will scribble a word of comment on each chapter of his nonsense, in such a way that, if you like, they can actually be numbered.

1. First of all then, having assured us that ten acute conclusions have validated his constatation (his whole style is gay with such blossoms as these), he assumes as generally accepted that the version of the New Testament now in common use is Jerome's, though it is known to be neither Cyprian's nor Hilary's nor Ambrose's nor Augustine's nor Jerome's,[5] for he has different readings; much less is it the version which he tells us he has corrected, for things are found in it which he condemns, in respect not only of the wording but of the sense. And this is the base of his theological argument.

2. He imagines, and assumes as proved, that I publicly correct and alter the Vulgate text, whereas I leave that intact and untouched and have turned into Latin what is found in the Greek copies, pointing out as I go along the agreements or disagreements of our own text; not seldom preferring what is in these copies of ours, correcting anything corrupt, explaining ambiguities, elucidating obscurities, and changing anything that is notably barbarous in expression, because I understand that very many people are so disgusted by the prodigious errors (which however are nearly always the translator's work and not the authors') that they cannot bring themselves to read the Scriptures. Nor for that matter have all mortals such an iron digestion that they can endure the style of it. But if we simplify our language for the benefit of ignorant and simple folk, should we not help educated readers too by purifying the language? In any case, if this critic of mine wishes nothing whatever to be published that differs from the Vulgate text in common use, it will not be lawful to publish the New Testament in Greek as the Greeks use it, unless it has first been corrected against our published Vulgate, for fear that someone will detect some disagreement. Who is mad enough to say any such thing? We must do away forthwith with St. Ambrose's version or paraphrase, whichever it is, of the Pauline Epistles, which differs extensively from our version; we must do away with Jerome's too, which differs from it in a number of places. And then most of our manuscripts must be done away with, because as a rule they differ among themselves. Observe too the disagreement between your friend and Augustine, whom he seems to think no one else has read. Augustine declares[6] that he has actually been helped by the difference between copies, since what is obscure in one version is more clearly rendered in another; we cannot all do all things. This man supposes that all confidence in Scripture is brought to an end, if the difference in reading is made public, and would rather the most manifest blunders were left in the sacred text than that two or three foolish old men who are hard to please should take offence. Yet St. Jerome was not in the least deterred from this line of enquiry by the fact that the change of some small word or other in the prophet Jonah[7] made almost the whole population rebel against their bishop, and pours scorn on those gods so dependent on gourds who are shaken by so small a change, although Augustine had written and told Jerome the story as though it were a serious matter. Why, let that severe critic of yours answer me just this one question: should we wish on behalf of God's church that she should read the books of Holy Scripture in a truly accurate text or no? If he admits that it is desirable, let him tell us whether he admits that sundry errors are imported into those books every day by the ignorance of correctors or the negligence of scribes. If this cannot be denied, why does he not welcome these efforts of mine, which contribute more than anything else to the double object of mending corruptions and preserving from corruption what is correct? For there is no denying that there are corruptions in most of our manuscripts – in fact, in almost all. Then let him tell us whether it is important that the Scriptures should be correctly understood or no. If he thinks it is important, why does he condemn my efforts, which have explained so many passages that even he, learned as he is, never understood before? Let him read my work

[4] The date suggests that Erasmus composed his answer as he read the letter; cf par. 91 and the general lack of exact references, careful argumentation, and organization. [Tr]

[5] Following a commission by Pope Damasus I, from 382 Jerome revised the Latin New Testament in the light of Greek texts. Later he translated the Old Testament anew from the Hebrew. In the 'Apologia' prefixed to the 1516 edition of his New Testament Erasmus had correctly pointed out that Jerome was the editor rather than the translator of the New Testament. [Tr] There were several fourth- and fifth-century Hilaries who were later sainted; Erasmus is probably referring to Hilary of Poitiers. [Ed]

[6] See the beginning of the *Quaestiones in Heptateuchem* 1 (CC 33:1); *De civitate Dei* 11.19. [Tr] See also above, 32. [Ed]

[7] In Jonah 4:6 God provides some shade for the weary prophet in the form of a common plant – a gourd, according to the Vulgate. In Jerome's translation the plant was an ivy, and Augustine reported that this unaccustomed word, when used by a bishop, had caused a disturbance among his flock in the city of Oea. In his reply Jerome tries to clarify the nature of that plant for which Latin apparently had no name; see Jerome's Ep[istle] 112.22, in reply to Augustine's Ep[istle] 71. [Tr]

through and deny if he can that what I say is true.

3. He says that many people have tried to undermine and do away with the Vulgate text, some to add elegance of style, others to exclude error, but that all attempts have failed. Is the man not ashamed of such palpable nonsense? Let him produce one person who has tried this – unless perhaps he will put forward the sole name of Lefèvre.

4. He writes that among all the Latin and Greek scholars who abound in Paris and Germany and England and Scotland no one has dared to attempt this, although has lately made the attempt, criticizing this edition of mine and carping at it here and there.[8]

5. And who can fail to see how openly false it is to say that in these countries there are so many men skilled in Latin and Greek? – especially in Scotland, while of Italy he says nothing. This makes me suspect that the man is a Scot.

6. Then what is more foolish than this line of argument? "In Paris there are a great many learned philosophers; it is therefore forbidden for this or that individual to attempt any innovation in philosophy". Let there be many thousands of them: even so one person must make a start. And none the less I suppose that in all that multitude I am not absolutely last, as far as knowledge of the two tongues is concerned.

7. He says that Lorenzo [Valla] was the start of the trouble; as though Lorenzo had translated the New Testament, or Jerome had not done the same thing long before his time.

8. Then he is most foolishly indignant because I subject Christ's words to the rules of Donatus[9] – just as though Christ had spoken in the exact words used by our translator. On the contrary, as it is known that the apostles wrote Greek, though not very correctly, I have not changed a single letter in the language they used; much less have I wished to bring Christ's words under the rule of law.

9. It is ridiculous too to make me responsible for the rules of grammar, as though it were I who am the authority for good Latin, rather than authors who wrote before the birth of Christ.

10. "Erasmus reckons this decree unworthy", says he. Quite the contrary: it is the papal decretals[10] which lay down that a document shall be rejected as spurious if a manifest blunder is detected in it, and another decree[11] carefully legislates for public instruction in the three ancient languages as being essential for the understanding of Scripture.

11. His standard for the purity of Latin is ancient usage, as Augustine wrote; as though I used any other standard, or the translator wrote in the style of his Ancients. The next thing, I suppose, will be a demand that we should all adopt his own flowers of style.

12. And all through this discussion he confuses elegance of language, which is a question for grammarians, with eloquence and with poetic style, as though there were no difference, and asserts that the way we should express ourselves depends entirely on the precedent of Holy Scripture, finding fault in passing with all those sainted authors whose writing is most unlike the example set by the language of the apostles. If we are not allowed to write in any other fashion, how dare he write this stammering stuff himself and use so many monstrous expressions, none of which is to be found in the writings of the apostles?

13. Meanwhile he dreams up the idea that the Latin translator produced what we now have under the inspiration of the Holy Spirit, though Jerome himself in his preface [to the Pentateuch] openly testifies that each translator renders to the best of his ability what he is capable of understanding.[12] Otherwise, Jerome himself would be grossly irreligious, in that he is not afraid to find fault sometimes with what we have in this edition.

14. In order to prove that all eloquence must be sought from Holy Scripture, he produces Jerome as his authority, although [in *Prologus in Ieremiam*] Jerome credits some of the prophets with uneducated language and Paul with ignorance of Greek, and that too in more than one passage.

15. We believe that Augustine likewise had the assistance of the Holy Spirit in expounding the books of Scripture; and yet [in his *Retractiones*] he revises his work and wishes it to be read with a critical eye.

16. Besides which, the objection he raises against himself, following Jerome, that the saints were more eloquent in their mother tongue than in any other, is thus dissolved by our expert logician. "If it is a question", says he, "of the flatulent and windy verbiage admired by the world, I at least do not refuse to call the saints inarticulate. But if the saints meant rustic barbarism when they criticized the prophets, it is right in our day to have a higher opinion of them". As though the

[8] In his commentary on the Pauline Epistles he had criticized an interpretation in Erasmus' New Testament of 1516. [Tr]

[9] The grammar of Aelius Donatus was so popular in the Middle Ages that his name came to connote grammar in general. [Tr]

[10] Erasmus was probably recalling *Decreta* part 1 distinctio 9 chs 3-6 in the *Corpus iuris canonici*. This quotes Augustine admitting errors in his own works and insisting that, in order to be authoritative, the text of Scripture must be freed from errors, using Hebrew and Greek as a basis. Erasmus may also have thought of Jerome's preface [to his edition of the Gospels] which acknowledges the papal request to revise the New Testament. [Tr]

[11] It dated from the Council of Vienna, 1311-12, but is slightly misrepresented here. [Tr]

[12] See above, 30. [Ed]

word 'eloquence' changed its meaning when wrongly used, or as though we thought the apostles foolish and rustic in their statements of principle, in which the most important part of eloquence is to be found, or as though Cyprian's style must be windy verbiage because it is unlike the language of the prophets.

17. He then concludes this elegant syllogism by telling us that all the folly and falsehood of the poets must be rejected, in order to secure the truth of his conclusion. It goes like this (and I quote the precise words, so let no one suspect me of fabricating my charges): "The sole source for purity of language, for ornament, for elegance or eloquence, lies in Holy Scripture alone". But what has eloquence in prose or verse to do with grammar? This is where the amphora started that suddenly turned out to be a storage-jar [Horace *Ars Poetica* 21, 22]. St. Augustine [in *De ordine* 1.8.24] on the other hand, to whom he refers, tells his friend Licentius to return to his familiar Muses. And Jerome [in *Adversus Rufinum* 1.16] makes himself familiar with Cicero's dialogues to get himself a more abundant style. Did any of the Ancients draw his style from any other source than the works of orators and poets? Who ever attempted to enrich his vocabulary out of Holy Scripture? Finally, has anyone by despising the poets immediately achieved eloquence of this sacred and prophetical variety?

18. And surely anyone can see that this famous argument of his contains manifest blasphemy. He says that the only elegance is to be found in Holy Scripture; does this mean that only elegance is to be found there? Yet what Augustine says, whom he quotes as an authority, is not the same as what this man meant – although he is too illiterate to express what he did mean. For Augustine argues, not that eloquence is to be found solely in Holy Scripture, but that it does not lack eloquence, while possessing wisdom whose handmaid he thinks eloquence should be, although he admits it is eloquence of a different kind. And yet he calls in question whether Scripture should be credited with any share of eloquence, though of its other virtues he has no doubt.

19. To ignore for the moment that it does not immediately follow, if you can produce a certain number of rhetorical figures from the writings of the apostles, that perfect eloquence is to be found in them, since Jerome and Origen and Chrysostom are often offended by their inversions, their uncompleted arguments, and the other drawbacks of their style; but in apostles we do not expect Aristotelian or Platonic philosophy, any more than wealth or servants, and equally we do not expect eloquence.

20. After that, he strings together three prodigious lies when he says, pointing at me, "What then can a man now have in mind who tries to bring back into the daylight the version of Lorenzo Valla that was condemned long ago, except to make the language of Holy Scripture look despicable and inept?" To begin with, everyone knows it to be false that Lorenzo made a version of Holy Scripture. Still more false is it that his annotations were condemned long ago. Falsest of all, his remark that anyone who publishes them is trying to make the language of Holy Scripture look despicable. On the contrary, it is made both more luminous and more attractive by the removal of portentous errors, imported into it by his own old friends.

21. Then he lets fly against me and makes a tremendous fuss because in a proverb somewhere I compared Holy Scripture in passing to those Silenus figures spoken of by Alcibiades,[13] although the same view is held in different language by every orthodox theologian. What comparison could be more appropriate? And this man speaks as though no one but he understands the Scriptures – because he is innocent of anything in the way of culture! – and as though I were incapable of achieving any of the discoveries of which he is so proud.

22. And look at the shameless falsehoods which he aims at me, declaring that by this comparison I make a mock of Holy Scripture! When all that I say there aims at the praise and glory of Christ and of his holy word, as must be obvious to all who read what I write. A fine example of that heavenly eloquence that he and he alone has acquired – without opening the poets, from his studies in Holy Writ! – the virtue of which is to make shameless attacks with a lot of trumped-up charges against another man's reputation.

23. It is the same folly that makes him say I deprive Holy Writ of its eloquence, when in so many passages I speak highly of it. I am concerned with nothing but the translation; and if I have any fault to find with the apostles, I state openly that it lies in their language, and even so, I do not criticize or correct it.

24. Our self-appointed inquisitor ordains that all the poets shall be thrown away, although, as I say [in paragraph 17], Augustine tells his friends to go back to them and so often quotes them with respect; nor is he alone in this. And why mention the poets, as though it was with their aid that I corrected the New Testament rather than on the authority of ancient and orthodox Fathers who are read with approval by the whole church?

25. After this he invokes all the authority of a

[13] Satyrs and Sileni were part men, part beasts – at first men with horse's ears, later men with goat's legs and tail – in Greek mythology, associated with the Dionysiac cult. Silenus was also seen as a dispenser of homely wisdom. In *Adagia* (III iii 1), Erasmus' collection of 3000 proverbs, he draws an analogy between Scripture and Alcibiades' comparison of Socrates to Silenus in that both "love to appear utterly uninformed and ignorant" (*Symposium* 218d). [Ed]

certain Thomas (I cannot think it is Aquinas), who wrote a commentary on Boethius' *Consolation of Philosophy*, to prove his assertion that all the poets should be thrown away, because [in *Consolation* 1.1.3] Boethius speaks of the torn garments of the Muses. He does not notice that, ragged as they are, they tell him what he is to write, and that he relaxes in lyric verse all through his book; nor does he drive away all the Muses, but only those of the theatre, and not even them completely, but only while he is in such great grief, which needs a more powerful remedy. I will forgive anyone who looks down on the Muses as Boethius looked down on them; but this man rejects poetry as gold and jewels are rejected by donkeys.

26. Furthermore, while Boethius called the elegiac Muses "all in rags" because they bear all the outward marks of sorrow, our friend adapts the epithet to poetry as a whole, and says they are called ragged in two ways, actively because they tear men's minds to rags and passively because they rest on no unbroken basis of reason. Both remarks are equally absurd.

27. He then goes further and, since elegance of style depends not on reason but on authority, he challenges me to put forward two examples, one from the poets and one from Holy Scripture, and stand or fall by the result. I therefore put forward that phrase from the Apocalypse "He that is and was and is to come" [Revelation 4:8] – words which are attributed to St. John, so let us have no quibbling about the translation; and the other from the poets "Well begun is half done" [Horace *Epistles* 1.2.40].

28. Not but what he has forgotten all this time that Augustine speaks of more eminent authors, meaning classics like Plautus, Sallust, Cicero, and others like them, and says that elegance of style depends upon their authority and not on the Holy Spirit. And yet the language of the apostles does not conform to their authority.

29. Not to mention, at the same time, that when Augustine lays it down, following Quintilian, that good writing has a threefold purpose, to instruct, to entertain, and to move the reader, this man refers it to the authority of St. Thomas.[14] And who can deny that we owe this to the Holy Spirit, when he without the Holy Spirit gives so much entertainment – though he does not instruct us, or move us except to laughter?

30. He reasons moreover, in his idiot fashion, as follows: "Hitherto the church has used this version: if the version is done away, the church did not possess the Holy Spirit". I will now reason in my turn, thus: "Ambrose did not possess this version: he therefore did not possess the Holy Spirit".

[14] *De doctrina christiana* 4.12.27, but Augustine's quotation is closer to Cicero *Orator* 21.69 than to Quintilian 3.5.2. [Tr]

31. On the contrary, the gift of the Spirit is given more lavishly, the more the church acquires of other good things. In the old days she had no literature and no eloquence, and she lacked wealth and power; now she has both, but it does not follow that Christ has deserted his spouse.

32. That countrified and simple style in which the New Testament was left to us by the apostles suited those early days; nowadays perhaps it is fitting that we should have it in neater dress, provided it be simple still.

33. And all the time, all through this argument, the solecisms which we find in our Latin New Testament, and even the errors which his old friends have introduced in no small number, are ascribed by him to the authority of the Holy Spirit – with barefaced impudence, for it would be improper to do such a thing even with the apostles.

34. Finally, he settles the question with a syllogism more than worthy of Chrysippus: "Eloquence stems from authority; it is therefore not a science. From the authority of the lesser judges or the greater? Not from the lesser; from the greater therefore. But no man is greater than the Holy Spirit. It is unlawful therefore to make any innovations in the New Testament". Who can read such stuff and not roar with laughter?

35. Besides this, he makes a malicious attack on a statement in a certain letter of mine to Dorp[15] that the leaders of the church have been more concerned with a knowledge of the ancient tongues than with sophistic or Aristotelian philosophy, since in particular they took steps to encourage the tongues as being absolutely necessary, but did nothing of the sort for sophistic philosophy; in fact, it is called in question in the *Decreta*, some great authorities disapproving of it. At this point, he accused me of a triple falsehood. "Not at all", he says, "every wise man teaches that without philosophy it is impossible to understand the Scriptures". But out of this large party, he does not produce a single name. If he did produce one, it would not touch me, for I am speaking of the warnings conveyed in the *Decreta*.

36. Secondly, he admits that the study of philosophy has aroused doubts, but not, he says, disapproval. That is exactly what I say. A subject, therefore, which has been encouraged by decree and never doubted is much more reliable.

37. He also denies that the study of philosophy has ever been disapproved of by eminent authorities. He will not deny it if he reads Origen, Jerome, Ambrose.

38. But then he argues against me on this point as

[15] Erasmus is referring to a letter he wrote to his colleague at Louvain, Maarten van Dorp (professor of philosophy, later rector of the university), in late May, 1515, defending the *Praise of Folly* against its detractors. Once written, the letter was included as a kind of preface to the book in most of its early editions. [Ed]

though I condemned the study of philosophy, when all I did was compare it with practice in the tongues. At least it cannot be denied that the gift of tongues was given to the apostles as something essential for the preaching of the Gospel; that they were given a knowledge of the philosophy of Plato or Aristotle is not on record – although a reasonable study of philosophy has my emphatic approval.

39. It is absurd that he should expect the interpreter, the man who makes a translation, to seek his style from the Holy Spirit without any reading of classical authors, and should deny that anyone can compass an explanation, which is really a more excellent gift of prophecy, except with the help of Aristotelian philosophy.

40. This first conclusion, as he calls it, he rounds off by saying that all poets were thieves and robbers, who came later. And yet most of the poets were before Christ; nor does he distinguish what a poet is, so that he seems to thrust Damasus, Gregory of Nazianzus, and Prudentius down into this class.[16]

41. Then, as though forgetting what he has just said, he admits that in the sacred books there is no elegance of style; but thus it seemed good to God, he says, to alter the style of the translators, although that is what Jerome did, when the Septuagint had already been accepted in the public usage of the church for nearly five hundred years. Besides which he was not afraid to alter a Hebraism too harsh for modern ears, which we can still see in Augustine's book on the idioms of the Old Covenant [*De locutionibus*].

42. "The man who denies", he says, "that this version is Jerome's flies in the face of the whole world, of every rank in the ministry, and of the whole established order. The Roman church herself confesses that her version is Jerome's, and sets his prefaces at its head". Those are his words. Let him substantiate what he asserts so boldly. The church of Rome has never pronounced on this point, and it is the consensus of scholars that this version is not Jerome's.

43. What then is the point of the abuse he levels at me? "No doubt they are all liars, and he alone is speaking the truth". As though I alone had said what thousands of scholars freely admit.

44. But Jerome's prefaces are added. Is that surprising, they being so informative? Though some of them are not Jerome's.

45. Then he expects me to make it clear that Jerome disapproves of some things which are found in my edition. Let him read Jerome for himself and convict me of falsehood if he can.

46. He says that the church cannot err. Is the church in error instantly if there is a corruption in your copy of the text? And yet some things can happen to the church of which she has no previous experience. And I maintain, not that in this translation [the Vulgate] there is anything that can undermine the orthodox faith, but that there are defects which it is worth while to point out. Read my own version, and if you do not find hundreds of passages which you, good scholar as you are, have hitherto misunderstood, have the law on me to your heart's content.

47. "You are a stumbling-block to the world", he says, "with your innovations in things that all accept". Not at all: all men of the highest station and character are grateful to me, and the dogs who barked to begin with bark no more when they have read my work. A few conceited people take offence, who would not have it thought that there is anything they did not know.

48. "Granting", says he, "that there are errors in the text, it was not right to publish them for ordinary people". On the contrary, there is every reason to publish things that all men ought to know.

49. "A private person", he says, "without authorization cannot make a new translation or correct an old one". In the first place, I think that I, like others, have the right, if I have made any progress in theology, to make it publicly known, having been co-opted into a faculty of theology [at Louvain]. Secondly, I am not making a new version; I translate the Greek; and so far as I am concerned, the old version is still there for all men's use, as it always was. Last but not least, let us assume that I have no authority: does this mean that, while the ignorant are free to corrupt the sacred text, I may not correct it unless a synod has been summoned first? Suppose I were a bishop or a cardinal, what has that to do with it? The business in hand calls not for a mitre or a red hat, but for skill in the tongues.

50. There is another absurdity, where he says that this is the version which refuted Jerome Hus[17] and Wycliffe; whereas the former was burnt and not confuted, and the latter's books were not condemned until after his death.[18] And even if what he says were quite true, does it follow that it is unlawful to remove any error that may have crept into the Scriptures?

51. "If there is any error in them", he says, "it should have been corrected in accordance with the ancient testimony of the Fathers". And yet what he

[16] Prudentius is the greatest poet of Christian antiquity; Gregory did write many poems, but is better known as a theologian. Pope Damasus I was primarily concerned with placing the text of Scripture, the creed, and the institution of the papacy on solid foundations. [Tr]

[17] A slight confusion: Jerome of Prague and Jan Hus were both burned during the Council of Constance. [Tr]

[18] While five bulls issued by Gregory XI in 1377 suspected John Wycliffe of heresy and listed a number of specific statements due to be investigated, a longer list of errors was drawn up by the Council of Constance in 1415, which declared him a heretic and ordered his remains to be dug up and his books to be burned. [Tr]

demands is exactly what I have done; only this has escaped his notice, because he has not glanced at my book.

52. "Leprosy", he says, "must be shown to the priest, whose business it is to pass judgment" [Leviticus 13:49]. Quite right; and that is why I submitted my work to Leo the Tenth, who had encouraged me to undertake it. And he, by the agency of two cardinals, approved my efforts. When he thinks fit, he will entrust to some person of his choice the task of having my books corrected by the learned. This is a province which I do not take upon myself, although I have paved the way to it.

53. As for the point he makes about the seventy separate cells,[19] he does not perceive that the force of this falls on Jerome, who makes fun of them as the constructions of some anonymous forger. If their version is attributed to the Holy Spirit, Jerome is impious, who calls it somewhere a forgery; and yet this verdict of Jerome's is accepted by the church in respect of several books of the Old Covenant.

54. The same wisdom is evident in his remark that the Greeks falsified their texts when they split off from the Roman church. And what, pray, was the reason why they should corrupt them all? Moreover, their separation from the Roman church being quite recent, how comes it that their modern texts and their very ancient ones are in agreement?[20] How comes it that Origen and Basil and Chrysostom – and Latin Fathers too, Ambrose, Jerome, Hilary, Cyprian – are in accord with their falsified texts and disagree with ours? Did the Greeks falsify at one stroke the texts used by all these authors?

55. Moreover, where I had objected [paragraph 10], following the papal decrees, that the true text of the New Testament ought to be checked against the Greek copies, he admits that in ancient times this was appropriate, but says that nothing could be less so now. And the reason he gives is their separation. As though the revolt of the Greeks had made any difference to their text of the Gospels!

56. But if the fact that the Greeks have split off from the Roman church is a valid reason for mistrusting the Greek text of the Bible, it was equally illicit in Jerome's day to correct the Old Testament out of the Hebrew texts, for the Jewish people had already rebelled, not from the Roman church but from Christ himself, which I consider somewhat more damnable.

57. Last but not least, if we are to put our trust exclusively in the books of Greeks who are not schismatics, it is precisely their texts that I follow for preference; but they do not differ from the schismatics' copies.

58. But his master-stroke of impudence is that, whereas I had written that it is more difficult for a Greek text to be corrupted than for one of ours, he makes out that I said it was impossible for Greek codices to be damaged in any way; and though the reason I adduced was the difficulty of Greek script, which is made up not merely of letters but of ligatures and accents, this liar says the reason I gave was that the Greek language allows no scope for falsehood. What monstrous effrontery – especially as my letter still exists and has been printed more than once!

59. And on this point he maintains that I contradict Augustine [*De haeresibus* 30], who wrote that Luke was the only gospel accepted by Greek heretics. What is it to us, if the Greeks had their heretics? Is it a reason for corruption in Latin texts, that heretics have arisen among the Latins? I myself in this work follow none but orthodox authorities; and even so, there are places where it would be right to give heretics too a hearing. What new critical spirit have we here?

60. He attacks me for stating that the Greeks do not differ from the Roman church in those doctrines which are set forth in the books of the New Testament, and that the only points in dispute are in ancient times the word *homusius* and nowadays certain questions of liturgy and the jurisdiction and poverty of the Roman pontiff. "Let the man read Augustine's *De haeresibus*", says he, "and he will learn what he has been ignorant of hitherto". What sort of argument, if you please, is this? Everybody knows that various heresies arose among the Greeks even before they recognized the Roman church, and yet in those days they were reputed orthodox. I am talking about schism, and the questions on which those Greeks differ from us who have separated themselves from the Roman See.

61. If, however, he contends that the Greeks did manipulate their texts, at least the passages they corrupted were those which appeared to undermine their schismatic opinions. Then let him produce one single passage which can be suspect on those grounds. In actual fact, if anything can arouse suspicion in the Greek texts, it will be above all the passages which were thought to tell in favour of the Arians or the school of Origen; for the whole of Greece seems to have been united in such hatred or jealousy of them in particular that, although their authors have taken from Origen as their source almost everything they tell us that is worth having, they seem to have had nothing so much at heart, none the less, as the complete destruction of everything he wrote – which would have

---

[19] Occupied by the translators of the Septuagint; see Jerome *Praefatio in Pentateuchem*, also quoted in *Adversus Rufinum* 2.25. [Tr] For Jerome's scoffing, see above, 30. [Ed]

[20] The Eastern or Greek Orthodox Church centered in Constantinople broke with the Western or Roman Catholic Church in 1054 under Pope Leo IX, catalyzed by territorial disputes over Sicily. [Ed]

been enough, even in isolation, to give us an understanding of Holy Scripture. I overlook for the moment the way in which he tells me to read Augustine on heresies as though he were the only man who had ever read it, or as though I could not read it unless instructed to by him, or as though I do not in fact cite evidence from that work in several places.

62. We have surveyed the keen thinker and the brilliant writer, and I cannot refrain from giving you at the same time an example of the wit. This is the kind of elegant sally in which this facetious fellow, the Graces' favourite son, indulges at my expense. "Jerome remarks", says he,

> that there are as many different texts as there are copies.[21] Some men follow one copy and some another; which is our poor translator to take as his authority? At any rate, my dear Jerome, saint as you are, it was to no purpose that Pope Damasus drove you to work so hard, when there was in existence a Greek copy faultless at all points, which our translator has now unearthed. O my dear Jerome, what a blinking night-owl you were, if you could not find such a copy as our friend, a mere beginner, has now found!

Such are his words, and as I recall them I think of Hercules at Lindus,[22] and how he enjoyed the flood of abuse as he sat at dinner. In the old days there were as many different texts as there were copies, and now it is not so. So what did Jerome follow in correcting the text? And another point: did I really depend on a single copy?

63. Again, repeating his initial assumption that by my new translation I wish to do away with the old, he recommends to me the rule of Augustine,[23] who

> in the canonical writings follows the authority of the great majority of churches, which should include of course those which were important enough to have apostles as their bishops and to have epistles addressed to them. A man will therefore observe this limitation in the canonical books: he will prefer those which are accepted by all catholic churches to those which certain of them do not accept, and among those which are not accepted by all churches he will prefer those received by more numerous and important churches to those held by churches which are fewer and less authoritative. If however he finds that some are held by the majority of churches and others by the more important ones, though such a thing is not easy to find,

and so forth. From all this he infers that my translation can carry no weight at all. But how am I affected by what is said in this passage about the rejection or acceptance of books, and not about the correction of the text? Otherwise, why did Augustine himself accept Jerome's version, which was entirely new? And besides, what scope will be left for this rule of Augustine's, if the only thing all the churches are allowed to accept is what has already been accepted by the church of Rome? Not that I am against Augustine, but because it is clear that he did not recognize the authority of the Roman See which we now accord it; all the more so as, when writing to Innocent, he addresses him as brother and gives no hint of his supreme eminence,[24] but treats him as a colleague.

64. After this he proceeds as though I thought there were some falsehood or folly in those Scriptures in which I admit that there is some obscurity. On the contrary, if there is anything false or foolish in the copies, it is attributable not to the apostles but to the old cronies of this muck-raking critic. And in any case I make no changes that affect the solid basis of the faith.

65. He instructs me therefore that I ought to have sent my book to the supreme pontiff for him to decide whether it should be suppressed or published. On that argument every book ought to be sent to the supreme pontiff, for every book might contain matter of offence for someone. But Thomas never did such a thing, nor did Scotus, nor for that matter did Augustine or Jerome. They published first, and the approval followed, and was not asked for. And furthermore, as I do not uproot the old version, but by publishing a revision of it make easier for us not only to possess it in a purer form but to understand it better, how could I suspect that there would be malignant critics like this man, ready to take offence at a work that would benefit everyone? If anyone had cause to fear a stumbling-block, it was those that are weak; yet on their side no cause of stumbling has arisen. All this trouble has been stirred up solely by two or three people of the class commonly accounted perfect, who when my book was not yet

[21] In the preface, addressed to Pope Damasus I, of his edition of the Gospels. [Tr]

[22] *Adagia* II v 19. Hercules killed and ate two oxen belonging to a peasant at Lindus in the island of Rhodes, and maintained that the owner's curses made his meat taste all the sweeter. [Tr]

[23] *De doctrina christiana* 2.8.12. [Tr]

[24] There is little substance to Erasmus' claim, except that Augustine and other bishops quite properly addressed Pope Innocent I as brother. [Tr]

published poisoned the minds of simple folk everywhere and condemned what as yet they knew nothing of, rousing prejudice against my work before it was known what good it could do. It is their fault, not mine, if any man has been offended.

66. Again, that I should have dared to dedicate it to Leo the Tenth, he calls temerity. "The poets", he says, "show brazen temerity in dedicating their worst obscenities to those who are endowed with the highest positions in the church". And why did our muck-raker suddenly drag the poets in at this point? Or who pray are those poets who dedicate their filth to bishops? Far from that, I dedicated my work to the pope in response[25] to a letter to me from himself; nor did he think it too much to read a large part of it with his own eyes. Men of the greatest authority can testify that having read it he gave it the highest praise in the hearing of the cardinals and scholars who were with him. And, as I said before, he sent me an answer by the agency of two cardinals.

67. In any case, what does he mean by 'authorize'? Put through such tests that there is no error left? If that is the law, nothing we have is authorized outside the canonical Scriptures. Nor is that what I asked of Leo. I merely draw men's attention, leaving the decision to scholars, if they have found something more correct.

68. After these declamatory flights he spreads himself in a more agreeable field and portrays for us the gifts of a translator out of Augustine and Thomas, but all the time confusing at every point the gift of the tongues or of interpretation and the gift of prophecy, which according to Paul [1 Corinthians 14:10] are different gifts. He declares that no one can translate Scripture unless he is provided with the gift of the Holy Ghost. And yet I have shown that St. Jerome's view was different, though he is the translator of both Testaments.

69. Besides this, while there is, I suppose, no one today arrogant enough to claim that he has the gift of prophecy or of the tongues, it is rash to pass judgment on the spirit of other men. I have striven to convey the very truth, following in the footsteps of the orthodox Fathers, nor have I set any goal before me save the reader's profit and Christ's glory. As I toiled, from time to time I sought the guidance of the Holy Spirit; at least there was no lack of good intentions. Further, what angel was it gave you the idea that the Spirit's aid was denied me as I sought to do good, while you fancy he was one of your privy council as you penned these scurrilous attacks – attacks, moreover, on a work you have never even seen? Nor is the identity of your paraclete[26] concealed from me. He who poured calumnies on a work that did not yet exist – he was your inspiration in criticizing a work you had not read, if we can call it criticism to spew what filth you please over something you've never seen.

70. He declares it unlawful for any man to teach without public authorization. Does it not satisfy him that I have the same authorization that Thomas had? (Not that I would compare myself with him.) Does it not satisfy him if I do it at the urgent request of the best of prelates and on encouragement from the pope himself? Though Thomas for that matter is not concerned with publishing texts, but with public sermons or lectures.

71. He maintains that Jerome did not dare undertake a version of Holy Scripture, except on orders from Damasus. What effrontery the man has! On whose authority then did he translate the Pentateuch?[27] At the request of a certain Desiderius, was it not? Was it Damasus put him up to translate the books of Esdras? Read his preface, and let this featherpate blush for his mistakes. And then Tobit: surely he was put up to that by Chromatius and Heliodorus? But why need I refute his falsehoods one by one, seeing that the New Testament was the only thing Jerome revised at the request of Pope Damasus?

72. It is known therefore that the New Testament was revised at the request of Pope Damasus; but it is not known that he approved Jerome's revision. For you cannot approve something of which you have no knowledge – especially as this fellow thinks everything should be rejected that has not achieved endorsal (to adapt his own flowers of speech) in published instruments.

73. Though Damasus does not lay this task upon him by virtue of being supreme pontiff of the world. Whether he was such a thing I leave an open question; the name at least in those days had not yet been heard, so far as one can gather from the writings of all the early Fathers.[28] He lays the task as bishop of

[25] This is probably a confusion; cf above, par. 52. [Tr]

[26] Here and in pars. 74 and 85 we find probably the first hints at Erasmus' conviction that his growing difficulties in Louvain were caused in the first place by Jan Briart of Ath, theologian and chief administrative officer of the University of Louvain. [Tr] By 'paraclete' Erasmus does not mean the Holy Spirit but Lee's mentor Briart, whom he later calls the "spirit that suborns him" and his "guardian angel". [Ed]

[27] The dedicatory preface to Damasus (cf par. 62) does not mention his translations of books of the Old Testament, but cf Epistles 35-6, 56. The following references to three prefaces inserted in Jerome's Bible also do not refer to an order from Damasus. [Tr]

[28] Damasus was not a pope in the sense we know it today; there were, for example, other bishops in Damasus' day called 'popes', such as Epiphanius of Constantia, Jerome's opponent. However, Damasus was the first 'pope' to declare Rome the 'apostolic see', founded by St. Peter, and while in 380 Christian orthodoxy

upon Jerome as being hitherto a Roman; for it was in Rome that he was both baptized and ordained to the priesthood.

74. Meanwhile there is another surprising fact: this scandalmonger, or the spirit that suborns him, has never so much as mentioned Lefèvre d'Étaples, who showed earlier and greater audacity than I ever have, and that too without authorization either from the pope, whom I had informed by letter of what I was setting out to do before I set out, or from the authority conferred on all who are accepted as professors of divinity. From this it is clear that he does not so much dislike the result as wish to attack the man who produced it.

75. So, having accomplished this to his heart's content, he goes on to make trouble about a remark in my letter to Dorp that "Jerome sometimes cannot refrain from an outburst of indignation against Vigilantius, from levelling insults against Jovinian and bitter invective against Rufinus". This he interprets as a savage and wanton attack on Jerome, as though I meant that he was wrong in so doing, or as though Jerome while still alive was exempt from all human failings, and indeed as though every man of good will did not sometimes wish that Jerome had a little more of this mildness in him.

76. Then again, rejecting a remark of mine that in what I write I never reflect on any man's reputation, he objects that in a number of passages I dissent from Thomas, from the Master of the Sentences [Pierre Lombard], from [Nicholas of] Lyra, from Hugo [or Hugh] of Saint-Cher, as though no one could dissent without insulting or attacking the reputation of his opponent. Could anything be more idiotic? And yet, if I do dissent, it is with a prior expression of respect for those to whom such respect is due, among whom I do not reckon Lyra or Saint-Cher. And if some do accord them less weight than they used to, there was no reason why to preserve their authority we must always follow a false view.

77. He says they would not tolerate it, if they were still alive. Very well: let him who like a second Elisha [2 Kings 2:9] has succeeded to their spirit play their part for them if he can.

78. Then he thinks it an unanswerable argument against me that in my notes on Jerome I poke fun in passing at a certain Franciscan [Henry Standish], while I do this without naming any names, and there is such a large crowd of Franciscans for whom such fun would be appropriate. If one were to tell a story of a man's ignorance without mentioning his name, must one be thought to insult all one's fellow-creatures?

79. What follows, to be quite honest, I simply do not understand, but I will copy his own words with the bloom still on them: "I might add", says he,

> that he is wrong in thus attacking this Franciscan. It is men greedy for position or reputation, hungry for coin, empty-headed, full of words and wind, who see to it that our text of Jerome should be thus mutilated and corrupt. If some copies are corrupt through scribal error, let them be corrected against ancient texts (for I reckon some can still be found that were written in Jerome's own day), and let us not have new ones made which destroy the elegance of Jerome and his eloquence and meaning.

Those are his words.

80. My first question is: by these elegant words "hungry for coin, empty-headed, full of words and wind" and so forth, does he mean to describe the Franciscans?

81. Secondly, is he saying that I mutilated Jerome, when I have added a great deal to earlier editions and cut away nothing except wrong headings in a number of places?

82. And then, am I inviting a new Jerome, and not rather restoring the ancient one? Are some people so crass that they think what they are reading now is Erasmus and not Jerome?

83. Again, do they suppose that I have corrected Jerome from any source other than very ancient copies, which might well be thought to have been written in the age of Jerome himself, did any such thing exist? And even so, I have not been satisfied with single copies. In this department at least very good scholars have done more work than might be thought possible.

84. What are these things that overflow Jerome's elegance and eloquence and meaning? Unless you find nothing elegant except what smacks of your own style ...

You see, my dear Maarten, what a lot of nonsense there is in that small book. Though even so I have noted a few points out of many, and already repent the waste of time. And yet he is so self-confident that he dares to make you the judge whether he has said anything silly, though there are rather more silly things in his book than there are words. Such are the men who set up to teach Erasmus! And yet this is that famous book which he laboriously completed on the basis of those ten conclusions which had passed, he says, through the hands of many men, and which he proposed to dedicate to some outstanding figure; and he tells us to share such valuable material with faithful and right-thinking friends. Then he summons anyone who is willing to take him on into the ring, and demands an antagonist – though we ought to

was declared to be the doctrines of the bishops of Rome and Alexandria, a synod called by Damasus in 382 officially pronounced the primacy of Rome over the Eastern Church. [Ed]

respect the eminent researches of so great a scholar, for they cannot be interrupted without great loss to the world. It would be truer to say that the poor man has a foul itch and wants someone to scratch himself against; and any man of sense will not go near him. I, to be sure, do not yet dislike the man enough to wish to expose him to the jeers of the learned world, though that is what he wants. Pray tell him, my dear Lips, to use his spare time more fruitfully in the future. If he is sound at heart, he will accept your warning and amend; if his mind is too far gone, leave him to his distemper. I hope you will devote yourself to reading sacred authors, in preference to wasting your best years on this sort of rubbish.

Farewell. 1518, 7 May

Thomas More

Sir Thomas More (1477-1535), humanist writer and chancellor of England, is best remembered today as the man who preferred beheading to recognizing King Henry VIII as head of the Church of England.

More was the son of the lawyer John More, who was later knighted and appointed judge of the King's Bench; he received his childhood education not only at St. Anthony's in Threadneedle Street, the best school in the City, but at the house of John Morton, archbishop of Canterbury, chancellor of England, and future cardinal. As a result of Morton's interest in the boy's education, he was sent to Oxford University, where he studied Latin and formal logic for two years before being brought back to London to study law in 1494. He was admitted to the bar in 1501 and began practicing law, but was unsure whether his interests lay in the law; he spent four years at a Carthusian monastery testing his vocation for the priesthood, but finally decided on a secular career. Still, he kept up his theological studies on the side, began every day of his life with extended prayer, and habitually wore a hair shirt.

He married Jane Colt in 1504 or 1505, and educated her in music and Latin to make her a proper hostess; when she died, perhaps in childbirth, in 1511, he remarried within weeks, and gave his new wife, Alice Middleton, a similar training (minus the Latin). The picture of the classic 'control freak' this paints is not inaccurate; born to rule, More quickly rose from lawyer to undersheriff of London (1518), undertreasurer (1521, the year he was knighted), speaker of the House of Commons (1523), high steward at Oxford (1524) and Cambridge (1525), chancellor of the duchy of Lancaster (1527), and, at the age of 51, chancellor of England (1529).

All this while he was King Henry's 'tame humanist', an unofficial courtier to whom the king looked for counsel on the intellectual and cultural issues of the day. Between 1513 and 1518 he had worked on (but never finished) *The History of King Richard III*; in 1516 he published his Latin *Utopia*, a fantasy that allowed him to explore crucial social issues like education, penology, religion, and women's rights – and that created a new literary genre, much imitated all over Europe. He had also become close friends with the Dutch humanist Erasmus, and created permanent rooms for his friend in his London home, before moving to Chelsea in 1524; it was at More's house that Erasmus wrote *The Praise of Folly*, whose Latin title (*Moriae encomium*) makes it also, punningly, "The Praise of More".

Just as More was being promoted to the high rank of chancellor, the seeds of his downfall were being sown. King Henry sought to convince More that his marriage to Catharine of Aragon was null and void in 1527, and More found himself unable to agree; in 1529 his first act as chancellor of England was to indict his predecessor Cardinal Wolsey for treason in connection with Henry's divorce; in 1530 he refused to sign the letter pressuring the pope to annul the marriage, and in 1531 he attempted to resign the chancellorship when the English clergy proclaimed Henry their supreme head. When the divorce was finalized in 1533 and Henry married Anne Boleyn, More refused to attend the wedding, and in 1534 he was imprisoned for treason; he was tried, found guilty, and sentenced to the traitor's death of drawing, hanging, and quartering (which Henry commuted to beheading) in 1535. Humanists all across Europe, Protestant and Catholic alike, protested the execution and mourned his death; More was canonized by Pope Pius XI in 1935, and celebrated by Robert Bolt in the play *A Man for All Seasons* in 1960.

More became involved in polemics in 1528, when Bishop Tunstall commissioned him to read all of the heretical writings in English and pronounce upon them; the result was the *Dialogue Concerning Heresies* (1529), excerpted below. Tyndale replied in *Answer unto Sir Thomas More's Dialogue* (1531), and More wrote his longest book, the two-volume *Confutation of Tyndale's Answer* (1532-1533) in response; he also defended his own enforcement of the antiheresy laws in two further books in 1533.

The authoritarianism of More's book remains largely medieval, and thus not so much a substantial as a rhetorical modernization of translation theory. More shows a slight modern leaning in his willingness to tolerate English Bible translations (though even that is hardly more modern than Jerome or Augustine), but his modernity is most obvious in his demystificatory and above all dialogical argumentation (though his dialogue form is hardly more modern than Plato). His interlocutor, called only the Messenger, gives a highly persuasive articulation to the tabooed 'seditious' or 'heretical' notions More is attacking – thus introducing into the argument its own potential 'confutation'. The Messenger, whom More modelled on a tutor to the children of one of his friends just outside London, has come in contact with Lutheranism at the university and comes to More with his questions and confusions; he remains a Catholic but is strongly drawn to the Protestant idea that the written word of the Bible supersedes even the ancient practices of the church. The Messenger voices what we would have to call the wave of the future, the spirit of the pragmatic, commonsensical, demystificatory middle class that was steadily to expand its hegemony until it more or less ruled the world; and in this historical sense, despite the argumentative bludgeoning he takes from More, the Messenger triumphs 'in' (or beyond) the dialogue: the history of the last four centuries has conditioned More's readers to take the Messenger's side.

Whether the Clergy of This Realm Have Forbidden All the People to Have Any Scripture Translated into our Tongue
From *A Dialogue Concerning Heresies and Matters of Religion* (1529)

The .xiv. chapter

> The author answers the doubt moved [raised] before in the .xi. chapter concerning the constitution provincial[1] and that the clergy is therein far from the fault that is imputed to them in that point showing; also that the clergy has not forbidden the Bible to be made and read in English.

But now to the matter we were in hand with. You said you would make answer for the law whereby the clergy of this realm have forbidden all the people to have any scripture translated into our tongue, which is as I said in my mind an evil made law.

Marry said I that is soon answered. Lay the charge to them that made it.

Marry said he so I do. For who made that constitution but they?

Surely said I nobody else – nor they neither.

No said he? What every man knows it.

Verily said I many men talk of it, but no man knows it. For there is none such indeed. There is of truth a constitution that speaks of such matter, but nothing of such fashion. For you shall understand that the great archheretic Wycliffe – whereas the whole Bible was long before his days by virtuous and well-learned men translated into the English tongue, and by good and godly people with devotion and soberness well and reverently read – took upon him of a malicious purpose to translate it anew.[2] In which translation he purposely corrupted that holy text, maliciously planting therein such words as might in the readers' ears serve to the proof of such heresies as he went about to sow; which he not only set forth with his own translation of the Bible, but also with certain prologues and glosses which he made thereupon. And these things he so handled (which was no great mastery) with reasons probable and likely to lay people and unlearned, that he corrupted in his time many folk in this realm. And by other ill books which he made in Latin, being after borne into Bohemia and there taught by Jan Hus and others, he was the occasion of the utter subversion of that whole realm both in faith and good living, with the loss also of many a thousand lives. And as he began again the old heresies of those ancient heretics whom and whose errors the church of Christ had condemned and sub-

[1] The reference is to the 'Constitution' of Archbishop Thomas Arundel, which the two speakers have been discussing for several pages. In regard to translations, it decrees:

> We resolve therefore and ordain that no one henceforth on his own authority translate any text of Holy Scripture into English or any other language by way of a book, pamphlet or tract, and that no book, pamphlet or tract of this kind whether already recently composed in the time of the said John Wycliffe or since, publicly or privately, under pain of the greater excommunication, until the translation shall have been approved by the diocesan of the place, or if need be by a provincial council. [Ed]

[2] John Wycliffe probably did not actually write the Bible translation usually attributed to him; his active sponsorship and perhaps direct guidance of the project did however link it closely to his name. Before the Wycliffite translation, the Bible had appeared in English, but the manuscripts were extremely rare and few are likely to have seen them. The translations "by good and godly people with devotion and soberness well and reverently read" were probably psalms and liturgical passages and other incidental texts taken from the Bible (events in the life of Jesus, for example) that had existed in popular vernacular translations for centuries. [Ed]

dued many diverse ages before, so does Luther again begin to set up his. For all that he has, in effect he has of him. Saving that, lest he should seem to say nothing of his own, he added some things of himself of such manner as there was never heretic before his days, neither so wicked that he would for sin, nor so foolish that he dared for shame write, say, or I trow [believe] think the like.

I long said he to hear some of them, for the man is taken for wiser than the mean, so madly as men bear him in hand.

Well said I that shall we see soon when we come thereto. But for our present purpose, after it was perceived what harm the people took by the translation, prologues, and glosses of Wycliffe, and also of some other that after him helped to set forth his sect, then for that cause – and for as much as it is dangerous to translate the text of scripture out of one tongue into another as holy Saint Jerome testifies[3] – for as much as in translation it is hard always to keep the same sentence [meaning] whole – it was I say for these causes at a council held at Oxford provided [decreed] upon great pain [under punishment of law] that no man should from then forth translate into the English tongue or any other language of his own authority, by way of book, libel [booklet], or treatise, nor no man openly or secretly read any such book, libel, or treatise newly made in the time of the said John Wycliffe or since, or that should be made any time after, till the same translation were by the diocesan [bishop], or if need should require by a provincial council approved. And this is a law that so many so long have spoken of, and so few have in all this while wrought to seek whether they say truth or no. For I trow that in this law you see nothing unreasonable. For it neither forbids the translations to be read that were already well done of old before Wycliffe's days, nor damns his because it was new, but because it was nought [worthless], nor prohibits new to be made, but provides that they shall not be read if they be mismade, till they be by good examination amended, except they be such translations as Wycliffe made and Tyndale that the malicious mind of the translator had in such wise handled it that it were labour lost to go about to mend them.

I long by my truth said he and even sit on thorns till I see that constitution. For not myself only but every man else has ever taken it far otherwise, that ever I have heard spoken thereof till now. But surely I will see it myself ere I sleep.

You shall be sooner eased said I. For I cannot suffer to see you sit so long on thorns. And therefore you shall see it by and by.

And therewith I fetched him forth the constitutions provincial with Lyndwood thereupon and turned him to the place in the title de magistris. Which when himself had read he said he marvelled much how it happened that in so plain a matter men be so far abused to report it so far wrong.

This grows said I partly by malice, partly by sloth and negligence, in that folk be more glad to believe and tell forth a thing that may sound to the dispraise of the clergy than to search and be sure whether they say true or no.

The .xv. chapter

The messenger moves against the clergy that, though they have made no law thereof, yet they will indeed suffer no English Bible in any man's hand, but use to burn [are in the habit of burning] them where they find them, and sometimes to burn the man too. And for example he lays one Richard Hunne, showing that the chancellor of London murdered him in prison and after hanged him, saying that he hanged himself, and after condemned him of heresy because he had an English Bible, and so burned the Bible and him together; whereunto the author answers.

I suppose said he that this opinion has rather grown another way, that is to wit by the reason that the clergy, though the law serve them not therefore, do yet indeed take all translations out of every layman's hand. And sometime with those that be burned or convicted of heresy, they burn the English Bible without respect to whether the translation is old or new, bad or good.

Forsooth said I if this were so, then were it in my mind not well done. But I believe you mistake it. Howbeit what you have seen I can not say. But myself have seen and can show you Bibles fair and old written in English, which have been known and seen by the bishop of the diocese and left in laymen's hands and women's to such as he knew for good and catholic folk, that used it with devotion and soberness.[4] But of truth all such as are found in the hands of heretics they use to take away. But they do cause none to be burned as far as ever I could wit [tell], but only such as be found faulty. Whereof many be set forth with evil prologues or glosses maliciously made by Wycliffe and other heretics.[5] For no good man would I ween

[3] Jerome does not, of course, call the translation of scripture 'dangerous' – only difficult. See above, p. 25-30. [Ed]

[4] More may be referring to two English Bibles bequeathed in 1507 to Coventry churches by a wealthy local mercer. F. F. Bruce suggests that the translation may in fact have been the second edition of the Wycliffite Bible, probably done by John Purvey (see above, pp. 53-57). [Ed]

[5] For the prologue to the second edition of the Wycliffite Bible, see "On Translating the Bible", above, pp. 54-57.

[think] be so mad as to burn up the Bible wherein they found no fault, nor any law that let [prevented] it to be looked on and read.

Marry said he but I have heard good men say that even here in London not many years ago, in the days of the bishop that last died, they burned up as fair Bibles in English as any man has lightly seen, and thereto as faultless for aught that any man could find, as any Bible is in Latin. And yet besides this they burned up the dead body of the man himself, whom themselves had hanged in the bishop's prison before, making as though the man had hanged himself. And of the burning of his body had they no colour [grounds to conceal the truth], but only because they found English Bibles in his house. Wherein they never found other fault but because they were English.[6]

Who told you this tale said I?

Forsooth diverse honest men said he that saw it, and especially one that saw the man hanging in the bishop's prison ere he was cut down. And he told me that it was well and clearly proved that the chancellor and his keepers had killed the man first and than hanged him after. And that they had laid heresy to him only for hatred that he sued a praemunire against diverse persons, for a suit taken about a mortuary in the audience of the archbishop of Canterbury. And then they proved the heresy by nothing else but by the possession of a good English Bible. And upon heresy so proved against him whom they had hanged, lest he should say for himself, they burned up the holy scripture of God, and the body of a good man therewith. For I have heard him called a very honest person and of a good substance.

Forsooth said I of good substance he was, I think well worth a thousand marks. And of his worldly conversation among the people I have heard none harm. But surely as touching his faith toward Christ, methinks I may be bold to say that he was not honest. And as touching truth in words, he that has told you this tale was not so honest indeed as methinks you take him for.

Why said he do you know the matter well?

Forsooth said I so well I know it from top to toe, that I suppose there be not very many men that know it much better. For I have not only been diverse times present myself at certain examinations thereof, but have also diverse and many times sundrily talked with almost all such except the dead man himself as most knew of the matter. Which matter was many times in sundry places examined. But especially at Baynard's Castle one day was it examined at great length, and by a long time every man being sent for before, and ready there all that could be found that anything could tell or that had said they could anything tell in the matter. And this examination was had before diverse great lords spiritual and temporal and other of the king's honourable counsel, sent thither by his highness for the nonce [express purpose] of his blessed zeal and princely desire borne to the searching of the truth.[7] Whereunto his gracious mind was much inclined, and had been by a right honourable man informed, that there was one had showed a friend of his that he could go take him by the sleeve that killed Hunne – for Richard Hunne was his name whom you speak of. I was also myself present at the judgement given in Poules, whereupon his books and his body were burned. And by all these things I very well know that he of whom you have heard this matter has told you tales far from the truth ...

The .xvi. chapter
The messenger rehearses some causes which he has heard laid by some of the

Without this prologue and marginal glosses, the translation was not necessarily associated with Wycliffe. Tyndale's New Testament also had a famous preface attacking the Catholic church. [Ed]

[6] The Richard Hunne case had been well-known among the London populace for almost a decade when More wrote his *Dialogue*. In 1514 Hunne had refused to pay the local priest the mortuary tax to bury his infant son; he had then been arrested and, after accusing the clergy of violating the Statute of Praemunire, found hanged by his belt on a spike in the Tower Prison at Lambeth. The Statute was a hotly debated law governing the assignation of legal jurisdiction to the ecclesiastical or secular authorities in civil cases; Hunne apparently felt he was not being prosecuted by the proper authorities. The chancellor of London, Dr. William Horsey, was accused of murdering Hunne, but was staunchly supported by the bishop of London, Richard FitzJames (the "bishop last died" [d. 1522] referred to earlier in the paragraph). After Hunne's death 'heretical writings' were found in his house, and his body was tried for heresy, found guilty and burned. [Ed]

[7] Baynard's Castle was a royal palace overlooking the Thames that was destroyed in the Great Fire of 1666. King Henry VIII presided over this meeting, which revolved around the Statute of Praemunire: which had jurisdiction over the inquiry into Chancellor Horsey's handling of the Hunne affair, the English monarchy (in the person of Henry) or the church (in the person of Cardinal Wolsey)? In a decision that points forward to Henry's break with the church a few years later, he settled the matter by peremptorily assuming jurisdiction and pardoning Horsey. Wolsey was dismissed from office the following year, in 1529, for attempting to engineer Henry's divorce from Catharine of Aragon, and died just in time to avoid trial for treason; in 1533 Henry married Anne Boleyn and broke with Rome. When More, who had succeeded Wolsey as Lord Chancelor, refused to convert to Anglicanism, he was put to death. [Ed]

> clergy, wherefore the scripture should not be suffered in English; and the author shows his mind that it were convenient to have the Bible in English; and therewith ends the third book.

Sir said your friend yet for all this can I see no cause why the clergy should keep the Bible out of laymen's hands that can [speak] no more but their mother tongue.

I had went [thought] said I that I had proved you plainly that they keep it not from them. For I have showed you that they keep none from them but such translation as be either not yet approved for good or such as be already reproved for nought, as Wycliffe's was and Tyndale's. For as for other old ones that were before Wycliffe's days remain lawful, and be in some folk's hands had and read.

You say well said he. But yet as women say somewhat [to some extent] it was always that the cat winked when her eye was out.[8] Surely so is it not for nought that the English Bible is in so few men's hands, when so many would so fain have it.

That is very truth said I. For I think that though the favourers of a sect of heretics be so fervent in the setting forth of their sect that they let [forbear] not to lay their money together and make a purse among them for the printing of an evil made or evil translated book, which though it happen to be forbidden and burned yet some be sold ere they be spied, and each of them lose but their part, yet I think there will no printer lightly be so hot [eager] to put any Bible in print at his own charge, whereof the loss should lie whole in his own neck, and then hang upon a doubtful trial whether the first copy of his translation was made before Wycliffe's days or since. For if it were made since, it must be approved before the printing. And surely how it has happened that in all this while God has either not suffered or not provided that any good virtuous man has had the mind in faithful wise to translate it and thereupon either the clergy or at the least wise some one bishop to approve it, this can I nothing tell [I cannot tell at all]. But howsoever it be, I have heard and hear so much spoken in the matter, and so much doubt made therein, that peradventure it would let [hinder] and withdraw any one bishop from the admitting thereof, without the assent of the remnant. And whereas many things be laid [alleged] against it, yet is there in my mind not one thing that more puts good men of the clergy in doubt to suffer it than this that they see sometimes much of the worse sort more fervent in the calling for it than them whom we find far better. Which makes them to fear lest such men desire it for no good, and lest if it were had in every man's hand, there would great peril arise, and that seditious people should do more harm therewith than good and honest folk should take fruit thereby. Which fear I promise you nothing fears [does not scare] me, but that whosoever would of their malice or folly take harm of that thing that is of itself ordained to do all men good, I would never for the avoiding of their harm take from other the profit which they might take, and nothing deserve to lose. For else if the abuse of a good thing should cause the taking away thereof from other that would use it well, Christ should himself never have been born nor brought his faith into the world, nor God should never have made it neither, if he should for the loss of those that would be damned wretches have kept away the occasion of reward from them that would with help of his grace endeavour them to deserve it.

I am sure said your friend you doubt not but that I am full and whole [fully and wholly] of your mind in this matter that the Bible should be in our English tongue. But yet that the clergy is of the contrary and would not have it so, that appears well in that they suffer it not to be so. And over that I hear in every place almost where I find any learned man of them, their minds all set thereon to keep the scripture from us. And they seek out for that part every rotten reason that they can find and set them forth solemnly to the show [on display], though five of those reasons be not worth a fig. For they begin as far as our first father Adam, and show us that his wife and he fell out of paradise with desire of knowledge and conning [learning] [Genesis 3:22-23]. Now if this would serve, it must from the knowledge and study of scripture drive every man, priest and other, lest it drive all out of paradise. Then say they that God taught his disciples many things apart, because the people should not hear it.[9] And therefore they would [wish] the people should not now be suffered to read all. Yet they say further that it is hard to translate the scripture out of one tongue into another – and especially, they say, into ours. Which they call a tongue vulgar and barbarous. But of everything especially they say that scripture is the food of the soul. And that the common people be as infants that must be fed but with milk and pap [Hebrews 5:12-13, 1 Corinthians 3:1-3]. And if we have any stronger meat it must be chammed [chewed] before by the nurse and so put into the baby's mouth. But methinks though they make us all infants, they shall find many a shrewd brain among us that can perceive chalk from cheese well enough, and if they would once take us our meat in our own hand. We be

---

[8] I.e., a one-eyed cat can't help but wink. The implication is that the bishops can't help but pretend that they want the people to have the Bible in English due to pressure from the Reformers. [Ed]

[9] Mark 4:33-34, a passage commonly cited to defend the authority of ecclesiastical tradition even when it deviates from scripture. [Ed]

not so evil toothed but that within [once in] a while they shall see us cham it ourselves as well as they. For let them call us young babies and they will, yet by God they shall for all that well find in some of us that an old knave [fool] is no child.

Surely said I such things as you speak is the thing that as I somewhat said before puts good folk in fear to suffer the scripture in our English tongue. Not for the reading and receiving, but for the busy chamming thereof, and for much meddling with such parts thereof as least will agree with their capacities. For undoubtedly as you spoke of our mother Eve, inordinate appetite of knowledge is a means to drive any man out of paradise. And inordinate is the appetite when men unlearned, though they read it in their language, will be busy to ensearch [seek out] and dispute the great secret mysteries of scripture, which though they hear they be not able to perceive. This thing is plainly forbidden us that be not appointed nor instructed thereto. And therefore holy Saint Gregory of Nazianzus, that great solemn doctor, sore touches and reproves all such bold busy meddlers in the scripture, and shows that it is in Exodus by Moses ascending up upon the hill where he spoke with God and the people tarrying beneath [Exodus 24:15, 18], signified that the people be forbidden to presume to meddle with the high mysteries of holy scripture, but ought to be content to tarry beneath and meddle none higher than is meet for them, but receiving from the height of the hill by Moses that what is delivered them, that is to wit the laws and precepts that they must keep, and the points they must believe, look well thereupon and often, and meddle well therewith. Not to dispute it but to fulfill it. And as for the high secret mysteries of God, and hard texts of his holy scripture, let us know that we be so unable to ascend up so high on that hill, that it shall become us to say to the preachers appointed thereto as the people said unto Moses, hear you God and let us hear you [Exodus 20:19]. And surely the blessed holy doctor Saint Jerome greatly complains and rebukes that lewd [uneducated] homely manner that the common lay people, men and women, were in his days so bold in the meddling, disputing, and expounding of holy scripture. And shows plainly that they shall have evil proof therein that will reckon themselves to understand it by themselves without a reader.[10] For it is a thing that requires good help and long time and a whole mind given greatly thereto. And surely since as the holy apostle Saint Paul in diverse of his epistles says, God has by his holy spirit so instituted and ordained his church that he will have some readers and some hearers, some teachers and some learners [Ephesians 4:11], we do plainly pervert and turn upside down the right order of Christ's church when the one part meddles with the other's office. Plato the great philosopher especially forbids such as be not admitted thereunto nor men meet therefor to meddle much and embusy themselves in reasoning and disputing upon the temporal laws of the city, which would not be reasoned upon but by folk meet therefor and in place convenient.[11] For else they that can not very well attain to perceive them begin to mislike, dispraise, and condemn them. Whereof follows the breach of the laws and disorder of the people. For till a law be changed by authority, it rather ought to be observed than condemned. Or else the example of one law boldly broken and set at nought waxes a precedent for the remnant to be used like[wise]. And commonly the best laws shall worst [deteriorate] like much of the common people, which most long (if they might be heard and followed) to live all at liberty under none at all. Now if Plato, so wise a man, thought this good in temporal laws – things of men's making – how much is it less meet for every man boldly to meddle with the exposition of holy scripture, so devised and indicted [inspired] by the high wisdom of God that it far exceeds in many places the capacity and perceiving of man. It was also provided by the Emperor in the law civil that the common people should never be so bold to keep disputations upon the faith or holy scripture, nor that any such thing should be used among them or before them.[12] And therefore as I said before, the special fear in this matter is lest we would be too busy in chamming of the scripture ourselves, which you say we were able enough to do. Which undoubtedly the wisest and the best learned, and he that therein has by many years bestowed his whole mind, is yet unable to do. And then far more unable must he needs be that boldly will upon the first reading, because he knows the words, take upon him therefore to teach other men the sentence [meaning] with peril of his own soul and other men's too, by the bringing men into mad ways, sects, and heresies, such as heretics have of old brought up and the church has condemned. And thus in these matters if the common people might be bold to cham it as you say and to dispute it, then should you have the more blind the more bold, the more ignorant the more busy, the less wit the more inquisitive, the more foolish the more talkative of great doubts and high questions of holy scripture and of God's great and secret

[10] See section 29 of Jerome's 22nd letter, the famous discussion of asceticism: "If there is anything of which you are ignorant, if you have any doubt about Scripture, ask one whose life commends him, whose age puts him above suspicion, whose reputation does not belie him, etc". (W. H. Fremantle's translation). [Ed]

[11] More is probably thinking of the *Republic*, e.g. 479d-480a, 484a-499e, 539cd, 590d-592a. [Ed]

[12] The law More is referring to Justinian borrowed from the Emperor Marcian. [Ed]

mysteries, and this not soberly of any good affection but presumptuously and unreverently at meat and at meal. And there, when the wine were in and the wit out, would they take upon them with foolish words and blasphemy to handle holy scripture in more homely manner than a song of Robin Hood.[13] And some would as I said solemnly take upon them like as they were ordinary readers[14] to interpret the text at their pleasure and therewith fall themselves and draw down others with them into seditious sects and heresies, whereby the scripture of God should lose his honour and reverence, and be by such unreverent and unwitting demeanour among many people quite and clean abused, unto the contrary of that holy purpose that God ordained it for. Whereas if we would no further meddle therewith, but well and devoutly read it, and in that that is plain and evident as God's commandments and his holy counsels endeavour ourselves to follow with help of his grace asked thereunto, and in his great and marvelous miracles consider his godhead, and in his lowly birth his godly life and his bitter passion exercise ourselves in such meditations, prayer, and virtues as the matter shall minister us occasion, [ac]knowledging our own ignorance where we find a doubt, and therein leaning to the faith of the church, wrestle with no such text as might bring us in a doubt and weresty [confusion] of any of those articles wherein every good Christian man is clear; by this manner of reading can no man nor woman take hurt in holy scripture. Now then the things on the other side that unlearned people can never by themselves attain, as in the Psalms and the Prophets and diverse parts of the Gospel, where the words be sometimes spoken as in the person of the prophet himself, sometimes as in the person of God, sometimes of our saviour Christ, not always of one fashion, but sometimes as God, sometimes as man, sometimes as head of this mystical body, his church triumphant in heaven, sometimes as in the person of his sensual parts of his own body, otherwhile in the person of some particular part of his body mystical; and these things with many others often times interchanged, and suddenly sundry things of diverse matters diversely mingled together – all these things which is not possible for unlearned men to attain unto, it were more than madness for them to meddle withal, but leave all these things to them whose whole study is beset thereupon, and to the preachers appointed thereunto, which may show them such things in time and place convenient with reverence and authority, the sermon so tempered as may be meet and convenient always for the present audience. Whereunto it appears that our saviour himself and his apostles after him had ever special respect. And therefore as I say forsooth I can in no wise agree with you that it were meet for men unlearned to be busy with the chamming of holy scripture, but to have it chammed unto them. For that is the preacher's part, and theirs that after long study are admitted to read and expound it. And to this intent, weigh all the words as far as I perceive of all holy doctors that anything have written in this matter. But never meant they as I suppose the forbidding of the Bible to be read in any vulgar tongue. Nor I never yet heard any reason laid [proposed] why it were not convenient to have the Bible translated into the English tongue, but all those reasons, seemed they never so gay and glorious at the first sight,[15] yet when they were well examined they might in effect for aught that I can see as well be laid against the holy writers that wrote the scripture in the Hebrew tongue and against the blessed evangelists that wrote the scripture in Greek, and against all those in like wise that translated it out of every of those tongues into Latin, as to their charge that would well and faithfully translate it out of Latin into our English tongue. For as for that our tongue is called barbarous is but a fantasy. For so is, as every learned man knows, every strange language to others. And if they would call it barren of words, there is no doubt but it is plenteous enough to express our minds in anything whereof one man is used [accustomed] to speak with another. Now as touching the difficulty which a translator finds in expressing well and lively the sentence of his author, which is hard always to do so surely but that he shall sometimes [di]minish either of the sentence or of the grace that it bears in the former tongue, that point has lain in their light that have translated the scripture already either out of Greek into Latin or out of Hebrew into any of them both [either of them], as by many translations which we read already to them that be learned appears. Now as touching the harm that may grow by such blind Bayards[16] as will when they read the Bible in English be more busy than will become them. They that touch that point harp upon the right string, and touch truly the great harm that were likely to grow to some folk; howbeit not by the occasion yet of the English translation, but by the occasion of their own lewdness

[13] Robin Hood became a kind of ideological shifter in this period, with the Reformers (beginning with Tyndale a decade before) accusing the clergy of tolerating pagan legends of Robin Hood while banning devout vernacular translations of the Bible, and the Catholics (More at their head) associating the popularity of the Robin Hood tales with the populism of the Reformation. [Ed]

[14] 'Ordinary reader' here means precisely the opposite of what we would take it to mean: a lecturer on law at the Inns of Court, a learned man appointed to use his authority to restrain possible interpretations. More was himself an 'ordinary reader' at two different inns. [Ed]

[15] I.e., no matter how gay and glorious they might have seemed at first sight. [Ed]

[16] Common name for a horse; part of a proverbial expression signifying reckless behaviour. [Ed]

and folly, which yet were not in my mind a sufficient cause to exclude the translation and to put other folk from the benefit thereof, but rather to make provision against such abuse and let a good thing go forth. No wise man were there that would put all weapons away because manquellers [murderers] misuse them. Nor this letted not [did this prevent] as I said the scripture to be first written in a vulgar [vernacular] tongue. For the scripture as I said before was not written but in a vulgar tongue such as the whole people understood nor in any secret cyphers but such common letters as almost every man could read. For neither was the Hebrew nor the Greek tongue nor the Latin neither any other speech than such as all the people spoke. And therefore if we should lay [argue] that it were evil done to translate the scripture into our tongue because it is vulgar and common to every English man, then had it been as evil done to translate it into Greek or into Latin, or to write the New Testament first in Greek or the Old Testament in Hebrew, because both those tongues were as very vulgar as ours. And yet should there by this reason also not only the scripture be kept out of our tongue, but over [in addition to] that should the reading thereof be forbidden both all such lay people and all such priests too as can no more than their grammar and very scantily that? All which company, though they can understand the words, be yet as far from the perceiving of the sentence in hard and doubtful texts as were our women if the scripture were translated to our own language. Howbeit of truth seldom has it been seen that any sect of heretics has begun of such unlearned folk as nothing could else but [as could only speak] the language wherein they read the scripture, but there has always commonly these sects sprung of the pride of such folk as had with the knowledge of the tongue some high persuasion in themselves of their own learning besides. To whose authority some other folk have soon after, part of malice, part of simpleness, and much part of pleasure and delight in new-fangledness, fallen in and increased the faction. But the head has ever commonly been either some proud learned man, or at the least beside the language some proud smatterer [dabbler] in learning. So that if we should for fear of heretics that might hap[pen] to grow thereby keep the scripture out of any tongue, or out of unlearned men's hands, we should for like fear be fain to keep it out of all tongues and out of learned men's hands too, and wot [know] not whom we might trust therewith. Wherefore there is as methinks no remedy but if any good thing shall go forward, somewhat [something] must needs be adventured. And some folk will not fail to be nought. Against which things provision must be made, that as much good may grow and as little harm come as can be devised, and not to keep the whole commodity from any whole people because of harm that by their own folly and fault may come to some part. As though a lewd surgeon would cut off the leg by the knee to keep the toe from the gout, or cut off a man's head by the shoulders to keep him from the toothache. There is no treatise of scripture so hard but that a good virtuous man, or women either, shall somewhat find therein that shall delight and increase their devotion; besides this that every preaching shall be the more pleasant and fruitful unto them when they have in their mind the place of scripture that they shall there hear expounded. For though it be, as it is indeed, great wisdom for a preacher to use discretion in his preaching and to have a respect unto the qualities and capacities of his audience, yet lets that [yet that hinders] nothing but that the whole audience may without harm have read and have ready the scripture in mind that he shall in his preaching declare and expound. For no doubt is there but that God and his Holy Spirit has so prudently tempered their speech through the whole corpus of scripture that every man may take good thereby and no man harm, but he that will in the study thereof lean proudly to the folly of his own wit. For albeit that Christ did speak to the people in parables and expounded them secretly to his especial disciples, and sometimes forbore to tell some things to them also because they were not as yet able to hear them, and the apostles in like wise did sometimes spare to speak [refrain from speaking] to some other [Mark 4:33-34, John 16:12]; yet lets all this nothing [yet none of this prevents] the translation of the scripture into our own tongue, any more than in the Latin. Nor it is any cause to keep the corpus of scripture out of the hands of any Christian people so many years fastly [firmly] confirmed in faith, because Christ and his apostles used such provision in their utterance of so strange and unheard mysteries, either unto Jews, pagans, or newly christened folk, except we would say that all the expositions which Christ made himself upon his own parables unto his secret servants and disciples withdrawn from the people should now at this day be kept in like wise from the commons, and no man suffered to read or hear them but those that in his church represent the state and office of his apostles. Which there will I wote well no wise man say [which I know well no wise man will say], considering that those things which were than commonly most [more commonly than most] kept from the people be now most necessary for the people to know. As it well appears by all such things in effect, as our saviour at the time taught his apostles apart. Whereof I would not for my mind withhold the profit that one good devout unlearned layman might take by the reading, not for the harm that a hundred heretics would fall in by their own wilful abuse, any more than our saviour letted for the weal of such as would be with his grace of his little chosen flock to come into this world and be *lapis offensionis et petra scandali* – the stone of stumbling and the stone of falling[17] – and ruin to all the wilful wretches in the world beside. Finally methinks that the constitution provincial of which we spoke right [just] now has determined this question already. For when the clergy therein agreed that the English Bibles should remain which were translated before Wycliffe's days, they consequently did agree that to have the Bible in English was none hurt [harm]. And in that they forbade any new translation to be read till it were approved by the bishops, it appears well thereby that their intent was that the bishop should approve it if he found it faultless, and also of reason amend it where it were faulty; but if the man were a heretic that made it, or the faults such and so many as it were more easy to make it all new than mend it. As it happened for both points in the translation of Tyndale.

Now if it so be that it would haply be thought not a thing meetly to be adventured to set all on a flush [flood] at once and dash rashly out holy scripture in every lewd fellow's tease,[18] yet thinks me there might such a moderation be taken therein as neither good virtuous lay folk should lack it nor rude and rash brains abuse it. For it might be with diligence well and truly translated by some good Catholic and well-learned man, or by diverse [several] dividing the labour among them, and after[wards] conferring their several parts together each with other. And after that might the work be allowed and approved by the ordinaries [bishops or their deputies], and by their authorities so put unto print as all the copies should come whole unto the bishop's hand. Which he may after his discretion and wisdom deliver to such as he perceives honest, sad [sober, serious], and virtuous, with a good [ad]monition and fatherly counsel to use it reverently with humble heart and lowly mind rather seeking therein occasion of devotion than of disputation. And providing, as much as may be [possible], that the book be after the decease of the party brought again and reverently restored unto the ordinary. So that as near as may be devised, no man have it but of the ordinary's hand, and by him thought and reputed for such as shall be likely to use it to God's honour and merit of his own soul. Among whom if any be proved after to have abused it, then the use thereof to be forbidden him, either forever or till he be waxen wiser.

Martin Luther

Martin Luther (1483-1546) was the founder of the sixteenth-century Reformation and the first great spokesperson for the modern 'masses' – the emergent middle classes for whom the various Reformed churches were designed. As the translator of the German Bible, he is widely regarded as the father of the German literary language, and his pronouncements on translation in the 'Circular Letter', especially the passage on "going out and asking the mother in her house, the children in the street, the ordinary man at the market", are still taught in German schools.

Luther was born to Hans and Margarethe Luther (or Luder) in Eisleben, and soon moved with them to Mansfeld, where his father worked in the management of the local copper mines and, by 1491, became a town councillor. Hans Luther had high ambitions for his son and in 1501 sent him to the University of Erfurt to become a lawyer, where Luther took his B.A. in 1502 and M.A. in 1505. Then, however – in terror, as he later recalled, of a thunderstorm in particular but more generally, as Erik Erikson suggests in *Young Man Luther*, of his own unruly temperament – he decided to join the Augustinian monastery in Erfurt. His father was furious, and later lectured Luther on the commandment to honour one's father and mother; but Luther was determined to be a monk, and threw himself into the monastic life with repressed passion.

His life as a monk was not, however, what one would imagine: he was soon selected for advanced theological studies at the newly founded University of Wittenberg, and after taking a 'biblical baccalaureate' degree in 1509 he began teaching; in 1512 he received a doctorate of theology and succeeded his Augustinian mentor Johann von Staupitz in the chair of biblical theology. He is said to have instigated the Reformation between lectures; by 1517, when he nailed his famous 95 theses to the Wittenberg door (and, more importantly, when they were printed up and circulated all over Europe), he had developed an extensive following among both the middle classes and the German princes and knights, who were desirous of expanding their administrative freedom from Roman control.

In the ensuing five years, during which Luther was excommunicated and called before various tribunals to recant (which he refused to do), he was protected by his powerful supporters, but also disturbed at the social unrest his theological rebellion was inspiring among the peasants; and for the next few years, culminating in the Thuringian peasant revolt of 1525, he preached and published avidly against revolution. That same year he married Katherina von Bora, a former nun, and broke with Erasmus, who had until then been

[17] 1 Peter II. [Au] See 1 Peter 2:8, a quotation from Isaiah 8:14. [Ed]

[18] I.e., to cause every unlearned reader unnecessary bother and irritation. [Ed]

a reluctant and cautious admirer. Also that year, Luther's long-time protector, the Saxon elector Frederick the Wise, died and was succeeded by John, another devout supporter of Luther; this changing of the guard, as it were, seemed to mark Luther's triumph over the Catholics, and in the next few years he supervised the reorganization of the Saxon church. This Reformed church was first called Lutheran by Luther's enemies, and Luther himself denied to his dying day that he was a 'Lutheran'; but gradually the name stuck and was accepted by his partisans.

Luther published his German New Testament in 1522, and his German Bible in 1534: the massive labour proceeded slowly due to Luther's many other activities. The New Testament was largely translated in hiding at the castle of Wartburg, where Luther had fled (after a faked kidnapping) following the Edict of Worms, which declared him an outlaw and proscribed his writings. Deprived of his books, disguised as 'Knight George', bearded and fat, Luther combatted gray bouts of depression by writing exegetical works and working on his translation, increasingly with the help of loyal supporters like Philip Melanchthon. As he relates in the 'Circular Letter', below, once published his Testament (like all of his other writings) was banned – but slightly revised and republished without Luther's name by Hieronymus Emser, it achieved great popularity.

It is one of the great ironies of the history of Western translation theory that orthodox translation theory should be repeatedly defended in wild, shaggy, 'rebellious' letters like this one – that, for example, Luther should feel just as compelled to take vicious potshots at the Catholic defenders of Jerome's Vulgate translation as Jerome had felt to snipe at his detractors 1135 years before; and that the central issue, whether to translate word for word or sense for sense, should be exactly the same, unchanged by a millennium of medieval theology, in the two documents.

Luther's most important contribution to translation theory lies in what might be called his 'reader-orientation'. When he formulates the standard principle that translations should be made out of good target-language words, idioms, syntactic structures, and the like, for example, he doesn't idealize or objectify language, as Augustine had done – doesn't treat the target language as a stable sign-system whose internal coherence must be respected when transferring source-language meanings into it. Instead he personalizes it, humanizes it, blends it with the vitality of his own sense of self. In so doing, significantly enough, he socializes it: what he internalizes is no solipsistic fantasy-system but language as social communication, language as what people like him (members of his class) say to each other in real-life speech situations.

Circular Letter on Translation (*Sendbrief vom Dolmetschen*, 1530)
Translated by Douglas Robinson

Wenzeslaus Link![1] May the God of all Christians shower his grace and charity upon you.

Wise King Solomon writes in Proverbs 11:26, "Whoever withholds corn, the people shall curse him; but blessing shall be upon the head of him who sells it". Which should actually be understood to mean everyone who can serve the general good of Christendom. And Jesus calls a faithless servant a lazy wretch for the same thing, for burying his money in the ground [Matthew 25:24-30]. So here I am with this circular letter, which I have at hand because of a good friend, and I guess I know what I have to do with it if I don't want to be cursed by the Lord and his congregation: publish it. There's been so much talk about my translation of the Old and New Testaments, and the enemies of the truth have tried so hard to pretend that the text has been changed or falsified in so many places, and as a result so many simple-minded Christians (even some learned ones with no Hebrew or Greek) have either dismissed it or hated it, that I'm hoping this letter will at least thwart the godless in the exercise in their vices and buck up the pious in the exercise of their scruples. So tell every lover of truth to read this work with an open heart and to pray to God for a true understanding of the holy scriptures, for the good and the growth of all Christendom. Amen.

To Nuremberg, September 15, 1530

Dear N, my upright, circumspect, open-minded friend.

Grace and peace in Christ! My dear friend, I got your letter with the two questions that you wanted me to answer. The first one was why I translated Paul's words in Romans 3:28, which in Latin read *Arbitramur hominem iustificari ex fide absque operibus*, as *Wir halten, das der mensch gerecht werde on des gesetzs werck, allein durch den glauben*, or (literally) "We hold that (the) man becomes rectified without the law's work, alone/only through (the) believing". You say the papists are getting themselves all worked up over the fact that Paul never wrote the word *sola* (*allein* or 'alone/only'), and who am I to be adding things to the word of God, etc. The second was whether the departed saints pray for us, since we

[1] Luther sent his circular letter to this old friend, a Nuremberg priest, for publication. [Tr/Ed]

read that the angels pray for us, etc.[2]

Well, on that first question, why don't you just tell your papists for me that if I had thought for one second that the papists, even all the papists in the whole wide world, could translate a single chapter of the Bible without making hash of the thing, I would have eaten humble pie and asked them to help me translate the New Testament. But it was plain to me as the nose on my face that not a man jack among them knew how to speak German correctly, much less translate it, so I saved them and myself the trouble. Note what's happening, though. They're learning to speak and write German from my translation, and so in a sense stealing my language, which they hardly knew a word of before. But do they thank me for it? No they do not. They use it against me. But I don't hold it against them. I'm flattered to have taught these ungrateful pups to talk right.

And, second, you can tell them that I've put the New Testament into German conscientiously and to the best of my ability; never forced anybody to read the thing, but left it up to them, and I did it all to help those who couldn't do it better themselves. Nothing's stopping anybody from making a better one. Whoever doesn't want to read it can leave it lay; I'm not going to beg or praise anybody for it. It's my Testament and my translation and nobody can take it away from me. If I've made mistakes in it anywhere (and I'm not aware of doing so, and you can bet I'd never mistranslate a single letter of it out of mischief), I'm still not going to let the papists sit in judgment on it. Their ears are too long and their hee-hawing too feeble for that job. I know perfectly well what it takes in the way of skill, hard work, good sense, and understanding to be a good translator, but they know less than the miller's beast, for they've never even tried it.

They say when you work in public, everybody's a critic, and that's certainly been true for me. All these people who can't even talk right, let alone translate, try to teach *me* how to do it! And if I'd asked them how to translate the first two words of Matthew 1:1, *Liber Generationis*,[3] not one of them could've said jack, yet these fine journeymen would pronounce judgment on the whole Bible. St. Jerome faced the same thing when he did his Latin translation: everybody knew better than him how to do it, and people bitched and moaned about his work as weren't fit to shine his shoes. It takes a heap of patience to try to do any public service; everybody's got to be Mister Knowitall and get everything bass-ackwards, teaching everyone and knowing nothing. That's just the way they are; a leopard can't change his spots.

I'd like to see just one papist put his money where his mouth is and try his hand at translating one of Paul's letters or one of the prophetic books without using Luther's German language and translation. What fine-sounding German we'd hear then! We've already seen what happens when some bungler from Dresden figures he'll 'touch up' my New Testament (I refuse to utter his name in my books any more; he's got a higher judge than me now, and besides, he's well enough known as it is).[4] He recognized that my German is sweet and good and knew plenty well that he couldn't do it any better himself, but still he wanted to drag it in the mud, so he rushed out and grabbed my New Testament, almost word for word as I had it, ripped out my preface and commentary and rubbed out my name, wrote his own name and preface and commentary in their place, and is now selling my New Testament under his name! Dear children, how it pained me when the governor in his ghastly preface condemned Luther's New Testament and forbade anyone to read it, while ordering everyone to read the bungler's New Testament – which is the exact same one Luther made!

You think I'm making this up? Go get both Testaments, Luther's and the bungler's, open them up in front of you, and compare them – it'll be pretty clear who translated both of them. The few places he changed and patched up, even though I may not always like the results, don't really hurt the text all that much, so that it's never really seemed to me worth the bother to attack it in print. But I did have to laugh at the high and mighty wisdom that trashes my translation and condemns it and bans it when it's published under my name, but makes everybody read it when it's published under some other name. Tell me, is it something to be proud of, to shove somebody's book in the mire, then to steal that book and publish it under your own name, and so to try and make a name for yourself with another man's work, which you despise? But God's his judge now. For me it's enough, and it makes me glad, that (as St. Paul too boasts [Philippians 1:18]) even my enemies need my work, and that Luther's book (though without Luther's name, under his enemies' name) is being read. What better revenge could I hope for?

And so back to the matter at hand: if that papist of yours won't get off your back about this 'sola-only'

[2] This translation excerpts Luther's answer to the first question only. [Tr/Ed]

[3] *The book of the generation [of Jesus Christ]*, in King James, or, as the Revised Standard has it, *The book of the genealogy of Jesus Christ.* [Tr/Ed]

[4] Luther is referring to one Hieronymus Emser (d. 1527), who had critiqued Luther's translation in 1523, then, using his critique to get Duke Georg von Sachsen-Meißen to ban Luther's edition, published his own German version, heavily dependent on Luther's, in 1527. The 'higher judge' is God, before whom Luther imagines him having appeared three years before. [Tr/Ed]

business, tell him that Doctor Martin Luther *wants* it that way, and if he doesn't like it, he can shove it. *Sic volo, sic iubeo, sit pro ratione voluntas.*[5] For we don't want to sit at the papists' feet and learn from them; we would teach them, and judge them, strut our stuff before those jackasses, boast before them like Paul before his crazy saints.[6] They're doctors? So am I! They're learned? So am I! They're preachers? So am I! They're theologians? So am I! They're disputants? So am I! They're philosophers? So am I! They're dialecticians? So am I! They're lecturers? So am I! They write books? So do I!

And let me boast further: I can interpret the psalms and the prophets, and they can't. I can translate, and they can't. I can pray, and they can't. And, not to put too fine a point on it, I understand their own dialectic and philosophy better than any one of them, and know for a fact that not one of them understands his Aristotle.[7] If there's a single one of them that can understand a prologue or a chapter out of Aristotle aright, I'll eat my hat. And I'm not exaggerating. I was trained in their arts from childhood and know exactly how deep and wide they run. And they know it, too – they know that I know and can do everything they can. But those heathens treat me like some kind of outsider, like somebody who just blew into town about three seconds ago and hasn't yet seen or heard their schtick. So they strut around like cocks of the walk, flaunting their knowledge and teaching me things that I learned about twenty years ago in school, as if I should howl and whine with every bitch on the block. I've known for seven years that horseshoe nails are made of iron.

So that's my answer to your first question; and let me urge you to give these jackasses no other answer to their useless braying about the word *sola* than that Doctor Luther wants it that way, and he's a greater doctor than all the popish doctors put together, amen. From now on they're beneath my contempt, people (I almost said jackasses) like that. For they've got shameless little weasels among them that've never even learned their own sophistry,[8] people like Doctor Smith[9] and Doctor Silverspoon[10] and their ilk; and yet they jump all over me on this thing that is not only above all sophistry but also, as St. Paul says [1 Corinthians 1:20], above all the wisdom and the reason in the world. Truly, a jackass hardly needs to open his mouth to sing – you recognize him by his ears.

But let me tell you and our own people why I wanted to use *sola* in Romans 3:28 – or actually, why I used not *sola* but *solum* or *tantum* there. That's how closely these jackasses pore over my text! Still, I've used *sola fide* elsewhere, and do want both of them, *sola* and *solum*. I've worked hard in my translation to make my German pure and clear. And sometimes we looked for just the right word for two weeks, three, four weeks, and even then didn't always find it. In the Book of Job Melancthon and Aurogallus and I sometimes managed to turn out three miserable lines in four days. Now that it's all translated, of course, it's easy as pie to read. Anyone can skim over three or four pages without stumbling *once*, and never even realizing what stumps and stones used to lie in what now looks as smooth as a planed board. Nobody noticed how hard we had to sweat and fret to remove those stumps and stones and smooth it out so nicely. It's easy to plow when the field is cleared. But to pull out the wood and the stumps and get the field ready for the plow? Nobody wants that job. Working for the good of the world is a thankless task. Even God, what with the sun and the heavens and the earth, and the sacrifice of his son – even he can't win the world's gratitude. It's the world; that's just the way it is, in the devil's name, and can do no different.

Anyway, working as I did on my translation I hardly needed papists to tell me that the Latin and Greek texts of Romans 3:28 had no *solum* in them. It's true: those four letters, s-o-l-a, aren't there, and the jackasses stare at letters like a monkey at a new suit. What they can't see is that it fits the meaning of the text, and if you want to want to translate it into strong and clear German, you've got to put it in there. You see, I wanted to speak German, not Latin or Greek, since German was the language I was translating into. And see, that's the way we do it in German, when we are talking about two things, one of which we're affirming and the other denying: we use the word *allein* or 'alone' or 'only' or 'just' alongside 'not' or 'no'. For example, we say "The peasant only brings corn, no money". Or "Nope, ain't got no money, only corn". Or "I've just eaten, haven't had anything to drink yet". Or "The only thing you've done is write it, you haven't proofread it yet?" There are lots of phrases like that in everyday speech.

[5] "Thus do I want it, thus do I command it; let my will be reason enough". Juvenal, *Satires* 6:223. [Tr/Ed]

[6] Here and in the mock exchange in the next few lines Luther is adapting 2 Corinthians 11:21-23. [Tr/Ed]

[7] Aristotle so dominated the scholastic thinking of the late Middle Ages that he was a favourite point of attack for the Reformers. [Tr/Ed]

[8] A common Reformation derogation of scholasticism. [Tr/Ed]

[9] Johan Fabri from Leutkirch, bishop of Vienna, who was the son of a smith (hence Luther's nickname for him). He was one of Luther's most vigorous opponents and a proponent of the Catholic Restoration in Germany. [Tr/Ed]

[10] Johan Dobneck from Wendelstein, an enemy of Luther's who wrote a scurrilous biography of him. His nickname Cochläus reminds Luther of the Latin word *cochlear* 'spoon'. [Tr/Ed]

So even if the Latin and the Greek might not use *sola* in these sentences, the German does. That's the way German works. You've got to have an *allein* to bring the 'not' or 'no' out more fully and clearly. If you try to say "The peasant brings corn, no money", the "no money" lacks punch, sounds weak and puny compared to "The peasant only brings corn, no money" The *allein* (or 'only') helps the 'no' out, makes it clear, full-bodied German speech. Only an idiot would go ask the letters of the Latin alphabet how to speak German, the way these dumbasses do. You've got to go out and ask the mother in her house, the children in the street, the ordinary man at the market. Watch their mouths move when talk, and translate that way. Then they'll understand you and realize that you're speaking *German* to them.

Jesus says, for example, in Matthew 12:34, *Ex abundantia cordis os loquitur*. If I followed those jackasses, they would probably set the letters before me and have me translate it, "out of the abundance of the heart the mouth speaketh".[11] Tell me, is that how any real person would say it? Who would understand such a thing? What on earth is the "abundance of the heart"? Anybody who said that would probably mean he had too large a heart, or too much heart – and even that doesn't sound right. For "abundance of the heart" sounds about as good in ordinary speech as "abundance of the house", or "abundance of the stove", or "abundance of the bench". What the mother in her house and the common man would say is something like: "speak straight from the heart". This is the kind of ordinary phrasing that I've always striven for, but alas, haven't always managed to find. The letters of the Latin alphabet make it pretty hard to speak good German.

Or when the traitor Judas says in Matthew 26:8, *Ut quid perditio haec?* and in Mark 14:4, *Ut quid perditio ista unguenti facta est?* If I followed those lemmings the literalists, I'd have to render that latter question "Why was this waste of the ointment made?"[12] What kind of talk is that? Whoever talks about "making a waste of the ointment"? You make a mess, not a waste, and anybody who heard you talking about making a waste would naturally think you were actually making something, when in fact you were unmaking it – though that still sounds pretty vague (nobody unmakes a waste either). If this sounds right in ordinary speech, why don't these people come forward and retranslate the New Testament into this fine, pretty talk, and leave Luther's Testament alone? I mean, then the full extent of their skill would really see the light of day! What a real person would say, of course, is "What a waste!" or "What a shame to waste that ointment!" Then the listener would understand that Mary Magdalene has squandered the ointment, at least according to Judas, who would have been more sparing with it.

Item: the angel greets Mary with the words, "Greeted be thou, Mary, full of grace, the Lord with you!"[13] Here again the Latin letters have done the translating. Would we say that? Who would ever say "you're full of grace" – and who would understand it? Full of beer, maybe, or full of money; but not full of grace. So I translated it *Maria du holdselige*, (literally) "Mary you sweet-blessed one", or "sweet Mary", to give Germans a chance to think about what the angel's greeting meant. But this drove the papists out of their tiny minds with rage. They said I'd ruined the angel's greeting – even though I still hadn't found the best German for the word. Of course, if I had used the best German for it, something like *Gott grüße dich, du liebe Maria*, (literally) "God greet you, you dear/beloved Mary", or "God sends his love, Mary honey" (that is after all what the angel means, and that's what he would have said if he'd been speaking German or English), they probably would have gone and hanged themselves out of the "abundance of their devotion" to Mary, just because I so horribly abused the greeting.

But what do I care if they rant and rave? I won't stand in their way if they want to translate that way; but you won't catch me translating like them. If somebody doesn't like my way, he can ignore it and do it however he wants, just so long as I don't have to look at it. Nor do they have to answer for my translation. Hear the difference for yourself: I want to say, *du holdselige Maria*, sweet, mild Mary, *du liebe Maria*, dear, beloved Mary, and let them say, *du voll Gnade Maria*, you full of grace Mary. Anybody who speaks German knows what a wonderful heart-wrenching word that is, *liebe*: *du liebe Maria, der liebe Gott, der liebe Kaiser, der liebe Fürst, der liebe Mann, das liebe Kind*.[14] Is there another language that can say *liebe* in such a wonderfully tender way, so that the heart brims over with joy at the mere saying of it, as in German?

I'm sure St. Luke brought all his mastery of Hebrew and Greek to bear on finding the best possible Greek word, *kecharitomeni*, for the angel's Hebrew word. And the angel Gabriel probably spoke to Mary as he did to Daniel, whom he called *hamudoth* and *isch hamudoth, vir desideriorum*, which is to say, "dear Daniel" [Daniel 9:23, 10:11, 19]. That's the way the angel Gabriel talks, as we see in the Book of

---

[11] Which is precisely what King James' translators did. [Tr/Ed]

[12] Again, following the King James Version. [Tr/Ed]

[13] Luke 1:28, translated literally from Luther's German. [Tr/Ed]

[14] Dear Mary, dear God, dear emperor, dear prince, dear man, dear child. *Liebe* is literally 'lovey', 'beloved'. [Tr/Ed]

Daniel. Now if I wanted to translate this like the jackasses insist, literally, I'd have to say "Daniel, you man of desires". Doesn't that sound great! Of course, "man of desires" is perfectly recognizable English. The only problem is that it means something rather different from what the angel Gabriel meant, like "O Daniel, who lustest after women" or "Hey, horny Daniel". Pretty wonderful translation, huh? If I let the letters go their merry way and try to determine what the Hebrew speaker *meant* by *isch hamudoth*, I find that the true meaning is something like "Dan my man", "sweet Mary", "June honey", "you great big gorgeous hunk of a man", and the like. You see, the translator has to store up lots of words, so he'll have plenty to choose from if one doesn't always sound right.

And why should I go on and on about translation? If I wanted to trace every one of my words back to its original germ or idea, it would take me a year to write it. Whatever it takes to translate, I've done it, and I'm not going to let any wet-behind-the-ears papist jackasses and dumbasses line up and take potshots at me. Anybody who doesn't like my translation, let me give you a little helpful hint: *don't read it!* And I say, the devil take anybody who doesn't like it or who corrects it without my knowledge or against my will. If anybody's going to correct it, I'll do it myself. And if I don't do it, everybody else should leave my translation alone. You got something to do with your life? Then go do it and have a nice day.

This much I can say with a clear conscience: I worked hard and faithfully on that translation, and never had no ulterior motives about it neither. I've never asked for a plug nickel in return for the work I did (nor got none). And I wasn't out for my own fame and glory, either, God knows. I did it all to help my dear fellow Christians, and for the glory of the Man Upstairs, who fills every hour of my life with so many blessings that even if I'd translated a thousand times more and faster I still wouldn't have earned the right to an instant of this life or a single good eye. Everything I am and have is through his grace and mercy, yea, through his dear blood and sour sweat, and that's why, God willing, everything I do, with joy and from the heart, must be to his greater glory. Let the bunglers and the papist asses run me down, fine, but the devout Christians sing my praises, mine and our Lord Jesus Christ's, of course, and I feel amply rewarded if only Jesus finds in me his faithful labourer. I want nothing from the papist asses, they're not fit to judge my work, and it would cut me to the quick if they were ever to praise me. Their vilifications are my finest praise. That's why I'll be a doctor, and a damn fine paragon of a doctor at that, from now till the Judgment Day, and they'll never take that name away from me, no way.

Now, true, I didn't always let the letters go their merry way. Me and my assistants studied them very carefully, so that when a lot seemed to be riding on a passage I stuck to the letter and didn't deviate from it quite so freely. In John 6:27, for instance, Jesus says "Him hath God the Father sealed".[15] This would sound better if it said "God has marked this man", or better still, "This here's the fella God meant". But there I thought it better to do violence to the German language than to stray from the word. Oh well, translation's not for everybody, never mind what the crazy saints say. You've got to be upright, devout, faithful, hard-working, God-fearing, Christlike, learned, experienced, and disciplined to do it right. That's why I say no false Christ or camp-follower will ever be a good translator, as was made amply clear in the translation of the prophets published at Worms.[16] They worked hard on that translation, but it still owes a lot to my German, partly because there were Jews working on it who didn't think much of Jesus. Good translators, too, and hard-working, but that's not always enough.

That's that about translation and the way people talk, then. Not that I put all my trust in the way people talk, though, and followed it, for instance in inserting *solum*-only into that phrase in Romans 3:28; the text itself required it, St. Paul's meaning with all its high authority compelled me to add that word. After all, he is dealing with the main tenet of Christian doctrine, that we are put right by believing in Jesus, without all the works of the law, and that, no matter how good and useful and efficient those works are, the *law* (God's law and word, remember) will never put us right. He gives the example of Abraham, who was put so completely right without works that even the greatest work that had yet been commanded by God up till that time, which took precedence over all other works, circumcision, couldn't put him right; rather he was made righteous without circumcision or any other work through faith alone, as St. Paul writes in Romans 4:2, "If he was put right by the things he did, he has something to boast about. But he cannot boast before God".[17] And if you thus so completely 'circumcise' works, cut them off like a foreskin (and that must be the meaning of the idea that faith alone puts you right), then whoever would talk straight about the circumcision of works must say: faith alone and not works put us right. The thing itself forces us to talk like that – the thing, and also the way people talk. So tell me: it irritates some people to say that faith alone puts us right, since then we may decide that we don't have to do good works. But what should we say instead? Isn't it far more irritating when St. Paul himself doesn't say "faith alone"

---

[15] King James Version. [Tr/Ed]

[16] Published by Hans Denk and Ludwig Hätzer in 1527. [Tr/Ed]

[17] Today's English Version. [Tr/Ed]

but goes down even deeper and comes up even dirtier with his "apart from works of law"? And in Galatians 2:16, "not justified by works of law",[18] and other places too, all through the epistles. So you won't find "faith alone" in your concordance, but "apart from works of law" is so gross, so irritating, so disgraceful, that no amount of concordances is going to help it. How much more easily will people learn not to do good works from hearing preachers talk about works with such gaunt, stark phrases as "apart from works, without works, not by works"? Isn't that pretty irritating, to preach "apart from works, without works, not by works"? So why shouldn't it be irritating when I preach "through faith alone"?

And what's more irritating still, St. Paul doesn't just chuck plain old ordinary works, he chucks the works of the law itself, which some people might think means he's cursing and condemning the law and letting them do whatever evil they please, as in Romans 3:8, "And why not do evil that good may come?" as a camp-follower in our own time began. Should we disown an irritating passage like this of St. Paul's and not talk freely and freshly about faith? My friend, we're willing to suffer and to teach that irritation with St. Paul, and to set ourselves so strongly against works and to cast ourselves on faith alone, for no other reason than to irritate people, to trip them up, so that they will learn to understand that they can't get right through good works – that the only way is through Christ's death and resurrection. And if you can't get right through good works, how much less of a chance do you have through evil works and without the law! So you can't conclude that, since good works don't help, maybe evil works will, any more than you can conclude that, since the sun won't help a blind man see, maybe the night and darkness will.

What amazes me is that people can get so hung up on a thing like this that's plain as day. Tell me, is Christ's death and resurrection our work, something we do, or not? No way is it our work, nor is it the work of a single law. But it is Christ's death and resurrection alone that make us free from sin and righteous, as Paul says in Romans 4:25: "He was given over to die because of our sins, and was raised to life to put us right with God."[19] And tell me further: with what work do we grab and hold onto Christ's death and resurrection? It can't be an external work; it has to be the eternal faith in our hearts. That alone, all alone, and apart from all works, will grab onto the kind of death and resurrection that can be preached according to the Gospel.

So what good does it do to rant and rave and burn people as heretics, if the matter is basically so clear and so obvious and so undeniably *there*, that faith in Christ's death and resurrection seizes us, apart from all works, and that that death and that resurrection are our life and our salvation? If it's so obvious that faith alone brings, grabs, gives us that life and that salvation, why shouldn't we say so? It's no heresy that faith alone seizes Christ and gives us life; but it's heresy to say it. Ain't it absurd? They know the thing is right but punish talk about the same thing as if it were wrong – as if anything could be right and wrong at the same time.

Nor am I the only one, nor even the first one, to say that faith alone puts us right. Ambrose, Augustine, and many others have said the same thing. And anyone who wants to read St. Paul with understanding has to say the same. What else could you say? Paul's words are too strong – and they won't tolerate a single work, not one. And if it's no work, then it must be faith alone. O what a fine, useful, unirritating lesson it would be that taught people they could be put right by faith *or* works! That would be like saying that it's not Christ's death alone that takes away our sins, but our works have something to do with it too. Wouldn't that be a fine way of honouring Christ's death, to say that it gets helped out by our works, and that works can do for us what his death does to make us good and strong like him? It's the devil in these people that can't help disgracing the blood of Christ.

So okay: since the thing itself makes us say that faith alone puts us right, and the way people talk teaches us to express it like this; since I have before me the example of the holy fathers and the danger that the people will cling to works and miss out on faith and lose Jesus, especially now, when people have been raised for so long on works and have to be torn away from them by main force – given all this, it's not only right but absolutely essential that we speak out loud and clear: faith alone without works puts us right. My only regret is that I didn't add the word 'any' to it, twice, "without any works of any laws", to give it its full clarity. So it's going to stay in my New Testament, and no matter how crazy all those papist asses get they'll never get me to take it out. That's enough of that. I'll deal further with this, God willing, in my booklet *De iustificatione*.[20]

William Tyndale

William Tyndale (c. 1490/94-1536) was without question the most influential Bible translator in the English language; the three major English Bible translations of the sixteenth and

[18] This and the previous quote from the Revised Standard Version. [Tr/Ed]

[19] Today's English Version. [Tr/Ed]

[20] "On Justification", never finished. [Tr/Ed]

seventeenth centuries, the Geneva Bible, the Douay-Rheims Bible, and the King James Bible, were all heavily indebted to his uncompleted work of the 1520s and 30s.

Born in Gloucestershire, Tyndale attended Oxford University, then became an instructor at Cambridge University, where he fell in with a group of humanists who began to reshape his thinking about religion. By 1521 he was convinced that the Bible should be the source of all Christian beliefs and practices, and that everyone should therefore be able to read it in his or her native language. He began to translate the New Testament shortly thereafter, first in England, then, when the authorities there prevented his work, in Germany, with financial support from wealthy London merchants. The New Testament was finished and published in 1525, at first in Cologne, and after it had been suppressed by Catholic authorities there, in Worms.

Despite bans and book-burnings, it was enormously popular, and sold over 50,000 copies in the first ten years of its existence – the ten years or so till Tyndale's execution for heresy in 1536. He managed to elude the authorities who sought him for heresy for several years on the Continent, working on his Old Testament when he could; when he was captured in Antwerp it was not yet completed.

Along with John Wycliffe, Tyndale was one of the hottest targets of Sir Thomas More's pen in the *Dialogue Concerning Heresies*: not only was he More's contemporary, who had fled More's legal jurisdiction to the Continent in order to break the law by translating the Bible into English, he was More's immensely *popular* contemporary, who was successfully engaged in doing that whereof More's Messenger only spoke. It was only fitting, therefore, that Tyndale should publish an answer to More's dialogue, two years after it appeared, in 1531; More published a confutation of Tyndale's answer the next year, in 1532.

How Happeneth That Ye Defenders Translate Not One Yourselves?
From *An Answer to Sir Thomas More's Dialogue* (1531)

The Fourteenth Chapter

MORE. Wycliffe was the occasion of the utter subversion of the realm of Boheme, both in faith and good living, and of the loss of many a thousand lives.[1]

TYNDALE. The rules of their faith are Christ's promises; and the rule of their living, God's law. And as for loss of lives, it is truth that the pope slew, I think, a hundred thousand of them, because of their faith, and that they would no longer serve him: as he slew in England many a thousand, and slew the true king and set up a false, unto the effusion of all the noble blood and murdering up of the commonality, because he should be his defender.

MORE. The constitution of the bishops is not that the scripture shall not be in English, but that no man many translate it by his own authority, or read it, until they had approved it.[2]

TYNDALE. If no translation shall be had, until they give licence or till they approve it, it shall never be had. And so it is all one in effect, to say there shall be none at all in English, and to say, till we admit it; seeing they be so malicious that they will none admit, but feign all the cavillations they can, to prove it were not expedient: so that if it be not had spite of their hearts, it shall never be had. And thereto, they have done their best to have had it enacted by parliament, that it should not be in English.

The Fifteenth Chapter

He jesteth out Hunne's death with his poetry, wherewith he built Utopia. "Many great lords came to Baynard's castle", (but all nameless) "to examine the cause"[3] as the credible prelates, so well learned, so holy, and so indifferent, which examined Bilney and Arthur, be also nameless ...

The Sixteenth Chapter

The messenger asketh him, "If there be an old lawful translation before Wycliffe's, how happeneth it that it is in so few men's hands, seeing so many desire it?"[4] He answereth,

[1] See 76, above. [Ed]

[2] See 77, above. Tyndale is paraphrasing; More's actual text reads:

> it was I say for these causes at a council held at Oxford provided upon great pain that no man should from then forth translate into the English tongue or any other language of his own authority, by way of book, libel, or treatise, nor no man openly or secretly read any such book, libel, or treatise newly made in the time of the said John Wycliffe or since, or that should be made any time after, till the same translation were by the diocesan, or if need should require by a provincial council approved. [Ed]

[3] Paraphrasing again: "And this examination was had before diverse great lords spiritual and temporal and other of the king's honourable counsel". See More, above, 78. [Ed]

[4] Messenger: "Surely so is it not for nought that the English Bible is in so few men's hands, when so many

"The printer dare not print it, and then hang on a doubtful trial, whether it were translated since or before; for it were translated since, it must be first approved".

What may not M. More say, by authority of his poetry? 'There is a lawful translation that no man knoweth'; which is as much as no lawful translation. Why might not the bishops show which were that lawful translation, and let it be printed? Nay, if that might have been obtained of them with large money, it had been printed, ye may be sure, long ere this. But, sir, answer me hereunto: how happeneth that ye defenders translate not one yourselves, to cease the murmur of the people, and put to your own glosses, to prevent heretics? Ye would, no doubt, have done it long since, if ye could have made your glosses agree with the text in every place. And what can you say to this, how that, besides they have done their best to disannul all translating by parliament, they have disputed before the king's grace, that it is perilous and not meet, and so concluded that it shall not be, under a pretence of deferring it of certain years: where M. More was their special orator, to feign lies for their purpose.

MORE. Nothing discourageth the clergy so much, as that they of the worst sort most calleth after it.[5]

TYNDALE. It might well be, Pharisees full of holiness long not after it; but publicans, that hunger after mercy, more sore desire it. Howbeit, it is in very deed a suspect thing, and a great sign of a heretic, to require it.

Then he juggleth with allegories. Sir, Moses delivered them all that he had received of God, and that in the mother tongue; in which all that had the heart thereto studied, and not the priests only, as thou mayest see in the scripture. And the apostles kept nothing behind; as Paul testified (Acts xx.), how he had showed them all the counsel of God, and had kept nought back. Should the lay people less hearken unto the expositions of the prelates in doubtful places, if the text were in their hands when they preached? ...

And when he maketh so great "difficulty and hardness in Paul's epistles"; I say, it is impossible to understand either Peter or Paul, or aught at all in the scripture, for him that denieth the justifying of faith in Christ's blood.[6] And again, it is impossible to understand in the scripture more than a Turk, for whosoever hath not the law of God written in his heart, to fulfil it: of which point, and of true faith too, I fear me that you are void and empty, with all your spirituality, whose defender ye have taken upon you to be, for to mock out the truth for lucre and [ad]vantage.

Juan Luis Vives

Juan Luis Vives (1492/93-1540), also known in his day by his Latin name Johannes Lodovicus Vives, was a Spanish humanist who studied under Erasmus and later became his colleague at the University of Louvain – and who tutored Mary, princess of Wales, and lectured at Oxford until he was imprisoned in 1527 for opposing Henry VIII's divorce from Vives' countrywoman Catharine of Aragon. He is best remembered today for his pedagogical works, but he also achieved renown for his philosophical and psychological treatises.

Vives was born the son of a draper in Valencia, Aragon. Luis and Blanca Vives were *marranos* or converted Jews who lived under constant suspicion throughout Vives' childhood – the family had to flee Valencia when Vives was seven because a clandestine synagogue had been discovered in the home of his great-uncle's widow Castellana Guirot. In 1524 Vives' father was found guilty of heresy by the Spanish Inquisition, and four years later his mother, who had died in 1508, was convicted of heresy posthumously and exhumed from her grave; his youngest sister, also, who had been raised a Jew and had married a Jew, was condemned by the Inquisition some time before 1524. The four older Vives children, including Juan (the second-born), were raised Christians, and the family was publicly Christian, but may have continued to practice Judaism secretly.

The year after Vives' mother's death, in 1509, he entered the University of Paris to study philosophy; in 1512 left Paris for Bruges, where he wrote several religious works; and in 1519 he was appointed professor of philosophy at the University of Louvain. Having dedicated his commentary on Augustine's *City of God* to Henry VIII, he was invited (probably at the instigation of Catharine of Aragon and Thomas More) to come to England

---

would so fain have it". More:

> Yet I think there will no printer lightly be so hot to put any Bible in print at his own charge, whereof the loss should lie whole in his own neck, and then hang upon a doubtful trial whether the first copy of his translation was made before Wycliffe's days or since. For if it were made since, it must be approved before the printing.

See More, above, 79. [Ed]

[5] "Yet is there in my mind not one thing that more puts good men of the clergy in doubt to suffer it than this that they see sometimes much of the worse sort more fervent in the calling for it than them whom we find far better". See More, above, 79. [Ed]

[6] This is Luther's argument; see above, 88-89. [Ed]

by Cardinal Wolsey. He spent the years from 1523 to 1527 as preceptor to Mary Tudor, for whom, commissioned by Queen Catherine, he wrote *The Instruction of a Christian Woman* (1523), an early treatise on women's education. During the same period he held a lectureship at Corpus Christi College, Oxford, where he was granted a doctorate in civil law. Having sided with Queen Catharine in Henry's divorce action, he was imprisoned for six or eight weeks and then released, on condition that he leave England. The next decade of his life, during which he wrote *De Tradendis Disciplinis* (1531) and *De Ratione Dicendi* (1533), he spent at Bruges; after two years in Paris from 1536 to 1538, he returned to Bruges, where he died in 1540 at the age of 47.

Vives was very much a man of the Renaissance, opposing scholasticism and defending the inductive method, arguing for modern methods of education (especially the study of nature as opposed to the ancient authorities) and for extending education to women (albeit in ways that seem blatantly sexist to us today). His remarks on the types and pedagogical uses of translation are not uniquely innovative in the early sixteenth century, but they crystalize Renaissance attitudes toward translation with clarity.

Practice in Writing
From *On Education* (*De Tradendis Disciplinis*, 1531)
Translated by Foster Watson

Practice in writing is a great help. "The pen", says Cicero, "is the best teacher and producer of speech".[1] Therefore, as soon as they have learnt syntax, let the pupils translate from the mother-tongue into Latin, and then back again into the mother-tongue. Let them begin with short passages, which can be gradually increased in length day by day. The same kind of exercises can be done in Greek, although I should prefer that pupils learned to translate from Greek authors rather than to translate from our language into Greek. It is right to draw attention to the fact that a translator must be well equipped in both languages; still he must receive most practice in the language into which he is translating. But it is impossible to fully translate words of which one does not know the meaning. The works of Aristotle will be badly translated by a man who is not a philosopher and those of Galen by a man who is not a doctor.

The pupils should likewise be well exercised in explaining difficult passages of great writers. For this requires great attention. Concentration is thus strengthened and the mind is sharpened, and the judgment becomes more active. Strange to say there are some people who do not understand how to write down what they would be well able to speak; this happens, as far as I can discover, because a wandering and unsettled mind is capable of sufficient attention for speech, but not for understanding what is written; it cannot support the strain of collecting and, as it were, compelling itself.

Added to this there must be practice in comparing writers, together with the expressions in which they agree, and in which they differ; for the general practice of language cannot be all limited to fixed rules. Let pupils write an easy letter, or tale, let them amplify a short sentence or a maxim, render a proverb into another language, and write a poem in prose, stripping it of all metre, an exercise which Crassus often practised, as we find mentioned in Cicero.[2] Laurentius Valla and Raphael Volaterranus employed the same method when they were translating Homer. Though I approve of this practice for boyish ignorance, I do not sanction it as an adequate rendering of a great writer, since in such a translation the greatest part of the beauty of the words is taken away. Let the pupil write at first few exercises, but let the master see that those are done correctly, then let him proceed to further exercises; style does not come by painful labour, but rather by careful and diligent exercise, so that the small beginnings which conduce so greatly to the whole (more than we believe even) may not escape our careful notice. Let scholars keep what they have written in earlier months, in order to compare it with that written in later months, so that they may perceive the progress made and persevere in the way in which they see they have made improvement.

Translation and Interpretation
From *On the Right Way of Speaking* (*De ratione dicendi*, 1533)
Translated by Mary Jean Thomas

Translation is the changing of words from one language to another while preserving the meaning. In some of these *only the meaning* is looked to, in others only the *phrasing and style*, as when someone attempts to translate Demosthenes or the orations of Tully or the poetry of Homer or Vergil into another language. The appearance and color of speaking in them is preserved completely. There has been too little understanding on the part of men who have done this of how great a difference there is in languages. For no language is so copious and varied that it can respond throughout to the figures and conformations of another, even the most infantile ones. "Not everything derived from the Greeks follows in our language",

[1] From Quintilian. [Tr]

[2] See Dr. Lawrence Humphrey, *de Interpretatione*. [Tr]

says M. Fabius, "just as they often have wanted to signify their words in our language and have not been able to".[3] There is a third kind of translation where *both the matter and the words are considered*; that is where the words bring strength and grace to the meaning either by themselves, joined with others, or by the whole speech itself.

Those translations where only the meaning is preserved are to be interpreted freely, and the translator should be forgiven for omitting certain things which do nothing toward bringing out the meaning, or for adding what aids the meaning. Nor are figures and schemes of one language to be expressed in the other, much less what is idiomatic. Nor do I see why it is pertinent to admit solecisms or barbarisms, just so you represent the meaning in the words. Certain ones have done this in translating Aristotle and the holy scriptures.

In order to find the most suitable language, the translator may add or subtract. He may put two words for one or one for two. One should take as his example Cicero's little book *de Universitate* and Theodorus Gaza as the best in interpretation. For Gaza in the first volume of Aristotle's *de Animalibus* turns λύσωμα to *aequamentum et discrimen* [an equaling and distinction], στρυφνόν to *austerum* [harsh] and *acerbum* [bitter].[4] Thus he expresses one word by two. And in the same book where there appears δοκεῖ δέ ὁ σπόγγος ἔχειν τινά αἴσθησιν. Σημεῖον δέ ὅτιχαλεπώτερον ἀποσπᾶται οὐ μη γίγνεται λαθρα ἴως ἡ κίνησις ὡς φασί he adds on his own *ut avulsores* [as those who tear off]. Then in that book he changes τά καλούμενα ὁλοθούρια to *et quae tota simplici mitioreque testa operte vertibula appel-lantur, et calli, aut tubera* [and which in all simplicity and gentleness are called covered vessel joints, and callouses or protruberances]. In the same way, those things congruent to the Latin he expresses as such even if little else is had by inserting the Greek such as ὠτός δέ μέ ρος τὸ μέν ἀνῶνυμον τὸ δέ λόγος which he translated *auris pars exterior, cui est nomen auriculae, parte constet exteriore pinna, inferiore fibra* [part of the outer ear, to which belongs the name of auricle, consists in parts in the outer wing and the inner fiber].

Seneca, in his book about *Tranquility of Life*, calls tranquility *euthumian* at the beginning. "For it is not", he says, "necessary to change and translate words in regard to the form of the thing spoken about. Something must be signified by the name which has the force of the Greek appellation, not the face" [Seneca *De tranquillitate* 2.3]. However, I will not easily agree that the interpreter take such great liberties upon himself unless he has first explored and ascertained that he is not mistaken in the art and the matter he treats. It should be a just work.

In *interpretations* it is not only advantageous, but of prime necessity, as much in the whole of life as in all the disciplines and arts, that they at each moment be faithful. Interpretations are made false either by ignorance of the language or the subject spoken about. For words are finite, things infinite, and so by the similitude of words, which is called synonymity, many are misled. Ignorant interpreters are deceived about the truth of the matter and they deceive others who themselves believe the words and style belong to that art or that particular to that author. So you may see certain ones in translating Aristotle or Galen have administered the business with little felicity and from too little respect for the work because they were not as versed in philosophy and medicine as was the work.

In those interpretations in which the matter and words are considered, the tropes and figures and the other ornaments of speech should be preserved the same insofar as it can be done. Otherwise, you should at least attempt a similarity in the force and decor so that words congruent to the second language produce the same force and grace as they did in the first language. In this matter there has been great error in the translating of Aristotle, as much in all his works as in the *Elenchii*, as we have demonstrated elsewhere. It would be most useful to the language if skillful interpreters would dare to give some foreign figure or trope its own citizenship, so long as it is not too far removed from the customs and conditions of the later language. Sometimes it would even be useful, in imitation of the first language and, as it were, mother tongue, to invent or form some apt word in the latter, or daughter, language so that both are made rich. Gaza, a Greek, did this well in Latin. Just anyone should not think himself free to do this. It is better in such practice to be more sparing and meticulous than daring and profuse.

There are certain translations of meanings in which even the words must be considered very exactly so that sometimes, if it can be done, they are rendered exactly – such as in the most difficult passages and those very obscure to the understanding. There are very many of these in Aristotle which one must leave to the judgment of the reader. The same is also true in public and private matters of great importance and in the mysteries of holy things which are contained in the sacred books. Here the translator should not interpose his own judgment.

Proper names of men and of places should translate in that form from one language to another, not be

---

[3] Quintilian *Institutes* 2.14.1. See above, 19-20. [Ed]

[4] I leave the Greek untranslated here in order to illustrate the point Vives is trying to make: that a translator often expands or condenses the number of words. Furthermore, I did not have access to the Gaza translation and the quoted passages do not coincide with the Loeb texts of Aristotle's *Parts of Animals*. [Tr]

changed to the force of signification. You should not translate *Aristotle* as 'Highest End', or *Plato* as 'Wide', or *Israel* as 'Supplantor'. The Greeks and Romans left foreign names in their origin and nature, only inflecting them to the forms of their own languages. Rightly Lucian derides that historian (and many others) who changed Roman names into Greek, so that he made Saturn *Chronos* and did other names in the same way.

It is perfectly permissible, as I have said, to delete or to add a letter or syllable where it renders the word appropriate and congruent to the language, so that where they say *Catullus* in Latin, they say *Katlos* in Greek; *Fabius Valens* in Latin becomes *Phabian Hualos* in Greek. *Quintus* becomes *Kointos*; *Thyberem*, *Thymbron*; *Tullius*, *Tullion*; *Caligula*, *Kalligolan*; *Lucius*, *Leukion*.[5] And in my judgment, they act distastefully who derive Roman names from Greek writing, as when they want *Rhoman* to be aspirated because they aspirate in Greek those words which begin in *rho*. Certain names received in the language have various forms. One should use them according to custom. The Roman says *Carthaginian*; the Greek says *Karchedona*. The Roman says *Agrigentus*; the Greek says *Akrigas*.

Proper names which have passed to some language through a medium are taken from the latter, not the first. The foreign words from the east and south came to the Romans by the teaching of the Greeks. From the north and west, however, words came to the Greeks through the Romans. Therefore, the Romans spoke in the Greek manner what the Greeks taught them, and the Greeks spoke in the Roman manner what they accepted from Rome. Both inflected the words a little according to their own methods of pronunciation. This can also be seen in our vulgar tongues. The Spanish and Italians, because they know about German words through the French, pronounce Germanic regions and cities not as the Germans themselves, but as the French. Those who force Latin speech to pronounce Hebraic names according to the Hebrews seem to me to do violence to the nature of things. So noble a speech as Latin does not accept absurd twistings of the palate, of the tongue, of the whole mouth, and what Hebrew Latin has taken from the Greeks retains the Greek form. In nature the transition from extremes is not easy, but the transition from things nearby or similar is easy. Further, the Latin Churches received almost all the holy scriptures from the Greeks and the use of the names prevails from the Septuagint, which is congruent and in conformity to the Greek language and to Latin, which was born from Greek. Besides, the Hebrews themselves do not pronounce the names of nations as do those mentioned above who would have Latins use Hebrew pronunciations. The Hebrews write so that what they say about the kings of Persia, Medora, and Egypt and about the areas and places on the globe will be clear to the Hebrew reader.[6]

The translation should follow one style or another. If there is some strength in the style of the author, it should be carried over in the interpretation, such as when you translate the *Golden Ass* of Apuleius you should imitate that jocular style most apt to moving one to laughter. Otherwise you should follow your own inclination, letting your own best nature be your guide – provided you are rightly instructed. If possible you should compete with your model so that the speech you receive is returned better, more appropriate, and more agreeable to the subject and to the listeners. That especially is best which is most relevant and most profitable. Do not do as some depraved souls who, induced by vanity, burden a correct, brilliant, and honest style with all sorts of curls and ornaments so that from the easy and pleasing they produce something heavy and bothersome. And what of those who spoil the elegance and splendor of the original style by obscure, drawn out, and humble words and figures, and by excessive displays in affectation of eloquence, showing no judgment of what should be the nature and force of the speech? They think that style by far the best which they crammed full of the rarest or most exquisite or most antiquated words.

Where you have preserved the charm of the style most exactly and where you have interpreted the words most properly, the translation will be best and preferable, for one's model should be represented truly. An example of this kind of translation is Cicero's little book *de Universitate*, part of the *Timaeus* of Plato, which I would propose to students as the best model of translating.

All poetry is much more freely interpreted than prose speech because of the necessity of meter. One is permitted to add, to subtract, and to change in poetry, and this may be done very freely when the ideas are most important and what we especially want is that the integrity of them remain. Cicero in the second book of *de Gloria* (I shall bring forth one example instead of several) interprets a verse of Homer from the *Iliad* as, "Who once destroyed the Trojans falls on his sword". He omitted two Greek words in the translation because they added nothing to its meaning.

---

[5] A list of Roman proper names, some with famous referents: Gaius Valerius Catullus the Roman poet, Fabius Valens and Caligula the Roman emperors. [Ed]

[6] These references to Hebrew, the only place in Vives' works suggesting proficiency in that language, have been taken to indicate that he may have attended a Hebrew school as a boy. [Ed]

Etienne Dolet

Etienne Dolet (1509-1546) was a French humanist printer, translator, and scholar who is often referred to as the first martyr of the Renaissance, and specifically as the first martyred *translator*: he was tortured and burned at the stake on charges of atheism and heresy incurred in a translation.

Since Dolet wasn't the only such 'heretic' in the era, however, it may be that he was in fact executed for aggravating the wrong people: he was a hot-tempered, quarrelsome man who loved learning and loathed priests and had a knack for making bitter enemies. After his studies at the universities of Paris, Padua, and Venice, he settled at the University of Toulouse; banished from Toulouse, he moved to Lyon, where he ran afoul of the law by killing a painter. He was thrown in prison but pardoned by the king, who declared the act justifiable homicide.

Like many Renaissance thinkers, Dolet in his writings walked a narrow line between orthodoxy and various brands of heterodoxy; he protected himself so well that it is still impossible to determine whether he was the atheist he was accused of being or just a Protestant of some sort. He publicly encouraged people to read the Bible in the vernacular, a seditious act associated with Protestantism, and as a printer published many Calvinist works (this was one of the 'crimes' that led to his first arrest in 1542; but he was also denounced by Calvin (along with the Roman Catholic Church).

His scholarly fame rests on a highly influential commentary on the Latin language (1536-1538), which helped transform Latin scholarship; he also wrote works assimilating his classical mentors Cicero and Cato to sixteenth-century France. The book on Cato, in which he proclaimed himself a Christian moralist of the Catonian stripe, was the first book he published as a printer; later books included his own translations and editions of classical authors, the New Testament and Psalms, and the works of his good friend François Rabelais – a more radical thinker and writer who was less abrasive than Dolet, and avoided his fate.

The actual legal record of his arrest, conviction, and execution is a bit hazy; probably the charges against him were largely trumped up. Central to the accusation that led to his execution was mistranslation: he had translated a dialogue then widely attributed to Plato, *Axiochus*, and the theological faculty at the Sorbonne seized upon a specific passage where Socrates seems to be saying that there is nothing after death, and thus to be denying the immortality of the soul. Since this was an impossible charge for the Sorbonne to lay at the feet of the divine Plato, they accused Dolet of mistranslating, specifically by adding three words, "rien du tout", to the passage – words that today look much like Luther's *allein*, a slight intensification of the author's meaning: "et quand tu seras decedé, elle n'y pourra rien aussi, attendu que tu ne seras plus *rien du tout*" ("whereas you will no longer be *anything at all*"). This, according to the official censure, "is wrongly translated and is contrary to the intentions of Plato, in whose work neither in the Greek nor in the Latin are there these words *rien du tout*". This accusation seems to have been the sole basis for the charge of blasphemy, the prime count of the three on which Dolet was convicted and executed.

His five principles of good translation are not original with him (they do not develop much on the similar lists offered by Leonardo Bruni and King Duarte of a century before), but they were influential. Certainly Dolet's fate at the hands of the theological faculty of the Sorbonne has endeared him to anxious translators everywhere.

The Way to Translate Well From One Language into Another (*La maniere de bien traduire d'une langue en aultre*, 1540)
Translated by James S Holmes

To translate well from one language into another requires in the main five things.

In the first place, the translator must understand perfectly the sense and matter of the author he is translating, for having this understanding he will never be obscure in his translations, and if the author he is translating is difficult in any way he will be able to render him easy and entirely understandable. And without further ado I shall give you an example of this. In the first book of Cicero's *Questions Tusculanes* is the following passage: 'Animum autem animam etiam fere nostri declarant nominari. Nam & agere animam, & efflare dicimus; & animosos, & bene animatos: & ex animi sententia. Ipse autem animus ab anima dictus est.'[1]

Translating this work of Cicero's,[2] I remarked as follows. 'One need not dwell at all on the difference,' I said, 'between the terms *animus* and *anima*. For the Latin expressions containing the two terms make clear

[1] "Others however justify the soul and breath as we Romans practically do – the name explains this, for we speak of 'giving up the ghost' and 'expiring' and of 'spirited people' and 'people of good spirit' and 'to the best of one's belief'; moreover the actual word for 'soul' has come from the word for 'breath' in Latin" (J. E. King's translation). [Ed]

[2] Dolet's translation of the *Tusculan Disputations*, which appeared a few years later, in 1543. [Tr]

to us that they mean practically the same thing. It is certain that *animus* is said for *anima*, and that the *animus* expresses itself through the *anima*, as if one would say that the vital principle and its manifestations are the source of the spirit, and that same spirit is an effect of the said vital principle.' Tell me, you who know Latin, whether it would have been possible to translate this passage well without a deep understanding of Cicero's sense. Know then that it is important and necessary for every translator to fathom perfectly the sense of the author he is turning from one language into another. And without that he cannot translate reliably and faithfully.

The second thing that is required in translating is that the translator have perfect knowledge of the language of the author he is translating, and be likewise excellent in the language into which he is going to translate. In this way he will not violate or diminish the majesty of the one language or the other. Do you believe that a man can translate any of Cicero's orations well into French if he be not perfect in the Latin and French tongues? Bethink you that every language has its own properties, turns of phrase, expressions, subtleties, and vehemences that are peculiar to it. If the translator ignores the which, he does injustice to the author he is translating, and also to the language he is turning him into, for he does not represent or express the dignity and richness of the two tongues which he has taken in hand.

The third point is that in translating one must not be servile to the point of rendering word for word. And if someone does that, he is proceeding from poverty and lack of wisdom. For if he has the qualities aforesaid (which he needs in order to be a good translator), he will give thought to meanings without regarding the order of words, and set to work in such a way that the author's intention will be expressed while preserving precisely the property of the one and the other language. And it is too great a precision (or should I say stupidity, or ignorance?) to begin one's translation at the beginning of the sentence: if by changing the order of the words you can express the intention of him you are translating, no one can reprove you for it. Here I do not want to overlook the folly of some translators who submit to servitude in lieu of liberty. That is to say, they are so foolish as to make an effort to render line for line or verse for verse. By which mistake they often corrupt the sense of the author they are translating and do not express the grace and perfection of the one and the other language. You should diligently avoid this vice, which demonstrates nothing but the translator's ignorance.

The fourth rule, which I shall give at this place, is more to be observed in languages not reduced to an art than in others. Not yet reduced to a fixed and accepted art I call such languages as French, Italian, Spanish, that of Germany, of England, and other vulgar tongues. Should it therefore happen that you translate a Latin book into one or another of these (even into French), you should avoid adopting words too close to Latin and little used in the past, but be content with the common tongue without introducing any new terms foolishly or out of reprehensible curiousness. If some do so, do not follow them in this, for their arrogance is of no worth, and is not tolerable among the learned. From this do not understand me to say that the translator should entirely abstain from words that are not in common use, for it is well known that the Greek and Latin languages are much richer in terms than is French. The which often forces us to use rare words. But it should be done only out of sheer necessity. I am further well aware that some might say that most terms in the French language have been derived from the Latin, and that if our predecessors had the authority to introduce them, we moderns and our descendants may do the same. Let all that be debated by babblers, but the best thing is to follow the common tongue. I shall treat this point more amply, with further illustration, in my *Orateur françoys*.

Let us now move on to the fifth rule that should be observed by a good translator. The which is of such great import that lacking it any composition is ponderous and displeasing. But what does it consist of? Nothing other than the observation of rhetorical numbers[3]: that is to say, a joining and arranging of terms with such sweetness that not alone the soul is pleased, but also the ear is delighted and never hurt by such harmony of language. I speak of these rhetorical numbers more copiously in my *Orateur*, hence I shall not discourse of them further here. But here I do advise the translator to have a care for them, for without observing numbers one cannot be admirable in any composition whatsoever, and without them thoughts cannot be serious and have their required and legitimate weight. For do you think that it is enough to have correct and elegant terms without a good joining of them? I say to you that it is just as in a confused heap pf various kinds of precious stones, the which cannot display their luster because they are not properly arranged. Or just as when various musical instruments are badly played by performers who are ignorant of the art of music and know little of its tones and measures. In fine, there is little splendour in words if their order and pattern be not as it should be. And for that in times past the Greek orator Isocrates was esteemed above all, and likewise Demosthenes. Among the Latins Mark Tully Cicero was a great observer of numbers. But do not think that orators should observe them more than historiographers. And that being true, you will find that Caesar and Sallust kept their numbers no less than

---

[3] Dolet's term is 'oratorical numbers'. Today we would probably talk about 'style.' [Tr]

Cicero. The conclusion in this regard is that without closely observing numbers an author is nothing, and if he does observe them he cannot fail to become renowned for eloquence, providing he also is precise in his choice of words, serious in his thoughts, and ingenious in his arguments. These are the points of a perfect orator, one truly arrayed in all glory of eloquence.

Elizabeth Tudor

Queen Elizabeth I (1533-1603, reigned 1558-1603) was not only a famous patron of the arts, foster-mother of the Elizabethan Age in English literature; she was herself, as Roger Ascham informs us in *The Schoolmaster*, below, an accomplished poet and translator.

Born to King Henry VIII and his ill-starred second wife Anne Boleyn, Lady Elizabeth suffered a childhood filled with sudden and baffling reversals of fortune that almost invariably threatened her very life. Her mother, who had catalyzed the protestant revolution in England, was beheaded when Elizabeth was not quite three, ostensibly for adultery, but probably because she had not given Henry a son. Her younger half brother, Edward VI, the son of Jane Seymour, whom Henry married after beheading her mother, was crowned king at age ten (Elizabeth was fourteen) at his father's death, but died five years later of tuberculosis. During that period, in Elizabeth's late teens, Thomas, Lord Seymour, husband of her stepmother Catherine Parr (Henry's last wife, who survived him), was accused of plotting to marry Elizabeth and overthrow his brother the Lord Protector; Elizabeth narrowly escaped being accused as his co-conspirator and executed with him. As the Protestant successor to the throne she was a potential threat to her older sister Mary I, the Catholic daughter of Catharine of Aragon, and during Mary's reign – characterized by ruthless persecutions of Protestants, whence the byname 'Bloody Mary' – was once imprisoned in the Tower on a trumped-up charge. She survived these crises largely by making herself as invisible and harmless as possible, and by giving to all queries "an answer answer-less", a habit that would see her through many subsequent crises as queen.

She was crowned queen at 25 and reigned for 45 years – the 'Virgin Queen' who had vowed since she was eight (when her father had executed her cousin and stepmother, Catherine Howard) that she would never marry, and never did. Her passionate nature made her difficult to work with, but endeared her to the English people, to whom she also brought a period of extended prosperity. She loved dramatic demonstrations of her power, political intrigues, and the theatre, and the Elizabethan period is today associated with the defeat of the Spanish Armada and the work of writers like Christopher Marlowe, William Shakespeare, and Francis Bacon; she was also on quite a few hit lists, and thwarted numerous attempts on her life, at least three planned by Mary, Queen of Scots, her cousin. In 1580 Pope Gregory XIII opined that it would be no sin to rid the world of her. Her uncanny ability to evade such plots and generally to have her way in anything she set out to accomplish, which had a good deal to do with an astute sense of character that enabled her to surround herself with brilliant and loyal advisors, gave her an almost supernatural reputation all across Europe.

Many of the young Lady Elizabeth's translations seem to have originated as 'schoolwork' – assigned by her tutor at the instruction of her stepmother, Queen Catherine Parr, at whose house she continued to live after her half brother Edward's ascension to the throne – and the texts she chose or was given to translate by and large reflect the kind of classical education Roger Ascham would recommend for young boys several decades later: orations by Isocrates, a dialogue by Xenophon, one of Seneca's letters. Two of her best-known translations, however, were of far less obvious texts by Queen Margaret of Navarre, who was renowned for her learning, Protestant sympathies, and political acumen. Both of the French originals were apparently harmless religious pieces; but the religious controversies that surrounded their author made them anything but harmless choices for a princess of eleven and fifteen years, respectively, to translate.

The diffident tone of her remarks is heavily overdetermined: it was the tone prescribed not only for translators but for females and for children as well, and Lady Elizabeth was all three; but beyond that, her self-deprecating prudence was the mask that enabled her to survive seventy years of what her subject William Shakespeare called "outrageous fortune".

Letter to Catherine Parr
Preface to Her Translation of Queen Marguerite of Navarre, 'The Glasse of the Synnefull Soule' (1544)

To our most noble and virtuous queen Catherine, Elizabeth, her humble daughter, wishes perpetual felicity and everlasting joy.

Not only knowing the effectuous will and fervent zeal, the which your highness has towards all godly learning, as also my duty towards you, most gracious and sovereign princess, but knowing also that the wit of a man or a woman wax dull and unapt to do or understand anything perfectly, unless it be always occupied upon some manner of study. Which things considered, have moved so small a portion as God has lent me, to prove what I could do. And, therefore, have I ... translated this little book out of French rhyme into English prose, joining the sentences together, as well as the capacity of my simple wit and small learning could extend themselves.

The which book is entitled or named, 'The Mirror, or Glass, of the Sinful Soul', wherein is contained, how she (beholding and contemplating what she is) does perceive how, of herself and her own strength, she can do nothing that good is, or that, through his incomprehensible love, grace, and mercy, she (being called from sin to repentance), does faithfully hope to be saved. And although I know that, as for my part which I have wrought in it (as well spiritual as manual), there is nothing done as it should be, ... yet do I trust also ... that the file of your excellent wit and godly learning ... shall rub out, polish, and mend (or else cause to mend) the words (or rather the order of my writing), the which I know, in many places, to be rude, and nothing done as it should be. But I hope that, after to have been in your grace's hands, there shall be nothing in it worthy of reprehension, and that in the meanwhile no other (but your highness only) shall read it, or see it, lest my faults be known of [by] many. Then shall they be better excused (as my confidence is in your grace's accustomed benevolence) than if I should bestow a whole year in writing or inventing ways for to excuse them.

Praising God Almighty, the Maker and Creator of all things, to grant unto your highness the same New Year's day, a lucky and prosperous year, with prosperous issue, and continuance of many years in good health and continual joy, and all to his honour, praise, and glory.

From Ashridge, the last day of the year of our Lord God, 1544.

The Study of a Woman
From Preface to Her Translation of Queen Marguerite of Navarre, *A godly Medytacyon of the christen Sowle* (1548)

If thou do throughly read this work (dear friend in the Lord), mark rather the matter than the homely speech thereof, considering it is the study of a woman, which has in her neither cunning [knowledge] nor science, but a fervent desire that such one may see what the gift of God the creator does when it pleases him to justify [make righteous] a heart. For what is the heart of a man, concerning his own strength, before he has received the gift of faith? Thereby only has he knowledge of the goodness, wisdom, and power of God. And as soon as he through that faith knows pithily the truth, his heart is anon full of charity and love. So that by the ferventness thereof, he excludes all fleshly fear and firmly trusts in God ...

O happy and fortunate gift which causes a man to possess a grace so desired. Alas, no man could this understand, only by such gift God had given it him ... Therefore gentle reader, with a godly mind, I beseech thee patiently this work to peruse which is but small in quantity, and taste nothing but the fruit thereof. Praying to God full of all goodness, that in thy heart he will plant the lively faith. Amen.

Mikael Agricola

Mikael Agricola (c. 1510-1557) was a Finnish Reformer whose translations of parts of the Bible and Finnish primer and catechism almost singlehandedly created the Finnish literary language.

Little is known of Agricola's early life. As his Latin surname ('Farmer') suggests, he was the son of a farmer; he attended the Latin school in Viipuri, the largest city in Karelia (ceded to the Soviet Union in 1940), was appointed scribe to Bishop Martin Skytte around 1528, and was ordained in the early 1530s. The bishop sent him to Wittenberg in 1536, apparently with the express purpose of learning from Luther how to go about translating the Bible into Finnish, and for three years he did indeed work with Luther (who called him 'Grickel') and Philip Melanchthon. Upon his return to Finland in 1539 he began (or continued) work on the Finnish Bible while serving as rector of the Turku School and, for the last seven years of his life, as bishop. Sweden was at war with Russia from 1555 to 1557, and Agricola was sent to Moscow as part of the peace delegation; he died in 1557 immediately upon his return, apparently of exhaustion from the journey.

Agricola never did complete the translation he envisaged of the entire Bible; however, in addition to a primer (the first book published in Finnish), a catechism, and several liturgical works, he managed to translate a scriptural prayer book (1544), the New Testament (1548), and collections of psalms and prophecies (1551). As he notes in his preface to the New Testament, below, very little had been written in Finnish when he undertook his translations; in order even to begin it he was compelled to invent an orthography and coin numerous new words. The result was necessarily uneven, and his register shifts from the solemn to the bathetic, from the altar to the barnyard, often make for comical reading.

Of theoretical interest in Agricola's preface to the New Testament is the attention he gives to dialectal differences in the construction of a literary language for Bible translation. The Finnish east/west tension that Agricola summarizes historically has been critical for the development of a Finnish literary language: Agricola, a Karelian, did his Bible translations while living in Turku in the West, and defends his use of Western dialectal forms; in the nineteenth century another polemic raged over whether the *Kalevala* was originally a western or an eastern epic.

Preface to the New Testament (1548)
Translated by Douglas Robinson

Here, then, dear Christian reader, and dear Finnish Tavastian, Karelian,[1] or whatever friend of the Lord Jesus you may be, are the books of the New Testament translated into Finnish, partly from the Greek, partly from books in Latin, German, and Swedish, according to the gifts given us by the spirit and grace of our Lord Jesus Christ. Since until our times the language of this land is hardly ever used in books or letters, I offer you now this Testament, though who knows with what favor it will be received in our Lord's eyes. And you should know that the New Testament was first written by the Evangelists and Apostles in the Greek language, except for the Gospel According to St. Mark and St. Paul's Epistle to the Hebrews, which are thought to have been written in Hebrew.[2] But when Rome converted to the Christian faith, the New Testament was translated into Latin, the language that was used in Rome. Now that the Christian faith and Christendom have spread from Rome up through Germany, England, Denmark, and Sweden to here, and to other provinces that were once under the power of the Roman Church, the Holy Bible, the Word and worship of God, and the liturgy till now have been in Latin one and all, both here and in all those provinces. But every church service should have been held in the language understood by the people in each individual province where the faith was received, so that, just as Christ came to save everybody, so too should his words, which he gave us for our salvation, be open and accessible to everyone and hidden from no one, as they have been till now (much worse) at great risk to our souls. For St. Paul in 1 Corinthians 14 says that nothing should be spoken in the church but what will work for the understanding and salvation of all. As he says of himself, "in public worship I would much rather speak five words that people can understand and be helped by, than ten thousand words in a foreign language".[3] But this is what has happened since time immemorial with Latin. That's why it has been so common for priests in our parishes, some understanding a little Latin and some none at all, to be (God help us and save us!) mean and lazy teachers of the word, as many still are today. But there's many a fool in a holy place, more's the pity. And some seldom or never bother to prepare their sermons or teach the people to say the Lord's Prayer, let alone the greater tenets of our faith, though the highest office of the priest is to teach the people the catechism and the word of God. And others still are so wicked out of lust for false glory, profit, or envy that they will not look to their own duties nor allow others to read God's word, of which Jesus spoke many times and severely in Luke 11[:52], saying, "Woe to you experts in religion! For you hide the truth from the people. You won't accept it for yourselves, and you prevent others from having a chance to believe it". Now lest a single priest or teacher from this day forward hide his laziness behind an ignorance of Latin or Swedish, and thus neglect his duties as a teacher, therefore this New Testament has been translated from the simple text that the evangelists and apostles wrote. Comments have also been added in the margins and under chapter headings, so that readers with little practice in understanding the Holy Bible might better grasp its meaning and pass it on to others. For the text itself is the very words of God's Holy Spirit, but the prefaces and commentary have been added for clearer understanding. And some of the words may at first sound strange and taste bitter upon the tongue, but in time and with usage they will become sweeter. And if this translation please not everyone, let the all-wise Judge read it, as St. Jerome writes to Pammachius in *De optimo genere interpretandi*, where among other things he says, *simplex translatio potest errorem habere, non crimen.*[4]

Now someone may say, "Oh how I wish I knew how and when the Finnish people became Christians". Let me answer briefly: in the Year of Our Lord 1150 Erik Jedvardsson (he whom we now call St. Erik) was proclaimed king in Sweden, and that same year he began to think about spreading the Christian faith to

[1] Häme (formerly called by its Latin name Tavastia) is a province in southwestern Finland, Karelia a province in southeastern Finland; in Agricola's day this address was a way of saying "Finns east and west", or "all Finns". [Tr/Ed]

[2] Incorrectly. Jesus spoke Aramaic, and the four gospels in that sense might be read as 'translations' into Greek; but Mark wrote in Greek. The author of the letter to the Hebrews, long erroneously identified as Paul, is unknown. [Tr/Ed]

[3] 1 Corinthians 14:19. See above, 16. The Living Bible translation has been modified slightly here to reflect Agricola's euphemistic reference not to 'unknown' but to 'foreign' languages. [Tr/Ed]

[4] In Paul Carroll's translation: "a simple version like mine may contain errors but not mistakes of criminal proportion". See above, 25. [Tr/Ed]

Finland as well.[5] And so he gathered a great army and, taking St. Henry with him, who was then bishop of Uppsala, went to war against the Finns, also called suomalaiset,[6] conquered them, had mercy upon them and befriended them, and bade the Word of God be preached unto them. And when he went back to Sweden he left St. Henry here as bishop and preacher; the next year Henry, who was an Englishman by birth, was struck dead.[7] Thenceforth until this day, the Latin language has been used in this bishopric as in others, in churches, parishes, and worship services, as is publicly attested by the old church Bibles still found in churches today. And this is how the Finns were first converted to Christianity. But in the Year of Our Lord 1248 another king named Erik, Erik Eriksson, sent a great army here to Finland under the command of his son-in-law Birger Jarl, and conquered the Tavastians.[8] But he oppressed and persecuted them until they converted to Christianity and let themselves be baptized. To these converts he guaranteed peace for their souls and their possessions; but to those who did not convert he gave no peace until they accepted the Christian faith. And in this fashion the Tavastians or hämäläiset first became Christians. Further let it be known that in the Year of Our Lord 1293, the Marsk of Sweden Torgils gathered an army and sent it into Karelia, for the Karelians were continually harming Tavastia and all of Finland. Just as they had always caused much harm to Christianity. At that time the Karelians were conquered by the Swedes, who then built the fortress and city of Viipuri in order to curb the Karelians and Russians.[9] And thus were the Karelians too converted to Christianity. The reader will note that the coast-dwellers of Finland, in the provinces of Porvoo and Raasepori along the southern coast and the archipelago and Kalanti and Ostrobothnia along the western coast, who still speak Swedish today, originally came from Sweden or Gotland.[10] And because those pagan unChristianized Finns who lived inland desired, as was their wont, to harm the coast-dwelling Swedes, the latter might well have gone to Sweden by boat or ship to seek help and safety among their in-laws and friends. This is why they were Christians long before the other dwellers in this Finnish bishopric and land. Finally, while these peoples speak different dialects or idioms, in order that all of these provinces, each of which speaks a little of the others' dialects – in order, I say, that this entire bishopric be called Finland, the mother as it were of the others (for she first became Christian, and

---

[5] Little is known of Erik Jedvardsson; the crusade he launched into Finland is largely legendary. Sweden at the time was a loose federation of provinces. Toward the end of the Viking Age, early this millennium, the Swedes (centered in Uppland, around Uppsala, just north of Stockholm) ruled the federation, and king Olof Skötkonung (reigned c. 994-c. 1022) converted all Sweden to Christianity; but the Goths in the south rose up against them in the mid-eleventh century, and by 1130 Sverker from East Gotland was declared king. Erik Jedvardsson was a Swedish 'pretender' who called himself king of Sweden but in fact only ruled in Svealand; Erik's and Sverker's descendants alternated on the throne, which soon came to be established in Stockholm, for half a century. After Erik was murdered in 1160 he was canonized as the patron saint of Sweden. [Tr/Ed]

[6] Agricola has it the other way around: *suomalaiset* (the Finns' word for themselves) who are also called Finns. [Tr/Ed]

[7] Uppsala was one of five Swedish bishoprics; in the late thirteenth century it was joined by a sixth in Åbo, or (in Finnish) Turku, where Agricola was to be named bishop in 1550; and in 1554 Swedish King Gustav I Vasa divided Finland into two bishoprics and named Agricola bishop of Turku, Paavali Juusten bishop of Viipuri. Henry was an English missionary who had been appointed to the prestigious Uppsala bishopric, and legend has it that he accompanied Erik on his crusade to Finland. According to legend he was killed by a peasant named Lalli around 1160, and was canonized as the national saint of Finland in the late 12th century. [Tr/Ed]

[8] Birger Jarl (or Earl) was the most powerful man in Sweden after the king, and the king's right-hand man, especially in military affairs. Birger was actually Erik's brother-in-law (Erik married Birger's sister), not son-in-law. [Tr/Ed]

[9] The Russians and the Swedes had been fighting over Finland for over a century, and even the Danes had invaded Finland around the turn of the twelfth and thirteenth centuries. Duke Jaroslav of Novgorod had begun colonizing Karelia in the 1220s, pursuing the same policy of forced baptisms that the Swedish kings were practicing in the west, and from the 1220s to the 1240s the Swedish kings brought all the influence of the Roman Catholic Church to bear to prevent this intervention in what they saw as their sovereign territory. Agricola does not mention Birger Jarl's failed invasion of Karelia in 1240, when he was defeated by a duke of Novgorod. The fortress Birger had built in Turku was designed for the eventual goal of seizing all of Finland for Sweden, a goal realized by Torgils Knutsson, Marsk or Marshal of Sweden, half a century later. The war with Novgorod lasted until 1323, when the border between Russia and Finland was agreed upon and Finland officially became a part of Sweden. [Tr/Ed]

[10] Porvoo (Swedish Borgå) and Raasepori (Swedish Raseborg) are near Helsinki; the Turku archipelago surrounds the southwestern tip of Finland; Kalanti (Swedish Calandi) is on the southern west coast, Ostrobothnia (Latin for Eastern Bothnia, on the eastern shore of the Gulf of Bothnia) on the northern west coast. Still today there are towns in Ostrobothnia where the Swedish-speaking natives speak no Finnish. [Tr/Ed]

the provincial mother church and episcopal seat are located here in Turku), this New Testament has mainly been written in Finnish.[11] Inevitably phrases and words from other languages have been included as well.[12] And it is no wonder that there are so many languages in this bishopric; for while the territory of Finland is one single bishopric, it is also divided into seven provinces, as Jacobus Zeiglerus Landanus writes. The first and foremost of them is North and South Finland.[13] The second Satakunta upper and lower. The third Häme or Tavastia. The fourth Karelia. The fifth Uusimaa. The sixth Raasepori. The seventh Ostrobothnia, without Kalanti, etc. And because so many provinces and dialects are to be found in this land and bishopric, and each has some excellent proverbs or forms of speech, let no Christian and godly person who reads this book take offense if this recently begun Finnish translation have some part that is wrong or strange or horrible – which is to say, *new. Nam nihil simul inceptum, et perfectum esse constat.*[14] But if in future some friend of the Lord's should know how to translate it better, he is free to do so; only beware lest he lose his temper. Let every wise man and unlearned man, priest and layman, and the entire Finnish people, each in his or her separate capacity, be advised to pay close heed to the words of God written in this book, remaining ever watchful in them, pondering them, remembering them, and living according to them until the life ever after, which Jesus Christ grant us all. AMEN.

[11] The gist of this rather convoluted argument is that, since 'Finland' (then technically only the region around Turku in the southwest, also called Finland-Proper) is the mother of all 'Finns' (who inhabit the bishopric that is roughly coterminous with modern Finland), and because the episcopal seat is in Turku, Agricola has translated the New Testament into the Turku dialect of Finnish rather than the Karelian dialect with which he himself grew up. This is an argument for a standard or hegemonic dialect: Agricola is arguing that the only way to unify the bishopric linguistically (and culturally and politically) is by translating the New Testament into the dialect of the dominant region, which he insists is 'Finland' or the southwest. A good case might have been made for adopting the Karelian dialect as the basis of standard Finnish, especially since a second episcopal seat was established there six years after the publication of this translation, and the Finns had first migrated into the region through Karelia; political reasons probably made Turku the more obvious choice, with its geographical and cultural proximity to Sweden and the Catholic (later Lutheran) religious authorities it represented. [Tr/Ed]

[12] For 'inevitably' Agricola has *coska tarue on anonut* "because (or whenever) need has requested". He means that there weren't (always) enough Finnish words to satisfy his translational needs, and so he had to use Latinisms and Sveticisms and other loan words. [Tr/Ed]

[13] Or Finland-Proper, the area around Turku in southwestern Finland. [Tr/Ed]

[14] "For nothing is simultaneously started and perfected". [Tr/Ed]

Joachim du Bellay

Joachim du Bellay (1522?-1560) was a French poet who led, with Pierre de Ronsard, the literary group known as La Pléiade and wrote the group's manifesto, "The Defense and Illustration of the French Language".

Du Bellay was born into a noble family near Lirè, France, but lost both parents at an early age and was raised by a somewhat neglectful brother. In his early twenties he met Jacques Peletier at Poitiers, where he had gone to study law; Peletier had just published his French translation of Horace's *Ars Poetica* and was propounding the theories of literature and translation that du Bellay and Ronsard were soon to be advancing under the banner of La Pléiade. *The Defense*, which du Bellay wrote at the age of 27 in response to Thomas Sebillet's *Art Poétique* (1548), was written very much in the spirit of Horace's pronouncements on translation and imitation: one should imitate freely, not translate slavishly. It was written in haste, and has not stood up to modern criticism quite as well as its immense reputation and influence would warrant; ironically enough, for example, in 1904 Pierre Villey showed that whole segments of the piece had been translated almost verbatim – slavishly! – from Sperone Speroni's *Dialogo delle lingue* (1542).

Du Bellay published his first sonnets, inspired by Petrarch, around the same time; shortly thereafter he traveled to Rome with his cousin, Cardinal Jean du Bellay, whose secretary he remained until 1557, when he returned to Paris. His *Antiquités de Rome* and *Regrets*, the latter considered his finest work, were published in 1558, two years before his death at 37.

Du Bellay's essay is the source of the French word for translation, *traduction* – based on a misreading of Bruni's 'On the Correct Way to Translate', du Bellay took *traduction* or 'betrayal' to be equivalent to translation (a reading that in any case fit his brief nicely), and the word stuck in French (and other romance-language) usage.

The Defense and Illustration of the French Language (*La Déffence et Illustration de la langue françayse*, 1549)
Excerpted and translated by James Harry Smith and Edd Winfield Parks

Book I Chapter I
The Origin of Languages

If Nature (of whom some famous person, not without reason, has expressed doubt whether she should be called mother or stepmother) had given to men a general will and assent, in addition to the numberless comforts that have come from her, the inconstancy of humans would not have needed to forge so many forms of speech. This diverse confusion may rightly be called a tower of Babel. For languages are not born out of themselves, like herbs, roots, trees, some frail and weak, others healthy and strong, and more able to carry the weight of human conceptions: but all their power is born in the world by the will and arbitrary act of man. This, it seems to me, is a good reason that one should not praise one language and condemn another, for all of them have the same origin, the imagination of man, and have been formed with the same judgment, for the same end: that we may signify to one another the concepts and thoughts of our minds. It is true that in course of time some, because they have been more carefully governed, have become richer than others; but that ought not to be attributed to the felicity of the languages, but solely to the ingenuity and industry of men. For all that nature has created, all the arts and sciences, in all quarters of the world, are in force to the same end; but, because men are of diverse wills, they speak and write differently. In this regard, I cannot enough blame the stupid arrogance and foolhardiness of some of our nation who, being anything but Greeks or Latins, disparage and reject with more than stoic scorn everything written in French; and I cannot marvel enough at the opinion of certain scholars who think that our vernacular is incapable of good literature and erudition, as if an invention ought to be judged good or bad on expression alone. I have not attempted to satisfy the former. As to the latter I am perfectly willing, if it be possible, to make them change their opinion, by certain considerations that I want briefly to set forth; not that I feel myself more 'clairvoyant' in this, or in other matters, than they, but that the affection which they bear to alien languages does not allow them the desire to give sound and complete judgment to their own.

Chapter III
Why the French Language is Not So Rich as the Greek and Latin

And if our language is not as copious and rich as the Greek or Latin, that ought not to be imputed to any fault of the language, as if it of itself could ever be other than poor and sterile: but the fault ought rather to be laid to the ignorance of our ancestors, who (as someone has said in speaking of the ancient Romans), holding in higher respect doing well than talking well, and preferring to leave to their posterity the examples, rather than the rules, of virtuous action, deprived themselves of the glory of their high deeds, and us of the fruit of the imitating of them: and in the same way have left us our language so impoverished and naked that it needs the ornaments and (if I may so speak) the pens of others. But who would say that Greek and Latin had always been of that excellence which we see in the times of Homer, of Demosthenes, of Virgil, of Cicero? And if these authors had considered that, for whatever diligence and cultivation might be expended, their languages would never bear fruit, would they have striven so hard as they have to bring them to the point where we now see them? I can say the same thing of our language, which begins now to flower without bearing fruit, or rather, like a plant stem, has not yet flowered, so far is it from having brought forth all the fruit that it might very well produce. This is certainly not the fault of its nature, which is as fertile as are others, but the fault of those who have had it in charge and have not cultivated it sufficiently: like a wild plant, in the very desert where it had come to life, without watering or pruning (or in any way protecting it from the brambles and thorns which overshadowed it), they have left it to grow old and almost die. If the ancient Romans had been as neglectful of the cultivation of their language, when it first began to swarm, certain it is that in such a short time it could not have grown so great. But they, like good farmers, first transplanted it from a wild to a domestic soil; then, in order that it might the more quickly and better bear fruit, cutting from around it the useless branches, they replaced them with sound and serviceable ones; and, masterfully drawing upon Greek, they rapidly engrafted what they took and made it similar to their own trunk that thenceforth it appeared not adopted, but natural. And so were produced in Latin flowers and fruits colored with that high eloquence, with numbers, with the artful liaison, with all those things which, not so much by its own nature as by artifice, every language customarily produces. If the Greeks and Romans, more diligent in the cultivation of their languages than we in that of ours, did not find in theirs, except with great labor and application, any grace, any number, finally, any eloquence, we ought not to wonder if our vernacular is not as rich as it might be, nor to take occasion to berate it as a low thing, and of little worth. The time will come, and I hope for such a bright destiny for France, that this noble and puissant kingdom will obtain in her turn the reins of monarchy, and that our language – (if with Francis I the French language was not completely buried) which now is beginning to throw out its roots, rise from the ground, and lift itself with such pride and grandeur – may equal even those of Greece and Rome, producing like them Homers, Demosthenes, Virgils, Ciceros, as France has several times produced Pericles, Nicias, Alcibiades, Themistocles, Caesars, Scipios.

Chapter IV
That the French Language is not As Poor as Many Think It

I do not, nevertheless, think our vernacular, even as it is now, is so vile and abject as the ambitious admirers of Greek and Latin hold it, who do not think anything good, and who reckon even Pitho, goddess of Persuasion, unable to call anything good, except it be in a foreign tongue and one not understood by the common vulgar. And whoever will look well at it will find that our French language is not so poor that it cannot render faithfully what it borrows from others; so unproductive that it cannot, of itself, bear a fruit of good invention, through the industry and diligence of its cultivators, if any of them are found such friends to their country and to themselves that they are willing to devote themselves to it. But to whom, after God, are we to render thanks for such a blessing, but to our good king and sire, Francis, first of that name, and first in all virtues. I say first because he has, in his noble realm, been the first to restore all the arts and sciences in their ancient dignity: and he has carried our language from a rude and unpolished state into an elegant one, where, if not so ample as it might be, it is at least a faithful interpreter of all the others; the proof of which is that the Greek and Latin philosophers, historians, physicians, poets, orators, are all now in French. What shall I say of the Hebrews? The sacred letters bear sufficient witness to what I maintain. I shall lay by the ignorant arguments of those who contend that the mysteries of theology ought not to be uncovered, almost as though they were profaned by being put into the tongues, as those who sustain the contrary opinion assert. For this discussion is not germane to what I am trying to do, which is alone to show that our language did not have at its birth the gods and stars so hostile that it may not one day attain the excellence and perfection of the other languages, only provided that all the sciences can accurately and amply be negotiated in it, as one is able to see in such a large number of Greek and Latin books, nay more, even in Italian, Spanish, and others, translated into French by many an excellent pen, in our time.

Chapter V
That Translations Are Not Enough to Give Perfection to the French Language

Nevertheless this laudable toil of translating does not seem to me alone a sufficient means of raising our vernacular to be the equal and paragon of other more famous languages. I mean to prove this so clearly that no one, I think, will contradict it, without being manifestly a calumniator of the truth. In the first place, there is a close agreement between all the better writers on rhetoric, that there are five departments of good speaking: invention, elocution, disposition, memory, and pronunciation. But since the last two of these are not acquired by the advantage of language so much as they are given to each according to the facility of his nature, augmented and supported by studious exercise and constant diligence; moreover, since 'disposition' depends more upon the discretion and good judgment of the orator than upon particular rules and precepts (for the exigencies of time, the circumstances of place, the situation of the audience, and the variety of occasions are numberless); I shall content myself with speaking of the first two, invention and elocution. The office then of the orator is to speak eloquently and at length of each thing proposed. But this faculty of speaking thus of all things can only be acquired by the perfect comprehension of knowledge, which has been the first concern of their Roman imitators. It is necessary that these two languages be understood by those who wish to acquire that abundance and that richness of invention, the first and principal piece of harness for the orator. Once arrived at that point, the faithful translators can grandly serve and assist those who have not the unique accomplishment of devoting themselves to foreign languages. But the elocution is certainly the most difficult part, and without it all other things remain useless, similar to a sword still encased in its scabbard; elocution, by which principally an orator is judged most excellent, and one type of speaking better than another, as it is called eloquence itself; the virtue of which consists in using proper and ordinary words, and words not foreign to common usage, and in using metaphors, allegories, comparisons, similes, personification, and other figures and ornaments, without which all oratory and poems are bare, deficient and debilitated. I will never believe that one can learn all that from translations, because it is impossible to translate it with the same grace that the author has put into it: because each language has something indefinably individual only to itself; and if you make an effort to render its innate character into another language, observing the law of translation, so that it is not expanded at all beyond the limits of the author, your diction will be constrained, turgid, and without charm. This being so, if you read a Latin translation of Demosthenes or Homer, a French translation of Cicero or Virgil, in order to see if they will engender such sentiments, even as Proteus, they will transform you into diverse shapes from what you feel reading the authors in their own languages. You will think that you are crossing the heated Mountain of Aetna on the cold summit of the Caucasus. And what I say of the Greek and Latin tongues can reciprocally be said of all the vulgar tongues, of which I need cite only Petrarch, of whom I venture to say that, if Homer and Virgil came to life, and undertook to translate him, they could not do so with the same grace and naturalness that he has in his Tuscan dialect. Nevertheless men in our time have attempted to make him speak French. Here in brief are the reasons which have made me feel that the work and industry of translators, however useful to instruct those ignorant of languages foreign to their knowledge, is not sufficient to give to our own language that perfection and, as painters say of their pictures, that finishing touch, which we desire. And if the reasons that I have cited do not seem strong enough, I will produce, for my guarantors and defenders, the ancient Roman authors, principally poets and orators, who (since Cicero has translated some books of Xenophon and of Aratus, and Horace laid down the precepts for good translation) have attended to this part more for their own study and particular profit, rather then to give it to the world for the amplification of their language, to their own glory, and the profit of others. Whoever has seen works of that time in translation (I mean Cicero and Virgil, and that fortunate century of Augustus), cannot be able to give the lie to what I say.

Chapter VI
Of Bad Translators and of Not Translating the Poets

But what shall I say of those who are truly more worthy of being called traducers than translators? Since they betray those whom they attempt to make known, defrauding them of their glory, and by the same means seducing the ignorant readers, showing them the white for the black; who, in order to acquire the name of scholars, credit themselves with translating from languages of which they have never understood the first elements, such as Hebrew and Greek; and still better to show themselves off, they seize upon the poets, the class that certainly, if I knew, or desired to translate, I would address myself to as little as possible because of that divine invention, which they have more than other authors, that grandeur of style, magnificence of words, gravity of sentences, audacity and variety of figures, and a thousand other splendors of poetry: in brief, that energy and incomparable spirit which is in their works, that the Latins call genius. All of which things can hardly be expressed in translation, any more than a painter can represent the soul with the body of the person whom he attempts to represent from nature. What I say is not addressed to those who, at the command of princes and great lords, translate the most famous Greek and Latin poets; because the obedience that one owes to such personages does not permit any excuse in such endeavors; but truly I desire to speak to those who, light-heartedly, undertake such tasks thoughlessly, and acquit themselves in the same manner. O Apollo! O Muse! To profane thus the sacred relics of antiquity! But I shall not say another word. Those, however, who wish to do work worthy of a place in their own language, must leave this labor of translation, especially of poets, to those who inevitably distill more boredom than glory from a thing that is laborious and without profit, I dare to say useless, nay even pernicious, for the enrichment of their language.

Chapter VII
How the Romans Have Enriched Their Language

If the Romans (some one will say) did not conquer by the labor of translation, by what means then did they so enrich their language, even almost to equality with the Greek? By imitating the better Greek authors, transforming themselves through them, devouring them; and, after having digested them well, converting them into blood and nurture; each taking to himself according to his nature and the argument which he wishes to choose, the best author, all of whose rarest and most exquisite virtues they observe diligently, appropriating and embodying these, like engraftments, as I have said before, to their language. That caused the Romans to build those sublime writings that we delight in and admire so greatly, counting some equal, others preferable, to the Greek. And what I say Cicero and Virgil well prove, whom gladly I always name among the Latins, of whom the one, as he was entirely given over to the imitation of the Greeks, so reproduced and truly expressed the meaning of Plato, the vehemency of Demosthenes, and the racy charm of Isocrates, that Molon of Rhodia, hearing him speak one time, exclaimed that he was introducing Greek eloquence to Rome. The other so well imitated Homer, Hesiod, and Theocritus, that it has since been said that he surpassed one of these three, equalled another, and approached so near to the third that if felicity of the theme used had been equal, the palm would have been in doubt.[1] I ask you then, you authors who busy yourselves only with translations, if those famous authors had trifled with translations, would they have raised their language to the excellence and eminence where we now see it? Do not think, then, that however much

---

[1] As is clear from Aulus Gellius (22, above), the ancients thought of Virgil as having 'translated from' or 'imitated' Homer in the *Aeneid*, Hesiod in the *Georgics*, and Theocritus in the *Bucolics*. [Ed]

diligence and industry you may employ in that endeavor, you will be able to make our language, now prostrate, lift up its head and get up on its feet.

Chapter VIII
To Enlarge French Literature By Imitation of the Ancient Greek and Latin Authors

Write himself, then, must he who wishes to enrich his language, write in imitation of the best Greek and Latin authors; at all their best qualities, as at a fair target, direct the aim of his style; for it cannot be doubted that the great part of the art is contained in imitation; and as it was for the ancients most praiseworthy to invent well, so it is most profitable well to imitate them, even for those whose language is not yet plentiful and rich. But he must understand, who wishes to imitate, that it is no easy thing to follow well the excellent qualities of a good author, as if to transform oneself with him, for nature has so wrought even those things which appeal, most similar, that by some mark or feature they can be distinguished. I say this because there are many in every literature who, without penetrating to the secret, innermost part of an author whom they have approached, adapt themselves solely to first appearances, and spend themselves rather on the beauty of words than on the might of the real content. And certainly, as it is not vicious, but greatly laudable, to borrow from another language sentences and words, and to appropriate them to one's own; so it is greatly reprehensible, and must seem odious to every reader of a liberal, cultivated nature, to see, in the same language, such an imitation, such a one as that of some of the learned, even, who think themselves better in proportion as they resemble an Héroët or a Marot. I charge you (O you who desire the enlargement of your literature and its excellence over the others) not to imitate headlong, as recently someone has said, its most famous authors, as ordinarily do the great part of our French poets, a practice certainly as faulty as it is of no worth to our vernacular: for that is not another thing but to give it (O tremendous liberality) what it already has. I would that our language were so rich in models of its own that we should have no need of recourse to others. But if Virgil and Cicero had been content to imitate the authors of their literature, what should we have had of Latin, beyond Ennius or Lucretius, beyond Crassus or Antonius?

Book II, Chapter IV
What Types of Poems the French Poet Should Choose

Read then, and re-read, O future poet, handle lovingly, night and day, the exemplary Greek and Latin poets; then leave all those old French poets to the Jenix Floranx of Toulouse and to the Puy of Rouen; such as rondeaux, ballades, virelays, chants royal, chansons, and other such groceries, which corrupt the taste of our language and only serve to bear testimony to our ignorance. Devote yourself to pleasant epigrams, not as made today, by a mob of tellers of new tales, who, in a poem of ten lines, are content to have said nothing which gives value in the first nine lines, provided in the tenth there appear a laughable thing: but to the imitation of a Martial, or of some other excellent poet; if liveliness does not satisfy you, mingle the profitable with the pleasant. Distill with a pen flowing and not scabrous, these plaintive elegies, after the example of an Ovid, a Tibullus, and a Propertius, mingling into it sometimes some of these ancient fables, no small ornaments of poetry. Sing to me those odes, yet unknown to the French muse, on a lute well tuned to the sound of the Greek and Roman lyre, not without a single line in which appears some trace of rare but authentic lore. Material for that the praises of the gods and of great men will furnish you, and the deathward tread of earthly things, and the disquiet of youth: love, the unrestrained rites of wine, and all good cheer. Above all, take care that the type of poetry be far away from the vulgar, enriched and made illustrious with proper words and vigorous epithets, adorned with grave sentences, and varied with all manner of colorful and poetic ornaments: not as a *Laissez la Verde Couleur*, *Amour avecques Psyches*, *O Combien est Heureuse*, and other such works, more worthy of being called native chansons than odes or lyrical verse. For epistles are not a genre which greatly enriches our language, because they are concerned with familiar and domestic things, unless you wish to make them in imitation of elegies, like Ovid's, or sententious and grave poems, like Horace's. As much might I say to you of satires, which the French, I know not why, have labelled cock-and-bull stories, and which I also advise you to avoid, as I desire you to be strangers to evil gossip; unless you desire to follow the example of the ancients in heroic verse (that is to say, in verses varying from ten to eleven syllables, as well as from eight to nine), under the name of satire, and not of that inept appellation of *cock-and-bull* story, to censure with moderation the vices of our time, and not call by name vicious persons. You have for model Horace, who according to Quintilian held first place among satirists. Let me hear those beautiful sonnets, the learned and pleasant invention of the Italians, conforming to the ode, and differing from it only in that the sonnet has certain fixed and limited verse forms; whereas the ode can run through all manner of verse forms, even to the invention of new forms at will, as in Horace, who has sung, according to the grammarians, in nineteen forms of verse. For the sonnet, then, you have Petrarch and other modern Italians. Sing for me on a resonant musette and on a well-jointed flute some pleasant rustic eclogues, after the manner of Theocritus and of Virgil;

poets of the sea can follow the example of a Sannazar, that delightful Neopolitan. If it please the Muses, may we have in all the kinds of poetry that I have named, many imitations such as the Eclogue on the birth of a son to Monsieur le Dauphin, to my mind, one of the best small works that Marot has ever written. Adopt also into the French family those easy-flowing and graceful hendecasyllabics[2] as written by Catullus, by Pontano, and by Second, which you can write as in Latin, save for quantity, since French has not long and short syllables. As to comedies and tragedies, if the king and the country desire them reestablished in their ancient dignity, which place the farces and moralities have usurped, I am indeed of the opinion that you should employ yourself on these, and if you wish to make for the enrichment of your language, you know where you can find the models.

Anna Cooke

Anna Cooke Bacon (1528-1610), one of five remarkable daughters of Sir Anthony and Lady Anne Fitzwilliam Cooke and mother of Francis Bacon, was a learned and gifted writer and translator who largely put by her gifts out of deference to her 'estate' as a woman.

The passage below is excerpted from her prefatory letter, addressed to her mother, to a translation she did of the Italian sermons of a contemporary theologian, Bernardino Ochino, at age 22, while still single and living with her parents.

The Study of Italian Justified
From Preface to Her Translation of Bernadine Ochine, *Fouretene sermons* (1550?)

Since the Original of whatsoever is, or may be converted to, any goodness in me has freely proceeded (though as the minister [representative] of GOD) of your Ladyship's mere careful and motherly goodness, as well procuring all things thereunto belonging, as in your many and most Godly exhortations, wherein among the rest it has pleased you, often, to reprove my vain study in the Italian tongue, accompting [accounting] the seed thereof to have been sown in barren, unfruitful ground ... I have ... perceived it my duty to prove how much the understanding of your will could work in me towards the accomplishing of the same. And for that I have well known your chief delight, to rest in ... exalting wholly the glory of God: ... I have taken in hand to dedicate unto your Ladyship this small number of sermons ... to the end it might appear that your so many worthy sentences touching the same have not utterly been without some note in my weak memory .... [I]t may please your Ladyship to vouchsafe that this my small labor may be allowed at your hands, under whose protection only it is committed with humble reverence, as yielding some part of the fruit of your motherly admonitions, in this my willing service. Your Ladyship's daughter most boundenly obedient,

A. C.

Jacques Peletier

Jacques Peletier du Mans (1517-1582) was a French humanist poet, translator, and scholar whose work proved influential for a group of poets that called themselves La Pléiade, most particularly Joachim du Bellay, whose 'Defense and Illustration of the French Language' is printed above.

Du Bellay's powerful argument for the enrichment of French culture through the free imitation of ancient Greek and Roman works was indebted to Peletier's preface to his translation of Horace's *Ars poetics* (1545); Peletier later expanded on his claims there in *L'art poétique française* (1555), though never with the imagistic and polemical brilliance of du Bellay.

Of Translation
From *The French Poetic Art* (*L'art poétique française*, 1555)
Translated by David G. Ross

The truest form of imitation is translation, for imitating is nothing else than wanting to do what another has done. The translator does likewise; he submits, not only to another's invention, but to his arrangement, and even to his style to the extent that the translator can and the character of the target language permits, because the effectiveness of a writing quite often depends on the quality of its words and phrases, the omission of which strips the author of his elegance and cheats him of his meaning. In consequence, translation is a labor more of work than of praise. For if you work well and true, you are deemed to have but redone the first work, and the lion's share of the glory remains with the original. If you express yourself badly, the blame falls on you alone. Why, if your author has written badly, you will still be considered a man of bad judgment for not having chosen a good example. In short, a translator is never seen as the author. But do I wish for all that to discourage translators? Not at all, nor even less to deprive them of the praise they have earned by being in part the conduit through which France has begun to taste worthy things. And they even have one consolation: if they translate worthy material well, their author's name will make their own live on. Indeed, it is certainly no small thing to have

[2] Poems with eleven-syllable lines. [Ed]

one's name appear in the right place. Quite often, moreover, it is the inventors who risk being outlasted by the translators, since a good translation is worth much more than a bad invention. Furthermore, well-done translations can much enrich a language. For the translator will be able to provide French with a beautiful phrase from Greek or Latin, and introduce to his community the gravity of the sentences, the majesty of the clauses, and the styles of the foreign language, two very propitious points, as they approach common beliefs. But, in particular cases, the translator must, in my opinion, be somewhat wary, for example, with new words, which are so recognizable and suspect. A translator who is not already known for doing good work does not receive the same indulgence with words as one with whom readers are used to dealing. For this reason the job of translator is more poorly regarded. It is true that one may, when one's author is excellent – and the prudent man takes good care not to translate any other kind – use completely new words, provided that one is certain there is no alternative and that they do justice to the author. For a translator's excessive use of paraphrase, that is of circumlocution, is too great an annoyance, and it strips the value from the author's clever labors. Translation thus has a place among our arts, because it is made from art, nay it is so artistic that only a few comprehend its rules. Why, I could not be more amazed at those who, in seeking to criticize word-for-word translation, seek to avail themselves of the authority of Horace when he said, "Nec verbum verbo curabis reddere, fidus Interpres".[1] It is certain there that Horace is speaking to a point completely different from their own, namely that, with regard to the subject of poetry – and not of translation, a subject for which he provided few guidelines and held little regard – when we choose a well-known section of an author's material, we make it our own if, among other people, we do not resolve to repeat the passage word for word, as would a faithful translator. I have already touched on this subject in the section on the subject of poetry. And so I distinctly want to clarify Horace's argument, as I have seen our grammarians interpret it differently from the way he intended it, and have always schooled myself in explaining the thoughts of poets, reading them for pleasure in my most devoted studies. As one example among others, I came upon this passage in Virgil's third eclogue, which reads, "Et longum, formose, vale: vale, inquit, Iola". The commentators say either that the fourth foot of the verse is a dactyl and hear, "le vale, inquit I, ola"; or that it is a spondee and one must hear, "le va, leinquit I, ola". The poet's inspiration was to make the first 'vale' long, imitating the speech of the lass Philide. For Menelaus says, "Philide cried at my leaving; and if she said a long farewell, farewell she said". Indeed, those who wish to show their affection through tears intentionally speak slowly. To this end, the poet used 'vale' twice: once with the normal, short pronunciation and the second with the long pronunciation of the weeping girl. I have detailed this example in passing, as much because artistic things are never inappropriate when discussing art, as to demonstrate again the cleverness of my Virgil. I know that these noble commentators have, for many years already, been unable to understand the hundredth section of his work, where they betray their ignorance clearly through what they make of the final, short 'vale', thereby breaking the rule of synalepha.[2] That would amount to two liberties without cause or reason. And again I have worked to demonstrate that what I said elsewhere is true, namely that short Latin and Greek syllables must be pronounced short, and the long ones long. In relation to our discussion, word-for-word translations are without elegance, not because they're against the law of translation, but only because two languages are never identical in phraseology. Ideas are common to the understanding of all men, but words and speech patterns are specific to nations. Furthermore, let no one quote Cicero to me, a man who did not speak highly of the conscientious translator, because I truly do, and I expect nothing else, except when the translator must preserve the natural quality of the language into which he is translating. Nevertheless, I most certainly maintain that, in what the two languages portray, nothing must be lost of the author's phrases, nor even of the primacy of his words, given that his meaning and subtility often consist of them. For he who could translate sentence for sentence and word for word all of Virgil into French verse would be worthy of extraordinary acclaim. How, indeed, can a translator better fulfill his duty than by always approximating as closely as he can the author to whom he is obligated. Think, then, how magnificent it would be to see a second language echo all the elegance of the first, while still maintaining its own integrity. Yet, as I have said, it cannot be done.

Roger Ascham

Roger Ascham (1515-1568) was a British humanist best remembered today for his theories of education in the posthumously published *Scholemaster* (1570), excerpted below. He was one of the first to stress the importance of educating the whole person and not just the intellect – let alone just the skill of Latin composition.

[1] "Nor trouble to render word for word, faithful translator". See Horace, above, 15. [Ed]

[2] The coalescence of two vowels into one, as in "th' Elysian fields". [Ed]

Ascham entered Cambridge University at the age of fourteen; he eventually took his M.A. in Greek there, and was elected a fellow of St. John's. His interest in Greek placed him at the centre of the Renaissance resurgence of interest in that language, and from 1548 to 1550 he served as Greek and Latin tutor to Lady Elizabeth, whom he praises for her diligence and proficiency in the passage below. He remained close to the court for the last two decades of his life, first as English ambassador to the Habsburg emperor Charles V, then as Latin secretary to Edward VI and sometime secretary to Queen Elizabeth, whom he helped to continue her study of Greek during the first ten years of her reign.

The Ready Way to the Latin Tongue
From *The Schoolmaster* (1570)

The second book.

After that your scholar, as I said before, shall come indeed, first, to a ready perfectness in translating; then, to a ripe and skillful choice in marking out his six points, as,

1. *Proprium.*
2. *Translatum.*
3. *Synonymum.*
4. *Contrarium.*
5. *Diversum.*
6. *Phrases.*

Then take this order with him: Read daily unto him some book of Tully, as the third book of Epistles chosen out by Sturmius, *de Amicitia*, *de Senectute*, or that excellent Epistle containing almost the whole first book *ad Q[uintum] fra[trem]*;[1] some comedy of Terence or Plautus; but in Plautus, skillful choice must be used by the master, to train his scholar to a judgement, in cutting out perfectly over old and improper words; *Caes[ar's] Commentaries*[2] are to be read with all curiosity, in specially without all exception to be made, either by friend or foe, [for in it] is seen the unspotted propriety of the Latin tongue, even when it was, as the Grecians say, in ἀκμῄ, that is, at the highest pitch of all perfectness; or some orations of T[itius] Livius, such as be both longest and plainest.

These books I would have him read now a good deal at every lecture [lesson]; for he shall not now use daily translation, but only construe again, and parse, where you suspect is any need; yet let him not omit in these books his former exercise in marking diligently and writing orderly out his six points. And for translating, use [get in the habit of] you yourself, every second or third day, to choose out some Epistle *ad Atticum*,[3] some notable common place out of his orations, or some other part of Tully, by your discretion, which your scholar may not know where to find, and translate it you yourself into plain natural English, and then give it him to translate into Latin again; allowing him good space and time to do it, both with diligent heed and good advisement. Here his wit shall be new set on work; his judgement, for right choice, truly tried; his memory, for sure retaining, better exercised, than by learning anything without the book; and here, how much he has profited shall plainly appear. When he brings it translated unto you, bring you forth the place of Tully: lay them together; compare the one with the other; commend his good choice, and right placing of words; show his faults gently, but blame them not oversharply; for, of such missings, gently admonished of, proceeds glad and good heed-taking; of good heed-taking springs chiefly knowledge, which after grows to perfectness, if this order be diligently used by the scholar and gently handled by the master; for here shall all the hard points of grammar both easily and surely be learned up, which scholars in common schools, by making of Latins, be groping at with care and fear, and yet in many years they scarce can reach unto them. I remember, when I was young, in the North, they went to the Grammar school, little children; they came from thence great lubbers: always learning, and little profiting; learning without book, everything, understanding within the book little or nothing. Their whole knowledge, by learning without the book, was tied only to their tongue and lips, and never ascended up to the brain and head, and therefore was soon spit out of the mouth again. They were, as men, always going, but ever out of the way; and why? For their whole labour, or rather great toil without order, was even vain idleness without profit. Indeed, they took great pains about learning, but employed small labour in learning; when by this way prescribed in this book, being straight, plain, and easy, the scholar is always labouring with pleasure, and ever going right on forward with profit; always labouring I say, for, or [ere] he have construed, parsed, twice translated over by good advisement, marked out his six points by skillful judgement, he shall have necessary occasion to read over every lecture [lesson] a dozen times at the least. Which, because he shall do always in order, he shall do it always with pleasure. And pleasure allures love; love has lust to labor; labor always obtains his purpose, as most truly both Aristotle in his *Rhetoric* and Oedipus

[1] Cicero (also called 'Tully') wrote *De amicitia* ('On Friendship') and *De senectute* ('On Old Age') in 45-44 B.C.E.; *Ad Quintum fratrem* was a collection of letters "to his brother Quintus". [Ed]

[2] The commentaries of Julius Caesar on the Gallic and Civil Wars. [Ed]

[3] A collection of Cicero's letters to Atticus in sixteen books. [Ed]

in Sophocles do teach, saying, πᾶν γάρ ἐκπονούμενον ἅλισκε.[4] and this oft reading, is the very right following of that good counsel which Pliny does give to his friend Fuscus, saying, *Multum, non multa*.[5] But to my purpose again:

When, by this diligent and speedy reading over, those forenamed good books of Tully, Terence, Caesar, and Livy, and by this second kind of translating out of your English, time shall breed skill, and use shall bring perfection, then you may try, if you will, your scholar with the third kind of translation; although the two first ways, by mine opinion, be not only sufficent of themselves but also surer, both for the master's teaching and scholars' learning than this third way is: which is thus. Write you in English some letter, as it were from him to his father, or to some other friend, naturally, according to the disposition of the child, or some tale, or fable, or plain narration, according as Aphthonius begins his exercises of learning, and let him translate it into Latin again, abiding in such place where no other scholar may prompt him. But yet, use you yourself such discretion for choice therein, as the matter may be within the compass, both for words and sentences, of his former learning and reading. And now take heed lest your scholar do not better in some point than you yourself, except [unless] you have been diligently exercised in these kinds of translating before:

I had once a proof hereof, tried by good experience, by a dear friend of mine, when I came first from Cambridge, to serve the Queen's Majesty, then Lady Elizabeth, lying at worthy Sir Ant. Denys in Cheston. John Whitney, a young gentleman, was my bedfellow, who willing by good nature and provoked by mine advice, began to learn the Latin tongue, after the order declared in this book. We began after Christmas; I read unto him Tully *de Amicitia*, which he did every day twice translate, out of Latin into English, and out of English into Latin again. About S. Lawrence tide [August 10] after, to prove how he profited, I did choose out Torquatus' talk *de Amicitia*, in the later end of the first book *de Finibus* because that place was the same in matter, like in words and phrases, nigh to the form and fashion of sentences, as he had learned before in *de Amicitia*.[6] I did translate it myself into plain English, and gave it him to turn into Latin: which he did, so choicely, so orderly, so without any great miss in the hardest points of grammar, that some in seven years in Grammar schools, yea, and some in the universities too, cannot do half so well. This worthy young gentleman, to my greatest grief, to the great lamentation of that whole house, and specially to that most noble Lady, now Queen Elizabeth herself, departed within few days out of this world ...

There be six ways appointed by the best learned men, for the learning of tongues, and increase of eloquence, as

1. *Translatio linguarum.*
2. *Paraphrasis.*
3. *Metaphrasis.*
4. *Epitome.*
5. *Imitatio.*
6. *Declamatio.*

All these be used, and commended, but in order, and for respects as person, hability, place, and time shall require. The five last be fitter for the master than the scholar; for men, then for children; for the universities rather than for Grammar schools; yet nevertheless, which is fittest in mine opinion for our school, and which is either wholly to be refused or partly to be used for our purpose, I will, by good authority, and some reason, I trust particularly of every one, and largely enough of them all, declare orderly unto you.

Translatio Linguarum.[7]

Translation is easy in the beginning for the scholar, and brings also much learning and great judgement to the master. It is most common, and most commendable of all other exercises for youth; most common, for all your constructions in Grammar schools be nothing else but translations; but because they be not double translations, as I do require, they bring forth but simple and single commodity, and because also they lack the daily use of writing, which is the only thing that breeds deep root, both in the wit, for good understanding, and in the memory, for sure keeping of all that is learned. Most commendable also, and that by the judgment of all authors, which entreat of these exercises. Tully in the person of L. Crassus, whom he makes his example of eloquence and true judgement in learning, does not only praise specially and choose this way of translation for a young man, but does also discommend and refuse his own former wont, in exercising *Paraphrasin* and *Metaphrasin*.[8] *Paraphrasis* is to take some

---

[4] Rhet. 2, In Oedip., Tyr. Epist. lib. 7. [Au] See book two of Aristotle's *Rhetoric*, Sophocles' *Oedipus Rex*, and Plato's seventh *Letter*. Ascham's "labour always obtains his purpose" is a rough translation of the Greek, which says "for everything is obtained by labour". [Ed]

[5] "Much, not many". Ascham is referring to Pliny's suggestion (in Betty Radice's translation) "that a man should be *deeply, not widely*, read". See Pliny's letter to Fuscus Salinator, above, 19. [Ed]

[6] Torquatus is one of the speakers in *De amicitia*; Ascham excerpted one of his speeches for Whitney. For an excerpt from *De finibus bonorum* see 10-12, above. [Ed]

[7] The translation of languages. [Ed]

[8] See Cicero, 7, above. Cicero does not exactly 'discommend' paraphrase and metaphrase, or rephrasing and rewording Latin texts. He does recommend

eloquent Oration, or some notable commonplace in Latin, and express it with other words; *Metaphrasis* is to take some notable place out of a good poet, and turn the same sense into meter, or into other words in prose. Crassus, or rather Tully, mislikes both these ways, because the author, either orator or poet, had chosen out before the fittest words and aptest composition for that matter, and so he, in seeking other, was driven to use the worse.

Quintilian also prefers translation before all other exercises; yet having a lust to dissent from Tully (as he does in very many places, if a man read his rhetoric over advisedly, and that rather of an envious mind, than of any just cause) does greatly commend *Paraphrasis*, crossing spitefully Tully's judgement in refusing the same; and so do Ramus and Talaeus even at this day in France too.[9] But such singularity, in dissenting from the best men's judgments, in liking only their own opinions, is much misliked of [by] all them that join with learning, discretion, and wisdom. For he that can neither like Aristotle in logic and philosophy nor Tully in rhetoric and eloquence will, from these steps, likely enough presume, by like pride, to mount higher, to the misliking of greater matters: that is either in religion, to have a dissentious head, or in the commonwealth, to have a factious heart; as I knew once a student in Cambridge, who, for a singularity, began first to dissent, in the schools, from Aristotle, and soon after became a perverse Arian, against Christ and all true religion; and studied diligently Origen, Basileus, and St. Jerome, only to glean out of their works the pernicious heresies of Celsus, Eunomius, and Helvidius, whereby the Church of Christ was so poisoned withall.[10]

But to leave these high points of divinity, surely, in this quiet and harmless controversy, for the liking or misliking of *Paraphrasis* for a young scholar, even as far as Tully goes beyond Quintilian, Ramus, and Talaeus in perfect eloquence, even so much, by mine opinion, come they behind Tully, for true judgement in teaching the same.

Plinius Secundus, a wise Senator of great experience, excellently learned himself, a liberal patron of learned men and the purest writer, in mine opinion, of all his age, I except not Suetonius, his two schoolmasters Quintilian and Tacitus, nor yet his most excellent learned uncle, the Elder Plinius, does express in an epistle to his friend Fuscus many good ways for order in study; but he begins with translation, and prefers it to all the rest; and because his words be notable, I will recite them.

> *Utile in primis, ut multi praecipiunt, ex Graeco in Latinum, & ex Latino vertere in Graecum: Quo genere exercitationis, proprietas splendor verborum, apta structura sententiarum, figurarum copia & explicandi vis colligitur. Praeterea, imitatione optimorum, facultas similia inueniendi paratur: & quae legentem, fefellissent, transferentem fugere non possunt. Intelligentia ex hoc, & iudicium acquiritur.*[11]

You perceive how Pliny teaches that by this exercise of double translating is learned, easily, sensibly, by little and little, not only all the hard congruities of grammar, the choice of aptest words, the right framing of words and sentences, comeliness of figures and forms, fit for every matter, and proper for every tongue, but that which is greater also, in marking daily, and following diligently thus, the step of the best authors, like invention of arguments, like order in disposition, like utterance in elocution, is easily gathered up; whereby your scholar shall be brought not only to like eloquence, but also to all true understanding and right judgement, both for writing and speaking. And where Dionys[ius] Halicarnassaeus has written two excellent books, the one, *De delectu optimorum verborum* ['On Choosing the Best Words'], the which, I fear, is lost, the other, of the right framing of words and sentences [*On the Arrangement of Words*], which remains yet in Greek, to the great profit of all them that truly study for eloquence, yet this way of double translating shall

translating into Latin rather than reworking Latin texts, but *paraphrasis* and *metaphrasis* are Quintilian's terms for that reworking, not Cicero's. See Quintilian, above, 19-20. [Ed]

[9] Petrus Ramus (Pierre de la Ramée) and Audomarus Talaeus (Omer Talon) both taught an original blend of Ciceronian rhetoric and Aristotelian logic at the Collège de l'Ave Maria in France. Both were highly controversial figures; Ramus was banned from teaching Aristotelian logic for several years, and two years after Ascham wrote this treatise was murdered. In the lines that follow Ascham expresses his horror at such 'dissentious' behaviour. [Ed]

[10] The Arian heresy was propounded early in the fourth century C.E. by the Alexandrian religious leader Arius; its major tenet was that Jesus was not God but a created being. Though ruthlessly persecuted throughout the fourth century, it survived in some forms until the seventh century. There were two first-century Roman senators named Helvidius Priscus, father and son; both were known not for religious heresies so much as for their opposition to emperors, the father to Vespasian, who put him to death, the son to Domitian. The son was known as a Stoic philosopher; Ascham may be referring to him. [Ed]

[11] See Pliny the Younger above, 18, from the sentence beginning "The most useful thing" to the end of the paragraph. [Ed]

bring the whole profit of both these books to a diligent scholar, and that easily and pleasantly, both for fit choice of words and apt composition of sentences. And by these authorities and reasons am I moved to think this way of double translating, either only or chiefly, to be fittest for the speedy and perfect attaining of any tongue. And for speedy attaining, I durst venture a good wager, if a scholar in whom is aptness, love, diligence, and constancy, would but translate after this sort [in this fashion] one little book in Tully, as *De senectute* ['On Old Age'], with two epistles, the first *Ad Q[uintum] fra[trem]* ['To his brother Quintus'] the other *Ad Lentulum* ['To Lentulus'], the last save one in the first book; that scholar, I say, should come to a better knowledge in the Latin tongue than the most part do that spend four or five years in tossing all the rules of grammar in common schools. Indeed this one book with these two epistles is not sufficient to afford all Latin words (which is not necessary for a young scholar to know) but it is able to furnish him fully, for all points of grammar, with the right placing, ordering, and use of words in all kind of matter. And why not? For it is read that Dion [Chrysostom] Prusaeus, that wise philosopher and excellent orator of all his time, did come to the great learning and utterance that was in him by reading and following only two books, *Phaedon Platonis* and Demosthenes' most notable oration Περί παραπρεσβείας.[12] And a better and nearer example herein may be our most noble Queen Elizabeth, who never took yet Greek nor Latin grammar in her hand after the first declining of a noun and a verb, but only by this double translating of Demosthenes and Isocrates daily, without missing every forenoon, and likewise some part of Tully every afternoon, for the space of a year or two, has attained to such a perfect understanding in both the tongues, and to such a ready utterance of the Latin, and that with such a judgement, as they be few in number in both the universities, or elsewhere in England, that be in both tongues comparable with her Majesty. And to conclude in a short room [space] the commodities of double translation, surely the mind by daily marking, first, the cause and matter; then, the words and phrases; next, the order and composition; after the reason and arguments; then the forms and figures of both the tongues; lastly, the measure and compass of every sentence, must needs by little and little draw unto it the like shape of eloquence as the author does use which is read.

And thus much for double translation.

[12] Plato's *Phaedo* and Demosthenes' 'The False Legation'. [Ed]

Etienne Pasquier

Etienne Pasquier (1529-1615) was a French lawyer and historian best known in his day for his successful defence of the University of Paris in a suit brought by Jesuits who wanted to teach there; he is best remembered since his death for his monumental ten-volume history of France *Recherches de la France* (1560-1621), and for his posthumously published correspondence (1619), which provides a wealth of information about the political and cultural issues of the day.

Pasquier studied law under famous humanist scholars, one of whom was Jacques Cujas, to whom the first letter printed below is addressed. He was called to the bar in Paris at age 20; several years later he defended a wealthy young widow in court, and married her in 1557. He began his *Recherches* while convalescing from an illness in 1560, and continued to work on them for the next fifty years, most of the rest of his life. The fame he garnered from the University of Paris case brought him many influential clients, and in his late forties and early fifties he began to be appointed to judgeships: commissioner of the assize court in Poitiers (1579) and Tours (1583), and advocate general in the Chambre des Comptes in Paris (1585).

In 1604 he retired from the law to write, completing in the last ten years of his life several books of the *Recherches*, a study of the Code of Justinian (of which he writes to Jacques Cujas), some poems and works of biblical exegesis.

Letter to Jacques Cujas (1576)
Translated by David G. Ross

To Monsieur Cujas, Counselor of the Parlement de Grenoble and Doctoral professor of law at the Université de Bourges

Although I have no knowledge of you except as a celebrated citizen and what the reading of your written eruditions has given me,[1] yet having found an appropriate occasion to write you, I do not wish to let it slip, hoping by this gesture to make an overture of friendship, one whose foundation will be all the more solid as it is based on virtue. Monsieur Loisel[2] told me that upon your recent arrival in this city, he welcomed you with the last three books of the Code[3] in old French, which I had lent him, and that you were eager to

[1] A strange claim: Pasquier had studied under Cujas. [Ed]

[2] Another former student of Cujas. [Ed]

[3] The Codex Justinianus, codified by Justinian I. The

receive word on the matter, as you were working on some sort of commentary. I am aggrieved that you then seized them on your own authority, and, it must be said, with sovereign power, so that my consent was not required. I am assured that they could not be better employed than in the hands of someone who is, all at once, an expert in the civil law usage of Greek, Latin, and French. And no matter how much you desire from these books, you will get it, for, it is worthy of mention, our French ancestors have already taken care to clarify in the language of the day the most hidden secrets of the Roman Constitutions.

Do not think, moreover, that what you see in this translator[4] is common to the many others who have in the same capacity translated into our vernacular the Bible, most of Aristotle's works, Livy, the volumes of St. Augustine's *City of God*, and a multitude of others, of which I have seen some as complete books in the library established by our great King François at Fontainebleau and the rest in other libraries as the opportunity presented itself.

It is true that their works have been lost and will continue to be lost as time passes. Not that they all wrote well according to the standards of their eras, but that is the profit we derive from a vexing translation. I know well that a well-done translation does precious little to make our fellow citizens understand the beautiful and noble ideas of foreigners, unless it travels far from our own. But I cannot say, for it would be untrue, that there is a more unrewarding task than translation, which goes so unrecognized by posterity. The translator is a slave; he wracks his brains to follow the footprints of the author he is translating, devotes his life to it, and employs every graceful turn of phrase with currency among his peers, in order to conform as closely as possible to the meaning of the other. Nevertheless, the translator's language changes little by little over time, and one day, as if we had given him a new gown, we no longer wish to make use of the old one. That is why, as the old vernacular vanishes, we discard old translations and wish to return to the original books, be they Greek or Latin, that were translated. And it is only the inventors who are perpetuated. For while the vernacular continues to change, it is up to us to make use of the originals, indeed we are obliged to read them to mine them further for ideas if they merit it. Cicero, the great orator, wished to translate some Greek books. Did they survive? By no means, although he was the father of fine rhetoric. I will demonstrate this with a quite familiar example from our own heritage. Has our good *Romant de la Rose* gotten lost due to its ancientness? The first to put a hand to the work was Guillaume de Lory around the time of Phillipe Auguste, and the person who finished it, Jean Clopinet called 'de Meun', lived under the reign of St. Louis.[5] The best translator our French ancestors produced was Master Nicole Oresme, who, as a reward for his labors, was given the bishopric of Lisieux by King Charles V. For it was the former who translated into our vernacular Aristotle's *Physics*, *Politics*, and *Ethics*, as well as several other books that were given a most favorable reception. Today, however, you only see the few vestiges of his work that have been collected in various libraries, like the remains of a shipwreck from long ago.

By contrast, there are no learned men among us who do not read the written eruditions of his contemporary, Master Alain Chartier,[6] nor any who do not take up *Romant de la Rose*, which, with the same intentions, Clément Marot wanted to dress in French by mixing old and modern language together. What then causes this discrepancy? It is easy to provide the reason. Oresme only used the language of his time in his translations, a language which is lost, requiring us to return to the original author. As for Lory, Meun, and Chartier, although their language is entombed in the sepulchre of our age, yet their beautiful phrases and ideas cannot perish, for those who desire to profit from them are constrained by necessity to read and reread their works, like the bees who tend lovely flowers, to find what they cannot elsewhere. I do not wish for all that to deter anyone of our age from translating, for, while a translator does little to enshrine his name in posterity, he brings a great benefit to the living. In summary, you will use the translation that I am sending as Virgil used the works of the good Ennius *Ex stercore aurum* ["Out of filth, gold"] with the understanding that if, in your studies of law, you should again want of the services of this humble servant, I will not be stingy in my assistance. As for me, I have begun to research the history of France. And for this reason, I have called my work *Recherches*.[7] The task ahead is great and requires perusing several old books. If you have any on this subject, would you do me the service of

Code had been available in French translation since the Middle Ages, and the first three books were printed in French in 1550; Pasquier owned several manuscripts, and loaned them out freely. Cujas published a Latin translation of the Code in 1577. [Ed]

[4] Not named in the manuscripts. [Ed]

[5] Pasquier clearly thinks of the *Roman de la Rose* as an original creation by Guillaume de Lorris, who did in fact write the first one-fifth of the poem around 1240. Philip II reigned somewhat earlier than Lorris's writing, from 1179-1223, and Jean de Meun finished the poem somewhat later than the reign of Louis IX (1226-1270). See Jean de Meun, above, 47. [Ed]

[6] Pasquier is mistaken: Alain Chartier was born in 1385, three years after Oresme's death. [Ed]

[7] Pasquier had published the first two books of *Les Recherches de la France* in 1560 and 1565. [Ed]

sharing them with me, on the condition that I will return them to you, just as I would entreat you to return mine, as soon as you are done. Farewell.

Letter to Odet de Tournebus[8] (1576)
Translated by David G. Ross

To Monsieur Tournebus, Counselor in the court of the Parlement de Grenoble

So you want me to render Cicero in French. Please note the power you have gotten over me. There is nothing I detest as much as the translating profession. Not that I feel this way on some fanciful notion, for it is the conduit by means of which we share in the beautiful ideas of old authors; but among the labors of the mind, I think none more unenjoyable or unrewarding than it. Not only do we as translators subjugate our pen to a foreign language and enslave our minds to the tyranny of another, but I fear that our translations do not pass on to our survivors; instead they die with our own vernacular, which changes every hundred years, thereby remaining entombed in the gloom of a long history. And, for my part, I do not want one of the Church's mere eighty-nine year leases to be part of my stay; rather, I want a legacy, which, if not rich, is mine to perpetuate with the hope of leaving it for all time to my descendants. When our inventions merit it, howsoever the vernacular have changed, others are obliged to return to us for lack of other means. Indeed, if our words are troublesome for their obsolescence, those who survive us will conform them to modern speech, so that the people are not deprived of the worthy subject. This does not happen to the translator, who only borrows the clothing, which, after a long lapse of time, becomes too stale and is discarded to return to the original authors, be they Greek or Latin, whose approved languages are perpetuated over many centuries to our day. In addition, languages do not correspond to each other in their form of expression, and what is becoming in one language will be awkward when transplanted in another. In this way, just as there are many things in Latin that cannot be duplicated in our French with the same elegance, so are there many in French that even Cicero, should he be reborn, would be unable to render with the same grace in Latin. I grant you that, as the Romans lived under a government of the people, while we live under a monarch and his royalty, our regulations and administration have nothing in common with theirs. For we in effect adopt a Latin air when we speak French while employing the words 'sénat' [senate], 'sénateur' [senator], 'consul', 'consulat' [consulate], 'tribun' [tribune], 'édile' [aedile, magistrate], 'préteur' [lender], 'dictateur' [dictator], and 'proconsul', which are drawn from the soil of democracy, others that come in tow, such as 'comices' [assembly], 'oraison' [oration], 'concion' [discourse], 'auspices', 'centurions', 'gladiateurs' [gladiators], and a thousand others of the same vintage. I mean to say that these words provide no more edification to the French people, not reared under Roman law and custom, than if they read them in Latin. And if, to see ourselves as cleverer than our peers, we seek to adapt words of our own heritage, instead of those above, to effect a given meaning and discover that we have such words in our lexicon together with their Latin counterparts, I believe that we become even less intelligible, and that, while thinking we have earned the thanks of the people, we make ourselves the object of their mockery. Such is the fate of those who wish to conform Latin words, whichever they be, to our French usage. Moreover, there are other Latin words that one would not know how to translate – for example: 'Rostra' [rostrum, speaker's platform], 'Forum', 'Circus', 'Maximus' [the Great], 'Flamen' [priest], and a multitude of others that escape my memory – so that it is truly like the expression: "You have a tiger by the tail".[9] For no matter where you direct your thoughts, you will not know which option to choose.

To demonstrate the point, I will content myself with proffering the first two words of the subject that I have introduced for myself: one Cicero, called by the Romans a 'great orator', and the defense he presented for Milo,[10] which they called an 'oration'.[11] How in French do we use the word 'orateur'? It is the bishops and prelates who, in letters sent to kings and princes, assume the role of "their humble 'orateurs'" and repeat the word in devotions and prayers. And, in a similar case, if you say the word 'oraison' to the man in the street, he will never suppose it applies to pleading a cause, but only to the prayers we offer to God and the Saints. If I call Cicero an 'avocat' [lawyer], as we today call those who litigate, there is no one so unversed in history that he would not realize the dishonor I did to the dignity of the former's bygone office. Indeed, Tacitus, or the contemporary who used his name in writing *Dialogue on Orators*, showed clearly

[8] Odet de Tournebus (or Turnèbe) was a young lawyer in the Parlement de Paris who died young of the violent fever. He published in his short lifetime several works written by his father Adrien Turnèbe, who died when he was twelve, including, in 1576, a commentary on Cicero's orations that he dedicated to Pasquier, along with a request that Pasquier translate a speech of Cicero's into French – the request that occasioned this letter. He also wrote Latin and French poetry and a five-act drama. [Ed]

[9] Literally, "You have the wolf by the ears". [Tr]

[10] In 52 B.C.E., for the murder of Clodius. [Ed]

[11] *Orator/orateur* and *oratio/oraison* come from the Latin verb *orare* "to speak, pray, beseech". [Ed]

that the great glory of public speaking had by then mostly decayed, because those who practiced it were called 'avocats' instead of 'orateurs'. In a similar vein, if I suggest as a solution the noun 'plaidoyer' [litigant] – as I intend to do – there is still no doubt that I will incur the censure of many who will find this word too base for the grandeur of the occasion. This means that I am obliged to say and admit that a translator must choose of two extremes, for he either writes for those who understand the Latin language or for those who do not. If he does the first, he would seem to act in vain, because the reader would sooner drink the water at the fountain's source. If he does the second, there is a significant danger that, in permitting ourselves to make a Cicero understood to the reader, we will not live up to our expectations, and thus will be forsaken by both. As a result, our work falls into the hands of a clutch of curious people, whom, as they are fewer in number than the other two groups, I make a great effort to please by wracking my brains in this type of writing. Furthermore, such minds are usually more difficult to please than others. All these particulars can have great effect in dissuading us from translating. But, when you add to that how much the art of eloquence in its totality was more familiar to the Romans that it is to us, there is a surfeit of cause for us to worry. The Romans dealt with a people who delighted in words; their only subject of dedication was the public speech, each expecting it to promote his stature. And for this reason, they had special teachers who explained to them how to embellish their language; the countenances and expressions of good speaking; and the way to rouse the passions within us, to operate with the hearts of the people, to capture the good-will of the most ill-natured and unsociable, to galvanize and assuage us, and to excite the listeners, either to anger or to compassion and pity. And to avoid the censure of the audience, they went all out to please them, devoting time to many frivolous superfluities that calm us even as readers. But, in our case, we must ply our trade before solemn judges, obliging us to be more reserved. We expect our speeches to have more muscle and less flab. If we took the liberty of cajoling, as did the majority of these ancients, beyond what is normally permitted, we would be providing everyone with comic material. I give you as an example none other than the instant speech, in which Cicero, with the mark of greatness, displayed all the power of his eloquence. Good God! How many liberties did he take there that would be not just poorly received in our parliament, but scorned – as though anyone would try it! In consequence, their habit of employing their ideas and words in a pleasing fashion taught them to vary their language in many ways; it is perhaps not in us to make a vocation of speaking as they did. And yet, you hound me to death to conduct an experiment in translation on this very speech. You are in truth asking me to jeopardize my reputation in language before all, by making my first attempt on one of Cicero's masterpieces. To that I may say, for it is true, that in the same way as Alexander the Great would not want to be depicted in flat painting or in relief by anyone except the painter Apelles or the engraver Lysippus, both of whom were giants in their arts, so is it forbidden to all to try portraying Cicero, except he who is another Cicero is his own language. I will do it nonetheless, knowing I will be, like Icarus,[12] plummeting from above to the rocks below, for having wanted to bring my wings to close to the heat of our great sun; I will be pleased to displease myself, not just to please you, but also because I do not wish to imply that our vernacular is so limited that it has not sufficient properties to render many things of Latin, if not with completeness, at least with a certain elegance and purity.

In conclusion, should there be anything to criticize in what I will present, let it be imputed to the wretchedness and poverty of my own mind rather than to anything in our French language. Why, if I cannot satisfy each and everyone, the same disaster will befall me, the translator, as does the author. And, as his diligence and industry, applied to organize his speech well, will fail its purpose, so will I fail mine, whatever effort I may have devoted to translating him. Nevertheless, just as Milo invoked the good wishes of Cicero for the occasion, so I resolve that if this work of mine should fall into the hands of a group of honorable intellects, they will be satisfied that I did my best for my friends, among whom I want all to know that you occupy one of the highest places and that your entreaties are like commands to me; I, like a vassal to his lord, cannot disobey without committing the crime of treason. Farewell.

Margaret Tyler

Little more is known of Margaret Tyler (fl. 1578) than that, as she herself tells us in another dedicatory letter, she once worked as a servant for Lord Thomas Howard's parents – not enough to explain her extraordinary boldness in undertaking to translate a *romance*, a literary form viewed with horror by all good Renaissance fathers and husbands and assiduously kept from their daughters and wives. Renaissance

[12] In Greek myth, Daedalus and his son Icarus were imprisoned by King Minos; Daedalus engineered their escape by building wings for the two of them out of wax and feathers, but Icarus flew too close to the sun, which melted the wax in his wings, and he fell to his death. Daedalus escaped to Sicily. [Ed]

women were not supposed to be learned; if they were learned, they were supposed to read, not write; if they wrote, they were supposed to translate others' works, not create original literature; and if they translated, they were supposed to work on religious texts, not romances. Margaret Tyler broke most of these rules, and defends herself against blame in this preface.

M.T. to the Reader
Preface to Her Translation of Diego Ortunez de Calahorra, *A mirrour of princely deedes and knighthood* (1578)

Thou hast here, gentle reader, the history of Trebatio an emperor in Greece: whether a true story of him indeed or a famed fable, I wot not, neither did I greatly seek after it in the translation, but by me it is done into English for thy profit and delight ... For I take the grace thereof to be rather in the reporter's device than in the truth of this report, as I would that I could so well impart with thee the delight which myself finds in reading the Spanish; but seldom is the tale carried clean from another's mouth. Such delivery as I have made I hope thou wilt friendly accept, the rather for that it is a woman's work, though in a story profane, and a matter more manlike than becomes my sex. But as for the manliness of the matter, thou knowest that it is not necessary for every trumpeter or drumstare [drummer] in the war to be a good fighter. They take wage only to incite others though themselves have privy maims, and are therefore recurless. So gentle reader if my travail in Englishing this author may bring thee to a liking of the virtues herein commended, and by example thereof in thy princes and countries quarrel to hazard thy person and purchase good name, as for hope of well deserving myself that way, I neither bend myself thereto nor yet fear the speech of people if I be found backward. I trust every man holds not the plow, which would the ground were tilled; and it is no sin to talk of Robin Hood though you never shot in his bow; or be it that the attempt were bold to intermeddle in arms, so as the ancient Amazons did, and in this story Claridiana does, and in other stories not a few, yet to report of arms is not so odious but that it may be borne withal, not only in you men which yourselves are fighters but in us women, to whom the benefit in equal part appertains of your victories, either for that the matter is so commendable that it carries no discredit from the homeliness of the speaker, or for that it is so generally known that it fits every man to speak thereof ... The invention, disposition, trimming, and what else in this story is wholly another man's, my part none therein but the translation ... So that the question now arises of my choice, not of my labour, wherefore I preferred this story before matter of more importance. For answer whereto, gentle reader, the truth is that as the first motion to the kind of labour came not from myself, so was this piece of work put upon me by others, and they which first counseled me to fall to work took upon them also to be my taskmasters and overseers lest I should be idle, and yet because the refusal was in my power, I must stand to answer for my easy yielding ... But my defence is by example of the best, amongst which many have dedicated their labours, some stories, some of war, some physic, some law, some as concerning government, some divine matters, unto diverse ladies and gentlewomen. And if men may and do bestow such of their travails upon gentlewomen, then may we women read such of their works as they dedicate unto us, and if we may read them, why not farther wade in them to the search of a truth. And then much more why not deal by translation in such arguments, especially this kind of exercise being a matter of more heed than of deep invention or exquisite learning, and they must needs leave this as confessed, that in their dedications they mind not only to borrow names of worthy personages, but the testimonies also for their further credit, which neither the one may demand without ambition nor the other grant without overlightness: if women be excluded from the view of such works as appear in their name, or if glory only be sought in our common inscriptions, it matters not whether the parties be men or women, whether alive or dead. But to return, whatsomever the truth is, whether that women may not at all discourse in learning, for men lay in their claim to be sole possessors of knowledge, or whether they may in some manner that is by limitation or appointment in some kind of learning, my persuasion has been thus, that it is all one for a woman to pen a story, as for a man to address his story to a woman. But amongst all my ill-willers, some I hope are not so strait [strict] that they would enforce me necessarily either not to write or to write of divinity. Whereas neither durst I trust mine own judgement sufficiently, if matter of controversy were handled, nor yet could I find any book in the tongue which would not breed offence to some, but I perceive some may be rather angry to see their Spanish delight turned to an English pastime, they could well allow the story in Spanish, but they may not afford it so cheap, or they would have it proper to themselves. What natures such men be of, I list not [do not want to] greatly dispute, but my meaning has been to make other partners of my liking ... And thus much as concerning this present story, that it is neither unseemly for a woman to deal in, neither greatly requiring a less staid age than mine is. But of these two points gentle reader I thought to give thee warning, lest perhaps understanding of my name and years, thou mightest be carried into a wrong suspect [suspicion] of my boldness and rashness, from which I would gladly free myself by this plain excuse, and if I may deserve thy good favour by like labour, when the choice is mine own I will have a special regard of thy liking.

So I wish thee well,
Thine to use, M.T.

Michel de Montaigne

A French courtier best known for his *Essays*, Michel Eyquem de Montaigne (1533-1592) was one of the strongest early voices of what we now call the modern era: skeptical, open-minded, a spokesman for religious tolerance and human-centered morality, he is credited with inventing the literary form of the essay.

Montaigne was born in the family castle near Bordeaux, France, which had been bought by his paternal great-grandfather, and which had brought with its purchase a noble title. His father, like his ancestors, was a wealthy merchant, and he gave his eight children (of whom Michel was the oldest) the best education money could buy. Montaigne spoke only Latin until he was six, when he was allowed to learn French; after his education in Bordeaux and Toulouse, he served without enthusiasm for thirteen years as a lawyer in the Parlement de Bordeaux, part of the king's highest court of justice, where he met the most important person in his life, Étienne de La Boétie. Their friendship, which both characterized as extraordinarily, even mysteriously close, only lasted four or six years, for La Boétie soon contracted dysentery and died; Montaigne mourned him the rest of his life.

Indeed Montaigne's biographers speculate that, had La Boétie lived, Montaigne would not have written his essays. He married Françoise de La Chassaigne in 1656, two years after La Boétie's death, but was not fond of his wife and indeed thought of marriage (and the fathering of six children, all but one of whom died in infancy) as a social duty. His father died in 1568, leaving him lord of Montaigne; in 1570, at the age of 37, he sold his position at the Parlement and retired to the family castle to write his essays. He planned to spend the rest of his life there, but in 1581 was elected mayor of Bordeaux; wanting to decline the honour, he was ordered to accept by Henry III, and served two two-year terms, the second of which was characterized by civil strife between Protestant and Catholic forces. He was a relatively efficient mayor; as a skeptical Catholic who had long argued for religious tolerance and attempted to mediate between the two factions, he was well-suited to his office. He was later thrown in the Bastille, during a visit to his publisher in Paris in 1587, by Protestants who suspected him of being a spy for Henry of Navarre. His last four years, from 1588 to 1592, he spent in retirement, attended by Marie de Gournay, a young admirer who upon his death became his literary executrix.

The bulk of his essays were written in the decade or so between his retirement from the Parlement de Bordeaux and his election as mayor of Bordeaux; he did write thirteen new essays in the eighties, publishing them in the fifth edition (1588), which he had gone to Paris to see through the press when he was arrested. His earlier essays are more negative, more critical of human frailties, his later (those written after 1578) more optimistic and concerned with human possibilities; but all of his essays are characterized by an integrity of feeling, a willingness to tie discursive form not to ancient models but to his own shifting moods. He wrote 'essays' in the root meaning of the word, exploratory gropings toward understanding, tentative probings of issues and problems – including the problem of his own inquiring mind.

'On Cannibals', one of Shakespeare's primary sources for *The Tempest*, is in some ways a peculiar entry in an anthology of translation theory. It is not 'about' translation, although Montaigne does mention a specific translation problem at the end; what it is 'about' is cross-cultural communication and understanding, specifically between 'civilized' Europe and the 'uncivilized' New World, and the various pressures on Europeans to understand the 'cannibals' and on the 'cannibals' to adapt to the customs of their European colonizers. Montaigne is concerned with the consequences of translating not texts, but people: of converting 'cannibals' into imitation Europeans.

We Call Barbarous Anything That is Contrary to Our Own Habits

From 'On Cannibals' ('Des cannibales', 1580)
Translated by J. M. Cohen

Having surveyed, during his invasion of Italy, the marshalling of the army that the Romans had set out against him, King Pyrrhus remarked: "I do not know what barbarians these are" – for so the Greeks called all foreign nations – "but the ordering of the army before me has nothing barbarous about it". The Greeks said the same of the forces with which Flaminius invaded their country; and Philip also, when from a little hill he saw the orderly arrangement of the Roman camp, set up in his kingdom under Publius Sulpicius Galba.

We see from this how chary we must be of subscribing to vulgar opinions; we should judge them by the test of reason and not by common report.

I had with me for a long time a man who had lived ten or twelve years in that other world which has been discovered in our time, in the place where [Nicolas Durand de] Villegaignon landed [in 1555, in south-eastern Brazil], and which he called Antarctic France. This discovery of so vast a country seems to me worth reflecting on. I should not care to pledge myself that another may not be discovered in the future, since so many greater men than we have been wrong about this one. I am afraid that our eyes are bigger than our stomachs, and that we have more curiosity than understanding. We grasp at everything, but catch nothing except wind ...

This man who stayed with me was a plain, simple fellow, and men of this sort are likely to give true testimony. Men of intelligence notice more things and view them more carefully, but they comment on them; and to establish and substantiate their interpretation, they cannot refrain from altering the facts a little. They never present things just as they are but twist and disguise them to conform to the point of view from which they have seen them; and to gain credence for their opinion and make it attractive, they do not mind adding something of their own, or extending and amplifying. We need either a very truthful man, or one so ignorant that he has no material with which to construct false theories and make them credible: a man wedded to no idea. My man was like that; and besides he has on various occasions brought me seamen and merchants whom he met on his voyage. Therefore I am satisfied with his information, and do not inquire what the cosmographers say about it.

We need topographers to give us exact descriptions of the places where they have been. But because they have this advantage over us, that they have seen the Holy Land, they claim the additional privilege of telling us news about all the rest of the world. I would have everyone write about what he knows and no more than he knows, not only on this, but on all other subjects. One man may have some special knowledge at firsthand about the character of a river or a spring, who otherwise knows only what everyone else knows. Yet to give currency to this shred of information, he will undertake to write on the whole science of physics. From this fault many great troubles spring.

Now, to return to my argument, I do not believe, from what I have been told about this people, that there is anything barbarous or savage about them, except that we all call barbarous anything that is contrary to our own habits. Indeed we seem to have no other criterion of truth and reason than the type and kind of opinions and customs in the land where we live. There we always see the perfect religion, the perfect political system, the perfect and most accomplished way of doing everything. These people are wild in the same way as we say that fruits are wild, when nature has produced them by herself and in her ordinary way; whereas, in fact, it is those we have artificially modified, and removed from the common order, that we ought to call wild. In the former, the true, most useful, and latter we have bastardized them, and adapted them only to the gratification of our corrupt taste. Nevertheless, there is a special savour and delicacy in some of the uncultivated fruits of those regions that is excellent even to our taste, and rivals our own. It is not reasonable that art should win the honours from our great and mighty mother nature. We have so loaded the riches and beauty of her works with our inventions that we have altogether stifled her. Yet, wherever she shines forth in her purity, she makes our vain and trivial enterprises marvellously shameful.

> *Et veniunt ederae sponte sua melius,*
> *surgit et in solis formosior arbutus antris,*
> *et volucres nulla dulcius arte canunt.*[1]

With all our efforts we cannot imitate the nest of the very smallest bird, its structure, its beauty, or the suitability of its form, nor even the web of a lowly spider. All things, said Plato, are produced either by nature, or by chance, or by art; the greatest and most beautiful by one or other of the first two, the least and most imperfect by the last.

These nations, then, seem to me barbarous in the sense that they have received very little moulding from the human intelligence, and are still very close to their original simplicity. They are still governed by natural laws and very little corrupted by our own. They are in such a state of purity that it sometimes saddens me to think we did not learn of them earlier, at a time when there were men who were better able to appreciate them than we. I am sorry that Lycurgus and Plato did not know them, for I think what we have seen of these people with our own eyes surpasses not only the pictures with which poets have illustrated the golden age, and all their attempts to draw mankind in the state of happiness, but the ideas and the very aspirations of philosophers as well. They could not imagine an innocence as pure and simple as we have actually seen; nor could they believe that our society might be maintained with so little artificiality and human organization.

This is a nation, I should say to Plato, in which there is no kind of commerce, no knowledge of letters, no science of numbers, no title of magistrate or of political superior, no habit of service, riches or poverty,

[1] "The ivy grows best when it grows wild, and the arbutus is most lovely when it grows in some solitary cleft; birds sing most sweetly untaught". Propertius, I, ii, 10. [Tr]

no contracts, no inheritance, no divisions of property, only leisurely occupations, no respect for any kinship but the common ties, no clothes, no agriculture, no metals, no use of corn or wine. The very words denoting lying, treason, deceit, greed, envy, slander, and forgiveness have never been heard. How far from such perfection would he find the republic that he imagined: "men fresh from the hands of the gods" [Seneca *Letters*, 90].

Hos natura modos primum dedit.[2] ...

Not knowing how costly a knowledge of this country's corruptions will one day be to their happiness and repose, and that from intercourse with us will come their ruin – which, I suppose, is far advanced already – three men of their nation – poor fellows to allow themselves to be deluded by the desire for things unknown, and to leave the softness of their own skies to come and gaze at ours – were at Rouen at the time when the late King Charles the Ninth visited the place. The King talked with them for some time; they were shown our way of living, our magnificence, and the sights of a fine city. Then someone[3] asked them what they thought about all this, and what they had found most remarkable. They mentioned three things, of which I am sorry to say I have forgotten the third. But I still remember two. They said that in the first place they found it very strange that so many tall, bearded men, all strong and well armed, who were around the King – they probably meant the Swiss of his guard – should be willing to obey a child, rather than choose one of their own number to command them. Secondly – they have a way in their language of speaking of men as halves of one another – that they had noticed among us some men gorged to the full with things of every sort while their other halves were beggars at their doors, emaciated with hunger and poverty. They found it strange that these poverty-stricken halves should suffer injustice, and that they did not take the others by the throat or set fire to their houses.

I talked to one of them for some time; but I had an interpreter who followed my meaning so badly, and was so hindered by stupidity from grasping my ideas, that I could hardly get any satisfaction from him. When I asked the visitor what advantage he gained by his superior position among his own people – for he was a captain and our sailors called him the king – he said, the privilege of marching first into battle. And by how many men was he followed? He pointed to a piece of ground, to indicate that they were as many as would fill a space of that size. It might have been four or five thousand. And when there was no war, did all his authority cease? He answered that it remained, and that when he visited the villages that depended upon him, paths were cleared for him through their thickets, so that he could travel at his ease. All this does not seem too bad. But then, they do not wear breeches.

[2] "These are the first laws that nature gave". Virgil, *Georgics*, II, 20. [Tr]

[3] Montaigne himself. [Tr]

Gregory Martin

Gregory Martin (c. 1540-1582) was the primary translator of the first English Roman Catholic Bible, the so-called Douay-Rheims Bible. The New Testament was published in 1582, the year of his death (he did not quite live to see it in print); the Old Testament was not published until 1609-1610. A fine scholar of Greek and Hebrew, for doctrinal reasons he translated the New Testament as literally as possible from Jerome's Latin Vulgate, the official Bible of the Roman Catholic church.

Martin was born in Maxfield, Sussex, but we know nothing of his childhood until he was nominated one of the first scholars at the recently founded St. John's College at Oxford (1557). Taking his M.A. in 1564, he spent six years as tutor to the children of Thomas, Duke of Norfolk; but living in England meant living a secret life, practising Protestantism in public but Roman Catholicism in private, since upon her ascension to the throne in 1558 Elizabeth had banned all Catholic observances. In 1570 he renounced Protestantism and moved to the English College founded by William Allen in Douay, where he studied theology and was ordained priest in 1573. He travelled widely, helped Allen establish the English College in Rome from 1576 to 1578, when he returned to Rheims (where the College moved that year to escape persecution) as public professor and reader of divinity. He died of tuberculosis in Rheims while his New Testament was at the printer's.

Martin's translation was attacked heavily by his Protestant compatriots in England, of course, most notably in the 1580s by William Fulke (see below), and the Douay-Rheims Bible was suppressed, banned, often systematically sought out and destroyed, for two centuries. Many of his phrasings, however, influenced the translators of King James in the early seventeenth century; and his version remained the standard Roman Catholic Bible for English readers (revised in 1752 by Bishop Richard Challoner) until the publication of the Confraternity translation in the mid-twentieth century.

Another book Martin published in the year of his death was *A Discoverie of the Manifold*

Corruptions of the Holy Scriptures by the Heretikes of Our Daies, which sought to clear the way for a favourable reception of his New Testament by attacking Protestant translations. The following year, in 1583, William Fulke published a paragraph-by-paragraph confutation of Martin's *Discovery*, two passages from the preface to which appear below. Fulke's polemic is structured almost dialogically, giving first Martin's paragraph and then his own rebuttal, so that he actually reprints Martin's entire book one paragraph at a time. In his 1589 confutation of Martin's preface to the Rheims New Testament Fulke again attacks Martin paragraph by paragraph, but this time does not reprint the actual text of Martin's preface. The debate between these two scholars, short snippets of which are reprinted here, offers valuable insight into the clash between Protestantism and Roman Catholicism in an English context at the late sixteenth century, and thereby also into the stakes of Bible translation in an era of religious upheaval. To aid the reader in following this debate, each paragraph has been numbered.

Five Sundry Abuses or Corruptions of Holy Scripture
From the preface to *A Discovery of the Manifold Corruptions of the Holy Scriptures by the Heretics of Our Days, Specially the English Sectaries, and of their Foul Dealing Herein, by Partial and False Translations to the Advantage of their Heresies, in the English Bibles Used and Authorized Since the Time of Schism* (1582)

1. As it has been always the fashion of heretics to pretend scriptures for show of their cause, so has it been also their custom and property to abuse the said scriptures many ways in favour of their errors.

2. One way is, to deny whole books thereof, or parts of books, when they are evidently against them. So did (for example) Ebion all St. Paul's epistles, Manicheus the Acts of the Apostles, Alogiani St. John's Gospel, Marcion many pieces of St. Luke's Gospel, and so did both these and other heretics in other books, denying and allowing what they list, as is evident by St. Irenaeus, St. Epiphanius, St. Augustine, and all antiquity.

3. Another way is to call into question at the least and make some doubt of the authority of certain books of holy scriptures, thereby to diminish their credit. So did Manicheus affirm of the whole New Testament that it was not written by the apostles; and peculiarly of St. Matthew's Gospel, that it was some other man's under his name, and therefore not of such credit, but that it might in some part be refused. So did Marcion, and the Arians, deny the epistle to the Hebrews to be St. Paul's, Epiph. lib. 2 haer. 69, Euseb. lib. 4. hist. c. 27; and Alogiani the Apocalypse to be St. John's the Evangelist, Epiph. et August. in haer. Alogianorum.[1]

4. Another way is to expound the scriptures after their own private conceit and fantasy, not according to the approved sense of the holy ancient fathers and Catholic church. So did Theodorus Mopsuestites (Act. Synod 5.) affirm of all the books of the prophets, and of the Psalms, that they spoke not evidently of Christ; but that the ancient fathers did voluntarily draw those sayings unto Christ, which were spoken of other matters.[2] So did all heretics that would seem to ground their heresies upon scriptures, and to avouch [vouch for] them by scriptures expounded according to their own sense and imagination.

5. Another way is to alter the very original text of the holy scripture, by adding, taking away, or changing it here and there for their purpose. So did the Arians in sundry places, and the Nestorians in the first epistle of St. John, and especially Marcion, who was therefore called *Mus Ponticus*, the mouse of Pontus, because he had gnawn (as it were) certain places with his corruptions, whereof some are said to remain in the Greek text until this day.[3]

6. Another way is to make false translations of the scriptures, for the maintenance of error and heresy. So did the Arians (as St. Jerome notes in xxvi. Esa.) read and translate Proverb viii. [8:22] *Dominus creavit me in initio viarum suarum*, that is, "The Lord created me in the beginning of his ways", so to make Christ, the wisdom of God, a mere creature.[4] St. Augustine also, Lib. V. cont. Julian. c. 2 ['Against Julian' 5.2], notes it as the interpretation of some Pelagian, Gen. iii. *Fecerunt sibi vestimenta* for *perizomata*, or *campestria*, that is, "They made themselves garments"; whereas the word of the scripture is, breeches or aprons, proper and peculiar to cover the secret parts.[5]

---

[1] They were right: Paul did not write Hebrews and John the Evangelist did not write the Book of Revelation. The abbreviated references are to Epiphanius, 2.69; Eusebius, *Ecclesiastical History* 4.27; Epiphanius and Augustine on the heresy of the Alogiani. [Ed]

[2] This position, now accepted by all Christian exegetes, was first advanced by Theodore in the early 5th century and attacked as heretical by many centuries of ecclesiastical councils. [Ed]

[3] The Nestorians were a Christian sect founded by Nestorius. Pontus was the region in northeastern Anatolia, Asia Minor, from which Marcion came. [Ed]

[4] The 'Wisdom' (*hokma*) personified in the Proverbs 8 as a woman (probably from eastern mystery religions) was associated typologically with Jesus throughout the Middle Ages and into the modern era; this did cause some interpretive difficulties, as the Proverbs text does describe Wisdom as 'created' by God. [Ed]

[5] Aug. ep. 89 et lib. 1. de pec. mer. cap. 11. [Au] Augustine, letter 89, and *De peccatorum meritis et remissione* ['On the Earning and Remission of Sins'] 1.11 (411/12). See Genesis 3:7. [Ed]

Again, the selfsame heretics did read falsely, Rom. v. *Regnavit mors ab Adam usque ad Moysen etiam in eos qui peccaverunt in similitudinem praevaricationis Adae*; that is, "Death reigned from Adam to Moses, even on them that sinned after the similitude of the prevarication of Adam" [Romans 5:14]; to maintain their heresy against original sin, that none were infected therewith, or subject to death and damnation, but by sinning actually, as Adam did. Thus did the old heretics ...

7. Must such difficulties and diversities be resolved by chopping and changing, hacking and hewing, the sacred text of holy scripture? See into what perplexities wilful heresy and arrogancy has driven them. To discredit the vulgar Latin translation of the Bible, and the Fathers' expositions according to the same (for that is the original cause of this), and besides that they may have always this evasion, "It is not so in the Hebrew, it is otherwise in the Greek", and so seem jolly fellows and great clerks unto the ignorant people. What do they? They admit only the Hebrew in the Old Testament, and the Greek in the New, to be the true and authentical text of the scripture. Whereupon this follows, that they reject, and must needs reject, the Greek of the Old Testament (called the Septuagint) as false, because it differs from the Hebrew. Which being rejected, thereupon it follows again, that wheresoever those places so disagreeing from the Hebrew are cited by Christ or the evangelists and apostles, there also they must be rejected, because they disagree from the Hebrew; and so yet again it follows that the Greek text of the New Testament is not true, because it is not according to the Hebrew verity, and consequently the words of our Saviour and writings of his apostles must be reformed (to say the least), because they speak according to the Septuagint, and not according to the Hebrew.

8. All which must needs follow, if this be a good consequence, "I find it not in Moses, nor in the Hebrew, therefore I struck it out", as Beza does and says concerning the foresaid words, *qui fuit Cainan*.[6] This consequence therefore let us see how they will justify; and withal let them tell us, whether they will discredit the New Testament because of the Septuagint, or credit the Septuagint because of the New Testament; or how they can credit one and discredit the other, where both agree and consent together; or whether they will discredit both for credit of the Hebrew; or rather, whether there be not some other way to reconcile both Hebrew and Greek, better than Beza's impudent presumption. Which if they will not maintain, let them flatly confess that he did wickedly, and not (as they do) defend every word and deed of their masters, be it never so heinous, or salve it at the least.

9. Alas! how far are these men from the modesty of the ancient fathers, and from the humble spirit of obedient Catholics, who seek all other means to resolve difficulties, rather than to do violence to the sacred scripture; and when they find no way, they leave it to God. St. Augustine, concerning the difference of the Hebrew and the Greek, says often to this effect, that it pleased the Holy Ghost to utter by the one that which he would not utter by the other.[7] And St. Ambrose thus: "We have found many things not idly added of the seventy Greek interpreters".[8] St. Jerome,[9] though an earnest patron of the Hebrew (not without cause, being at that time perhaps the Hebrew verity indeed) yet gives many reasons for the differences of the Septuagint; and concerning the foresaid places of St. Luke, he does give a reason thereof, both for the seventy, and for the evangelist that followed them, neither doubting of the truth thereof, nor controlling them "by the authority of Moses" (as Beza speaks), that is, by the Hebrew. Others say concerning Cainan, that Moses might leave him out in the genealogy of Shem by the instinct of the same spirit, that St. Matthew left out three kings in the genealogy of our Saviour [Matthew 1]. Where if a man would control the evangelist by the Hebrew of the Old Testament that is read in the books of the Kings, he should be as wise and as honest a man as Beza. Lastly, venerable Bede thinks it sufficient in this very difficulty of Cainan to marvel at it reverently, rather than to search it dangerously.[10] And thus far of picking quarrels to the original text, and their good will to alter and change it as they list, if they might be suffered.

10. Which also may be proved by all their false translations (being the principal point I mean to speak of) most evidently. For as now they translate falsely to their purpose, because they cannot alter the text; so would they, if it were possible, have the text agreeable to their translation. For example, he that translates 'ordinances', when it is in the original Greek text

---

[6] The *qui fuit Cainan* (lit. "from whom was Cainan") controversy revolved around the discrepancies between the genealogies in Genesis 11:10, which does not mention Cainan, and Luke 3:36, which does. [Ed]

[7] Lib. 18 de Civit. cap. 43, 2 lib. de Doct. Chr. cap. 15. [Au] *The City of God* 18.43; *On Christian Doctrine* 2.15.22 (see Augustine, above, 34). [Ed]

[8] Hexaemeron. Lib. III. cap. 5. Opera. Vol. I. p. 42. [Hartshorne] See Ambrose's *On the Six Days of Creation* 3.5. [Ed]

[9] Comment. Hieronymi in Isaiae xxviii. Opera, Vol. III. pp. 237, 238.; Praefat. Hieronymi in Paralipom. Opera, Vol. I. pp. 1022, 1023. [Hartshorne] See Jerome's commentary on Isaiah 28, and his preface to the paralipomena. See also the letter to Pammachius, above, 23-30. [Ed]

[10] Praef. in Act. Apost. [Au] Bede's preface to Acts. [Ed]

'justifications' and 'traditions', he would rather that it were 'ordinances' also in the Greek; but because he cannot bring that about, he does at the least what he can, to make the ignorant believe it is so, by so translating it.

11. And this of all other is the most fine and subtle treachery against the scriptures, to deceive the ignorant readers withal (which St. Paul calls "the secret things of dishonesty and adulterating of the word of God" [2 Corinthians 4], as it were mingling water with wine, like false vintners), when they give them for God's word, and under the name of God's word, their own words, and not God's, forged and framed, altered and changed, according to differences of times, and variety of new opinions, and diversity of humours and spirits, diversely and differently, one heretic not only correcting his fellow every day, but one eagerly refuting and refelling another: Bucer and the Osiandrians and Sacramentaries against Luther for false translations; Luther against Münster, Beza against Castalio, Castalio against Beza, Calvin against Servetus, Illyricus both against Calvin and Beza. The puritans control the grosser Calvinists of our country; yea, the later translations of the selfsame heretics control the former exceedingly, not only of oversights but of wilful falsifications; as is notorious in the later editions of Luther and Beza, and in our English Bibles set forth in diverse years, from Tindal [Tyndale] their first translator until this day; yea (which is more) the English translators of Beza's New Testament control him and his translation, which they protest to follow, being afraid sometimes and ashamed to express in English his false translations in the Latin.[11]

The Holy Scriptures Ought Not be Read Indifferently of All
From 'The Preface to the Reader', *The New Testament of Jesus Christ* (1582)

1. The Holy Bible long since translated by us into English, and the Old Testament lying by us for lack of good means to publish the whole in such sort as a work of so great charge and importance requires, we have yet through God's goodness at length fully finished for thee (most Christian reader) all the NEW TESTAMENT, which is the principal, most profitable and comfortable piece of Holy Writ; and, as well for all other institution of life and doctrine, as specially for deciding the doubts of these days, more proper and pregnant than the other part not yet printed.

2. Which translation we do not for all that publish upon erroneous opinion of necessity that the Holy Scriptures should always be in our mother tongue, or that they ought, or were ordained by God, to be read indifferently of all, or could be easily understood of everyone that reads or hears them in a known language; or that they were not often through man's malice or infirmity pernicious and much hurtful to many; or that we generally and absolutely deemed it more convenient in itself, and more agreeable to God's word and honour or edification of the faithful, to have them turned into vulgar tongues, than to be kept and studied only in the ecclesiastical learned languages. Not for these nor any such like causes do we translate this sacred book, but upon special consideration of the present time, state, and condition of our country, unto which diverse things are either necessary or profitable and medicinable now that otherwise in the peace of the Church were neither much requisite nor perchance wholly tolerable.

3. In this matter, to mark only the wisdom and moderation of holy Church and the governors thereof on the one side, and the indiscreet zeal of the popular, and their factious leaders, on the other, is a high point of prudence. These latter, partly of simplicity, partly of curiosity, and specially of pride and disobedience, have made claim in this case for the common people, with plausible pretences many, but good reasons none at all. The other,[12] to whom Christ has given charge of our souls, the dispensing of God's mysteries and treasures (among which Holy Scripture is no small store) and the feeding his family in season with food fit for every sort, have neither of old nor of late ever wholly condemned all vulgar versions of Scripture, nor have at any time generally forbidden the faithful to read the same; yet they have not by public authority prescribed, commanded, or authentically ever recommended any such interpretation to be indifferently used of all men.

4. The Armenians say they have the Psalter and some other pieces translated by St. Chrysostom into their language, when he was banished among them;[13] and George the Patriarch [Gregory II of Cyprus], in writing his life, signifies no less. The Sclavonians affirm they have the Scriptures in their vulgar tongue, turned by St. Hierom,[14] and some would gather so much by his own words in his epistle to Sophronius,[15] but the place indeed proves it not. Vulpilas surely gave the Scriptures to the Goths in their own tongue, and

[11] Dial. cont. Melan. Lind. dubit. p. 84, 96, 89. See Zuing. resp. 1. and Confess. Tigurinorum. Ibid. p. 83 97. The New Testament of the year 1580. Luke iii. 36. [Au]

[12] Mat. 24:45, 1 Cor. 4:1. [Au] Both passages proclaim the difference between true and false servants of God. [Ed]

[13] Bib. Sacl. li. 4. [Au] Saint John Chrysostom was exiled (largely for preaching against the misuse of wealth) to Cucusus, Armenia, for roughly the last four years of his life. [Ed]

[14] Hiero. ep. 134. [Au] Letter 134 (to Augustine in 416) of Jerome, here called Hierom by Martin. [Ed]

[15] Sophronius was Jerome's middle name and occasional pseudonym; he did not write any letters *to* Sophronius. [Ed]

that before he was an Arian.[16] It is almost three hundred years since James Archbishop of Genoa is said to have translated the Bible into Italian. More than two hundred years ago, in the days of Charles V, the French king, was it put forth faithfully in French, the sooner to shake out of the deceived people's heads the false heretical translations of a sect called Waldenses.[17] In our own country, notwithstanding the Latin tongue was ever (to use Venerable Bede's words)[18] common to all the provinces of the same for meditation or study of Scriptures, and no vulgar translation commonly used or occupied of the multitude, yet there were extant in English even before the troubles that Wycliffe and his followers raised in our Church, as appears as well by some pieces yet remaining as by a provincial Constitution of Thomas Arundel Archbishop of Canterbury,[19] in a Council held at Oxford, where strait [strict] provision was made that no heretical version set forth by Wycliffe or his adherents should be suffered, nor any other in or after his time be published or permitted to be read, being not approved and allowed by the Diocesan before [in advance], alleaging [allying, calling on as an ally] St. Hierom for the difficulty and danger of interpreting the holy Scripture out of one tongue into another, though by learned and Catholic men. So also it is there insinuated that neither the translations set forth before that heretic's time nor other afterward being approved by the lawful ordinaries, were ever in our country wholly forbidden, though they were not (to say the truth) in quiet and better times (much less when the people were prone to alteration,[20] heresy, or novelty), either hastily admitted or ordinarily read of the vulgar, but used only, or specially, of some devout religious and contemplative persons, in reverence, secrecy, and silence, for their spiritual comfort.

5. Now since Luther's revolt also, diverse learned Catholics, for the more speedy abolishing of a number of false and impious translations put forth by sundry sects, and for the better preservation or reclaim of many good souls endangered thereby, have published the Bible in the several languages of almost all the principal provinces of the Latin Church; no other books in the world being so pernicious as heretical translations of the Scriptures, poisoning the people under colour of divine authority, and not many other remedies being more sovereign against the same (if it be used in order, discretion, and humility) than the truth, faithful, and sincere interpretation opposed thereunto.

6. Which causes the holy Church not to forbid utterly any Catholic translation, though she allow not the publishing or reading of any absolutely and without exception, or limitation: knowing by her divine and most sincere wisdom, how, where, when, and to whom these her Master's and Spouse's gifts are to be bestowed to the most good of the faithful; and therefore neither generally permits that which must needs do hurt to the unworthy not absolutely condemns that which may do much good to the worthy. Whereupon the order which many a wise man wished for before was taken by the Deputies of the late famous Council of Trent[21] in this behalf and confirmed by supreme authority that the holy Scriptures, though truly and Catholicly translated into vulgar tongues yet may not be indifferently read of all men, nor of any other than such as have express licence thereunto of their lawful Ordinaries, with good testimony from their curates or confessors, that they be humble, discreet, and devout persons, and like to take much good, and no harm thereby. Which prescript[ion], though in these days of ours it cannot be so precisely observed as in other times and places, where there is more due respect of the Church's authority, rule, and discipline;[22] yet we trust all wise and godly persons will use the matter in the meanwhile with such moderation, meekness, and subjection of heart as the handling of so sacred a book, the sincere senses of God's truth therein, and the holy Canons, Councils, reason, and religion do require.

William Fulke

William Fulke (before 1538-1589) is best remembered for his fierce Protestant polemics

[16] Vulpilas or Ulfilas translated the Bible into Gothic from the Septuagint c. 350 C.E.; there is no indication that he was ever not an Arian. [Ed]

[17] Martin is apparently referring to fourteenth-century revisions of the Arsenal Bible (done at Acre c. 1250) or Guyart des Moulins's *Bible Historiale* (c. 1317, with many revisions over the next two centuries). The Waldenses (or Valdenses, or Vaudois, or Valdesi), reputedly founded by one Valdes or Peter Waldo in 12th-century France to follow Jesus in a life of poverty and simplicity, were later associated with a Protestant group on the Franco-Italian border. A Waldensian translation of the Bible into Flemish was done before 1200. [Ed]

[18] Li. 1 hist. Angl. 1.1. [Au] Martin is referring to the first page of book one of Bede's *The Ecclesiastical History of the English People* (731/32). [Ed]

[19] For further discussion of Arundel's provincial constitution, see More, above, 76-77. [Ed]

[20] I.e., changing or deviating from the accepted interpretation of the Bible. [Ed]

[21] The Council of Trent (1545-1563), the 19th ecumenical council of the Roman Catholic Church, helped consolidate the church by clarifying Catholic doctrine against the assaults of the Protestants. [Ed]

[22] Martin writes this in exile in Rheims, where he has fled to escape Elizabeth's strict ban on Roman Catholicism: so far from being 'duly respected' in England, the church is banned. [Ed]

against what he liked to call the 'Romish sect' – not only in print, as in the two extracts appearing here, but in frequent public disputations. Nothing is known of Fulke's parents or childhood, apart from the fact that his father wanted him to be a lawyer and sent him, upon his graduation from St. John's College, Cambridge (1555), to Clifford's Inn, where he spent six or more years ostensibly studying the law but paying more attention to the sciences. Sometime in the early sixties he returned to Cambridge, where, despite his father's disapproval and withdrawal of financial support, he studied theology and ancient languages. He took a Master's degree in 1564 and a Bachelor of Divinity some years after, and was elected fellow of his college; but, suspected of Puritanism, due partly to his argumentative nature, partly to the people he associated with, he was driven from his college. Undaunted by the loss of institutional affiliation, he began to hold forth in lectures and public debates, which seem to have been well-attended.

Around this time he attracted the attention of the Earl of Leicester, who was much taken by Fulke and did a great deal to advance his career, appointing him rector of two different parishes in 1571 and 1573 and attaching him to the suite of the Earl of Lincoln when the latter was sent as British ambassador to Paris. Upon his return to England in 1578 he was appointed master of Pembroke College, where he remained the rest of his life, devoting a good deal of his time to the vindication of the Protestant faith.

As with Gregory Martin's paragraphs, above, to which he responds, Fulke's paragraphs have been numbered to facilitate reconstruction of the paragraph-by-paragraph debate.

That None Of These Five Abuses are Committed By Us

From the preface to *A Defence of the Sincere and True Translations of the Holy Scriptures into the English Tongue, Against the Cavils of Gregory Martin* (1583)

1. Whether these five abuses have been common to all heretics, and whether it has been the fashion of all heretics to pretend scriptures for show of their cause, though I will spare now to inquire of,[1] as a thing wherein learned men at the first sight may espy the great skill that Martin pretends to have in discerning of heretics and heresies; yet will I show (by the grace of God) that none of these five abuses are committed by us or our catholic [universally valid and true] translations, and that the Popish heretics are, in some sort or other, guilty of them all.

2. First, we deny no one book of the canonical scripture that has been so received of the Catholic church for the space of 300 years and more, as it has been often proved out of Eusebius, St. Jerome, and other ancient authorities; but the Papists, in advancing apocryphal books to be of equal credit with the canonical scriptures, do in effect deny them all. Besides that, to add unto the word of God is as great a fault as to take away from it, the one being forbidden under as heavy a curse as the other. Those blasphemies of Pighius[2] and Eccius,[3] the one calling the Holy Scripture a nose of wax and a dumb judge, the other terming the Gospel written to be a black Gospel and an inky divinity; and that of Hosius,[4] acknowledging none other express word of God, but only this one word *ama*, or *dilige*, 'love thou'; what other thing do they import, but a shameless denial of all books of the Holy Scripture in deed, howsoever in word they will seem to admit them?

3. We neither doubt of the authority of any certain book of the Holy Scriptures, neither call we any of them into question; but with due reverence do acknowledge them all and every one to be of equal credit and authority, as being all inspired of God, given to the church for the building up thereof in truth, and for the avoiding of fables and heresies. But the Papists, arrogating to their Pope authority to allow or refuse any book of Holy Scripture, and affirming that no Scripture has authority but as it is approved by their church, do bring all books of the Holy Scripture into doubting and uncertainty with such as will depend upon their Pope and Popish Church's authority, which they affirm to be above the Holy Scriptures, saying they might as well receive the Gospel of Nicodemus as of St. Mark, and by the same authority reject the Gospel of St. Matthew, as they have done the Gospel of St. Bartholomew. These blasphemous assertions although some of them would colour or mitigate with gentle interpretations, yet there is no reasonable man but sees into what discredit and uncertainty they must needs bring the authority of the canonical books of Holy Scripture with the simple and ignorant.

4. We expound not the Scriptures after our own

[1] I.e., I will not go to the trouble to inquire into it now. [Ed]

[2] Pighius, Hierarch. Eccles. Assertio, Lib. III. cap. 3. fol. 80, edit. 1538. [Au] Book 3, chapter 3, folio 80 of the 1538 edition of Pighius' 'Assertion of Church Hierarchy'. [Ed]

[3] Eck. Apologia pro Principibus Catholicis. Fol. 74 b. Antverp. 1542. [Au] Folio 74 of the 1542 edition of Eckius' 'Apologia for Catholic Principles'. [Ed]

[4] Hosii Opera, De Expresso Dei Verbo. Tom. I. p. 628. [Au] Hosius, 'On the Express Word of God', vol. 1 p. 628. [Ed]

private conceit and fantasy; but, as near as God gives us grace, according to the plain and natural sense of the same, agreeable unto the rule or proportion of faith, which being approved by the ancient fathers, and catholic Church of Christ, in all matters necessary to eternal salvation: not bringing a new and strange sense, which is without the Scriptures, to seek confirmation thereof in the Scriptures (as the manner of heretics is rightly noted by Clemens[5]); but out of the Scriptures themselves seek we the exposition of such obscure places as we find them, being persuaded with St. Augustine,[6] that nothing in a manner is found out of those obscure and dark places, which many not be found to be most plainly spoken in other places. And as for the approved sense of the holy ancient fathers, and catholic Church of the eldest and purest times, if the Papists dare stand unto it for the deciding of many of the most weighty controversies that are between us, there is no doubt but they should soon and easily be determined, as has been showed in divers and many treatises, written against them. In which if any thing be brought so plainly expounding the Scripture against their Popish heresies, as nothing can be more express nor clear, then they are driven to seek new and monstrous expositions of those fathers' interpretations; or else they answer, "They are but those fathers' private expositions"; appealing to the catholic Church's interpretation, which is nothing else but their own private conceit and fancy, having no record to prove that catholic Church's interpretation but the present heretical opinions of this late degenerated anti-Christian congregation. And when they have discoursed never so much of the catholic Church's interpretation, they reduce and submit all men's judgments to the determination of their councils, and the decrees of the councils to the approbation of their Pope; which, as he is oftentimes a wicked man of life, so is he ignorant and unlearned in the Scriptures; to whose most private censure the Holy Scriptures themselves, and all sense and exposition of them, is made subject, under colour [on the pretense] that Christ, praying for Peter that his faith should not fail in temptation, gave all Popes such a prerogative, that they could not err in faith; though they were wicked of life, void of learning, ignorant in the Scriptures, destitute of the Spirit of God; as is proved most invincibly by example of diverse popes that have been heretics, and maintainers of such errors as are not now in controversy between us (lest they should say we beg the principle), but of the sect of the Arians, Monothelites, Eutychians, Saducees, and such other.

5. The original text of the Holy Scripture we alter not, either by adding, taking away, or changing of any letter or syllable, for any private purpose; which were not only a thing most wicked and sacrilegious, but also vain and impossible. For, seeing not only so many ancient copies of the original text are extant in diverse places of the world, which we cannot, if we would, corrupt, and that the same are multiplied, by printing, into so many thousand examples; we should be rather mad than foolish, if we did but once attempt such a matter, for maintenance of any of our opinions. As also it is incredible that Marcion, the mouse of Pontus, could corrupt all the Greek copies in the world (as Lindanus, of whom you borrowed that conceit, imagines), in those places in which he is charged by Tertullian. For Marcion's heresy was not so generally received by the Greek Church, that all men would yield unto him; neither was Tertullian so sound of judgment in the Latin Church, that whatsoever he judged to be a corruption in Marcion, must of necessity be so taken. But if adding and detracting from the Scripture be proper notes of heretics, who can purge Stephen Gardiner and Gregory Martin? – the one, for adding unto a verse of the psalm this pronoun *se, himself*, to prove the carnal presence, citing it thus, *Escam se dedit timentibus eum*, "He gave himself to be meat to them that fear him"; whereas the words of the prophet, according to the Hebrew, Greek, and Latin, are no more but, *Escam dedit*, "He has given meat",[7] &c. – the other, in his fond book of schism,[8] citing this text out of 1 Cor. x. as many Papists do against the certainty of faith, *Qui stat, videat ne cadat*, "He that stands, let him take heed he fall not"; whereas not only the truth of the Greek, but even the vulgar Latin translation has, *Qui se existimat stare*, "He that thinks or supposes that he stands, let him take heed that he fall not" [1 Corinthians 10:12]. But of such additions and detractions, used by the Romish rats, far worse than the mice of Pontus, we shall have more occasion to speak hereafter.

6. As touching false and heretical translations, which is the chief argument of this book, I doubt not but, by

[5] Clem. Alexandr. Stromatum VII. p. 890. Ed. Potter. Venet. 1757. [Hartshorne] Book seven of Clement of Alexandria's *Stromateis* or 'Miscellanies'. [Ed]

[6] Augustinus de Doctrina Christiana. Lib. II. 14. [Au] Augustine's *On Christian Doctrine* 2.14. See above, 34. [Ed]

[7] "Wherein (in the sacrament of the altar) God instituted *memoriam mirabilium suorum, et escam se dedit timentibus eum; that is to say*, 'a memory of his marvels, and gave himself meat to them that lovingly fear him'". Gardiner's "Detection of the Devil's Sophistrie, wherein he robs the unlearned people of the true belief in the most blessed Sacrament of the aulter". London, 1546. fol. 69. b. See Psalm 111:4-5. [Hartshorne]

[8] Martin's "Treatise of Schism, showing that all Catholics ought in any wise to abstain altogether from heretical Conventicles, viz. their Prayers, Sermons, &c." Douay, 1578. [Hartshorne]

the grace of God, to clear our English translators from any wilful corruptions for the maintenance of any error or heresy; such as were those of the Arians and Pelagians, which Gregory Martin, as though he uttered some great piece of skill, does so diligently express. I shall have occasion also to show, that the Papists themselves of our times, maintaining their corrupt vulgar translation against the truth of the original texts of Greek and Hebrew, are most guilty of such corruption and falsification; whereof although they be not the first authors, yet, by obstinate defending of such errors, they may prove worse than they which did first commit them. For the authors of that vulgar translation might be deceived, either for lack of exact knowledge of the tongues, or by some corrupt and untrue copies which they followed, or else perhaps that which they had rightly translated, by fault of the writers and negligence of the times might be perverted; but these men frowardly justifying all errors of that translation, however they have been brought in, do give plain testimony that they are not led with any conscience of God's truth, but wilfully carried with purpose of maintaining their own errors; lest, if they did acknowledge the error of the Romish Church in that one point, they should not be able to defend any one iota of their heresy, whose chief colour is the credit and authority of that particular and false Church, rather than any reason or argument out of the holy Scriptures, or testimony of the most ancient Christian and catholic Church ...

7. Who allows, or who can abide chopping and changing, or hacking and hewing, the sacred text of holy Scriptures? As for the perplexities, whereunto you feign that wilful heresy and arrogance has driven us, is of your weaving; for (God be praised!) we can well enough with good conscience and sound knowledge, that may abide the judgment of all the learned in the world, defend both the Hebrew text of the Old Testament and the Greek text of the New; not of purpose to discredit the vulgar Latin translation and the expositions of the Fathers, but to fetch the truth, upon which the hope of our salvation is grounded, out of the first fountains and springs, rather than out of any streams that are derived from them. And this we do agreeable to the ancient Fathers' judgments. For who knows not what fruitful pains St. Jerome took in translating the Scripture out of the original tongue? Neither would he be dissuaded by St. Augustine,[9] who although he misliked that enterprise at the first, yet afterward he highly commended the necessity of the Greek and Hebrew tongue for Latin men, to find out the certain truth of the text in the infinite variety of the Latin interpretations; for thus he writes, *De Doct. Christ.* lib. 2, cap. 11: *Contra ignota signa propria magnum remedium est linguarum cognitio. Et Latinae*, &c.

> Against unknown proper signs the knowledge of tongues is a great remedy. And truly men of the Latin tongue, whom we have now taken in hand to instruct, have need also of two other tongues unto the knowledge of the divine Scriptures, namely, the Hebrew and the Greek, that recourse may be had unto the former copies, if the infinite variety of the Latin interpreters shall bring any doubt; although we find oftentimes in the books Hebrew words not interpreted, as *Amen*, *Alleluia*, *Racha*, *Osanna*, &c.,

and a little after, *Sed non propter haec pauca, &c.*

> But not for these few words which to mark and inquire of it is a very easy thing, but for the diversities (as it is said) of the interpreters, the knowledge of those tongues is necessary. For they that have interpreted the Scriptures out of the Hebrew tongue into the Greek tongue may be numbered, but the Latin interpreters by no means can be numbered. For in the first times of the faith, as a Greek book came into every man's hand, and he seemed to have some skill in both the tongues, he was bold to interpret it. Which thing truly has more helped the understanding than hindered, if the readers be not negligent; for the looking upon many books has oftentimes made manifest sundry obscure or dark sentences.[10]

This is St. Augustine's sound judgment of the knowledge of tongues and diversity of interpretations, for the better understanding of the Scriptures. But let us see what be the absurdities that you gather of our defending the original texts of both the tongues. First, we must needs reject the Greek of the Old Testament, called Septuagint, as false, because it differs from the Hebrew, where it is not only different in words, but also contrary in sense. Why should we not? But if it retain the sense and substance, although it express not the same words, we need not reject it. St. Jerome,[11] who was required by Paula and Eustochium to expound the prophets, not only according to the truth of the Hebrew, but also after the translation of the

[9] De Doctrina Christiana, Lib. II. cap. 11, 12. Opera, Vol. III. pp. 24, 25. [Hartshorne] See Augustine, above, 32-33. [Ed]

[10] See Augustine, above, 32. [Ed]

[11] Comment. Hieronymi in Nahum. cap. 1. Opera, Vol. III. p. 1567. [Hartshorne] Chapter 1 of Jerome's commentary on Nahum. [Ed]

Septuagint, whereof he diverse times complains, upon the 1st of Nahum says expressly, that it was against his conscience always to follow the same. *Ignoscite prolixitati*, &c.

> Pardon me that I am so long, for I cannot, following both the story and the tropology or doctrine of manners, comprehend both briefly; most of all, seeing that I am so greatly tormented or troubled with the variety of the translation, and against my conscience sometimes I am compelled to frame a consequence of the vulgar edition,

which was the Septuagint.[12] This was St. Jerome's opinion of the Septuagint translation. But upon rejection of that translation (say you) it follows, that wheresoever those places, so disagreeing from the Hebrew, are cited by Christ, or the evangelists and apostles, there also they must be rejected, because they disagree from the Hebrew; and so the Greek text of the New Testament is not true, and consequently the words of our Saviour and writings of his apostles, speaking according to the Septuagint, must at least be reformed. It is an old saying, and a true, that one inconvenience being granted, many do follow; and so you may heap up a hundred after this manner. But for answer I say, that neither our Saviour, nor his apostles, citing any place out of the Old Testament, do bring anything disagreeing in sense and substance of matter (the purpose for which they allege it considered) from the truth of the Hebrew text. Therefore there is no need that the LXX. [Septuagint] in those places should be rejected. Although our Saviour Christ, speaking in the Syrian tongue, is not to be thought ever to have cited the text of the LXX., which is in Greek.[13] And his apostles and evangelists, using that text, regard the substance of the sentence, and not the form of words. For many times they cite not the very words of the Greek LXX. neither; and St. Jerome, *in Catalogo script. Eccles.* ['Toward a Catalogue of Ecclesiastical Writings'], which is set as a preface to St. Matthew's Gospel, tells you expressly, that in the Hebrew example of St. Matthew, which he had, wheresoever the evangelist St. Matthew, either in his own person, or in the person of our Lord and Saviour, uses the testimonies of the Old Testament, he follows not the authority of the seventy translators, but the Hebrew, of which these are two places: "Out of Egypt have I called my son" [Matthew 2:15, quoting Hosea 11:1], and "he shall be called a Nazarite".[14] See you not what a perilous perplexity we are in by defending both the Hebrew text of the Old Testament, and the Greek of the New, when neither are contrary to the other?

8. No whit of that does follow by striking out *qui fuit Cainan*, because it is not found in Moses; and therefore we have nothing to do to justify your vain consequence, grounded upon an absurdity of your own devising. But we must tell you, whether we will discredit the New Testament because of the Septuagint! No, not for a thousand millions of Septuagints, nor for all the world will we credit the Septuagint against the truth of the Old Testament. But whatsoever is cited out of the LXX. in the New, is not contrary to the Hebrew in the Old; and therefore the way of reconciliation is easily found, without discrediting both, or either of both, in those places. And in this place, which is a mere corruption, borrowed out of the corruption of the Septuagint, or a Judaical addition, Genesis xi., I think there is no better way of reconciling than to strike it clean out, as Beza has done; which generation neither is in the Hebrew verity, nor in your own vulgar Latin translation, either Genesis xi., or 1 Par. i.[15] Beside that it makes a foul error in the computation of time, adding no less than two hundred and thirty years between Arphaxad and Sala,[16] more than the Hebrew verity, or the vulgar Latin agreeing therewith, does number. And therefore he was more presumptuous, that out of the corrupt and false text of the Septuagint added the same unto the genealogy in St. Luke, than Beza, which by the authority of Moses removed the same. If you will still persist to defend the authority of the Septuagint against the Hebrew verity, which like an atheist you deride, at leastwise defend your own vulgar Latin translation of the Old Testament, and deliver yourself out of that perplexity in which you would place us between the Hebrew of the Old and the Greek of the New Testament; seeing no less doubts entangles you between the Latin of the New, and the Latin of the Old, differing altogether alike as the Greek and the Hebrew do.

---

12 Jerome's references to a "vulgar edition" in the letter to Pammachius, above (26, 27, 29), are unclear. Jerome's translator Paul Carroll took them to refer to Jerome's own Vulgate translation, which was not yet written; Fulke takes them to refer to the Septuagint. [Ed]

13 Jesus and his followers are thought to have spoken Aramaic, a northwestern or north-central Semitic language that appears in the Old Testament books of Daniel and Ezra; Syriac was a dialect of East Aramaic. [Ed]

14 Matthew 2:23 ('Nazarene', someone from Nazareth), misquoting Judges 13:5 ('Nazarite', ancient Jewish ascetic). Jerome treats both passages in his letter to Pammachius, above, 27. [Ed]

15 The two Old Testament books of Chronicles, perhaps because they were initially left out of the Biblical canon, were given the Greek title *Paralipomena* or 'Things Omitted'. [Ed]

16 Or, as most English translations have it, Arpachshad (the father) and Shelah (the son). See Genesis 11:10-12. [Ed]

9. Here of pity you will show unto us a piece of learning, how the fathers reconcile the said Hebrew and Greek without violence to the text, as they do always, or else leave the matter to God.

First, St. Augustine, *De Civitate*, lib. 18, cap. 43, *De Doct. Chr.* lib. 2, cap. 15, of their agreement, notwithstanding they were separated into several cells, gathers, that those Septuagints were inspired with the same prophetical spirit of interpreting, that the prophets were in foreshowing.[17] But this does St. Jerome utterly deny, and derides the ground of this imagination, those seventy-two cells at Alexandria, as a fable and a lie.[18] That St. Ambrose says, "we have found that many things are not idly added of the seventy Greek interpreters";[19] we confess as much, where their addition serves for explication of that which is contained in the Hebrew; and so means Ambrose; not that they had authority to add anything which Moses had omitted. And we acknowledge with St. Jerome, that there may be many reasons given for the difference of the one from the other.

10. You shall never be able to prove by any translation of ours (though perhaps in some we may err) that we have any purpose either to falsify the truth, or to change the text, though it were possible for us. In translating we have dealt with a good conscience, albeit not always peradventure we have attained to the full truth, which in translating out of one tongue into another is a very hard point thoroughly to observe. Your example of 'ordinances' translated for that which in the Greek is 'justifications' and 'traditions', when you show where and by whom it is so translated, you shall receive an answer. In the meantime I say, a translator that has regard to interpret for the ignorant people's instruction may sometimes depart from the etymology or common signification or precise turning of word for word, and that for diverse causes. You yourselves translate not *ecclesia* always 'the church', but sometimes the assembly; nor *seniores*, 'elders', but seniors, or ancients. Neither would you translate *presbyter* always 'a priest', if you translated the Old Testament. In the story of Susannah you would not call them priests, that laid wait for her honesty and life; yet in your vulgar Latin they are called priests [Luke 8:3]. So are they called πρεσβντεροι in Greek in the New Testament, which you turn sometimes priests, sometimes ancients, and sometimes seniors.

11. By false translations wilfully and of purpose to falsify the truth of God's word is as gross and as abominable treachery as to corrupt the very text; although I think St. Paul, speaking of the covertures, or cloaks of dishonesty, and adultering of the word of God, 2 Cor. iv. means a further cunning than false translations [2 Corinthians 4:2]. That those whom you call heretics find fault with one another's translations, they do none otherwise than you Popish heretics. Do not you, Gregory Martin, in the 7th chapter and 33rd section of this book, find fault with all the Catholics, as you term them, that translate *sheol*, *sepulchrum*, 'a sepulchre', and not always 'hell'? If Bucer or Zuinglius do justly observe any error in Luther, or Luther in Münster, or Beza in Castalio, the Anabaptist, or Calvin in Servetus, the horrible heretic, yea, and if froward and schismatical Illyricus can discover any error committed by Calvin and Beza, the truth loses nothing, when the errors of men are found out, by what means soever. That you speak of the puritans controlling the grosser Calvinists of our country, I know not what you mean, neither do I think you can justify your words, for translation of the Scriptures. Where you say, the later translations of the selfsame heretics control the former exceedingly, not only of oversights, but of wilful falsifications, it is a wilful and impudent slander; yet you blush not to say, it is notorious. How, I pray you? You answer, In the later editions of Luther and Beza, and in our English Bibles set forth in diverse years, from Tyndal, their first translator. That Luther, Beza, and the later translators of the English Bibles, have corrected some small faults that have escaped in their former editions, it may be granted. But do Luther and Beza therefore accuse themselves, or the later English translators the former, of wilful falsifications? I think those brute beasts, to whom Ambrose[20] ascribes the art of making syllogisms (if they could speak), would not conclude thus brutishly. Certain it is that Balaam's ass did reason substantially [Numbers 22:21-33]. But much more, you say, the English translators of Beza's New Testament do control him and his translation, being sometimes afraid and ashamed to express his false translations. If it be so, they are more modest than you, which seem to be afraid or ashamed of nothing so much, as lest you might seem to fail in unshamefacedness. But to the purpose. If they think Beza (as all men may err) has somewhat trodden awry, is it a fault to avoid his step, or a proud controlling or accusing him of falsification? Nevertheless, whereinsoever Luther, Beza, or the English translators have reformed any of their former oversights, the matter is not so great that it can make a heresy. Yea, if you were of St. Augustine's judgment, you would acknowledge that the multitude and diversity of translations is for the benefit of them that be ignorant in the tongues,

[17] See Augustine, *City of God* 18.43 and *On Christian Doctrine* 2.15 (for which see above, 34). [Ed]

[18] Praefat. in Pentateuch. [Au] For this remark from Jerome's *Preface to the Pentateuch*, see above, 30. [Ed]

[19] Hexam. lib. 3. cap. 6. [Au] Ambrose, *On the Six Days of Creation* 3.6. [Ed]

[20] Hexam. lib. 6, cap. [Au] Ambrose, *On the Six Days of Creation* 6.4. [Ed]

yea, and of them also that be learned in them oftentimes, that of diverse men's translations they may judge which is the aptest.[21]

The Holy Scriptures Should Always Be in Our Mother Tongue
From 'Confutation of the Rhemists' Preface', *Confutation of the Rhemist Testament* (1589)

1. If the whole Bible had been translated by you, and that long since, into the English tongue, it is marvel that it has lain so long by you, for lack of good means to publish it. You have published books of as great charge, and much less importance, within these eight and twenty years; but such, indeed, by which you had more hope to win unto your credit and cause than you have by the Holy Bible, though you perverted it with never so partial translation, and poisoned it with never so heretical and blasphemous annotations, as you have done your edition of the New Testament. You were wont to boast of the zeal of Popes, cardinals, and other great prelates of the Romish sect for the conversion of our nation unto their obedience. Were they also so straight-laced that none of them can find in their purses to bear the charges of printing a work so necessary, or at leastwise profitable, as you hold the translation of the Scriptures to be for the maintenance of the Catholic religion? Or do you not rather, as the family of love used to do, for their works, craftily beg of your favourers in England larger exhibition upon colour of printing your translation of the Bible? When it is not hard to gather that you were purposed indeed to set it forth, and would use such means as you may, in those parts, the forbearing of the money, though your printer took it upon interest, might be paid for in the sale of one impression, although it so might happen that a number of them were confiscated, or miscarried in the ways, as chanced to some of these your books. But whoso sees what unnecessary charge you have put yourselves unto in printing this your translation of so large a volume[22] may easily perceive you set it not forth for poor men's profit, and that by so excessive price, of so small a part of the whole Bible, you mean to discourage your friends from waiting for all the rest: what advantage you have in this part, for deciding the doubts of these days, we shall examine in the several places where you pretend to take it.

2. You are afraid to give over your old impudent proposition that ignorance of the Scriptures is the mother of Popish devotion. And therefore you hold it an erroneous opinion "That the holy Scriptures should be always in our mother tongue, or that they ought, or were ordained by God, to be read indifferently of all". Whereas it is certain that the Holy Scripture of the Old Testament was by God's ordinance first written in the mother-tongue of the Jews, and the New Testament in the Greek tongue, which was the mother-tongue to a great part of the world, and that language, which was most generally understood among the Gentiles, unto whom the Gospel was preached. Our Saviour Christ commands not only a reading, as you yourselves confess, but also a deep search of the Scriptures, unto all the Jews indifferently. Paul commands the education of Timothy in knowledge of the Scriptures from his infancy [2 Timothy 3:15]. Which authorities prove that the Holy Scriptures were ordained by God to be read and known indifferently of all, and therefore ought to be translated into the mother tongues of all nations, that all may read and know them. Another erroneous opinion they account it to think that the Scriptures can be easily understood of everyone that reads or hears them in a known language, which if it were admitted, yet it follows not that the Scriptures ought not to be in a known language because they cannot be easily understood of everyone that reads or hears them, but rather that everyone that reads or hears them ought more diligently to study and exercise himself in them, more often hear and read them, and more fervently pray to God for aid of his Spirit, that he may understand them.[23] And yet it is certain that albeit some places of the Scripture are not easy to be understood of all men, yet there are many parts of them, and so many as are able to instruct us unto salvation, so plain and easy, as they may be understood of everyone that reads or hears them. And of this judgment is Augustine, answering this objection of the obscurity of the Scriptures:

> Therefore has the Holy Ghost magnifically and wholesomely so tempered the holy Scriptures that by plain and open places he might prevail against famine: by dark places, he might wipe away loathsomeness. For nothing almost is gathered out of those obscurities which is not found most plainly uttered in some other place.

– *De doct. Christ. lib. 2, cap. 6.*[24] And in the chapter immediately before, he shows that by reason of the diversity of languages, the same sound of words, not serving all nations, the Scriptures were translated into

[21] De Doct. Christ. lib. 2 cap. 11. [Au] See Augustine, above, 32. [Ed]

[22] The Rheims New Testament comprised 745 pages of annotated translation, a 22-page preface, and 27 pages of other unpaginated apparatus (keys, glossaries). [Ed]

[23] I.e., even if it is true that the Scriptures are sometimes difficult to understand, what follows from that is not that they should be kept in Latin but that the lay public should be trained in their correct interpretation. [Ed]

[24] See Augustine, above, 32. [Ed]

divers tongues, that they might be generally known.

> Whereof it is come to pass that even the holy Scriptures, by which so great diseases of men's wits are helped, being proceeded from one tongue, which might conveniently spread over all the world, through divers languages of the interpreters, being dispersed far and wide, might become known of the nations to their salvation.[25]

By both of which places, it is evident that Augustine deemed it more convenient in itself, and more agreeable to God's word, honour, and edification of the faithful, to have the Scripture turned into vulgar tongues than to be kept and studied in any learned language whatsoever. Now why you should account any one tongue, more than other, to be ecclesiastical, you are able to give no sound reason, seeing God has called his Church of all tongues and nations, and sanctified them all, to the preaching of the Gospel and praise of his name. As for the Latin tongue, which you would most willingly have to be counted an ecclesiastical tongue, it was for many hundred years after Christ the common vulgar and popular tongue in most part of the west Churches, of those nations that were subject to the Roman empire. And why it is now ecclesiastical that then was vulgar, I know no cause but that Antichrist, whose tongue it is, blasphemously challenging to be the head of the Church has chosen and authorized it to be ecclesiastical in contumely of all other languages which the Holy Ghost, descending upon the Apostles, in cloven tongues, has consecrated to the preaching of Christ Jesus and to the magnifying and setting forth of the great praises of God. That through man's malice, or infirmity, the Scriptures are often made pernicious and hurtful to many, it is no greater reason to keep them from the knowledge of most men than it were to deprive all men from meat and drink because many do abuse them to the destruction of both their bodies and souls. As for the special consideration that procured this edition, when you express it, we may better judge of it. In the meantime, we can conceive none others but that which is the practice of many heretics, when you could not altogether suppress the knowledge of the Holy Scriptures, whereby your errors are discovered, you thought it the next way for your purpose, by your partial translations, as much as you could, to obscure them, and by your heretical annotations to pervert them, that the one should make them unprofitable and the other hurtful.

3. The wisdom of the Popish Synagogue and the governors thereof is the wisdom of the old serpent, and of the children of this world, who are often wiser in their kind than the children of light, with whom it is a high point of prudence to provide for themselves by any unjust means whatsoever. So have the Popish clergy always endeavoured, by depriving the common people of the reading of holy Scriptures and following their predecessors the Jewish lawyers [Sadducees], have taken away the key of knowledge, of the same policy, that they did, lest their wickedness being commonly discovered by the light, they should lose that estimation which through blind ignorance they have commonly obtained. They who have made claim for the common people in this case, whom, of your charity, you call the populace and their seditious leaders, of godly zeal and true simplicity, not of curiosity, pride and disobedience, have both made it, and justified it, with better reasons can be alleged, than the authority of God in the Old Testament, and of Christ, our Saviour and his Apostles in the New, and the practice of the primitive church, and the consent of the most ancient and approved Fathers of the same, which have been brought to prove that the Holy Scriptures ought to be known of all Christians! But the Governors of the Popish Antichristian Church, arrogating to themselves the name and dignity of the dispensing of God's mysteries and treasures, among which, as you confess, the Holy Scriptures are no small store; by maintaining that ignorance is the mother of devotion, declare, if they could, that they would willingly abolish all knowledge of the Holy Scriptures from the common people's hearts. And whereas you say, "that of old, they have not ever condemned all vulgar versions of the Scripture, nor generally forbidden the faithful to read them"; let the registers of bishops be searched, where it will appear that many have been accused and condemned as heretics for having, reading, or hearing the holy Scriptures in the English tongue, without any exception taken against the truth of the translation. And that the governors of the Popish Church "have not by public authority prescribed, commanded, or authentically ever recommended any interpretation of Scripture into the vulgar tongue to be indifferently used of all men"; they have declared sufficiently thereby that they were not the ministers of God and Christ, nor successors of his apostles, nor of the ancient fathers of the primitive church, all of whom, by public and lawful authority, always prescribed, commanded, and authentically recommended, as the Holy Bible and the writings of the fathers are most plentiful witnesses, the Holy Scriptures of God to be known, read, and understood of all Christians indifferently, and without exception of any; which of necessity implies the translation of the same into all vulgar languages, without which it is not possible for all sorts of Christians to read them, know them, and understand them.

4. Seeing the Armenians were converted to the faith long before Chrysostom went among them, it is

[25] See Augustine, above, 32. [Ed]

not to be doubted but that they had the whole Scriptures in their vulgar tongue long before this time.[26] And their confession lately set forth does plainly argue that they have the whole Bible in their own language at this day. To justify that the Sclavonians say of Hieronym's translation into their tongue, his own words are these: "I say not this that I would bite my predecessors, or think that anything is to be detracted from them, whose translation being most diligently corrected, I have given long ago to the men of my language". Now the Sclavonians were the men of Hieronym's language, or mother-tongue, as he testifies himself of the place of his nativity, *in catalogo*;[27] for whose use he might translate the vulgar Latin Bible, which was according to the Septuagint, after he had most diligently corrected it. But if this place prove it not sufficiently, at least he says plainly that the Scriptures were translated into the tongues of many nations. *Prefat. ad Damasum in evangelia* ['Preface to Damasus on the Gospel']. Besides these, the Syrians, Arabians, and Ethiopians had of ancient time the holy Scriptures in their several languages.[28] The Spaniards of ancient time had the Old Testament translated into their mother tongue. Walafridus [Strabo] testifies that the Dutch tongue is the same which was the language of the Goths and Gethes, into which, since the days of Ulphilas, by whom they were first converted, some wise man of that nation translated the holy Scriptures. *De reb. eccles. cap. 7* ['On Ecclesiastical Matters', ch. 7]. In our own country, not only the Saxon translations of diverse parts of the Holy Scriptures but the testimony of Bede, whom you quote and cite most impudently, does prove that vulgar translations of the Holy Scriptures in his time were commonly used and occupied by the multitude. His words are these:

> This island at this present, according to the number of books in which the law of God is written, does search out and confess, one and the self-same knowledge of the highest truth, and of the true height in five tongues; namely, of the Angles, Britons, Scots, Picts, and Latins, which in meditation of the Scripture is made common to all the rest.

He means that men of all the four nations studied the Scriptures by help of the Latin tongue, and such commentaries and treatises of the elder Fathers as were written therein. But he says expressly that the knowledge of the highest truth, which is not to be found but in the Holy Scriptures, and according thereunto was both searched out and confessed in the mother tongue of the other four nations, by whom he means the Christians unlearned in the Latin tongue.

That the Scriptures were current in English, both before and after Wycliffe's time, and not of his translation, beside your conjecture out of Lyndwood, is manifestly proved by many ancient written copies of the English Bible, differing in translation, yet to be showed, of which Wycliffe's translation could be but one. Notwithstanding that the Pharisaical clergy condemned the reading of them for heresy, let the acts of public writings remaining in the Registers testify. And of what devilish policy they kept the laws of God in secrecy and silence, which he commanded to be uttered in all places and times, to the edifying of all sorts of Christians, howsoever you seek to smooth and cover it, God's children do plainly espy it.

5. How pernicious heretical translations of the Scriptures are which poison the people under colour of divine authority; if we had not learned sufficiently by the corruptions of old heretics, this translation of yours does give plentiful testimony, which being helped forward with heretical annotations, as it were with stings, to make way for the poison to enter, has no small force to deceive the simple. But the best is, we are assured that they shall not prevail finally, but in them whom the Lord acknowledges not for his.[29] In the meantime, not only the remedy of true and sincere translation, out of the fountain and original text, is to be opposed, but also the fraud of the adversary, as occasion serves, to be discovered and laid open.

6. The Popish Church arrogating to herself divine wisdom, in restraining that which God has left to be

[26] The Armenians were converted to Christianity in 300, over a century before Chrysostom was exiled there, by St. Gregory the Illuminator (240-332). Unfortunately for Fulke's supposition, he converted them not with Bible translations and catechisms but by converting the Arsacid king Tiridates III, who then simply decreed that all his subjects must be baptized. The Armenian Bible was undertaken by Mesrop Mastoc and two pupils c. 405/6, while Chrysostom was still in Armenia, and probably finished soon after. [Ed]

[27] Jerome was born in what was recently Yugoslavia, and his Slavic native language would have been closely related to that spoken by the Sclaveni. *In Catalogo scriptorum Ecclesiasticorum* is Jerome's preface to St. Matthew's Gospel. [Ed]

[28] There were at least two ancient Syriac translations of the Bible, the Old Syriac (pre-fifth-century) and the Peshitta, possibly done by Rabbula, Bishop of Edessa, c. 411-35. Scholars speculate that Arabic translations of the entire Bible may have existed before Islam; the earliest known translation is of the prophetic books by the priest El-Alam from the ninth or tenth century. Ethiopic translations probably date from the fifth or sixth century; the only extant mss are from the sixteenth to eighteenth centuries. [Ed]

[29] I.e., the 'stings' of Catholic translations will only poison those whom God rejects, Catholics. [Ed]

most free and general, declares that she is the Babylonical harlot, the spouse of Antichrist [Revelation 18], who exalts himself above all divine authority and controls the wisdom of God in everything that is contrary to his devilish presumption: as in the use of images, of the cup in the Lord's Supper, of marriage in the Church ministers, of meats in times made by him more religious, and such other.[30] The true Church of God teaches the true use of the Scriptures, even out of the Scriptures themselves, and discourages not men from reading of them, as it were from a dangerous discourse, whereby they are like to take harm, knowing that none but spiders can suck poison out of wholesome flowers, which poison yet is not in the good flowers, but in the evil nature of the spider. The Holy Scriptures, learned even from a man's infancy, are able to make him wise unto salvation, and being well studied of the man of God, are able to make him perfect and ready unto all good works, and to execute every part of his office. – *2 Tim. 3.15 &c.*

John Florio

John Florio (1553?-1625), the renowned translator of Montaigne's *Essays*, was for most of his life a teacher of foreign languages in London and the companion of most of the well-known writers of the day; critics have suggested that Shakespeare's Holofernes in *Love's Labour's Lost* was a satire on Florio, and it is certain that Shakespeare drew heavily on Florio's translation of Montaigne's 'On Cannibals' in writing *The Tempest*.

Florio was born to a Florentine Protestant, Michelangelo Florio, who fled persecution in his native Italy and arrived in England some time in the 1540s. His father, like him a language teacher and translator, was also like him in being hot-headed and impetuous (during Florio's childhood he was cut off by his patrons for gross immorality) – both personality traits that lend verve and excitement to the Montaigne translations.

Florio grew up in Oxford, and around 1576 became tutor in foreign languages to the son of the Bishop of Durham, Emmanuel Barnes; in 1581 he matriculated at Magdalen College, Oxford, where he also taught foreign languages. Over the next two decades he did a number of translations, mostly from the Italian, threw himself body and soul into the literary intrigues of London, where he moved at some point in the period, and composed an Italian-English dictionary (1598).

His translation of Montaigne was completed and licensed to Edward Blount in 1599, but the book did not appear until 1603; it was immediately received, and continues today to be regarded, as a brilliant rendition of Montaigne's quirky, angular style. That same year, he was appointed reader in Italian to Queen Anne; the next year, gentleman-extraordinary and groom of the privy chamber, a position he retained until 1620, when he fled London due to the plague, to Fulham, where he resided until his death in 1625.

The Epistle Dedicatory
From translation of Montaigne's *Essays* (1603)

To the Right Honorable my best-best Benefactors, and most-most honored Ladies, Lucy [Russell] Countess of Bedford; and her best-most loved-loving Mother, Lady Anne Harington

Strange it may seem to some, whose seeming is misseeming, in one worthless patronage to join two so severally all-worthy ladies. But to any in the right it would be judged wrong to disjoin them in aught who never were nearer in kind than ever in kindness. None dearer (dearest ladies) I have seen, and all may say to your honorable husbands, than you, to you than your honorable husbands; and than to other than either is to the other. So as were I to name but the one, I should surely intend the other; but intending this dedication to two, I could not but name both. To my last birth, which I held masculine (as are all men's conceits that are their own, though but by their collecting; and this was to Montaigne like Bacchus,[1] closed in, or loosed from his great Jupiter's thigh) I the indulgent father invited two right honorable godfathers, with the one of your noble ladyships to witness. So to this defective edition (since all translations are reputed females, delivered at second hand; and I in this serve but as Vulcan, to hatchet this Minerva from that Jupiter's big brain[2]) I

[30] Fulke refers to heated doctrinal controversies between Protestants and Catholics over idolatry, the nature of Jesus' presence in communion, clerical celibacy, and the nature of feast and fast. [Ed]

[1] Bacchus, Roman god of wine; in the original Greek story, when Semele was six months pregnant with Dionysus/Bacchus, sired on her by Zeus, she refused to sleep with Zeus, who in a rage consumed her with lightning. Hermes rescued the fetus and sewed him up in Zeus's thigh, whence he was delivered three months later; thus Dionysus's byname 'twice-born'. [Ed]

[2] Minerva, Roman goddess of wisdom; in the original Greek story, Zeus lusted after the Titaness Metis ('counsel'), and when she would not give herself to him, swallowed her whole. Several months later, suffering from a severe headache, he had Hephaestus (Roman Vulcan) split open his skull with an axe, and out sprang Athene (Minerva), fully armed for battle. [Ed]

yet at least a fondling foster-father, having transported it from France to England; put it in English clothes; taught it to talk our tongue (though many times with a jerk of the French jargon); would set it forth to the best service I might; and to better I might not than you that deserve the best. Yet hath it this above your other servants: it may not only serve you two, to repeat in true English what you read in fine French, but many thousands more, to tell them in their own what they would be taught in another language. How nobly it is descended, let the father in the ninth chapter of his third book ['Of Vanity'] by letters testimonial of the Roman Senate and city bear record: how rightly it is his, and his beloved, let him by his discourse in the eighth of his second ['Of the Affection of Fathers to their Children'], written to the Lady of Estissac (as if it were to you concerning your sweet heir, most motherly affected Lady Harrington) and by his acknowledgement in this first to all readers give evidence, first that it is *de bonne foy* ['in good faith'], then more than that, *c'est moy* ['it's me']: how worthily qualified, embellished, furnished it is, let his fair-spoken and fine-witted daughter by alliance pass her verdict, which she need not recant. Herehence to offer it into your service, let me for him but do and say, as he did for his other-self, his peerless pair Steven de Boetie, in the 28th of this first ['Nine and Twenty Sonnets of Steven de La Boetie, to the Lady of Grammont'], and think he speaks to you my praise-surmounting Countess of Bedford, what he there speaks [Diane d'Andoins] to the Lady of Grammont Countess of Guissen: since as his master poet said,

> – *mutato nomine, de te*
> *Fabula narratur:* – Hor. ser. lib. i. *Sat.*
> i. 69[3]

> Do you but change the name,
> Of you is said the same:

So do her attributes accord to your demerits; whereof to run a long-breathed career, both so fair and large a field might invite me, and my in-burning spirits would incite me, if I were not held in by your sweet reining hand (*who have ever held this desire, sooner to exceed what you are thought, then be thought what you are not*) or should I not prejudice by premonstration your assured advantage, *When your value shall come to the weighing*. And yet what are you not that may excel? What weight would you not elevate in true balance of best judgments? More to be followed by glory, since you fly it; which yet many good fellow: most to be praised, for refusing all praises; which yet will press on virtue; will she, nill she. In which matter of fame (and that exceeding good) well may you (I doubt not) use the word which my author here (I fear) usurpeth:

> – *Virésque acquirit eundo.* – Virg. *Aen.*
> 1. 4, 175.[4]

> The further that she goeth,
> The more in strength she groweth:

Since (as in the original) if of his virtue or glory, more of yours, his archpoet might verify.

> *Ingrediturque solo, & caput inter*
> *nubila condit:* – 177.

> She (great and good) on earth doth move,
> Yet veils her head in heaven above:

But being by your limitless moderation locked in limits (*who more desire, nothing may be said, than too much*) though I can never say too much; as he of Carthage,[5] so I of your praiseworthiness, were better to say nothing than too little. For this in hand (if it may be so honored to kiss your Honor's gracious hand) if any grace or good be either afforded to it, or deserved by it, all that by the father, foster-father, and all that are of kin or kind unto it, must be to your Honor, grace, and goodness imputed and ascribed. For (that I may discharge me of all this, and charge you with your own; pardon Madame my plainness) when I with one chapter found myself overcharged, whereto the charge or choice of an honorable person, and by me not-to-be denied benefactor (noble and virtuous Sir Edward Wotton) had engaged me (which I finished in your house) your Honor having deigned to read it, without pity of my failing, my fainting, my labouring, my languishing, my gasping for some breath (O could so honorable be so pitiless? Madame, now do I flatter you?), yet commanded me on (and let me die outright ere I do not that command). I say not you took pleasure at shore (as those in this author) to see me sea-tossed, weather-beaten, shipwrecked, almost drowned (Mon. lib. iii. *c.* 1).[6] Nor say I like this man's Indian King, you checked with a sour-stern countenance the yearnful complaint of your drooping, near-dying subject (lib. iii. *c.* 6).[7] Nor say (as he allegeth out of others) like an ironically modest virgin, you

---

[3] Horace, *Satires* 1.69. [Ed]

[4] Virgil's *Aeneid*, book 1, chapter 4, line 175. The next quote is from line 177. [Ed]

[5] Aeneas, Virgil's hero, whom Dido, legendary founder of Carthage, wished to marry and make king; Mercury brought him the message that he was to depart immediately, and he did, withstanding her bitter reproaches in silence. See book four of the *Aeneid*. [Ed]

[6] Montaigne's *Essays*, Book 3, Chapter 1: 'Of Profit and Honesty'. [Ed]

[7] Book 3, chapter 6: 'Of Coaches'. [Ed]

induced, yea commanded, yea delighted to see me strive for life, yet fall out of breath (lib. ii. *c*. 23).[8] Unmerciful you were, but not so cruel. (Madame, now do I flatter you?) Yet this I may and must say, like in this Frenchman's report, our third in name, but first and chief in fame, K. Edward, you would not succour your black, not son, but servant, but bade him fight and conquer, or die (lib. i. *c*. 41).[9] Like the Spartan imperious mother, a shield indeed you gave me, but with this word. *Aut cum hoc; aut in hoc* (*Giou. Imp. Mar Pes.*). I must needs say while this was in doing, to put and keep me in heart like a captive cannibal fattened against my death, you often cried *coraggio* ['Courage!'] and called *ça ça* ['Yes, do that!'], and applauded as I passed, and if not fet me in, yet set me on, even with a siren's *o tresloüable Ulisse* (Mont. li. ii. *c*. 16).[10] O Madame who then spoke fair? As for me, I only say, as this man's embossed Hart out of hart (lib. ii. *c*. 11),[11] I sweat, I wept, and I went on, till now I stand at bay; howsoever, I hope that may yet save me which from others strangles others, I mean the collar you have put about my neck with your inscription, *Noli me caedere, nam sum Dianae* ["Do not kill/beat me, for I am Diana's"]. Yet nor can you deny, nor I dissemble, how at first I pleaded this author's tedious difficulty, my self-known insufficiency, and others' more leisureful ability. But no excuse would serve him that must serve without excuse. Little power had I to perform, but less to refuse what you imposed; for his length you gave time; for his hardness you advised help; my weakness you might bid do its best; others' strength you would not seek-for-further.

To the Courteous Reader
From his translation of Montaigne's *Essays* (1603)

Shall I apologize translation? Why but some hold (as for their freehold) that such conversion is the subversion of universities. God hold with them, and withhold them from impeach or impair. It were an ill turn, the turning of books should be the overturning of libraries. Yea but my old fellow Nolano told me, and taught publicly, that from translation all science had its offspring. Likely, since even philosophy, grammar, rhetoric, logic, arithmetic, geometry, astronomy, music, and all the mathematics yet hold their name of the Greeks; and the Greeks drew their baptising water from the conduit pipes of the Egyptians, and they from the well-springs from the Hebrews or Chaldees. And can the well-springs be so sweet and deep; and will the well-drawn water be so sour and smell? And were their countries so ennobled, advantaged, and embellished by such deriving; and doth it drive our noblest colonies upon the rocks of ruin? And did they well? and proved they well? and must we prove ill that do so? Why but learning would not be made common. Yea but learning cannot be too common, and the commoner the better. Why but who is not jealous, his mistress should be so prostitute? Yea but this mistress is like air, fire, water, the more breathed the clearer; the more extended the warmer; the more drawn the sweeter. It were inhumanity to coop her up, and worthy forfeiture close to conceal her. Why but scholars should have some privilege of preeminence. So have they; they only are worthy translators. Why but the vulgar should not know all. No, they cannot for all this; nor even scholars for much more: I would, both could and knew much more than either doth or can. Why but all would not be known of all. No nor can; much more we know not than we know; all know something, none know all; would all know all? they must break ere they be so big. God only; men far from God. Why but pearls should not be cast to swine; yet are rings put in their noses; and a swine should know his sty, and will know his meat and his medicine, and as much beside, as any swine doth suppose it to be marjoram. Why, but it is not well divinity should be a child's or old wife's, a cobbler's, or clothier's tale or table talk. There is use, and abuse; use none too much; abuse none too little. Why but let learning be wrapped in a learned mantle. Yea but to be unwrapped by a learned nurse; yea, to be lapped up again. Yea, and unlapped again. Else, hold we ignorance the mother of devotion; praying and preaching in an unknown tongue; as sorry a mother, as a seely [simple] daughter; a good mind perhaps, but surely an ill manner. If the best be meet for us, why should the best be barred? Why but the best wrote best in a tongue more unknown; nay in a tongue more known to them that wrote, and not unknown of them that speaks more learned. Yea such perhaps, as Quintilian's orator; a learned man I warrant him, for I understand him never a word. Why but let men write for the most honor of the writer. Nay, for most profit of the reader; and so haply, most honor. If to write obscurely be perplexedly offensive, as Augustus well judged; for our own not to write in our own but unintelligible is haply to fewer and more critical, but surely without honor, without profit, if he go not, or send not an interpreter; who else what is he but a translator? Obscure be he that loves obscurity. And therefore

[8] Book 2, chapter 23: 'Of Bad Means Employed to a Good End'. [Ed]

[9] Book 1, chapter 41: 'That a Man Should Not Communicate His Glory'. There Montaigne tells the story of the Battle of Crécy (1346) in the Hundred Years' War, decisively won by King Edward III of England and his son, Edward the Black Prince. [Ed]

[10] Book 2, chapter 16: 'Of Glory'. Montaigne is here quoting in French from the sirens' song to Odysseus in book twelve of the *Odyssey*; Florio renders the address "Ulisses thrice-renowned". [Ed]

[11] Book 2, chapter 11: 'Of Cruelty'.

willingly I take his word, though wittingly I do mistake it, *translata proficit.*[12] Why but who ever did well in it? Nay, who did ever well without it? If nothing can be now said, but hath been said before (as he said well) if there be no new thing under the sun. What is that that hath been? That that shall be (as he said that was wisest). What do the best then, but glean after others' harvest? borrow their colors, inherit their possessions? What do they but translate? perhaps, usurp? at least, collect? if with acknowledgement, it is well; if by stealth, it is too bad; in this, our conscience is our accuser, posterity our judge; in that our study is our advocate, and you readers our jury. Why but whom can I name, that bare a great name for it? Nay who great else, but either in part, as Plato and Aristotle out of many; Tully, Plutarch, Pliny out of Plato, Aristotle and many; or of purpose, as all that since have made most know the Greek, and almost the Latin, even translated their whole treatises? Why Cardan maintaineth, neither Homer's verse can be well expressed in Latin, nor Virgil's in Greek, nor Petrarch's in either. Suppose Homer took nothing out of any, for we hear of none good before him, and there must be a first; yet Homer by Virgil is often so translated as Scaliger conceives there is the armor of Hercules most puissant put on the back of Bacchus most delicate; and Petrarch, if well tracked, would be found in their footsteps, whose very garbage less poets are noted to have gathered. Why but that Scaliger thinks that Ficinus by his rustical simplicity translated Plato, as if an owl should represent an eagle, or some tara-rag player should act the princely Telephus[13] with a voice as ragged as his clothes, a grace as bad as his voice. If the famous Ficinus were so faulty, who may hope to [e]scape foot-free? But for him and us all let me confess, as he here censureth; and let confession make half amends, that every language hath its genius and inseparable form; without Pythagoras his metempsychosis it cannot rightly be translated.[14] The Tuscan altiloquence, the Venus of the French, the sharp state of the Spanish, the strong significancy of the Dutch cannot from here be drawn to life. The sense may keep form; the sentence is disfigured; the fineness, fitness, featness diminished, as much as art's nature is short of nature's art, a picture of a body, a shadow of a substance. Why then belike I have done by Montaigne as Terence by Menander, made of good French no good English. If I have done no worse, and it be no worse taken, it is well. As he, if no poet, yet am I not thief, since I say of whom I had it, rather to imitate his and his author's negligence than any back-biter's obscure diligence. His horse I set before you, perhaps without his trappings, and his meat without sauce. Indeed in this specially find I fault with my master, that as Crassus and Antonius in Tully,[15] the one seemed to condemn, the other not to know the Greeks, whereas the one so spoke Greek as he seemed to know no other tongue; the other in his travels to Athens and Rhodes had long conversed with the learnedest Grecians: so he, most writing of himself, and the worst rather than the best, disclaimeth all memory, authorities, or borrowing of the ancient or modern; whereas in course of his discourse he seems acquainted not only with all, but no other but authors; and could out of question like Cyrus or [Julius] Caesar call any of his army by his name and condition. And I would for us all he had in this whole body done as much as in most of that of other languages my peerless dear-dearest and never sufficiently commended friend hath done for mine and your ease and intelligence. Why then again, as Terence, I have had help. Yea, and thank them for it, and think you need not be displeased by them that may please you in a better manner. Why but essays are but men's school-themes pieced together; you might as well say, several texts. All is in the choice and handling. Yea marry; but Montaigne, had he wit, it was but a French with ferdillant, legier, and extravagant. Now say you English wits by the staidest censure of as learned a wit as is among you. The counsel of that judicious worthy Counsellor (honorable Sir Edward Wotton) would not have embarked me to this discovery, had not his wisdom known it worth my pains, and your perusing. And should or would any dog-toothed critic or adder-tongued satirist scoff or find fault, that in the course of his discourses, or web of his essays, or entitling of his chapters, he holdeth a disjointed, broken and gadding style; and that many times they answer not his titles, and have no coherence together, to such I will say little, for they deserve but little; but if they list [wish], else let them choose, I send them to the ninth chapter of the third book, folio 596 ['Of Vanity'], where himself preventeth their carping, and foreseeing their criticism answereth them for me at full. Yet are there herein errors. If of matter, the author's; if of omission, the printer's; him I would not amend, but send him to you as I found him: this I could not attend; but where I now find faults, let me pray and entreat you for your own sake to correct as you read; to amend as you list.

[12] Lit. "transferred [things] are useful"; *translata* here meant metaphors, but Florio deliberately read it to mean translated things, translations. [Ed]

[13] In Greek mythology, illegitimate son of Heracles and Auge, who was daughter of Aleus, king of Tegea, and later wife of King Teuthras of Mysia; Telephus later inherited the Mysian throne. [Ed]

[14] I.e., translation is like Pythagoras' theory of metempsychosis or the transmigration of souls: the meaning is the soul that leaves one verbal body and is transplanted into another. [Ed]

[15] In Cicero's *On the Orator*; see above, 7. [Ed]

But some errors are mine, and mine by more than translation. Are they in grammar or orthography? as easy for you to right as me to be wrong; or in construction, as misattributing him, her, or it, to things alive, or dead, or neuter; you may soon know my meaning, and eftsoons use your mending; or are they in some uncouth terms, as entrain, conscientious, endear, tarnish, comport, efface, facilitate, amusing, debauching, regret, effort, emotion, and such like; if you like them not, take others most commonly set by them to expound them, since there they were set to make such likely French words familiar with our English, which well may bear them. If any be capital in sense mistaking, be I admonished, and they shall be recanted. Howsoever, the falseness of the French prints, the diversities of copies, editions and volumes (some whereof have more or less than others), and I in London having followed some, and in the country others; now those in folio, now those in octavo, yet in this last survey reconciled all; therefore or blame not rashly or condemn not fondly[16] the multitude of them set for your further ease in a table (at the end of the book) which ere you begin to read, I entreat you to peruse: this printer's wanting a diligent corrector, my many employments, and the distance between me and my friends I should confer with, may extenuate, if not excuse, even more errors. In sum, if any think he could do better, let him try; then will he better think of what is done. Seven or eight of great wit and worth have assayed, but found these essays no attempt for French apprentices or Littletonians. If this done it may please you, as I wish it may, and I hope it shall, I with you shall be pleased: though not, yet still I am the same resolute John Florio.

George Chapman

George Chapman (1559/60-1634) wrote poetry and drama, and even shared Ben Jonson's cell in 1605 for writing a play that King James found offensive to Scotland; but he is best remembered for his translation of Homer, which remained the standard version at least until Pope's translation a century later – and a century after that, in 1815, it still inspired John Keats to write his famous sonnet, 'On First Looking into Chapman's Homer'.

Chapman attended Oxford University for a time without taking a degree; in his mid-twenties accepted a job in London in the household of Ralph Sadler; and in his early thirties participated in military action on the Continent. Most of his poetry and drama displays a fascination with the warrior-hero, from his paean to Sir Walter Raleigh in *De Guiana, Carmen Epicum* in 1596 to such late tragedies as *Bussy d'Ambois* (1607), *The Conspiracy, and Tragedie of Charles Duke of Byron* (1608), and *The Widdowes Tears* (1612).

And of course the warrior-hero figures centrally in Homer as well. Chapman published the first seven books of his *Iliad* in 1598, along with part of book 18 ('Achilles' Shield'), and the first twelve in 1609; the complete translation appeared in 1611, and the *Odyssey* followed five years later, in 1616. In addition to his imprisonment for sedition, Chapman was imprisoned twice for debt, once in 1600 and again in 1612, after the death of Prince Henry, who had promised to subsidize his Homeric translations.

His remarks on translation from the preface to the 1611 *Iliad* are notable less for their specific content than for their tone – for the impassioned defence of Homer and attack on Chapman's detractors, and for the earnest "I don't care what anybody says, I'm *okay*" defence of his own translation.

The Preface to the Reader
From his translation of the *Iliad* (1611)

Of all books extant in all kinds, Homer is the first and best. No one before his, Josephus affirms, nor before him, saith Velleius Paterculus, was there any whom he imitated, nor after him any that could imitate him. And what poesie may be no cause for detraction from all the eminence we give him, Spondanus (preferring it to all arts and sciences) unanswerably argues and proves. For to the glory of God and the singing of his glories (no man dares deny) man was chiefly made. And what art performs this chief end of man with so much excitation and expression as poesie – Moses, David, Salomon, Job, Esay [Isaiah], Jeremy [Jeremiah], &c. chiefly using that to the end abovesaid? And since the excellence of it cannot be obtained by the labor and art of man (as all easily confess it), it must needs be acknowledged a divine infusion. To prove which in a word this distich in my estimation serves something nearely:

> Great poesie, blind Homer, makes all see
> Thee capable of all Arts, none of thee.

For out of him, according to our most grave and judicial Plutarch, are all arts deduced, confirmed or illustrated. It is not therefore the world's vilifying of it that can make it vile, for so we might argue and blaspheme the most incomparably sacred. It is not of the world indeed, but (like truth) hides itself from it. Nor is there any such reality of wisdom's truth in all human excellence as in poets' fictions – that most vulgar and

[16] I.e., neither blame rashly nor condemn foolishly. [Ed]

foolish receipt [recipe] of poetical licence being of all knowing men to be exploded (accepting it as if poets had a tale-telling privilege above others), no artist being so strictly and inextricably confined to all the laws of learning, wisdom and truth as a Poet. For were not his fictions composed of the sinews and souls of all those, how could they defy fire, iron, and be combined with eternity? To all sciences, therefore, I must still (with our learned and ingenious Spondanus) prefer it, as having a perpetual commerce with the divine Majesty, embracing and illustrating all his most holy precepts and enjoying continual discourse with his thrice perfect and most comfortable spirit. And as the contemplative life is most worthily and divinely preferred by Plato to the active, as much as the head to the foot, the eye to the hand, reason to sense, the soul to the body, the end itself to all things directed to the end, quiet to motion and eternity to time, so much prefer I divine poesie to all worldly wisdom. To the only shadow of whose worth, yet I entitle not the bold rimes of every apish and impudent braggart (though he dares assume anything); such I turn over to the weaving of cobwebs, and shall but chatter on molehills (far under the hill of the Muses) when their fortunat'st [most fortunate] self-love and ambition hath advanced them highest. Poesie is the flower of the Sun and disdains to open to the eye of a candle. So kings hide their treasures and counsels from the vulgar – *ne evilescant* ["So as not to become debased"], saith our Spondanus. We have example sacred enough that true poesie's humility, poverty and contempt are badges of divinity, not vanity. Bray then, and bark against it, yet wolf-faced wordlings, that nothing but honours, riches and magistracy, *nescio quos turgide spiratis* (that I may use the words of our friend still) *qui solas leges Justinianas crepatis; paragraphum unum aut alterum, pluris quam vos ipsos facitis &c.*[1] I for my part shall ever esteem it much more manly and sacred in this harmless and pious study to sit till I sink into my grave than shine in your vainglorious bubbles and impieties – all your poor policies, wisdoms and their trappings at no more valuing than a musty nut. And much less I weigh the frontless detractions of some stupid ignorants that, no more knowing me than their own beastly ends, and I ever (to my knowledge) blest from their sight, whisper behind me vilifyings of my translation[2] – out of the French affirming them, when both in French and all other languages but his own our with-all-skill-enriched poet is so poor and unpleasing that no man can discern from whence flowed his so generally given eminence and admiration. And therefore (by any reasonable creature's conference of my slight comment and conversion) it will easily appear how I shun them and whether the original be my rule or not. In which he shall easily see I understand the understandings of all other interpreters and commenters in places of his most depth, importance and rapture. In whose exposition and illustration if I abhor from the sense that others wrest and rack out of him, let my best detractor examine how the Greek word warrants me. For my other fresh fry, let them fry in their foolish galls – nothing so much weighed as the barkings of puppies or foisting hounds, too vile to think of our sacred Homer or set their profane feet within their lives' lengths of his thresholds. If I fail in something, let my full performance in other some [something else] restore me – haste spurring me on with other necessities. For as at my conclusion I protest, so here at my entrance, less than fifteen weeks was the time in which all the last twelve books were entirely new translated – no conference had with anyone living in all the novelties I presume I have found. Only some one or two places I have showed to my worthy and most learned friend, M. Harriots, for his censure how much mine own weighed: whose judgement and knowledge in all kinds I know to be incomparable and bottomless – yea, to be admired as much as his most blameless life and the right sacred expense of his time is to be honoured and reverenced. Which affirmation of his clear unmatchedness in all manner of learning I make in contempt of that nasty objection often thrust upon me:– that he that will judge must know more than he of whom he judgeth, for so a man should know neither God nor himself. Another right learned, honest and entirely loved friend of mine, M. Robert Hews, I must needs put into my confessed conference touching Homer, though very little more than that I had with M. Harriots. Which two, I protest, are all, and preferred to all. Nor charge I their authorities with any allowance of my general labour, but only of those one or two places which for instances of my innovation, and how it showed [looked] to them, I imparted. If any tax me for too much periphrasis or circumlocution in some places, let them read Laurentius Valla and Eobanus Hessus, who either use such shortness as cometh nothing home to Homer, or, where they shun that fault, are ten parts more paraphrastical than I. As, for example, one place I will trouble you (if you please) to confer with the original and one interpreter for all. It is in the end of the third book, and is Helen's speech to Venus fetching her to Paris from seeing his cowardly combat with Menelaus – part of which speech I will here cite:

Οὕνεκα δή νῦν οἶον ᾿ΑλέξανδρονΜενέλαος Νικήσας, &c.[3]

[1] "You who make a noise about Justinian laws alone breathe some turgidly; you make more of one paragraph or another than you [are] yourselves." Edward Capps III's translation. [Ed]

[2] Chapman had been publishing individual books of his *Iliad* for over a decade, since 1598. [Ed]

For avoiding the common reader's trouble here, I must refer the more Greekish to the rest of the speech in Homer, whose translation *ad verbum* [literally] by Spondanus I will here cite, and then pray you to confer [compare] it with that which followeth of Valla:

> Quoniam verò nunc Alexandrum Menelaus
> Postquam vicit, vult odiosam me domum abducere,
> Propterea verò nunc dolum (ceu dolos) cogitans advenisti?
> Sede apud ipsum vadens, deorum abnega vias,
> Neque unquam tuis pedibus revertaris in coelum,
> Sed semper circa eum aerumnas perfer, et ipsum serva
> Donec te vel uxorem faciat, vel hic servam, &c.[4]

Valla thus:

> Quoniam victo Paride, Menelaus me miseram est reportaturus
> ad lares, ideo tu, ideo falsa sub imagine venisti, ut me
> deciperes ob tuam nimiam in Paridem benevolentiam; eò
> dum illi ades, dum illi studes, dum pro illo satagis, dum
> illum observas atque custodis, deorum commercium reliquisti
> nec ad eos reversura es ampliús; adeò (quantum suspicor)
> aut uxor eius efficieris, aut ancilla, &c.[5]

Wherein note if there be any such thing as most of this in Homer; yet only to express (as he thinks) Homer's conceit for the more pleasure of the reader he useth this overplus *dum illi ades, dum illi studes, dum pro illo satagis, dum illum observas atque custodis, deorum commercium reliquisti*. Which (besides his superfluity) is utterly false. For where he saith, *reliquisti deorum commercium*, Helen saith, Θεῶν δ᾿ ἀπόλειπε κελεύθους, *deorum autem abnega*, or *abnue, vias*, ἀπειπεῖν (*vel* ἀπόειπεῖν as it is used poetically) signifying *denegare* or *abnuere*;[6] and Helen (in contempt of her too much observing men) bids her renounce heaven and come live with Paris till he make her his wife or servant – scoptically [skeptically] or scornfully speaking it, which both Valla, Eobanus and all other interpreters (but these *ad verbum*) have utterly missed. And this one example I thought necessary to insert here to show my detractors that they have no reason to vilify my circumlocution sometimes when their most approved Grecians, Homer's interpreters, generally hold him to fit to be so converted. Yet how much I differ, and with what authority, let my impartial and judicial reader judge – always conceiving how pedantical and absurd an affectation it is in the interpretation of any author (much more of Homer) to turn him word for word, when (according to Horace and other best law-givers to translators[7]) it is the part of every knowing and judicial interpreter not to follow the number and order of words but the material things themselves, and sentences to weigh diligently, and to clothe and adorn them with words and such a style and form of oration as are most apt for the language into which they are converted. If I have not turned him in any place falsely (as all other his interpreters have in many and most of his chief places); if I have not left behind me any of his sentence [meaning], elegance, height, intention and invention; if in some few places (especially in my first edition, being done so long since and following the common tract) I be something paraphrastical and faulty – is it justice in that poor fault (if they will needs have it so) to drown all the rest of my labour? But there is a certain envious windfucker,[8] that hovers up and down, laboriously engrossing all the air with his luxurious ambition and buzzing into every ear my detraction – affirming I turn Homer out of the Latin only, &c – that sets all his associates and the whole rabble of my maligners on their wings with him

---

[3] *Iliad* 3.402-410. In Robert Fitzgerald's translation these lines read:

> Is it because
> Meneláos has beaten Aléxandros
> and, hateful though I am, would take me home,
> is that why you are here in all your cunning?
> Go take your place beside Aléxandros!
> Leave the bright paths the gods take over heaven
> and walk no more about Olympos! Be
> unhappy for him, shield him, till at last
> he marries you – or, as he will, enslaves you.

[4] "Since now, after Menelaus defeated Alexander [Paris], he wishes to lead hateful me home, now you have come planning a trick? Sit down by my side, give up the ways of the gods, nor ever will you ever turn back to heaven with your feet, but always endure hardships near him, and keep him until he should either make you his wife or his maidservant, etc." Edward Capps III's translation. [Ed]

[5] "Since with Paris defeated, Menelaus is about to carry wretched me to our home gods, you have come here under a false guise so that you may deceive me because of your excessive benevolence toward Paris; while you are present and devoted to him, while you are satisfying his wishes, while you are preserving him, you have left the proper business of the gods, nor are you about to return to them any time soon; there (I suspect) you will either become his wife or his maidservant." Edward Capps III's translation. [Ed]

[6] The 'overplus' passage beginning with *dum* is the series of "while you are ..." phrases in note 5, above. The "where he saith" contrast is "left the proper business of the gods" in Valla and "denied/rejected/spoke away the ways/paths of the gods" in Homer. [Ed]

[7] See Horace, above, 15; also Cicero, above, 9. [Ed]

[8] I.e., windhover or kestrel, a species of hawk. [Ed]

to bear about my empair[ment] and poison my reputation. One that, as he thinks, whatsoever he gives to others he takes from himself, so whatsoever he takes from others he adds to himself. One that in this kind of robbery doth like Mercury, that stole good and supplied it with counterfeit bad still.[9] One like the two gluttons, Philoxenus and Gnatho, that would still empty their noses in the dishes they loved that no man might eat but themselves. For so this castrill [kestrel], with too hot a liver and lust after his own glory, and to devour all himself, discourageth all appetites to the fame of another. I have stricken: single[10] him as you can. Nor note I this to cast any rubs or [s]plashes out of the particular way of mine own estimation with the world, for I resolve this with the wilfully obscure:

> *Sine honore vivam, nulloque numero ero.*
> Without men's honors I will live, and make
> No number in the manless course they take.

But to discourage (if it might be) the general detraction of industrious and well-meaning virtue, I know I cannot too much diminish and deject myself; yet that passing little that I am, God only knows – to whose ever-implored respect and comfort I only submit me. If any further edition of these my silly endeavors shall chance, I will mend what is amiss (God assisting me) and amplify my harsh comment to Homer's far more right and mine own earnest and ingenious love of him. Nothwithstanding, I know the curious and envious will never sit down satisfied. A man may go over and over till he come over and over, and his pains be only his recompence: every man is so loded [guided] with his particular head, and nothing in all respects perfect but what is perceived by few. Homer himself hath met with my fortune in many maligners, and therefore may my poor self put up without motion. And so little I will respect malignity and so much encourage myself with mine own known strength and what I find within me of comfort and confirmance (examining myself throughout with a far more jealous and severe eye than my greatest enemy, imitating this:

> *Judex ipse sui totum se explorat ad unguem, &c.*) –[11]

that after these *Iliads* I will (God lending me life and any meanest means) with more labour than I have lost here and all unchecked alacrity dive through his *Odysses*. Nor can I forget here (but with all hearty gratitude remember) my most ancient, learned and right noble friend M. Richard Stapilton, first most desertful [deserving] mover in the frame of our Homer. For which (and much other ingenious and utterly undeserved desert) God make me amply his requiter and be his honorable family's speedy and full restorer. In the mean space [meantime], I entreat my impartial and judicial reader that all things to the quick he will not pare, but humanely and nobly pardon defects, and if he find anything perfect receive it unenvied.

Miles Smith

Miles Smith (d. 1624), bishop of Gloucester and a distinguished classical scholar and Orientalist, was a key member of the committee appointed by King James I to make a new version of the Bible, based on several earlier translations. In addition to working on the translation, Smith was assigned the task of writing the preface to the new Bible – excerpted below.

Smith, the son of a butcher, entered Corpus Christi College, Oxford, around 1568, where he took his B.A. (1573), M.A. (1576), B.D. (1585), and D.D. (1595). Beginning in 1576 he served as petty canon or chaplain of Christ Church, prebendary of Hinton in Hereford cathedral, and (upon completion of his doctorate of divinity in 1595) prebendary of Exeter cathedral. King James, himself an amateur theologian (author of *Daemonologie*) and translator (of a long work by the French Huguenot author Guillaume de Salluste, Seigneur de Bartas), rewarded Smith for his labour on the new English Bible with the bishopric of Gloucester.

In January 1604, having succeeded Queen Elizabeth less than a year before, King James authorized 54 scholars to undertake an extensive revision of existing English translations from the past century or so: the partial translation done by William Tyndale (1525), the Whitchurch Great Bible (1539), the Calvinist Geneva Bible (1562), the Bishops' Bible (1568), and the Catholic Rheims New Testament (1582). In order to ensure that the new 'translation' would in fact be a revision of these previous translations, James (or possibly a scholar designated by him, Richard Bancroft, Bishop of London and soon to be Archbishop of Canterbury) drew up a list of fifteen rules for the committee to follow, and the first required them to follow the Bishops' Bible (a revision and expansion of Tyndale) as closely as possible: "The ordinary Bible read in

---

[9] Mercury (Greek Hermes), god of merchants, was known as a thief; his first act as a boy was to steal twelve cows from Apollo and, once discovered, claim he sacrificed them to the twelve gods (including himself). [Ed]

[10] I.e., separate or single out, distinguish, chase separately. [Ed]

[11] "The judge himself explores his entire self to the quick, etc." Edward Capps III's translation. [Ed]

the Church, commonly called the Bishops' Bible, to be followed, and as little altered as the truth of the original will admit". This commission is also reflected in the preface, below:

> Truly (good Christian reader) we never thought from the beginning that we should need to make a new translation, nor yet to make of a bad one a good one ... , but to make a good one better, or out of many good ones, one principal good one, not justly to be excepted against; that hath been our endeavour, that our mark.

In fact, the 47 scholars who eventually did the work exceeded this commission, rewriting earlier translations extensively, and even to some extent retranslating from the original languages.

For the next fifty years, the Authorized Version competed with the Calvinist 'Geneva' Bible for dominance in England; generally considered by scholars of the day to be the worst of the predecessors to the Authorized Version, the Geneva Bible had nevertheless been around for a half-century longer and did not easily yield in the churches to the newcomer. By the early eighteenth century, however, the Authorized Version was established as *the* Bible of the English-speaking Protestant world. And as is well known, its influence on English literature has been enormous; Willis Barnstone writes:

> It shaped the poetry of Milton as earlier versions had entered into the grandeur of Shakespeare's speech. No poet of stature after the early seventeenth century has not been profoundly affected by its diction, syntax, and musical cadences, not to mention its content. Wordsworth and even free-thinking Shelley, pious though tormented Hopkins, profanely reverent Dylan Thomas, and T.S. Eliot after his conversion are more recent children of the King James Bible.

The tone and tenor of Smith's preface are familiar from previous Protestant defences of Bible translation from the hundred years preceding (Tyndale, Luther, Fulke), giving Biblical justification for making the Scriptures available to the ordinary people in the vernacular and responding to Catholic accusations of flagrant misinterpretation.

The Translators to the Reader
Preface to the *Authorized Version* of the Bible (1611)

Happy is the man that delighteth in the Scripture, and thrice happy that meditateth in it day and night.

But how shall men meditate in that which they cannot understand? How shall they understand that which is kept close in an unknown tongue? As it is written, *Except I know the power of the voice, I shall be to him that speaketh a barbarian, and he that speaketh shall be a barbarian to me.*[1] The Apostle excepteth no tongue; not Hebrew the ancientest, not Greek the most copious, not Latin the finest. Nature taught a natural man to confess that all of us in those tongues which we do not understand are plainly deaf; we may turn the deaf ear unto them. The Scythian counted the Athenian, whom he did not understand, barbarous; so the Roman sees the Syrian, and the Jew (even S. Hierome himself calleth the Hebrew tongue barbarous, belike because it was strange to so many), so the Emperor of Constantinople calleth the Latin tongue barbarous, though Pope Nicolas do storm at it; so the Jews long before Christ called all other nations *Lognazim* [foreign], which is little better than barbarous. Therefore as one complaineth that always in the Senate of Rome there was one or other that called for an interpreter; so lest the Church be driven to the like exigent, it is necessary to have translations in a readiness. Translation it is that openeth the window, to let in the light; that breaketh the shell, that we may eat the kernel; that putteth aside the curtain, that we may look into the most holy place; that removeth the cover of the well, that we may come by the water, even as Jacob rolled away the stone from the mouth of the well, by which means the flocks of Laban were watered [Genesis 29:10]. Indeed without translation into the vulgar tongue, the unlearned are but like children at Jacob's well (which was deep) without a bucket or something to draw with: or that person mentioned by Isaiah [29:11] to whom when a sealed book was delivered, with the motion, *Read this, I pray thee*, he was fain to make this answer, *I cannot, for it is sealed.*

While God would be known only in Jacob, and have his name great in Israel, and in none other place, while the dew lay on Gideon's fleece only, and all the earth besides was dry; then for one and the same people, which spake all of them the language of Canaan, that is, Hebrew, one and the same original in Hebrew was sufficient. But when the fullness of time drew near, that the Sun of righteousness, the Son of God should come into the world, whom God ordained to be a reconciliation through faith in his blood, not of the Jew only, but also of the Greek Prince (Greek for descent and language) even of Ptolemy Philadelph King of Egypt, to procure the translating of the Book of God out of Hebrew into Greek. This is the translation of the Seventy Interpreters, commonly so called, which prepared the way for our Saviour among the

[1] 1 Corinthians 14:11. See Paul, above, 16. [Ed]

Gentiles by written preaching, as Saint John Baptist did among the Jews by vocal. For the Grecians being desirous of learning, were not wont to suffer books of worth to lie moulding in kings' libraries, but had many of the servants, ready scribes, to copy them out, and so they were dispersed and made common. Again, the Greek tongue was well-known and made familiar to most inhabitants in Asia, by reason of the conquest that there the Grecians had made, as also by the colonies which thither they had sent. For the same causes also it was well understood in many places of Europe, yea, and of Africa too. Therefore the word of God being set forth in Greek, becometh hereby like a candle set upon a candlestick, which giveth light to all that are in the house, or like a proclamation sounded forth in the marketplace, which most men presently take knowledge of; and therefore that language was fittest to contain the Scriptures, both for the first preachers of the Gospel to appeal unto for witness, and for the learners also those times to make search and trial by. It is certain that that translation was not so sound and so perfect, but that it needed in many places correction; and who had been so sufficient for this work as the apostles or apostolic men? Yet it seemed good to the Holy Ghost and to them to take that which they found (the same being for the greatest part true and sufficient) rather then by making a new, in that new world and green age of the Church, to expose themselves to many exceptions and cavillations, as though they made a translation of the Seventy to serve their own turn, and therefore bearing witness to themselves, their witness not to be regarded. This may be supposed to be some cause why the translation of the Seventy was allowed to pass for current. Notwithstanding, though it was commended generally, yet it did not fully content the learned, no not of the Jews. For not long after Christ, Aquila fell in hand with a new translation, and after him Theodotion, and after him Symmachus: yea, there was a fifth and sixth edition, the authors whereof were not known. These with the Seventy made up Hexapla, and were worthily and to great purpose compiled together by Origen. Howbeit the edition of the Seventy went away with the credit, and therefore not only was placed in the midst by Origen (for the worth and excellence thereof above the rest, as Epiphanius gathereth) but also was used by the Greek fathers for the ground and foundation of their commentaries. Yea, Epiphanius above named doth attribute so much unto it that he holdeth the authors thereof not only for interpreters, but also for prophets in some respect;[2] and Justinian the Emperor, enjoining the Jews his subjects to use specially the translation of the Seventy, rendreth this reason thereof, because they were as it were enlightened with prophetical grace. Yet for all that, as the Egyptians are said of the Prophet to be men and not God and their horses flesh and not spirit [Isaiah 31:3]: so it is evident (and Saint Hierome affirmeth as much[3]) that the Seventy were interpreters, they were not prophets; they did many things well, as learned men; but yet as men they stumbled and fell, one while through oversight, another while through ignorance, yea, sometimes they may be noted to add to the original, and sometimes to take from it; which made the apostles to leave them many times, when they left the Hebrew, and to deliver the sense touching the Greek translations of the Old Testament.

There were also within a few hundred years after CHRIST translations many into the Latin tongue; for this tongue also was very fit to convey the Law and the gospel by, because in those times very many countries of the West, yea of the South, East, and North, spoke or understood Latin, being made provinces to the Romans. But now the Latin translations were too many to be all good, for they were infinite (*Latini Interpretes nullo modo numerari possunt*, saith S. Augustine[4].) Again they were not out the Hebrew fountain (we speak of the Latin translations of the Old Testament) but out of the Greek stream, therefore the Greek being not altogether clear, the Latin derived from it must needs be muddy. This moved S. Hierome, a most learned father, and the best linguist without controversy [unquestionably] of his age, or of any that went before him, to undertake the translating of the Old Testament, out of the very fountains themselves; which he performed with that evidence of great learning, judgement, industry and faithfulness that he hath forever bound the Church unto him in a debt of special remembrance and thankfulness.

Now though the Church were thus furnished with Greek and Latin translations, even before the faith of CHRIST was generally embraced in the Empire (for the learned know that even in S. Hierome's time, the Consul of Rome and his wife were both ethnics, and about the same time the greatest part of the Senate also) yet for all that the godly-learned were not content to have the Scriptures in the language which themselves understood, Greek and Latin (as the good lepers were not content to fare well themselves, but acquainted their neighbours with the store that God had sent, that they also might provide for themselves [2 Kings 7:9]) but also for the behoof and edifying of the unlearned which hungered and thirsted after righteousness, and had souls to be saved as well as they, they provided translations into the vulgar for their countrymen, insomuch that most nations under heaven did

[2] See above, 22. [Ed]

[3] See above, 30. [Ed]

[4] "Those who have translated them into Latin are innumerable" (Robertson's translation). *On Christian Doctrine* 2.11.16; see above, 32. [Ed]

shortly after their conversion hear CHRIST speaking unto them in their mother tongue, not by the voice of their minister only, but also by the written word translated. If any doubt hereof, he may be satisfied by examples enough, if enough will serve the turn. First S. Hierome saith, *Multarum gentiu linguis Scriptura ante translata, docet falsa esse quae addita sunt, &c., The Scripture being translated before in the languages of many Nations, doth show that those things that were added* (by Lucian or Hesychius) *are false*. So S. Hierome in that place [*Preface to the Four Gospels*]. The same Hierome elsewhere affirmeth that he, the time was, had set forth the translation of the Seventy, *suae linguae hominibus*, for his countrymen of Dalmatia. Which words not only Erasmus doth understand to purport, that S. Hierome translated the Scripture into the Dalmatian tongue, but also Sixtus Senesis, and Alphonsus à Castro (that we speak of no more), men not to be excepted against by them of Rome, do ingenuously confess as much.[5] So, S. [John] Chrysostom, that lived in S. Hierome's time, giveth evidence with him: *The doctrine of S. John* (saith he) *did not in such sort* (as the Philosophers did) *vanish away: but the Syrians, Egyptians, Indians, Persians, Ethiopians, and infinite other nations being barbarous people, translated it into their (mother) tongue, and have learned to be (true) philosophers*, he meaneth Christians. To this may be added Theodorit [of Mopsuestia], as next unto him both for antiquity and for learning. His words be these, *Every country that is under the sun is full of these words* (of the apostles and prophets) *and the Hebrew tongue* (he meaneth the Scriptures in the Hebrew tongue) *is turned not only into the language of the Grecians, but also of the Romans, and Egyptians, and Persians, and Indians, and Armenians, and Scythians, and Sauromatians, and briefly into all the languages that any nation useth*. So he. In like manner, Ulpilas is reported by Paulus Diaconus and Isidore [of Seville] (and before them by Sozomen) to have translated the Scriptures into the Gothic tongue; John Bishop of Seville by Vasseus, to have turned them into Arabic, about the year of our Lord 717; Beda by Cistertiensis, to have turned the Psalter into Saxon; Efnard by Trithemius to have abridged the French psalter, as Beda had done the Hebrew, about the year 800; King Alfred by the said Cistertiensis to have turned the Psalter into Saxon; Methodius by [Johannes] Aventinus (printed at Ingolstad) to have turned the Scriptures into Sclavonian; Valdo, Bishop of Frising by Beatus Rhenanus, to have caused about that time the Gospels to be translated into Dutch-rhythm, yet extant in the Library of Corbinian; Valdus, by diverse [authorities] to have turned them himself, or to have gotten them turned into French, about the year 1160; Charles the 5. of that name, surnamed The Wise, to have caused them to be turned into French, about 200 years after Valdus's time, of which translation there be many copies yet extant, as witnesseth Beroaldus. Much about that time, even in our King Richard the second's days, John Trevisa translated them into English, and many English Bibles in written hand are yet to be seen with diverse [people], translated as it is very probable in that age. So the Syrian translation of the New Testament is in most learned men's libraries, of Widminstadius's setting forth, and the Psalter in Arabic is with many, of Augustinus Neibiensis' setting forth. So Postel affirmeth, that in his travail he saw the Gospels in the Ethiopian tongue; and Ambrose Thesius allegeth the Psalter of the Indians, which he testifieth to have been set forth by Potken in Syrian characters. So that, to have the Scriptures in the mother-tongue is not a quaint conceit lately taken up, either by the Lord Cromwell in England, or by the Lord Radzewił in Polonie [Poland], or by the Lord Ungadius in the Emperor's dominion, but hath been thought upon, and put in practice of old, even from the first times of the conversion of any nation; no doubt because it was esteemed most profitable to cause faith to grow in men's hearts the sooner, and to make them to be able to say with the words of the Psalm [48:8], *As we have heard, so we have seen.*

Now the Church of Rome would seem at the length to bear a motherly affection towards her children, and to allow them the Scriptures in their mother tongue; but indeed it is a gift, not deserving to be called a gift, an unprofitable gift; they must first get a license in writing before they may use them, and to get that, they must approve themselves to their confessor, that is, to be such as are, if not frozen in the dregs, yet soured with the leaven of their superstition.[6] Howbeit, it seemed too much to Clement the 8. that there should be any license granted to have them in the vulgar tongue, and therefore he overruleth and frustrateth the grant of Pius the fourth. So much are they afraid of the light of the scripture (*Lucifugae Scripturarum*, as Tertullian speaketh) that they will not trust the people with it, no not as it is set forth by their own sworn men, no not with the license of their own bishops and inquisitors. Yea, so unwilling they are to communicate the Scriptures to the people's understanding in any sort, that they are not ashamed to confess, that we forced them to translate it into English against their wills. This seemeth to argue a bad

[5] I.e., not only Protestants but Catholics too admit that Jerome translated into Dalmatian as well as Latin. [Ed]

[6] I.e., before they could gain access to an English Bible translation they had to have written certification that they were good Catholics – as seen from a highly partisan Protestant point of view. [Ed]

cause, or a bad conscience, or both. Sure we are that it is not he that hath good gold that is afraid to bring it to the touchstone, but he that hath the counterfeit; neither is it the true man that shunneth the light, but the malefactor, lest his deeds should be reproved; neither is it the plain dealing merchant that is unwilling to have the weights, or the meteyard brought in place, but he that useth deceit. But we will let them alone for this fault, and return to translation.

Many men's mouths have been open a good while (and yet are not stopped) with speeches about the translation so long in hand, or rather perusals of translations made before; and ask what may be the reason, what the necessity of the employment: Hath the Church been deceived, say they, all this while? Hath her sweet bread been mingled with leaven, her silver with dross, her wine with water, her milk with lime? (*Lacte gypsum male miscetur*[7], saith S. Irenaeus) We hoped that we had been in the right way, that we had had the oracles of God delivered unto us, and that though all the world had cause to be offended and to complain, yet that we had none. Hath the nurse holden out the breast, and nothing but wind in it? Hath the bread been delivered by the fathers of the Church, and the same proved to be lapidosus, as Seneca speaketh? What is it to handle the word of God deceitfully, if this be not? Thus certain brethren. Also the adversaries of Judah and Jerusalem, like Sanballat in Nehemiah [4:3], mock, as we hear, both at the work and workmen, saying: *What do these weak Jews, &c. will they make the stones whole again out of the heaps of dust which are burnt? Although they build, yet if a fox go up, he shall even break down their stony wall.* Was their translation good before? Why do they now mend it? Was it not good? Why then was it obtruded to the people? Yea, why did the Catholics (meaning Popish Romanists) always go in jeopardy for refusing to go to hear it? Nay, if it must be translated into English, Catholics are fittest to do it. They have learning, and they know when a thing is well, they can *manum de tabula*. We will answer them both briefly; and the former, being brethren, thus, with S. Hierome, *Damnamus veteres? Minime, sed post priorum studia in domo Domini quod possumus laboramus.* That is, *Do we condemn the ancient? In no case: but after the endeavours of them that were before us, we take the best pains we can in the house of God.* As if he said, Being provoked by the example of the learned that lived before my time, I have thought it my duty to assay whether my talent in the knowledge of the tongues may be profitable in any measure to God's Church, lest I should seem to have laboured in them in vain, and lest I should be thought to glory in men (although ancient) above that which was in them. Thus S. Hierome may be thought to speak.

And to the same effect say we, that we are so far off from condemning any of their labours that travailed before us in this kind, either in this land or beyond sea, either in King Henry's time, or King Edward's (if there were any translation, or correction of a translation in his time) or Queen Elizabeth's of ever-renowned memory, that we acknowledge them to have been raised up of God, for the building and furnishing of his Church, and that they deserve to be had of [by] us and of [by] posterity in everlasting remembrance. The judgement of Aristotle [*Metaphysics* ch. 2] is worthy and well known: If Timotheus had not been, we had not had much sweet music; but if Phrynis (Timotheus his master) had not been, we had not had Timotheus. Therefore blessed be they, and most honoured be their name, that break the ice, and glueth onset upon that which helpeth forward to the saving of souls. Now what can be more available thereto, than to deliver God's books unto God's people in a tongue which they understand? Since of a hidden treasure, and of a fountain that is sealed, there is no profit, as Ptolemy Philadelph wrote to the rabbis or masters of the Jews, as witnesseth Epiphanius[8]; and as S. Augustine saith [*City of God* 19.7]: *A man had rather be with his dog then with a stranger* (whose tongue is strange unto him). Yet for all that, as nothing is begun and perfected at the same time, and the later thoughts are thought to be the wiser; so, if we building upon their foundation that went before us, and being helped by their labours, do endeavour to make that better which they left so good; no man, we are sure, hath cause to mislike us; they, we persuade ourselves, if they were alive, would thank us. The vintage of Abiezer, that struck the stroke: yet the gleaning of grapes of Ephraim was not to be despised. See Judges 8. verse 2. Jehoash the king of Israel did not satisfy himself till he had smitten the ground three times; and yet he offended the Prophet for giving over then [2 Kings 13:18-19]. Aquila, of whom we spoke before, translated the Bible as carefully and as skillfully as he could; and yet he thought good to go over it again, and then it got the credit with the Jews, to be called ἀκρίβειαν, that is, accurately done, as Saint Hierome witnesseth. How many books of profane learning have been gone over again and again, by the same translators, by others? Of one and the same book of Aristotle's *Ethics*, there are extant not so few as six or seven several [different] translations. Now if this cost may be bestowed upon the gourd, which affordeth us a little shade, and which today flourisheth, but tomorrow is cut down [Jonah 4:6-11]; what may be bestown, nay what ought we not to bestow upon the vine, the fruit whereof

[7] "Milk mixes badly with lime". [Ed]

[8] See above, 22. [Ed]

maketh glad the conscience of man, and the stem whereof abideth forever? And this is the word of God, which we translate. *What is the chaff to the wheat*, saith the Lord [Jeremiah 23:28]? *Tanti vitreum, quanti verum margaritum* (saith Tertullian), if a toy of glass be of that reckoning with us, how ought we to value the true pearl? Therefore let no man's eye be evil, because his majesty's is good; neither let any be grieved that we have a prince that seeketh the increase of the spiritual wealth of Israel (let Sanballats and Tobiahs do so, which therefore do bear their just reproof) but let us rather bless God from the ground of our heart, for working this religious care in him, to have the translations of the Bible maturely considered of and examined. For by this means it cometh to pass, that whatsoever is sound already (and all is sound for substance, in one or other of our editions, and the worst of ours far better then their authentic vulgar) the same will shine as gold more brightly, being rubbed and polished; also, if any thing be halting, or superfluous, or not so agreeable to the original, the same may be corrected, and the truth set in place. And what can the King command to be done, that will bring him more true honour then this? And wherein could they that have been set a work, approve their duty to the king, yea their obedience to God, and love to his saints more, than by yielding their service, and all that is within them, for the furnishing of the work? But besides all this, they were the principal motives of it, and therefore ought least to quarrel it: for the very historical truth is, that upon the importunate petitions of the Puritans, at his Majesty's coming to this crown, the conference at Hampton Court having been appointed for hearing their complaints; when by force of reason they were put from all other grounds, they had recourse at the last, to this shift, that they could not with good conscience subscribe to the Communion book, since it maintained the Bible as it was there translated, which was as they said, a most corrupted translation. And although this was judged to be but a very poor and empty shift; yet even hereupon did his Majesty [James] begin to bethink himself of the good that might ensue by a new translation, and presently after gave order for this translation which is now presented unto thee. Thus much to satisfy our scrupulous brethren.

Now to the latter we answer: that we do not deny, nay we affirm and avow, that the very meanest translation of the Bible in English, set forth by men of our profession (for we have seen none of theirs of the whole Bible as yet) containeth the word of God, nay, is the word of God. As the king's speech which he uttered in Parliament, being translated into French, Dutch, Italian and Latin, is still the king's speech, though it be not interpreted by every translator with the like grace, nor peradventure so fitly for phrase, nor so expressly for sense, everywhere. For it is confessed, that things are take their denomination of the greater part; and a natural man [Horace] could say, *Verium ubi multa nitent in carmine, non ego paucis offendor maculis, &c.*, A man may be counted a virtuous man, though he have made many slips in his life (else, there were none virtuous, for *in many things we offend all* [James 3:2]), also a comely man and lovely, though he have some warts upon his hand, yea, not only freckles upon his face, but also scars. No cause therefore why the word translated should be denied to be the word, or forbidden to be current, notwithstanding that some imperfections and blemishes may be noted in the setting forth of it. For whatever was perfect under the sun, where apostles or apostolic men, that is, men endued with an extraordinary measure of God's spirit, and privileged with the privilege of the infallibility, had not their hand? The Romanists therefore in refusing to hear, and daring to burn the Word translated, did no less than despite the spirit of grace from whom originally it proceeded, and whose sense and meaning, as well as man's weakness would enable, it did express. Judge by an example or two. Plutarch writeth, that after that Rome had been burnt by the Gauls, they fell soon to build it again: but doing it in haste, they did not cast the streets, nor proportion the houses in such comely fashion, as had been most sightly and convenient; was Catiline therefore an honest man, or a good patriot, that sought to bring it to a combustion? or Nero a good Prince, that did indeed set it on fire? So, by the story of Ezra [3:12], and the prophecy of Haggai [2:3] it may be gathered, that the temple built by Zerubbabel after the return from Babylon was by no means to be compared to the former built by Solomon (for they that remembered the former, wept when they considered the latter) notwithstanding, might this latter either have been abhorred and forsaken by the Jews, or profaned by the Greeks? The like we are to think of translations. The translation of the Seventy dissenteth from the Original in many places, neither doth it come near it, for perspicuity, gravity, majesty; yet which of the apostles did condemn it? Nay, they used it (as it is apparent, and as Saint Hierome and most learned men do confess) which they would not have done, nor by their example of using it, so grace and commend it to the Church, if it had been unworthy the appellation and name of the word of God. And whereas they urge for their second defense of their vilifying and abusing of the English Bibles, or some pieces thereof, which they meet with, for that heretics (forsooth) were authors of the translations (heretics they call us by the same right that they call themselves Catholics, both being wrong) we marvel what divinity taught them so. We are sure Tertullian was another mind: *Ex personis probamus fiden, an ex fide personas?* Do we try men's faith by their persons? we should try their persons by their faith. Also S. Augustine was of another mind: for he lighting upon certain rules made by Tychonius a Dantist, for the better understanding of the word, was not ashamed to make use of them, yea, to insert them into his own book, with giving commendation to them so far forth as they were worthy to be commended, as is to be seen in S. Augustine's third book *De doctrina Christiana* [*On Christian Doctrine*]. To be short, Origen, and the whole Church of God for certain hundred years, were of another mind; for they were so far from treading under foot (much more from burning) the translation of Aquila a proselyte, that is, one that had turned Jew; of Symmachus, and Theodotion, both Ebionites, that is, most vile heretics, that they joined them together with the Hebrew original, and the translation of the Seventy (as hath been before signified out of Epiphanius) and set them forth openly to be considered of and persuaded by all. But we weary the unlearned, who need not know so much, and trouble the learned, who know it already.

Yet before we end, we must answer a third cavil and objection of theirs against us, for altering and amending our translations so oft; wherein truly they deal hardly, and strangely with us. For to whom ever was it imputed for a fault (by such as were wise) to go over that which he had done, and to amend it where he saw cause? Saint Augustine was not afraid to exhort S. Hierome to a Palinodia or recantation; the same S. Augustine was not ashamed to retract, we might say revoke, many things that had passed him, and doth ever glory that he seeth his infirmities. If we will be sons of the truth, we must consider what it speaketh, and trample upon our own credit, yea, and upon other men's too, if either be any way hindrance to it. This to cause; then to the persons we say, that of all men they ought to be most silent in this case. For what varieties have they, and what alterations have they made, not only of their service books, portesses and breviaries, but also of their Latin translation? The service book supposed to be made by S. Ambrose (*Officium Ambroseianum*) was a great while in special use and request: but Pope Hadrian calling a Council with the aid of Charles the Emperor, abolished it, yea, burnt it, and commanded the service book of Saint Gregory universally to be used. Well, *Officium Gregorianum* gets by this means to be in credit, but doth it continue without change or altering? No, the very Roman service was two fashions, the new fashion, and the old (the one used in one church, the other in another) as is to be seen in Pamelius a Romanist, his preface, before Micrologus[9]. The same Pamelius reporteth out of Radulphus de Rivo, that about the year of our Lord, 1277, Pope Nicolas the third removed out of the churches of Rome the more ancient books (of service) and brought into use the missals of the Friars Minorites, and commanded them to be observed there; insomuch that about an hundred years after, when the above named Radulphus happened to be at Rome, he found all the books to be new (of the new stamp). Neither was there this chopping and changing in the ancient times only, but also of late: Pius Quintus himself confesseth, that every bishopric almost had a peculiar kind of service, most unlike to that which others had; which moved him to abolish all other breviaries, though never so ancient, and privileged and published by bishops in their dioceses, and to establish and ratify that only which was of his own setting forth, in the year 1568. Now, when the father of their church, who gladly would heal the sore of the daughter of his people softly and slightly, and make the best of it, findeth so great fault with them for their odds and jarring; we hope the children have no great cause to vaunt of the uniformity. But the difference that appeareth between our translations and our often correcting them is the thing that we are specially charged with; let us see therefore whether they themselves be without fault this way (if it be to be counted a fault, to correct) and whether they be fit men to throw stones at us: *Olandem major parcas insane minori*, they that are less sound themselves, ought not to object infirmities to others. If we should tell them that Valla, Stapulensis, Erasmus, and Vives found fault with their vulgar translation, and consequently wished the same to be mended, or a new one to be made, they would answer peradventure, that we produced their enemies for witnesses against them; albeit, they were in no other sort enemies, than as S. Paul was to the Galatians [4:16], for telling them the truth; and it were to be wished that they had dared to tell it them plainlier and oftener. But what will they say to this, that Pope Leo the tenth allowed Erasmus translation of the New Testament, so much different from the vulgar, by his apostolic Letter and Bull; the same Leo exhorted Pagnuin to translate the whole Bible, and bare whatsoever charges was necessary for the work? Surely, as the apostle reasoneth to the Hebrews [7:11, 8:7], that if the former Law and Testament had been at all points allowable, to small purpose had labour and charges been undergone about framing of a new. If they say, it was one Pope's private opinion, and that he consulted only himself; then we are able to go further with them and to aver that more of their chief men of all sorts, even their own Trent-champions Pavia and Vega, and their own Inquisitors, Hieronymus ab Oleastro, and their own Bishop Isidorus Clarius, and their own Cardinal Thomas a Vio Caietan do either make new translations themselves or follow new ones of other men's making, or note the vulgar interpreter for halting; none of them fear to dissent for him, nor yet to except against him. And call they this a uniform tenor

[9] The *Micrologus ecclesiasticis observationibus* (973-1072) was a medieval commentary on the liturgy. [Ed]

of text and judgement about the text, so many of their worthies disclaiming the new received conceit? Nay, we will yet come nearer the quick: doth not their Paris edition differ from the Louaine, and Hentenius his from them both, and yet all of them allowed by authority? Nay, doth not Sixtus Quintus confess, that certain Catholics (he meaneth certain of his own side) were in such humor of translating the Scriptures into Latin, that Satan taking occasion by them, though they thought of no such matter, did strive what he could, out of so uncertain and manifold a variety of translations, so to mingle all things, that nothing might seem to be left certain and firm in them, &c? Nay further, did not the same Sixtus ordain by an inviolable decree, and that with the counsel and consent of his Cardinals, that the Latin edition of the Old and New Testament, which the Council of Trent would have to be authentic, is the same without controversy which he then set forth, being diligently corrected and printed in the Printing-house of the Vatican? Thus Sixtus in his Preface before his Bible. And yet Clement the eighth, his immediate successor, publisheth another edition of the Bible, containing in it infinite differences from that of Sixtus (and many of them weighty and material) and yet this must be authentic by all means. What is to have the faith of our glorious Lord JESUS CHRIST with Yea and Nay, if this be not? Again, what is sweet harmony and consent, if this be? Therefore, as Demaratus of Corinth advised a great King, before he talked of the dissensions among the Grecians, to compose his domestic broils (for at that time his Queen and his son and heir were at deadly feud with him) so all the while that our adversaries do make so many and so various editions themselves, and do jar so much about the worth and authority of them, they can with no show of equity challenge us for changing and correcting. But it is high time to leave them, and to show in brief what we proposed to ourselves, and what course we held in this our perusal and survey of the Bible. Truly (good Christian reader) we never thought from the beginning that we should need to make a new translation, nor yet to make of a bad one a good one (for then the imputation of Sixtus had been true in some sort, that our people had been fed with gall of dragons instead of wine, with whey instead of milk), but to make a good one better, or out of many good ones, one principal good one, not justly to be excepted against; that hath been our endeavour, that our mark. To that purpose there were many chosen that were greater in other men's eyes then in their own, and that sought the truth rather then their own praise. Again, they came or were thought to come to work, not *exercendi causa* (as one saith) but *exercilati*, that is, learned, not to learn: For the chief overseer and ἐργοδιώκτης under his Majesty, to whom not only we, but also our whole Church was much bound, knew by his wisdom, which thing also Nazianzen taught so long ago, that it is a preposterous order to teach first and to learn after, yea that τό ἐν πιθῷ κεραμίαν μανθάνειν to learn and practice together is neither commendable for the workman nor safe for the work. Therefore such were thought upon, as could say modestly with Saint Hierome, *Et Hebraeum Sermonem ex parte didicimus, and in Latino pene ab ipsis incunabulis &c. detriti sumus, Both we have learned the Hebrew tongue in part, and in the Latin we have been exercised almost from our very cradle.* S. Hierome maketh no mention of the Greek, wherein yet he did excel, because he translated not the Old Testament out of Greek, but out of Hebrew. And in what sort did these assemble? In the trust of their own knowledge, or of their sharpness of wit, or deepness of judgement, as it were in an arm of flesh? At no hand. They trusted in him that hath the key of David, opening and no man shutting; they prayed to the Lord the Father our Lord, to the effect that S. Augustine did: *O let thy Scriptures be my pure delight, let me not be deceived in them, neither let me deceive by them* [*Confessions* 11.2]. In this confidence, and with this devotion did they assemble together; not too many, lest one should trouble another; and yet many, lest many things haply might escape them. If you ask what they had before them, truly it was the Hebrew text of the Old Testament, the Greek of the New. These are two golden pipes, or rather conduits, wherethrough the olive branches empty themselves into the gold. The same Saint Hierome affirmeth, and Gratian hath not spared to put into his decree, that *as the credit of the Old books* (he meaneth of the Old Testament) *is to be tried by the Hebrew volumes, so of the New by the Greek tongue*, he meaneth by the original Greek. If truth be to be tried by these tongues, then whence should a translation be made, but out of them? These tongues therefore, the Scriptures we say in those tongues, we set before us to translate, being the tongues wherein God was pleased to speak to his Church by his prophets and apostles. Neither did we run over the work with that posting haste that the Septuagint did, if that be true which is reported of them, that they finished it in 72 days [Josephus *Antiquities* 12]; neither were we barred or hindered from going over it again, having once done it, like S. Hierome, if that be true which himself reporteth, that he could no sooner write any thing, but presently it was caught from him, and published, and he could not have leave to mend it;[10] neither, to be short, were we the first that fell in hand with translating the Scripture into English, and consequently destitute of former helps, as it is written of Origen, that he was the first in a manner that put his hand to write commentaries upon the Scriptures, and

[10] See Jerome's letter to Pammachius, 24, above. [Ed]

therefore no marvel, if he overshot himself many times. None of these things: the work hath not been huddled up in 72 days, but hath cost the workmen, as light as it seemeth, the pains of twice seven times seventy-two days and more: matters of such weight and consequence are to be speeded with maturity; for in a business of moment a man feareth not the blame of convenient slackness. Neither did we think much [hesitate] to consult the translators or commentators, Chaldean, Hebrew, Syrian, Greek, or Latin, no nor the Spanish, French, Italian, or Dutch [German]; neither did we disdain to revise that which we had done, and to bring back to the anvil that which we had hammered; but having and using as great helps as were needful, and fearing no reproach for slowness, nor coveting praise for expedition [quickness], we have at the length, through the good hand of the Lord upon us, brought the work to that pass that you see.

Some peradventure would have no variety of senses to be set in the margin, lest the authority of the Scriptures for deciding of controversies by that show of uncertainty should somewhat be shaken. But we hold their judgement not to be so sound in this point. For though whatsoever things are necessary are manifest, as S. Chrysostom saith,[11] and as S. Augustine, *In those things that are plainly set down in the Scriptures, all such matters are found that concern faith, hope, and charity* [*On Christian Doctrine* 2.9]. Yet for all that it cannot be dissembled, that partly to exercise and whet our wits, partly to wean the curious from loathing of them for their everywhere-plainness, partly also to stir up our devotion to crave the assistance of God's spirit by prayer, and lastly, that we might be forward to seek aid of our brethren by conference, and never scorn those that be not in all respects so complete as they should be, being to seek in many things ourselves, it hath pleased God in his divine providence here and there to scatter words and sentences of that difficulty and doubtfulness, not in doctrinal points that concern salvation (for in such it hath been vouched that the Scriptures are plain) but in matters of less moment, that fearfulness would better beseem us than confidence, and if we will resolve, to resolve upon modesty with S. Augustine (though not in this same case altogether, yet upon the same ground) *Melius est dubitare de occultis, quam litigare de incertis*, it is better to make doubt of those things which are secret than to strive about those things that are uncertain.[12] There be many words in the Scriptures, which be never found there but once (having neither brother nor neighbor, as the Hebrews speak), so that we cannot be holden by conference of places. Again, there be many rare names of certain birds, beasts, and precious stones, etc. concerning which the Hebrews themselves are so divided among themselves for judgement, that they may seem to have defined this or that, rather because they would say something, they because they were sure of that which they said, as S. Hierome somewhere saith of the Septuagint. Now in such a case, doth not a margin do well to admonish the Reader to seek further, and not to conclude or dogmatize upon this or that peremptorily? For as it is a fault of incredulity to doubt of those things that are evident; so to determine of such things as the Spirit of God hath left (even in the judgement of the judicious) questionable can be no less than presumption. Therefore as S. Augustine saith, that variety of translations is profitable for the finding out of the sense of the Scriptures: so diversity of signification and sense in the margin, where the text is not so clear, must needs do good, yea, is necessary, as we are persuaded.[13] We know that Sixtus Quintus expressly forbiddeth that any variety of readings of their vulgar edition should be put in the margin (which though it be altogether the same thing to that we have in hand, yet it looketh that way) but we think he hath not all of his own side his favorers for this conceit. They that are wise had rather have their judgements at liberty in differences of readings than to be captivated to one, when it may be the other. If they were sure that their high priest had all laws shut up in his breast, as Paul the second bragged, and that he were as free from error by special privilege, as the dictators of Rome were made by law inviolable, it were another matter; then his word were an oracle, his opinion a decision. But the eyes of the world are now open, God be thanked, and have been a great while; they find that he is subject to the same affections and infirmities that others be, that his skin is penetrable, and therefore so much as he proveth, not as much as he claimeth, they grant and embrace.

Another thing we think good to admonish thee of (gentle reader) that we have not tied ourselves to a uniformity of phrasing, or to an identity of words, as some peradventure would wish that we had done, because they observe that some learned men somewhere have been as exact as they could that way. Truly, that we might not vary from the sense of that which we had translated before, if the word signified the same thing in both places (for there be some words that be not of the same sense everywhere) we were especially careful, and made a conscience, according to our duty. But, that we should express the same notion in the same particular word; as for example, if we translate the Hebrew or Greek word once by *purpose*, never to call it *intent*; if one where *journeying*, never *traveling*; if one where *think*, never *suppose*;

[11] In his commentary on 2 Thessalonians 2. [Ed]

[12] *De Genesi ad litteram imperfectus liber* 8.5. [Ed]

[13] Augustine, *On Christian Doctrine* 2.14; see above, 33. [Ed]

if one where *pain*, never *ache*; if one where *joy*, never *gladness*, &c. Thus to mince the matter, we thought to savour more of curiosity the wisdom, and that rather it would breed scorn in the atheist, than bring profit to the godly reader. For is the Kingdom of God become words or syllables? Why should we be in bondage to them if we may be free, use one precisely when we may use another no less fit, as commodiously? A godly Father in the primitive time showed himself greatly moved, that one of newfangledness called κράββατον σκίμτους, though the difference be little or none; and another reporteth, that he was much abused for turning *cucurbita* (to which reading the people had been used) into *hedera*. Now if this happen in better times, and upon so small occasions, we might also be charged (by scoffers) with some unequal dealing towards a great number of good English words. For as it is written of a certain great philosopher, that he should say that those logs were happy that were made images to be worshipped; for their fellows, as good as they, lay for blocks behind the fire: so if we should say, as it were, unto certain words, Stand up higher, have a place in the Bible always, and to others of like quality, Get ye hence, be banished for ever, we might be taxed peradventure with S. James his words, namely, *To be partial in ourselves and judges of evil thoughts* [James 2:4]. Add hereunto, that niceness in words was always counted the next step to trifling, and so was to be curious about names too; also that we cannot follow a better pattern for elocution than God himself; therefore he using diverse words in his Holy Writ and indifferently for one thing in nature, we, if we will not be superstitious, may use the same liberties in our English versions out of Hebrew and Greek, for that copy or store that he hath given us. Lastly, we have on the one side avoided the scrupulosity of the Puritans, who leave the old ecclesiastical words, and betake them to other, as when they put washing for baptism, and congregation instead of church: as also on the other side we have shunned the obscurity of the Papists, in their *azimes*, *tunic*, *rational*, *holocausts*, *praepuce*, *pasche*, and a number of such like, whereof their late translation is full, and that of purpose to darken the sense, that since they must needs translate the Bible, yet by the language thereof, it may be kept from being understood. But we desire that the Scripture may speak like itself, as in the language of Canaan, that it may be understood even of [by] the very vulgar.

Many other things we might give thee warning of (gentle reader) if we had not exceeded the measure of a preface already. It remaineth that we commend thee to God, and to the spirit of his grace, which is able to build further then we can ask or think. He removeth the scales from our eyes, the veil from our hearts, opening our wits that we may understand his word, enlarging our hearts, yea correcting our affections, that we may love it above gold and silver, yea that we may love it to the end. Ye are brought unto fountains of living water which ye digged not [Genesis 26:15]; do not cast earth into them with the Philistines, neither prefer broken pits before them with the wicked Jews [Jeremiah 2:13]. Others have laboured, and you may enter into their labours; O receive not so great things in vain, O despise not so great salvation: Be not like swine to tread under foot so precious things, neither yet like dogs to tear and abuse holy things. Say not to our Saviour with the Gergesites, Depart out of our coasts [Matthew 8:34]; neither yet with Esau sell your birthright for a mess of potage [Hebrews 12:16]. If light be come into the world, love not darkness more then light; if food, if clothing be offered, go not naked, starve not yourselves. Remember the advise of Nazianzen, *It is a grievous thing* (or dangerous) *to neglect a great fair, and to seek to make markets afterwards*; also the encouragement of S. Chrysostom, *It is altogether impossible that he that is sober (and watchful) should at any time be neglected*; lastly, the admonition and menacing of S. Augustine, *They that despise God's will inviting them, shall feel God's will taking vengeance of them*. It is a fearful thing to fall into the hands of the living God [Hebrews 10:31]; but a blessed thing it is, and will bring us to everlasting blessedness in the end, when God speaketh unto us, to hearken; when he setteth his word before us, to read it; when he stretcheth out his hand and calleth, to answer, Here am I; here we are to do thy will, O God. The Lord work a care and conscience in us to know him and serve him, that we may be acknowledged of him at the appearing of our Lord Jesus Christ, to whom with the Holy Ghost be all praise and thanksgiving. Amen.

Miguel de Cervantes Saavedra

Soldier, slave, novelist, playwright, and poet, Miguel de Cervantes Saavedra (1547-1616) is generally regarded the greatest writer in Spanish literature; his *Don Quixote* is one of the classics not only of Spanish but of modern European literature.

Born near Madrid, fourth of seven children, to a barber-surgeon and his wife who were members of the minor gentry, Cervantes received some education (we are not certain where or how much), but did not attend university; instead, in 1569, at the age of 21, he went to Italy, where he may have served for a short time as chamberlain in a cardinal's household. In 1570 he enlisted in a Spanish infantry regiment stationed in Naples, then a Spanish possession, to fight the Turks;

according to all reports he fought bravely and, in the 1571 battle that broke the Turkish control of the Mediterranean, was wounded in his left hand (which never recovered) and chest.

The next few years he spent mostly in Naples, still a soldier; in 1575 he was sailing for Spain when his ship was captured by Barbary pirates and Cervantes and his brother Rodrigo were sold into slavery in Algiers. Since he was carrying letters of recommendation to the King, his value as a slave was inflated and his captivity prolonged – but the letters may also have saved him from torture and even death after any one of his four attempted escapes. Rodrigo was freed in 1577, but it was 1580 before his family could raise the 500 gold escudos to ransom Miguel.

Cervantes returned to Spain in hopes that his bravery might bring him some compensation, but to no avail; he spent the rest of his life in straitened circumstances and unsatisfying employment. In the early 1580s he had an illegitimate daughter (his only child, Isabel) by a married woman; in 1584 he married a woman 18 years his junior, Catalina de Salazar y Palacios. She owned a small property in La Mancha, and he set about writing, first *La Galatea* (1585), a novel, then anywhere between nine and thirty plays, none of which was a theatrical success.

In 1587 he was forced to seek employment outside the theatre, and became a commissary of provisions for the Spanish Armada – an unpleasant task, since it required him to requisition foodstuffs from rural communities, but it did involve a good deal of travel through Andalusia that he later put to good use in *Don Quixote* and elsewhere. This job lasted a year or so, until the defeat of the Armada by the English; given his sloppy bookkeeping he might have lost the job anyway, and the next decade and a half saw him bouncing from job to job, or job possibility to job possibility, wrangling with the court over unpaid salaries and taxes, even spending a year in debtor's jail from 1597 to 1598 – which may have been where he first dreamed up Don Quixote.

That romantic gentleman first saw print in 1605, and was an instant sensation, soon spreading Cervantes' name all across Europe. Unfortunately, he sold the publication rights to his printer, and never collected a penny in royalties on the first part. He lived mostly on patronage in the remaining years of his life, publishing his *Novelas exemplares* ('Exemplary Novels', 1613), *Viaje del Parnaso* ('Voyage to Parnassus', 1614), *Ochos comedias, y ocho entremeses nuevos* ('The Interludes', 1614), part two of *Don Quixote* (1615), from which the excerpt below is taken, and *Los trabaios de Persiles y Sigismunda, historia setentrional* ('The Labours of Persiles and Sigismunda, A Northern Story', published posthumously in 1617). He wrote the dedication to *Los trabaios* three days before he died in April, 1616, bidding the world farewell with a moving peace of mind.

Cervantes has Don Quixote pronounce on translation, famously, shortly upon arriving in Barcelona in chapter 62 of the second part. The image of the translation as the reverse side of a Flemish tapestry will recur throughout the history of translation theory, most notably in August Wilhelm von Schlegel.

Viewing Flemish Tapestries From the Wrong Side
From *Don Quixote*, Part II (1615)
Translated by Walter Starkie

Don Quixote wished to go for a stroll through the city without ceremony and on foot, for he feared that the boys would persecute him if he went on horseback. So, he and Sancho, with two other servants Don Antonio gave him, went out for a walk. As they were going down a street, Don Quixote lifted his eyes and saw inscribed over a door in very large letters, 'Books printed here', which greatly pleased him, for he had never before seen any printing and longed to know how it was done. He went in with all his followers and saw them drawing off the sheets in one place, correcting the proofs in another, setting up the type in this, and revising in that – in short, all the processes that are to be seen in a large printing house. Don Quixote went up to one department and asked what they were doing there. The workmen duly explained, and he watched with wonder and passed on. Then he approached another man and asked him what he was doing, and the workman replied: "Sir, that gentleman you see there", and he pointed out a fine-looking fellow of dignified appearance, "has translated an Italian book into our Castilian language, and I am setting it up for the press".

"What is the title of the book?" asked Don Quixote.

"Sir", replied the author, "the book in Italian is called *Le Bagatelle*".

"And what corresponds to *Le Bagatelle* in our Castilian?" asked Don Quixote.

"*Le Bagatelle*", said the author, "is, we might say, trifles in our tongue, and though this book is humble in its title, it has good solid things in it".

"I know a little Italian", said Don Quixote, "and pride myself on singing some of Ariosto's stanzas. But tell me, sir – and I do not ask this to test your knowledge – have you ever come across the word *pignata* in your reading?"

"Yes, often", replied the author.

"And how do you translate it into Castilian, sir?" asked Don Quixote.

"How else", answered the author, "but by stew?"

"Bless me!" exclaimed Don Quixote. "How advanced you are in the Tuscan tongue! I would lay a good wager that when the Tuscan tongue has *piace*, you say 'please', and when it has *piu*, you say 'more', and you translate *su* by 'above' and *giu* by 'beneath'".

"Yes, so I translate them, certainly", said the author, "for these are their proper equivalents".

"Yes, I'll dare swear that you are not appreciated by the world, which is forever loath to reward intellect and merit. What abilities are lost here! What talents neglected! What virtues unappreciated! But yet, it seems to me that translating from one tongue into another, unless it be from those queens of tongues, Greek and Latin, is like viewing Flemish tapestries from the wrong side, for although you see the pictures, they are covered with threads that obscure them so that the smoothness and the gloss of the fabric are lost. And translating from easy languages does not signify talent or power of words, any more than does transcribing or copying one paper from another. By that I do not wish to imply that this exercise of translation is not praiseworthy, for a man might be occupied in worse things and less profitable occupations. I except from this observation two famous translators; the one, Doctor Cristóbal de Figueroa for his *Pastor Fido*,[1] and the other Don Juan de Jáuregui for his *Aminta*,[2] for they leave you doubting which is the translation and which the original".

Jean Chapelain

Jean Chapelain (1595-1674) was a French poet and literary critic and sometime translator who is best remembered today as a kind of cultural politician: a prime mover in the founding of the French Academy, his word carried enormous weight in the determination of 'quality' (and thus social status and royal support) among contemporary writers.

Chapelain was not highly regarded as a poet – his reputation in his own day was as a conversationalist at Catherine de Vivonne's famous salon (the Hotel de Rambouillet) – but his early translation (in his mid-twenties) of Mateo Alemán's recent picaresque novel *Guzmán de Alfarache* attracted a good deal of attention, and he became a protégé of the influential poet and critic François Malherbe. His poetic production included a collection of odes and an epic poem, *La Pucelle* (first twelve cantos in 1656, last twelve posthumously in 1882).

In the book wars between the ancients and the moderns, Chapelain was a proponent of the moderns, and argued strenously for an empirical approach to literature, as opposed to the blind application of 'universal' standards and principles derived from Greek and Roman sources. He was very active in the Academy that he helped Cardinal Richelieu to found; it was his idea for the Academy to commission a dictionary of the French language, and when Richelieu wanted Corneille censured for *Le Cid* (1638) – ostensibly on stylistic and grammatical grounds, more likely because Corneille defended Spain (with which France was at war) and the duel – Chapelain drafted the document.

One of his many correspondents was Pierre-Daniel Huet, author of *De interpretatione* (1661), another activist in favour of deriving rules (in Huet's case, for translation) from actual cases rather than ancient authorities. In their letters to each other Huet and Chapelain tisked their tongues at Nicolas Perrot d'Ablancourt, in their view a renegade translator who simply flouted the rules; interestingly, however, his contempt for translation and willingness to abridge and expand, planish and polish Alemán's book in French points unmistakably ahead to what would later be derided as the 'beautiful infidelity' of d'Ablancourt's work.

To the Reader
Preface to *Le Gueux, ou la vie de Guzmán d'Alfarache* ('The Rogue, or the life of Guzmán de Alfarache', 1619-1620)
Translated by David G. Ross

Translating is an abject thing, and translation in those who practice it presupposes a servility of spirit and a depreciation of intellect. The noble disdain the exercise, and one rarely sees an intellect well-disposed to great things embrace it except as a pastime, nor a translated work have a long or celebrated life. Learned antiquity made almost no use of it, rather each book was read in its own language; and of the copious hundred thousand books with which the scholar Ptolemy had built his library,[1] there is only a record of one Dares Phrygius and one Dictys Cretensis whose monuments have

---

[1] *Il pastor fido* ('The Faithful Shepherd', 1590) is a tragicomic play written by the Italian playwright Giovanni Battista Guarini, translated into Spanish by Cristóbal de Figueroa. Richard Fanshawe's 1647 translation of the play into English prompted John Denham's 1648 poem 'To Sir Richard Fanshawe Upon His Translation of Pastor Fido', printed below. [Ed]

[2] Juan de Jáuregui y Aguilar translated Tasso's *L'Aminta* in 1573. [Ed]

[1] The famous library at Alexandria, based on Aristotle's private library, was planned by Ptolemy I Soter and established by Ptolemy II Philadelphius. [Ed]

passed on to posterity via other languages. The *Phaenomena* of Aratus were a beginner's effort from Cicero's childhood,[2] which the latter himself did not value, and what one sees of Valerius Flaccus' *Argonautica* is only a translation of the subject and disposition, not of the words. Neither the comedy nor the tragedy survived from Greece to Rome except with this license, and the surviving idylls always granted it to themselves. Of all the versions with which our mongering age now abounds, only Plutarch's has equaled its original; no other can be found that brought little or much fame to its author, with all deference to Viginère. And, indeed, I am of the opinionated opinion – whatever the interested parties say about it – that acquaintance with two languages, when it is perfect (which is all that can be advanced to improve this business), is not sufficient to improve the reputation of a man except as a good grammarian; abject honor, servile ambition. Nevertheless, I do not for all that want to censure or prohibit the practice; for, on the contrary, I deem it to be useful to everyone and necessary to many whom books translated into their native language teach an acquaintance with innumerable things of which they would be deprived as a result of their ignorance of the language in which they are written. But I mean that those who trouble themselves with it must not promise themselves any commendation for competency or doctrine (which is the only copious praise that literature can give to its sucklings), given that neither one nor the other can be called idioms, which are the agents of the sciences, but only of those sciences that have their own natural principles and undoubted proofs.

Having always been of this opinion, I am aware of nothing that would be more repugnant to my taste than this profession, and I could sooner be sold on marvelous humbug than I would ever be near to seeing myself subjected to it. I do not pretend to say that my ambition raises me too high and that it makes me believe the enterprise beneath my ability and strengths; for it is true that I only exercise myself with language to provide myself with pleasure and not with grief. I was of this state of mind when the esteem that I had caused some friends of mine to have for the Spanish *Guzmán*[3] spiritedly carried them to the point of daring to speak importunately until I was made to undertake the translation. The power that they have over my soul and actions has gently forced me to this work and perhaps made me abandon better to content them. Believe me that it is a command that I was given, and I say so without pretense; my name, which I am hiding for the aforementioned motive, must relieve you of any suspicion. Now, of these two ills, it is a sort of blessing to discover oneself with the lesser; the misery of this occupation is much more tolerable when one discovers a good, well-received subject, which *Guzmán* was at its birth with so much fortune that not just all of Spain, but, no exaggeration, all of Europe held it in such great esteem as to consider it the best of all that had ever been done in the genre, and observers have, in its introduction, remarked with amazement at the circulation it had: in seven years, twenty-five licensed editions were done of the first part alone, not counting counterfeits, and at least fifty thousand volumes of it were distributed. This peculiarity, perhaps base and unworthy of this occasion, bears irreproachable witness to the general opinion regarding its worth. But my personal opinion does not go so far, and – do not think I am selling you my wares for more than they are precisely worth – I will tell you frankly what I think of it. *Guzmán* is on the whole a rich conception and a well-conceived satire in the footsteps of Lucian and Apuleius in their *The Golden Ass*,[4] and, more immediately, in those of *Lazarillo de Tormés*,[5] which was its prototype. None of these last equals it in ingenuity, richness, or variety, just as it does not approach a single one in doctrine or features of erudition. What excellence it has is an accurate description of the world's malversions – as we experience at present in all capacities – using particular circumstances from which it derives with such familiarity and such clarity that there is nothing more to be desired; stories therein are hardly ever told unadorned, and digression is a license that it allows itself, and wisely so, for there lies the benefit of its reading. Speaking of specifics, on the other hand, as there are any number of beautiful pieces, so are there some that do not satisfy me and for which I would desire more discrimination and less sordidness from the author. I noticed somewhere therein what one of the era's noble and amusing intellects made of Spanish writers: that his words are full of repetitions; that there is sometimes roguery in his roguery, that his illations [inferences] are often scarcely reasonable and sometimes not at all; that his digressions are too frequent and too long-winded to avoid disrupting the flow of the discourse, putting the reader off the scent, and disgusting him on the first encounter; that the ideas he has on every subject are little beyond the ordinary; that one only rarely sees him make a witticism or a pun – he is

[2] Cicero translated Aratus' most famous poem, the *Phaenomena* on astronomy, into Latin in *de Natura Deorum* 2.41 (44 B.C.E.). [Ed]

[3] *Vida y hechos del picaro Guzmán de Alfarache, atalaya de la vida humana* (1599-1605), early picaresque novel by the Spanish novelist Mateo Alemán. [Ed]

[4] Lucian was the supposed author of a surviving fragment called *Lucius, or the Ass*, on which Lucius Apuleius partly based his *Metamorphoses*, known in English as *The Golden Ass*. [Ed]

[5] *Lazarillo de Tormés* (1554), the first picaresque novel, published anonymously in Spain. [Ed]

ill at ease for the most part; but these are still only superficial blemishes and small holes, which do not prevent this globe from being round. Indeed, although it is not close to perfect, the good still exceeds the bad by a great deal, which is the stamp and imprint of good books, among which there are none to be found that is so perfect that there is not still something to criticize. But if the learned find this work to be inferior to those of the past, they will at the same time be able to wonder at the deficiency of the age and impute the shortcoming to it, for the work is the best that was done. And how neither *Euphormio*[6] nor *Justine*[7], which followed it, approaches it; they would lose outright to such a formidable opponent; it comes out on top no matter how you look at it. There you have what I think of *Guzmán*, turning to the undertaking of which the goal of my labor has been to show not all there was, but all that could please. So, to treat it thus, I often found myself constrained to abridge useless things and add necessary ones, above all in the relationship between judgments, which are quite disconnected in the original and hold together rather well in this copy. Therefore, I say to you without temerity that it has nothing good that is not here, that it has nothing bad that herein appears, and that what it should have said is usually here. There were indeed places where, against my own judgment and with extreme necessity, I had to follow the author or instead ruin his composition and interweaving, especially in those where he resumes and repeats previously discussed matters. That cannot slip by without shocking the sensitive, and I regret that he was inaccurate and unmindful, thereby compelling me to embrace his errors. I have however remedied this as much as possible, to the point of being able to say that they are less oppressive. Additionally, for the proverbs with which this book is strewn, I translated them not word for word, for they would have turned out awkward, but by other, equivalent proverbs to the extent that the French language was able to provide them, and, lacking these, by the moral of each. Also, there were no phrases peculiar to the Spanish that I translated into French likenesses, retaining the properties of the language to the point of affecting its baseness, as that way of writing would have it. And, understand, what you will perhaps like the least – if you do not censure it yet – respecting the base and artless ways of speaking, is what was most troublesome for me. But if, when he turns to raillery, you find me inferior – as I frankly admit, such places may exist – you will recall that banter and biting lines, always having either affected terms or harmonies, can only lose their elegance in translation; there are always constraints, and languages in these encounters have their properties that are unsuitable for others. He who will deem me prolix and my volume much larger than the original, who will censure me for superfluity and for an affectation of grandiloquence, if he will only consider that any work of concise style, of obscure and hidden meaning, in short, of laborious interpretation like this one, cannot be translated as succinctly, for the sake of being understood, and in as few words as its original. Another, yet unavoidable fault will be noticed in this translation: the names of cities that have been inserted herein, which in Spanish are of great effect and by themselves engross the minds of the natives so as to make them find the adventures pleasant; it is not so with foreigners, on whom what one succeeds in recounting has almost no effect, as the named places are unknown. This is approximately the good and the bad of my translation, which I anticipate must be underrated from the very first or perhaps censured with superficial opinions as useless, since, they will say, it has already been done once, and as easy, since I will have been able to use that completed version. To this my honor obliges me to respond that, in the first place, without disturbing the sorry memory of Chappuis,[8] who put his hand to it, in everyone's estimation he was unsuccessful, and so much so that if his first works had ever earned him a name, this last takes it from him without redemption. It was not malice that got him, for the good fellow always proceeded in good faith, but it is true that this morsel was a bit too delicate for his palate, and the merest trifle was enough to bowl him over. So the knowledge of his bad work in this and the complaints that I saw articulated by all of the understanding made me resolve – having as I did to bring the second work of the same author to light, an extraordinary and unique piece, not to wrong this one – to redo the first anew and to delay the misery that this moil must give me for the benefit that would accrue to the public of delivering them both to it from the same pen and the same ink – and done well, if I dare to say so without presumption. I have thus rebuilt it anew with your benefit alone in mind, dear Reader. Regarding the second point that I might have used the first translation, I let you reflect whether I would want to make use of something that I, along with everyone, reject as bad, and that, to recognize it at all as such, I am making a resolution to recommence rather than to correct, which would be to deceive you and to deceive

[6] John Barclay's *Euphormionis Lusinini Satyricon*, a Petronian satire on the Jesuits, was published in 1603-7. [Ed]
[7] Probably Marcus Junianus Justinus' *Trogi Pompeii Historiarum Philippicarum epitoma* (1613), translated into English by Robert Codrington as *The History of Justine, Taken Out of the Four and Forty Books of Trogus Pompeius* (1654).

[8] Gabriel Chappuis translated the first part of *Guzmán* into French; his partial translation appeared posthumously, in 1625. [Ed]

myself. If I wanted to make use of it, it would be either of easy passages or, instead, of difficult ones: as for the easy ones, No! for facile things are facile and do not require any assistance; as for the difficult ones, a stronger No, since if he had met with the difficulties in a way that merited his imitation, he would have all the more sense with the easy things and, in consequence, would have done well everywhere, which runs counter to common sense and to the opinion of the very people who made this objection. Here, I effusively swear to you that during all my work, and over the course of the six previous years, I neither read nor even saw Chappuis's work, so completely that I am able to make this solemn oath to you, lest some impression remain of me that is not good, which might impede my judgment and deprive my inspiration of its freedom. But without other arguments or oaths, I refer those who would have me enter into an odious competition, if they are up to it, to the inspection of ticklish passages and to the comparison of places on which each of us has worked, where I am sure that a little inspection will illustrate my labor and his ignorance. But if they will not or if they cannot deliver this, let them read the second part; it is a brand new topic, which has been neither seen nor touched by others, and which I cannot be charged with having stolen or borrowed from anyone. The way that I handled it will prove beyond rejoinder that even for the first one I had neither the effect nor the idea of such vileness. And the notes that I did, as much for my personal satisfaction as for your benefit, Reader – the instant translation concerning the most difficult areas, which are set forth in the footnotes – will further serve to make you recognize that my work is of quite another sort than that of others, accurate in quite another way, and crafted by quite another type for your benefit and satisfaction. So what I am giving you is a complete body replete with all its members to the extent possible, without blemish or any fault that could rightly shock you. It is divided into two parts. The first has had so many celebrators of its quality that it is pointless here to recite the commendations; you cannot be so inexperienced with books that you do not know its value. Of the second, as of the one that has been seen less and that has fallen into but a paltry few hands, I will tell you that you will see it surpass your expectations and even your desires; for if the other has deserved to have itself imitated by so many authors and to be followed by one of the conceived scheme, the one that comes next, if it did not end his misfortunes, would deserve not one but one hundred sequels in witness of its perfection. I will say nothing more about it in order to have the author say here what, at the publication of the first part, he put in front thereof under the title of

Brief Announcement

Joseph Webbe

Joseph Webbe (before 1612-1633) was an English physician and grammarian who was best known for his controversial advocacy of a colloquial method of teaching languages, including Latin and Greek.

We know next to nothing about his life prior to the publication in 1612 of a Latin treatise on astrology; apparently he took an M.A. and a Ph.D. somewhere on the continent, possibly at the University of Padua. Some time before 1620 he published his English translation of *The Familiar Epistles of Cicero*, and some time before 1622 he returned to England, where he began to propound his unprecedented approach to language learning, in *An Appeal to Truth* in 1622, *A Petition to the High Court of Parliament, in the Behalf of Auncient and Authentique Authors* in 1623 (here he claims that his method has found favour with King James I), and *Vsus et Authoritas* in 1626.

Webbe's argument 'concerning art and use' revolves around the best way to learn Latin – from grammarians, through 'art', or by speaking it after the model of their own writings, through 'use'. Having himself been raised speaking only Latin, and benefitted greatly from it, Webbe argues strenuously for the latter course.

His remarks on translation arise from his desire to explain why modern society is slipping away from a close familiarity with the 'custom of the ancients': not only do moderns reduce ancient Latin to the 'art' or logic of grammar and invent new words and phrasings, they also (especially the less learned) translate word for word 'into other languages' – a reference, apparently, to the phenomenon of interference, by which, say, an English-speaker learning Latin contaminates the Latin s/he speaks with English word order. In this desperate attempt to hold fast to a dying Latin tradition, Webbe clings to Ciceronian usage against Cicero's own precepts; for while Cicero did warn against translating word for word, his preference was for translating freely and creatively so as precisely to develop new words and phrasings in Latin.

Perceiving the Custom of the Ancients
From *An Appeal to Truth, Concerning Art and Use* (1622)

And to this purpose Cominius says, If we would follow the example of ancient authors, orators, historians, and poets, either in Latin or in Greek, and should be exercised in their custom of speaking, which we find within their writings, there is no doubt but we may arrive unto their very heights of elegancy.

But, there are four especial reasons, alleged by my author, why few or none perceive the custom of the ancients.

First, they put whatsoever they would speak word for word into another language, in the same order wherein they speak it in their own. Now, though this may in some fall out well, yet there are many speeches, sentences, proverbs, sayings, and authorities, of two words only, or of more, which, translated into three or four languages, are to be set down in every one after a diverse order, and other words are to be received. For every tongue has proper and peculiar words, which are neither agreeable to other tongues nor liable to translation; by which the eleganter sayings, the graver sentences, and the more usual proverbs are especially composed. Wherefore they are deceived which speak according to the order of other languages, which is known to be much used, and most among the unlearned.

Secondly: though such as follow grammar, and are a middle sort of scholars, do not always translate verbally [literally], yet they speak not by the order and custom of the ancients, but place their words after a grammatical order and construction; rather obeying the rules and precepts of grammarians than the custom of the ancients and the judgment of hearing, which is contrary to the precepts of Cicero.

Thirdly: though the learned sort, and such as would be called poets, and orators, translate not always word for word, nor do everywhere observe a grammatical construction, yet they come not near the Latin elegancy, as having been brought up from their childhood by the art of grammar and analogy. They take a pride to frame new words, without regard unto the judgment of the ear, which though they be sometimes placed according to the order of the ancients, yet are they harsh and without elegancy, because they are not moderated and measured by the ear, as their ancestors would have them.

Fourthly: the greater part of men, and especially of the learneder sort, are ashamed forsooth to speak in the same words, and in the same order placed, that the ancients spoke them, lest it might be cast in their teeth that they knew not how to speak of themselves without using the ways and words of others.

Suzanne du Vegerre

Nothing is known about Suzanne du Vegerre other than that she published a book entitled *Admirable Events, selected out of four bookes, written in French by John Peter Camus* in 1639. Her preface underscores the standard (male) position on romances during the period, and thus stands in stark opposition to Margaret Tyler's preface of fifty years earlier; it is significant for the history of translation theory, however, that she chooses to combat romances not by ignoring them (translating something else, say) but by doing a propagandistic translation of four of them in one. Her book might be thought of as the first volume of *Reader's Digest Condensed Books* – except that her condensation is ideologically motivated, designed to give the reader only the unornamented truth by omitting everything 'entertaining' in the original.

The Author's Epistle to the READER
Preface to her translation of John Peter Camus, *Admirable Events* (1639)

The enterprise which I have taken in hand is to wrestle, or rather to encounter, with those frivolous books which may all be comprised under the name of Romance, which would require the hands which fables attribute to Briareus,[1] or the strength which Poets give unto Hercules; the hands of that giant to handle so many pens and the vigour of that hero to undergo so painful a labour; but what cannot a courage do, animated by a zeal of pleasuring his neighbour, and provoked by desire to advance the light of virtue, and to lessen vice. O why has not my pen the virtue to cure the wounds that these wicked books cause in this world? or at least why cannot it devour these monsters, which the writers of those aforesaid works, mere enchanters of minds, cause to appear in the forms of books? ... [A]t least if these my labours could cure those who are miserably infected with often viewing these pamphlets; if the loss of so much time may be called employment, I should not think my labour spent in vain, nor my pen unprofitable. But when I see this mischievous tree, which I strive to cut down, casting forth so many branches as I lop off, and doing like the vine, which never sprouts so well as when it is cut, it makes me fear a labour like unto that of Danaides, or of Sisyphus ...[2]

Now to overthrow so many fabulous books, I undertake not my combat directly, as if I were confuting heresies, for it is not needful that I should trouble myself to prove the obscurity of darkness, nor to show

---

[1] Briareus was one of three hundred-armed and fifty-headed giants in Greek mythology called Hecatoncheires, sons of Uranus and Gaia. [Ed]

[2] The Danaids in Greek mythology (Danaus and his daughters) once attempted to bring water to a city under siege in leaky buckets. Sisyphus was condemned by the Judges of the Dead to roll a huge boulder up a hill and over the other side; whenever he neared the top, however, it rolled back down and he had to start over. [Ed]

the falsehood of these romances, adventures, chivalries, and other such trash ... By what manner do I then labour to overcome my adversaries? it is by diversion, setting relations true and beneficial, in the place of those that are profane, ... to the end that those whose great leisure causes to seek wherewith to employ their time may find wherewithall to entertain their desires.

Even as truth is constant, so falsehood is wavering and differing, and is capable of more different forms than the *materia prima* [primal matter], or the Proteus of poets, which is the cause that these authors, who love vanity and follow after lies, set forth their works in as many fashions as they please ... [I]n brief, they stuff them with so many baits that the licoriceness of the sauce makes them lose the taste of the meat, which of itself is without flavour or relish, and most commonly hurtful; whereas narrations of things which have truly happened are tied to more subjection, for ... conscience obliges to keep faithfully to the ground and body of the history: ... the author is strictly tied to the bounds of probability, out of which he may not swerve a nail's breadth without discrediting the whole work. For although fables, parables, and poetical fictions do sometimes hide in them good precepts, and many serious examples, yet the instructions lose much of their credit when they are mixed amongst vain inventions ...

Now amongst the multitude of these writings, which like unto reeds have nothing but a pleasing verdure and a fair show of stately words, hollow and empty without any solid substance, there are one kind which may be called an ant's nest, a seed-plot or nursery of these wanton inventions, and that is it which bears the title of tales and novels ... full of so much licentiousness and dishonesty that it is pity to see these books in the hands of youth, who suck this Heraclean [Herculean] honey (sweet but venomous) through the sight ...

... But to say in general what mine opinion is of these and all such like confused heaps of frivolous relations, I cannot better compare them than to dainty garden knots and borders which have serpents hidden under their flowers, or unto fine fields: pleasing unto the eye, but full of hemlock and aconitum,[3] or unto sallets, wherein are poisonous herbs, or unto those fine goldsmiths' works, wherein are inferred base metals and counterfeit stones ... or unto the horse of Troy, out of which came armed soldiers, by whom that beautiful city was turned into ashes. I say not this so much to disgrace my adversaries as to give testimony to truth.

Now (my dear reader) it is this kind of books which I strive to supplant by these singular Events, which I here offer unto thy view ... [T]hou shalt here find natural beauties without art, I mean, examples which borrow all their grace and worth from the force of truth which upholds them, and whose testimonies are seen in the times, places, and persons:

All these Events, which I call singular, as well for being rare and notable, as for having no connection the one with the other, each one making its body, have as it were undertaken either to cry down a vice or to extol a virtue. The end I aim at, as being (also the end of all good history) to withdraw from evil and to excite unto good, ... adding a few words, short but pressing, like to so many spurs, which prick forward to well doing, and so many bits which hold back from the doing of evil, sometimes showing the recompence of goodness and sometimes the punishment of vice, to the end that love and fear may support the good and retain the bad in their endeavors....

As for the manner I am to advertise thee, that I study as much as I can for brevity ... I keep close to the matter, and give little liberty unto my thoughts to spread into digressions, if they be not necessary, and as it were bred in the subject, by reason whereof I have weaned myself from the sweet milk of poesie, and have abstained from putting any verses in these Events. I have also taken away the other graces, as apostrophes, dialogisms, complaints, speeches, conferences, letters, orations; in brief, all that might enlarge or embellish so that in comparison of our other relations, these are but abridgements of histories, and as it were skeletons, nothing remaining but the bones of each event, stripped of the ornaments which might have set forth their bodies in a far fairer hew. There be minds which soil in reading a history of great length, human patience being not of any great extent; but when Events are set down in such a manner as the end is not far from the beginning, this is it which encourages the reader, and both gives him a desire of seeing further and also eases him in reading ...

This book of Events is a garland made of many flowers, a honey composed of many herbs, whose juices are different, a treacle made of divers ingredients, and wherein the serpent of vice is seasoned with so many antidotes that in lieu of hurting, it will do good ...

If I did write these histories rather to please men than to benefit my neighbour, it may be I should be fain to fear their censures and seek to conjure or appease their bad humours. But should I entertain such a thought as to purchase reputation in this world, then would I set myself in another posture, and would give unto my pen a subject more flashing and ranging ...

Examples of good and evil have a like virtue (provided) they meet with a disposition according in the souls of them that see them. For many read books for curiosity, others for variety, or to pass time, and for want of other employment, another with envy, few

---

[3] The aconites are poisonous plants; the species *Aconitum Napellus* in English is called either monkshood or wolfsbane. [Ed]

with sincerity, few with a desire to profit, and to put in practise the good instructions they find therein ...

But let them say on, some good souls (nevertheless) whose dispositions are inclined to virtue will be glad to find profitable admonitions set down and sweetly mingled with varieties of pleasures fitting their humour. And therefore I have strove by the help of my pen to publish examples worthy to be noted, to the end that we may grow wise by the good or evil hap of others. This is the mark aimed at by all these Events, which I have gathered in the great field of the world. It is your part, dear reader, to extract honey out of the hardest stone, oil out of the flint, studying a reformation of manners in this school of human actions. Remembering always that the secret (and if I may so say) the great work of prudence and justice is to avoid evil and to embrace good.

John Denham

Sir John Denham (1615-1669) was one of the most popular English poets of the mid-seventeenth century, and his popularity, based on his meditative and didactic landscape poetry, continued well into the eighteenth century.

He was educated for the law courts at the University of Oxford and was even admitted to the bar, but he never practised law; he made his fame and fortune as a writer, translating the first six books of the *Aeneid* while still at Oxford (not published until 1656) and making his name with a tragedy in blank verse in 1641 and a long poem in 1642. His reputation has subsequently dimmed, but his poetry was greatly admired by critics and imitated by poets for a century after his death.

During the roughly two decades of the Civil War, from 1642 to 1660, Denham was an ardent activist in the cause of Charles II. He was high sheriff of Surrey at the outbreak of war, and was appointed governor of Farnham Castle, where he was taken prisoner by William Waller; he was soon released and allowed to retire to Oxford, where he amused his royalist friends with satires on the parliamentarians. He spent two years on the Continent with the exiled royal family, where he gambled away what remained of his money. With the restoration of the monarchy Charles rewarded him with a knighthood, the job of surveyor-general of works, and election to the Royal Society; he later served as a Member of Parliament. When after the death of his first wife he remarried in 1665, scandal followed: his eighteen-year-old wife (he was fifty) became the lover of the Duke of York, Denham had a fit of madness and appeared before the king calling himself the Holy Ghost, and his wife died soon after under suspicious circumstances, claiming that she had been poisoned (a post mortem showed no trace of poison). Hated by the populace for his alleged murder of his wife, generally disliked at court, Denham spent the remaining years of his life the hapless butt of lampooners, who accused him of everything from murder to plagiarism.

In addition to his own poems and translations, Denham wrote the fifth act for Katherine Philips' translation of Corneille's *Horace*, which had remained unfinished at her death in 1663 (published in 1669) and contributed verses to Richard Fanshawe's translation of Guarini's *Pastor Fido*, the preface to which appears below.

"To Sir Richard Fanshaw Upon His Translation of Pastor Fido" (1648)

Such is our pride, our folly, or our fate,
That few but such as cannot write, translate.
But what in them is want of art, or voice,
In thee is either modesty or choice.
While this great piece, restored by thee doth stand
Free from the blemish of an artless hand.
Secure of fame, thou justly dost esteem
Less honour to create, than to redeem.
Nor ought a genius less than his that writ,
Attempt translation; for transplanted wit,
All the defects of air and soil doth share,
And colder brains like colder climates are:
In vain they toil, since nothing can beget
A vital spirit, but a vital heat.
That servile path thou nobly dost decline
Of tracing word by word, and line by line.
Those are the laboured births of slavish brains,
Not the effects of poetry, but pains;
Cheap vulgar arts, whose narrowness affords
No flight for thoughts, but poorly sticks at words.
A new and nobler way thou dost pursue
To make translations and translators too.
They but preserve the ashes, thou the flame,
True to his sense, but truer to his fame.
Fording his current, where thou find'st it low
Let'st in thine own to make it rise and flow;
Wisely restoring whatsoever grace
It lost by change of times, or tongues, or place.
Nor fettered to his numbers and his times,[1]
Betray'st his music to unhappy rhymes.
Nor are the nerves of his compacted strength
Stretched and dissolved into unsinewed length:
Yet after all (lest we should think it thine)
Thy spirit to his circle dost confine.
New names, new dressings, and the modern cast,

[1] I.e., the quantity and quality of his metrical feet. [Ed]

Some scenes, some persons altered, had out-faced
The world, it were thy work; for we have known
Some thanked and praised for what was less their own.
That master's hand which to the life can trace
The airs, the lines, and features of a face,
May with a free and bolder stroke express
A varied posture, or a flatt'ring dress;
He could have made those like, who made the rest,
But that he knew his own design was best.

Preface to *The Destruction of Troy* (1656)

There are so few translations which deserve praise that I scarce ever saw any which deserved pardon; those who travel in that kind, being for the most part so unhappy as to rob others without enriching themselves, pulling down the fame of good authors without raising their own. Neither has any author been more hardly dealt with than this our Master; and the reason is evident, for what is most excellent is most inimitable; and if even the worst authors are yet made worse by their translators, how impossible is it not to do great injury to the best? And therefore I have not the vanity to think my copy equal to the original, nor (consequently) myself altogether guiltless of what I accuse others; but if I can do Virgil less injury than others have done, it will be in some degree to do him right; and indeed, the hope of doing him more right is the only scope of this essay, by opening this new way of translating this author to those whom youth, leisure, and better fortune makes fitter for such undertakings.

I conceive it a vulgar error in translating poets, to affect being *Fidus Interpres*;[2] let that care be with them who deal in matters of fact, or matters of faith. But whosoever aims at it in poetry, as he attempts what is not required, so he shall never perform what he attempts; for it is not his business alone to translate language into language, but poesie into poesie; and poesie is of so subtle a spirit, that in pouring out of one language into another, it will all evaporate; and if a new spirit be not added in the transfusion, there will remain nothing but a *caput mortuum*,[3] there being certain graces and happinesses peculiar to every language, which gives life and energy to the words; and whosoever offers [makes an attempt] at verbal [literal] translation shall have the misfortune of that young traveller who lost his own language abroad, and brought home no other instead of it: for the grace of the Latin will be lost by being turned into English words; and the grace of the English by being turned into the Latin phrase. And as speech is the apparel of our thoughts, so are there certain garbs and modes of speaking which vary with the times, the fashion of our clothes being not more subject to alteration than that of our speech; and this I think Tacitus means by that which he calls *sermonem temporis istius auribus accommodatum*: the delight of change being as due to the curiosity of the ear, as of the eye. And therefore if Virgil must needs speak English, it were fit he should speak not only as a man of this nation, but as a man of this age; and if this disguise I have put upon him (I wish I could give it a better name) fit not naturally and easily on so grave a person, yet it may become him better than that fool's-coat wherein the French and Italian have of late presented him; at least, I hope, it will not make him appear deformed, by making any part enormously bigger or less than the life (I having made it my principal care to follow him, as he made it his to follow Nature in all his proportions). Neither have I anywhere offered such violence to his sense as to make it seem mine and not his. Where my expressions are not so full as his, either our language or my art were defective (but I rather suspect myself); but where mine are fuller than his, they are but the impressions which the often reading of him has left upon my thoughts; so that if they are not his own conceptions, they are at least the results of them; and if (being conscious of making him speak worse than he did almost in every line) I err in endeavouring sometimes to make him speak better; I hope it will be judged an error on the right hand, and such an one as may deserve pardon, if not imitation.

[2] 'Faithful translator'. Horace's famous term from the 'Art of Poetry'; see above, 15. [Ed]

[3] Lit. 'death's head' or skull; fig. worthless residue. [Ed]

Nicolas Perrot d'Ablancourt

Nicolas Perrot, sieur d'Ablancourt (1606-1664), was renowned in his day for his free translations of the classics – so renowned that Gilles Ménage (1613-1692) coined the phrase *les belles infidéles* to describe them.

D'Ablancourt was born to a family of famous lawyers, and was early trained in the law as well; having finished his classical studies at the early age of 13, he was admitted advocate of Parliament at 18. His father, Paul Perrot de la Saller, was a Protestant, but in his late teens Nicolas converted to Catholicism; his uncle Cyprian Perrot, who had played a part in the conversion, urged him to enter the priesthood, but Nicolas refused, and later, by his late twenties, converted back to Protestantism – a step that raised a furore which he waited out in Leiden, Holland, studying Hebrew.

Upon his return to Paris he devoted himself to study, but also made many influential friends among learned Parisian society, and in 1637 was made a member of the French Academy. He left Paris shortly afterward to escape the effects of war with the Hapsburgs, and retired to his family estate, Ablancourt, where he lived, mostly translating, till his death. His translations of Tacitus, Lucian, Caesar, Thucydides, Arrian, and others won him both great fame and, due to the liberties he took with them, scathing attacks from the classicists of his day. He was once asked why, since he seemed to intent upon making French originals out of Greek and Roman classics, he did not simply *write* French originals rather than pretending to translate; he replied that most so-called original works in French were but disguised translations, and that "to serve one's country a man ought rather to translate valuable authors than to write new books, which seldom contain anything new".

To Monsieur Conrart[1]
Dedication of French translation of Lucian (1654)
Translated by David G. Ross

To Monsieur Conrart
The King's Counselor and Secretary

Monsieur,
As things return to their origin and usually finish where they began, it was fitting to devote the last of my translations to one who received the first fruits thereof; and Minucius Felix having given rise to our friendship, Lucian should provide its fulfillment.[2] Moreover, it was necessary to place at the frontispiece of this work a name that expels any wrongful prejudice that one could feel toward it, and necessary that this author's debauchery be eclipsed by the virtue of Monsieur Conrart. It should be added that this book could not reasonably appear in public under any other auspices than your own, since you have contributed so much to bring it to the world, and your good counsel is the reason it sees the light of day in a more complete state. This is therefore not so much a gift, as a gesture of acknowledgement; yet it is a selfish acknowledgement, since it implores the protection of the one it acknowledges as its benefactor. And truly, Monsieur, since it is chiefly you who had me undertake this translation, you must share in the blame or in the praise that will result from it; besides, it will encounter enough monsters to battle at its birth to warrant a protector.[3] But so you cannot reproach me for having recklessly involved you in a quarrel that you could very well live without, I give you two weapons with which to defend yourself and to shelter us both from calumny.

All that can be said against me can be classified under two headings, that of the scheme and that of its implementation. For some will say that this author should not have been translated, others that he should have been translated differently. I want therefore to respond to these two objections, after having said something about Lucian that will serve as my justification and make clearer my reasons for translating it.

Lucian was from Samosata,[4] the capital of Commagene, and was not of high lineage; for his father, not having the means to support him, resolved to teach him a trade; but as the early signs were not propitious for him, he threw himself into letters with a dream that he relates at the beginning of this work. He himself says that he embraced the profession of barrister; but holding the wrangling and other vices of the bar in detestation, he took refuge in philosophy as if it were an asylum. His writings make it seem that he was a rhetorician, who made a profession of eloquence and who composed proclamations and harangues on diverse subjects, and even speeches; although we no longer have any of his making. He settled down first in Antioch, whence he passed to Ionia and Greece, then to Gaul and Italy, and later returned to his country via Macedonia. But it is clear that he lived some of the time in Athens, thereby acquiring its vices and virtues. Eventually, he withdrew from the labors of which I spoke, in order to devote himself to philosophy; that is why he complains somewhere that people wanted to ship him back in his old age. He lived ninety years, from before the reign of Trajan to past Marcus Aurelius, under whom he was held in great esteem and became the Emperor's comptroller in Egypt. Suidas wanted him to be thrown to the dogs, which was apparently slander to take revenge for Lucian's not having spared the first Christians in his jests any more than others. All the same, what he said may be, in my opinion, in reference to their charity and simplicity, which is more praise than insult; also, one must not expect an encomium of Christianity from a pagan. Some have believed him a Christian, but that is not apparent in this book. It is true that, for a foreigner, he knew much of our mysteries, although his proximity to Judaea and Christian

[1] Valentin Conrart was one of the prime movers in the founding of the French Academy (1634-1635) and the most famous 'tyrant' of the French language in his day, the self-appointed overlord of correct French spelling, grammar, and word order. [Ed]

[2] d'Ablancourt had published an anonymous translation of Marcus Minucius Felix in 1637; this is his first public acknowledgement that he was the translator. The translation of Lucian was not his last; he only temporarily intended for it to be. [Ed]

[3] For two reasons: Lucian was considered an immoral writer, and d'Ablancourt was considered an unfaithful translator. [Ed]

[4] Modern Samsat, Turkey. Lucian's native language was Syrian. [Ed]

commerce, together with his natural curiosity, made it possible for him to acquire all of this knowledge. Others would portray him as a paragon of wisdom and doctrine; but beyond the love for boys to which he was inclined and what little sentiment he had for divinity, he cannot be pardoned for having destroyed the reputations of the most important men with rumor, or rather their enemies, as his source. For although he could be excused by saying that it was not against us that he bore a grudge, but against those who took advantage of their name to hide their vices, it is evident that he never missed an occasion to traduce them and that he always subjected them to some slander in passing. Furthermore, the way he treats the most important matters makes it clear enough that he was not deeply involved in philosophy, and that he had only learned of it what was useful for his vocation of rhetorician, which was to speak for and against on all manner of subjects. But it cannot be denied that his was one of the wittiest minds of his century, being full of delicacy and embellishment, with a cheerful and playful disposition and the gallant manner that the ancients dubbed 'urbanity', let alone the clarity and purity of his style, together with his elegance and civility. I only find him coarse on the subject of love, whether that must be attributed to the nature of his time or of his character; but when he wishes to speak of it, he leaves the confines of probity and falls forthwith into the obscene, which is more the mark of a debauched than a gallant mind. He has some pompous aspects as well: he tries to say everything, and he does not always finish where he should, which is a vice arising from too much intellect and knowledge. But it is a great testimony to the merit and excellence of his works that they have been preserved for us, given what little affection one has for their author and the disappearance of so many other pieces from antiquity, which have been lost through either misfortune or neglect; and Christians must certainly have found that the works could do much more good than harm. Also, no man has ever better exposed the conceit and illusion of false gods, nor the pride and ignorance of philosophers, along with the weakness and fickleness of human affairs; and I doubt that there are better books in this regard. For he insinuates himself into one's mind through jest; and his morals are all the more useful, as they are pleasing. Moreover, one can learn a thousand quite interesting things herein; and it is like a bouquet of flowers picked from what was most noble among the ancients [anthology of antiquity]. I leave aside that the myths are treated here in an ingenious fashion, which is very suitable to ensuring their retention, and which is of no small help in the understanding of poets. Therefore, one must not find it odd that I translated, in imitation of several learned persons who have done Latin versions,[5] some from one dialogue and others from another; and I am all the less reproachable, as I abridged the coarsest sections and prettified certain places that were too unrestrained, whereupon I begin the justification of my conduct, for before you lies my scheme, justified quite well by the many benefits that could accrue to the public from reading this author. I will only say that I permitted his opinions to remain completely intact, because it would not otherwise be a translation, but I respond to the greatest outrages in the summary or the remarks, so that no harm will be done.

As the majority of things here are only witticisms and jests, which are different in every language, it was not possible to do a regular translation. There are even some pieces that could not be translated at all, like *Judgment of the Vowels* and two or three others, which treat the nature of Greek terms and cannot be understood beyond that.[6] All similes having to do with love speak of that of boys, which was not strange to Grecian morals, and which is horrifying to our own. At every turn, the author quotes from Homeric verses, which would nowadays be pedantic, let alone from the old, excessively hackneyed myths, from the proverbs, examples, and antiquated similes, which would at present make an impression quite contrary to his intention; for we are talking here about elegance, and not about erudition. It was thus necessary to change all that in order to have a pleasing result; otherwise, it would not be Lucian; and what is pleasing in his language, would be intolerable in ours. Moreover, as with beautiful faces, there is always something that we wish were not there, so with the best authors, there are sections that must be changed or clarified, particularly when things are only done to please; for one cannot then tolerate the slightest fault, and what little is lacking in refinement becomes annoying instead of enjoyable. Therefore, I do not always bind myself either to the words or to the reasoning of this author; and I adjust things to our manner and style with his goal in mind. Different times demand different reasoning as well as different words; and ambassadors are accustomed, for fear of appearing ridiculous to

[5] A Greco-Latin edition of Lucian had appeared in 1615, containing Latin translations by various hands, many of them imitating the Latin dialogues of Thomas More and Erasmus; d'Ablancourt used it but attacked it. In 1653, the year before this writing, Tanneguy Lefèbvre had published the Greek text and his own translation of Lucian's *Death of Peregrinus*. Lefèbvre, a Hellenist, attacked d'Ablancourt's translation of Lucian fiercely, saying the translator had gone mad; d'Ablancourt later asked him for advice with his translation of Thucydides. [Ed]

[6] In place of *Judgment of the Vowels* in d'Ablancourt's translation there appeared *Dialogue des Lettres de l'Alphabet*, a similar treatment of the French alphabet, attributed to Frémont d'Ablancourt. [Ed]

those they strive to please, to dressing themselves according to the fashion of the country where they are sent. Nonetheless, that is not really translation; yet it is worth more than translation; and the ancients did not translate any other way. That is how Terence worked with the comedies that he took from Menander, although Aulus Gellius does not allow them to be called translations; but the name is not important, provided we have the thing. Cicero did the same in *De Officiis*, which are only an approximate translation of Panaetius; and in those he did from the orations of Demosthenes and Aeschines, he says that he did not work as an interpreter but as an orator,[7] which is the same thing that I am obliged to say about Lucian's dialogues, although I did not give myself equal freedom everywhere. There are many places that I translated word for word, at least as much as can be done in an elegant translation; there were also some where I rather preferred what had to be said, or what I could say, to what he had said, in imitation of Virgil in what he took from Homer and Theocritus.[8] But I restrained myself nearly everywhere, without becoming involved in specifics that are no longer of our world.[9] I know well, however, that this will not please everyone, especially those who idolize all the words and thoughts of the ancients, and who do not believe a work is good if its author is still alive. For those types of people will whine as they did in the time of Terence.

Contaminari non decêre Fabulas,

How one must not falsify one's author, nor adulterate his theme; but I will use him to respond,

Faciunt nae intelligendo, ut nihil intelligant,
Qui cum hunc accusant, Naevium, Plautum, Ennium
Accusant, quos hic noster authores habet.
Quorum aemulari exoptat negligentiam
Potius, quàm istorum obscuram diligentiam.[10]

How well this "obscuram diligentiam" expresses the problem with these strict translations, which can only be understood after one has read the original![11]

There you have, Monsieur, what I had to say in my defense. I leave it to your mettle and cunning, not to mention your zeal and affection, to make use of these arms, which are more robust than brilliant, if your name is not enough to scatter the enemies and prevent them from emerging. Whatever happens, I will ascribe all the success of this work to the glory of my protector, and will remain throughout my life,

Monsieur,
Your very humble and very obedient servant,
Perrot Ablancourt

Adjusting Things to Accommodate the Subject
From Preface to French translation of *Thucydides* (1662)
Translated by David G. Ross

Among so many virtues are found some reproachable faults; first of all is obscurity, which is so great in his harangues, even to the eyes of Cicero, that this last says "Ipsae Illae Thucydidis conciones, ita multas habent obscuras abditasque sententias, vix ut intelligantur, quod est in oratione civili vitium vel maximum".[12] This arises as much from his preference for terms and phrases that are not in use, as from the difficulty in his constructions where no word is in its place, which adds vigor but detracts from clarity; he also heaps thought upon thought instead of separating them, something he also has in common with Tacitus, which is why, with regard to this subject, I refer the reader to the preface that I did for that author.[13] All that can be said in their defense is that they did not write for the

[7] 'Pro corona'. [Au] Demosthenes' oration, which Cicero translated as 'Pro corona', has been variously translated into English as *The Oration on the Crown* and *In Defence of Ctesiphon*. For Cicero, see above, 7-12, especially, for the interpreter vs. orator distinction, 9. Cicero wrote *De Officiis* ('On Moral Obligation') in 45-44 B.C.E. [Ed]

[8] "Partin reliquit, alia expressit, etc. Quod Graecum quidem mire quam suave est, verti autem neque potuit, neque debuit". A. Gell., 1.9 c 9. [Au] d'Ablancourt is quoting from the first paragraph of Aulus Gellius, above, 20. [Ed]

[9] I.e., things rooted in cultures long gone. [Ed]

[10] "They corrupt reason by dint of reasoning. For by reproaching it, they reproach the ancients, whom he has as guarantors, and of whose carelessness he prefers an imitation to the obscure exactness of others". [Au] This is Ross's translation of d'Ablancourt's free translation of Terence's prologue to *Andria* (*The Andrian Girl*, 166 B.C.E.). [Ed]

[11] An oblique reference to the translations of Louis-Isaac Le Maitre de Saci, the primary translator in the group that produced a French Catholic New Testament based on the Vulgate, who a decade or more later (1666-1668) would translate the Old Testament from the Vulgate while imprisoned in the Bastille for Jansenism. d'Ablancourt was bitterly opposed to the Jansenists, and heaped scorn on the academic (minutely and literally accurate) translations produced by Saci; at this writing Saci was at work on a French translation of Terence's *Andrian Girl* (1655). [Ed]

[12] "That the meaning of Thucydides' harangues is so hidden that one usually cannot make it out at all, which is a significant problem in communicating with the world". [Au] Ross's translation of d'Ablancourt's translation. The Cicero passage is taken from the *Orator* (9.30), excerpted above, 7. [Ed]

[13] d'Ablancourt translated Tacitus in 1640-1644. [Ed]

people, but for respectable sorts who take hints, and for whom something must remain to be guessed. But I do not want to engage in a defense of something that is equally removed from my style and my disposition, as well as from that of my age, which only likes what is natural and easy. Yet, that will serve as my excuse if I have taken certain liberties to cast light onto this darkness, and if I did not think myself obliged to imitate this author in his scheme. For to leave him his faults, as some would through an overstrict fidelity, and, on the other hand, to deny him his elegance, because rendering them is, in their opinion, impossible without offending the rules of translation,[14] would be to write *le Thucydide ridicule*,[15] which would have all of his faults and none of his virtues; it would be to change, if it is proper to say so, the thunderbolts of Pericles into the ice of the frozen north. If it were possible, it would be fitting for them to relight the fire and do like the Cyclops of myth by forging the thunderbolts of Jupiter "sonitumque metumque miscebant operi",[16] in order to sustain the glory of our author and the sublime style that is attributed to him. For this here is not so much the image of Thucydides but Thucydides himself, who has assumed another body, as it were through some form of metempsychosis; and from a Grecian is made a Frenchman who cannot bemoan a lack of resemblance when he appears less imperfect any more than a patient would to his doctor, who has, by virtue of his medicines, returned him to health and vigor. But the point[17] regarding the preservation of his character and the refusal to make Xenophon of Thucydides or Cicero of Tacitus is quite sensible, although those who deny this still have the excuse that they are providing an animated portrait, whose rough beauties they have changed into others more exquisite; but those strict translators produce only a carcass from a living body and make a monster from a miracle. Similar to those scholars of law spoken of in the Gospel, who only observe it in trifles and demur at charity and other, more onerous virtues. But it is better to be unfaithful in the small in order to be faithful in the great.[18] There you have what I had to say in defense of somewhat liberal translators, of whom I have been made a leader,[19] and whom a learned person seems to have made it his business to condemn quite recently.[20]

Our author is also accused of having left his subject matter disconnected, for having attached himself too assiduously to the sequence of events; but this cannot be attributed to him in my opinion, because death prevented him from putting the finishing touches on his work. As evidence of this, the eighth book, which he did not have the time to finish, transgresses the most in this regard, and does not even have any harangues, although there were ideal occasions for making some on the change of government.[21] And it certainly was a good reason to exercise one's pen, so it was not futile to compare oneself with Thucydides, as though one sought to compete with him with for eloquence, and I would prefer to lend him my fame to robbing him of his, since I take all the liberties I do only to support it. I have thus returned to their sections several digressive periods that interrupted the narration, as doing so did not remove anything from the meaning and only made things clearer.

This overstrict exactness, or the author's lack of opportunity to review his work, is indeed the cause of several repetitions and certain details that were useless or needless and of little importance, and that I thereby either set aside in the margin or neglected to translate. For as one cannot be too meticulous with things that deserve it, one cannot be too brief with the rest. I sometimes omit the resumptions at the end of topics as well, because they are hardly more pleasing to us then repetitions, besides which the sections highlight them, something that was unknown to the ancients, and that contributes much to the clarity of a work and greatly assists the reader.[22]

I will not comment here on the faults to which Dionysius of Halicarnassus[23] called attention, because they are essentially concerned with style and I avoided

---

[14] Referring especially, perhaps, to Huet's *De interpretatione* of the year before (1661); see below, 163-69. [Ed]

[15] Referring to a recent brief (1649-1657) vogue of burlesque satires of ancient authors. [Ed]

[16] Virgil, *Aeneid* 8.431-32: "mingles dreadful cries with their work". [Ed]

[17] Probably referring again to Huet; see below, 167-68. [Ed]

[18] See e.g. Matthew 25:14-30 or Luke 19:11-27 for the parable of the talents, or Luke 15:11-32 for the parable of the prodigal son. d'Ablancourt may be thinking specifically of Jesus' attacks on the Pharisees and scribes for their devotion to the letter of the law: e.g. Matthew 15:1-11, 23:1-31, Mark 7:1-23, Luke 11:37-52. [Ed]

[19] In the *Nouvelle allégorique*. [Au] By Antoine Furetière, in 1658. The *Nouvelle* is a satire on the contemporary French world of letters; d'Ablancourt appears in it as Capitaine Magnifique. [Ed]

[20] Huet, the year before; see below, 167. [Ed]

[21] That of the 400s. [Au] d'Ablancourt is referring to the coup of 411 B.C.E.. [Ed]

[22] The division of text into separate words, sentences, and paragraphs (what d'Ablancourt calls 'sections') was a relatively recent innovation, dating from the late Middle Ages. The ancients did mark the beginning and ending of chapters in the text; d'Ablancourt calls these indications 'resumptions'. [Ed]

[23] Dionysius comments on Thucydides in *On Thucydides*, the second letter to Ammaeus, and the lost *On Imitation* (excerpted in ch. 3 of the letter to Gnaeus Pompeius). [Ed]

them for the reasons I have mentioned; besides not all of them are genuine and some of those for which he is called to task are childish errors, to which no man was less subject; and those cited are not faults, but are only so when repeated too frequently.

I was forgetting something that I have already mentioned in my other translations, namely that I only translate those harangues directly that are fit to assume the airs of eloquence. The others, though too short, are better indirect, because one sees all at once what they are saying without the encumbrance of comings and goings, which are somewhat tiresome in the works of the ancients as they are not very graceful. It must still be added that I did not do any remarks on the harangues, because I did not feel obligated to vindicate myself for the liberties I took, as much because, concerning as they did the harmony of the embellishments, not a single defect could be tolerated, as because doing so offended neither the verity of the narration nor of the purpose of Thucydides. For he himself says that he contented himself with preserving the purpose of those who spoke and adjusting things to accommodate the subject, so that his example releases us from the scrupulousness that one would wish to require of us;[24] besides we are robbing him of enough elegancies to deliver him some by way of compensation. I have but one thing more to say, namely that I consulted Monsieur le Fèvre[25] on several problems, a man whose erudition is recognized by everyone; but I make mention of that in the remarks, so as not to cheat him of his glory.

Abraham Cowley

Abraham Cowley (1618-1667) was an English poet hugely admired in his own day as an adapter of the Pindaric ode to English poetry: his *Pindarique Odes* (1656) bring Pindar's poetic enthusiasm into a style exaggeratedly reminiscent of John Donne, with strikingly farfetched conceits, and a novel poetic form based on lines of uneven length.

A fervent royalist, Cowley was ejected from Cambridge, where he had studied and become a fellow, in 1643 by Cromwell's Parliament; he then joined the royal court at Oxford and followed them abroad in 1645 as cipher secretary to the Queen. For the next decade he served the royalist cause in various capacities, returning to England in 1656, four years before the restoration. He received few rewards from either Cromwell or the restored Charles II, however, and soon retired to Chertsey, where he tended his garden in both horticultural fact and contemplative essays reminiscent of Montaigne. He was also an amateur scientist who worked to further the cause of the Royal Society, publishing a monograph entitled *Proposition for the Advancement of Experimental Philosophy* in 1661. His defence of free imitation, below, provided John Dryden with his primary foil in the 1680 preface to Ovid.

Preface to *Pindarique Odes* (1656)

If a man should undertake to translate Pindar word for word, it would be thought that one madman had translated another; as may appear when a person who understands not the original reads the verbal traduction of him into Latin prose, than which nothing seems more raving. And surely rhyme, without the addition of wit and the spirit of poetry (*quod nequeo monstrare, & sentio tantum*[1]), would but make it ten times more distracted than it is in prose. We must consider in Pindar the great difference of time betwixt his age and ours, which changes, as in pictures, at least the colours of poetry; the no less difference betwixt the religions and customs of our countries; and a thousand particularities of places, persons, and manners, which do but confusedly appear to our eyes at so great a distance. And lastly (which were enough alone for my purpose), we must consider that our ears are strangers to the music of his numbers,[2] which sometimes (especially in songs and odes) almost without anything else makes an excellent poet; for though the grammarians and critics have labored to reduce his verses into regular feet and measures (as they have also those of the Greek and Latin comedies) yet in effect they are little better then prose to our ears. And I would gladly know what applause our best pieces of English poesie could expect from a Frenchman or Italian, if converted faithfully, and word for word, into French or Italian prose. And when we have considered all this, we must needs confess, that after all these losses sustained by Pindar, all we can add to him by our wit or invention (not deserting still his subject) is not likely to make him a richer man than he was in his own country. This is in some measure to be applied to all translations, and the not observing of it is the cause that all [translations] which ever I yet saw are so much inferior to their originals. The like happens too in pictures, from the same root of exact imitation; which being a vile and unworthy kind of servitude, is incapable of producing anything good or noble. I have seen originals, both in painting and poesie, much more beautiful then their

---

[24] Again, probably a reference to Huet. [Ed]

[25] Tanneguy Lefèbvre, classical scholar and father of Anne Dacier, excerpted below, 187-90. [Ed]

[1] "Because I can only know it intuitively, without being able to demonstrate it". [Ed]

[2] I.e., the quantity of his metrical feet. [Ed]

natural objects; but I never saw a copy better than the original, which indeed cannot be otherwise; for men resolving in no case to shoot beyond the mark, it is a thousand to one if they shoot not short of it. It does not at all trouble me that the grammarians perhaps will not suffer this libertine way of rendering foreign authors to be called translation; for I am not so much enamoured of the name translator, as not to wish rather to be something better, though it want yet a name. I speak not so much all this, in defence of my manner of translating, or imitating (or what other title they please) the two ensuing odes of Pindar; for that would not deserve half these words, as by this occasion to rectify the opinion of diverse men upon this matter. The Psalms of David (which I believe to have been in their original, to the Hebrews of his time, though not to our Hebrews of Buxtorfius's making, the most exalted pieces of poesie) are a great example of what I have said; all the translators of which (even Mr Sand[y]s himself; for in despite of popular error, I will be bold not to except him) for this very reason, that they have not sought to supply the lost excellencies of another language with new ones in their own; are so far from doing honour, or at least justice to that divine poet, that, methinks, they revile him worse then Shimei.[3] And Buchanan himself (though much the best of them all, and indeed a great person) comes in my opinion no less short of David, than his country does of Judaea. Upon this ground, I have in these two Odes of Pindar taken, left out, and added what I please; nor make it so much my aim to let the reader know precisely what he spoke, as what was his way and manner of speaking; which has not been yet (that I know of) introduced into English, though it be the noblest and highest kind of writing in verse; and which might, perhaps, be put into the list of Pancirollus among the lost inventions of antiquity. This essay is but to try how it will look in an English habit: for which experiment, I have chosen one of his Olympique, and another of his Nemean Odes, which are as follows.

Pierre Daniel Huet

Pierre Daniel Huet (1630-1721) was one of the foremost French scholars of his day, renowned as the translator of Longus and Origen and works of history, theology, literary criticism, and translation theory.

Huet was born to Daniel Huet, a magistrate who had converted to Protestantism, and Isabelle Pillon de Bertoville; but his father died when he was eighteen months old, his mother when he was six, and he was raised by neglectful foster parents, "far from home, blood, and education", as he later wrote in his memoirs. Educated by the Jesuits at Caen, he proved a brilliant student, and at 13 entered university, where he studied law (eventually taking a doctorate) and learned Greek and Hebrew on his own from a book he loved, Samuel Bochart's *Geographie* (1646); another contemporary book that left a lasting impression on him was Descartes's *Principia philosophiae* (1644).

He first won renown at age 18, with his Latin translation of Longus' Greek romance *Daphnis and Chloe* (1648); arriving in Paris shortly after, hoping to meet famous thinkers and literati, he met and became friends with Bochart and later, in 1652, accompanied him to Sweden, where Descartes had died two years previously. There Queen Christine begged him to stay and join her court, but he declined and returned to Caen – bearing, however, a transcription of Origen's 'Commentaries on St. Matthew', which he set about translating into Latin; the completed translation was not published until 1688. In the course of this work he wrote *De interpretatione* (1661), excerpted below – a study of the principles of translation that for seventeenth-century France was the final word upon the subject. He was accepted into salons with open arms, and when during this period he founded a society for the improvement of natural philosophy and anatomy, Louis XIV endowed it liberally; in 1670 the king appointed him tutor to the Dauphin. Despite the time-consuming nature of that post, which he held until 1680, he managed to publish books on the origin of the novel (1670) and the truth of the gospels (1679), and to edit a series of Greek and Latin classics for the Delphini series.

By the end of the decade Louis XIV wanted to appoint him to a higher post, and began hinting at a bishopric; through a series of confusions, however, the appointment did not arrive until 1685, and then led to a crossing of wires: Abbé Brulart de Sillery was supposed to become Bishop of Avranches, Huet Bishop of Soissons, but somehow each was appointed to the other's position. The intrigues and quarrels that ensued further postponed the appointment until 1992, when Huet became Bishop of Avranches at the age of 62. He did not, however, like the work load of his new job, which left him little time to study, and resigned after seven years, in 1699. Returning once again to Caen, he rejoined the Jesuits at the abbey of Fontenay, and would have lived out his life there

[3] A Benjamite kinsman of David's who took Absalom's side in his rebellion against his father David, and cursed him as a "man of blood" (2 Samuel 16:5-13); pardoned by David (19:16-23); later executed by Solomon (1 Kings 2:36-46). [Ed]

had various legal problems not obliged him to move back to Paris; there, in the Jesuit Maison Professé, he spent the last two decades of his life, writing histories of ancient navigation (1702) and the city of Caen (1716), a collection of poetry (1709), notes on the Vulgate Bible, and, after a severe and nearly fatal illness in 1712, his memoirs, the first volume of which was published in his lifetime (1718), the second posthumously (1722).

Concerning the Best Kind of Translation
From *De optimo genere interpretandi* (1661)
Translated by Edwin Dolin

To Andreas Grandorgaeus

Andreas, the excellence and depth of talent possessed by your brother, Jacob Praemontius, was great; his learning was distinguished and worthy of a free man; further, he exercised in literary matters a judgment so subtle that no one

> knew better how to separate a crude from
> a charming phrase.
> [Horace *Ars Poetica* 273]

To these qualities was joined remarkable sincerity of character together with seriousness moderated by a certain easy friendliness as well as a dependability almost unique for keeping friendships. From the time I was a boy I had an intimacy and association with him such that we were joined both in friendship and in every desire and also such that we had an entirely similar program of studies. But still our relationship had, as it were, a preordained rule to the effect that he, who was both older than I as well as more versed in all learning and wisdom, held the place of preceptor and teacher, while I was the student and listener. And so I obeyed, to the extent that I could, his very wise advice and never left his side without having become better or more learned; I strove to have fewer faults through his proven distinction, since I had come to him disposed by nature to indulge in excessive playfulness of temperament and to give vent to youthful impulsiveness. He softened the one by his sense of restraint and he blunted the other by his admonitions and precepts. In the same way the skill of farmers constrains a tree abounding in branches and luxuriating in leaves.

He was the first who held me back as I was going off to teachers of specious learning. He was not content to lead me back to the road; he pointed to the fountains themselves from which the lessons of sound learning were imbibed. When the disorderly brashness of childhood had been scraped from me, he instilled into my crude and rough mind the first awareness of refinement. And so I must refer to him what I have received from him, if I ever accomplish anything in literature. This is certainly not the case yet, as I recognize and, now that he has been taken away, I scarcely dare hope. When an encourager of his sort gave me heart and applied the spur, I had the capacity to aspire to great things of all kinds and, perhaps, to make progress, if life had continued for him. But in fact length of years for so remarkable a nature was in no way to be expected. Thus has it been constituted that everything that is best is frail and brief, while length of active life befalls easily to the worse. Now, though, deprived of that kind of assistance, what capacity should I suppose in myself to struggle towards the heights, much less attain them?

> I weep when I consider what sort of life
> will be mine afterwards
> And what loneliness.
> [Terence *Hecyra* 405-406 (3,3,45)]

All the same, I am revived by the following considerations: You have returned to your country truly a blood-brother of this very good man Jacob, a brother not simply in body and birth but also in sweetness of character; and your return seems, as it were, to make good the loss of Jacob:

> How delighted I am, when I see standing firm
> The survivors of this family.
> [Terence *Adelphi* 444-445 (3,3,90)]

Moreover, there is the not unimportant hope that you will be willing to take up as your own the relationships entered into by him and I am confident that you will not differ from him in the slightest on a matter where it is to your honor to be as much like him as possible. So, since you are perpetuating the distinction of your brother's learning in such a way that you have completed it by adding to it your own achievements, I beg you also to perpetuate his benevolence towards me, blooming in fact with new growth and kindness.

But I want to speak again of your brother. Courteous as always, he used to visit me almost every day and if he had made a note on any subject, he would share it with me, while if I had written something he would ask that it be read to him. Once, when he found me in my library surrounded by books and asked whether, given all the preparations I was working on something in particular, I replied that I was pushing around mill-wheels, I was translating Origen. He picked up the notebook in which I was writing the translation, read a few lines and, surprised by the carelessness of the writing, said, "These, I assume, are the first props and supports of your efforts; either you will take them down, when solid columns have arrived, or you will cover them with something attractive". Since I did not see clearly what he meant, I said, "What is the direction of your remark, Praemontius? Because I don't understand why this translation demands, as it were, a second translation". Agreeably, as was his custom, he said,

> I will not ask you to publish a second translation, no, only one, but one that is worthy both of you and of Origen, structured, of course, by means of a suitable arrangement of words and a smooth flow of language and reproducing the sublime and almost divine ideas of that great man with corresponding impressiveness. Surely those ideas should not be obscured by clumsy language and weakened by a charmless poverty of style. Moreover, I would not want anything to go out into the world from your hand not benefiting from your talent and hard work. I am concerned for your reputation just as if it were joined with my own and just as if public opinion about both our names were contained in yours alone.

I said, "I am very grateful for the concern you express, but be careful

> Lest in your zeal you make a mistake and, devoted,
> Introduce loathing for my books,
> [Horace *Epistles* 1.13.5]

which, nevertheless, you want everybody to like. Because I am apprehensive lest by carefully polishing the language of this work I gain possibly the reputation of being a writer who is not bad, while I am losing the reputation of being a good translator. But this second reputation is the one I ought most of all to strive to achieve at this time, while the reputation of being a good writer is, for the moment, of no importance. For my view of the matter is as follows: If anyone takes on the role of translator, his efforts should especially be focused, not on using his skill in writing, if by chance he has some such skill, and not on deceiving people with the charm of his language, but on displaying in his own words the author, whom he is trying to translate, as if the author were to be preserved in a mirror and picture. The translator should take away every deceptive ornament as if it were a covering or, rather, as if he were scrubbing off an overlying pigment from the original color".

In response Praemontius said,

> Your view is new to me, but I have no desire to dispute with you about it, since your view seems to me fairly close to the truth, if I am to say what I think. Because, as you distinguish so incisively, it's one thing to write beautifully, another thing to translate accurately, which up till now, in truth, had not occurred to me. However, I am concerned about how you can please people of this time, in whose eyes approximately the same approach to translation has gained favor which just now I was asking you to adopt and which you rejected. Therefore, since you have the audacity to disrupt a custom shared by nearly everyone and a point of view favored by nearly every vote, you need to take care that you do not seem to be acting thoughtlessly. And, in fact, if you listen to me, you will enclose in some brief essay what you think about the best kind of translation and, in addition, the arguments which have led you to your opinion. The discussion will be both quite pleasurable for our contemporaries to read and most definitely useful; because we know that from the time culture found rebirth and was won back from barbarism this eagerness for translation has attracted men of learning to such an extent that, as soon as they had achieved some skill in both languages, they immediately turned their attention to translating ancient authors. They did not believe they had acquired any degree of reputation among men of culture unless they had published some example of their learning by translating writings of the ancients. The more reason to look with wonder at the scene: while few or almost no rules have been articulated concerning translation and as each individual follows his own inclination, everyone has gone off in a different direction, so that there are about as many methods of translation as there are names of translators. Granted, for some years now the custom has generally prevailed, as I said, that even authors whose style is weak and whose writing is unimpressive are invested by translators with a distinctly generous flow of discourse and a dazzling web of words. So you will do something worthwhile, if you delimit this activity, translation, within precise boundaries and reduce it to order.

"Indeed I will do that", I said,

> given that this is what you urge me to do. But, since this project needs leisure and for the moment other matters demand my attention; and on the condition that you not require payment, as it were, of this debt on a day certain, I will give the subject attention so that you will say I am a tardy debtor, yes, but nevertheless a reliable one.

"I will be looking forward to what you are promising", he said, "and I will take care that, in addition, you think of me as a lender whose request for repayment is not annoying but who nevertheless is mindful of what is due him and persistent". Such were his words. Then, a few months after this agreement was established between us, a death both untimely and lamented by all good persons oppressed him.

> But what a man! The best I have seen in
> my life.
> [Terence *Phormio* 367 (2.3.19)]

In fact, I would certainly not be able to bear his loss, unless I were sustained by the persistence in my heart of the memory and recollection of the life I spent most peacefully with him and of the perfect harmony of our scholarly pursuits and our desires; and, further, unless I were nourished by the hope that you will become for us a second Praemontius. Indeed, so you may know more clearly that such is my conviction, I have taken the view that this whole essay, which was begun at his request and with his advice and which he was able to claim from me, has to do with you. So, if you please, accept it, whatever its value may be: you, as a fair judge will settle the dispute; I will very readily demur to your authority and that of your brother.

I have attributed the whole discourse about translation to Isaac Casaubon, both because of his prestige and his learning and because he seems at one time to have achieved a singular skill in this exercise. Let Casaubon himself testify that he wrote, in a separate book, an essay specifically devoted to clarifying this subject. However, this work was not published, whether because of the carelessness of those to whom this duty belonged or because of some chance event. Still, I do remember listening to Peter Puteanus, a very prominent man, when he said, a few days after Casaubon had published his Polybius, that Jacob August Thuanus and Fronto Ducaeus had come to Casaubon in the Royal Library, where Casaubon was director. We know by tradition that these two were great men, learned as much as any, and very close to Casaubon through long familiarity and friendship. Puteanus said that, when Thuanus had marvelously praised the political wisdom and military knowledge of Polybius and had declared openly the singular assistance he had received from him after he had begun to write the history of his own times, Fronto then extolled to the heights the efforts of Casaubon in cultivating Polybius. But what pleased them both the most, Puteanus declared, was the method of translation that he had used in translating this work. They believed, he continued, that it was not possible to decide easily whether Casaubon had translated Polybius or Polybius Casaubon. Puteanus went on to say that Fronto asked precisely what method of translation, beyond all others, met with his vigorous approval. When Casaubon had heard this question, according to Puteanus, there ensued a considerable discussion among the three concerning the best type of translation. For my part, I have set forth their whole discussion on this question in this book. But, so that I may the more speedily fulfill the obligation I have undertaken, let it be Casaubon himself whom we hear as he expounds the subject with the others.

CASAUBON. Just as the two of you say, excellent Fronto, and you, also, most worthy Thuanus, the reputation of Polybius is great and it may be – I'm not certain – the greatest among all those who have engaged in the writing of histories. As to what the two of you added, doubtless because of your kindness, namely, that I did not labor in vain when I edited and translated Polybius and that this labor was pleasing in your view, now indeed it is established, so far as I am concerned, that the fruit of my efforts is plentiful, since I have reached my goal, which was that my endeavors meet with your approval. I am all the more pleased in view of the fact that a very difficult project had been undertaken by me. For Cicero said it is distressing and very like torture to write with someone else's taste and not with one's own. Moreover, as to exactly what method I think ought especially to be used in translation and what theory should be followed, which, Fronto, is what you asked me about, I set forth my view in a short treatise that, if God provides me the means, I will publish with my commentary on Polybius.

FRONTO. Really, it is most fortunate that you have slipped into this topic and introduced reference to this treatise, because a great desire to savor it fully entered into me after you aroused our expectation in your preface to Polybius. Both of you know how many years now I have myself worked to the limit of my strength in this same testing ground, translation. But why should I wait for your treatise? Really now, what can be more pleasant in this interval of leisure, or more useful, than that this whole question concerning the best theory of translation be explained by you, Casaubon?

CASAUBON. A heavy burden is being put on me by you, Fronto. This subject involves difficult kinds of explanation; and even supposing I write well, that does not mean I can do the same in speaking. A more judicious procedure on your part, if I have written carefully and cogently on the topic, would have been to read it rather than to have chosen to hear what I am about to offer in a confused and facile oral presentation. So reflect, my excellent friend, on where you are driving me and understand that the blame will affect you as well as me, namely, that if I am not able to govern this particular province, perhaps some blame will be mine for having accepted the office; you, on the other hand, will incur quite possibly the greatest blame for having passed this office on to me.

THUANUS. I for one will accept the risk you are warning us about, because I understand your intelligence and learning. As for the quality of your intelligence and learning, you seem barely to have investigated it, because each of us is unknown to himself or, at any rate, you seem trying to keep it hidden. So do proceed, Casaubon; I certainly will in no way regret and neither will your friend, Fronto, the fact that we have propelled you into this discussion.

CASAUBON. That force you speak of, Thuanus, is that of being pulled and at the same time pushed where one does not want to go and where one will be not without danger. Still, I will suffer this injustice from you both, an injustice that you would surely blame, if you turn out to have demanded from me what I cannot do. But if, while responding to your zeal, I shall perhaps successfully conclude the project I undertook, you would still cite with praise my fluency and ease. Therefore, something that in my view should be done at the start of any discussion, so that the argument not wander aimlessly and digress, is that this whole theory of translation (*interpretatio*) needs to be allocated into specific divisions (*genera*); next, of these divisions certain parts that fit with our purpose must be, first of all, selected and then assigned each to its proper place; the remaining parts, which are irrelevant to our project, should be disregarded; then each item must be given its appropriate definition as well as limited and ratified by a precise description. Afterwards arguments that can be made against our analysis must be refuted: when these matters have been established, various translations (*interpretationes*) by various people will be submitted to examination and tested by our standard.

In the first place the term translation (*interpretatio*) is very widely known. Routinely included in this term is: Every form of discourse by which a matter not understood is made known. Also contained in this term is not merely translation from one language into another, but, in addition, commentaries, explanation of glosses, scholia, *metabolai* (variations), paraphrases, metaphrases, also *homoglottoi* (expressions in the same language), *alloglottoi* (expressions in a foreign language), and the other things of this kind. Further, the definition of this word has been extended to include the explanation of obscure areas of learning, the solution of riddles and dreams, the interpretation of oracles, the solution of a confused problem and, finally, the clarification of any matter not understood whatever. However, for us at this time what is meant by the word 'translation' (*interpretatio*) is, strictly speaking: the transfer of some discourse into another language. This happens generally for two reasons: first, for the purpose of learning a language and improving one's style, as is the case with beginners when they translate their native language into Latin or Latin into Greek as if they wished to communicate to experts in these languages a discourse commonly unknown. From these two causes two species arise. We omit the former, which does not concern us for the moment. The latter I define as follows: Discourse expressed in a better known language offering and reproducing discourse expressed in a less known language. This is the meaning I will use, if I may, for the word 'translation' (*interpretatio*) throughout this whole discussion.

Now there appears also to be two forms of this type. One form is when the translator (*interpres*) is concerned not merely with the author and the idea behind the author's words, but either is concerned for the reader's pleasure or his preoccupations or is indulging his own personality. A second form is when the translator has to do with a single author and his whole skill and application is devoted to presenting this author very accurately.

To the first form, as described above, seems to belong what the old Roman poets derived from the Greeks and expressed in Latin verses. Of this sort are what Ennius, Pacuvius, Accius and Atilius rendered into Latin from Aeschylus, Sophocles and Euripides; what Plautus, Terence, Caecilius, Afranius and Aquilius from Demophilus, Philemon, Diphilus, Epicharmus, Menander and Apollodorus; what Ovid and Germanicus from Aratus; what Cicero rendered from Aratus as well as from Homer, Aeschylus, Sophocles, Euripides and others and inserted here and there into his books; what Avienus and Rhemnius Fannius from the same Aratus and from Dionysius; what Catullus from Sappho and Callimachus; Varro of Atax from Apollonius; Cornelius Gallus from Euphorion; what Aubonius from a certain ancient poet, and what others have translated from others into Roman poetry. This type includes the orations of Cicero in which he gave Latinity to the orations of Aeschines and Demosthenes, not as a translator, but as a public speaker.[1] It includes the *Hexaemeron* of St. Ambrose in which he diligently explained the like-named book of St. Basil by rearranging its sequence and adding material from Origen and Hippolytus together with some of his own writings.

Also in this first category should be put 'epitome', when a translator encloses a somewhat free-wheeling author in certain limits; also *paraphrase*, a definition of which by Quintilian has been transmitted as follows, "I do not wish a *paraphrase* to be only a translation but a contest and rivalry concerning the same meanings".[2] Similar are *periphrasis* and *metaphrasis*. The latter produces a translation such that, as occasion arises, it either adds some thing or takes some thing

[1] See Cicero, above, 9. [Ed]

[2] See Quintilian, above, 20. [Ed]

away and reforges the discourse into another form: when Symeon Logotheta did this in reporting the lives of men distinguished for sanctity, his writings were called *Metaphrases*, while he himself earned the nickname "Metaphrastes". *Periphrasis* I define as that which describes in many words what can be said in one word or only a few. This is correctly named by Fabius [Quintilian] as a roundabout way of speaking or circumlocution. These definitions by Quintilian ought to apply not only to what is written in the same language by also to what is written in a foreign language *paraphrastically* and *periphrastically*. Moreover, whatever Ennius borrows from Homer, Vergil from Homer and also from Theocritus, Hesiod, Pindar, Theopompus, Peisander, Apollonius and Parthenius; whatever Aemilius Macer borrowed from Nicander, Varro from Menippus, Cicero from Panaetius in his books *De Officiis*, Livy from Polybius, Lynceus from Callimachus, Ovid from Parthenius of Nicaea, Cornelius Celsus from Hippocrates, Hyginus from Cornelius Alexander, Papinius from Antimachus, Valerius Flaccus from Apollonius, Apuleius from Lucius of Patrae, Boethius from Nicomachus Gerasensis in his *Musical Matters*, Martianus Capella from Aristides Quintilian, Joseph from the writers of Scripture, and Pseudo-Hegesippus and Gorionides from Joseph should certainly not be considered translations (*interpretationes*), because quite obviously their purpose was to imitate these authors or follow them, not translate them. A discussion about this method has no part in the present discourse.

But the second form, the one that must endeavor merely to reproduce diligently and very faithfully the author being translated (*interpretandum*), this form includes what I have translated from Polybius and you, Fronto, from Chrysostom, as well as what we see has been rendered through the efforts of more recent translators.

I think I have sufficiently shown how different are the kinds of translation (*interpretatio*). The next task is to select the best species of this genus, about which I said I would speak, and define it according to a specific concept. I say that the best method of translation is when the translator adheres very closely, first, to the meaning of the author, then also to the actual words themselves, if the capacities of the two languages permit, and finally, when he sketches the innate character of the author, insofar as can be done, and concentrates on one thing only, namely, faithfully to present him diminished in no way and increased in no way, but whole and very like himself in every way.

Now, since translation seems to be nothing other than the explicit image and likeness of the author and since a likeness should be considered best that represents the features, coloring, eyes, the whole shape, in short, of the face and condition of the body in such a way that he seems present when absent, since a portrayal surely is inept that portrays something other than it is, even though the portrayal expresses it as more beautiful and more pleasing to behold, it clearly follows that the translation which definitely is more excellent is not the one that prunes the author's extravagance or compensates for his dryness or brings light to his obscurity or corrects his faults or rearranges his confused sequence, but that which places the whole author before our eyes outlined in his native colors and prefers him either to be praised because of his virtues or, if he has deserved it, to be laughed at because of his specific vices. Because who, please, except a woman too fond of herself and wishing to please herself, would praise a mirror that disguises the face opposite it in such a way that, when you place opposite to it a face wan from pallor or dried up with leanness or shining with excessive redness, presents to you a rosy face or one full of health or one moderated by a pleasing brightness? Again, who would not laugh at, rather than fall in love with, a woman who presents as attractive a rouged face, false hair, artificial teeth and deceptive height?

Nature certainly has put a great love and enthusiasm for truth into the minds of human beings. We are all drawn and pulled by this love and we consider other things as less important than truth. Nor is there anyone of so dull a mind that he would be willing to be drawn into a false notion, even when it is a charming and pleasant one; who would allow himself to be deluded by sleight-of-hand and blinded by tricks? Who would not, as soon as he has perceived that he has been cheated, grow hot with resentment? What would I say is more similar to a mirror of this kind or to a woman sprinkled with paint than an adulterated translation that creates charm in an author by means of false coloring; which, if I may so speak, fattens the thin, dissolves the vanity of the bombastic, raises up the low or depresses the haughty? Let us suppose someone has undertaken to translate Thucydides, a writer obviously accurate in his words, concise, dignified, prolific in ideas, rapid, abrupt and fairly obscure. For so he is described by Cicero. Now suppose that this translator,[3] a man doubtless fluent by nature and capable of an eloquence steady, clear and sweet, softens the rapid energy of Thucydides, brightens his obscure speeches and abstruse ideas with a richer flow of discourse; adds stylistic beauties graciously and freely and constrains the author's uneven, rugged style into artful rhythms. Now also suppose a reader ignorant of Greek but burning with a desire to read Thucydides and to penetrate into his recesses takes up this sort of translation; obviously he will be trying to find Thucydides in

[3] Huet is probably thinking of d'Ablancourt here; see above, 157-61. [Ed]

Thucydides and will say that, in fact, a deception has been created for him by the translator or he will suppose either candor or judgment lacking in Cicero and Fabius, from whom he had heard that Thycydides is crowded, compressed, intense, rich in ideas more than in words.

Next, suppose some other man turns his attention to translating Xenophon, whom Cicero cites for his smoothness and elegance. Suppose this person is sober and serious, precise in his ideas, brief, penetrating and, in addition, not sufficiently open and clear. Let him express Xenophon not as Xenophon is, but as he wishes Xenophon to be. Let him dispose his language, not according to the model, Xenophon; rather, let him create Xenophon according to his own style of discourse; let him disturb Xenophon's smoothness and introduce vehemence; in short, let him make from an Attic honeybee an eagle. Whoever sees Xenophon redone and magically changed in this way, if he believes he has seen the genuine Xenophon and grasped him in his mind, well, his impressions have powerfully deceived him. I would wish Thucydides displayed just as he is, strong; Xenophon just as he is, quiet and charming; Herodotos, clear and diffuse; Isocrates, rhythmic, if it can be done; Demosthenes, exalted and serious; Plato, rich and imaginative in his expression; Aristotle, sinewy; Theophrastus, sweet; Heraclitus, if he were extant, dark. In brief, the translation should be like Proteus[4] and change himself into every marvelous shape that exists; more changeable than even the chameleon, he should transfer all external colors into himself, imbibe and acquire them.

So approval should rigorously be denied to that very learned man, who, because Cicero's richness and abundance marvelously pleased him, when he decided to translate Aristotle, an obviously dry and plain writer, amplified by means of a ciceronian style what had been written by Aristotle briefly and obscurely.

I have often wondered about this shameless tendency to distort the ancient writers and what caused it. My conclusion is that innate in each of us is love of himself, which the Greeks aptly designated with one word, *philautia*; self-love, commonly joined with ignorance of good things, created the audacity I am discussing. After disease of this type has settled into the minds of people there must occur unhealthy ideas; from them arise reckless attitudes, carried away by which this age has laid profane hands on ancient books that ought never to be touched except with reverence; and so our time has sold its trash as actually the work of glorious authors. Because, so long as a translator thinks well of himself and inordinately procures his own pleasure, he easily arrogates to himself the role of judge and makes decisions confidently about the author whom he has undertaken to render. So anything that does not suit his taste he spurns, substituting for it his own invention. Yet even if some of these inventions receive his personal vote, they are only maintained in place on condition that the translator decides to do so by allowing the offspring of his own mind to insinuate themselves into someone else's and drive out, often, the legitimate children. In order to resist this evil there must be removed, root and all, the valuation human beings form of themselves beyond what is in them. Each of us ought to restrain the extravagance of his style; deal with the writings of others and especially of the ancients with caution; and, finally, after we have carefully learned the role of translator, fulfill that role faithfully once we have accepted it, making no concessions to our particular temperaments. Anyone who behaves differently is a busybody, not a translator; he should be said to interpolate, not interpret.

THUANUS. Absolutely correct, Casaubon, and this was my view previously. Any time I had come across a translation of this sort – and I often came across them, since they are numerous at this time – I would grieve that naive young people were being so disgracefully deceived and I would be very annoyed that these obstacles were being set up and the road closed by those whom one would have expected to strengthen and improve the entrance way to the inner sanctuary of sacred and renowned antiquity. All the more, then, do I rejoice that you have come forward, you who have dared not merely to take this road, in spite of the obstacles, but also to open it up for others. Certainly concern about this situation was appropriate to you, a man famously learned in Greek and Roman literature, not to mention other disciplines; familiar with the whole classical tradition; equipped with a remarkable talent for this area and, most important, with a sharp and uncorrupted judgment. But

> I hesitate to praise you further openly and to your face
> Lest you suppose I do it more to flatter you than because I want to.
> [Quintilian *Institutiones Oratoriae* Book 10, chapter 5]

So, continue, please; and, since you urge a translator to be an unremitting companion of his author, explain whether you want him also to go with equal steps and follow *foot by foot*, that is, accompany one quantity of words with an equal quantity of words.

CASAUBON. That's where I was, excellent Thuanus. I was thinking this when you spoke. But from me you will hear something not favored by everybody. All the same, I will speak, since you two, for me,

[4] In Greek mythology, a shape-shifter who could see the future, but would only tell it if one held tight to him while he changed into a myriad of forms. [Ed]

will be worth all the thousands, which is what Antimachus of Clarus is supposed to have said to Plato. To resume, then: In general I assert that a word should be expressed by a word; even the placing of the words should be kept, provided such is permitted by the language that the translator is using. When, for example, for each Greek word a corresponding word in Latin does not occur, then certainly some additional word must be permitted and even several additional words, if the situation demands. Likewise, when Latin does not always allow the same sequence and position of words as does Greek, then obviously it is necessary that this arrangement of words must be changed. Finally, the conflict and incompatibility of the languages can create many other obstacles preventing the translator from stepping closely and precisely into the footsteps of his author.

Katherine Philips

Katherine Philips (1631-1664) – or as she was called in her lifetime, "the Matchless Orinda" – was an English poet known and beloved in her day as the poetess of friendship. Generally regarded as the first English woman poet, she wasn't, in the strict sense of the word; but as her somewhat hagiographical biographer writes in 1931, "in her, for the first time in the history of English letters, a woman was received into the select company of poets" (Philip Webster Souers, *The Matchless Orinda*).

She was born to prosperous middle-class parents, John and Katherine Fowler, in London on January 1, 1631 or 1632. Her father was a cloth merchant who died when Katherine was around eleven years old; she was first educated by a kinswoman who lived with them until she was eight, Mrs. Blackett, who later sang her praises as a precocious child, claiming that she had read the Bible from cover to cover before she turned four. At eight she was sent to Mrs. Salmon's school for girls, where she probably learned French and Italian but no Latin or Greek; at fifteen, four years after the death of her father, she was taken out of school to follow her mother to Wales, where they lived with her new stepfather, Sir Richard Phillipps of Picton Castle. She would live in Wales most of the rest of her short life; two years later (1648) she married James Philips, a man 37 years her senior who had previously been married to a daughter of Katherine's stepfather, and they settled in the tiny Welsh town of Cardigan.

Used to London and starved for society in rural Wales, she soon became an avid correspondent, in which role she largely orchestrated the Society of Friendship that is associated with her name: while her beloved Lucasia (Anne Owens) did live in nearby Orielton, most of the other members of this 'literary salon' communicated by letter rather than attending meetings. Upon all Society members, as upon herself, she bestowed classical names, which she almost invariably used for them in her poems and letters. Poliarchus, to whom the collection of letters excerpted below was written, was Sir Charles Cotterell.

Raised a Puritan and married to another who held several prominent posts in Cromwell's government, Katherine Philips at some point in the twelve years between her marriage and the restoration became an Anglican and a royalist, as were most of her Society members; the Platonic idealism of the Society has been seen as her attempt to rise above (or repress) the shifting political allegiances in which she was caught. During those years she also became a mother: her son Hector was born in 1655 but died almost immediately, and her daughter Katherine was born the year after.

With the restoration in 1660, Katherine Philips quickly emerged from her local fame to become the Matchless Orinda, the most celebrated woman poet of her day. It is likely, in fact, that her growing fame as a royalist poet helped smooth her husband's transition from life as a tool of Cromwell and a speculator in Crown lands to life as a loyal subject of the king. Also instrumental in James Philips' royal pardon may have been Orinda's new patron Poliarchus, King Charles' master of ceremonies Sir Charles Cotterell. Cotterell wrote a little poetry and did a little translating, and admired Orinda's poems greatly; soon after meeting him Katherine Philips made him her literary mentor and patron. Her letters to him from Dublin, where she spent more than a year attending to her husband's business matters (he was claiming Irish land in compensation for her father's business investment before his death in 1642), provide one of the fullest accounts we have of seventeenth-century life in England and Ireland.

While in Dublin she also began translating Pierre Corneille's *La Mort de Pompée* (1643), somewhat diffidently at first, but soon with much encouragement from prominent people in Dublin society; she completed the translation and saw it performed to much acclaim in Dublin early in 1663. Since the Dublin printing of the translation sold out quickly, a London bookseller reprinted it the same year, and it went through four more editions by 1710, the year her complete poems were published.

She returned to Wales in the summer of 1663, but missed the excitement of Dublin; and while working in secrecy on a translation of Corneille's *Horace* (1641), she was also agitating for a trip to London. Finally she devised a business matter with which she could help her husband, and he gave her permission to go in March, 1664; but in June of that year she contracted small-pox in London and died, at the age of 33. Her translation of *Horace*, unfinished at her death, was completed by John Denham and performed, again to much acclaim, in 1667/8 and 1668/9.

Philips may have been the first woman ever to write a 'book' on translation – although that is a problematic description of what she did in several ways. In the first place, she didn't exactly write *Letters from Orinda to Poliarchus* as a book; it was a collection of actual letters written to her patron Sir Charles Cotterell published several decades after her death. In the second, the book is not exactly 'about' translation – certainly it is not a theoretical treatise about translation such as Huet had written in France two years earlier. Still, it was – or the letters from which it was compiled were – written by a translator, through the epistolary voice of a translator, and revolves around the practical problems she faces, emotional and technical, in translating into English Corneille's *La mort de Pompée* (1643), which had appeared just two decades before she wrote.

Translating Pompey
From *Letters from Orinda to Poliarchus* (1705)

Dublin, Aug. 20, 1662

... But of this in a little time more at large, when I shall have greater cause, and too much leisure for such reflections. I will now inform you of my adventures here. My good fortune has favoured me with the acquaintance of my Lord Orrery [Roger Boyle]: he is indeed a man of great parts, and agreeable conversation; and has been so extremely civil to me that were he not a most obliging person, I am sure he could not excuse it to his own judgment. By some accident or another my scene of Pompey fell into his hands, and he was pleased to like it so well that he sent me the French original; and the next time I saw him so earnestly importuned me to pursue that translation that to avoid the shame of seeing him who had so lately commanded a kingdom become a petitioner to me for such a trifle, I obeyed him so far as to finish the act in which that scene is; so that the whole third act is now English. This I the rather did, hoping to undeceive him in the partial opinion he had of my capacity for such an undertaking; and not doubting but he would have dispensed with my farther trouble therein. But he no sooner had it than (I think to punish me for having done it so ill) he enjoined me to go on; and not only so, but bribed me to be contented with the pains by sending me an excellent copy of verses, which, were I not conscious of my own unworthiness, would make me rather forget the subject than disbelieve the compliments of his Lordship's muse. But I have undergone as great a temptation to vanity from your tongue and pen as he can give me; and yet I hope neither of you shall ever make me forget myself so much as to take pride in anything but the having Poliarchus[1] for my friend. I will by my next send you my Lord's verses, on condition that in exchange you will let me have a copy of your translation of *Le Temple de la Morte*;[2] his Lordship is in love with the original, and you will infinitely oblige me in putting it in my power to show him your excellent version of it. To bribe you yet farther, I will send you mine of Pompey as fast as I do it; and because this is no great temptation, I will send you some translations from Virgil by Mr Cowley. You will wonder at my Lord's obstinacy in this desire to have me translate Pompey, as well because of my incapacity to perform it as that so many others have undertaken it; but all I can say or do is to no purpose, for he persists in his request, and will not be refused. The best on it is that having sent him one act already, I will take day enough for the rest. But I have wearied you as much with this story as he has me with commands which I am so unable to perform. He knows you, for he speaks of you with a good deal of honour and esteem, and therein, much more than by all his compliments to me, has not only discovered his judgment, but obliged, &c.

Orinda

September 17, 1663

... But let me not forget to tell you before I conclude that I have seen the second and fourth acts of Pompey that was translated by the wits,[3] and have read and considered them very impartially; the expressions are some of them great and noble, and the verses smooth;

---

[1] Sir Charles Cotterell, master of ceremonies for the royal court. The name Poliarchus was taken from John Barclay's *Argenis* (1621). [Ed]

[2] 'The Temple of Death', by Phillipe Habert. Cotterell's translation does not survive. [Ed]

[3] The so-called 'court wits' at the court of Charles II. This translation has since come to be known as that by the 'persons of honour', and it was a group effort: Edmund Waller seems to have translated the first act and Charles Sackville, Lord Buckhurst, the fourth; Philips lists Sir Charles Sedley and Sir Edward Fillmore as translators of two other acts, and tradition names one Sidney Godolphin as author of the fifth. Godolphin has not been traced. [Ed]

yet there is room in several places for an ordinary critic to show his skill. But I cannot but be surprised at the great liberty they have taken in adding, omitting and altering the original as they please themselves. This I take to be a liberty not pardonable in translators, and unbecoming the modesty of that attempt; for since the different ways of writing ought to be observed with their several proprieties, this way of garbling authors is fitter for a paraphrase than a translation; but having assumed so great a licence, I wonder their verses are anywhere either flat or rough,[4] which you will observe them not seldom to be; besides, their rhymes are frequently very bad, but what chiefly disgusts me is, that the sense most commonly languishes through three or four lines, and then ends in the middle of the fifth: for I am of the opinion that the sense ought always to be confined to the couplet, otherwise the lines must needs be spiritless and dull. I wish you could procure me the third and fifth acts, for I long to see them, especially the third, which I take to be the most noble and best written in the French. I am impatient likewise to hear your thoughts of that translation. You know me as far from envy as those gentlemen are above it, and therefore will not impute the freedom I have taken in these remarks to that or any other passion but purely to my opinion, and the liberty I take of telling it to so intimate a friend as Poliarchus; for after all I really think the worst of their lines equal to the best in my translation. If that play had tired the spectators as much as my letter has you, they would have given it but a cold reception; but you, I know, will pardon all the troubles that you have created to yourself, and encouraged from her that is more than anybody in the whole world, &c.

Orinda

John Dryden

John Dryden (1631-1700) was the predominant English literary figure of his day: poet, dramatist, translator, and critic, his influence on English literature for the next century or two was massive, and his pronouncements on translation are often cited (erroneously, as this volume testifies) as the first systematic theory of translation in the West.

He was born to a reasonably wealthy country gentleman who sided with Parliament against the king in 1642, when civil war broke out. He received the classical education characteristic of his class and gender, and in 1650 entered Trinity College, Cambridge, where he was graduated in 1654. In 1649, at 18, he had written and published a poem honouring Oliver Cromwell; in 1660 and 1661, at ages 29 and 30, he wrote two long poems celebrating the restored monarch Charles II, and was welcomed into the king's stable of public poets. In 1663 he married Lady Elizabeth Howard, with whom he eventually had three sons. In 1668 he was appointed poet laureate, the premier poet in that stable, and over most of the remaining three decades of his life this was the role he played best: a kind of poetic publicity secretary to the king.

For the next twelve years, however, most of his work was for the theatre. He was a shareholder in Thomas Killigrew's repertory company for the bulk of that period, and turned out about a play a year, some of which, like *All For Love* (1677), are still performed. In 1681, however, King Charles began to find himself in political trouble due to public fears that his Catholic brother James would succeed him. The Earl of Shaftesbury led the Whig party in a campaign to smear James as treasonous and replace him with Charles's illegitimate Protestant son; the king managed to turn public opinion against the Whigs and had Shaftesbury himself jailed for treason. Dryden, the king's poet laureate, jumped into the fray with both feet, lambasting the Whigs ferociously in a succession of brilliant verse satires and developing a reputation as one of the finest satirists of his day.

In 1685 James II ascended to the throne, and Dryden, ever the public poet, converted to Catholicism and retained the laureateship; when James abdicated three years later, however, Dryden's political credibility was gone, and he lost the laureateship to a poet he had savaged in verse several years before, Thomas Shadwell. He wrote a few more plays and collaborated on a dramatic opera, but increasingly turned his hand to translation: having translated Ovid in 1680, he now translated Juvenal and Persius for the publisher Jacob Tonson, and in 1694, after those works had proved financially successful, Tonson commissioned an English translation of Virgil. Completed and published three years later in 1697, this was Dryden's last major work: he died in 1700, and was buried in the Poets' Corner of Westminster Abbey, between Geoffrey Chaucer and Abraham Cowley.

Like his contemporaries John Denham, Abraham Cowley, and the Earl of Roscommon, Dryden was engaged in the gentlemanly search for secular principles of translation; and for him, as for them, 'gentlemanly' largely meant 'amateurish', meant refusing to put on scholarly airs – meant, in fact, resisting the temptation

[4] I.e., since the wits translated so freely, it is surprising that they could not iron out all the flat and rough spots normally generated by excessive fidelity. [Ed]

to write lengthy knit-browed treatises on the subject, as Lawrence Humphrey had in *Interpretatio linguarum* (1559), as Charles Batteux would in *Principes de littérature* (1743), and as Alexander Frazer Tytler would in *Essay on the Principles of Translation* (1797).

Still, Dryden's (undeserved) reputation today as the 'first translation theorist' reflects a movement in his remarks toward system – a movement that motivates the writing of a handful of pages rather than a whole book, and that does not knit his brow, does not drive him into impenetrable thickets of jargon, both of which factors surely contribute to his continuing reputation among modern readers. His three 'new' terms for translation, metaphrase, paraphrase, and imitation, for word-for-word, sense-for-sense, and 'free' translation, were far from new; first theorized for translation in ancient Alexandria (by Philo) and Rome (by Quintilian), they were rediscovered in the Renaissance and used repeatedly by authors from Roger Ascham in 1570 to Pierre-Daniel Huet in 1661. Still, Dryden remains an attractive and accessible popularizer of this long tradition.

The Three Types of Translation
From 'Preface' to *Ovid's Epistles* (1680)

All translations, I suppose, may be reduced to these three heads.

First, that of metaphrase, or turning an author word by word, and line by line, from one language into another. Thus, or near this manner, was Horace his *Art of Poetry* translated by Ben Jonson. The second way is that of paraphrase, or translation with latitude, where the author is kept in view by the translator, so as never to be lost, but his words are not so strictly followed as his sense; and that too is admitted to be amplified, but not altered. Such is Mr Waller's translation of Virgil's Fourth *Aeneid*. The third way is that of imitation, where the translator (if now he has not lost that name) assumes the liberty, not only to vary from the words and sense, but to forsake them both as he sees occasion; and taking only some general hints from the original, to run division on the groundwork, as he pleases. Such is Mr Cowley's practice in turning two Odes of Pindar, and one of Horace, into English.[1]

Concerning the first of these methods, our master Horace has given us this caution:

> *Nec verbum verbo curabis reddere, fidus*
> *Interpres* ...[2]
>
> Nor word for word too faithfully translate;

as the Earl of Roscommon has excellently rendered it. Too faithfully is, indeed, pedantically: 'tis a faith like that which proceeds from superstition, blind and zealous. Take it in the expression of Sir John Denham to Sir Richard Fanshaw, on his version of the *Pastor Fido*:

> That servile path thou nobly dost decline,
> Of tracing word by word, and line by line:
> A new and nobler way thou dost pursue,
> To make translations and translators too:
> They but preserve the ashes, thou the flame,
> True to his sense, but truer to his fame.[3]

'Tis almost impossible to translate verbally [literally], and well, at the same time; for the Latin (a most severe and compendious language) often expresses that in one word, which either the barbarity or the narrowness of modern tongues cannot supply in more. 'Tis frequent, also, that the conceit is couched in some expression, which will be lost in English:–

> *Atque iidem venti vela fidemque ferent.*[4]

What poet of our nation is so happy as to express this thought literally in English, and to strike wit, or almost sense, out of it?

In short, the verbal copier is encumbered with so many difficulties at once, that he can never disentangle himself from all. He is to consider, at the same time, the thought of his author, and his words, and to find out the counterpart to each in another language; and, besides this, he is to confine himself to the compass of numbers, and the slavery of rhyme. 'Tis much like dancing on ropes with fettered legs: a man may shun a fall by using caution; but the gracefulness of motion is not to be expected: and when we have said the best of it, 'tis but a foolish task; for no sober man would put himself into a danger for the applause of escaping without breaking his neck. We see Ben Jonson could not avoid obscurity in his literal translation of Horace, attempted in the same compass of lines: nay, Horace himself could scarce have done it to a Greek poet:-

> *Brevis esse laboro, obscurus fio*:[5]

either perspicuity or gracefulness will frequently be wanting. Horace has indeed avoided both these rocks in his translation of the three first lines of Homer's *Odysseis*, which he has contracted into two:–

[1] See above, 161-62. [Ed]

[2] See above, 15. [Ed]

[3] See above, 155. [Ed]

[4] "And the same winds bear away your sails and your loyalty". Ovid, *Heroides* 7.8. [Ed]

[5] "I strive to be brief, I become obscure". Horace, 'Art of Poetry' 25-26. [Ed]

Dic mihi musa virum captae post tempora Trojae,
Qui mores hominum multorum vidit, et urbes.

Muse, speak the man, who, since the siege of Troy,
So many towns, such change of manners saw.

EARL OF ROSCOMMON.

But then the sufferings of Ulysses, which are a considerable part of that sentence, are omitted:–

῞Ος μάλα πολλά πλάγχθη.[6]

The consideration of these difficulties, in a servile, literal translation, not long since made two of our famous wits, Sir John Denham and Mr Cowley, to contrive another way of turning authors into our tongue, called, by the latter of them, imitation. As they were friends, I suppose they communicated their thoughts on this subject to each other; and therefore their reasons for it are little different, though the practice of one is much more moderate.[7] I take imitation of an author, in their sense, to be an endeavour of a later poet to write like one who has written before him, on the same subject; that is, not to translate his words, or to be confined to his sense, but only to set him as a pattern, and to write, as he supposes that author would have done, had he lived in our age, and in our country. Yet I dare not say, that either of them have carried this libertine way of rendering authors (as Mr Cowley calls it) so far as my definition reaches; for in the *Pindaric Odes*, the customs and ceremonies of ancient Greece are still preserved. But I know not what mischief may arise hereafter from the example of such an innovation, when writers of unequal parts to him shall imitate so bold an undertaking. To add and to diminish what we please, which is the way avowed by him, ought only to be granted to Mr Cowley, and that too only in his translation of Pindar; because he alone was able to make him amends, by giving him better of his own, whenever he refused his author's thoughts. Pindar is generally known to be a dark writer, to want connection (I mean as to our understanding), to soar out of sight, and leave his reader at a gaze. So wild and ungovernable a poet cannot be translated literally; his genius is too strong to bear a chain, and Samson-like he shakes it off. A genius so elevated and unconfined as Mr Cowley's was but necessary to make Pindar speak English, and that was to be performed by no other way than imitation. But if Virgil, or Ovid, or any regular intelligible authors be thus used, 'tis no longer to be called their work, when neither the thoughts nor words are drawn from the original; but instead of them there is something new produced, which is almost the creation of another hand. By this way, 'tis true, somewhat that is excellent may be invented, perhaps more excellent than the first design; though Virgil must be still excepted, when that *perhaps* takes place. Yet he who is inquisitive to know an author's thoughts will be disappointed in his expectation; and 'tis not always that a man will be contented to have a present made him, when he expects the payment of a debt. To state it fairly; imitation of an author is the most advantageous way for a translator to show himself, but the greatest wrong which can be done to the memory and reputation of the dead. Sir John Denham (who advised more liberty than he took himself) gives his reason for his innovation, in his admirable Preface before the translation of the Second *Aeneid*: *Poetry is of so subtile a spirit, that, in pouring out of one language into another, it will all evaporate; and, if a new spirit be not added in the transfusion, there will remain nothing but a caput mortuum.*[8] I confess this argument holds good against a literal translation; but who defends it? Imitation and verbal [literal] version are, in my opinion, the two extremes which ought to be avoided; and therefore, when I have proposed the mean betwixt them, it will be seen how far his argument will reach.

No man is capable of translating poetry, who, besides a genius to that art, is not a master both of his author's language, and of his own; nor must we understand the language only of the poet, but his particular turn of thoughts and expression, which are the characters that distinguish, and as it were individuate him from all other writers. When we are come thus far, 'tis time to look into ourselves, to conform our genius to his, to give his thought either the same turn, if our tongue will bear it, or, if not, to vary but the dress, not to alter or destroy the substance. The like care must be taken of the more outward ornaments, the words. When they appear (which is but seldom) literally graceful, it were an injury to the author that they should be changed. But since every language is so full of its own proprieties that what is beautiful in one is often barbarous, nay sometimes nonsense, in another, it would be unreasonable to limit a translator to the narrow compass of his author's words: 'tis enough if he choose out some expression which does not vitiate the sense. I suppose he may stretch his chain to such a latitude; but by innovation of thoughts, methinks he breaks it. By this means the spirit of an author may be transfused, and yet not lost: and thus 'tis plain that the reason alleged by Sir John Denham has no farther force than to expression; for thought, if it be translated

[6] "Who was very much tossed [on the sea]". *Odyssey* 1.1. [Ed]

[7] Denham was more moderate than Cowley. [Ed]

[8] See above, 156. [Ed]

truly, cannot be lost in another language; but the words that convey it to our apprehension (which are the image and ornament of that thought), may be so ill chosen as to make it appear in an unhandsome dress, and rob it of its native lustre. There is, therefore, a liberty to be allowed for the expression; neither is it necessary that words and lines should be confined to the measure of their original. The sense of an author, generally speaking, is to be sacred and inviolable. If the fancy of Ovid be luxuriant, 'tis his character to be so; and if I retrench it, he is no longer Ovid. It will be replied, that he receives advantage by this lopping of his superfluous branches; but I rejoin, that a translator has no such right. When a painter copies from the life, I suppose he has no privilege to alter features and lineaments, under pretence that his picture will look better: perhaps the face which he has drawn would be more exact, if the eyes or nose were altered; but 'tis his business to make it resemble the original. In two cases only there may a seeming difficulty arise; that is, if the thought be notoriously trivial or dishonest; but the same answer will serve for both, that then they ought not to be translated:–

> ... *Et quae*
> *Desperes tractata nitescere posse, relinquas.*[9]

Thus I have ventured to give my opinion on this subject against the authority of two great men, but I hope without offence to either of their memories; for I both loved them living and reverence them now they are dead. But if, after what I have urged, it be thought by better judges that the praise of a translation consists in adding new beauties to the piece, thereby to recompense the loss which it sustains by change of language, I shall be willing to be taught better, and to recant. In the meantime it seems to me that the true reason why we have so few versions which are tolerable is not from the too close pursuing of the author's sense, but because there are so few who have all the talents which are requisite for translation, and that there is so little praise and so small encouragement for so considerable a part of learning.

To apply, in short, what has been said to this present work, the reader will here find most of the translations with some little latitude or variation from the author's sense. That of *Oenone to Paris* is in Mr Cowley's way of imitation only. I was desired to say that the author [Aphra Behn], who is of the fair sex, understood not Latin. But if she does not, I am afraid she has given us occasion to be ashamed who do.

For my own part, I am ready to acknowledge that I have transgressed the rules which I have given; and taken more liberty than a just translation will allow. But so many gentlemen whose wit and learning are well known being joined in it, I doubt not but that their excellencies will make you ample satisfaction for my errors.

Steering Betwixt Two Extremes
From 'Dedication of the *Aeneis* (to John, Lord Marquess of Normanby, Earl of Musgrave)' (1697)

On the whole matter, I thought fit to steer betwixt the two extremes of paraphrase and literal translation; to keep as near my author as I could, without losing all his graces, the most eminent of which are in the beauty of his words; and those words, I must add, are always figurative. Such of these as would retain their elegance in our tongue, I have endeavoured to graff[10] on it; but most of them are of necessity to be lost, because they will not shine in any but their own. Virgil has sometimes two of them in a line; but the scantiness of our heroic verse is not capable of receiving more than one; and that too must expiate for many others which have none. Such is the difference of the languages, or such my want of skill in choosing words. Yet I may presume to say, and I hope with as much reason as the French translator [Jean Regnauld de Segrais], that, taking all the materials of this divine author, I have endeavoured to make Virgil speak such English as he would himself have spoken, if he had been born in England, and in this present age. I acknowledge, with Segrais, that I have not succeeded in this attempt according to my desire: yet I shall not be wholly without praise, if in some sort I may be allowed to have copied the clearness, the purity, the easiness, and the magnificence of his style. But I shall have occasion to speak further on this subject before I end the Preface ...

I am also bound to tell your Lordship, in my own defence, that, from the beginning of the First *Georgic* to the end of the last *Aeneid*, I found the difficulty of translation growing on me in every succeeding book. For Virgil, above all poets, had a stock, which I may call almost inexhaustible, of figurative, elegant, and sounding words: I, who inherit but a small portion of his genius, and write in a language so much inferior to the Latin, have found it very painful to vary phrases, when the same sense returns upon me. Even he himself, whether out of necessity or choice, has often expressed the same thing in the same words, and often repeated two or three whole verses which he has used before. Words are not so easily coined as money; and yet we see that the credit not only of banks but of exchequers cracks, when little comes in, and much goes out. Virgil called upon me in every line for some new word: and I paid so long, that I was almost bankrupt; so that the latter end must needs be more

[9] "And what he thinks his touch will never turn to gold, that he lets alone" (E.C. Wickham's translation; Horace, 'Art of Poetry', l. 140-41. [Ed]

[10] I.e., graft, here figuratively, 'to set or fix firmly'. [Ed]

burdensome than the beginning or the middle; and, consequently, the Twelfth *Aeneid* cost me double the time of the First and Second. What had become of me, if Virgil had taxed me with another book? I had certainly been reduced to pay the public in hammered money, for want of milled; that is, in the same old words which I had used before: and the receivers must have been forced to have taken anything, where there was so little to be had.

Besides this difficulty (with which I have struggled, and made a shift to pass it over), there is one remaining, which is insuperable to all translators. We are bound to our author's sense, though with the latitudes already mentioned; for I think it not so sacred, as that one iota must not be added or diminished, on pain of an *Anathema*. But slaves we are, and labour on another man's plantation; we dress the vineyard, but the wine is the owner's: if the soil be sometimes barren, then we are sure of being scourged; if it be fruitful, and our care succeeds, we are not thanked; for the proud reader will only say, the poor drudge has done his duty. But this is nothing to what follows; for, being obliged to make his sense intelligible, we are forced to untune our own verses, that we may give his meaning to the reader. He who invents is master of his thoughts and words: he can turn and vary them as he pleases, till he renders them harmonious; but the wretched translator has no such privilege: for, being tied to the thoughts, he must make what music he can in the expression; and, for this reason, it cannot always be so sweet as that of the original. There is a beauty of sound, as Segrais has observed, in some Latin words, which is wholly lost in any modern language. He instances in that *mollis amaracus*, on which Venus lays Cupid, in the First *Aeneid*. If I should translate it *sweet marjoram*, as the word signifies, the reader would think I had mistaken Virgil: for those village words, as I may call them, give us a mean idea of the thing; but the sound of the Latin is so much more pleasing, by the just mixture of the vowels with the consonants, that it raises our fancies to conceive somewhat more noble than a common herb, and to spread roses under him, and strew lilies over him; a bed not unworthy the grandson of the goddess.

If I cannot copy his harmonious numbers, how shall I imitate his noble flights, where his thoughts and words are equally sublime? *Quem*

... quisquis studet aemulari,
... caeratis ope Daedalea
Nititur pennis, vitreo daturus
Nomina ponto.[11]

[11] "Whomever he is eager to emulate, he tries on feathers waxed through the skill of Daedalus, gives his name to the glassy sea." Horace Odes 4.2.2. Edward Capps III's translation. [Ed]

What modern language, or what poet, can express the majestic beauty of this one verse, amongst a thousand others?

Aude hospes, contemnere opes, et te
quoque dignum
Finge deo ...[12]

For my part, I am lost in the admiration of it: I contemn the world when I think on it, and myself when I translate it.

Lay by Virgil, I beseech your Lordship, and all my better sort of judges, when you take up my version; and it will appear a passable beauty when the original Muse is absent. But, like Spenser's false Florimell made of snow,[13] it melts and vanishes when the true one comes in sight. I will not excuse, but justify myself, for one pretended crime, with which I am liable to be charged by false critics, not only in this translation, but in many of my original poems; that I latinize too much. 'Tis true, that, when I find an English word significant and sounding, I neither borrow from the Latin, nor any other language; but, when I want at home, I must seek abroad.

If sounding words are not of our growth and manufacture, who shall hinder me to import them from a foreign country? I carry not out the treasure of the nation, which is never to return; but what I bring from Italy, I spend in England: here it remains, and here it circulates; for, if the coin be good, it will pass from one hand to another. I trade both with the living and the dead, for the enrichment of our native language ...

Wentworth Dillon, Earl of Roscommon

The fourth earl of Roscommon (1633?-1685) was an English translator and poet of whom Samuel Johnson wrote that "he improved taste, if he did not enlarge knowledge, and may be numbered among the benefactors to English literature", and whom Alexander Pope called the only moral writer of King Charles II's reign:

Unhappy Dryden! – in all Charles's days
Roscommon only boasts unspotted lays.

Born in Ireland the son of Sir James Dillon, Roscommon was raised a Protestant (his father had

[12] "Guest of mine, be strong to scorn wealth and so mould yourself that you also may be fit for a God's converse." Evander to Aeneas in Virgil's *Aeneid* 8.364. W. F. Jackson Knight's translation. [Ed]

[13] Spenser, *Faerie Queen* 3.8.5-9. [Ed]

been converted from Catholicism by Archbishop Ussher, primate of Ireland) and educated privately; when his uncle Thomas Wentworth, lord deputy under Charles I, was executed during the Civil War, he was sent to university at Caen in Normandy. He stayed on the Continent until the restoration in 1660, and was warmly welcomed upon his return by Charles II, who also restored to him all honours, properties, and lordships possessed by his forefathers in 1641. In 1661 he became a member of the Irish Parliament; in 1662 he married Lady Frances Boyle, and in 1674 Isabella Boynton, but died childless. In the 1670s, living in London, he attempted to found a literary academy based on the one in Caen, and while the idea did not exactly take hold, the meetings inspired numerous translations and Roscommon's own 'Essay on Translated Verse' (1684); John Dryden and other writers of the day occasionally attended meetings as well.

Roscommon was an active but rather selective translator; in addition to Virgil's sixth eclogue and two of Horace's odes and a few other literary bits and pieces, he translated Horace's *Art of Poetry* (1680), which Dryden quoted in his preface to Ovid, published the same year. His poetry was highly regarded in his day; today he is largely remembered as the author of the 'Essay on Translated Verse'.

An Essay on Translated Verse (1684)

Happy that author whose correct essay
Repairs so well our old Horatian way,
And happy you, who, by propitious fate,
On great Apollo's sacred standard wait,[1]
And with strict discipline instructed right,
Have learned to use your arms before you fight.
But since the press, the pulpit, and the stage
Conspire to censure and expose our age,
Provoked too far, we resolutely must
To the few virtues that we have be just.
For who have longed, or who have laboured more
To search the treasures of the Roman store,
Or dig in Grecian mines for purer ore?
The noblest fruits, transplanted, in our isle
With early hope and fragrant blossoms smile.
Familiar Ovid tender thoughts inspires,
And nature seconds all his soft desires;
Theocritus does now to us belong,
And Albion's[2] rocks repeat his rural song.
Who has not heard how Italy was blest,
Above the Medes, above the wealthy East?
Or Gallus' song, so tender, and so true,
As ev'n Lycoris might with pity view![3]
When mourning nymphs attend their Daphne's hearse,[4]
Who does not weep that reads the moving verse?
But hear, oh, hear, in what exalted strains
Sicilian muses through these happy plains
Proclaim Saturnian times,[5] our own Apollo reigns.

When France had breathed, after intestine broils,
And peace and conquest crowned her foreign toils,
There, cultivated by a royal hand,
Learning grew fast, and spread, and blest the land;
The choicest books that Rome or Greece have known,
Her excellent translators made her own;
And Europe still considerably gains,
Both by their good example and their pains.
From hence our gen'rous emulation came,
We undertook, and we performed the same.
But now we show the world a nobler way,
And in translated verse do more than they.
Serene and clear, harmonious Horace flows,
With sweetness not to be expressed in prose;
Degrading prose explains his meaning ill,
And shows the stuff, but not the workman's skill;
I, who have served him more than twenty years,
Scarce know my master as he there appears.
Vain are our neighbours' hopes, and vain their cares,
The fault is more their language's than theirs:
'Tis courtly, florid, and abounds in words,
Of softer sound than ours perhaps affords;
But who did ever in French authors see
The comprehensive English energy?
The weighty bullion of one sterling line,
Drawn to French wire, would through whole pages shine.
I speak my private but impartial sense,
With freedom, and (I hope) without offence;
For I'll recant, when France shows me wit,
As strong as ours, and as succinctly writ.
'Tis true, composing is the nobler part,
But good translation is no easy art;
For though materials have long since been found,
Yet both your fancy and your hands are bound,
And by improving what was writ before,
Invention labours less, but judgment more.

---

[1] Apollo was the Greek god of divine distance, who presided over religious law, prophets, and oracles; Roscommon refers to him in his aspect as the god of music, poetry, and the dance. [Ed]

[2] I.e., England's. [Ed]

[3] Lycoris was the name the Roman poet Cornelius Gallus gave his mistress Volumnia in his poems. [Ed]

[4] In Greek mythology, Daphne was pursued by Apollo, whom she fled by having her father the river-god change her into a laurel; Apollo made the laurel the symbol of poets and triumphant conquerors. Ovid tells the story in book one of the *Metamorphoses*. [Ed]

[5] I.e., a new golden age. [Ed]

The soil intended for Pierian seeds[6]
Must be well purged from rank pedantic weeds.
Apollo starts, and all Parnassus shakes,[7]
At the rude rumbling Baralipton makes.
For none have been with admiration read,
But who, beside their learning, were well-bred.

The first great work (a task performed by few)
Is that yourself may to yourself be true:
No masque, no tricks, no favour, no reserve;
Dissect your mind, examine every nerve.
Whoever vainly on his strength depends,
Begins like Virgil, but like Maevius ends:
That wretch, in spite of his forgotten rhymes,
Condemned to live to all succeeding times,
With pompous nonsense and a bellowing sound
Sung lofty Ilium tumbling to the ground.
And, if my muse can through past ages see,
That noisy, nauseous, gaping fool was he;
Exploded, when, with universal scorn,
The mountains laboured and a mouse was born.

Learn, learn, Crotona's brawny wrestler[8] cries,
Audacious mortals, and be timely wise!
'Tis I that call, remember Milo's end,
Wedged in that timber which he strove to rend.

Each poet with a different talent writes,
One praises, one instructs, another bites;
Horace did ne'er aspire to epic bays,[9]
Nor lofty Maro stoop to lyric lays.
Examine how your humour[10] is inclined,
And which the ruling passion of your mind;
Then seek a poet who your way does bend,
And choose an author as you choose a friend:
United by this sympathetic bond,
You grow familiar, intimate, and fond;
Your thoughts, your words, your styles, your souls agree,
No longer his interpreter, but he.

With how much ease is a young muse betrayed,
How nice the reputation of the maid!
Your early, kind, paternal care appears,
By chaste instruction of her tender years.
The first impression in her infant breast
Will be the deepest and should be the best.
Let no austerity breed servile fear,
No wanton sound offend her virgin ear.
Secure from foolish pride's affected state,
And specious flattery's more pernicious bait,
Habitual innocence adorns her thoughts,
But your neglect must answer for her faults.

Immodest words admit of no defence,
For want of decency is want of sense.
What mod'rate fop would rake the park for stews[11]
Who among troops of faultless nymphs may choose?
Variety of such is to be found;
Take then a subject proper to expound:
But moral, great, and worth a poet's voice,
For men of sense despise a trivial choice:
And such applause it must expect to meet,
As would some painter, busy in a street,
To copy bulls and bears, and ev'ry sign
That calls the staring sots to nasty wine.

Yet 'tis not all to have a subject good;
It must delight us when 'tis understood.
He that brings fulsome objects to my view
(As many old have done, and many new)
With nauseous images my fancy fills,
And all goes down like oxymel of squills.[12]
Instruct the list'ning world how Maro sings
Of useful subjects and of lofty things:
These will such true, such bright ideas raise,
As merit gratitude as well as praise;
But foul descriptions are offensive still,
Either for being like or being ill.
For who, without a qualm, hath ever looked
On holy garbage, though by Homer cooked,
Whose railing heroes and whose wounded gods
Make some suspect he snores as well as nods?
But I offend – Virgil begins to frown,
And Horace looks with indignation down;
My blushing muse with conscious fear retires,
And whom they like implicitly admires.

On sure foundations let your fabric rise,
And with attractive majesty surprise,
Not by affected, meretricious arts,
But strict harmonious symmetry of parts,
Which through the whole insensibly must pass,

[6] Pieria in North Thessaly was thought to be the home of the Muses; Pierian thus usually refers to poetry or learning. [Ed]

[7] Mt. Parnassus in Greek was thought of as sacred to Apollo and the muses, hence to poetry. [Ed]

[8] Milo(n) of Croton (late 6th century B.C.E.), famous Greek wrestler whose name has become a byword for great strength. According to legend he died attempting to split a tree: he got his hand caught in the split and was trapped there until devoured by wolves. [Ed]

[9] Bay-wreaths given ancient poets as rewards; fig. fame, reputation. [Ed]

[10] I.e., temperament. The four humours (liquids) or 'ruling passions' were blood (sanguine temperament), yellow bile (choleric temperament), phlegm (phlegmatic temperament), and black bile (melancholic temperament). [Ed]

[11] I.e., prostitutes. [Ed]

[12] A medicinal potion made from the bulb of the sea-onion (squill) mixed with a vinegar-honey syrup (oxymel). [Ed]

With vital heat to animate the mass, –
A pure, an active, an auspicious flame,
And bright as heav'n from whence the blessing came.
But few, oh few souls, preordained by fate,
The race of gods have reached that envied height;
No rebel titan's sacrilegious crime,[13]
By heaping hills on hills can thither climb.
The grisly ferry-man of hell denied
Aeneas entrance, till he knew his guide;[14]
How justly then will impious mortals fall,
Whose pride would soar to heav'n without a call!

Pride, of all others the most dangerous fault,
Proceeds from want of sense or want of thought.
The men who labour and digest things most
Will be much apter to despond than boast.
For if your author be profoundly good,
'Twill cost you dear before he's understood.
How many ages since has Virgil writ!
How few are they who understand him yet!
Approach his altars with religious fear,
No vulgar deity inhabits there:
Heav'n shakes not more at Jove's imperial nod
Than poets should before their Mantuan God.[15]
Hail, mighty MARO! may that sacred name
Kindle my breast with thy celestial flame,
Sublime ideas and apt words infuse;
The muse instruct my voice, and thou inspire the muse!

What I have instanced only in the best
Is in proportion true of all the rest.
Take pains the genuine meaning to explore,
There sweat, there strain, tug the laborious oar.
Search ev'ry comment that your care can find,
Some here, some there may hit the poet's mind.
Yet be not blindly guided by the throng;
The multitude is always in the wrong.
When things appear unnatural or hard,
Consult your author, with himself compared;
Who knows what blessing Phoebus may bestow[16]
And future ages to your labour owe?
Such secrets are not easily found out,
But, once discovered, leave no room for doubt.
Truth stamps conviction in your ravished breast,
And peace and joy attend the glorious guest.

Truth still is one; truth is divinely bright;
No cloudy doubts obscure her native light:
While in your thoughts you find the least debate,
You may confound, but never can translate.
Your style will this through all disguises show,
For none explain more clearly than they know:
He only proves he understands a text,
Whose exposition leaves it unperplexed.
They who too faithfully on names insist
Rather create than dissipate the mist,
And grow unjust by being overnice,
For superstitious virtue turns to vice.
Let Crassus' ghost and Labienus tell
How twice in Parthian plains their legions fell,
Since Rome hath been so jealous of her fame,
That few know Pacorus' or Monoeses' name.

Words in one language elegantly used
Will hardly in another be excused,
And some that Rome admired in Caesar's time
May neither suit our genius nor our clime.
The genuine sense, intelligibly told,
Shows a translator both discreet and bold.
Excursions are inexpiably bad,
And 'tis much safer to leave out than add.
Abstruse and mystic thoughts you must express
With painful care but seeming easiness,
For truth shines brightest through the plainest dress.
Th' Aenaean muse, when she appears in state,
Makes all Jove's thunder on her verses wait,
Yet writes sometimes as soft and moving things
As Venus speaks or Philomela sings.[17]
Your author always will the best advise:
Fall, when he falls; and when he rises, rise.
Affected noise is the most wretched thing
That to contempt can empty scribblers bring.
Vowels and accents, regularly placed
On even syllables, and still the last,
Though gross, innumerable faults abound,
In spite of nonsense never fail of sound.
But this is meant of even verse alone,
As being most harmonious and most known;
For if you will unequal numbers try,
There accents on odd syllables must lie.
Whatever sister of the learned nine[18]
Does to your suit a willing ear incline,
Urge your success, deserve a lasting name,
She'll crown a grateful and a constant flame.
But if a wild uncertainty prevail,

[13] Prometheus was the rebel titan punished by Zeus for giving fire to humans. [Ed]

[14] In book six of Virgil's *Aeneid*, Charon ferries Aeneas across the Styx to the land of the dead. [Ed]

[15] I.e., Virgil, from Mantua, Italy, referred to as MARO in the next line. [Ed]

[16] A name of Apollo (god of poetry) in his aspect of sun-god. [Ed]

[17] Jove (Jupiter), Roman god of thunder; Venus, Roman god of love; Philomela was raped by Zeus and punished for it by a jealous Hera, who tore out her tongue and turned her into a mockingbird. [Ed]

[18] I.e., the nine muses, Clio (history), Euterpe (tragedy, flute-playing), Thalia (comedy), Melpomene (tragedy, lyre-playing), Terpsichore (lyric poetry, dancing), Erato (lyric poetry, hymns), Polymnia (dancing, geometry), Urania (astronomy), and Calliope (epic poetry). [Ed]

And turn your veering heart with ev'ry gale,
You lose the fruit of all your former care
For the sad prospect of a just despair.

A quack, too scandalously mean to name,
Had by man-midwif'ry got wealth and fame;
As if Lucina[19] had forgot her trade,
The lab'ring wife invokes his surer aid.
Well-seasoned bowls the gossip's spirits raise,
Who, while she guzzles, chats the doctor's praise.[20]
And largely what she wants in words supplies
With maudlin eloquence of trickling eyes.
But what a thoughtless animal is man,
How very active in his own trepan![21]
For greedy of physicians' frequent fees,
From female mellow praise he takes degrees,
Struts in a new unlicensed gown, and then,
From saving women falls to killing men.[22]
Another such had left the nation thin,
In spite of all the children he brought in.
His pills as thick as hand granadoes[23] flew,
And where they fell, as certainly they slew.
His name struck ev'rywhere as great a damp
As Archimedes through the Roman camp.
With this the doctor's pride began to cool,
For smarting soundly may convince a fool.
But now repentance came too late for grace,
And meager famine stared him in the face.
Fain would he to the wives be reconciled,
But found no husband left to own a child;
The friends that got the brats were poisoned too;
In this sad case what could our vermin do?
Worried with debts and past all hope of bail,
Th'unpitied wretch lies rotting in a jail,
And there, with basket alms scarce kept alive,
Shows how mistaken talents ought to thrive.

I pity from my soul unhappy men,
Compelled by want to prostitute their pen,
Who must, like lawyers, either starve or plead,
And follow, right or wrong, where guineas lead;
But you, Pompilian,[24] wealthy, pampered heirs,
Who to your country owe your swords and cares,
Let no vain hope your easy mind seduce,
For rich ill poets are without excuse.
'Tis very dangerous tamp'ring with a muse:
The profit's small, and you have much to lose;
For, though true wit adorns your birth or place,
Degenerate lines degrade th' attainted race.
No poet any passion can excite,
But what they feel transport them when they write.
Have you been led through the Cumaean cave,[25]
And heard th' impatient maid divinely rave?
I hear her now; I see her rolling eyes;
And panting, lo! the god, the god, she cries;
With words not hers, and more than humane sound,
She makes th' obedient ghosts peep trembling through
the ground.
But though we must obey when heaven commands,
And man in vain the sacred call withstands,
Beware what spirit rages in your breast;
For ten inspired ten thousand are possessed.
Thus make the proper use of each extreme,
And write with fury, but correct with phlegm;[26]
As when the cheerful hours too freely pass,
And sparkling wine smiles in the tempting glass,
Your pulse advises and begins to beat
Through every swelling vein a loud retreat.
So when a muse propitiously invites,
Improve her favours and indulge her flights;
But when you find that vigorous heat abate,
Leave off, and for another summons wait.
Before the radiant sun a glimmering lamp,
Adult'rate metals to the sterling stamp,
Appear not meaner than mere humane lines,
Compared with those whose inspiration shines;
These nervous, bold; those languid and remiss;
There, cold salutes; but here a lover's kiss.
Thus have I seen a rapid, headlong tide,
With foaming waves the passive soan[27] divide,
Whose lazy waters without motion lay,
While he, with eager force, urged his impetuous way.

The privilege that ancient poets claim,
Now turned to license by too just a name,
Belongs to none but an established fame,
Which scorns to take it. –
Absurd expressions, crude, abortive thoughts,
All the lewd legion of exploded faults,
Base fugitives, to that asylum fly,
And sacred laws with insolence defy.
Not thus our heroes of the former days
Deserved and gained their never fading bays;
For I mistake, or far the greatest part
Of what some call neglect was studied art.

[19] Lucina was a light-bringing goddess who presided over childbirth; Juno and Diana were often referred to with the surname Lucina. [Ed]

[20] I.e., the man sets up as a midwife, delivers a baby well enough, then the godparent spreads the word of his skill to her drinking buddies – with eloquent tears, as the next two lines make clear. [Ed]

[21] I.e., undoing. [Ed]

[22] I.e., because women praise him, he thinks he's a real doctor ('takes degrees') and begins dispensing medicines that kill the people who take them. [Ed]

[23] I.e., hand grenades. [Ed]

[24] A term of contempt applied to a large, corpulent man. [Ed]

[25] Location of the Sybilline oracle (the 'impatient maid' of the next line) of Apollo. [Ed]

[26] I.e., with the phlegmatic or calm humour. [Ed]

[27] Meaning unclear; possibly 'sound'. [Ed]

When Virgil seems to trifle in a line,
'Tis like a warning-piece, which gives the sign
To wake your fancy and prepare your sight,
To reach the noble height of some unusual flight.
I lose my patience when, with saucy pride,
By untuned ears I hear his numbers tried.[28]
Reverse of nature! shall such copies, then,
Arraign th' originals of Maro's pen,
And the rude notions of pedantic schools
Blaspheme the sacred founder of our rules!

The delicacy of the nicest ear
Finds nothing harsh or out of order there.
Sublime or low, unbended or intense,
The sound is still a comment to the sense.

A skillful ear in numbers should preside,
And all disputes without appeal decide.
This ancient Rome and elder Athens found,
Before mistaken stops debauched the sound.

When, by impulse from heaven, Tyrtaeus sung,
In drooping soldiers a new courage sprung;
Reviving Sparta now the fight maintained,
And what two generals lost, a poet gained.[29]
By secret influence of indulgent skies,
Empire and poesy together rise.
True poets are the guardians of a state,
And, when they fail, portend approaching fate,
For that which Rome to conquest did inspire
Was not the vestal, but the muse's fire;[30]
Heaven joins the blessings; no declining age
E'er felt the raptures of poetic rage.

Of many faults rhyme is perhaps the cause;
Too strict to rhyme, we slight more useful laws;
For that in Greece or Rome was never known,
Till, by barbarian deluges o'erflown,
Subdued, undone, they did at last obey,
And change their own for their invaders' way.

I grant that from some mossy idol oak,
In double rhymes our Thor and Woden spoke;
And by succession of unlearned times,
As bards began, so monks rung on the chimes.

But now that Phoebus and the sacred nine
With all their beams on our blessed island shine,
Why should not we their ancient rites restore,
And be what Rome or Athens were before?

Have we forgot how Raphael's num'rous prose
Led our exalted souls through heavenly camps,[31]
And marked the ground where proud apostate thrones
Defied Jehovah? Here, 'twixt host and host,
(A narrow but dreadful interval)
Portentous sight! before the cloudy van
Satan with vast and haughty strides advanced,
Came tow'ring armed in adamant and gold.
There bellowing engines, with their fiery tubes,
Dispersed ethereal forms, and down they fell
By thousands, angels on archangels rolled;
Recovered, to the hills they ran, they flew,
Which (with their pond'rous load, rocks, waters, woods)
From their firm seats torn by the shaggy tops,
They bore like shields before them through the air,
Till more incensed they hurled them at their foes.
All was confusion; heaven's foundations shook,
Threat'ning no less than universal wrack,
For Michael's arm main promontories flung,
And overpressed whole legions weak with sin;
For they blasphemed and struggled as they lay,
Till the great ensign of Messiah blazed,
And, armed with vengeance, God's victorious Son
(Effulgence of eternal deity),
Grasping ten thousand thunders in his hand,
Drove th' old original rebels headlong down,
And sent them flaming to the vast abyss.

O may I live to hail the glorious day,
And sing loud paeans through the crowded way,
When in triumphant state the British muse,
True to herself, shall barb'rous aid refuse,
And in the Roman majesty appear,
Which none knew better, and none come so near.

Aphra Behn

Aphra Behn (1640-1689) was a striking figure in seventeenth-century England: a strong, resolute woman who spied for Charles II, made a good living writing for the London theatre, and wrote what may be the first English novel (*Oroonoko*, 1688), she was vilified mercilessly for her 'forwardness' in invading the exclusively masculine public sphere, yet also much admired

---

[28] I.e., when I hear his poetic meter tested or criticized. [Ed]

[29] The Spartans conquered the Messenians in two wars, probably from about 735 to 715 and from 660 to sometime around the end of the 7th century. According to legend, the Spartans were unable to defeat the Messenians in the second war until the poet Tyrtaeus bolstered their spirits with militaristic poetry. [Ed]

[30] The vestal fire in Rome (and many other ancient civilizations) was thought to be the embodiment of the sacred king, and was tended by virgins thought of as its wives. [Ed]

[31] This stanza is a paraphrase of book six of John Milton's *Paradise Lost* (1667, seventeen years before this writing). 'Num'rous prose' refers to Milton's verse form; Raphael recaps this history for Adam in books five to eight. [Ed]

and much imitated.

Her childhood is obscure; almost certainly of middle-class origins, she was possibly orphaned, probably adopted by a family named Amis, with whom she travelled to the English colony of Surinam (soon to become Dutch Guiana) in the late 1650s. There she had the experiences on which she based *Oroonoko*, and met and fell in love with William Scot, a shadowy intelligence type who seems to have been spying for either England or Holland or both (and doubling and tripling for each). Her open love affair with him scandalized the English authorities on the island, and she was sent home, where she married a London merchant of Dutch extraction named Behn (pronounced 'Ben'), who died in 1666. When her erstwhile lover, who was now working openly for Holland, sent a message to the English government offering to sell information on Dutch troop and ship movements if Aphra were sent as messenger, she became a spy. Unfortunately, the English coffers were empty, and Behn was kept in Holland for several months with no pay, with the result that, upon her return to England, she was thrown in debtor's prison.

In 1671 Behn began to write for the London theatre in financial need, and soon distinguished herself with her forthright wit and racy scenes – scenes that were widely accepted from male playwrights but that shocked seventeenth-century society when they came from a woman's pen. Fortunately for Behn, her shock value drew audiences and her dialogue kept them coming back, and she was able to cash in on her popular success to withstand the intrigues and the slanders (especially that of 'prostitute') that sought to drive her out of the business.

With the collapse of the theatre in the late 1680s, Behn turned to translation and prose fiction to make a living – and wrote her translations and novels (and, as a sideline, translation theory and literary criticism) with the same boldness she had shown in her dramatic career. Here too she drew vicious attacks from her male peers; in 1685, for example, William Prior tore into her 'paraphrase' of Ovid's letter of Oenone to Paris (in Dryden's 1680 collection):

The Female Wit, who next convicted stands,
Not for abusing Ovid's Verse, but Sands';
She Might have learn'd from the ill-borrow'd Grace,
(Which little helps the Ruin of her Face)
That Wit, like Beauty, triumphs o'er the Heart,
When more of Nature's seen, and less of Art:
Nor strive in Ovid's Letters to have shown
As much of Skill, as Lewdness in her own.
Then let her from the next inconstant Lover,
Take a new Copy for a second Rover:
Describe the Cunning of a Jilting Whore,
From the ill Arts her self has us'd before;
Thus let her write, but Paraphrase no more.

Behn was the first woman to write a separate treatise on translation (as opposed to a preface), her 20-page 'Essay on Translated Prose' (1688), excerpted below; it stood as a kind of postmortem on her translation of Fontenelle's *Entretiens sur la Pluralité des Deux Mondes* (1686), and was intended, as she herself says, to complement the Earl of Roscommon's 'Essay on Translated Verse' of four years before.

Behn's most important work on translation, however, lies not in the 'Essay' (two-thirds of which deals with Fontenelle rather than translation) but in the prefaces, especially in the tonal ease with which she dismisses ancient demands of translational fidelity.

Translating French Into English
From 'An Essay on Translated Prose' (1688)

The general applause this little book of the discovery of several new worlds has met with, both in France and England in the original, made me attempt to translate it into English. The reputation of the author (who is the same that wrote *The Dialogues of the Dead*), the novelty of the subject in vulgar languages, and the author's introducing a woman as one of the speakers in these five discourses were further motives for me to undertake this little work; for I thought an English woman might adventure to translate anything a French woman may be supposed to have spoken. But when I had made a trial, I found the task not so easy as I believed at first; therefore, before I say anything either of the design of the author or of the book itself, give me leave to say something of translation of prose in general. As for translation of verse, nothing can be added to that incomparable essay of the late Earl of Roscommon;[1] the nearer the idioms or turn of phrase of two languages agree, 'tis the easier to translate one into the other. The Italian, Spanish, and French are all three at best corruptions of the Latin, with the mixture of Gothic, Arabic, and Gaulish words. The Italian, as it is nearest the Latin, is also nearest the English; for its mixture being composed of Latin and the language of the Goths, Vandals, and other northern nations who overran the Roman Empire and conquered its language with its provinces, most of these northern nations spoke the Teutonic, or dialects of it, of which the English is one also; and that's the reason that the English and Italian learn the language of one another sooner

[1] See Roscommon, above, 176-80. [Ed]

than any other; because not only the phrase but the accent of both do very much agree. The Spanish is next of kin to the English, for almost the same reason; because the Goths and Vandals having overrun Africa, and kept possession of it for some hundred of years, where mixing with the Moors, no doubt, gave them a great tincture of their tongue. These Moors afterward invaded and conquered Spain; besides Spain was before that also invaded and conquered by the Goths, who possessed it long after the time of the two sons of Theodosius the Great, Arcadius and Honorius. The French, as it is most remote from the Latin, so the phrase and accent differs most from the English. It may be it is more agreeable with the Welsh, which is near akin to the Basbriton and Biscagne languages, which is derived from the old Celtic tongue, the first that was spoken amongst the ancient Gauls, who descended from the Celts.

The French therefore is of all the hardest to translate into English. For proof of this there are other reasons also: And first, the nearer the genius and humour of two nations agree, the idioms of their speech are the nearer; and everybody knows there is more affinity between the English and Italian people than the English and the French, as to their humours; and for that reason, and for what I have said before, it is very difficult to translate Spanish into French; and I believe hardly possible to translate French into Dutch. The second reason is, the Italian language is the same now as it was some hundred of years ago, so is the Spanish, not only as to the phrase, but even as to the words and orthography; whereas the French language has suffered more changes this hundred years past, since Francis the First, than the fashions of their clothes and ribbons, in phrase, words, and orthography. So that I am confident a Frenchman a hundred years hence will no more understand an old edition of Froissart's history than he will understand Arabic. I confess the French arms, money, and intrigues have made their language very universal of late, for this they are to be commended: it is an accident which they owe to the greatness of their king, and their own industry, and it may fall out hereafter to be otherwise. A third reason is, as I said before, that the French being a corruption of the Latin, French authors take a liberty to borrow whatever word they want from the Latin, without farther ceremony, especially when they treat of sciences. This the English do not do, but at second-hand from the French. It is modish to ape the French in everything. Therefore, we not only naturalize their words, but words they steal from other languages. I wish in this and several other things, we had a little more of the Italian and Spanish humour, and did not chop and change our language as we do our clothes, at the pleasure of every French tailor.

In translating French into English, most people are very cautious and unwilling to print a French word at first out of a new book, till use has rendered it more familiar to us; and therefore it runs a little rough in English to express one French word by two or three of ours; and thus much as to the ease and difficulty of translating these languages in general. But as to the French in particular, it has as many advantages of the English as to the sound as ours has of the French as to the signification; which is another argument of the different genius of the two nations. Almost all the relatives, articles, and pronouns in the French language end in vowels, and are written with two or three letters. Many of their words begin with vowels; so that when a word after a relative, pronoun, or article ends with a vowel and begins with another, they admit of their beloved figure *apostrophe*, and cut off the first vowel. This they do to shun an ill sound; and they are so musical as to that, that they will go against all the rules of sense and grammar rather than fail; as for example, speaking of a man's wife they say, *son epouse*, whereas in grammar it ought to be *sa epouse*; but this would throw a Frenchman into a fit of a fever to hear one say, by way of apostrophe, *s'epouse*, as this makes their language to run smoother, so by this they express several words very shortly, as *qu'entend je?*, in English, What do I hear? In this example, three words have the sound but of one, for sound prevails with them in the beginning, middle and end. Secondly, their words generally end in vowels, or if they do not, they do not pronounce the consonant, for the most part, unless there be two together, or that the next word begins with a vowel. Thirdly, by the help of their relatives, they can shortly and with ease resume a long preceding sentence in two or three short words; these are the advantages of the French tongue, all which they borrow from the Latin. But as the French do not value a plain suit without a garniture [decoration], they are not satisfied with the advantages they have, but confound their own language with needless repetitions and tautologies; and by a certain rhetorical figure peculiar to themselves, imply twenty lines to express what an Englishman would say with more ease and sense in five; and this is the great misfortune of translating French into English: if one endeavours to make it English standard, it is no translation. If one follows their flourishes and embroideries, it is worse than French tinsel. But these defects are only comparatively, in respect of English. And I do not say this so much to condemn the French as to praise our own mother tongue, for what we think a deformity, they may think a perfection; as the Negroes of Guinea think us as ugly as we think them. But to return to my present translation:

I have endeavoured to give you the true meaning of the author, and have kept as near his words as was possible; I was necessitated to add a little in some places, otherwise the book could not have been understood. I have used all along the Latin word *axis*, which is axle-tree in English, which I do not think so proper a word in a treatise of this nature; but 'tis what is generally understood by everybody. There is another word in the two last nights which was very uneasy to me, and the more so for that it was so often repeated, which is *tourbillion*, which signifies commonly a whirlwind; but Monsieur Descartes understands it in a more general sense, and I call it a whirling; the author hath given a very good definition of it, and I need say no more, but that I retained the word unwillingly, in regard of what I have said in the beginning of this preface.

I know a character [description] of the book will be expected from me, and I am obliged to give it, to satisfy myself for being at the pains to translate it; but I wish with all my heart I could forbear it; for I have that value of the ingenious French author that I am sorry I must write what some may understand to be a satire against him ...[2]

Recasting, Not Translating
From Fontenelle's 'Preface to the History of Oracles' (1688)

Not long since there fell into my hands a small book written in Latin, *de Oraculis Ethnicorum*, or *Of the Heathen Oracles*, composed by Mr Van-Dale, Doctor of Physic, and printed in Holland, in which I found that the author has strenuously refuted the commonly received opinion that the ancient oracles were delivered by demons, and that they ceased wholly at the coming of Jesus Christ. The whole work appeared to me to be full of knowledge in antiquity and profound learning, which gave me a great curiosity to translate it, that the ladies and those gentlemen who do not much care to read Latin might not be deprived of so agreeable and useful a discourse. But I reflected that a translation of this book (though excellent in its original) would not be so good, if too closely turned into French. For Mr Van-Dale wrote only for the learned, and had reason to neglect those ornaments and softnesses which they do not esteem; he cites a great number of passages very faithfully, and his versions are wonderful exact when he translates from the Greek; he enters also into a discussion of many points of criticism, which, though they are not always necessary, yet they are always curious; and this he does to gratify the learned, who care little for flourishing reflections, discourses of morality, or pleasant wit.

Besides, Mr Van-Dale makes no difficulty very often to interrupt the thread of his discourse and to introduce other things which present themselves; and from one digression he sometimes passes to another, and so perhaps to a third. And herein he does not amiss, since those for whom he writes are fitted for the fatigue of reading, and this learned disorder does not at all embarrass or perplex them. But those for whom I design this translation would have been very ill accommodated if I had taken this method: the ladies, and the major part of the men of this country are indeed more pleased with the graces and turns of expression and thought than with the most exact enquiries and profoundest arguments. And being very fond of ease, they desire to read books written in a facile method, that they may be the less obliged to a troublesome attention. For this reason, I laid by the thoughts of translating and thought it would be better, preserving the foundation and principal matter of the work, to give it altogether another form. And I confess that no man can extend this liberty farther than I have done; for I have changed the whole disposition of the book, and have retrenched whatever appeared to me either of too little profit in itself or of too little pleasure to make amends for that little profit. I have not only added all the ornaments I could think of, but many things which prove or clear up what is in question upon the same subject, and the same passages which Mr Van-Dale furnished me withal. I argue sometimes in a manner contrary to his, and I have not been scrupulous to insert many reasons wholly my own. In fine, I have new cast and modelled the whole work, and have put it into the same order as I should have done at first (to have pleased my particular view) had I had so much knowledge as Mr Van-Dale; but, since I am far from it, I have borrowed his learning and ventured to make use of my own wit and fancy (such as it is) to adorn it. Nor should I have failed to have pursued his method had I had to do with the same persons as he had. And if it shall happen that this comes to his knowledge, I beseech him to pardon the liberty I have taken, since it will serve to show the excellency of his book. For certainly what belongs to him will still appear extremely fine, though it have passed through my hands.[3]

Gottfried Wilhelm Leibniz

Gottfried Wilhelm Leibniz (1646-1716) was a German mathematician and philosopher who also served as a political, pedagogical, technological, and general advisor to royalty. Something of an intellectual jack-of-all-trades, Leibniz invented differential and integral calculus, perfected base-2 or binary numeration, helped develop the science of geology, wrote a history of the earth, developed a method for the

[2] Behn continues on for another 13 pages, giving her 'character' of the book. [Ed]

[3] She goes on for another four pages to describe the book. [Ed]

desalinization of water, etc. – there is hardly a transitional project of the late seventeenth century to which Leibniz did not significantly contribute.

Leibniz was born to a pious middle-class Lutheran family and received a humdrum education at the Nicolai School; his father, however, who died when he was six, possessed an extensive library, where Leibniz obtained his true education. In 1661 he entered the University of Leipzig as a law student, and soon came into contact with the pathbreaking thought of the day – Descartes, Galileo, Thomas Hobbes, Francis Bacon – and began to dream of reconciling these thinkers with both Aristotelian scholasticism and his own Lutheranism. He took his law degree and applied for a doctorate of law in 1666, at the age of 20, but was denied on the basis of youth; moving to Nuremberg, he wrote a dissertation and was granted a doctorate and a professorship, the latter of which he refused.

Soon after, he entered the service of the prince elector, archbishop of Mainz, Johann Philipp von Schönborn, as a legal adviser: the beginning of his long career advising royalty on virtually everything under the sun. Whatever his specific job title (librarian, historian, councillor, court adviser), he always quickly found ways of making himself useful in a wide variety of fields, from religion to the waging of war, from hydraulics to education and the formation of a German academy. He knew most of the greatest scientists of his era personally and corresponded and disputed with them all (he wrote letters to 600 correspondents) – always, of course, in the service of his electoral employer and the Lutheran God. His abiding philosophical opponent was René Descartes, whose theories, he claimed, led to atheism; his metaphysical theories, including the principle of sufficient reason and the concept of the monad, are among the most influential philosophical developments of the period.

Leibniz's remarks on translation appear in his programmatic call for the "use and improvement of the German language" in 1697 – a nationalistic linguistics that consolidates Renaissance theories of linguistic richness, purity, and brilliance and looks ahead to German romantics like Wilhelm von Humboldt.

Enriching the German Language
From *Impartial Thoughts Concerning the Use and Improvement of the German Language* (*Unvorgreifliche Gedanken, betreffend die Ausübung und Verbesserung der deutschen Sprache*, 1697)
Translated by Douglas Robinson

56. This brings me to what is required of language in its day-to-day use – what in fact the gentlemen of the Productive Society, the Crusca, and the French Academy considered of primary importance,[1] and indeed what is of unquestionable importance from the start: not so much a language's origin or antiquity, nor any hidden messages, skills, or knowledge it may contain, but rather its ordinary use in speech and writing. It is here that the *richness*, *purity*, and *brilliance* of the German language should appear, three essential qualities of any language.[2]

57. *Richness* is the first and most essential of these, and consists in there being no dearth but if anything a superfluity of useful and forceful words to serve every eventuality, so that anything one wants to say can be said powerfully, properly, and colourfully.

58. One says of the Chinese that their writing is rich due to their manifold signs, but that their speech and vocabulary are poor due to the well-known fact that their writing does not correspond to their speech; and it appears that the superfluity of signs on which their writing is based is that much more of a detriment to the cultivation of their speech, since the paucity and ambiguity of their words often forces them to stop mid-sentence to explain themselves and clear up uncertainties by drawing signs in the air with their fingers.[3]

59. To be sure any language, no matter how poor, can in the end say *everything* – although it is said that there are barbaric peoples to whom one cannot communicate God's word. Still, while everything can ultimately be communicated through circumlocution and description, such prolixity deprives both the speaker and the listener of all passion and power in the speaking, by damming the feeling up too long. It is as if one were to take a tourist eager to see many beautiful palaces and drag him around to look at all the nooks and crannies in a single room; or as if one were to count like people who (according to Weigel in his

[1] The Fruchtbringende Gesellschaft or 'Productive Society' was a literary academy founded in Weimar in 1617 by Ludwig, prince of Anhalt-Köthen, for the purification of the German language and the fostering of German literature. The Accademia della Crusca or 'Academy of the Chaff' was an Italian literary society founded in 1582 for the purification (separation of the chaff from the wheat) of Tuscan, the language of the Italian Renaissance. The Academie Française or French Academy was founded in 1635 by Cardinal de Richelieu. [Tr/Ed]

[2] These are classical requirements going back to Cicero and Quintilian, and much debated in the European Renaissance. Leibniz's German terms and their classical/Latin equivalents are *Reichtum* (*copia*), *Reinigkeit* (*puritas*), and *Glanz* (*splendour*). [Tr/Ed]

[3] The first German studies of Chinese ideograms appeared in 1667 and 1685 (the first grammar in 1703), and Leibniz followed them with great interest. [Tr/Ed]

Tetraktys[4]) can't count over three and have no words or numbers for 4, 5, 6, 7, 8, 9, etc., which would make calculation exceedingly tedious and difficult.

60. The true test of a language's superfluity or deficiency lies in the translation of good books from another language, for that shows what is lacking and what is available. This is why it was so valuable for the Productives and their followers to undertake translations as part of their programme, even though they didn't always choose the best books to translate.[5]

61. Not that I believe that there is a language in the world that is capable of rendering every word of another language into its own with the same force and with a *single* word. Cicero reproached the Greeks for having no word for the Latin word *ineptus*;[6] he too, however, often recognized the poverty of Latin. And, as I have shown in the past, we have no lack of words that cannot be translated into French without circumlocution. Even today the French cannot express what we call *Reiten* and the Latins call *equitare*[7] with a single word; and their translations of Tacitus or other excellent Latin works come nowhere near the concise power of the original.

62. Even so, the richest and most adept language is still the one that can best manage literal translations, that can follow the original step by step; and because, as was mentioned above, the German language falls short of this goal in no small way, especially in certain subject areas, out of the ordinary ones influenced by human wilfullness and arbitrariness, it is essential that we work together to ensure that we need no longer yield in this respect to others.

63. This may entail hunting up good German words that have fallen into disuse and so fail to come to mind at the critical juncture; or reviving archaic and obsolete words of particular worth; or naturalizing foreign terms of special merit; or, finally, when all else fails, coining or constructing new words that can only be put into circulation through the good judgment and reputation of other and worthier people, indeed of an entire community.

64. For German works, both by the Productives and by others, are full of good words that can be used with profit, but that never come to mind when one needs them. I remember noting once that the French word *tendre*,[8] if feelingly understood in specific contexts, might not be rendered at all badly with the German word *innig* or *herzinnig*.[9] The ancient Germans used *Innigkeit*[10] to mean devotion. Not that I think this German word can be used for the French on every occasion; still, it is worthwhile noting it for possible use whenever a good occasion arises.

65. In pursuance of this programme, I suggest that certain learned people be entrusted with appointing a committee for reviewing and inspecting good German writings, especially, say, those of Opitz – not only his verse works but those in prose as well, such as his *Hercynia* or his translations of *Argenis* and *Arcadia*.[11] Other profitable texts to be examined would include the 'illustrious author's' *Aramena* and *Octavia*,[12] von Stubenberg's translations, and others of similar quality, such as Zesen's *Ibrahim Bassa*, *Sophonisbe*, and other writings of his, though his wit sometimes overshot its mark. One can also find useful things in otherwise weak books; it would be beneficial, therefore, to begin with the best, then take what one can from more mediocre works.

66. Nor should one neglect the revival of discarded and disused but nevertheless intrinsically sound words and idioms. To this end profitable use may be made of writings from the last century, like the works of Luther and other theologians, resolutions of the old Parliamentary Diet, regional and municipal ordinances, old notarial documents and other spiritual and secular writings, even Reynard the Fox, Rollenhagen's *Froschmäuseler*, the German Rabelais [Fischart] and *Amadis*, *The Austrian Theuerdank*, the Bavarian Aventin, the Swiss Stumpf and Paracelsus, the Nurembergian Hans Sachs, and other compatriots.[13]

---

[4] Erhard Weigel, under whom Leibniz had studied math in 1664, claimed that the base-4 system (which he called the Tetraktys) was the only natural and useful one. Leibniz is on shaky ground in ridiculing base-4, since he has gone down in history as the major theological proponent of the base-2 or binary system: for him 1 was God and 0 was the void. [Tr/Ed]

[5] Among the members of the Productive Society were Dietrich von Werder, who translated Tasso's *Jerusalem Liberated* and Aristo's *Orlando Furioso*, Wilhelm von Kalchheim-Lohausen, who translated Sallust, and, most famous of the group, Martin Opitz, who translated Seneca's *Troades* (1625), Sophocles' *Antigone* (1636), the Psalms (1637), and much more. [Tr/Ed]

[6] Silly, tasteless, out of place. [Tr/Ed]

[7] To ride (horses). [Tr/Ed]

[8] Tender, fond, affectionate. [Tr/Ed]

[9] Intimate, warm, heartfelt, tender, affectionate (lit. inward, heart-inward). [Tr/Ed]

[10] In modern German warmth, tenderness, intimacy (lit. inwardness). [Tr/Ed]

[11] *Schäferei von der Nymphe Hercynia* ('Pastoral of the Nymph Hercynia', 1630); Opitz translated John Barclay's political novel *Argenis* (1621) from Latin into German in 1626/31, and reworked an earlier translation of Sir Philip Sidney's prose narrative *Arcadia* (1590) in 1638. [Tr/Ed]

[12] The 'illustrious author' (*durchlauchtigste Autor*) was Anton Ulrich. Leibniz is punning on the title of the first novel he mentions, *Die durchleuchtigste Syrerin Aramena* ('The Luminous Syrian Aramena', 1669-1673). [Tr/Ed]

[13] *Reynard the Fox* ('Reinke de Vos', 1498), a story written in Low German. The Spanish prose romance *Amadis of Gaul* appeared in many versions, but the best

67. And in connection with the Swiss, let us not in our betterment of the German language forget that people's excellent old German idiom. I ask, for example, how one might concisely and precisely translate *foedus defensivum & offensivum* into German.[14] I doubt not but that our admirable authors of good modern German works will find no lack of accurate and attractive translations for this phrase taken from international law; but I do doubt whether any of the new translations will be more pleasing to the ear or vigorous on the tongue than the Swiss *Schutz- und Trutzverbündnis*.[15]

68. As for naturalization, in the right circumstances it should not be overlooked either – any more for languages than for peoples. Rome became great and powerful by absorbing the alien. Holland has grown as much by the influx of people as of its waters; the English language takes in everything, and if every lessor were to demand his own back, the Englishman would be like the crow in Aesop's fable, stripped of all his finery.[16] We Germans have had less need of such than others, but even we must not entirely renounce this profitable right.

69. There are, however, certain steps to follow in naturalization, for just as it is easier for individuals to adopt beliefs and customs the closer they are to ours, so also in the adoption of foreign words one would sooner borrow from languages of Germanic origin, and especially from the Dutch, than from Latin and her daughters.

70. And if English and Norwegian are a bit more distant from us than Dutch, and thus more suitable for the study of origins than for the improvement of language, there is no law that prevents us from putting them to this and other uses.

71. As for Dutch, if our Germans had the right to appoint representatives to rule the mother city of this German plantation or colony,[17] and for this purpose to have experts study and protect the Dutch language and its writings, then one could see clearly what demands to make upon it and what is already acceptable for incorporation into German. The same might be said about the Low German and other dialects: the Low-German word *Schlump*,[18] for example, as in "Es ist nur ein Schlump", which the French call *hasard*, is often not entirely inappropriate.

Anne Dacier

Anne Dacier (1654-1720) was a French scholar who won an immense following all over Europe for her French translations of the *Iliad* (1699) and the *Odyssey* (1708).

She was given a classical education by her father, the French humanist Tanneguy Lefèbvre; her classical education began at age 11 when, during the lessons her father was giving her brother, she would sit in the next room sewing and provide her brother answers to questions that stumped him. She soon outstripped her brothers and became her father's associate; once she was able to convince him that a French translation of Quintus Curtius Rufus he much admired was in fact seriously flawed.

In 1672 her father died, and the following year she moved to Paris, where at the age of 20 she published an edition of Callimachus (1674). When this edition came to the notice of Pierre-Daniel Huet, who was then tutor to the dauphin, he asked her to prepare other Latin editions for the dauphin's use; after some resistance, she agreed, and edited what became a famous series of them, *ad usum Delphini* – for the use of the dauphin. In 1683 she married one of her father's classicist students, André Dacier, and he helped her edit the series. She had translated Anacreon and Sappho into French before her marriage, in her twenties, and the critical response was enormously favourable; her annotated French translation of Terence's comedies appeared in 1688, again to much acclaim; but her reputation was sealed by prose translations of Homer, which appeared between 1699 and 1711.

Dacier's Homer translations landed in the midst of the famous quarrel of the ancients and moderns, then raging in France and England, and

known was Garci Rodrígez de Montalvo's (1508), which was translated into English in 1567 and into German from 1569 to 1595. *Der östereicher Theuerdank* ('The Austrian Theuerdank', 1517) is an allegorical poem begun by Maximilian I and completed by Melchior Pfinzig. [Tr/Ed]

[14] Lit. defensive and offensive league or federation; a mutual defense league. [Tr/Ed]

[15] Lit. defence and offence alliance; the translation is lent force by the *Schutz/Trutz* rhyme. [Tr/Ed]

[16] In 'The Vain Crow', a crow finds some peacock feathers, sticks them in amongst his own, and tries to strut with the peacocks; the peacocks strip him of his borrowed finery, so he tries to go back with the crows, who shun him for his erstwhile pretensions. [Tr/Ed]

[17] This is a rather chauvinistic account of Dutch history. In the period during which the Netherlands came closest to being a 'German plantation or colony', in the tenth and eleventh centuries, there was no German state to 'plant' or colonize it. It was ruled by the Teutonic Holy Roman emperors until the Concordat of Worms (1122), but they did not colonize it; they inherited it from the declining Frankish Empire. [Tr/Ed]

[18] Stroke of luck; the phrase in the next line means "That was pure luck". [Tr/Ed]

immediately placed her on the side of the ancients, against such figures as Charles Perrault and Bernard de Fontenelle (author of the text Aphra Behn had translated into English a decade earlier). One of Dacier's most famous works on the subject was *Des Causes de la corruption du goût* ('Of the Causes of the Corruption of Taste', 1714), an attack on la Motte, who had recently professed himself unimpressed with the *Iliad*.

The high esteem in which she was held in her lifetime and after was rare for women of her day; not surprisingly, perhaps, she herself shared the prevalent assumption that, in the verse from Sophocles that she once wrote in a German scholar's book, "Silence is the ornament of the female sex". She was frequently asked to translate and annotate parts of the Bible, but always refused, invoking Paul's injunction against women speaking in church. Still, she continued to publish well-received translations and scholarly and polemical works, and in 1684 was inducted into the Academy of Ricovrati at Padua.

Her comments on translation in the remarkable 60-page preface she attached to her *Iliad* (and that John Ozell translated into English for inclusion in the English *Iliad* he and two other translators did in 1712) are striking in the verve of her prose style and the breadth of her learning, both superior to the more famous prefaces of John Dryden (and lacking only his knack for the nifty synthesis of opposed positions). She underscores the inaccessible beauty of Homer and the necessary failure of any modern translation; debates the virtues of prose and verse translations of Homer (she favours prose); insists she is translating not for the learned reader who can read Homer in the original but for the "greater number, in respect of whom this poet is as it were dead"; and distinguishes 'servile' from 'noble and generous' translations, a distinction roughly between word-for-word and sense-for-sense translations, except that a 'noble' translation stays true to the 'letter' or formal qualities of the original too, "and by means of its bold, but true, strokes, becomes not only a faithful copy of its original, but even a second original; which cannot be executed but by a solid, noble, and fruitful genius".

My Condemnation

From preface to translation of *L'Iliade d'Homère* (1699)
Translated by John Ozell

But this mixed composition, the source of these beauties, is unknown to our tongue; it does not, at all, allow of these different turns; it knows not what to do with a mean, hard, or disagreeable word; it has no treasure in reserve, to conceal what is defective; it neither has those numerous particles to support its words, nor that different harmony, proceeding from the various ranging of terms; and consequently, it is incapable of expressing most of the beauties which shines in that poem. This is my condemnation,[1] and a very just one too, if I am tried with rigor; for, I own, in every verse in Homer I find a beauty, a force, a harmony, a grace, which it has been impossible for me to preserve.

To what purpose was it, then, to attempt a thing I could not succeed in? I will here give my reasons; perhaps they may make a tolerable excuse.

The wonders of Homer's style, and the beauties he has drawn from his tongue, are not the most valuable part of his poetry; there are beauties above those of the language, and such as cannot fail moving those who are not altogether insensible. The most barbarous nations, who have no notion of fine poetry, or the energy and harmony of language, could not forbear being sensible of the loftiness of his ideas, the majesty of his subject, that beautiful nature which reigns throughout every part of him, and the surprising variety of his character, which differ very much, even in the same kind of virtues. For instance, Ulysses and Nestor, both of them men of profound prudence, are not the same. Achilles, Diomedes, and Ajax, all of them brave, are yet so in a different manner. The Indians and the Persians have Homer translated into their languages; and it is positively said, there is a Chaldaic or Syriac translation of him. I am of opinion, a French translation may be as good as those, and better preserve most of the beauties of the style, or give a better sense of them.

Besides, I do not write for the learned, who read Homer in his own tongue; they know him better than I pretend to; I write for those who do not know him, that is, for the greater number, in respect of whom this poet is as it were dead; I write also for those who learn to read him, and are to take pains to understand him before they can be sensible of his beauties.

As for the first of them, that is, those who are deprived of the pleasure of reading him in Greek, let them give me leave here to make a comparison, which, by letting them see the judgment I make myself of my work, will put my translation out of the reach of their censure, and secure the original from their contempt. Can images be more properly made use of than when we speak of the father of poetry?

Let us then suppose, that Helen died in Egypt, that she was there embalmed, according to the best skill of the Egyptians, and that her body, being preserved to our days, was now brought into France. The mummy would not claim all the admiration which Helen when

[1] I.e., this is the condemnation of me (of my translation). [Ed]

living attracted at her return from Troy,[2] when all the people flocked along the way she was to pass, to see that famous beauty, which had armed Europe against Asia, and made Troy the funeral-pile of so many heroes; yet would she not fail to excite some curiosity, and afford some satisfaction. We should not behold those sparkling eyes, that complexion enlivened by the most natural sprightly colours, that grace, those charms, which enflamed so many lovers, and even thawed the frost of old age; but still we should perceive the exactness and the beauty of her features, we should guess at the[3] largeness of her eyes, the smallness of her mouth, the arch of her fine eyebrows; we should discover her noble and majestic shape; and the imagination, struck by those precious remains, would advance so far as to conceive that she, who still retains a beauty in the arms of death, must certainly have been[4] like the immortal goddesses, during her life.

This is the most impartial idea I can give of my translation; I own, it is not Homer alive and animated, but still it is Homer; there will not be found in him that energy, that grace, that life, those ravishing charms, and that fire, which warms all that comes near it; but every feature, and the admirable symmetry of all his parts will be picked out; nay, I dare be so bold as to hope, he will still retain lively colours enough to make it doubtful for a moment whether there are not yet some remains of life in him. In a word, it is Homer, and Homer much less altered than in the translations that have been hitherto made, which have so strangely disfigured him, that he is no longer to be known.

Some will say, there is a surer way of approaching to the original, which is to translate it into verse; for, as they allege, poets are to be translated into verse, to retain their fire. This would certainly be best, were it practicable; but to believe it possible is a mistake, capable, in my opinion, of demonstration. I have made bold, heretofore, to assert it, in my Preface to Anacreon; and since then, I have been fully confirmed in my judgment, by the little success the translations in verse have met with. The misfortune of those translations cannot be owing to any want of genius in those writers, since some of them are in possession of a great reputation, and owe that reputation to poetry. Therefore, it arises from the thing itself, wherein it is impossible to succeed; and convincing reasons may be given for it.

A translator, in prose, may say all that Homer has said; this he can never do in verse, especially in our tongue, where he must of necessity be always altering, retrenching, adding. Now, what Homer has thought and said, though rendered in a plainer and less poetical manner than he has done, is certainly much better than what those who translate him in verse are forced to lend him.

This is my first reason. There is another, which is the same I have already explained. Our poetry is not capable of expressing all the beauties of Homer, and soaring to his height; it may follow him in some select places; it may successfully hit off two, four, or six of his verses, as has been done by Mr Despreaux in his Longinus, and by Racine in some of his tragedies; but, at length, the connection will be so weak that nothing will be more languid. And what can be imagined meaner than a cold and flat piece of poetry, wherein nothing is tolerable that is not excellent? I could make this very obvious by examples, but that they are common, and every man may convince himself of this truth. Nay, I am not afraid to say, and could be able to prove it, that poets translated into verse cease to be poets.

Virgil was wont to say,[5] it had been easier to have wrested Hercules's club from him than to steal a verse from Homer by way of imitation. If Virgil found it a matter of such difficulty in his tongue, we may conclude it impossible in ours. I wish I may be mistaken; I shall be very well pleased to see a good translation of Homer in verse, and shall be the first to applaud that miracle; but I question whether any poet who has thoroughly read the original, and fully discovered all its strength and beauty, will venture at it.

It is not so in prose, which can follow all the poet's notions, retain the beauty of his images, say all he has said; and if at any time it is obliged to lend something to him, which must be done but very rarely, as being dangerous, it only borrows from him whatsoever it lends him; and, even under its plainness and mediocrity, fails not to support itself. I do not say I have performed all this, I only say it may be done in prose. Aristotle himself was sensible that prose is no enemy to epic poetry, since he writes that the *epopeia* makes use of prose as well as verse;[6] and it were easy to prove the truth of that assertion, by the nature of poetical imitation. Plato, in the third book of his *Commonwealth* [*Republic* (386c-387a)], has put into prose 30 verses of the beginning of the *Iliad*; and though he has changed the imitation into plain narration, yet nevertheless it engages and pleases. What then would it have been, had he retained the imitation; that is, had

[2] Dictys Cretensis, lib. 6. When it was known that Helen was come thither, many, both men and women, flocked from all parts, desiring to see her, for whose sake almost all the world had been engaged in war. [Au]

[3] These are the words of Constantin Manasses, in his description of Helen. [Au]

[4] This character the old men of Troy give her, in the third book of the Iliad. [Au]

[5] *Facilius Herculi clavum, quam Homero versum subtipese.* [Au]

[6] Aristotle deals with epic poetry in chapters 23, 24, and 26 of the *Poetics*; nowhere does he consider the possibility that an epic might be written in prose. [Ed]

he, instead of saying, like an historian, such and such a person said so and so, introduced the persons themselves speaking?

We must then be content with prose for translating of the poets, and endeavour to imitate the Hebrews, who having no poetry (that is, a sort of speech confined to a certain number of feet, and long or short syllables) have made a sort of poetry of their prose, by means of a more beautified, more sprightly, and a more figurative language; and it has succeeded so well, that nothing represents more lively ideas to the mind than the canticles, the psalms, and some passages in the prophets.

It is certain that prose, supported by and composed with art, will come nearer to poetry than a translation in verse; and Strabo says ῾Ο πεζός λόγος, ὁ γέ κατεσκευασμένος μίμημα τοῦ ποιητικοῦ ἐστί: "Well-wrought prose is an imitation of poetry". Then he shows how the first writers, such as Cadmus, Pherecydes, Hecateus imitated poetry in their writings; Λύσαντες τό μέτρον, τ᾽ ἄλλα δέ φυλάξαντες τά ποιητικά: "Only breaking the measure, and retaining all the other poetical beauties". Therefore Dionysius Halicarnasses teaches how compositions in prose may be made to resemble the style of the finest poems. But I do not think it enough to say that prose may come near to poetry; I will go yet farther and affirm that in case of translation, which is the matter in hand, there is sometimes such a niceness, a beauty, and an energy in prose as poetry cannot come near. The books of the prophets and the psalms, even in the Vulgate, are full of such passages, as the greatest poet in the world could not put into verse without losing much of their majesty and pathos.

When I speak of a translation of prose, I do not mean a servile translation, I mean a noble and generous translation which, adhering strictly to the way of thinking in the original, searches out the beauties of its language and represents the images without retailing the words. The first sort of translation becomes unfaithful through too scrupulous a faithfulness; for it loses the spirit to preserve the letter, which is the work of a cold and barren genius; whereas the other, though chiefly aiming to retain the spirit, yet fails not, in it greatest liberties, to retain the letter; and by means of its bold but true strokes becomes not only a faithful copy of its original, but even a second original; which cannot be executed but by a solid, noble, and fruitful genius.

What I have here said is to undeceive some persons who, being unacquainted with the nature and beauty of writings, have more particularly a very disadvantageous and false notion of translations. They fancy it is a servile imitation, wherein the flower of wit and fancy have no share; in a word; that there is no creation. This is certainly a gross mistake; translation is not like the copy of a picture, wherein the copier is tied down to the features, the colours, the proportions, the contours, and the attitudes of the original he follows; all this is quite otherwise, a good translator is not so confined; he is, at most, like a statuary [sculptor] who works after a picture, or like a painter who copies after a piece of statuary; he is like Virgil, who describes the Laocoon from the marble original, that wonderful piece, which he had before him.[7] In this imitation, as in all others, the soul, full of those beauties it intends to represent, and inebriated with the pleasing vapours arising from those abundance springs, is to suffer itself to be ravished and transported by that foreign enthusiasm; and to make it its own, and so to produce very different representations and expressions, though resembling the others. It is not perhaps altogether impossible to make this intelligible, by a comparison borrowed from music. We daily see musicians who, well skilled in their art, sing the notes of the tunes that are set before them, with the greatest nicety and exactness, without committing the least fault; and yet the whole is one entire fault, because being dull and having no genius, they take not the spirit that went to the composing of those tunes, and therefore do not add those flourishes and graces, which are, as it were, the soul of them; whereas we see others, who being more sprightly, and of a happier genius, sing those tunes with the same spirit with which they were composed, retain all their beauty, and make them appear almost another thing, though they are the same. This, if I mistake not, is the difference between good and bad translations; the one, by a low and servile imitation, give the letter, without the spirit; the other by a free and noble imitation, retains the spirit, without departing from the letter; and makes quite a new thing of that which was already known.

To return to Homer; I have already taken notice that I do not translate him for those that read him in his own tongue; as for the rest, I mean those who are utterly unacquainted with him, or those who begin to read him in the original, I dare flatter myself that my labour will not be lost, but will serve to make him known to the former, and intelligible to the latter: Homer is not so easy as is imagined. It is generally believed that so soon as we have got a smattering in the Greek tongue, we are in a condition to understand him; but it is a great mistake. Casaubon, that learned and sure critic, who had written comments on this poet, which doubtless are lost, says in his notes upon Strabo: *Neque enim divinum hunc poetam omnes intelligunt*, all men do not understand this divine poet. This I have often found by experience myself. I have read Homer several times; for I am as fond of him as the philosopher Arcesilaus was, who never failed to read some

[7] From book two of the *Aeneid*. [Ed]

passage of this poet, night and morning, and always said, when he took up his book, he was going to his love. Yet, notwithstanding this mighty passion, and this long acquaintance, if I understand him tolerably, it was only by labouring to make him understood by others. When we read only for ourselves, we are often satisfied with a slight and superficial perusal; but when we read for others, the obligation we lie under of giving clear and distinct ideas makes us stop to drive deeper into the subject, and necessity then serving as a spur to the mind, causes it to discover those beauties and meanings which cursory reading had not permitted it to take notice of. However, notwithstanding all my application, I am persuaded, I am not free from mistakes. Good things are performed with much toil and trouble, and faults are very easily committed. But it being very usual to impute to Homer the faults and meannesses of his translators, I desire at least that those which have escaped me may not be ascribed to him. I declare Homer is innocent of them, and that they are all to be put to my account.

Joseph Addison

Joseph Addison (1672-1719) was a leading essayist, poet, and dramatist in late-seventeenth- and early-eighteenth-century England, best known today in the collocation 'Addison and Steele': he and Richard Steele were the prime movers of the periodicals *The Tatler* and *The Spectator*, and have come down to us as models of neoclassical opinion and prose style.

Born the son of the Reverend Lancelot Addison, he received his boyhood schooling in local schools before being sent at the age of fourteen to the Charterhouse in London, where he met Richard Steele. In 1687 both boys went on to Oxford, where Addison became a demy or foundation scholar of Magdalen College in 1689, took his M.A. in 1693, and became a fellow in 1697 – a post he held for fourteen years, until 1711.

Addison's career as a statesman began in the late nineties, when his 'Poem to His Majesty' (1695) brought him to the attention of powerful Whigs around William and Mary as someone who could be useful to the crown. In 1697 he wrote a highly acclaimed preface for John Dryden's translation of Virgil's *Georgics*. From 1699 to 1704 he travelled in Europe on a treasury grant, writing widely circulated letters back about his meetings with European diplomats and men of letters and his impressions of French drama and opera. Upon his return to England, he moved more firmly into circles of power, notably into the Kit-Cat Club, an association of Whig statesmen and literary figures like Steele and William Congreve. He was frequently asked to write poems on political events and issues, and soon after arriving home was appointed John Locke's successor as commissioner of appeals in excise. The next year he became undersecretary to the secretary of state for southern affairs, a powerful and highly paid position in the Whig government.

About this time he also began to collaborate with Steele, whom he helped with loans and a prestigious appointment as editor of the London *Gazette*; they even roomed together for a while. Their first collaboration was on a play called *The Tender Husband* (1705), and by 1709, after Addison had been elected to Parliament and had served two years as Irish secretary, on Steele's new paper *The Tatler*. The next year the Tories ousted the Whigs from power, and while Addison kept his seat in Parliament, he lost his paying job as undersecretary, and began to devote most of his time to literary pursuits. Steele closed down *The Tatler* in January, 1711, but two months later founded *The Spectator*, an even more successful venture that in its prime sold 3000 copies a day. He had earlier written an English opera libretto (*Rosamond*, 1707), hiring Thomas Clayton to write the music; in 1713 he wrote *Cato*, an enormously successful tragedy that both the Whigs and the Tories read as a political allegory favouring their party.

Queen Anne died in 1714 and the Whigs returned to power, bringing Addison with them as secretary of the regents (who ruled the country until King George I from Hannover was crowned). He was appointed secretary of state in 1717, but resigned the following year due to ill health, and died the year after that. He did not marry until late in life; his wife, the dowager countess of Warwick, gave him a comfortable cushion of affluence for his last years.

The essay below, from the second month of *The Spectator*'s operation, is an early treatment of the translation of opera librettos and other musical lyrics that in its insistence on the 'genius' of each nation strikingly anticipates the translation theories of the romantics a century later.

National Accents
Spectator no. 29 (April 3, 1711)

> --------- Sermo lingua concinnus utraque
> Suavior, ut Chio nota si commixta Falerni
> est. – Hor.[1]

[1] "But a style where both tongues make a happy blend has more charm, as when the Falernian wine is mixed with Chio" (H. Rushton Fairclough's translation; Horace *Satires* 1.10.23-24). [Ed]

There is nothing that has more startled our English audience than the Italian recitativo at its first entrance upon the stage. People were wonderfully surprised to hear generals singing the word of command, and ladies delivering messages in music. Our countrymen could not forbear laughing when they heard a lover chanting out a *billet-doux*, and even the superscription of a letter set to a tune. The famous blunder in an old play of "*Enter a King and two Fiddlers solus*" was now no longer an absurdity, when it was impossible for a hero in a desert, or a princess in her closet, to speak anything unaccompanied with musical instruments.

But however this Italian method of acting in recitativo might appear at first hearing, I cannot but think it much more just than that which prevailed in our English opera before this innovation: the transition from an air to recitative music being more natural than the passing from a song to plain and ordinary speaking, which was the common method in Purcell's operas.

The only fault I find in our present practice is the making use of the Italian recitativo with English words. To go to the bottom of this matter, I must observe that the tone, or (as the French call it) the accent of every nation in their ordinary speech is altogether different from that of every other people; as we may see even in the Welsh and Scotch, who border so near upon us. By the tone or accent, I do not mean the pronunciation of each particular word, but the sound of the whole sentence. Thus it is very common for an English gentleman, when he hears a French tragedy, to complain that the actors all of them speak in a tone; and therefore he very wisely prefers his own countrymen, not considering that a foreigner complains of the same tone in an English actor.

For this reason, the recitative music in every language should be as different as the tone or accent of each language; for otherwise, what may properly express a passion in one language will not do it in another. Everyone who has been long in Italy knows very well that the cadences in the recitativo bear a remote affinity to the tone of their voices in ordinary conversation; or, to speak more properly, are only the accents of their language made more musical and tuneful.

Thus the notes of interrogation, or admiration, in the Italian music (if one may so call them) which resemble their accents in discourse on such occasions are not unlike the ordinary tones of an English voice when we are angry; insomuch that I have often seen our audiences extremely mistaken as to what has been doing upon the stage, and expecting to see the hero knock down his messenger, when he has been asking him a question; or fancying that he quarrels with his friend, when he only bids him good-morrow.

For this reason the Italian artists cannot agree with our English musicians, in admiring Purcell's compositions, and thinking his tunes so wonderfully adapted to his words; because both nations do not always express the same passions by the same sounds.

I am therefore humbly of opinion that an English composer should not follow the Italian recitative too servilely, but make use of many gentle deviations from it, in compliance with his own native language. He may copy out of it all the lulling softness and dying falls[2] (as Shakespeare calls them), but should still remember that he ought to accommodate himself to an English audience; and by humouring the tone of our voices in ordinary conversation, have the same regard to the accent of his own language as those persons had to theirs whom he professes to imitate. It is observed that several of the singing birds of our own country learn to sweeten their voices, and mellow the harshness of their natural notes, by practising under those that come from warmer climates. In the same manner I would allow the Italian opera to lend our English music as much as may grace and soften it, but never entirely to annihilate and destroy it. Let the infusion be as strong as you please, but still let the subject matter of it be English.

A composer should fit his music to the genius of the people, and consider that the delicacy of hearing, and taste of harmony, has been formed upon those sounds which every country abounds with: in short, that music is of a relative nature, and what is harmony to one ear, may be dissonance to another.

The same observations which I have made upon the recitative part of music may be applied to all our songs and airs in general.

Signor Baptist Lully acted like a man of sense in this particular. He found the French music extremely defective and very often barbarous; however, knowing the genius of the people, the humour of their language, and the prejudiced ears he had to deal with, he did not pretend to extirpate the French music and plant the Italian in its stead; but only to cultivate and civilize it with innumerable graces and modulations which he borrowed from the Italian. By this means the French music is now perfect in its kind; and when you say it is not so good as the Italian, you only mean that it does not please you so well, for there is scarce a Frenchman who would not wonder to hear you give the Italian such a preference. The music of the French is indeed very properly adapted to their pronunciation and accent, as their whole opera wonderfully favours the genius of such a gay airy people. The chorus in which that opera abounds gives the parterre[3] frequent opportunities of joining in concert with the stage. This inclination of the audience to sing along with the actors so prevails with them that I have sometimes known

[2] *Twelfth Night* 1.1.7. [Ed]

[3] I.e., the parquet circle, the rear seats in an opera house or theater. [Ed]

the performer on the stage do no more in a celebrated song than the clerk of a parish church, who serves only to raise the psalm, and is afterwards drowned in the music of the congregation. Every actor that comes on the stage is a beau. The queens and heroines are so painted that they appear as ruddy and cherry-cheeked as milkmaids. The shepherds are all embroidered, and acquit themselves in a ball better than our English dancing-masters. I have seen a couple of rivers appear in red stockings; and Alpheus,[4] instead of having his head covered with sedge and bullrushes, making love in a fair full-bottomed periwig, and a plume of feathers, but with a voice so full of shakes and quavers that I should have thought the murmurs of a country brook the much more agreeable music.

I remember the last opera I saw in that merry nation was *The Rape of Proserpine*,[5] where Pluto, to make the more tempting figure, puts himself in a French equipage, and brings Ascalaphus along with him as his *valet de chambre*. This is what we call folly and impertinence; but what the French look upon as gay and polite.

I shall add no more to what I have here offered, than the music, architecture and painting, as well as poetry and oratory, are to deduce their laws and rules from the general sense and taste of mankind, and not from the principles of those arts themselves; or in other words, the taste is not to conform to the art, but the art to the taste. Music is not designed to please only chromatic ears, but all that are capable of distinguishing harsh from disagreeable notes. A man of an ordinary ear is a judge whether a passion is expressed in proper sounds, and whether the melody of those sounds be more or less pleasing.

Alexander Pope

Alexander Pope (1688-1744) was an English poet, satirist, and translator best remembered for his eminently quotable couplets, and for his brilliant translations of Homer, which earned him the vast fortune of £10,000 and made him independently wealthy.

Pope's father was a wholesale linen merchant in London who retired from the linen business the year Alexander was born. Raised a Roman Catholic, Pope was later to make powerful and influential friends (and patrons) among other Catholics; but in childhood his religion kept him out of the local schools, and apart from some lessons from local Catholic priests and a few stints in Catholic schools, he was largely (and extensively) self-educated.

Pope's growth was stunted by some undiagnosed childhood disorder (possibly Pott's disease), and at full adult height he was only four feet six inches (137 cm) tall, with a curvature of the spine that made him look a bit hunchbacked. He suffered intensely from constant headaches, and in general his health was never good; but his health problems only served further to direct his activities to reading and writing.

Pope published *An Essay on Criticism* at the age of 23, in 1711, and instantly won almost universal acclaim; the first two cantos of *The Rape of the Lock* appeared the next year, and the year after that, in 1713, he announced his intention to undertake a translation of Homer. The first volume of the *Iliad*, whose preface is excerpted below, contained four books and appeared in 1715; the entire epic appeared five years later, in 1720. Pope was 32. Pope then asked William Broome, who had helped him annotate the *Iliad*, and Elijah Fenton to help him translate the *Odyssey*, which appeared in 1725 and 1726; Broome later complained that Pope underpaid him for his work, which amounted to nearly half of the epic.

Pope's Homer has been attacked as unhomeric, and certainly it sounds more like Pope, and generally like an eighteenth-century Englishman, than it does like an ancient Greek; but as Ezra Pound wrote of him in 1916, "out of fashion though he is, he has at least the merit of translating Homer into *something*" – that is, into a highly stylized and personalized idiom that is grounded in its own era, as opposed to the bland, inoffensive translationese some translators prefer. His remarks on translation justify this practice.

Pope's political sympathies as a Catholic were Tory rather than Whig, and toward the end of Queen Anne's reign this began to influence his literary affiliations as well. Addison and Steele, with whom he had once been close, became increasingly distant, and along with other Whigs at Butler's Coffee House they commissioned a rival *Iliad* from Thomas Tickell, whose translation of book one appeared two days after Pope's; but Pope also formed new close associations with Tory writers like Jonathan Swift and John Gay. As he grew increasingly weary of the embattled life of a wit, he gradually withdrew from it, moving to Chiswick in 1716 and to a villa on the Thames in Twickenham in 1718, where he was to live until his death 26 years later. At the same time he

---

[4] Alpheus was the ancient river god of the Peloponnese; the story of Alpheus and Arethusa is told in book five of Ovid's *Metamorphoses*. The rivers in red stockings are presumably actors playing Alpheus as well. [Ed]

[5] *The Rape of Proserpine* (*Raptus Proserpinae*) was an epic poem by the Roman poet Claudian; the opera based on it (1728) was composed by John Galliard, with a libretto by Lewis Theobald. [Ed]

sharpened his satire of the literati in numerous short pieces and *The Dunciad* (1728, 1729, 1743). His *Essay on Man* (1733-1734) was intended to be a mature reflection on nature, ethics, and society, but it was immediately attacked, with a good deal of justification, as shallow and derivative. In the mid-thirties he published a total of ten imitations of Horatian satires – close enough to Horace to permit the publication of the original Latin verses *face-à-face* with the English, but also far enough to allow him to take potshots at contemporary Whigs and the crass commercialism he associated with them. A blank-verse epic entitled *Brutus* remained unfinished at his death.

The Chief Characteristic of Translation
From preface to the *Iliad* (1715)

Having now spoken of the beauties and defects of the original, it remains to treat of the translation, with the same view to the chief characteristic. As far as that is seen in the main parts of the poem, such as the fable, manners, and sentiments, no translator can prejudice it but by willful omissions or contractions. As it also breaks out in every particular image, description, and simile, whoever lessens or too much softens those takes off from this chief character. It is the first grand duty of an interpreter to give his author entire and unmaimed; and for the rest, the diction and versification only are his proper province, since these must be his own, but the others he is to take as he finds them.

It should then be considered what methods may afford some equivalent in our language for the graces of these in the Greek. It is certain no literal translation can be just to an excellent original in a superior language; but it is a great mistake to imagine (as many have done) that a rash paraphrase can make amends for this general defect; which is no less in danger to lose the spirit of an ancient by deviating into the modern manners of expression. If there be sometimes a darkness, there is often a light in antiquity, which nothing better preserves than a version almost literal. I know no liberties one ought to take but those which are necessary for transfusing the spirit of the original and supporting the poetical style of the translation; and I will venture to say, there have not been more men misled in former times by a servile dull adherence to the letter than have been deluded in ours by a chimerical, insolent hope of raising and improving their author. It is not to be doubted that the fire of the poem is what a translator should principally regard, as it is most likely to expire in his managing; however it is his safest way to be content with preserving this to his utmost in the whole, without endeavouring to be more than he finds his author is in any particular place. 'Tis a great secret in writing to know when to be plain, and when poetical and figurative; and it is what Homer will teach us if we will but follow modestly in his footsteps. Where his diction is bold and lofty, let us raise ours as high as we can; but where his is plain and humble, we ought not to be deterred from imitating him by the fear of incurring the censure of a mere English critic. Nothing that belongs to Homer seems to have been more commonly mistaken than the just pitch of his style: some of his translators having swelled into fustian in a proud confidence of the sublime; others sunk into flatness, in a cold and timorous notion of simplicity. Methinks I see these different followers of Homer, some sweating and straining after him by violent leaps and bounds (the certain signs of false mettle), others slowly and servilely creeping in his train, while the poet himself is all the time proceeding with an unaffected and equal majesty before them. However, of the two extremes one could sooner pardon frenzy than frigidity: no author is to be envied for such commendations as he may gain by that character of style which his friends must agree together to call simplicity, and the rest of the world will call dullness. There is a graceful and dignified simplicity, as well as a bald and sordid one, which differ as much from each other as the air of a plain man from that of a sloven: 'tis one thing to be tricked up, and another not to be dressed at all. Simplicity is the mean between ostentation and rusticity.

This pure and noble simplicity is nowhere in such perfection as in the scripture and our author. One may affirm with all respect to the inspired writings that the divine spirit made use of no other words but what were intelligible and common to men at that time, and in that part of the world; and as Homer is the author nearest to those, his style must of course bear a greater resemblance to the sacred books than that of any other writer. This consideration (together with what has been observed of the parity of some of his thoughts) may methinks induce a translator on the one hand to give in to several of those general phrases and manners of expression, which have attained a veneration even in our language from their use in the Old Testament; as on the other, to avoid those which have been appropriated to the divinity, and in a manner consigned to mystery and religion.

For a further preservation of this air of simplicity, a particular care should be taken to express with all plainness those moral sentences and proverbial speeches which are so numerous in this poet. They have something venerable, and as I may say oracular, in that unadorned gravity and shortness with which they are delivered: a grace which would be utterly lost by endeavouring to give them what we call a more ingenious (that is a more modern) turn in the paraphrase.

Perhaps the mixture of some Graecisms and old words after the manner of Milton, if done without too much affectation, might not have an ill effect in a version of this particular work, which most of any other seems to require a venerable antique cast. But certainly the use of modern terms of war and government, such as platoon, campaign, junto, or the like (which some of his translators have fallen into) cannot be allowable; those only excepted, without which it is impossible to treat the subjects in any living language.

There are two peculiarities in Homer's diction that are a sort of marks or moles, by which every common eye distinguishes him at first sight: those who are not his greatest admirers look upon them as defects, and those who are seem pleased with them as beauties. I speak of his compound epithets and of his repetitions. Many of the former cannot be done literally into English without destroying the purity of our language. I believe such should be retained as slide easily of themselves into an English compound without violence to the ear or to the received rules of composition; as well as those which have received a sanction from the authority of our best poets and are become familiar through their use of them; such as the "cloud-compelling Jove", &c. As for the rest, whenever any can be as fully and significantly expressed in a single word as in a compounded one, the course to be taken is obvious.

Some that cannot be so turned as to preserve their full image by one or two words may have justice done them by circumlocution; as the epithet οἰνοσίφυλλος to a mountain would appear little or ridiculous translated literally 'leaf-shaking', but affords a majestic idea in the periphrasis: "The lofty mountain shakes his waving woods". Others that admit of differing significations may receive an advantage by a judicious variation according to the occasions on which they are introduced. For example, the epithet of Apollo, ἑκηβόλος or 'far-shooting', is capable of two explications: one literal in respect of the darts and bow, the ensigns of that god, the other allegorical with regard to the rays of the sun. Therefore in such places where Apollo is represented as a god in person, I would use the former interpretation, and where the effects of the sun are described, I would make choice of the latter. Upon the whole, it will be necessary to avoid that perpetual repetition of the same epithets which we find in Homer, and which, though it might be accommodated (as has been already shown) to the ear of those times, is by no means so to ours; but one may wait for opportunities of placing them where they derive an additional beauty from the occasions on which they are employed; and in doing this properly, a translator may at once show his fancy and his judgment.

As for Homer's repetitions, we may divide them into three sorts: of whole narrations and speeches, of single sentences, and of one verse or hemistitch.[1] I hope it is not impossible to have such a regard to these as neither to lose so known a mark of the author, on the one hand, nor to offend the reader too much on the other. The repetition is not ungraceful in those speeches where the dignity of the speaker renders it a sort of insolence to alter his words; as in the messages from gods to men, or from higher powers to inferiors in concerns of state, or where the ceremonial of religion seems to require it, in the solemn forms of prayers, oaths, or the like. In other cases, I believe the best rule is to be guided by the nearness or distance at which the repetitions are placed in the original: when they follow too close one may vary the expression, but it is a question whether a professed translator be authorized to omit any; if they be tedious, the author is to answer for it.

It only remains to speak of the versification. Homer (as has been said) is perpetually applying the sound to the sense, and varying it on every new subject. This is indeed one of the most exquisite beauties of poetry, and attainable by very few: I know only of Homer eminent for it in the Greek, and Virgil in Latin. I am sensible it is what may sometimes happen by chance, when a writer is warm, and fully possessed of his image: however, it may be reasonably believed they designed this, in whose verse it so manifestly appears in a superior degree to all others. Few readers have the ear to be judges of it, but those who have will see I have endeavoured at this beauty.

Upon the whole, I must confess myself utterly incapable of doing justice to Homer. I attempt him in no other hope but that which one may entertain without much vanity, of giving a more tolerable copy of him than any entire translation in verse has yet done. We have only those of Chapman, Hobbes, and Ogilby. Chapman has taken the advantage of an immeasurable length of verse, notwithstanding which there is scarce any paraphrase more loose and rambling than his. He has frequent interpolations of four or six lines, and I remember one in the thirteenth book of the *Odyssey*, ver. 312, where he has spun twenty verses out of two. He is often mistaken in so bold a manner that one might think he deviated on purpose if he did not in other places of his notes insist so much upon verbal trifles. He appears to have had a strong affectation of extracting new meanings out of his author, insomuch as to promise in his rhyming preface a poem of the mysteries he had revealed in Homer; and perhaps he endeavoured to strain the obvious sense to this end. His expression is involved in fustian, a fault for which he was remarkable in his original writings, as in the tragedy of *Bussy d'Amboise*, &c. In a word, the nature of the man may account for his whole performance; for he appears from his preface and remarks to have been of an arrogant turn, and an enthusiast in poetry. His own boast of having finished half the *Iliad* in less than fifteen weeks shows with what negligence his

[1] Half of a line of verse, broken by a caesura. [Ed]

version was performed. But that which is to be allowed him, and which very much contributed to cover his defects, is a daring fiery spirit that animates his translation, which is something like what one might imagine Homer himself would have writ before he arrived to years of discretion.

Hobbes has given us a correct explanation of the sense in general; but for particulars and circumstances he continually lops them, and often omits the most beautiful. As for its being esteemed a close translation, I doubt not many have been led into that error by the shortness of it, which proceeds not from his following the original line by line, but from the contractions above-mentioned. He sometimes omits whole similes and sentences, and is now and then guilty of mistakes which no writer of his learning could have fallen into, but through carelessness. His poetry, as well as Ogilby's, is too mean for criticism.

It is a great loss to the poetical world that Mr Dryden did not live to translate the *Iliad*. He has left us only the first book and a small part of the sixth, in which if he has in some places not truly interpreted the sense or preserved the antiquities, it ought to be excused on account of the haste he was obliged to write in. He seems to have had too much regard to Chapman, whose words he sometimes copies, and has unhappily followed him in passages where he wanders from the original. However, had he translated the whole work, I would no more have attempted Homer after him than Virgil, his version of whom (notwithstanding some human errors) is the most noble and spirited translation I know in any language. But the fate of great geniuses is like that of great ministers: though they are confessedly the first in the commonwealth of letters, they must be envied and calumniated only for being at the head of it.

That which in my opinion ought to be the endeavour of anyone who translates Homer is above all things to keep alive that spirit and fire which makes his chief character. In particular places, where the sense can bear any doubt, to follow the strongest and most poetical, as most agreeing with that character. To copy him in all the variations of his style, and the different modulations of his numbers. To preserve in the more active or descriptive parts a warmth and elevation; in the more sedate or narrative, a plainness and solemnity; in the speeches a fullness and perspicuity; in the sentences a shortness and gravity. Not to neglect even the little figures and turns on the words, nor sometimes the very cast of the periods. Neither to omit or confound any rites or customs of antiquity. Perhaps too he ought to include the whole in a shorter compass than has hitherto been done by any translator who has tolerably preserved either the sense or poetry. What I would farther recommend to him is to study his author rather from his own text than from any commentaries, how learned soever, or whatever figure they make in the estimation of the world. To consider him attentively in comparison with Virgil above all the ancients, and with Milton above all the moderns. Next these the Archbishop of Cambray's [Fenelón's] *Telemachus* may give him the truest idea of the spirit and turn of our author, and Bossu's admirable treatise of the epic poem the justest notion of his design and conduct. But after all, with whatever judgment and study a man may proceed, or with whatever happiness he may perform such a work, he must hope to please but a few, those only who have at once a taste of poetry and competent learning. For to satisfy such as want either is not in the nature of his undertaking; since a mere modern wit can like nothing that is not modern, and a pedant nothing that is not Greek ...

Charles Batteux

Charles Batteux (1715-1780) was a French professor of philosophy in the college royal whose scholarly works on literature and the fine arts, including the lengthy chapters on translations excerpted below, were extremely influential in his day, in France and across Europe; his *Cours de belles-lettres* (1750) was translated into English only ten years after its first publication. Toward the end of his life he was asked by the French government to write an elementary school curriculum for the military school; he did, in haste, but in 45 volumes. Their poor reception is said to have accelerated his death.

In addition to these scholarly works, Batteux did a respectable amount of translating: a two-volume French Horace, the moral writings of Epicurus, and the poetics of Aristotle, Horace, Vida, and Boileau.

Principles of Translation
From *Principles of Literature* (*Principes de littérature*, 1747-48)
Translated by John Miller

It is now in general agreed that translating the writings of the ancients is, if not the sole, at least the plainest, the shortest, and the surest means of becoming well acquainted with them and their language. It is also agreed that a translation ought exactly to express the original; that it should neither be too free nor too servile; that it should neither deviate into long circumlocutions, which weaken the ideas, nor adhere too strictly to the letter, which stifles the sentiment. But as these loose and general principles are but of small use when one comes to perfomance, we shall present some particulars to the younger class of readers, for whom these sheets are principally designed.

In translating, the chief difficulty lies not in comprehending the author's thought: this is usually attained by the assistance of good editions, of commentaries, and, above all, by examining the mutual relations and connections of the ideas: but when we come to express, in another language, the things, the thoughts, the expressions, the turns, the strain, of a work; to give the things, such as they are, without adding, diminishing, or misplacing; the thoughts, in their colors, their degrees, their shades; the turns, which impart fire, spirit, life, to the discourse; and to exhibit the expressions, natural, figurative, strong, copious, genteel, delicate, &c. and all this after a model rigorously strict, and yet would be obeyed without constraint; there is required, if not as much genius, at least as much taste, to translate well as to compose. Nay, perhaps even a greater degree is necessary.

The author who composes, wholly guided by a sort of instinct, is always free; and by his subject presenting him ideas, which he may accept or reject at his pleasure, is absolute master of his own thoughts and expressions. If the thought does not please him, or if the expression be not suitable to the thought, he may reject both: *quae desperat tractata nitescere posse, relinquit.*[1] The translator has nothing in his own power; he is obliged in everything to follow his author, and to submit to all his variations with an unreserved compliance. This may be conceived by the variety of strains necessarily found in the same subject, and still more in the same kind of writing. In a subject whose parts are regularly disposed, and placed in just harmony, we see the style rising and falling, softening and strengthening, contracting and extending, without any deviation from the unity of its fundamental character. Terence has, from one end to the other, a style perfectly adapted to comedy: it is always simple and elegant. But how different are the degrees of simplicity in the mouth of Simon, of Davus, of Pamphilus, of Myfis! how unlike are they when these actors are calm and affected! with one passion or with another! To express all these degrees, a translator must have thoroughly felt them; afterwards have the command, to an uncommon pitch, of the language which he wants to enrich with foreign spoils. What opinion then ought we not to have of a translation performed with success?

The first thing necessary to a person who intends to translate is thoroughly to understand the genius of the two languages which he proposes to handle. He may acquire this knowledge by a sort of perception resulting from the thorough acquaintance that he has with them. But would it be impertinent to throw some light upon the means of perception, and to examine whether there be no method to facilitate his labor, no criterion by which one may determine his success? ...

CHAP. III.
Rules of the art of Translating
A general principle

If it be true that we never deviate from the Latin arrangement but when we are forced so to do, either by the meaning itself, by the perspicuity of the expression, or by the harmony; it thence follows that we ought to return to the Latin order as often as we have not one of these three reasons; and so that all the Latin constructions are not exotic in French, nor all the French in Latin.[2] Languages are like men, who have one common nature which unites, and peculiarities which separate them. Thus, all the constructions which, established on the interest or point of view of the speaker, find, in the words of either language, no real obstacle to cause them to take another turn, ought to be preserved in the translation: and it will only be in the contrary case that one shall be obliged to change them, for fear of committing a Gallicism, if he writes Latin, or Latinism, if he writes French.

What is a Latinism? What is a Gallicism?

It is easy to answer these two questions, after what has been said. I am making a speech in Latin: instead of following the natural order of the sentiment, the habit I have contracted, in speaking French, of following another, on account of the indigence of that language, obliges one to make the same construction in the Latin phrase. I then commit a Gallicism. I should have said, *Praeclaras artes admiror*; but as, in French, I am accustomed to say, *J'admire les beaux arts*, 'I admire the polite arts'. I say also in Latin, *Admiror praeclaras artes*. And in speaking French and English, because I am entirely devoted to the reading of Latin authors, and say, *Felix est qui sapit*; I say likewise in French, *Celui la est heureux qui est sage*, 'He is happy who is wise'; I should have said, *Heureux celui qui est sage*, 'Happy is he who is wise'.

There is then a Gallicism in the Latin, when one follows in it the arrangement which the French took only on account of its peculiar constitution: and there is a Latinism in the French, when such Latin arrangements are followed in it as the French cannot easily admit. Thus a Latinism, an Anglicism, a Gallicism, a Hebraism, &c. signify only peculiarities of languages which have been, without reason, transferred into other languages.

---

[1] "And what he thinks his touch will never turn to gold, that he lets alone" (E.C. Wickham's translation). Horace, *Ars Poetica* l. 140-41. [Ed]

[2] It will be found that the most part of what follows is equally applicable to the English as to the French language, which general observation I choose to insert here that I may avoid the too frequent repetition of the same words in the text. [Tr]

As languages consist of two things, words, and their arrangements, they have also two sorts of peculiarities; that of the words, and that of their turns, and ways of expression; and, consequently, there is another sort of Gallicism in Latin, or Latinism in French: it is that which occurs in the words themselves, and which bears some resemblance with barbarism. For example, if one should Latinise a French word, and say, *Vivacitas ingenii*, *vivacite d'esprit*, 'liveliness of wit'; *vivacitas* is not native Latin in that sense: or, if one should Frenchify a Latin word not yet adopted by good custom, as *gloriole*, 'somewhat vainglorious'; *exprimer*, 'to express'; *telle coutume obtient*, 'such a custom prevails'; the words *exprimer*, *obtenir*, have a meaning which takes after the Latin. We are not talking here of that Gallicism, or Latinism, because we suppose the translator sufficiently master of the fundamentals of his language, and that he is acquainted with the words of it.

It follows from what has been said above, that the first principle of translation is, To leave the turns of expression such as they are in the author, when the two languages equally admit them ...

It is unnecessary to pursue the detail further. Let us draw from this principle some consequences, which may serve as so many particular rules of the art of translation. It follows,

I. That the order of the things, whether facts or reasonings, is not to be altered; since that order is the same in all languages; seeing it depends on the nature of man, rather than on the particular genius of nations.

II. That we ought also to preserve the order of the ideas, or at least of the members. There has been a reason, how nice soever to investigate, which has determined the author to use one arrangement rather than another. Perhaps it was the harmony; but it was also often the energy; though nothing that is energetical can be deficient in harmony. Cicero had said, *Neque potest is exercitum continerě imperator, qui seipsum non continet.* M. Flechier, who has translated that thought like an orator,[3] not having been able to preserve the order of the ideas, has at least preserved the order of the members: he has said, *Quelle discipline peut établir dans sons camp, celui qui ne peut regler sa conduite?* 'What discipline can he establish in his camp, who cannot regulate his own conduct?' He was too sensible of the energetic turn of Cicero's expression to say, *Un général qui ne regle point so conduite, ne peut regler une armée*: 'A general who cannot regulate his own conduct cannot regulate an army'. On the other side, if he had translated the sentence thus, *Un général ne peut regler une armée, qui ne peut se regler lui-meme*, 'A general cannot regulate an army who cannot regulate himself', he had committed a Latinism. So this example affords us a double lesson.

III. That the periods should be preserved, how long soever they be; because a period is but a thought, composed of several other thoughts, connected together by intrinsic relations; and this connection is the life of those thoughts, and the principal object of the speaker. In a period, the different members have a respect to each other, and their relations form a kind of harmony. If the phrases be interrrupted or divided, we may have indeed the thought; but then we have it without the coherence of principles, of consequences, of proof, or of comparison, which they had in the period, and which constituted its prevailing character. There are methods of reconciling everything. Periods, though suspended in their different members, have nevertheless pauses, where the meaning is almost finished, and which give the mind the relaxation it wants ...

IV. It follows, That all the conjunctions ought to be preserved. They are, as it were, the articulations of the members. One ought not to change their meaning, nor their position; and if there are cases in which they are omitted, it is only when the mind can easily dispense with the want of them, and when, advancing of itself from one phrase to another, the conjunction expressed would only interrupt, without being of service.

V. That all adverbs should be placed beside the verb, before or after, according as the harmony or energy permits. It is always on these two principles that their place is regulated in Latin.

VI. That symmetrical sentences be rendered with their symmetry, or in terms equivalent. Symmetry in discourse is a conformity of several ideas, or of several expressions. The symmetry of expressions may consist in the sounds, in the quantity of syllables, in the termination or length of the words, in the arrangement of the members. Here is a sentence of Cicero which has all these species of symmetry: *Nihil habet fortuna tua majus quam ut possis, nec natura melius quam ut velis, conservare quam plurimos. La nature et la fortune n'ont rien fait de meilleur, ni de plus grand pour vous, que de vous donner, l'une la volonté, l'autre le pouvoir de conserver des citoyens.* 'Your condition has nothing greater in it than to empower, nor your disposition better than to incline you to save the greatest numbers.' If one cannot render sound for sound, substantive, verb, adverb, adjective, as they are in the text, he ought, at least, to acquit himself by another sort of harmony.

VII. That bright thoughts, in order to preserve the same degree of clearness, should be nearly of the same extent of words. If they are contracted, there is danger of obscuring; if extended, of weakening their lustre:

---

[3] An allusion to Cicero's description of his own translation practices; see above, 9. [Ed]

Cui non conveniet sua res; ut calceus, olim
Si pede major erit, subvertet; si minor, uret.
[Horace, *Art of Poetry*]

Si je ne fais point m'ajuster a ma fortune, c'est un saulier trop etrait, qui me blesse, ou trop large, qui me fait tomber. 'If I cannot suit myself to my fortune, it will be a shoe so strait as to pinch, or so wide as to make me fall'.

VIII. That we must preserve the figures and forms of the thoughts, because the thoughts are the same in all minds: they are capable of taking everywhere the same arrangement, the same configuration, the same attitude. Thus we translate interrogations, antitheses, &c.

As to the figures and forms of words, such as metaphors, repetitions, cadences of names or of verbs, there is some difference to be observed: usually they may be replaced by equivalent expressions. For example, when Cicero says of a decree of Verres, that it was not *trabali clavo fixum*, we may say, that it was not *tellement cementé*, 'so cemented, rivetted, immoveably fixed', that, &c. If these figures cannot be transmuted, or replaced by equivalents, we must then resume the natural expression, and endeavour to transfer the figure to some other idea more susceptible of it, to that the phrase translated, taken altogether, may not lose any of the ornaments it had in the original.

IX. That the proverbs, which are popular maxims, and which are never but short pithy things, should be rendered by other proverbs, or by phrases so natural that they deserve to become such. As they are only concerning things whose use often recurs in company, all nations have a great many of them in common, if not as to expression, at least as to meaning; so one may almost always translate them. Madame Dacier has done so, very happily, in her translation of Terence.

X. That any paraphrase is faulty and imperfect; it is no longer translating, it is commenting. However, when there is no other way to communicate the meaning, necessity excuses the translator; one of the two languages is answerable for the defect.

XI. That we must entirely give up the expression in the text translated when the sense requires it for perspicuity, the sentiment for vivacity, or the harmony for delight. This consequence becomes a second principle.

XII. Ideas may, without ceasing to be the same, be presented under different forms, and be compounded or decompounded in the words used to express them. They may be presented by the way of verb, of adjective, of substantive, of adverb. The translator, if he be embarrassed, has these four methods of extricating himself. Let him take the scales, weight the expressions on either side, poise them every way, he will be allowed alterations, provided he preserve to the thought the same substance, and the same life. He will act only like a traveller, who, for his conveniency, exchanges sometimes one piece of gold for several of silver, sometimes several pieces of silver for one of gold.

Suppose we say in Latin, *Aspirante fortuna*, it will not be required of the translator to write, *La fortune le secondant*, 'Fortune assisting him'. He will be allowed to say, *Avec le secours de la fortune*, 'With fortune's aid'; he will change the participle into a substantive. *Arabes, si quid imperaret, praesti fuere*: *les Arabes se montrerent préts d'obéir à son ordre*; 'The Arabs were ready to obey his orders'. *Eram tunc, et vivebam, et sentiebam*, S. Aug.; *Alors j'avois l'étre, la vie, le sentiment*; 'I then existed, and was a living, and a rational being' [Augustine, *Confessions*].

If we meet, *fieri solet*, the verb may be changed into an adverb, and will throw aside its properties of a verb: *Il arrive ordinairement*; 'It usually happens'.

Itineri paratus et praelio; *Prét à la marche et au combat*; 'Ready for the march and for the fight'. This translation is not good French nor good English. Let us change the substantives into verbs: *Prét à marcher et a combattre*; 'Ready either to march or to fight'; or 'Ready both for marching and fighting'.

Sometimes the adjective will be changed into a verb. *Ad omne fortunae munus subsistite pavidi & suspiciosi*: *Quand la fortune vous présente ces faveurs, retenez votre avidité, defiez-vous, craignez*: 'At every boon of fortune, suspend your eagerness, distrust, fear'.

These are very simple expedients. I dare, however, undertake that they will never fail of producing their effect, and of opening to the perpelexed translator an outlet, which sometimes costs him a long and fruitless search when he follows the letter too close.

The French, it is said, are more sprightly in their discourse than the Latins. When they translate, they ought not to be so in a greater degree than their originals. Happy even if they be equally sprightly. The Latins had neither prepositions in the oblique cases of their nouns, nor auxiliaries in their verbs; they were nimble to run in the course. These auxiliaries are to us what servants and baggage are to an army. The Latins called them *impedimenta*, 'hindrances'.

To disencumber ourselves of them in part, we take the infinites rather than the other moods,[4] the participle, and especially the gerund: we shun passives, superlatives, certain conjunctives (as, *non seulement*, 'not only'; *mais encore*, 'but even'), when they too much lengthen the phrase: we cut off the pronouns from the Latin proper names; we shorten the encomiums usually added to them; we introduce loose and unconnected phrases, &c.

---

[4] This will not hold in English, where the infinitive has the particle *to* prefixed for distinction. [Tr]

Suspension is very conducive to vivacity of expression. We can introduce it, as we have said, by joining to the nominative of the verb what the Latins joined to the regimen, governed case, or object; or, when the phrase is of a certain extent, by taking the passive rather than the active; because, as we have also said, our passive admits the same order of the ideas as the Latin active.

All these expedients equally contribute to oratorial harmony; the greatest part of which consists in perspicuity and fervency of expression. A phrase which, with perspicuity, presents a beautiful meaning always pleases the ear. The latter is never dissatisfied but when we offer it sounds empty, overcharged, or ill matched. For we are not speaking of that harmony which consists in beauty of sounds. Of these the translator can only employ such as he finds in his own language.

As there are in all languages ways of speaking which are incapable of translation; such is this of La Fontaine:

> *Sixte en disait autant quand on le fit Saint Pere,*
> *Un citoyen de Mans, chapon de son metier:*[5]

we do not pretend that our observations can, in such a case, be of the least use. There are also certain things depending on the taste, and on the manners of the people, which cannot be transferred. For example: The Latins had a much greater licence of language than we. They had phrases and expressions which passed among them in genteel company, and which with us are low and mean. Sometimes a single one of these words or phrases would deform and disgrace a whole work of taste. How could we translate *Pastillos Rufillus olet, Gargonius hircum?*[6] or the waggish trick of Priapus, *Diffissá nate pepedi?*[7]

Elizabeth Carter (and Catherine Talbot and Thomas Secker)

Elizabeth Carter (1717-1806) was an English poet and translator, most famous among her contemporaries as the translator of the complete Epictetus. Her erudition was legendary in her day; Dr. Johnson, for example, bragged that he understood Greek better than anyone he knew except Elizabeth Carter.

Carter was born to the Rev. Nicholas and Margaret Carter at Deal in Kent. Her mother died when she was ten, and when her father remarried and had more children, she stayed on to help him raise and educate her half-brothers and -sisters; in her letters she frequently mentions the difficulty she has getting to an intellectual or artistic task when she has a dozen shirts to make, or some other domestic chore to attend to. She never married, in fact – by choice, not by necessity – and lived in the Deal house most of her life. Still, her father gave her exactly the same education he gave his other daughter and four sons, and taught her, among other things, Latin, Greek, and Hebrew; she later learned French, German, Italian, Portugese, and Arabic on her own, along with music, astronomy, history, and geography.

Carter published two volumes of poetry, *Poems upon Particular Occasions* in 1738 and *Poems on Several Occasions* in 1762, by which she is best remembered by scholars of the eighteenth century. But her contemporary reputation rested mainly on her translations: of Crousaz's critique of Pope's *Essay on Man* (1739) from the French, of Algarotti's *Sir Isaac Newton's Philosophy examined, for the use of the Ladies, in Six Dialogues, on Light and Colours* (1739) from the Italian, and of the complete works of Epictetus from the Greek (1757-58). She was also famously associated with the Bluestocking Circle, a renowned women's salon (attended also by some of the foremost male intellectuals of the day) organized by Elizabeth Montagu.

The suggestion to translate Epictetus came from Catherine Talbot (1721-1770), seconded by Thomas Secker (1693-1768), Bishop of Oxford, in early 1749. She had met Talbot, a woman three years her junior, in 1741; Talbot's father had died before her birth, and her mother had moved them in with Bishop Secker when her housemate Catherine Benson married him. Bishop Secker, who was appointed Archbishop of Canterbury the year after the translation appeared, in 1758, thus served as a kind of surrogate father to Catherine Talbot, who remained extremely important to Carter all her life; the two women kept up a voluminous

[5] These two lines are actually from two different fables. The first reads, in Marianne Moore's translation, "As Pope Sixtus had answered when offered the papal chair" (10.13.48); the second, also by Moore: "A citizen of Mans – capon some had dared say – " (8.21.5). [Ed]

[6] "Rufillus smells like a scent-box, Gargonius like a goat" (H. Rushton Fairclough's translation; Horace *Satires* 1.2.27, quoted 1.4.92). [Ed]

[7] Batteux is quoting from memory; the full quotation is "nam displosa sonat quantum vesica pepedi / diffissa nate ficus", or "For as loud as the noise of a bursting bladder was the crack [fart] when my fig-wood buttock split" (H. Rushton Fairclough's translation; Horace *Satires* 1.8.46-47). [Ed]

correspondence for several decades. After Talbot's death at the early age of 49, Carter also helped edit and publish a two-volume compendium of her friend's works, including an issue (#30, June 30, 1750) of Samuel Johnson's *Rambler* and a prayer-book entitled *Reflections on the Seven Days of the Week* (1770).

Carter began work on the translation in May of 1749, and worked on it at a fairly leisurely pace (due to her *lack* of leisure, in fact) over the next four years: the translation was complete in 1753, but publication was delayed by the writing of a life and notes for another four years, until 1757. Her evolving thought about translation – both its performance and its presentation to the public – can best be illustrated with snippets from her correspondence with the commissioners of her work, Catherine Talbot and the Bishop of Oxford.

Translating Epictetus
From Elizabeth Carter's correspondence with Catherine Talbot and Thomas Secker (1749-1757)

Elizabeth Carter to Catherine Talbot

Deal, June 20, 1749

I have really no patience with the translations I have inclosed you, for they appear to me neither sense nor language; but I had much rather give you proof that I can write obscure and bad English than that I could refuse to attempt at least anything which you command me.

Catherine Talbot to Elizabeth Carter

[Summer 1749]

I trust to your honour in venturing back two of your translations, which I send inclosed; for remember they are mine, and must be returned. I give you a thousand thanks for having thus far complied with my request, and I hope at leisure hours you will go on with the same excellent work.The Bishop of Oxford says your translation is a very good one; and, if it has any fault, it is only that of being not close enough, and writ in too smooth and too ornamented a style. Epictetus was a plain man, and spoke plainly; a translation that should express this would, he thinks, preserve more the spirit of the original, and give an exacter notion of it. The next day after I had your packet, he wrote down the two hasty translations I have inclosed to explain what he means. This is all he has to say, except that he much hopes you go on in a work you are well fitted for, and for which I hope to be much the wiser. Should you leave off now, I should almost be tempted to think that you take this critique amiss; but indeed if you knew how much I admire these speciments, you would, I am sure, gratify me with more, provided the application does you no harm, and does not hinder you from being employed in any way you like better. You will be so good to return me both your translations, and my Lord's, when you have compared them.

Elizabeth Carter to Catherine Talbot

[Summer 1749]

Return my most sincere thanks to my Lord for the instructions he has been so good to give me about Epictetus, which I will endeavor to observe. I have not done any more, for I really thought what I sent you so wretchedly ill translated that I had no heart to make any further attempt. I believe I had some important thing to say in defence of my passion for ornament, and to have drawn in poor Epictetus to assist me; but my head is really so confused that I cannot tell what I mean.

Catherine Talbot to Elizabeth Carter

[Summer 1749]

My Lord desires to hear all you can say in behalf of ornaments; but unless you can prove to him that Epictetus wore a laced coat, he will not allow you to dress him in one. You are welcome, I daresay, to the copy [of the Bishop's translations], and pray go on and translate.
– P.S.[1] Let me speak a word for myself: why would you change a plain, home, awakening preacher into a fine, smooth, polite writer, of what nobody will mind? Answer me that, dear Miss Carter.

Elizabeth Carter to Thomas Secker, Bishop of Oxford

[Summer 1749]

It must be acknowledged, my Lord, that the Enchiridion is merely plain common sense; but is not Arrian's Commentary much less simple? The reasoning often requires a much closer attention than the generality of readers are willing to bestow, and in some places appears even abrupt and unconnected; should it not, therefore, seem necessary to translate such a book rather in a paraphrastical way? With regard to style, one certainly ought not to introduce tropes and figures which the author himself never dreamed on; but if the sense is preserved, is it not lawful to endeavour to make him speak such a language as will make him appear natural and easy to those with whom he is taught to converse, rather than to retain any peculiar modes of his own country, which, to those who do not understand them, may appear uncouth and awkward: and moreover books of morality, which have no sacred authority to recommend them, will find it difficult to recommend themselves without some little external helps.

[1] In the Bishop's hand. [Ed]

Thomas Secker to Elizabeth Carter

Cuddesden, Sept. 13, 1749

Good Miss Carter,

This naughty girl [Miss Talbot] hath sealed up her packet without giving me notice; and so you must take what I have to say by itself. Arrian is not a commentator on Epictetus, as Simplicius is; but professes to exhibit his very conversations and discourses, as Xenophon doth those of Socrates; and a translator should represent him in our tongue such as he appears in his own, not indeed copying the peculiarities of the language he speaks in, but still preserving his genuine air and character, as far as ever is consistent with making him rightly understood. Where the terms of his philosophy are now become obscure, or the manners of his age and country unsuitable to ours, I allow the one to be cleared up, and the other softened, to a requisite degree, in the translation itself, and still more in a short note. Nay, some parts, those for instance where he digresses into logical niceties, provided a general notice be given of what nature they are, I think may be entirely passed over. Et quae desperas tractata nitescere posse, relinquis.[2] But with proper exceptions of this kind, every ancient writer should, in common justice, be laid before the modern reader, if at all, such as he is. And Epictetus in particular should, because he will make a better figure, and have more influence in his own homely garb than any other into which he may be travesti[ed] [disguised]. Abruptness and want of ornament very often add much force and persuasion to what is said. They show the speaker to be in earnest, which hath the greatest weight of anything; and the same sentiments delivered in a smooth and polite, a florid and panegyrical, or a formal and professional style are no longer the same. These last were the methods in vogue when Epictetus lived; and they had brought philosophy into disregard and disgrace. He saw it with grief; and reproved Messieurs les Philosophes with an honest zeal. Surely then we should be very careful to do nothing that may but seem to approach towards transforming him into one of these gentlemen. And I am fully persuaded that plain and home exhortations and reproofs, without studied periods and regular connections, in short, such as they might be supposed to come extempore from the fulness of the old man's good heart, will be more attended to and felt, and consequently give more pleasure, as well as do more good, than anything sprucer that can be substituted in their room [place]. I do not mean by all this to vindicate my own specimens. I confess myself to have bent the stick as strongly as I well could, the opposite way to yours. But I am content to divide the difference with you; which, perhaps, after we have both explained ourselves, will be no great one. Yet indeed, of the two, I think a rough and almost literal translation, if it doth but relish strongly of that warm and practical spirit which to me is the characteristic of this book, infinitely preferable to the most elegant paraphrase that lets it evaporate, and leaves the reader unmoved. I know you experience so much of this way of thinking in general that I may very safely trust you with the particular application of it; and therefore shall only add that I am, with high esteem, and every good wish,

Madam,

Your most obedient humble servant,

THO. OXFORD

Catherine Talbot to Elizabeth Carter

[Autumn 1749]

I am much of my Lord's mind (so far as I can judge from the manner in which things strike me) for energy, shortness, and plainness. I return you a thousand thanks for your goodness in providing me this high and useful entertainment; and so far as the application is not hurtful or disagreeable to you, should extremely wish you to go on. But in either of these cases I had rather learn Greek, Arabic, or Hottentot myself than put you on an unpleasant task, or give you an hour's headache.[3]

Elizabeth Carter to Catherine Talbot

[Autumn 1749]

You need be in no trouble about my head, for it is upon the whole much better, and receives no kind of injury from Epictetus. It is impossible I should find a study disagreeable which you are so obliging as to say gives you pleasure. I am only provoked with myself for doing it so awkwardly; however, I hope to make some improvement from the excellent instructions which my Lord has been so good to give me.

Thomas Secker to Elizabeth Carter

Saturday Night, Seven o'Clock,
March 31, 1753

Mr Foulis[4] translated the first book of Arrian's Epictetus some years ago, but hath proceeded no farther; and being told the other day that a new translation was in hand, wished success to it, and said he would further the sale of it as much as he could. This intelligence I have just now received from Dr. Wishart, Principal of

[2] "And what you think your touch will never turn to gold, that you let alone" (E.C. Wickham's translation, modified [from the 3rd to the 2nd person] to follow Secker's reworking of Horace, *Ars Poetica*, l. 140-41). [Ed]

[3] Carter frequently complains of splitting headaches in these letters. [Ed]

[4] She probably means one of the Foulis brothers, Andrew or Robert, both printers. [Ed]

Edinburgh College, to whom the Bishop of Norwich hath blabbed that the translator is a lady. It is a little premature; but be not grieved, good Miss Carter.

Elizabeth Carter to Catherine Talbot

[Autumn 1753]

I find, to my sorrow, that Mr Harris[5] insists on the translation of that wicked logical chapter from which my Lord had in great clemency absolved me. To be sure it would be an excellent piece of revenge to prevail on him to do it himself; but I really know not how to make him such a request; so I must even attempt to do it as well as I can. It is but leaving it just as unintelligible as I find it. I am greatly obliged to Mr Harris; and I hope my Lord will be so good, when he has an opportunity, as to mention my grateful acknowledgements of the favour he has done me ...

This has made the scheme public, however; and so this poor foolish translation, if it ever does appear, instead of the comfort of sneaking quietly through the world, and being read by nobody, will be ushered into full view, and stared quite out of countenance; but there are holes enough in the world for me to run my poor head into, whatever becomes of poor Epictetus.

Elizabeth Carter to Thomas Secker

[Summer 1755]

Your Lordship seems to be of opinion that this translation may do mischief, and I cannot help being a little alarmed and terrified about it. Epictetus, however well guarded in the translation, will, I fear, do but very little good to the unhappy people your Lordship mentions; and is it not therefore better that he should remain buried in Greek, where we may be pretty well assured he will do them but mighty little harm? Indeed I was always of opinion that the book would be of no use, but to those who the least need its assistance; but it never entered into my imagination that it would do anybody any hurt.

Catherine Talbot to Elizabeth Carter

[Summer 1755]

Now what I want to see in this edition is the right reasoning of Epictetus reduced by notes to those true Christian principles which alone can make them firm and sure, and practically useful ...

Many persons will study your book who scorn to look into the Bible: let them therefore be frequently pointed to the true source from whence all they can admire in the other is derived, and from which some passages are plainly taken.

You do not believe that any but good persons will read this book. Fine gentlemen will read it because it is new; fine ladies because it is yours; critics because it is a translation out of Greek; and Shaftesburian heathens because Epictetus was an honour to heathenism, and an idolater of the beauty of virtue.

With the cautions at which I have hinted, the English Epictetus will be a most excellent book, whatever objections I have made to the Greek one. There is a warmth and spirit in his exhortations that would do honour to better principles; and this set off with a keenness of wit and gaiety of humour that make him a delightful companion.

Elizabeth Carter to Catherine Talbot

[Summer 1755]

What shall I say to you, my dear Miss Talbot, upon the subject of Epictetus? Though I cannot help, in some instances, entertaining a more favourable opinion of him than you do, the probability which the Bishop of Oxford and you seem to think there may be of his doing mischief fill me with uneasiness and scruples. You say, indeed, that with proper notes and animadversions, the translation may be an excellent work. But it is surely a dangerous experiment to administer poison to try the force of an antidote. For my own part, I never had the least apprehension that an author who enjoins so strict a morality, who censures even the fashionable vices which fine gentlemen at present consider as mere trifles, and who discovers [displays] so deep a sense of religion, could be studied by bad people; or if he was, that the effect would be any other than the convincing them that there was nothing to be gained, though an infinite deal to be lost, by their turning heathens. At present I know not what to think. The Bishop of Oxford and you, I hope, will think for me.

Elizabeth Carter to Catherine Talbot

[1757/58]

A second edition, no doubt, may modestly be presumed from the encouragement which my Lord and you tell me the first is likely to receive from those promoters of the study of morality and Greek, the Irish Bishops and the two universities.[6] I should not have been so saucy if the Bishop of Oxford had not put it into my head. However, I am in very little pain about the matter; and Epictetus must comfort himself under the neglect of the universities by the civil treatment he meets with among the ladies.

[5] Possibly James Harris, a famous literary and philological scholar of the day. [Ed]

[6] The first run of 1800 copies was printed between June 1757 and April 1758, and by July of 1758 had to be supplemented with an additional 250. The translation netted Carter well over 1000 pounds in royalties, along with the bulk of her reputation among her contemporaries. [Ed]

I believe I did not tell you of one young man of large fortune (it is not long since he left the university), who being asked by another to subscribe, refused, with an affirmation that he would have done it, if the book had been some treatise of economy for the use of the ladies.[7] Is this not a most notable youth? And might not one be sure, by applying to him, of getting the best receipt [recipe] extant for making modern dumpling; for I believe he has much too good a taste to have been perverted at Oxford by the soups and sauces of the ancients.

Samuel Johnson

Samuel Johnson (1709-1784) was one of the most prominent figures in British intellectual life in the mid-eighteenth century. A critic, essayist, journalist, poet, educator, and lexicographer, he was one of the first British writers to elevate literary hackwork to the status of a fine art.

Johnson was born to Michael and Sarah Johnson in Lichfield, Staffordshire, a sickly child with weak eyes. His father was a prominent but poor bookseller in town who somehow managed to send his son to classical schools and on to the University of Oxford; Johnson was an enormously ambitious but dilatory student, and was to retain those somewhat contradictory qualities to the end of his life. Entering Pembroke College, Oxford, in 1728, he was forced to leave just over a year later, for financial reasons. In 1732 he signed on as undermaster in the grammar school at Market Bosworth, and loathed his work; soon thereafter a paid task was sent his way by his childhood friend Edmund Hector, that of translating into English Father Jeronimo Lobo's *A Voyage to Abyssinia* from a French version.

Johnson at this period in his life was not a pretty sight: dirt-poor, without prospects, his face horribly scarred by a childhood scrofula, aggressively lower-middle-class in speech and behaviour, and tortured by what would later (in our own century) be diagnosed as Obsessive-Compulsive Disorder (he could not pass through a doorway, or perform other simple functions, without lengthy and unpleasantly jerky ritualistic observances). Nevertheless in 1735 he managed to marry well, to a widow twenty years his senior named Elizabeth Porter, who came with a dowry of £700. With his wife's money he started a classical school for gentlemen near Lichfield, but the school never quite caught on, and after two years Johnson gave up.

In 1737, then, he moved to London, where he became a journalist, working for the *Gentleman's Magazine* and writing his own poetry and plays on the side. Always on the verge of abject poverty, always scrounging around for another way to make a few pence, Johnson wrote and wrote, and finally, in 1744, succeeded with a book on the life of his friend Richard Savage. This book and other works gradually built up his reputation in London, to the point where in 1745 he was asked by a consortium of London booksellers to write a dictionary of the English language. He published a *Plan* for the dictionary two years later, in 1747, and his play *Irene* was produced at Drury Lane Theatre by his former student David Garrick in 1749; but he was still virtually bankrupt, and in 1750 he began to publish *The Rambler*, a twopenny semiweekly sheet containing a single anonymous essay in a moral or instructive mode. This successful enterprise lasted two years, till 1752, the year his wife Tetty died.

Three years later, in 1755, his *Dictionary* appeared to much praise; with 40,000 entries, it was the first major English dictionary to use historical citations. It is best remembered today for the pugnacity of some of its definitions ("Oats: A grain, which in England is generally given to horses, but in Scotland supports the people"). In 1757 he began contributing his 'Idler' column to the *Universal Chronicle*, and in 1759 he began work on a novel based on his earlier translation of *A Voyage to Abyssinia*, entitled *The Prince of Abissinia* but better known as *Rasselas*; a kind of spiritual autobiography, it was immensely popular and translated into many languages in Johnson's own time and after.

In 1762 Johnson's financial problems were solved by a £300 per annum pension from the king; having defined 'pension' in his *Dictionary* as "pay given to a state hireling for treason to his country", he hesitated to accept it, but not for long. The next year, 53 years old, he met the 22-year-old James Boswell, who was later to write the famous *Life* of his friend and so cement one of the great friendships in literary history. A few years later, in 1765, his long-awaited eight-volume edition of Shakespeare appeared – a piece of quirky but first-rate editing and landmark criticism that was reviled by the romantics but is today highly respected by Shakespeare editors and critics.

Freed from the burdens of writing for a living, Johnson began to travel more, and also to play a more active role in politics, largely through political pamphlets. In 1777 a group of booksellers

[7] Surprisingly, perhaps, this young man was in the minority among the educated male elite, over 1300 of whom subscribed. [Ed]

asked him to write a series of lives of English poets, and this – including the life of Pope excerpted below – appeared between 1779 and 1781 to a barrage of criticism. Now in his seventies, Johnson was unfazed by the attacks; and *Lives of the English Poets* remains one of his most popular books.

The Art of Translation
The Idler 68/69 (1759)

Among the studies which have exercised the ingenious and the learned for more than three centuries, none has been more diligently or more successfully cultivated than the art of translation; by which the impediments which bar the way to science are, in some measure, removed, and the multiplicity of languages become less incommodious.

Of every other kind of writing the ancients have left us models which all succeeding ages have laboured to imitate; but translation may justly be claimed by the moderns as their own. In the first ages of the world instruction was commonly oral, and learning traditional, and what was not written could not be translated. When alphabetical writing made the conveyance of opinions and the transmission of events more easy and certain, literature did not flourish in more than one country at once, or distant nations had little commerce with each other; and those few whom curiosity sent abroad in quest of improvement delivered their acquisitions in their own manner, desirous, perhaps, to be considered as the inventors of that which they had learned from others.

The Greeks for a time travelled into Egypt, but they translated no books from the Egyptian language; and when the Macedonians had overthrown the empire of Persia, the countries that became subject to Grecian dominion studied only the Grecian literature. The books of the conquered nations, if they had any among them, sunk into oblivion; Greece considered herself as the mistress, if not as the parent of arts, her language contained all that was supposed to be known, and, except the sacred writings of the Old Testament, I know not that the library of Alexandria adopted anything from a foreign tongue.

The Romans confessed themselves the scholars [students] of the Greeks, and do not appear to have expected what has since happened, that the ignorance of succeeding ages would prefer them to their teachers. Every man who in Rome aspired to the praise of literature thought it necessary to learn Greek, and had no need of versions when they could study the originals. Translation, however, was not wholly neglected. Dramatic poems could be understood by the people in no language but their own, and the Romans were sometimes entertained with the tragedies of Euripides and the comedies of Menander. Other works were sometimes attempted; in an old scholiast there is mention of a Latin *Iliad*;[1] and we have not wholly lost Tully's version of the poem of Aratus; but it does not appear that any man grew eminent by interpreting another, and perhaps it was more frequent to translate for exercise or amusement than for fame.

The Arabs were the first nation who felt the ardour of translation: when they had subdued the eastern provinces of the Greek empire, they found their captives wiser than themselves, and made haste to relieve their wants by imparted knowledge. They discovered that many might grow wise by the labour of a few, and that improvements might be made with speed, when they had the knowledge of former ages in their own language. They, therefore, made haste to lay hold on medicine and philosophy, and turned their chief authors into Arabic. Whether they attempted the poets is not known; their literary zeal was vehement, but it was short, and probably expired before they had time to add the arts of elegance to those of necessity.

The study of ancient literature was interrupted in Europe by the irruption of the Northern nations, who subverted the Roman empire, and erected new kingdoms with new languages. It is not strange that such confusion should suspend literary attention; those who lost, and those who gained dominion, had immediate difficulties to encounter, and immediate miseries to redress, and had little leisure, amidst the violence of war, the trepidation of flight, the distresses of forced migration, or the tumults of unsettled conquest, to inquire after speculative truth, to enjoy the amusement of imaginary adventures, to know the history of former ages, or study the events of any other lives. But no sooner had this chaos of dominion sunk into order, than learning began again to flourish in the calm of peace. When life and possessions were secure, convenience and enjoyment were soon sought, learning was found the highest gratification of the mind, and translation became one of the means by which it was imparted.

At last, by a concurrence of many causes, the European world was roused from its lethargy; those arts which had been long obscurely studied in the gloom of monasteries became the general favourites of mankind; every nation vied with its neighbour for the prize of learning; the epidemical emulation spread from south to north, and curiosity and translation found their way to Britain.

He that reviews the progress of English literature will find that translation was very early cultivated among us, but that some principles, either wholly erroneous or too far extended, hindered our success from being always equal to our diligence.

---

[1] Possibly by Gnaeus Matius Calvena; it does not survive. [Ed]

Chaucer, who is generally considered as the father of our poetry, has left a version of Boethius on the *Comforts of Philosophy*, the book which seems to have been the favourite of the middle ages, which had been translated into Saxon by King Alfred, and illustrated with a copious comment ascribed to Aquinas. It may be supposed that Chaucer would apply more than common attention to an author of so much celebrity, yet he has attempted nothing higher than a version strictly literal, and has degraded the poetical parts to prose, that the constraint of versification might not obstruct his zeal for fidelity.

Caxton taught us typography about the year 1474. The first book printed in English was a translation. Caxton was both the translator and printer of the *Destruction of Troye* [by Raoul Lefevre], a book which, in that infancy of learning, was considered as the best account of the fabulous ages, and which, though now driven out of notice by authors of no greater use or value, still continued to be read in Caxton's English to the beginning of the present century.

Caxton proceeded as he began, and, except the poems of Gower and Chaucer, printed nothing but translations from the French, in which the original is so scrupulously followed that they afford us little knowledge of our own language: though the words are English, the phrase is foreign.

As learning advanced, new works were adopted into our language, but I think with little improvement of the art of translation, though foreign nations and other languages offered us models of a better method; till in the age of Elizabeth we began to find that greater liberty was necessary to elegance, and that elegance was necessary to general reception; some essays were then made upon the Italian poets, which deserve the praise and gratitude of posterity. But the old practice was not suddenly forsaken: Holland filled the nation with literal translation; and, what is yet more strange, the same exactness was obstinately practised in the versions of the poets. This absurd labour of construing into rhyme was countenanced by Jonson in his version of Horace; and whether it be that more men have learning than genius, or that the endeavours of that time were more directed towards knowledge than delight, the accuracy of Jonson found more imitators than the elegance of Fairfax; and May, Sandys and Holliday confined themselves to the toil of rendering line for line, not indeed with equal felicity, for May and Sandys were poets, and Holliday only a scholar and a critic.

Felltham appears to consider it as the established law of poetical translation that the lines should be neither more nor fewer than those of the original; and so long had this prejudice prevailed that Denham[2] praises Fanshaw's version of Guarini as the example of a new and noble way, as the first attempt to break the boundaries of custom, and assert the natural freedom of the Muse.

In the general emulation of wit and genius which the festivity of the Restoration produced, the poets shook off their constraint, and considered translation as no longer confined to servile closeness. But reformation is seldom the work of pure virtue or unassisted reason. Translation was improved more by accident than conviction. The writers of the foregoing age had at least learning equal to their genius; and, being often more able to explain the sentiments or illustrate the allusions of the ancients, than to exhibit their graces and transfuse their spirit, were, perhaps, willing sometimes to conceal their want of poetry by profusion of literature, and, therefore, translated literally, that their fidelity might shelter their insipidity or harshness. The wits of Charles's time[3] had seldom more than slight and superficial views; and their care was to hide their want of learning behind the colours of a gay imagination; they, therefore, translated always with freedom, sometimes with licentiousness, and, perhaps, expected that their readers should accept sprightliness for knowledge, and consider ignorance and mistake as the impatience and negligence of a mind too rapid to stop at difficulties, and too elevated to descend to minuteness.

Thus was translation made more easy to the writer, and more delightful to the reader; and there is no wonder if ease and pleasure have found their advocates. The paraphrastic liberties have been almost universally admitted; and Sherbourne, whose learning was eminent, and who had no need of any excuse to pass slightly over obscurities, is the only writer who, in later times, has attempted to justify or revive the ancient severity.

There is undoubtedly a mean to be observed. Dryden saw very early that closeness best preserved an author's sense, and that freedom best exhibited his spirit; he, therefore, will deserve the highest praise, who can give a representation at once faithful and pleasing, who can convey the same thoughts with the same graces, and who, when he translates, changes nothing but the language.

Translating Homer

From 'Life of Pope', in *Lives of the English Poets* (1779-81)

The train of my disquisition has now conducted me to

[2] See above, 155-56. [Ed]

[3] The so-called court wits of King Charles II in Restoration England, after 1660. They included Sir Edward Fillmore, Sidney Godolphin, Charles Sackville (Lord Buckhurst), Sir Charles Sedley, and Edmund Waller. [Ed]

that poetical wonder, the translation of the *Iliad*;[4] a performance which no age or nation can pretend to equal. To the Greeks translation was almost unknown; it was totally unknown to the inhabitants of Greece. They had no recourse to the barbarians for poetical beauties, but sought for every thing in Homer, where, indeed, there is but little which they might not find.

The Italians have been very diligent translators; but I can hear of no version, unless perhaps Anguillara's Ovid may be excepted, which is read with eagerness. The *Iliad* of Salvini every reader may discover to be punctiliously exact; but it seems to be the work of a linguist skilfully pedantic, and his countrymen, the proper judges of its power to please, reject it with disgust.

Their predecessors the Romans have left some specimens of translation behind them, and that employment must have had some credit in which Tully and Germanicus engaged; but unless we suppose, what is perhaps true, that the plays of Terence were versions of Menander, nothing translated seems ever to have risen to high reputation. The French, in the meridian hour of their learning, were very laudably industrious to enrich their own language with the wisdom of the ancients; but found themselves reduced, by whatever necessity, to turn the Greek and Roman poetry into prose. Whoever could read an author could translate him. From such rivals little can be feared.

The chief help of Pope in this arduous undertaking was drawn from the versions of Dryden. Virgil had borrowed much of his imagery from Homer, and part of the debt was now paid by his translator. Pope searched the pages of Dryden for happy combinations of heroic diction, but it will not be denied that he added much to what he found. He cultivated our language with so much diligence and art that he has left in his Homer a treasure of poetical elegances to posterity. His version may be said to have tuned the English tongue, for since its appearance no writer, however deficient in other powers, has wanted melody. Such a series of lines so elaborately corrected and so sweetly modulated took possession of the public ear; the vulgar was enamoured of the poem, and the learned wondered at the translation.

But in the most general applause discordant voices will always be heard. It has been objected by some, who wish to be numbered among the sons of learning, that Pope's version of Homer is not Homerical; that it exhibits no resemblance of the original and characteristic manner of the Father of Poetry, as it wants his awful simplicity, his artless grandeur, his unaffected majesty. This cannot be totally denied, but it must be remembered that "necessitas quod cogit defendit", that may be lawfully done which cannot be forborne. Time and place will always enforce regard. In estimating this translation consideration must be had of the nature of our language, the form of our metre, and, above all, of the change which two thousand years have made in the modes of life and the habits of thought. Virgil wrote in a language of the same general fabric with that of Homer, in verses of the same measure, and in an age nearer to Homer's time by eighteen hundred years; yet he found even then the state of the world so much altered, and the demand for elegance so much increased, that mere nature would be endured no longer; and perhaps, in the multitude of borrowed passages, very few can be shewn which he has not embellished.

There is a time when nations emerging from barbarity, and falling into regular subordination, gain leisure to grow wise, and feel the shame of ignorance and the craving pain of unsatisfied curiosity. To this hunger of the mind plain sense is grateful; that which fills the void removes uneasiness, and to be free from pain for a while is pleasure; but repletion generates fastidiousness, a saturated intellect soon becomes luxurious, and knowledge finds no willing reception till it is recommended by artificial diction. Thus it will be found in the progress of learning that in all nations the first writers are simple, and that every age improves in elegance. One refinement always makes way for another, and what was expedient to Virgil was necessary to Pope.

I suppose many readers of the English *Iliad*, when they have been touched with some unexpected beauty of the lighter kind, have tried to enjoy it in the original, where, alas! it was not to be found. Homer doubtless owes to his translator many Ovidian graces not exactly suitable to his character; but to have added can be no great crime if nothing be taken away. Elegance is surely to be desired if it be not gained at the expence of dignity. A hero would wish to be loved as well as to be reverenced.

To a thousand cavils one answer is sufficient; the purpose of a writer is to be read, and the criticism which would destroy the power of pleasing must be blown aside. Pope wrote for his own age and his own nation: he knew that it was necessary to colour the images and point the sentiments of his author; he therefore made him graceful, but lost him some of his sublimity.

The copious notes with which the version is accompanied and by which it is recommended to many readers, though they were undoubtedly written to swell the volumes, ought not to pass without praise: commentaries which attract the reader by the pleasure of perusal have not often appeared; the notes of others are read to clear difficulties, those of Pope to vary entertainment.

It has, however, been objected with sufficient reason that there is in the commentary too much of

---

[4] For Pope's own comments on this translation, see above, 193-95. [Ed]

unseasonable levity and affected gaiety; that too many appeals are made to the ladies, and the ease which is so carefully preserved is sometimes the ease of a trifler. Every art has its terms and every kind of instruction its proper style; the gravity of common critics may be tedious, but is less despicable than childish merriment.

Of the *Odyssey* nothing remains to be observed; the same general praise may be given to both translations, and a particular examination of either would require a large volume. The notes were written by Broome, who endeavoured not unsuccessfully to imitate his master.

Johann Gottfried von Herder

Johann Gottfried von Herder (1744-1803) was the primary forerunner of German romanticism, and a leading figure in its first flowering, the so-called *Sturm und Drang* (storm and stress) movement. His prophetic pronouncements on art, language, history, anthropology, political theory, and a host of other fields directly influenced all of the great romantic thinkers, from Goethe to the Grimm, Schlegel, and Humboldt brothers, and from Hegel to Dilthey.

Born to poor parents, Herder attended local schools but was able, in the summer of his eighteenth birthday, to enter the University of Königsberg, where he studied under two massively influential thinkers, Immanuel Kant and Johann Georg Hamann. Two years later, in 1764, he left Königsberg to take up a teaching job in Riga, Latvia, where he wrote his two early (and precocious) volumes, the fragments on recent German literature (1766-1767) excerpted below, and *Kritische Wälder* (1769), an aesthetic treatise on the beautiful.

In 1770, just turned 26, Herder visited Strasbourg and met Goethe, who was five years younger; their meeting was a momentous occasion in the lives of both men, and in some sense for the future of German thought. Herder's ideas on the classics, on Shakespeare, on German folk songs, and other topics overwhelmed Goethe with their persuasive force, and profoundly influenced his later work; Goethe would later, in 1776 (the year after he had himself been invited there), invite him to Weimar as general superintendant and consistory councillor, where in close collaboration with Goethe he did his most important work, and where he was raised to the nobility the year before his death, in 1802. Like Goethe, Herder was something of a polymath, working in ten or fifteen fields simultaneously and significantly affecting the future of each; also like Goethe, but a decade or so earlier, Herder underwent a conversion from *Sturm und Drang* to a serene Grecian classicism sometime in the late 1770s. Due to a number of difficulties, however, some financial, some personal – Herder was a headstrong man who deeply resented working in Goethe's shadow – the two men were gradually estranged toward the end of Herder's life.

Herder's early *Fragmente* claim in their main title to be 'On the More Recent German Literature'; in fact they deal constantly, and closely, with the full range of German translations, mostly from the classics. Herder, like most of his Renaissance and Enlightenment predecessors (especially Leibniz in this volume), is most centrally concerned with the improvement of German literature through translation, and devotes a good deal of attention to issues like German verse forms, the use of mythology, the role of criticism and philology in the development of a national literature, and so on. His theoretical pronouncements on translation are scattered through these more practical considerations, always in the enthusiastic, hopeful, and somewhat impatient tones of a 23-year-old man.

The Ideal Translator as Morning Star
From 'On the More Recent German Literature: Fragments' (*Über die neuere Deutschen Litteratur: Fragmente*, 1766-1767)
Translated by Douglas Robinson

The best translator must be the best critic; if only one could run that backwards as well, and bind the two together ...

Where is the translator who is at once philosopher, philologist, and poet? He shall be the morning star of a new day in our literature ...

And a second and higher level: if only there were translators who wouldn't just study their author in order to transfer the meaning of the original text into our tongue, "but would also seek out his characteristic tonalizations, would capture the soul of his writing style, indeed the very strokes of his pen, his phrases and colourings, his ruling disposition, the genius and the heart of his poetry".[1] To be sure, this is a lot to expect; but for my ideal translator, still not enough. Most translators want to add their own two bits to the translation, in the preface, in the critical notes, in the writer's biography; most laud the writer in their preface, or list the various editions of their author. Then they clutter up the notes with tedious explanations that underestimate the reader's intelligence, or else with quarrelsome

[1] Litt. Br. Th. 18. [Au] Herder is quoting from his own *Literary Letters*, part 18. [Tr/Ed]

attacks on other scholars that the reader couldn't care less about, or a junk drawer full of philological pedantry. Then they crown all this with a translation of the author's life, and the book is finished: for the translator, his daily bread; for the publisher, a product; for the bookbuyer a book in his library. But for literature? Nothing! or a crying shame. Zero or negative volume. But –

If someone were to translate Homer for us, the father of poetry – what a timeless contribution to German literature and an invaluable aid to writers of genius; what a precious gift to the muse of antiquity and to our own language. For just as Homer has long been the source of all divine and human wisdom, just as he was the focal point of Greek and Roman literature, so has he been the greatest original for our own. A Homeric translation can be all this as well, if only it will rise above mere efforts and *become* the entire life of a learned person, and so show us Homer as he is, and as he can be for us. How wonderfully the English have paved the way for us! Thomas Blackwell's *Investigation* into Homer's life and works (and alas! this precious book, so well received in England, is but half-translated into German) addresses the sublime mystery by which "a concourse of natural causes conspired to produce and cultivate that mighty Genius" of Homer.[2] With the true critical spirit Blackwell brings clarity to this question out of the mysteries of Greek literature and history, and so provides a key to Homer. This treatise should serve as introduction – an introduction that is never so needed as when we approach the most ancient, the most divine, the most untranslatable Homer. After this come the ancients' essential investigations into Homer: what all did he become for them? What can and should he be for us? How must we use him without abusing him – without ever actually *becoming* him?

This is a start; what about the translation? On no account should it be prettified, like the abomination of desolation wrought by these Bitaubean new translators.[3] The French, too proud of their national taste, assimilate everything to it rather than accommodating themselves to the taste of another time. Homer must enter France a captive, clad in the French fashion, lest he offend their eye; must let them shave off his venerable beard and strip off his simple attire; must learn French customs and, whenever his peasant dignity still shines through, be ridiculed as a barbarian. We poor Germans, on the other hand – lacking as we do a public, a native country, a tyranny of national taste – just want to see him as he is.

Nor can even the best translation reach this goal with Homer without notes and glosses in the highest critical spirit. We will gladly make this journey with the translator, if only he would take us with him to Greece and show us the treasures he has found. Unaccustomed as we are to this sort of travel, even in part uninclined to it, he must be our tour guide, point things out to us – not as tourists interested in word thefts or tired old legends out of schoolbooks, but as pilgrims seeking the great state secrets of Greek literature. One knows what French glosses on the ancients come to: dissections of individual (often inessential) beauties, written to provide their readers with amusement, recreation, and entertainment. One knows how pedants elucidate the classics. But one also knows Grimm's notes on *Anacreon*, Ebert's on Young, and can envision from this dim dawning the coming of the day – how through Homer a public might be educated in the Greek taste. I wouldn't want such a translation to lack hexameters, let alone poetry; but they should be hexameters and poetry in the Greek style, if only to give us the opportunity to discern how far behind our own language and poetry lag. The task I set is a difficult one; but at least it will produce *some* sort of transposition of Homer's untranslatable beauties.

Language as Maiden
From 'On the More Recent German Literature: Fragments' (*Über die neuere Deutschen Litteratur: Fragmente*, revised edition, 1768)
Translated by Douglas Robinson

A language before all translations is like a maiden who has not yet lain with a foreigner and borne a child of mixed blood: for the time being she is still pure and innocent, a true image of the character of her people. She is also poor, obstinate, and unruly; and as she is, so is the original and national language.

Alexander Fraser Tytler

Alexander Fraser Tytler, Lord Woodhouselee (1747-1813), was a Scottish historian best known for his accessible syntheses of other people's work; a contemporary, Lord Cockburn, remarked that "his lectures were not marked either by originality of matter or by spirit, but though cold and general they were elegant and judicious". Born in Edinburgh the oldest son of William and Ann Tytler of Woodhouselee, he attended school in Edinburgh until 1763, when he was sent to an academy in Kensington; two years later, in 1765, he entered the University of Edinburgh, where he

[2] *Enquiry into the Life and Writings of Homer* (1735; facsimile reprint New York: Garland, 1970), 4. Herder translates this passage loosely (perhaps from memory) into German, rephrasing it in question form. [Tr/Ed]

[3] Referring to Paul Bitaubé, a contemporary of Herder's who had recently published prose translations of Homer into French. [Tr/Ed]

studied law. Called to the Scottish bar in 1770, he began to display an interest – but not much talent – in literature; in 1780 he was appointed joint professor (with John Pringle) of universal history at Edinburgh, and in 1786 received the full appointment. In addition to the 1791 *Principles of Translation* essay, he published in the eighties and nineties several volumes of local, legal, and universal history, and in 1802 moved on to a judgeship: that year he was appointed to the bench of the court of session, and in 1811, two years before his death at 67, he was constituted a lord of justiciary. Lord Cockburn describes him further:

> Tytler was unquestionably a person of correct taste, a cultivated mind and literary habits, and very amiable, which excellently graced, and were graced by, the mountain retreat whose name he transferred to the bench. But there is no kindness in insinuating that he was a man of genius ...

His *Essay on the Principles of Translation* is, like all of his work, bland, inoffensive, unoriginal, but extremely accessible, and is often cited as the last expression of the Enlightenment spirit in the theory of translation.

The Proper Task of a Translator
From *Essay on the Principles of Translation* (1791)

Chapter I

If it were possible accurately to define, or, perhaps more properly, to describe what is meant by a *good translation*, it is evident that a considerable progress would be made towards establishing the rules of the *art*; for these rules would flow naturally from that definition or description. But there is no subject of criticism on which there has been so much difference of opinion. If the genius and character of all languages were the same, it would be an easy task to translate from one into another; nor would anything more be requisite on the part of the translator than fidelity and attention. But as the genius and character of languages are confessedly very different, two opinions have thence arisen regarding the proper task of a translator. On the one hand, it has been affirmed that it is the duty of a translator to attend only to the sense and spirit of his original, to make himself perfectly master of his author's ideas, and to communicate them in those expressions which he judges to be best suited to convey them. It has, on the other hand, been maintained that, in order to constitute a perfect translation, it is not only requisite that the ideas and sentiments of the original author should be conveyed, but likewise his style and manner of writing, which, it is supposed, cannot be done without a strict attention to the arrangement of his sentences, and even to their order and construction.[1] According to the former idea of translation, it is allowable to improve and to embellish; according to the latter, it is necessary to preserve even blemishes and defects; and to these must likewise be superadded the harshness that must attend every copy in which the artist scrupulously studies to imitate the minutest lines or traces of his original.

As these two opinions form opposite extremes, it is not improbable that the point of perfection should be found between the two. I would therefore describe a good translation to be *That in which the merit of the original work is so completely transfused into another language as to be as distinctly apprehended, and as strongly felt, by a native of the country to which that language belongs as it is by those who speak the language of the original work.*

Now, supposing this description to be a just one, which I think it is, let us examine what are the laws of translation which may be deduced from it.

> It will follow,
>
> I. That the translation should give a complete transcript of the ideas of the original work.
>
> II. That the style and manner of writing should be of the same character with that of the original.
>
> III. That the translation should have all the ease of original composition.

Under each of these general laws of translation are comprehended a variety of subordinate precepts, which I shall notice in their order, and which, as well as the general laws, I shall endeavour to prove, and to illustrate by examples ...

---

[1] Batteux *de la Construction Oratoire*, Par. 2. ch. 4. Such likewise appears to be the opinion of M. Huet:

> *Optimum ergo illum esse dico interpretandi modum, quum auctoris sententiae primum, deinde ipsis etiam, si ita fert utriusque linguae facultas, verbis arctissimè adhaeret interpres, et nativum postremo auctoris characterem, quoad ejus fieri potest adumbrat; idque unum studet, ut nulla cum detractione imminutum, nullo additamento auctum, sed integrum, suique omni ex parte, simillimum, perquam fideliter exhibeat. – Universè ergo verbum de verbo exprimendum, et vocum etiam collocationem retinendum esse pronuncio, id mode per linguae qua utitur interpres facultatem liccat.*

Huet. de Interpretatione, lib. 1. [Au] See Batteux, above, 197-98, and Huet, above, 167. [Ed]

Chapter II

In order that a translator may be enabled to give a complete transcript of the ideas of the original work, it is indispensably necessary that he should have a perfect knowledge of the language of the original and a competent acquaintance with the subject of which it treats. If he is deficient in either of these requisites, he can never be certain of thoroughly comprehending the sense of his author ...

But a translator, thoroughly master of the language, and competently acquainted with the subject, may yet fail to give a complete transcript of the ideas of his original author ...

Where the sense of an author is doubtful, and where more than one meaning can be given to the same passage or expression (which, by the bye, is always a defect in composition), the translator is called upon to exercise his judgment, and to select that meaning which is most consonant to the train of thought in the whole passage, or to the author's usual mode of thinking, and of expressing himself. To imitate the obscurity or ambiguity of the original is a fault;[2] and it is still a greater to give more than one meaning, as D'Alembert has done in the beginning of the Preface of Tacitus ...

Chapter V

Next in importance to a faithful transfusion of the sense and meaning of an author is an assimilation of the style and manner of writing in the translation to that of the original. This requisite of a good translation, though but secondary in importance, is more difficult to be attained than the former; for the qualities requisite for justly discerning and happily imitating the various characters of style and manner are much more rare than the ability of simply understanding an author's sense. A good translator must be able to discover at once the true character of his author's style. He must ascertain with precision to what class it belongs; whether to that of the grave, the elevated, the easy, the lively, the florid and ornamented, or the simple and unaffected; and these characteristic qualities he must have the capacity of rendering equally conspicuous in the translation as in the original. If a translator fail in this discernment, and want this capacity, let him be ever so thoroughly master of the sense of his author, he will present him through a distorting medium, or exhibit him often in a garb that is unsuitable to his character ...

The characteristic of the language of Homer is strength united with simplicity. He employs frequent images, allusions, and similes; but he very rarely uses metaphorical expression. The use of this style, therefore, in a translation of Homer, is an offence against the character of the original. Mr Pope, though not often, is sometimes chargeable with this fault; as where he terms the arrows of Apollo "the feather'd fates", Iliad, l. 68., a quiver of arrows, "a store of flying fates", Odyssey, 22. 136: or instead of saying that the soil is fertile in corn, "in wavy gold the summer vales are dress'd", Odyssey, 19. 131;[3] the soldier wept, "from his eyes pour'd down the tender dew". Ibid. 11. 486.

Virgil, in describing the shipwreck of the Trojans, says,

Apparent rari nantes in gurgite vasto;[4]

which the Abbé des Fontaines thus translates: "A peine un petit nombre de ceux qui montoient le vaisseau purent se sauver à la nage".[5] Of this translation Voltaire justly remarks, "C'est traduire Virgile en style de gazette. Où est ce vaste gouffre que peint le poête, *gurgite vasto?* Où est l'*apparent rari nantes?* Ce n'est pas ainsi qu'on doit traduire l'Eneide". *Voltaire, Quest. sur l'Encyclop. mot Amplification.*[6]

If we are thus justly offended at hearing Virgil speak in the style of the Evening Post or the Daily Advertiser, what must we think of the translator who makes the solemn and sententious Tacitus express himself in the low cant of the streets, or in the dialect of the waiters of a tavern? ...

But a translator may discern the general character of his author's style, and yet fail remarkably in the imitation of it. Unless he is possessed of the most correct taste, he will be in continual danger of presenting an exaggerated picture or a caricatura of his original. The distinction between good and bad writing is often of so very slender a nature, and the shadowing of

---

[2] M. Huet, however, thinks otherwise, and his opinion is a necessary consequence from the strict method of interpretation for which he contends: *Verbum ambiguè dictum est, et duplicem admittit explicationem. – Certè res in medio posita ut erat, ita debuit consistere, et verbum anceps ancipiti verbo reddi, ipsaque sententiae ambiguitas repraesentari.* De Opt. Gen. Interpret. p. 27. Edit. Lond. 1684. [Au] See Huet, above, 168. [Ed]

[3] It is well known that the greater part of the *Odyssey* was not translated by Pope himself, but by some assistants, whom he employed and paid for their labours; but having revised the whole, and published the work under his own name, he is justly responsible for all its faults. [Au] See Pope, above, 193-95. [Ed]

[4] From book one of Virgil's *Aeneid*: lit. "appeared scattered crewmen, in whirlpool desolate", or in W. F. Jackson Knight's translation, which is closer to the one Voltaire attacks, "Some of the crew could be seen, one here one there, swimming in the waste of water". [Ed]

[5] The French reads literally: "In distress a small number of those who climbing the vessel try to save themselves by swimming". [Ed]

[6] "This is to translate Virgil in the style of the gazette. Where is the vast gulf the poet paints, *gurgite vasto*? Where is the *apparent rari nantes*? This is no way to translate the *Aeneid*". [Ed]

difference so extremely delicate, that a very nice perception alone can at all times define the limits. Thus, in the hands of some translators, who have discernment to perceive the general character of their author's style, but want this correctness of taste, the grave style of the original becomes heavy and formal in the translation; the elevated swells into bombast, the lively froths up into the petulant, and the simple and naif degenerates into the childish and insipid.[7] ...

Chapter IX

It now remains that we consider the third general law of Translation.

In order that the merit of the original work may be so completely transfused as to produce its full effect, [it is necessary, not only that the translation should contain a perfect transcript of the sentiments of the original, and present likewise a resemblance of its style and manner, but that the translation should have all the ease of original composition.]

When we consider those restraints within which a translator finds himself necessarily confined with regard to the sentiments and manner of his original, it will soon appear that this last requisite includes the most difficult part of his task.[8] It is not easy for one who walks in trammels to exhibit an air of grace and freedom. It is difficult, even for a capital painter, to preserve in a copy of a picture all the ease and spirit of the original; yet the painter employs precisely the same colours, and has no other care than faithfully to imitate the touch and manner of the picture that is before him. If the original is easy and graceful, the copy will have the same qualities, in proportion as the imitation is just and perfect. The translator's task is very different: he uses not the same colours with the original, but is required to give his picture the same force and effect. He is not allowed to copy the touches of the original, yet is required, by touches of his own, to produce a perfect resemblance. The more he studies a scrupulous imitation, the less his copy will reflect the ease and spirit of the original. [How then shall a translator accomplish this difficult union of ease with fidelity? To use a bold expression, he must adopt the very soul of his author, which must speak through his own organs.[9]...]

If the order in which I have classed the three general laws of translation be their just and natural arrangement, which I think will hardly be denied, it will

---

7 ----- *Sectantem levia nervi*
Deficiunt animique: professus grandia turget:
Serpit humi tutus nimium timidusque procellae. –
In vitium ducit culpae fuga, si caret arte.
Hor. *Ep. ad Pis.* [Au]

From Horace's *Art of Poetry*: "One promises the grand style, and is bombastic; another, oversafe and fearful of the storm, creeps along on the ground ... Effort to avoid a fault may lead astray, if it be not guided by art" (E.C. Wickham's translation). [Ed]

8 Tytler here quotes at length from Batteux in the original French; the quoted passage appears above, 196, from "but when we come to express, in another language" to "What opinion then ought we not to have of a translation performed with success?". [Ed]

9 The following observations by Cowper, though loosely thrown out, and a little deficient in precision of thought, contain much matter deserving of a translator's attention:

> There are *minutiae* in every language, which, transfused into another, will spoil the version. Such extreme fidelity is in fact unfaithful. Such close resemblance takes away all likeness. The original is elegant, easy, natural; the copy is clumsy, constrained, unnatural: To what is this owing? To the adoption of terms not congenial to your purpose, and of a context such as no man writing an original work would make use of. Homer is everything that a poet should be. A translation of Homer so made will be every thing a translation of Homer should not be. Because it will be written in no language under heaven. It will be English, and it will be Greek, and therefore it will be neither. He is the man, whoever he be (I do not pretend to be that man myself), he is the man best qualified as a translator of Homer, who has drenched, and steeped, and soaked himself in the effusions of his genius, till he has imbibed their colour to the bone, and who, when he is thus dyed through and through, distinguishing between what is essentially Greek and what may be habited in English, rejects the former, and is faithful to the latter, as far as the purposes of fine poetry will permit, and no farther: this, I think, may be easily proved. Homer is everywhere remarkable either for ease, dignity, or energy of expression; for grandeur of conception, and a majestic flow of numbers. If we copy him so closely as to make every one of these excellent properties of his absolutely unattainable, which will certainly be the effect of too close a copy, instead of translating, we murder him. Therefore, after all ***** has said, I still hold freedom to be indispensible. Freedom I mean with respect to the expression; freedom so limited, as never to leave behind *the matter;* but at the same time indulged with a sufficient scope to secure the spirit, and as much as possible of the manner. I say as much as possible, because an English manner must differ from a Greek one, in order to be graceful, and for this there is no remedy. Can an ungraceful, awkward translation of Homer be a good one? No: but a graceful, easy, natural, faithful

follow that in all cases where a sacrifice is necessary to be made of one of those laws to another, a due regard ought to be paid to their rank and comparative importance. The different genius of the languages of the original and translation will sometimes make it necessary to depart from the manner of the original in order to convey a faithful picture of the sense; but it would be highly preposterous to depart, in any case, from the sense for the sake of imitating the manner. Equally improper would it be to sacrifice either the sense or manner of the original (if these can be preserved consistently with purity of expression) to a fancied ease or superior gracefulness of composition. This last is the fault of the French translations of D'Ablancourt, an author otherwise of very high merit. His versions are admirable, so long as we forbear to compare them with the originals: they are models of ease, of elegance, and perspicuity; but he has considered these qualities as the primary requisites of translation, and both the sense and manner of his originals are sacrificed, without scruple, to their attainment.[10]

Novalis

Friedrich Leopold, Baron von Hardenberg (1772-1801), who took his penname Novalis from his family's former name De Novali, was one of the bright lights of German romanticism; unfortunately, he died in his late twenties of tuberculosis.

Novalis' parents were Protestant nobility from Lower Saxony. In 1790 he matriculated at the University of Jena to study law, and there met Friedrich von Schiller, who would become another major figure in German romanticism; the next year he transferred to the University of Leipzig, where he met Friedrich von Schlegel, later a prominent romantic philosopher and critic and the younger brother of August Wilhelm von Schlegel, to whom the letter printed below is addressed. Completing his studies at the University of Wittenberg in 1793, several years later he was appointed auditor to the government saltworks in Weissenfels, where in 1799 he became a mine inspector.

He was engaged to be married twice, once in 1794 to the fourteen-year-old Sophie von Kühn, who died of tuberculosis in 1797 before they were married, and again in 1798 to Julie von Charpentier; this time he was the one to die of tuberculosis before they could be wed. His first great poetic work, *Hymns to the Night* (1800), was written out of sorrow for Sophie.

All of the work Novalis is remembered for today was written in the last three or four years of his life, including the mythical romance *Heinrich von Offerdingen* (1802), the utopian social-theological essay 'Christendom or Europe' (1799), and the two collections of philosophical fragments, one of which appears below: *Blütenstaub* ('Pollen', 1798) and *Glauben und Liebe* ('Faith and Love', 1798).

Novalis makes the first tentative attempt to systematize the emerging romantic theory of translation in 1798, in his collection of philosophical fragments *Blütenstaub* ('Pollen'). By itself his tripartite system is fairly unprepossessing – it is of interest to us today largely because it so clearly anticipates Goethe's dialectic of almost two decades later – but Novalis does begin to twist the mainstream trichotomy in unmistakably romantic ways, moving past the mainstream concern for segmental units (word-for-word, sense-for-sense) to the visionary acts of grammatical ordering, transformation, and mythical integration.

Translating Out of Poetic Morality (1797)
From a Letter to A. W. Schlegel
Translated by Douglas Robinson

Weissenfels: the 30th November 1797.

... Well-meaning as the reviewer of your Shakespeare undoubtedly is, his review is anything but poetry. What could *not* be said about your Shakespeare – especially if one is willing to go to extremes? It is among translations what 'W. Meister'[1] is among novels. Do we have anything yet that even comes close? We Germans have been translating for so long, and the bent toward translating is so ingrained in us as a nation – there is, after all, no German writer of any substance who has not also been a translator, who in fact has not puffed himself up as much over his translations as over his original works – and yet there is nothing we are more ignorant about than translation. In Germany translation could become both a science and an art; and for the scientific observer, your Shakespeare would make an excellent canon. We are the only nation (barring the

---

version of him, will not that be a good one?
Yes: Allow me but this, and I insist upon it,
that such a one may be produced on my
principles, and can be produced on no other.
Cowper's Letters. [Au]

[10] The following apology made by d'Ablancourt of his own version of Tacitus, contains, however, many just observations; from which, with a proper abatement of that extreme liberty for which he contends, every translator may derive much advantage. [Au] See d'Ablancourt, above, 157-61. [Ed]

[1] Goethe's novel *Wilhelm Meisters Lehrjahre* ('Wilhelm Meister's Apprenticeship', 1794-1796). [Tr/Ed]

Romans) who feel so irresistably driven to translate and who have learned so immensely from it. Hence the many similarities between late-Roman literary culture and our own. This drive is a sign of the German people's primordial nobility – a sign of that blend of the cosmopolitan and the forcefully individual that is true Germanness. Only for us have translations been expansions. One submits to true translation out of a kind of poetic morality, out of the sacrifice of one's own desires – out of a genuine love of beauty and the literature of the fatherland. To translate is to write poetry, every bit as creative an undertaking as writing one's own works – and harder, and rarer.

In the end all poetry is translation.

Grammatical, Transformative, and Mythic Translations
From *Blütenstaub* ('Pollen', 1798)
Translated by Douglas Robinson

68. A translation is either grammatical, or transformative, or mythic. Of these, mythic translations are translations in the noblest style: they reveal the pure and perfect character of the individual work of art. The work of art they give us is not the actual one, but its ideal. These translations do not yet exist in any full or completed form; but there are clear traces of them in the spirit of many critical and descriptive pieces on works of art, or wherever a poetic spirit is thoroughly melded with a philosophical mind. In part, Greek mythology is a translation of this sort of a national religion; the Madonna of modern times is another such myth.

Grammatical translations are translations in the ordinary sense of that word. They require a good deal of learning but no more than expository writing skills.

Transformative translations, when they are authentic, body forth the sublimest poetic spirit; but they verge constantly on travesty, as in Bürger's iambic Homer, Pope's Homer, or French translations generally. In fact, the true translator of this sort must be an artist himself, must be flexible enough to give us the idea of the whole any way he likes. He must be the poet's poet: must be able to give voice simultaneously to his own *and* the poet's idea.

The genius of all humankind stands in very much the same relationship to every individual human.

Books are not the only things that can be translated by these three methods: anything can.

August Wilhelm von Schlegel

August Wilhelm von Schlegel (1767-1845), German scholar, critic, translator, and poet, was along with his brother Friedrich one of the most influential figures in the spread of German romanticism.

Born the son of a Lutheran minister, Schlegel studied classical philology and aesthetics in Göttingen, and by his late twenties (the mid-1790s) was writing actively for various periodicals, including Schiller's *Die Hören*; in 1798 he and his brother Friedrich founded the famous romantic periodical *Athenäum*, which they edited for two years. The same year he was appointed extraordinary (assistant) professor at the University of Jena and began his verse translation of Shakespeare; by 1810 he completed 17 plays, and the project was completed in the 1820s and 30s by Ludwig Tieck and others. He also translated extensively from the romance languages, including Calderón (1803-1809) and Dante. He was an Orientalist of note as well, and in the 1820s established Sanskrit studies in Germany, setting up a Sanskrit printing press and publishing a three-volume 'Indian Library' (*Indische Bibliotek*) of major literary works.

In 1796 Schlegel married Caroline Michaelis, the most brilliant and prominent woman among the German romantics; in 1803, however, she left him for his younger colleague at Jena, Friedrich W. J. Schelling, who had just published his groundbreaking book *System of Transcendental Idealism* a few years earlier at the age of 25. Caroline Schlegel's divorce and remarriage sparked an intricate web of intrigues among the romantic scholars then at Jena, and that combined with a concurrent quarrel with his mentor Johann Gottlieb Fichte, also at the time living in Jena, drove Schelling to a professorship at the University of Würzburg.

Schlegel too left Jena shortly after his divorce, joining Madame de Staël on her travels through Germany, Italy, France, and Sweden; in 1813-1814 he served in that last country as press secretary to the crown prince Bernadotte. In 1818 he accepted the post that he would hold until his death, professor of literature at the University of Bonn.

Schlegel's views on translation, written in his late twenties – indeed, as he himself later noted, it was his first extended piece of writing – were very much in the air in the last decade of the eighteenth century and the first two decades of the nineteenth; himself heavily influenced by Herder, Schlegel would in turn influence Novalis, Goethe, Schleiermacher, and others, with the result that the decades around the turn of the nineteenth century became in Germany one of the most striking confluences of theoretical activity in the history of the West.

Noble Rust
From 'Dante: On the *Divine Comedy*' (*Dante – Über die Göttliche Komödie*, 1791)
Translated by Douglas Robinson

I have sought to germanize Dante as faithfully as possible, for there is nothing in this poet that is without weight, and despite the enormous liberties he allows himself in language and expression there is a conscientious clarity to his thought. He was never willing to give up a single line of what he had to say – which explains why the constraints of metre so often drove him to deform constructions, use odd terms and phrases, and mangle words. I originally thought I would have to translate into rhyme and even, as far as possible, into Dante's *terza rima* rhyme scheme, lest I wrest him, as it were, out of his element.[1] Despite all my labours of love, however, it goes without saying that much was lost. I have not hesitated to use foreign and semi-archaized expressions and to allow rough spots in the language and verse form, but rather have actively sought to reproduce the character of the original as it struck me. To soften or prettify it would have been to destroy it.

The translation of poetry must be controlled by whether one directs one's efforts toward the work or its author. There are works, typical of highly refined eras, that reveal little of who the artist as person *is*, only what he *can do* – that empower us to judge only of his talents. Poetic perfection is the only goal of these works, and should be their only criterion of excellence. Aesthetic defects *per se* are irrelevant. In these cases, then, why should the translator not be permitted to spare his reader these defects, to smooth over the rough spots, to clarify obscurities, to rectify misrepresentations, to touch things up? On the other hand, the more identical the work's character is with its creator, the more it is a reflex imprint of his inner self, the more dutybound the translator is to render faithfully his idiosyncratic faults, his obstinacy, the gaps and misdirections in his education – for all these things are psychologically and morally significant, and often intimately intertwined with his noblest features. We want to perfect the work of art; we want the man as he is.

One sign numismatists use to determine the authenticity of an old coin is what is called 'noble rust' (*aeruga nobilis*), which on a copper coin is more valuable to an expert than gold; anyone who wished to polish it off would be taken at the very least for an ignoramus. This sign of antiquity is the only thing counterfeiters have been unable to duplicate. And there is a similar rust on people – on heroes, philosophers, and poets – which attests to something of astonishing importance, that their greatness is no mere result of culture and upbringing: that in an age of manuscripts, inexperience, and naivety they overcame these lacks on their own. Only an erstwhile Frenchman would coldly polish off that rust while describing or translating the work, just so he could smugly show off his shiny penny. Enough of this! And who's to say it won't be newly struck on the next coin?

For us, Dante's habit of mixing Latin into his poems lends many passages a comic air; his contemporaries must have responded differently. Not only were both languages more closely related in that period, their boundaries less clearly drawn than they are today; Latin also seemed more dignified than Italian, which was called the *lingua volgare*, while the former was used by scholars,[2] by the court, by the church, and in the mass. Thus Dante believed that a poem of so sacred a subject would be ennobled by the use of Latin. Besides, the words themselves often harboured something mysterious and reverence-inspiring that would have been lost in a translation into the vernacular.

At Once Faithful and Poetic
From *Something on Shakespeare In Connection with Wilhelm Meister* (*Etwas über Wilhelm Shakespeare bei Gelegen-heit Wilhelm Meisters*[3], 1796)
Translated by Douglas Robinson

More than thirty years ago, a writer [Christoph Martin Wieland] whose own fertility of spirit seemed to destine him least of all to become a translator undertook the Herculean task of germanizing the greater part of Shakespeare – and now his translations have become classics as well. The task was all the more daunting then, with fewer aids to knowledge of the English language and even in England little criticism on this often difficult, indeed here and there totally incomprehensible poet. Even so, his achievement was not

[1] What is distinctive about this meter, composed of ordinary eleven-syllable iambs, is its distribution into three-line *terzas*, so that the middle line in each stanza rhymes with the first and last lines of the next, thus looping lines and stanzas together into a long chain that comes to a close at the end of the poem by leaving the middle line of the last *terza* suspended. In German it was impossible to follow this rhyme scheme and still translate faithfully. Euphony helped solve this problem, since I was able to leave the middle line unrhymed and lose less than the Italian would have; this enabled me to germanize the main things, the poetry and its periods, its pauses, the distribution of its thought. [Au]

[2] In his *Convito* Dante apologizes at length for writing the commentary on his *canzone* in the *lingua volgare* rather than Latin. [Au] The *lingua volgare*, literally 'vulgar language' or vernacular, originally meant 'language of the people'. See Dante, above, 48. [Tr/Ed]

[3] Goethe's novel *Wilhelm Meisters Lehrjahre* ('Wilhelm Meister's Apprenticeship', 1794-1796). [Tr/Ed]

immediately recognized – not surprisingly, in fact, since our stage was then still largely dominated by vapid imitations of the French, and even our best plays were fashioned after the French model. Who would have guessed then that these barbarous, godlessly unruly plays, dimly rumoured to have been written by one William Shakespeare, would one day see the light of day on the German stage? Lessing, that staunch foe of prejudice, was the first to expose French tragedy for what it was, and to speak out forcefully on Shakespeare's behalf; and it was he who reminded the Germans, since they seemed to have forgotten, that they already had a translation of this great poet – a translation that, whatever its faults, had plenty to teach them before it was inevitably superseded by a better.[4]

He could not, of course, predict what the next few years would bring – what he himself would bring, in fact, through the heightened receptivity sparked by the style of his own plays, especially *Emilia Galotti*. When *Götz von Berlichingen*[5] appeared, that too, along with other things, inaugurated, both for better and for worse, a new era on our stage.[6] Not long before that he had lauded the peerless Briton in such glowing tones that his detractors, where not utterly convinced, were at least swept along with him; above all he drove home the truth that Shakespeare's work could not be measured by the rules and regulations of trendy prettification.[7]

As a result, just nine years after the appearance of Wieland's translation a new edition of that translation would no longer suffice; a need was felt for an improved German rendition of Shakespeare's collected works. Wieland himself was unable to take on this task, but fortunately it dropped into the lap of one of our most learned and cultivated literati [Johann Joachim Eschenburg], whose thorough grounding in English, unparalleled critical acumen, and painstaking perseverence gave the translation what it had thus far lacked, overall cohesion and detailed precision.

Now an even greater number of Shakespeare plays were openly venerated: they reached down from the stage and took possession of the viewer's soul, leaving behind an indelible impression. Our greatest actors found here a forum for their talents, which they had never before been so brilliantly inspired to develop.[8] He became more and more familiar to us, felt ever more at home in Germany. Even novices in foreign literature learned to utter his name with reverence, and one could assert boldly that the only people to whom he belonged more exclusively than the Germans were the English – for no other people, either in the original or in translation, have read him so extensively, studied him so profoundly, loved him so passionately, or admired him so perspicaciously.

Nor is this a mere passing fad; it is not that we have now grown accustomed to this form of dramatic poetry as we have of others, as we are always willing and able to accommodate ourselves to the customs and thought patterns of other nations. No, he is not foreign to us. We need not take a single step out of character in order to feel that he is 'wholly ours'. The sun can be blocked by fog, genius by prejudice; but until every last vestige of feeling for simplicity and truth is utterly extinguished among us, we will always return to him with love. His every indulgence meets with our own easy indulgence, for we are not naturally finicky (although we can be talked into it); the excesses of his imagination and feeling (is there anything in him *but* such excesses?) are precisely the ones to which we are ourselves most exposed, and his unique virtues are those valued above all others by every self-respecting German. By these I mean the virtues both

---

[4] In the *Hamburgische Dramaturgie*, p. 15. [Au] Lessing published that collection of brief drama reviews in 1767-1769; his tragedy *Emilia Galotti*, mentioned below, was performed in 1772. [Tr/Ed]

[5] Goethe's play published in 1771 and (revised) in 1773; modelled directly on Shakespeare as rendered by Wieland, the play inspired a Shakespeare cult in Germany and became the first great work of the romantic *Sturm und Drang* movement. [Tr/Ed]

[6] For worse, let it be understood, not at all through Shakespeare's or Goethe's doing. It has been argued that disregarding the conventional rules made it easier to write bad plays. Not true! That has always been exceedingly easy. It is true enough that many of our own day's theatrical bombs could not have been dropped in any earlier time. But there were also plenty of mediocre pieces of the old cut that have since been forgotten. And the topical and the nonsensical – these were even more numbingly boring. It doesn't matter what formal rules you obey if your subject is trivial. The Aristotelian unities have been commended and condemned, conserved and contested, deified and dirt-trodden – but all the unities in the world won't save the thousands of dreary courtly dramas and Russian family portraits from the oblivion they deserve. [Au] Schlegel's argument here is only implicit: it is a refutation of the notion that Shakespeare and Goethe, by breaking down the classical unities, have been directly responsible for the recent plethora of bad plays. [Tr/Ed]

[7] In his pamphlet 'On the German Race and Art'. [Au] Published in the late 1750s. [Tr/Ed]

[8] Not without pain do I recall Schröder playing Shylock, Hamlet, and Lear, and then, it is said, withdrawing from his public. [Au] Ludwig Friedrich Schröder was the greatest German actor of his age; as theater manager he was also responsible for introducing Shakespeare (also the early plays of Goethe and other Sturm und Drang playwrights) to the German stage. The 'withdrawal' Schlegel refers to may be his removal from Hamburg to Vienna in 1780; however, he returned in 1785 and was producing plays (among them his own) at this writing. [Tr/Ed]

of the poet and of the man, insofar as the one is revealed in the other, for in Shakespeare both are bound up intimately together: he wrote as he lived. In everything that poured forth from his soul[9] there lives and speaks an ancient simplicity, a deeply human authenticity, an unpretentious greatness, an innocence sacred and sure, a mildness godlike and true.

His life was gentle, and the elements
So mix'd in him, that Nature might stand up
And say to all the world: "This is a man!"[10]

The key to these glorious treasures is, of course, the English language – not a golden key, as Gibbon rightly calls the Greek language, but one alloyed from more metals than ours, and equally precious ones. No matter how common a knowledge of English is in Germany, it is rarely sufficient to keep one's pleasure from constantly being disrupted by Shakespeare's many difficulties – even, in some cases, to prevent one's being discouraged from reading him altogether. Even among those who can read him in his entirety (barring those passages where the English themselves need a commentary due to obsolete words, unknown allusions, or corrupt redactions), how few there are who can read him without stumbling, or can respond to his finer beauties, his subtle nuances of phrasing, on which the harmony of a poetic work rests, with a native feel and familiarity! How few are so proficient at English pronunciation that they can read him aloud with the proper force and grace! Yet these things must always enormously enhance the impression he makes, for poetry is not a dumbshow.

A reader of Shakespeare capable of all the above would certainly be willing, even if just for variety's sake, to take a break on native soil, in the cool shade of his poems – if only those poems could be transplanted without too severely damaging the beauty of their leafwork. Wouldn't a translation, then, be a desirable thing? "We already have one, and a good one it is, too, accurate and complete". True enough! We had to have that much before we could wish for more. The satisfaction of needs provokes a longing for luxury; the best there is is no longer good enough for us. If Shakespeare should and could only be rendered into prose, we would have to make do with the versions we already have. But he is a poet, in the sense also that he writes in verse. If only it were possible to reproduce him at once faithfully and poetically, to follow the letter of his meaning step by step and still grasp some fragment of his innumerable and unutterable beauties – which do not dwell in the letter but float above it like a breath of the spirit! It's worth a try. Plasticity is our language's finest quality, and it has already accomplished much along these lines that in other languages has either miscarried or met with less success. Never say die!

[9] Even in his nondramatic poems, especially in his sonnets, which were so long neglected that of all his editors Steevens and Malone were the first to feel it worth the trouble even to mention them, and then unfavourably. These poems breathe with a man's childlike instincts, even where the child's trifling wit distorts their phrasing. Hence their value: they seem to have been inspired, judging from the little we know of the poet's life, by a real-life friendship and love. [Au]

[10] *Julius Caesar* 5.5.73-75, slightly misquoted: "This *was* a man!" [Tr/Ed]

Poetic Translation an Imperfect Approximation
From 'The Works of Homer by Johann Heinrich Voss' (*Homers Werke von Johann Heinrich Voss*, 1796)
Translated by Douglas Robinson

Of all the languages into which prose and verse translations of Homer have been made, from the Syriac to the English, none can approach the original text with such happy fidelity as German. The very fact that the metrical art of the ancients, insofar as we know and can apply it, has only found a secure foothold in German gives it a distinct advantage over other languages, which may be more modern and even in part more elevated, but whose development has been less well-rounded. True enough, the Italians, the Spaniards, the French, and the English attempted to introduce Greek meters into their languages earlier than the Germans; but their attempts didn't catch on – indeed they are usually mentioned only as academic curiosities. Another prodigious advantage we have lies in our liberty to combine several primary concepts in a single word, a capacity that, like Latin itself, the romance languages lack almost entirely.

There are, however, other reasons that make these latter languages unsuitable for translating Homer in particular, despite their classical appearance and their Greek background. As their simple beginnings were coarse and crude, so has their later cultivation been utterly erudite – a product of the schools, not a blossom of enhanced nature. Their poetic (especially their epic) forms bore the stamp of Alexandrian artistic diligence. Their heroic verse was too haughty to regress back to the unadorned yet golden modesty, the familiarity and innocent purity of the ancient singers. I am not concerned here with the phraseological exercises of the moderns; but had the ancient Latin work in this area survived, we might well find the *Odyssey* of Livius Andronicus in all its laborious fidelity more homeric than the polished imitations of the Augustan era.

These ruminations bring us to a concern that gets more to the heart of the matter – indeed, on which everything else depends. There is in the spirit of our language, as in the character of our nation – if indeed the two are not one and the same thing – a most versatile malleability. The German passion to know the foreign truly and deeply; the German willingness to enter into the most exotic thought patterns and the most outlandish customs; the ardour with which Germans embrace authenticity of content, no matter how unusual the garb in which it appears – all this does often degenerate into a mania for imitation and a foolish predilection for the foreign, but it also always moves steadily toward a free appropriation of the best. By ruling out certain directions their national culture might have taken, our fellow European citizens have rendered themselves incapable of entering deeply into a uniquely foreign mode of being; as a result they are stuck with either domestic poverty or domestic wealth. The fact that they have among them so many supposed lovers of classical antiquity should not fool us; how many of them must first mentally dress a Greek or Roman up in some modish attire before they can find him attractive? Whereas the German inclination is unquestionably to read the ancients in their own sense, and the very fact that the mother tongue must act as go-between for every newly acquired image and mood is precisely what gives our language its advantage in translating them in their true spirit – necessarily in concert, though this is but a different aspect of the same quality.

This malleability can in fact be used to derive standards for a German translation of Homer, standards that it would be silly to apply to a French or even an English translation – though this only makes the undertaking that much more difficult and its successful completion that much more laudable. Language in itself is an inert tool; it waits upon the artist to unpack its potential with his deft touch. That this is not always an easy task is amply attested by the many miscarried attempts at a poetic translation of Homer, some of which were written by well-known authors like Bodmer, Stolberg, and Bürger (I mean his experiments with an iambic *Iliad*) just before or concurrently with the appearance of Voss's first *Odyssey*. At first this latter met deservedly with the unanimous approval of the experts. But experts make up a small minority of the populace, and it was not to be expected either that this translation would be enthusiastically taken up by the masses or that its translator would be adequately recompensed for it. Nevertheless, this foreseeable indifference failed to dampen Voss's noble ardour for his task, and twelve years later he enriched our literature for the second time with a completely revised *Odyssey* and a newly germanized *Iliad*. The human dedication, so rare in our day, and the scrupulous rigour with which this writer strove to attain that which he realized was perfection; the still more intimate acquaintaince with the ancients and the broader sphere of learned expertise, of which he had by then given so much proof; the mature self-reliance of a poetic spirit who in his *Luise*[11] knew how to apply the manner of the Ionian singer to simple and natural descriptions that were picked up from everyday life but yet remained pure, delicate, and beautiful; the painstaking work on the German hexameter, in the construction of which, at least rhythmically, and perhaps expressively as well, he surpassed even Klopstock, the master of this art – all this warranted the expectation that this new translation would leave scarcely anything to be desired, since its predecessor had already achieved so much. And if this expectation was not fully met, the fault probably lay more in the principles that guided Voss's work than in any deficiency in the way they were followed. Principles must be tested thoroughly; all the critic can do is object attentively to deviations, against which so many writers are protected by their careless haste.

As Wieland has so rightly noted (in the *Teutsche Merkur* 1795, p. 12), in a translation of Homer fidelity, or rather, to get away from the notion of literal precision so commonly associated with fidelity, *truth* must be the translator's highest, indeed virtually his only, mandate. There are works whose re-creation allows artistic discretion as much free play as their original production did. Even very divergent copies of these may have merit if, independent of their originals, they give their readers pleasure. This approach becomes more hazardous, however, when the work's attractions arise partly out of its author's unique personality – when the author has unwittingly represented not only external objects but his inner subjectivity as well. Nothing is singly or separably present in a single being; its characteristics are all wrapped up in a coherent whole, so that one can distinctly feel it, indeed almost see it, when their steadfast inwardness does not permit conceptualization. As a result even apparently minor alterations are enough to cast a false light over the whole work. In a word: individuality cannot be pieced out; it's an all or nothing affair.

What we admire and love in the *Iliad* and the *Odyssey* is not the poet's person, which indeed is not to be found on its own in heaven or on earth – which is to say, *anywhere*. The quest for his person has produced so many gloriously perverse interpretations of his poetry that one takes them for the felicitous effusions of an unusually gifted spirit, the willful concoctions of a fine mind. What makes Homer famous, what will maintain his fame among the entire human race in perpetuity, is not the man he was but the form of humanity he assumed, one of the greatest forms of its kind, impelled by a vast natural law. Homer

[11] Voss's *Luise* (1795) was a naturalistic portrait of the life of a country pastor; it inspired Goethe to write *Hermann und Dorothea*. [Tr/Ed]

is the spokesman of his age, and this lends him a greater distinction than his mere personality could ever attain. To clothe him in an alien form is thus to smear not an individual character, but a collective one. Distorted images of this most ancient of the ancients, the first Greek as it were, must inexorably lead to error regarding the entire course of Greek culture, for his childlike poetry fires and unfolds the germ of everything, the noblest and loveliest, to which this people has ever given rise. Nor may one believe that this entertaining poet will let himself be split off from the enlightening witness of antiquity; anyone who cannot understand this cannot enjoy him. We all know of beautiful souls who find in Homer a reflection of their own faces, and who labour to discover in him bedraggled beauties that simply aren't there. Only a person of banal taste could fail to recognize the ghastly mismatch between form and content in, say, Pope's translation – or better, Pope's parody.

But who can discern Homer as he truly is? To this end the worst approach is the philological one; with it even the countless writings to which learned Greeks devoted themselves would still leave much obscurity to spare – even if all of them had survived. But the double relationship of words, on the one hand outwardly to objects that we have never seen before, so that we have to come to know them through the words themselves, and on the other inwardly to a circle of images to which we have almost no hope of access, leaves us vulnerable to the most manifold deceptions. How easy it is to import later scientific developments back into a language that is entirely lacking in abstractions, or in precise concepts for anything dealing with the phenomenon or functioning of the inner person – a language that only distinguishes and combines fleeting sensory perceptions! The medium is all the more deceptive in that the forward march of culture has often taken the signified through a long series of shifts, while the signifier has remained the same. The impact of the poetic work depends in the end only marginally on the meaning of words and phrases as conveyed by the understanding; it is rather the living breath of speech, a plenitude of animated sounds, that most utterly sensitizes us to poetry – especially nature poetry, which always precedes the fine arts and the sciences. Our intuitive sense of these complexly intertwined stimuli, at once powerful and frail, is only unfailing and unmediated in our native language.

To a certain extent that sense can be acquired in a foreign language, even a dead one; but only by comparing the different ways it is used in everyday life, in familiar or lofty prose styles, and in the various poetic genres. With Homer's poetry we are lacking in all such points of comparison, for excepting the remnants of Hesiod, he stands alone in his era. We are completely in the dark as to the state of ordinary language in his time and region; and given the fact that his era still lacked a written prose literature, and as far as we know only possessed the one style of poetry, it is only through the relationship of Homer's poetic expression to this everyday usage that the magnitude of his poetry can be determined with certainty. To be sure we can surmise that the language of the Olympian muse and her followers did not diverge greatly from that of the rest of humanity, just as in general in those days the mythical world, the most ancient source of poetry, still lay close to the real one; but in specific cases it is often difficult to tell ornamentation from necessity, lofty flights of fancy from the purely sensory perception of truth ...[12]

This detailed analysis of individual passages, which the diligence of the excellent translator obliges the critic to undertake, has brought us to an issue about which we have heretofore deliberately said nothing, so as not to confuse the various factors involved. We have been considering Voss's work purely as an interpretation[13] of the Greek, not as its transposition into the German. The concept of translation contains both of these relationships. For a translation must enable a language to enter fully into the space of another, so as to follow not only its rules but those conventions as well that cannot be determined by general prescriptions. Given the multiple and incommensurable divergencies of languages, and the reliance of poetry not merely on overall meaning but on the subtlest nuances, all poetic translation must forever remain an imperfect approximation.

It goes without saying that every liberty allowed the original poet must be fully allowed the translator-poet as well, who is so greatly at a disadvantage. But it is equally obvious that every language has certain established bounds, primordial and deep-rooted limits, that cannot be overstepped without being quite rightly accused of speaking no true language at all, merely an argot of one's own concoction. No exigency is justification enough for taking the latter course. Were it truly impossible to give us an *Iliad* in pure German, unmarred by hellenisms, it would be better to renounce all attempts to attain one.

A recent subject of debate has been the extent of the individual's right to contribute to the development of the language. That individual writers, especially poets, can have an enormous shaping influence on their language is well attested by the history of languages. And much that has been decried at first as a corruptive influence has later entered the language and undeniably

[12] There follow twenty-odd pages of analysis of specific passages in Voss's translations. [Tr/Ed]

[13] *Dolmetschung*, meaning both interpretation and translation, here however specifically in the sense of rendering the contours of the original. [Tr/Ed]

ennobled it. We should not, therefore, reject without careful consideration proposals that an obvious gap in a language be filled with some new construction. Like all human devices, speech too, that fair deed of our higher destiny, strives incessantly for improvement, and the individual performs a true service in becoming an instrument of this collective yearning. That service has but a single indispensable proviso, that he not tear down while building up: the proposed innovation must not be at odds with what is already firmly established. If language were a mere hodgepodge of things similar and dissimilar, a formless mass, there would be no objection to one's changing or expanding it at will; every enrichment, without exception, would be an improvement. But it is not that; it is a coherent totality, or at least professes to be progressively becoming one. Everything in it is attracted or repelled according to the laws of resemblance and kinship; collective forms flow through it, breathe life into its clay, and bring a binding force to bear on it. The simpler, more inclusive and cohesive its laws are, the more perfect its organization will be; the greater the freedom that arises in line with these laws rather than in opposition to them, the better suited it will be to poetic use. Excessive positive legislation that leaves little or no space in which to develop original talents is a pernicious thing in language as in politics. If German is in truth as malleable as it is held up to be, this is not a problem for us, at least in comparison with some other languages. But that just makes us all the more cognizant of our obligation not to force anything upon it that is inimical to its nature, anything that it cannot melt down into homogenous matter. The ability to recreate oneself in the image of a foreigner is only truly praiseworthy when one has autonomy to retain in the process, and does in fact retain it. Malleability without one's own spirit – what would that be but a self-declared nullity?

Projecting Oneself into Foreign Mentalities
From *History of Classical Literature* (*Geschichte der klassischen Literatur*, 1802)
Translated by Douglas Robinson

The translation[14] of poetry is an exceedingly difficult art on whose principles one could write a lengthy treatise – if one had a good deal of grammatical and philological detail to start with. Let me however make just a few brief remarks on it now.

This art, barring a few exceptions, is actually a fairly recent invention, one reserved in fact for German constancy and fidelity. In antiquity the Romans – at least at first, while they were still, not without violence, modelling their language on Greek forms – seem to have made, as far as we can tell from a few fragments, reasonably faithful if also rather awkward and uneven translations of Greek poetry. In fact, translating started them off. Subsequently, in the so-called Golden Age of their poetry, once they had developed their own system of diction, they seem increasingly to have lost this ability; and if one was not content with free imitations, as was mostly the case, their translations became more mannered and nondescript. In addition, Greek and Latin are closely related, almost like two dialects of a main language – a situation in which poetic re-creation tends to be highly and almost effortlessly successful, as it is, for example, between the Italians and Spaniards. Other nations have impressed upon their poetry the rule-governed rigidity of a thoroughly conventional phraseology, thus making it flat-out impossible to translate poetry into their language – French, for example, and to a lesser degree contemporary English as well. It is almost as if they expected foreigners to conform their dress and behaviour to the local customs; as a result they never really get to *know* a foreigner. If they ever push themselves on past the comfort zone to maximum accuracy, they do it in prose, which changes everything: they leave us only the inert ingredients, for the breath of life has flown. Literality is not fidelity. Fidelity entails making the same or a similar impression, for impressions are the essence of the thing. Prose versions of poems are therefore reprehensible. Metre should never be mere outward ornamentation, nor is it ever in authentic poems; it is rather one of the most original and constitutive elements of poetry. Indeed, given that every metrical form has a differentiated meaning, and that, as is easily shown, each has a specific place or position in which it necessarily belongs (as in general a unity of form and essence is the goal of all art, the more thoroughly metrical forms permeate and reflect each other, the more perfect they become), one of the first principles of the art of translation must be to render a poem, so far as the target language allows, into the same meter as in the original. One is sorely tempted to break this rule, partly due to the great difficulties it entails, partly out of entrenched habit, and must make double the effort to obey it strictly. All one must do to make the apparently impossible come true is never despair of attaining what has thus far been unattainable. The German language has the great merit of being till now the only one in which new metres introduced from classical languages have succeeded so far as to enter general circulation – and the first efforts in this area were made no more than half a century ago, only recently even greater perfection has been achieved in this area, and there remains still much to be done.

[14] *Dolmetschung*; this word's usage was influentially restricted to the rendering of commercial and similar texts by Schleiermacher a decade later, in a 'lengthy treatise' much like the one Schlegel calls for here. See Schleiermacher, below, 226. [Tr/Ed]

These metres may seem to some, even after everything celebrated poets have done with them, of dubious value for the creation of original poetry, or at least of potentially popular poetry. In translating the classics, obviously, they are indispensable. In the area of accented rhymed verse, German translators have recently begun to cultivate the metrical forms of the Italians and Spaniards, whereas regrettably we earlier followed the French, later to some degree the English. If we would only obey the principle mentioned above, we could translate tolerably from every major language into our own.

Not that I mean for this to be viewed as a structural advantage of German alone; with a little determination and enthusiasm for the task at hand any other culture could become equally receptive to expanded variety. It's just that it is particularly strong in our language, due to the greater pains it has taken to emulate inwardly the agitations and vibrations of the soul that correspond to all external sequences: the willingness of the German national character to project itself into foreign mentalities, indeed to surrender utterly to them, is so integral to our language as to make it the deftest translator and mediator for everyone else. It goes without saying that in the end even the finest translation is at best an approximation to an indeterminable degree; for otherwise one would have to achieve precisely the same results with totally different tools and means, which is in the strict sense impossible. Hence Cervantes, whose inventive mind indisposed him to translation, compared poetic translation to the reverse side of a Brussels tapestry, where the figures remain recognizable but are distorted by the crisscrossing threads.[15] For most of the works he had before him, that would have been good enough; for what I have sought to offer you along these lines it is but a fair portent of better things to come.

The Speaking Voice of the Civilized World
From *History of Romantic Literature* (*Geschichte der romantischen Literatur*, 1803)
Translated by Douglas Robinson

After all the above, our language is still something of which we should be – not exactly proud, but at least aware: aware of what we so abundantly possess. And for this we have a collective characteristic to which we have been predisposed since time immemorial, but which could only be properly developed in a period of artistic growth. I mean the complex flexibility of our language, which suits it perfectly for nestling up close to the most varied foreign languages, following their contours, imitating their metres, virtually stealing their sounds. There are other languages that do not so much translate as produce stylized travesties, which reveal the extent to which they themselves are dominated only by stylization, not a true style. The Germans, on the other hand, faithful and upright as they are in all things, are also faithful translators. I won't stop here to enumerate our accomplishments in the appropriation of classical poetry and metre, as that would take me too far afield from my present purpose. But as far as the modern languages of Europe are concerned, with luck German can translate from all of them, and can contend as well with the monosyllabic brevity of English as with the mellifluent syllables of the south. It seems to have a special preference for the more closely related forms of the Nordic languages. "The German is innately driven", as Friedrich Schlegel says,

> to love the foreign; especially the beauty of the south draws him to it with its irresistable charms. Proud of his nobility and Nordic strength, he still yearns incessantly for the bright landscapes of the south, as if for his primordial home. This pull is as old as history itself. This it was that scattered the bands of German heroes all across the southern provinces of the Roman Empire. This it was that fettered Germany to Italy in the Middle Ages, and during the Crusades ultimately led to the attempt to conquer the Orient.[16] At present, with the political existence of the German nation in part completely altered, in part brought to utter wrack and ruin, that all-consuming pull can only surface in the domain of scholarship and art – a domain in which no fetters curb the human spirit's natural desire for expansion and conquest.[17]

So today we make peaceful raids into foreign countries, especially the south of Europe, and return laden with our poetic spoils.

Still, this skill and industry in translating that I have been calling our claim to fame is dismissed by many as a bad habit. They call it both the cause and the effect of intellectual laziness and servility, insisting that it deprives us of the ability to create and invent on our own. But it is easy to show that, on the contrary, translating poetry objectively *is* true writing, *is* creating anew. Indeed if someone were to discourage translating altogether, one would have to reply that there is nothing

[15] See above, 149. [Ed]

[16] Meaning anything east of Western Christianity – in this case Palestine. [Tr/Ed]

[17] The quote is taken verbatim from F. Schlegel's 'Beiträge zur Geschichte der modernen Poesie und Nachricht von provenzalischen Manuskripten' ('Contributions to the History of Modern Poetry and a Report on Provençal Manuscripts'), *Europa* I, 2, 49. [Au]

the human spirit *can* do but translate: everything it does is a form of translation. To develop this idea fully would again take us too far afield; suffice it to say that higher poetic re-creation has a nobler purpose than the production of ordinary workmanlike translations as a helping hand for a sorry literary tradition. It is designed for nothing less than the unification of the best qualities of all nationalities, to enter fully into their thoughts and feelings, and thus to build a cosmopolitan centre for all humanity. Universality, cosmopolitanism is the truly distinctive German characteristic. What for so long left us lacking in external brilliance, at least in comparison with more one-sided nations, but in fact for that very reason left the determined efficiency of other nations behind – our lack of direction, which gave us the positive power of directional versatility – must subsequently bring about our superiority. It is, therefore, no mere sanguine optimism to suppose that the time is not distant when the German language will become the speaking voice of the civilized world.

Johann Wolfgang von Goethe

Johann Wolfgang von Goethe (1749-1832) was one of the greatest of all German writers and, despite his later rejection of the movement, the major figure in German romanticism. Goethe towers over German culture and literature like Dante over the Italian, Shakespeare over the English, Pushkin over the Russian – and the fact that he paused here and there in his 133 volumes of collected works to remark upon translation has helped make the German theoretical tradition one of the world's richest bodies of work in the field.

Born into the upper middle class of Frankfurt am Main, son of a wealthy retired lawyer and the daughter of Frankfurt's mayor, Goethe grew up with what we would call every advantage – not only social and financial but cultural and intellectual as well, as his mother Katharine early fostered his love of imagination and make-believe. In 1765 he was sent to the University of Leipzig to study law like his father; while he went somewhat grudgingly, preferring to study classics at the University of Göttingen, he found kindred spirits among the faculty and cultural dons of the city, and thoroughly steeped himself in art and architecture, music and drama, ancient civilization, novels and fairy tales.

In 1768 poor health brought him home to Frankfurt, where during his long convalescence he steeped himself in mystical writings and introspective self-discovery. Upon his recovery his father sent him to study law at the University of Strasbourg, where he met the great German philosopher J. G. Herder, who was to shape his thought about poetry and culture profoundly. Having published two volumes of poetic apprenticework while still at Leipzig, he now began to bring out the highly charged, energetic work that made him famous and influenced an entire epoch, soon to be called *Sturm und Drang* or 'storm and stress': the Shakespearean play *Götz von Berlichingen* in 1771 and 1773, numerous lyrical hymns, and, most importantly, *The Sufferings of Young Werther* in 1774. *Werther*'s enormous popularity actually caused a rash of copycat suicides across Europe: dozens of restless, impassioned young men longed to die as romantically as their literary hero, and did.

In the midst of all his literary activities, including editing a literary review, Goethe was supposedly practising law; but when in 1775 Duke Charles Augustus of Weimar invited him to visit and encouraged him to stay, Goethe gladly dropped the law (and an unwelcome betrothal) and made Weimar his home – he lived there almost six decades, until his death in 1832. The young duke admired Goethe immensely and piled political responsibilities on him, eventually making him minister of state and raising him to the peerage; Goethe, feeling provincial and middle-class, struggled hard to acclimate himself to the court and aristocratic ways, and largely succeeded, partly with the help of his lover Charlotte von Stein, a court official's wife to whom Goethe wrote over 1500 love letters and many famous poems.

In 1786 he travelled hastily and in great hugger-mugger to Italy, in whose architecture and painting he found a Grecian serenity that soon converted him out of his youthful 'Gothic' or romantic sensibility to an Olympian classicism. The immediate literary products of this new stance were *Iphigenie auf Tauris* (1787), *Roman Elegies* (1788-1789), *Torquato Tasso* (1790), and the first fragments of *Faust* (1790), each of which individually and all of which collectively sealed his reputation as the major literary figure of the day. In 1788 he took Christine Vulpius into his home; they had several children and lived together until 1806 before he legally married her. In between inspecting mines, overseeing the issue of army uniforms and the implementation of irrigation schemes, and accompanying his duke to war in France (1792), he continued to write, from 1794 to 1805 in close collaboration with the great German dramatist Friedrich von Schiller, whose romanticism he deplored but whose poetic and philosophical sensibility he greatly admired. It was through Schiller, and after Schiller's death in 1805 through the Schlegel brothers in Jena, that Goethe began to integrate his early *Sturm und Drang* work with his more recent classicism, under the new rubric 'romanticism'; it cannot have hurt that he was regarded as the greatest romantic poet by the Schlegels and Novalis, who called him 'the viceregent of poetry upon earth'.

It is in this period that Goethe wrote his passing fragmentary, aphoristic remarks upon translation, which was of central concern to romantic thinkers: in his autobiography, *Dichtung und Wahrheit* (1811-1814), in his 1813 homage to the great German translator and novelist Wieland at his death, and, most importantly, in his attempt to bring together the East of Persian poetry with the West, *West-Östlicher Divan* (1819).

Goethe was also a scientist of some renown: a botanist, an anatomist, a psychologist, and a physicist who was widely respected in his own day for his achievements in those fields. This work was never as original as his poetry, however, and has not stood the test of time; what remains interesting about his scientific work today is his constant attention to the phenomenology of scientific discovery, his ongoing reflections on the psychology of his own work.

Goethe was now world-famous; pilgrims flocked to Weimar to meet him, speak with him, sit at his feet. Still he found time to write, notably on two projects that had engaged him all his adult life: having written *Wilhelm Meister's Apprentice Years* upon his arrival in Weimar in 1795-1796, he now wrote *Wilhelm Meister's Travels* (1821-1829); and having published fragments and part one of *Faust* in 1790 and 1808, he finished the poem a few months before his death with the famous couplet "The eternal-feminine / draws us onward".

Prose Translations
From *Poetry and Truth* (*Dichtung und Wahrheit*, 1811-14)
Translated by Robert R. Heitner

Then Wieland's translation appeared.[1] It was devoured, and put into the hands of friends and relatives with my recommendation. It was to the advantage of us Germans that several of the significant works of foreign nations were first adapted for us in a light and lucid way. The prose translation of Shakespeare, by Wieland and then Eschenburg, was suitable reading for everyone and could circulate quickly with great effect because it was generally understandable. I honor meter and rhyme, for that is what makes poetry poetry, but the part that is really, deeply, and basically effective, the part that is truly formative and beneficial, is the part of the poet that remains when he is translated into prose. This residue is the pure, complete substance, which a dazzling external form can simulate, when it is lacking, or conceal, when it is present. Consequently, when a youth's cultural development is just beginning, I consider prose translations more profitable than poetic ones. Boys, of course, feel obliged to make a joke of everything, and one can see how they are amused by the sound of words and the beat of syllables, and destroy the profound substance of the noblest works with a kind of parodistic mischievousness. Therefore I suggest for consideration whether a prose translation of Homer should not soon be undertaken. Of course, it would have to measure up to the present standards attained by German literature. I leave this and everything aforesaid to the discretion of our worthy pedagogues, whose broad experience best qualifies them in such matters. There is just one more thing I would mention in favor of my proposal, namely Luther's translation of the Bible. The fact that this excellent man transmitted a stylistically most varied work and its poetic, historical, imperious, didactic tone to us homogeneously in our mother tongue has benefited religion more than if he had tried to imitate precisely the special characteristics of the original. Efforts have been made subsequently, in vain, to render the Book of Job, the Psalms, and other songs enjoyable for us in their poetic form. A simple translation always remains best for the masses, who have to feel an effect. Those expert translations that compete with the original actually only serve as entertainment for scholarly circles.

[1] Of Shakespeare. Christoph Martin Wieland translated 22 Shakespeare plays between 1762 and 1766. [Ed]

The Two Maxims
From *Oration in Memory of Wieland, Our Noble Poet, Brother, and Friend* (*Rede zum Andenken des edlen Dichters, Bruders und Freundes Wieland*, 1813)
Translated by Douglas Robinson

There are two maxims for translation: the one requires that the foreign author be brought over to us so that we can look upon him as our own; the other that we cross over to the foreign and find ourselves inside its circumstances, its modes of speech, its uniqueness. As all educated people know well enough from exemplary models, both approaches have their strong points. Our friend, who here as elsewhere sought the middle path, tried to combine the two; but in borderline cases, as a man of feeling and taste, he preferred the former.

Translations
From *West-Östlicher Divan* (1819)
Translated by Douglas Robinson

There are three kinds of translation. The first familiarizes us with the foreign country on our own terms. For this, a simple prose translation is best; for as prose completely sublates every poetic property and drags poetic enthusiasm itself down to a common water-level, at least at first it serves us best precisely because it startles us with the wonders of the foreign right in the midst of our ordinary lives, our national at-homeness. Without our even realizing what is happening to us, it sparks in us a borrowed but nonetheless authentic elevation of spirit. This is the sort of impact Luther's Bible translation will have on readers of all eras.

It would have been beneficial for the *Nibelungen*, for example, to have been rendered into serviceable prose from the beginning, and marketed as a popular book; then we would have felt the full force of its strange, its solemn, its sombre, its sublime chivalric spirit. Whether this project is still a good idea, or even feasible, let those who are most familiar with such antiquities judge for themselves.

This approach is followed by a second epoch in which one seeks to project oneself into the circumstances of the foreign country, but in fact only appropriates the foreign meaning and then replaces it with one's own. I want to call this kind of era the *parodistic*, in the purest sense of that word. For the most part those who feel called to this sort of undertaking are gifted people, and in fact the French employ it whenever they turn their hands to the translation of poetry; Delille's work has examples of it by the hundred. The French, who invariably insist on making foreign words feel right on their tongues, do the same to feelings, thoughts, even things: they demand for every foreign fruit a surrogate grown in their own soil.

Wieland's translations, too, were of this sort; he too had his distinctive understanding and taste, which he assimilated to the ancient or other foreign culture at his own convenience. This brilliant man can be considered the representative of his time; his impact has been enormous because, once he had appropriated something and reframed it for others, if it pleased him it pleased and delighted his contemporaries as well.

But because one cannot abide long in either perfection or imperfection, and one transformation always leads to another, this second epoch brought us to a third, the last and highest of all. Here one seeks to make the translation identical with the original, so that the one would no longer be in the *stead* but in the *place* of the other.

This approach met with the strongest resistance at first, for in clinging so closely to his original the translator more or less relinquishes his own country's originality, and creates a 'third' for which the masses are not ready. Some education of their tastes is inevitably necessary before the translation will find its audience.

One such translator was Voss, who can never be praised highly enough. Voss failed to satisfy the public at first, but gradually they 'heard' their way into his style, made themselves at home in it. Those of us who have followed what has been happening, what new versatility has burgeoned among the Germans, what rhetorical, rhythmical, and metrical advantages are now available to clever and talented young writers, the appearance among us of germanized foreigners like Ariosto and Tasso, Shakespeare and Calderón, even twice and three times over[2] – we can only hope that literary history will record plainly who first set off down this path in the face of numerous and sundry obstacles.

Von Hammer has made similar efforts with Oriental masterpieces, whose formal contours are best followed closely. How much more profitable are the passages of our friend's translation of Ferdowsi than those of an adaptor – an example of which appears in the *Fundgruben*.[3] We believe that this manner of reworking a poet is the most unfortunate mistake a hard-working and competent translator can make.

Since these three epochs of translation can be repeated and reversed in every literature, however, and the approaches they represent can be employed simultaneously, there is still today a place for a prose translation of the *Shah-nemah* and the work of Nezami. One could skim through it quickly to get the main gist, to take pleasure in its historical, fabulous, and generally ethical elements, to become gradually more conversant with its moods and its habits of thought, until at last we grew akin to it, became, as it were, its blood-brothers.

Think of the quite decisive acclamation we Germans accorded a translation like that of the *Sakuntala*:[4] we can attribute its success to the ordinary prose into which the poem was broken down. Now, though, it is high time we had a translation of the third type, one that would follow the various dialects, rhythms, metres, and prose phrasings of the original and thus make it new for us, delightful and familiar in all its uniqueness. There is a manuscript of this eternal work in

---

[2] By Goethe's day Ariosto's *Orlando Furioso* (1516) had been translated as *Der Rasender Roland* by Werder (1626), Heinse (1781), and Gries (1804-1808). Tasso's (1544-1595) *Gerusalemme Liberata* (1581) had been translated as *Befreiter Jerusalem* by Werder (1632-1636) and Gries (1804-1808). Shakespeare's plays had been translated by Wieland between 1762 and 1766, by Eschenburg into prose in 1775-1782, by A. W. Schlegel between 1797 and 1810, and by Voss and his sons in 1818-1829. Calderón had been translated into German by Schlegel in 1803-1809. [Tr/Ed]

[3] Von Hammer's journal of Oriental studies, the *Fundgruben des Orients*. [Tr/Ed]

[4] Georg Forster translated Kalidasa's *Abhijnanasakuntala* from William Jones's English translation into German in 1791. [Ed]

Paris; some German living there could win our undying gratitude by undertaking such a task.

The English translator [Horace Wilson] of 'Messenger of the Clouds', or 'Meghadûta', is similarly deserving of our praise, if only because one's first exposure to such a work is always a landmark in one's life. His translation is, in fact, of the second era, paraphrastic and supplementary, cajoling the ear and the mind of the northeasterner with its five-footed iambs. Our own Kosegarten has translated a few verses directly from the original language, and so earned my gratitude, for his lines give us quite a different impression than the English version. In addition, the Englishman has indulged in the transposition of motifs, which the practised aesthetic eye instantly discerns and condemns.

Let us conclude these remarks with a word on why we call the third epoch the last. A translation that seeks to be identified with the original approximates, finally, the interlinear version; in its attempt to enhance our understanding of the original it leads us onward, drives us on toward the source text, and so finally closes the circle in which the alien and the familiar, the known and the unknown move toward each other.

The Translator as Matchmaker
From *Maximen und Reflexionen* ('Maxims and Reflections', 1826)
Translated by Douglas Robinson

In translating, quest toward the untranslatable; there you will catch your first glimpse of the foreign country and its language.

Translators should be thought of as busy matchmakers, praising a half-veiled beauty as worthy of our love: they excite an irresistible yearning for the original.

On Carlyle's German Romance (1828)
Translated by Ellen von Nardroff and Ernest H. von Nardroff

To clarify the title of this work we should point out that the volume contains samples of Romantic literature, including fairy tales, selected from works of German authors who have distinguished themselves in this style. There are stories of varying length by Musäus, Tieck, Hoffmann, Jean Paul Richter and Goethe, translated into flowing, graceful English. Particularly noteworthy are the introductory notes on each author. We commend them highly, as we do the author's earlier biography of Schiller,[5] and recommend them to our newspapers and journals their translation and publication, unless that has already been done unbeknownst to us. The biographical material is presented with care and provides essential knowledge about each author's character and its influence on his writings. Here, as in Schiller's biography, Mr Carlyle evidences an objective, clear and deep understanding of German literary matters. He makes the particular concerns of our nation his own, he gives every author his due, each in his own category, and thus resolves to some extent the conflicts unavoidable within the literature of any nation. For to live and to be active means forming factions and taking sides. No one is blamed for struggling to attain position and rank, which will furnish him a livelihood and provide him the influence to ensure further success.

This struggle within a nation often long obscures the literary horizon. The outsider, however, waits for the dust to settle, the haze to disappear and the fog to lift; then he can see those distant regions with their areas of light and shade distinctly, and he observes them with the serenity of one gazing at the moon on a clear night.

At this point I would like to recall a few observations which I wrote some time ago. Though it may be objected that I am repeating myself, I would hope that repetition may occasionally serve some purpose.

It is evident that the best poets and writers of all nations have for some time been concentrating their efforts on universal human concerns. In every specific literary mode, whether its content is historical, mythological, mystical or fictional, we increasingly see a writer's national and individual characteristics illuminated from within by these universal concerns.

Although a similar concern prevails in everyday life, pervades even what is brutal, savage, cruel, false, selfish and deceitful on this earth, and seeks to spread benevolence everywhere, we do not have the right to hope that universal peace will result. But we do have hope that unavoidable controversies will gradually become less acrimonious, wars less cruel and victory less arrogant.

What points and works toward this goal in the literatures of nations, is what all nations have to recognize. We must get to know the particular characteristics of nations to understand them, to be able to have dealings with them. For these idiosyncrasies are like language and currency: they not only facilitate dealing among nations, they make them possible.

The surest way to truly achieve[6] universal tolerance is to accept the particular characteristics of

[5] Published in London in 1825 and sent by Thomas Carlyle to Goethe, along with the *German Romances* volume, in April, 1827; Goethe reviewed the biography this same year. Carlyle had translated Goethe's *Wilhelm Meister* into English in 1824, and Goethe wrote an introduction to the German translation of the Schiller biography when it appeared in 1830. [Ed]

[6] Translation slightly modified; the Nardroffs have "to truly universal tolerance", omitting Goethe's verb, which is *erreichen*. [Ed]

individuals and whole peoples, yet at the same time to adhere to the conviction that the truly valuable is characteristized by its being part of all mankind. For some time now the Germans have been contributing to such mediation and mutual acceptance. He who studies German finds himself in the marketplace where all nations offer their wares. He plays the role of interpreter while enriching himself.

And that is how we should see the translator, as one who strives to be a mediator in this universal, intellectual trade, and makes it his business to promote exchange. For whatever one may say about the shortcomings of translations, they are and will remain most important and worthy undertakings in world communication.

The Koran says: "God has given each people a prophet in its own language". Thus every translator is a prophet among his people. Luther's translation of the Bible has had the greatest impact, even though critics quibble and carp to this day. And what is the purpose of that gigantic effort of the Bible Society, but to transmit the gospel to every people in its own vernacular?

Friedrich Schleiermacher

Friedrich Schleiermacher (1768-1834) was a German theologian who is generally credited with the creation of modern Protestant theology – what is commonly known as 'liberal' theology. Among philosophers he is known as the founder of hermeneutics, a romantic approach to interpretation (of the Bible as God's word, for example) based not on absolute universal truth but on each individual's inner feeling and intuition.

Schleiermacher came from a clerical family: his father was a military chaplain, and his mother had many clergymen in her ancestry. His later theological work was heavily influenced by two years he spent in his teens at a school run by the 'Herrnhuters' or Moravian Brethren, a pietistic sect that stressed the joys of salvation and an intimate relation with Jesus – rather than the gloomy emphasis on sin and carnality and the fear of the Lord that characterized much Lutheranism of the time. He later described his hermeneutical theology as Herrnhuterism "of a higher order". He attended the Moravian seminary at Barby for the two years after his graduation from the school, but hated the deathly dogmatism of the place, and in 1787 left there for the University of Halle, where he steeped himself in the philosophical works of Immanuel Kant – his first and lasting nudge in the direction of romanticism.

Upon passing his examinations in reformed theology in 1790, Schleiermacher moved through a series of jobs (including tutor, assistant pastor, and pastor) and wrote a series of books (including *On Religion* in 1799 and *Soliloquies* in 1800) that by 1804 would lead to his appointment as professor of theology at the University of Halle; fleeing Prussia in 1807 due to the invasion of Napoleon, he moved to Berlin, where he lectured and preached until his appointment to a professorship in the new university in 1810, a position he held until his death. The new university was largely planned by the great romantic philosopher and philologist Wilhelm von Humboldt, whom Schleiermacher befriended and helped with the plans.

Schleiermacher's theological writings were extremely controversial, and made him many enemies – as well as winning him many loyal friends and supporters. Some of his rivals even inflamed the Prussian king against him to the point of having him banished from the realm – an edict that was never enforced. Nevertheless, he had an immense impact on German religious culture, helping bring about a rapprochement not only between romantics and theologians – his project in *On Religion* – but between Prussian Lutherans and Calvinists as well. He was active in curricular reform for theological studies (*Brief Outline of the Study of Theology*, 1811) and permanent secretary of the Royal Academy of Sciences in Berlin, where he delivered thirteen important lectures between 1811 and 1830, the third of which, delivered June 24, 1813, was 'On the Different Methods of Translating'.

His importance for the romantic theory of translation cannot be overestimated. 'On the Different Methods of Translation' is the major document of romantic translation theory, and one of the major documents of Western translation theory in general. Schleiermacher argues dualistically, in a down-branching tree diagram that at every argumentative juncture splits off an unwanted branch, until only his lofty ideal is left: bringing the reader to the author, or training the target-language readership to accept, even to crave, translations steeped in the foreign flavour of their originals.

On the Different Methods of Translating (*Ueber die verschiedenen Methoden des Uebersezens*, 1813)
Translated by Douglas Robinson

Everywhere we look we meet up with the fact that utterances are rendered, in one form or another, from one language to another. If on the one hand this brings people halfway around the world from each other into contact, and allows a language to assimilate words and phrases from another language that hasn't been spoken in centuries, on the other hand we find this same phenomenon within the confines of a single language as well. For not only are the different regional dialects of a people and the different developmental stages of a language or dialect over the centuries in a strict sense different languages, requiring translation for communication between them; even contemporaries who speak the same dialect but come from different social classes and cultural backgrounds, especially when they do not often come into social contact with each other, require a similar mediation in order to communicate. And do we not frequently feel compelled to translate the speech of people who are quite like us but of a different cast of mind? – that is, if we feel that the same words in our mouth would take on a different meaning, or at least be weighted differently, more strongly or more weakly, in theirs, and that if we wanted to say what they meant, we would have to use totally different words and phrases. It will then come to us, as we bring this feeling into sharper focus, incorporate it into our thinking, that we are *translating*. Sometimes we even have to translate our own words, when they feel alien and we want to make them truly our own once again. Nor is this ability used only in transplanting into foreign soil the scholarly and artistic accomplishments of a language, so as to expand their sphere of influence; it is also used in trade between two peoples, and in diplomacy between independent governments, wherever two people wish to speak to each other on an equal footing without recourse to a dead language.

Needless to say, we do not intend here to cover everything included within the wide scope of this subject. The need to translate within one's language or dialect, a more or less fleeting emotional need, is too much restricted in its impact to the passing moment to require other guidance than that of gut feelings; if it were submitted to rule, it could only be the kind of rule that impels people to that moral state in which the mind is kept open to that which is more alien, less akin to oneself.

If, then, we set this aside and focus our attention on translation from a foreign language into our own, here too we can distinguish two kinds of translation – not absolutely discrete kinds, since that is rare, but, let us say, with overlapping boundaries; still, clearly enough distinguishable if one keeps their extremes in mind. The *interpreter* works in the world of commerce, while the *translator proper* works in the fields of scholarship and art. If these definitions seem arbitrary, given that interpretation usually means work with oral texts, translation work with written ones, forgive me; they not only fit the present need, but are actually not so far removed from the old definitions. Verbal art and scholarship require writing to render their works permanent; to interpret scholarly or artistic works orally would be as pointless as it seems impossible. In the business world, on the other hand, writing is only a mechanical contrivance; oral interaction is primary, and a written interpretation should in fact be regarded as a secondary transcription of an oral one.

Closely related to interpretation in spirit and nature are another two, which, however, due to the greater complexity of the objects with which they deal, tend toward the realm of translation, the one toward art, the other toward scholarship. Every transaction involving interpretation is a procedure that is comprehensible in both languages; and when a translation of purely narrative or descriptive writings entails a similar procedure, it has a good deal to do with interpretation. The less the author of the original text makes his presence felt in it – the more he has simply acted as the apprehending organ of an object and followed the order of space and time – the more closely does a rendering of the text approximate a mere interpretation. And so the translator of newspaper articles and ordinary travel brochures approaches the work of the interpreter, and may seem absurd if his work begins to feel more demanding and as a result he wants to be seen as having worked as an artist. Conversely, the more intensely the work is dominated by the author's unique ways of seeing and making connections, the more thoroughly it is ordered by free choice or personal experience, the more irresistibly it will move into higher artistic realms. The translator of this sort of work must then also bring a different set of powers and proficiencies to his task, and gain a different order of familiarity with the original author and language than the interpreter.

On the other hand, every transaction involving interpretation is generally the stipulation of a specific case, according to certain legal relationships; the verbal transfer takes place only for those participants sufficiently familiar with these relationships, which are articulated in both languages by law, by custom, or by bilateral agreement. Transactions by which new legal relationships are established, whatever the formal resemblances, are in fact different. The less susceptible these are to consideration as specific examples of a recognized general principle, the more scholarly knowledge and discretion is required to compose them, and the more technical and linguistic knowledge the translator will need to render them. On this double scale, then, the translator rises ever higher above the interpreter until he reaches the true realm of translation: where all work revolves around the cultural products of art and scholarship, characterized on the one hand by the author's free use of his personal combinatory powers, on the other by the spirit of the language, inscribed with an entire system of seeing and feeling; where the object reigns no more, but instead is itself ruled by thinking and feeling, indeed is objectified and thus comes into being only in and through speech.

How then shall we ground this significant distinction, which everyone discerns even in the gray middle areas, but which shines most brightly at the furthest extremes? In the business world one deals mostly with visible, or at least precisely defined objects; every transaction has in a certain sense an arithmetic or geometrical character, so that number and measure invariably lend a helping hand. True, some commercial concepts incorporate, in the ancients' phrase, the greater and the lesser and so find expression in a continuum of words that in ordinary speech remain hazy in denotation and volatile in connotation; but in the business world even these concepts soon settle into stable usage through law and custom. As a result, so long as the speaker doesn't make careless mistakes or try to deceive listeners with deliberate ambiguities, he will be plainly understandable to anyone well-versed in the subject and the language, with only trifling divergences in usage. As to the question of what expression in one language is equivalent to which in the other, here there is rarely any doubt that cannot be instantly settled. Translating in this field is thus a merely mechanical task that can be performed by anyone with a modest proficiency in both languages, and where, so long as obvious errors are avoided, there is little difference between better and worse renditions.

In the transplantation of artistic and scholarly works, on the other hand, two possibilities arise that alter the situation completely. For if everything in two languages corresponded exactly, one to one – word to word, concept to concept, inflection to inflection, connective to connective, and all corresponding elements with the same extension and relationships, so that the two languages were different only to the ear – then all artistic and scholarly translation aimed at conveying the contents of a written or spoken text would be precisely as mechanical as in the business world, and it would be said that, except for the impact of phonetics and intonation, every translation placed the foreign and the native reader in precisely the same relation to the original author and work.

But of course nothing like this is true of real languages, at least of those divergent enough that they cannot be considered dialects of the same language; and the greater the distance between the two languages either chronologically or genealogically, the less true it is that any given word in one will correspond precisely to one in the other, or that an inflection in one will unify the same complex of relationships as any conceivable counterpart in the other. Since this 'irrationality', as I call it, permeates every element in two languages, it will certainly affect every aspect of social intercourse as well, the realm of interpretation; but it presses far less forcefully upon the social, and might as well have no effect at all. There words signifying potentially significant objects and actions have already been validated, as it were; and any precautions an empty and overprudent sophistry might want to take against one word possibly assuming greater consequence than another are immediately damped out by the thing itself.

The situation is totally different in art and scholarship, and generally wherever thought, one with the word, reigns more securely than the thing of which the word is but an arbitrary and yet well-established sign. For how infinitely difficult and intricate the business becomes here! What accurate knowledge, what command of both languages it then requires! And how often, with a similar sovereign command of the subject matter and the languages involved, and sharing the belief that no perfect equivalent can be found, do two translators differ as to which rendering most closely approximates the original. This is equally true of the most vivid poetic images and of the most inward and universal scholarly terms.

But the second thing that makes translation a totally different business from mere interpretation is that, whenever speech is not bound to visible objects or outward facts that it is expected simply to verbalize, whenever in fact what speakers seek to verbalize is their own spontaneous thought processes, their relationship to language will be dual, and their speech will be rightly understood only insofar as this relationship is rightly apprehended.

On the one hand, all humans are under the sway of the language they speak; they and their entire thinking are a product of that language, so that it is impossible to think with complete clarity anything that lies beyond its boundaries. The gestalt of their concepts, the nature and the limits of those concepts' connectability – all this is prescribed for them by the language in which they were born and raised, which thus binds cognition and imagination.

On the other hand, all free-thinking people with any mental initiative at all also play their part in shaping their language. For how else but through such intervention could that language have grown from its raw primordial state to its more mature development in scholarship and art? In this sense, then, it is each person's vital force that moulds forth new forms out of the clay of language, at first purely for the fugitive purpose of communicating a fleeting state of consciousness; only some of these forms will take root in the language and, by shaping other users of the language, continue to spread. One might even say that it is only to the extent that speakers have this sort of transformative effect on language that they deserve to be heard beyond their immediate sphere. For the very repeatability of language, the fact that it can be reproduced identically a thousand times over, necessarily causes it to fade quickly; the only utterances that last are those that forge a new moment in the life of the language.

This is why every free and noble utterance asks to be perceived from two perspectives: on the one hand through the spirit of the language from whose elements it was made, as a representation bound and conditioned by that spirit and then vividly reproduced by it in the speaker; and on the other through the speaker's felt sense of it as his act, something that could only have emerged out of, and can only be explained as the product of, his essence. Indeed every utterance of this sort is only truly understood in the higher sense of that word when these two perspectives are apprehended in their dialectical linkedness, so that one knows which of the two is ascendent in any given segment (or the totality) of the discourse. One cannot understand the utterance as an action performed by the speaker unless one has an attendant gut sense of just how and where the power of language has laid hands upon that speaker, where the verbal lightning has snaked down out of the sky of thought, how and where the linguistic forms have seized and held the errant imagination. Nor can one understand the utterance as a product of language and as an externalization of its spirit unless, feeling that, say, only a Greek could have thought and spoken like that, only this language could have had this particular impact on a human mind, one also has the gut sense that only this author could have thought and spoken in this particular Greek mode: only he could hold and mould the language in just this way; only his living possession of the language's treasures, his ear for measure and euphony, his intellectual and imagistic powers could manifest themselves like this. And if understanding at this level is difficult enough in a single language, and requires a precise and profound penetration into the spirit of language and the author's unique character, how much more advanced an art will it not be to understand the products of a far foreign tongue!

To be sure, having mastered this art of understanding through the most ardent efforts, through the accumulation of extensive and exact knowledge of the language and the history of the people that speak it, and through the most sensitive and deeply felt criticism of individual works and their authors, a reader – and *only* this kind of reader – might want to make all this understanding of the great classics of art and scholarship available to his compatriots and contemporaries. But the closer this type of reader comes to his task, the more precisely he tries to define the goals of such work and the means available for pursuing those goals, the more buried he will feel in doubt and indecision. Given two people as far apart as the author of the original and the potential reader of the translation – people who don't even speak each other's language! – is it really advisable to bring them into a relationship as intimate as that between the author and the source-language reader? Suppose on the other hand that the translator desires only to provide the target-language reader with some simulacrum of his own pleasure and understanding, fraught, to be sure, with traces of his labours and feel for the foreign; how does he achieve the latter, let alone the former, with the means at his disposal? If the target-language readers are to understand, they must grasp the spirit of the language native to the author, they must be able to gaze upon the author's inimitable patterns of thinking and meaning; but the only tools the translator can offer them in pursuit of these goals are their own language, which nowhere quite corresponds to the author's, and his own person, his own inconsistently clear understanding of, and vacillating admiration for, the author. In this light, does translation not seem a foolish undertaking?

It is not surprising, then, that some should despair of ever reaching that goal – some even, if I may be permitted to say so, before they begin to think clearly about it – and have devised two other methods of making acquaintance with works in a foreign language, by which some of these difficulties are removed by force, others wisely circumvented. These methods arose not in quest of the true artistic and linguistic meaning of the works, but rather, on the one hand, out of intellectual necessity, and on the other as a display of their intellectual ingenuity; as a result, in both methods the idea of translation as we have explored it here is utterly renounced. The two are *paraphrase* and *imitation*.

Paraphrase would prevail over the irrationality of languages, but only mechanically: "If I can't find a word in my language that corresponds to one in the original", it says, "I still want to try and match its value by adding restricting and expanding modifiers". Thus it slogs its way heavily through piles of slack details, torn between a burdensome 'too much' and a torturous 'too little'. It may succeed in reproducing the content within narrowing margins of error, but in so doing it abandons all attempts to convey the impact of the original; for the living utterance has been rendered irrevocably inert, pushed beyond all sense that it might have sprung from the breast of a human being. The paraphrast manipulates the elements of both languages as if they were mathematical symbols, reducible to the same value by addition and subtraction; this manipulation prevents the apparition of the spirit of *either* language, the original or that transformed. If the paraphrase further attempts to indicate psychologically the vague and vanishing traces of thought connections, with parenthetical fillers that it drives in like road markers – thus seeking, especially in difficult works, to serve in lieu of a commentary – then it is even less of a translation.

Imitation, on the other hand, gives in to the irrationality of language, conceding that no exact duplication of a verbal art work can ever be made in another language, and that, given the divergence of languages, to which the divergence of so many other things is connected, there is nothing to do but rework the original as a kind of after-image, an imitation. This would be a whole whose parts diverge markedly from the parts that made up the original whole, but which approximates the impact of that original as closely as the different materials allow. An imitation of this sort is no longer that work itself, nor is it even an attempt to represent the spirit of its language effectively; it is far closer to the truth, in fact, to say that many new elements are introduced to displace the original's foreignness. An imitation is rather an attempt to take the differences of language, morals, and education into account in order to create a text whose effect on the target-language reader will be as close as possible to that of the original on the source-language reader. The imitator thus sacrifices the identity of the original work on the altar of similarity of effect. Believing that no unmediated relationship is possible between the original author and the reader of the imitation, the imitator will not work to bring them together, but will focus all his attention on the target-language readership, seeking to make an impression on them that is like that once made by the original on readers of its own language and era.

Of these two approaches, paraphrase is more commonly employed in scholarly translations, imitation in the fine arts; for just as everyone admits that a work of art loses its music, its lustre, its very art in the process of paraphrase, so is no one likely to have undertaken the folly of freely imitating the content of a scholarly masterwork. But neither approach can satisfy one who has been pierced through with the beauty of the original, who would extend the sphere of its influence to those who speak his language, and who conceives translation in the stricter sense. Given their deviation from this stricter sense, paraphrase and imitation cannot be explored more fully here; they are only here to mark off the boundaries of our true investigation.

But what paths are open to the true translator, one who would bring those two utterly unconnected people together, the source-language author and the target-language reader – and would aid the latter, without banishing him from the sphere of the target language, in attaining as accurate and thorough an understanding and enjoyment of the former? I believe there are only two. The translator either (1) disturbs the writer as little as possible and moves the reader in his direction, or (2) disturbs the reader as little as possible and moves the writer in his direction. The two approaches are so absolutely different that no mixture of the two is to be trusted, as that would increase the likelihood that the writer and reader would miss each other entirely; it is important, therefore, that one or the other be followed as closely as possible.

It should be immediately apparent, in any case, both that the two are very different and that they are in fact related. For in approach 1 the translator works to compensate for his readers' unfamiliarity with the source language, by sharing with them the very image and impression he has gained through familiarity with the work as written in the original language, and in so doing nudging them toward that (for them truly alien) position which he has come to occupy. If on the other hand – this would be approach 2 – the translation would voice a Roman author, say, in a German context, allowing him to address Germans as if he had originally been German, then its goal must not be to assimilate the author to the translator (with whom, after all, the former speaks not German but Latin) but to haul him bodily into the German reader's world, making him or her their peer. Approach 1 (reader-to-author) will achieve its own perfection when one can say that, had the Latin author learned German as well as the German translator has Latin, that author would have translated the original Latin work into German precisely as the translator did. Approach 2 (author-to-reader), on the other hand, in which the author is displayed not as he would have translated his own Latin work *into* German, but rather as he would have written *as* a German born and bred, has another standard of perfection: here one should be able to say that, were the German readers metamorphosed into experts on and contemporaries of the original author, they would feel about the work precisely as they do now – now that the author has become German – about the translation.

The author-to-reader method (2) is obviously what people mean when they say that a translation should read as if the author had originally written it in German; and it should be immediately clear just how different in every detail the translation process it entails must be when compared with that of the reader-to-author approach (1), and how incomprehensible and ineffectual the results would be if one were to change methods in the middle of a project. And I submit that these are the only two translation methods with a clearly defined goal; there is no third. In fact no other approach is possible. The source-language author and the target-language reader must either meet at a middle point, which is always that of the translator, or the one must cross over to the camp of the other. And only one of these two possibilities can properly be called translation; for the other could only occur if, in our example, the German readers possessed a perfect command of Latin, or, even better, if the Latin language perfectly possessed and transformed *them*.

Whatever else one says about translation after the letter and translation after the sense, translation faithful and free, and the other oppositions currently bandied about – all these, including those that claim to be different methods, must finally be referred back to the two named above, even if, in terms of accuracy and error, virtue and vice, the use of different methods will make a difference in our understanding of what is faithful and true to the sense, or of what is too literal or too free.

What I intend to do, therefore, is to set aside all specific questions on the subject already discussed at length by the experts, in order to explore the most general aspects of both methods, hoping to clear the ground for an understanding not only of the strong points and impediments of each, but of how each best realizes the goals of translation and where each reaches the limits of its applicability. A general overview of this sort leaves two things to be done, to which this treatise is but a mere introduction: one, a directive could be compiled for each method, with reference to the various types of utterance; and two, a comparison and evaluation of actual translations could be made, the finest efforts of translators following either method. Both investigations would shed a good deal of new light on the subject; but I must leave them for others, or at least for another occasion.[1]

The method of translation that seeks to give the German reader the impression he would get if he were able to read the work in the original language must naturally first specify how, in this simulational work, the original is to be understood. For there is one understanding that *should not* be simulated, another that *cannot* be.

The kind of understanding that should not be simulated is that found in the beginning foreign language student who blunders through the details of a text with great labour and loathing, never succeeding in rising above individual words and phrases to a clear view of the whole, never gaining a vivid sense of its cohesiveness. And as long as the educated portion of a country collectively lacks the experience of 'getting inside' a foreign language, those who are more advanced should be on guard against undertaking this sort of translation. For if they take their own understanding to be the norm, they will themselves be little understood, and thus will accomplish little; while if they take the common understanding to be the norm and seek to represent it in their translation, the clumsy result could not be hustled off the stage fast enough. In such an era, free imitations should first arouse and enhance a desire for the foreign, and paraphrases break ground for a more general understanding that will open doors for future translations.[2]

But there is another mentality that no translator can simulate. Picture those wonderful people whom Nature now and then sees fit to bring forth, as if to demonstrate her ability in individual cases to erase the boundaries between national sensibilities – people who feel so singularly drawn and akin to a foreign culture that they have utterly given themselves over to living and thinking in its language and its texts; and who, at least while caught up body and soul in that foreign world, allow their native language and whole native world to become alien. Or picture those who seem designed expressly, as it were, to represent the power of language in its entirety – people who learn languages easily, and for whom every language they learn is of equal value with all others; people who put on and take off languages like clothing. Both of these polyglot groups mark off a point at which translation becomes worthless. For their apprehension of foreign works shows no trace of interference from their native language, nor do they ever even reflect, utterly at home as they are in the language of the original, upon those works in their native tongue; what incommensurability

[1] He did not return to this task; perhaps the most monumental attempt to obey Schleiermacher's dual mandate in English is George Steiner's *After Babel* (1975). [Tr/Ed]

[2] This was still the overall German situation in the era of which Goethe is speaking (*From My Life* 3.111) when he calls for prosaic translations even of poetic works; these, he says, which are always more or less paraphrases, are beneficial in the education of youth. Up to here I can agree with him wholeheartedly; for in an era of that sort only the inventive germ of the foreign poetry can be made comprehensible, while its metrical and musical qualities can only be acknowledged. I cannot, however, believe that Voss's Homer and Schlegel's Shakespeare can be put to no better use than as entertainment for scholarly circles, any more than I can believe that yet another prose translation of Homer would even today be helpful in artistic and critical education; rather, we need a free adaptation like Becker's for children, and for adults young and old a metrical translation (which of course we do not yet have). I can think of nothing in between these extremes that would be educationally beneficial. [Au]

The passage from Goethe to which Schleiermacher is referring, printed above (222), had appeared two years before this writing, in 1811. Schleiermacher's German for 'inventive germ' is *Erfindung*, a translation of the Latin rhetorical term *inventio*, the imaginative selection of proper elements for a literary or rhetorical work; his reference is to this passage from Goethe (see above, 222):

> I honour metre and rhyme, for that is what makes poetry poetry, but the part that is really, deeply, and basically effective, the part that is truly formative and beneficial, is the part of the poet that remains when he is translated into prose. [Tr/Ed]

could they then feel between their thinking and the language in which they read? This means that no translation can either reach or represent their understanding. And just as it would be coals to Newcastle to translate for them, so do they smile with sympathy, down from their Olympian heights, on translators' efforts along these lines. For translations are made for those who are *not* their peers; if everyone could scale those heights, there would be no need for translation at all.

Translation, then, takes place in a middle ground between these two extremes, the 'should not' and the 'cannot'. The person whose image of and pleasure in the foreign text it is the translator's task to model for his reader is neither a beginning foreign language student nor a polyglot, but a person of similar education who is capable of reading the text in the original language; a person we call, in the best sense of the words, an enthusiast, a good judge; a person for whom the foreign language is familiar but forever foreign, who needs no longer, like beginning students of the language, translate every word and phrase into his native language before gaining a sense of the whole, but who remains constantly aware, even in his most tranquil enjoyment of its beauties, of its differences from his own native language.

To be sure, even when we have settled these points, we will still remain pretty much up in the air as to the definition and extension of this translational approach. All we can say for sure is that, just as a culture will only begin to feel the need for translations when the educated class is fairly conversant in foreign languages, so too will the birth of art and the gradual raising of artistic standards be keyed to the spread and enhancement of enthusiasm for and good judgment of foreign cultural productions among those groups who have trained their ears without specializing in the study of languages.

On the other hand, we cannot ignore the fact that the more receptive readers there are for such translations, the higher the difficulties inherent in this undertaking loom, especially in connection with a culture's most characteristic works of art and scholarship, which are, after all, the translator's most important objects. For given the historicity of language, it is impossible to know it truly without knowledge of its history. Languages are never invented, and all purely arbitrary efforts in them and on them are sheer folly; rather, they are unveiled, little by little, and scholarship and art are the faculties by which this unveiling is advanced and perfected.

Every fine mind shaped by the culture's perceptions through the medium of either art or scholarship itself works and shapes the language, and the resulting works thus contain a piece of the language's history. This creates for the scholarly translator great and often insuperable difficulties, for anyone who reads with sufficient knowledge an excellent piece of scholarship in the original will not easily miss the impact it has had on its language. He will see how some words and collocations, new and dazzling to him, have wormed their way into the language through this author's particular expressive needs and powers; and seeing this will significantly structure his impression of the work. Conveying this kind of perception to the target-language readers is essential for translation; otherwise they may miss a vital part of the author's intentions.

But how is this to be achieved? Suppose, for example, the translator wants to show forth the original work's shaping effect on its language, but the best equivalent for a certain new word in the original language is an old and worn-out one in his own; how then will he show it, except by substituting for the 'new' word (old in his tongue) the foreign idea it signifies, and thus sliding over into imitation? Even where he is able to render the new with the new, the best equivalent may be slightly divergent in collocation and derivation and thus fail to render the sense faithfully; how then is he to respect the immediate context without introducing extraneous connotations? He will have to console himself with the thought that there will be other passages where the author will have used older and more familiar words, and he will be able to make up for his present neglect there; in this way it may be possible to carry out in the translation as a whole what he has failed to carry out in specific cases. But what possible hope does the translator have of success in the total context of a great writer's verbal creativity – taking into consideration, for example, his use of etymological roots and connections in a complex body of interrelated texts? The target language's conceptual and expressive system is totally different from that in the source language; the two languages' etymologies, so far from running in parallel, criss-cross each other in the most whimsical directions. There is no earthly way, therefore, that the translator's use of language can ever cohere exactly as his author's does. Here, then, he must be content to achieve in individual details what he cannot achieve in the whole. He will have to trust his readers not to compare this work mentally with others, as its readers in the original might, but rather to take each as it comes, and even to praise him if in individual works (even sometimes in individual parts of those works) he is able to be consistent with regard to the most important objects, so that a single word is not inundated with a flood of wildly different proxies, nor do terms for a tight conceptual cluster in the original proliferate promiscuously in the translation.

These difficulties mostly turn up in translations of scholarly works; others appear in the translation of poetry and poetic prose, where a most excellent and indeed higher meaning resides in the musical elements of language as they are manifested in rhythm and tonal shifts. Everyone can feel the dissipation of art's finest spirit, the highest magic of its most perfect works, when its music goes unnoticed or, worse, is disfigured. Whatever the judicious reader finds unique in this respect, therefore – whatever seems deliberate, whatever seems to have an impact on sound qualities and the fine-tuning of feeling and thus on the mimetic and musical accompaniment of speech – all this will have to be rendered by our translator.

But how often (and it is nothing short of miraculous that one need not say *always*) does rhythmical and melodical fidelity not clash irreconcilably with propositional and grammatical fidelity! How hard it is, while shilly-shallying between this and that alternative, not to surrender to precisely the wrong one! How hard it is, for that matter, for the translator to find the occasions to restore impartially to his author what he has had to remove from him before, rather than repeatedly and unwittingly favouring one artistic aspect over the other because it is more to his own liking. For if he is more enamoured of art's ethical substance and its treatment, he will pay less attention to where he has violated the work's metrical and musical form; rather than seeking replacements for those formal elements, he will content himself with a rendition that plays into the facile and the paraphrastic. If on the other hand the translator is a musician or a skilled versifier, he will disregard the work's logic in order to lay claim to its music. The more entangled he becomes in this partisanship, the more distasteful he will find his work; and an overall comparison of the translation with its original will show that he has unwittingly approached that shabby classroom style that misses the forest for the trees. For if, out of a love for sound and rhythmic qualities and a desire to reproduce them materially in his translation, he renders heavily and offensively what is light and natural in the original language, he will end up making on the reader a totally different impression.

In reflecting upon his relationship with the language in which he is writing, and upon the relationship between his translation and his other works, the translator uncovers still other difficulties. Apart from those extraordinarily gifted people equally at home in several languages, and often as not more at home in a second language than their first – those, as mentioned earlier, for whom one cannot translate – everyone feels a certain strangeness in foreign languages, no matter how fluently they read them. How then shall the translator convey to his readers, in their native language, this feeling that the text before them truly is foreign?

To be sure, one might reply that this riddle was solved long ago, and that German translators have put the answer into better than adequate practice many times; for the more closely the translation follows the contours of the original, the more foreign it will seem to the reader. True enough, and it is easy to smile upon this procedure in general. Still, if one doesn't want such smiles to come too easily, if one wants to avoid throwing the baby of the great translation out with the bathwater of classroom blundering, one will have to grant that a certain attitude toward language is indispensable to this translation method: one that avoids the banal, certainly, but that also gives off an aura of impediment, of having been bent forcibly into the foreign semblance. To achieve this with both ingenuity and restraint, surely, without putting either oneself or one's language at a disadvantage, may be the greatest difficulty our translator will have to overcome.

In fact, there can hardly be a more astonishing form of self-abasement to which a good writer will knowingly submit. Who would not want his native language to appear in the resplendence most characteristic of his people and of each individual genre? Who would willingly breed mongrels when he could instead sire loving children in the pure image of their father? Who would publicly cripple his own verbal facility and grace in order to appear, at least at times, churlish and clumsy, and as offensive as is necessary to keep the reader aware of what is going on? Who would gladly be thought a bungler just because he took pains to stick as close to the foreign language as his own would allow – or be censured like parents who give their children to be raised by acrobats, because he would not train his language in its own native gymnastics but must inure it to alien and unnatural contortions? Who, finally, would willingly suffer being smiled upon pityingly by the greatest experts and authorities who cannot fathom his belaboured and reckless German unless they augment it with their Greek and Latin?

These are the renunciations every translator must inevitably make, these the risks he runs when, endeavouring to keep his language sounding foreign, he fails to observe the fine line between undesirable extremes (nor can he avoid those risks, for everyone draws the line differently). If in addition he reflects upon how inexorably one becomes inured to new usages, he may grow apprehensive at the thought that translating might introduce something alien and raw into the primal freedom of his work, so that the delicate touch of his native feel for language might be dulled. If he then reflects upon the vast multitude of imitators, and upon the indolence and mediocrity that reign among the literati, he must feel outraged at the quantities of lax and lawless behaviour – out-and-out bungling, inflexibility, linguistic corruption of every sort – for which he may be held accountable. For virtually the only ones who will not seek to exploit his endeavours for their own gain will be the very best and the very worst.

A common complaint is that this approach to translation must necessarily be detrimental to the purity and undisturbed inner growth of a language. We might want to set these complaints aside, reassuring ourselves that any disadvantages such an approach might have must necessarily be offset by advantages; after all, since there is no good without bad, wisdom lies in gaining as much as possible of the former while leaving behind as much as possible of the latter. Still, certain things do follow from this difficult task of representing the foreign in one's native language.

First, not every language is equally amenable to this kind of translation; it requires a language not too tightly bound by a classical idiom that repudiates everything beyond its pale. Languages that are bound in this way might seek to expand their boundaries through being spoken by foreigners who cannot get by in their native languages alone, or through the appropriation of foreign works in imitations, or perhaps even in translations in which the foreign author is brought over to the native reader – though these latter should in general be left to 'freer' languages more tolerant of deviations and innovations, the accumulation of which may under certain circumstances facilitate the development of a well-defined linguistic character.

Second, and perhaps less obviously – though still plainly enough – this type of translation is worthless if it is only practiced randomly and incidentally in a language. For clearly, the goal is not reached if the reader feels the breath of a *totally* foreign spirit upon him. Rather, if he is to catch a glimmer, even a very dim one, of the original language and the work's indebtedness to it, and is thus in some sense to be compensated for his inability to understand it, he must not only get the vague feeling that what he is reading sounds a little odd; it must also sound like some specific *other thing*, something definitely other – and that will only be possible if he is materially able to make numerous comparisons. For example, if he has read several texts translated in this way, and he knows that some are from other modern languages, others from classical ones, he will gradually develop an ear for the difference between the modern and the classical. But he will have to have read far more to distinguish Greek from Roman works, or Italian from Spanish ones. Nor is this yet the highest goal; for the reader of a translation will only approach parity with the superior reader of the original when he can intuit, and gradually come to apprehend clearly, the spirit not only of the language but also of the individual author. For this the reader must be a talented observer who is also willing to train his observations through study of far greater bodies of comparative materials. These materials will not be available if translations are done haphazardly of this or that masterwork in this or that genre – with the result that translations will give even the best educated readers but a most imperfect knowledge of the foreign. And that these readers should ever judge translations or originals properly? – unthinkable.

This type of translation requires, therefore, a comprehensive mode of operation, a transplantation of entire literatures into a given language. It also assumes meaning and value only among a people committed to making the foreign their own; indeed isolated efforts along these lines are valuable only as harbingers of a better developed and more concerted desire to undertake such a project, and if they fail to stimulate such a desire, they meet with opposition from the spirit of their language and their time – they can only be seen as miscarried efforts and may have little or no success. But even if this idea should catch on, one should not hold out too much hope that a translation of this type, no matter how brilliant, will win general acclaim. Given the many factors that have to be considered and the many difficulties that have to be overcome, it is impossible to avoid differences of opinion as to which parts of the task to privilege, which to deprivilege. And so scholars will form different schools of thought, and the reading public too will fall into different camps with allegiance to one or another scholarly group; and while the basic method may be the same, different translations of the same work will be conceived from different perspectives, making it impossible to say whether any given translation is superior or inferior to any other. One will only seem more successful in specific passages, others in other passages; the value of each translation in and of itself will always be relative and subjective. It is not until they are all collected and cross-referenced, therefore, and the various ways and passages in which individual translations valorize this or that approximation to or preservation of the original have been explored, that they will have truly fulfilled their task.

These are the difficulties that this method faces, and the imperfections that inhere in it. Even granting them, however, we cannot deny either the existence or the merit of the undertaking itself. There are two conditions for its success: that people (a) recognize the possibility and desirability of understanding the foreign works and (b) perceive their native language as possessing a certain flexibility. Where these conditions are met, translating in this way becomes a perfectly natural intervention in the overall cultural development, and as it retains an inalterable value, so too does it provide an undeniable pleasure.

But what about the opposite method (2) – that which would shelter the reader against all trouble and toil by whisking the foreign author magically into his unmediated presence? The requirement set by this method, that of displaying the source-language text as if the author had originally written it in the target language, is often articulated as the true translator's task, far nobler and purer than the other method; and there have been many individual efforts, some of them even producing masterpieces, that have clearly held this up as their goal. Given that till now this approach has unquestionably been less common than its disquieting and in many cases unsatisfactory counterpart (1), let us now see how things stand with this approach and determine whether it should not in fact become *more* common, even to the point of supplanting the other.

The first thing to say is that the translator's language has nothing to fear from this assimilative method. His first rule, stemming from his working relationship with a foreign language, must be never to permit himself anything that would not be permissible in a work originally written in his native language. Like anyone else, in fact, he is duty-bound to show the same care for that language's purity and perfection as the original author did for his, to emulate the free and easy style for which that author is praised. It is also certain that the best way to provide our compatriots with an accurate sense of what a writer has become for his language is to have him speak to them as we think he would have spoken in our own. This is especially true when our language is roughly at the same developmental stage at which he first found his. For example, we can in a sense imagine how Tacitus would have spoken had he become a German – or, to put that more precisely, how a German would have spoken who was for the German language what Tacitus was for the Latin. And how wonderful for you if you can in fact imagine this so vividly that Tacitus really does speak! But whether this could happen if you let him say the same things in German that the Roman Tacitus said in Latin – that's another question, and one that is hard to answer in the affirmative. For it is one thing to gain an accurate sense and set down a more or less accurate representation of the impact a man has had on his language, and quite another to guess at the turns his thoughts and their expression would have taken had he grown up thinking and expressing himself in another language.

The conviction that thoughts and expressions are inwardly and essentially identical is fundamental to the hermeneutics of all speech, and thus also to translation; how then can anyone who shares this conviction truly want to split a speaker off from the language to which he was born? Can he truly suppose that a person, or even a single chain of that person's thoughts, could ever be one and the same in two languages? And if that chain is different in a certain way in the two languages, can he really pretend to analyze it down to its innermost core, to disregard the constitutive role played by a language, and then as it were through a new chemical process compound this 'prelinguistic' core with the essence and the power of another language? This would be to disregard everything in a writer's work that has even remotely been shaped by what he has spoken and heard in his native language since infancy, and then to transport into the stripped-down singularity of his object-oriented way of thinking everything that might have resulted from speaking and hearing the target language from birth, or rather from his first exposure to the language, till he became capable of original thought and articulation in it. But it is about as likely that this transportation should actually succeed as it is that organic products will ever be synthetically compounded.[3] In fact one might say that the goal of translating as if the source-language author had originally written in the target language is not only unattainable, but intrinsically null and void. For anyone who recognizes the constitutive power of language, and its inseparability from the distinctive qualities of the people who speak it, must also admit that for every great author, the totality of his knowing and the expressive means at his disposal has for the most part been shaped with and through his language. No one inhabits his language mechanically or outwardly, as if strapped to it; no one can unharness his language at will like a team of horses and hook up another in its place. Original work can only be done in one's native language; how one might have written one's works in another language is a nonquestion that cannot even be raised.

Now, there are two quite common exceptions to my rule that may be advanced to counter my claims.[4] The first is that some people have learned to write in a single foreign language, even well enough to create philosophical and poetic works in it – and not just in isolated cases, either. Why not furnish a sure benchmark, then, by projecting this ability onto every author one wants to translate? The reason this won't work is that the ability is grounded in situations where the author could not have said the same thing in his native language – indeed sometimes where no one could. Think of the period during which the Romance languages were being formed: which language was native to people then? And who would deny that scholars felt more at home in Latin than in the vernaculars into which they were born? This example is even more complicated for specific intellectual needs and activities, for as long as a scholar's native vernacular

[3] Which is, of course, a technological reality today, through gene-splicing and similar procedures. [Tr/Ed]

[4] Schleiermacher's argumentation is muddled here. The two exceptions he speaks of are in fact identical: that people write in foreign languages. The tenor of his claims suggests what he fails to make explicit: that his first exception comprises people like Joseph Conrad and Samuel Beckett who have learned a *single* foreign language well enough to create great art in it (though he will also want to get around this), his second people like diplomats who have learned *many* foreign languages well enough to make polite conversation in them (but cannot use them to create great art). In my translation I have emphasized the single/many distinction just slightly. [Tr/Ed]

remains underdeveloped, the language that has channeled those needs and activities to the developing culture will serve in part as a native language. Grotius and Leibniz could not do philosophy in Dutch or German without becoming entirely different people. In fact, even if the root has withered and the new growth has been stripped off the old trunk, anyone who is not simultaneously committed to building up a language and creating a new era will be driven willy-nilly into the arms of a foreign language. Every fine and noble thought came to our great king,[5] for example, through a thoroughly internalized foreign language; he could not have written in German the philosophical and poetic works he wrote in French. It is unfortunate that the partiality for England felt by part of his family did not result in his learning English from an early age; not only was the last golden age of English literature then in full flower, but English is much closer to German than French. We can only hope that, had he received a proper classical education, he would rather have written his works in Latin than in French. In any case, the fact that the writing of original works in a foreign language is governed by specific conditions – that people only write in a foreign language what they cannot write in their own, and that they only do so in a certain language, not in a random string of them – cannot be used as evidence for a method of translation that would display what an author wrote in his native language as it would look had he written it in another.

The second exception, that some people can read and write original things in several foreign languages, seems initially more promising for this method. For who would argue with our diplomats and courtiers when they insist that the charming remarks that trip off their tongues in foreign languages are first conceived in those languages, rather than having been translated from poor old German? And as these people pride themselves on being able to produce these niceties and gallantries in every language with equal ease, this must mean that they also think in every language with equal ease, and each will be perfectly aware of how another would have said in French what he just said in Italian. The only problem is that this light discourse is alien to that domain where the deep root of a particular language powerfully thrusts forth mental shoots; it is more like watercress that an artificer grows without soil on a white cloth. This discourse is neither the sacred solemnity of a language nor its beautiful, well-measured play; rather, as increased travel nowadays has made every place a marketplace, so what we have here is the discourse of the marketplace, whether political or literary, or just convivial. As such it in fact lies outside the translator's bailiwick, and falls rather into that of the interpreter.

Now it sometimes happens that these light remarks are scrabbled together on paper and called a piece of writing, a work of light and agreeable manners that neither unlocks the depths of being nor nurtures the uniqueness of the culture. This sort of work should be translatable by these rules, but *only* this sort, only a work that could as easily have been conceived in another language; the rules of this method should have no further extension, except perhaps to those peripheral parts of more profound and imposing works, such as prefaces and dedications, that are often couched entirely in the world of light conviviality. The more fully the individual intertwined ideas in a work are infused with the uniqueness of a culture, or *a fortiori* with the imprint of a long-past era, the more meaningless those rules become.

For true as it remains in many ways that one cannot be considered educated and cosmopolitan without a knowledge of several languages, we must also admit that cosmopolitanism does not seem authentic to us if at critical moments it suppresses patriotism; and the same thing is true of languages. That highly generalized love of language that cares little what language (the native one or some other, old or new) is used for a variety of expressive purposes (mundane or sublime) is not the best kind of love for improving the mind or the culture. One Country, One Language – or else another: a person has to make up his mind to belong somewhere, or else hang disoriented in the unpleasant middle.

It is right, for example, that Latin should still be the written language of officialdom, to keep on reminding us that it was the native language of our scholarly and ecclesiastical forebears; it is salutary that such should also be the case in the scholarly world all across Europe, to facilitate communication. But even in that latter world it will only succeed to the extent that the text is entirely object-oriented, and has little truck with personal opinions and interconnections. The same is true of the Romance languages. Anyone required to write one of them in an official capacity will be perfectly aware that his thoughts in their first embryonic state are German, and that he merely begins to translate them early on, while the embryo is still being formed; and anyone who dedicates himself to scholarly writing in one of them will only find his task easy, unforced, and unaccompanied by covert translation when he feels utterly under the sway of the object.

To be sure, some write in Latin or one of the Romance languages for their own pleasure; and if their

[5] Frederick the Great, who had been dead for nearly three decades at this writing, was educated (like all German aristocrats of the day) by French tutors and wrote all his important work in French; he spoke only broken German and considered Goethe and other German writers barbarians. His father, King Frederick William I, imposed on him as a child a Spartan regimen that included army drill and religion but excluded Latin, poetry, philosophy, and music. [Tr/Ed]

intentions in this were to write as well and as originally in the foreign language as in their own, I would unhesitatingly pronounce it a wicked and magical art akin to going doubled,[6] an attempt at once to flout the laws of nature and to perplex others. But that is truly not their aim; their hobby is but an exquisite mimetic game with which to beguile away the hours out on the margins of philosophy and art. Writing in a foreign language is never original; rather remembrances of specific authors or of the manner of a certain era, which flesh forth as it were a collective persona, float before the soul almost like living simulacra that, when imitated on paper, give the writing direction and definition. This is also why this approach rarely produces anything of true value, except perhaps the mimetic accuracy it undeniably fosters. It also affords the reader much harmless enjoyment of a beloved work of art, since the person imitated so clearly shines through everywhere. If on the other hand, in defiance of nature and morality, a writer becomes a traitor to his native language by surrendering his verbal life to another, it is no false or affected self-mockery when he protests that he can no longer move about in that language; it is rather his attempt to vindicate himself by portraying himself as a wonder, a miracle surpassing all natural rule and order, and a relief to others that he at least does not go doubled like a ghost.

But we have held forth too long upon these bizarre matters, and have given the impression that our topic is writing in foreign languages rather than translating from them. The point is this. If it is not possible to write something original in a foreign language that at once needs and deserves artistic translation, or if such writing is an anomaly of a rare and miraculous order, then one cannot impose upon all translation the rule that it must render what the author himself would have written in the target language. There simply are no great numbers of bilingual authors that might serve as analogues for the translator's work; wherever a work is more than light entertainment or commercial prose, therefore, the translator will be forced to fall back almost entirely upon his own imagination. In fact, if a translator tells a reader, "Here's the book, just as the man would have written it had he done it originally in German", who could object if the reader replied, "I'm as indebted to you as I would have been had you brought me a picture of him as he would have looked had his mother conceived him by a different father"? For if the distinctive mind of the author of a truly scholarly or artistic work is the mother, the native tongue, the language of the 'fatherland', is the father. This or that clever artifice pretends to mysterious insights that no one has, and one can only enjoy them as unreservedly as the other type if one takes them as a game.

Just how limited the applicability of this method is – limited, in fact, in the field of translation almost to zero – is most clearly evident in view of the impossible binds in which it is entangled in individual branches of scholarship and the arts. If one admits what we discussed above, that even in everyday usage there are very few words in one language that correspond fully to their counterparts in another, so that one might be employed to precisely the same effect in every context in which the other appears, it is difficult to avoid the conclusion that the same is even more true of concepts, especially of philosophically charged ones – indeed of the bulk of philosophy proper. Here more than anywhere else, synchronic and diachronic diversity notwithstanding, every language embodies a single system of concepts whose contiguous, connective, and complementary relationships form a single whole, individual parts of which can never correspond to individual parts of other systems – not even, perhaps, God and To Be, the primordial noun and verb. For even universals, no matter how far they lie beyond the realm of particulars, are illumined and coloured by language.

This linguistic system is the well of all wisdom, from which everyone buckets out what can be reached by hand and helps to bring to light what glimmers just below. Only thus does the individual's wisdom come alive, only thus does it truly rule his being – which in any case is fused with his language. And so suppose the translator of a philosophical writer cannot make up his mind to contort the target language as far as possible toward the source language, so as to give the reader a feeling for the latter's conceptual system; suppose, even worse, that he wants to let his writer speak as if he had originally conceived his thoughts and words in the target language. Given the componential dissimilarity of languages, his only two alternatives are paraphrase (which won't serve his purpose, since a paraphrase can and will never look like a text originally written in the same language) and rebuilding his author's entire wit and wisdom within the target-language conceptual system, and thus transmuting every one of its individual parts – which has the effect of blinding the translator to the bounds of his own unchecked arbitrariness. It goes without saying, in fact, that no one with the slightest respect for philosophical aspirations and trends will ever let himself play such a lax game.

Let Plato[7] answer for my next shift, from the philosopher to the writer of comedies, the literary genre that is linguistically closest to the realm of convivial conversation. Indeed the comedy draws breath from the manners of the people and the period, and reflects

[6] *Doppeltgehen*, becoming one's own double so as to be physically present in two places at once. [Tr/Ed]

[7] In the *Republic* Plato shifted from the poet and the playwright, which he tolerated up to a point but then banished, to the philosopher-king; he makes a rather strange justifier of Schleiermacher's shift. [Tr/Ed]

them wonderfully in its language. Its primary virtue is a light and natural grace – and this is precisely the source of the extraordinary difficulties faced by the translator of the method discussed above, as every approximation to a foreign language does violence to those expressive virtues. Does the translator want to let a playwright speak as if he had originally written in the target language? Then there will be much he will not be able to say, much that is not native to the target culture and thus has no representation in its language. The translator is then faced with the choice between cutting those passages entirely (and thus undoing the power and form of the original whole) and putting something else in their place. Clearly, then, the blanket application of this formula to translations leads either to mere imitation or to an even more strikingly offensive and bewildering hodgepodge of translation and imitation that tosses the reader mercilessly to and fro like a ball, between his world and the foreign one, between the author's and the translator's invention and wit. Nor is there any pure pleasure for him in all this, only exhaustion and a spinning head.

Contrast with this the translator of the reader-to-author method, whose motivation to make such high-handed changes is nil because he must keep his reader conscious of the otherness of his author's world and language. His is the admittedly arduous task of supplying the reader with an awareness of this foreign world as economically as possible, while at the same time letting the greater ease and naturalness of the original shine through everywhere.

These two examples from opposite poles in scholarship and the arts clearly demonstrate just how poorly translation's true goal of unadulterated pleasure in foreign works is attained through a method that would breathe into the translated work the spirit of a language alien to it. Not to mention the fact that any given language is rhythmically distinctive in both prose and poetry, and that, if we buy into the fiction that the source-language author could have written in the target language, he should be made to do so in target-language rhythms – which would only deform his work the more, and so further circumscribe that awareness of its unique character that the translation affords.

In fact that fiction, which is the sole foundation of the author-to-reader approach, oversteps the very purpose of translational activities. In the reader-to-author approach, translation is essential for a people when only a few can gain a sufficient knowledge of foreign languages, and only a few more have a taste for foreign works. If those with taste could cross over and become those who know foreign langauges, translation of this sort would be pointless, and scarcely anyone would tackle such a thankless task.

Not so with the author-to-reader approach. This has nothing to do with necessity – rather with prurience and presumption. Never mind how widespread competence in foreign languages might be, never mind how wide open access is to the greatest works for every qualified person – translation would still be a major production that would draw bigger and bigger crowds, all agape to hear Cicero or Plato hyped as alive and writing in German today. And if someone were to sell us on the same thing not in his own native language, but in another foreign one, why then he would seem to us the world's greatest genius in the difficult and almost impossible art of blending together the spirits of two languages.

The only thing is that this would not, obviously, be translation in the strict sense of the word, nor would its aim be to provide the most accurate enjoyment possible of the works themselves; it would rather creep ever closer to imitation, and the only person capable of properly enjoying the works (or shams) of art it produced would be one who was already familiar with them in the original. Its true aim could only be to offer a detailed illustration of the interconnections between certain types of expressions and collocations in different languages, and in general to cast on the target language the light of a foreign author's unique spirit – but untied and cast adrift from his language.

If, then, diplomats speaking many languages fluently are engaged in no more than an elaborate and elegant game and the idea of the author writing originally in a foreign language rests on a fiction that is almost impossible to put into practice, it is not surprising that this author-to-reader approach should be employed so sparingly, and that, when it is, the results should only make it amply clear that it cannot become standard operating procedure. This explains also why only the greatest artists, who have earned a belief in their own miraculous powers – and who have by rights already discharged their duty to the world, and thus can afford to enter into a fascinating and somewhat dangerous game – can follow this method in their work. It is even less surprising that great artists who feel they are in a position to tackle such a task should look down on other translators' work with pity. For they believe that the fine and free arts are vested in them alone, and the others by comparison are practically interpreters (even if those others too serve a purpose, and a somewhat nobler one than interpreters). The others are found to be pathetic in their wasteful expenditure of art and effort on such an inferior and thankless business. This is why great artists are so quick with the advice that, instead of translations of this sort, one should make do with paraphrases, as interpreters too will do in difficult and disputable cases.

What next? Should we adopt this view and follow this advice? The ancients apparently did little translating in the proper sense of that word, and most modern countries, too, daunted by the difficulties of true translation, typically content themselves with imitation and paraphrase. Who would maintain that anything had ever been truly translated into French, from either the classical or the Germanic languages?

Eager as we Germans might be to bend an ear to this advice, we would certainly never take it. We have been driven to translation *en masse* by an inner necessity, the voice of our special calling, and we cannot turn back now; we must press on. Just as our soil may have become richer and more fertile, and our climate more agreeable and mild, through the repeated introduction of foreign plants, so do we feel that our language, which has languished under the weight of our Nordic inertia, can only flourish vigorously and fully develop its own potential through repeated exposure to the foreign. And concomitantly with this, it seems that our respect for the foreign and our mediatory nature together destine the German people to incorporate linguistically, and to preserve in the geographical center and heart of Europe, all the treasures of both foreign and our own art and scholarship in a prodigious historical totality, so that with the help of our language everyone can enjoy, as purely and as perfectly as a foreigner can, all the beauty that the ages have wrought.

This seems, in fact, to be the true historical goal of translation for all people in all periods, as it already is for Germans today. Only one method, however, will usher us toward that goal – bringing the reader to the author. Its pitfalls, which we have not sought to conceal, must be overcome as far as possible by art. We are already well on our way, but the bulk of the work lies ahead of us. Much apprentice work must be done before a few great works can come into being; all that glitters at first is not gold, and much will have to be superseded by superior attempts. Just how far individual artists have already begun to deal with the pitfalls of this approach, in part by truly overcoming them, in part by fortuitously meandering between them, many examples make amply clear. And if there are inferior talents working in the field as well, we shall not worry that their efforts might wreak havoc with our language. For let it be noted that any language into which so many works are translated harbours a special domain just for translations, and much must be allowed them that would not otherwise be permitted to see the light of day. Anyone who attempts to transplant these failed innovations further without collective authorization will have few followers, or none at all; and if, after a certain period (not too short), we want to close out the account, we can trust the assimilative process of language to reject any incompatible foreign bodies that met only a passing need.

On the other hand, we must not fail to recognize that much that is beautiful and powerful in our language was first created through translation – partly developed anew, partly recovered from oblivion. We speak too little, and chatter by comparison too much; and it cannot be gainsaid that for quite some time our writing style had been moving far too strongly in that latter direction, and that translation has helped considerably to return a more austere style to favour. If ever the time should come when our public sphere gives birth on the one hand to a more profound and linguistically accurate conviviality, and on the other to increased space for the speaker's talents, then we may have less need for the translator in the advancement of our language. May that day arrive before we have come full circle in the labours of translation!

Wilhelm von Humboldt

Karl Wilhelm, baron of Humboldt (1767-1835), was one of the most influential language scholars and educational reformers in Western history. His romantic conception of the creativity of language use was to have in our own century a powerful shaping influence on the transformational-generative theories of Noam Chomsky; and the central role he played in planning and founding the Friedrich-Wilhelms-Universität (nowadays the Humboldts-Universität) in Berlin made him in effect the father of the modern university.

Born to an officer in the army of Frederick the Great and his Huguenot wife, Humboldt and his younger brother Alexander, who was to become as influential in the fields of anthropology and biogeography as Wilhelm was in linguistics and pedagogy, were largely raised by their mother, especially after their father's death in 1779. Privately educated, the elder Humboldt was sent to the University of Jena, where he made lifelong friends with the German romantic poet, playwright, and philosopher Friedrich von Schiller. His increasing fame as a writer won him important political appointments in the Prussian government at Rome, beginning in 1801; in 1809 he was appointed Prussian minister of education, in which capacity he not only founded what has been called the first modern university (where Hegel was professor of philosophy and later rector, from 1818-1830, and Karl Marx was his student) but upgraded elementary education as well, raising standards for the training and certification of teachers.

His remarks on language and translation, printed below, are significant in that they ground German romantic translation theory far more fully and clearly than Goethe or Schleiermacher ever did in romantic theories of language, of which, in any case, Humboldt was the undisputed master. The main idea for Humboldt is that, just as every language is utterly unique and possesses its own special inner form, so too is every word unique and has no equivalent in any other language.

These romantic principles seem to sound the knoll of doom for translation, since they would appear to make equivalence and thus translation itself impossible. But Humboldt argues fairly traditionally first that translation, even if impossible, is an important tool for the broadening of the mind of both individuals and whole cultures; then, more ingeniously, that there is a 'mystical connection' between words and their referents. This connection is in ideas, the mystical intellectual liquid that holds external physical objects (the referents of words) in ideal solution, which in turn makes it possible to ground the uniqueness of words in something stable enough to permit translation. Implicit in this formulation is the universality of ideas, of the mind, which Humboldt – like other romantics – invokes in order to counteract the variability and local specificity of individual words, phrases, and languages.

The More Faithful, The More Divergent
From the introduction to his translation of Aeschylus' *Agamemnon* (1816)
Translated by Douglas Robinson

A poem of this inimitable nature is – and not just in the sense that all works of great originality are – untranslatable. It has often been remarked, and both linguistic research and everyday experience bear this out, that with the exception of expressions denoting material objects, no word in one language is ever entirely like its counterpart in another. Different languages are in this sense only synonymous: each one puts a slightly different spin on a concept, charges it with this or that connotation, sets it one rung higher or lower on the ladder of affective response. No one has ever assayed a synonym dictionary for the major languages, not even just for Greek, Latin, and German, inordinately useful as that would be – indeed a most attractive task, if it were ingeniously enough conceived. All we have are the fragments of such a dictionary in various writers' works.

So little is a word the mere sign of a concept, that without it the concept would never even be born, let alone apprehended. Words are the condensation of the shadowy intellect at work, like cirrus clouds forming in a clear sky. Soon they become separate beings, well-defined in character and form, empowered to influence the heart, and not without reproductive capabilities. If the origin of a word were analogous to the action of a single human being (which of course it could never be, since to utter a word one must be certain of its being understood, which means that language can only be thought of as the byproduct of a simultaneous reciprocation in which neither party is in a position to assist the other, rather each must internalize the entire dialogical effort), it would be most like the birth of an ideal form in an artist's imagination. Like the word, the ideal form can never be gleaned from anything actual; it emanates from a pure mental energy, ultimately in fact from nothing. But from that moment on it enters life and becomes actual and durable. What artist or genius, or anyone else for that matter, has not since early childhood created imaginary figures, with which he subsequently lived on more familiar terms than he did with actual ones?

And in this light, how could a word whose meaning is not directly grounded in sense perception be absolutely identical with a word in another language? There must be differences; and in fact if one closely compares the best, most painstakingly faithful translations, one is astonished at the divergences that appear where the translator sought only sameness and similitude. One could even argue that the more a translation labours to be faithful, the more divergent it becomes. For then it imitates minute details while shunning the purely general, and all it can do in the end is substitute one detail for another.

Still, we should not let this keep us from translating. On the contrary, translation, especially of poets, is one of a literature's most urgent tasks – in part so as to expose those who speak no foreign language to artistic and human forms that they would otherwise never know, a process by which every nation wins esteem; but in part also, and more especially, to augment the significance and expressivity of the native language. For the wonderful thing about languages is that they all suffice at first for everyday communicative needs, but then each can be infinitely complicated, enhanced, and ennobled by the spirit of the nation that works on it. It would not be too much to say that every language, even the patois of the most barbarous tribe, about which too little is known, is capable of expressing *everything*, from the sublime to the base, from the forceful to the tender – which should not, however, be taken to mean that one language is not inherently better than another, or that others are not unattainably great. But these notes slumber in them, as in an unplayed instrument, until the nation learns to bring them forth.

All linguistic forms are symbols: not the things themselves, nor conventional signs, but sounds that, through the spirit from which they emanated and continue to emanate, find themselves in an actual and if you like mystical relation with the things and concepts they represent – a relation stored in actual objects, dissolved, as it were, in ideas, and always subject, in a manner for which no bounds can be imagined, to alteration, definition, disjunction, and combination. These symbols can be charged with a higher, lower, or gentler sense by being thought and spoken, received and reproduced in particular ways, with the result that, without being overtly changed, the language is elevated to a higher and more developed state of self-representation. And as the mind of the language broadens, so does the mind of the entire nation.

Just to give a single example, think of how the imitation of Greek metres has enriched the German language, and of the many wonderful developments brought about in the German people (and not just the learned, either, but the masses as well, even women and children) since the Greeks in their authentic and undistorted form became their favourite reading matter. Klopstock's service to the German people through his first successful renditions of Greek metre is beyond words, not to mention Voss, who may be said to have imported classical antiquity into the German language. It is hard to imagine, in an era that was already highly sophisticated, a more powerful and salutary influence on a national cultural development than the solitary voice of Voss. For with his talent and determination, and his refusal to be daunted by new projects while working on the old, he invented the enduring forms in which the ancients will be reproducible in German for as long as that language is spoken; and while his work still leaves room for improvement, anyone who creates a true form may be certain that his work will endure. Indeed without such a form, even isolated eruptions of genius will remain inconsequential for further progress along the same lines.

But if translation is to appropriate for the language and spirit of its nation what it possesses either not at all or only in a different way, simple fidelity must be its first prerequisite. This fidelity must be directed at the true character of the original more than at distracting incidentals; for every good translation grows out of a simple, modest love for the original and the study born of that love, and to these things it must in the end return. Attendant upon this view, necessarily, is the importance of giving the translation a certain tinge of foreignness – and the boundary between this and obvious error is in this case easy to draw. So long as what is felt is not foreignness, but only the foreign,[1] the translation has attained its noblest goals; wherever foreignness per se shines through, and perhaps even leaves the foreign in shadow, there the translator reveals his inadequacy before the original. Here the unbiased reader's gut sense will not easily miss the dividing line. If in timid awe before the outlandish one goes further and seeks to shun the foreign – for as the saying goes, the translator must write as the original author would have written in the translator's language (an idea utterly blind to the fact that no scholarly or technical writer would ever have written the same things or in the same manner in another language[2]) – one then brings all translation, and all its usefulness to a language and a nation, to nought. For how else could it have come about that the Greeks and Romans have been translated into French, some of them even quite well according to the current style, but that all these translations have brought with them neither the merest whiff of the spirit of antiquity nor the slightest increase in the national understanding (since individual scholars are irrelevant here) of those authors?

To move on from these general remarks to my own work, as a translator I have tried to approach something like the simplicity and fidelity I have been describing above. With every new revision I have sought to eliminate more of what was not stated equally plainly in the text – for the impossibility of rendering the original's unique beauties all too easily tempts one to adorn it with alien trinkets that give it overall a divergent colour and sound. I have also guarded against ungerman and unclear phrasings, though in that latter respect one should not set unfair standards that might rule out greater benefits. A translation cannot and should not be a commentary. While it should contain no obscurities resulting from wishy-washy word choice or squint-eyed syntax, wherever the original only intimates without making itself clear, where it indulges in metaphors whose tenor is elusive, where it omits connective ideas, there the translator would do violence to the text by arbitrarily clarifying and so distorting it. The obscurity one sometimes finds in the writings of the ancients, most especially the *Agamemnon*, is born of the brevity and the boldness with which, scorning connective clauses, they string together thoughts, images, feelings, memories, and intuitions as they arise out of a profoundly agitated soul. The more thoroughly one penetrates the mood of a poet, his period, his characters, the more that obscurity vanishes and is replaced by a high clarity. And one must read a translation, too, almost as attentively, and not insist that whatever in the original language is sublime, vast, and outlandish become effortlessly and immediately intelligible in the translation. Still, effortlessness and clarity remain virtues that the translator attains only with great difficulty, and never through hard work or revision, but for the most part only through a fortuitous first inspiration; and I know all too well just how much my translation leaves to be desired in this respect.

---

[1] Humboldt's words for foreignness (*Fremdheit*) and the foreign (*das Fremde*) can mean also alienness and the alien, strangeness and the strange, perhaps even unfamiliarity and the unfamiliar. [Tr/Ed]

[2] Humboldt is here borrowing the critique of that 'saying' advanced three years before this writing by his friend Friedrich Schleiermacher, in 'On the Different Methods of Translating' (see above, 233-37). [Tr/Ed]

Anne-Louise-Germaine Necker, baronne de Staël-Holstein

Anne-Louise-Germaine Necker, baronne de Staël-Holstein (1766-1817), better known in her day and since as the Madame de Staël, was one of the most important and influential writers in the romantic era. A novelist, a playwright, a historian, a literary critic, an essayist, a memoirist, and a poet, Madame de Staël also maintained famous salons in Geneva and Paris.

She was born Anne-Louise-Germaine Necker in Paris, to Swiss parents; her father, Jacques Necker, was a banker who became Minister of Finance to Louis XVI, and her mother, Suzanne Curchod, held a literary and political salon. Germaine was bright and talkative, and early sat in on and participated in her mother's salon. She was married at 20 to Baron Erik de Staël-Holstein, the Swedish ambassador in Paris; but it was a marriage of convenience, and there was no love between the spouses. There were three children, Auguste, who became his mother's literary executor, Albert, and Albertine, who was reputedly fathered by Benjamin Constant. The couple were formally separated in 1797, one year after Albertine's birth.

She was early prolific, author of a romantic drama (*Sophie*, 1786), a tragedy (*Jane Grey*, 1790), and a critical study of Rousseau (1788) in her early twenties; the book on Rousseau made her reputation and swept her into the literary and political vortex of late-eighteenth-century Paris. A staunch supporter of the revolution, aligned with the Girondin faction, she also became romantically involved with Louis de Narbonne, a minister of Louis XVI, and fled with him to England in 1793, where she was effectively banished from polite society due to what were considered her scandalous morals and politics. Returning to Paris in 1794, after the Terror, she set up a salon and continued publishing brilliant and influential essays, increasingly on German romanticism – she was reading extensively in the works of Wilhelm von Humboldt and the Schlegel brothers. Shortly after her return she began a love affair with Benjamin Constant that was to last until the middle of the first decade of the nineteenth century; Constant seconded her interest in German romanticism.

Napoleon gained supreme power over France in 1799 as First Consul, and de Staël, Constant, and the anti-Napoleon circle of friends around them soon became a thorn in his side. She was too well-known internationally to throw in jail; instead in 1803 he had her banished from Paris, to a radius around the city of 40 miles. She and Constant repaired to the Necker house in Coppet, near Geneva, which remained her headquarters for the rest of her life. She also travelled widely in Europe, for several months with August Wilhelm von Schlegel. This period saw the publication of her novel *Corinne* (1807) and *De l'Allemagne* (1810), an enthusiastic cultural history of Germany that Napoleon had burned as an anti-French tract. She married a Swiss officer named Jean Rocca in 1811, but her safety was increasingly precarious in Napoleon's Europe, and she travelled around its peripheries for several years, in Russia, Finland, and Sweden, and finally in England, before returning to France in 1814, upon the Bourbon restoration. Quickly disillusioned with the Bourbons, however, she left for Coppet in 1815, where she was joined in 1816 by Lord Byron. Later that year she returned to Paris, where, despite declining health and suspicion from both the government and returning émigrés, she held her salon throughout the winter. By the next spring she was an invalid; by July, she was dead.

Her remarks on translation, published in 1816 in an Italian magazine, follow the German romantics in lauding the salutary effects of translation upon the native language and in decrying assimilative French translations.

On the Spirit of Translations (*De l'esprit des traductions* 1816)
Translated by David G. Ross

There is no more distinguished service that can be performed for literature than to transport the masterpieces of human intellect from one language to another. There are so few works of the first rate; genius in any genre whatsoever is so rare a phenomenon that if any modern nation were reduced to its own such treasures, it would be forever poor. Moreover, of all the forms of commerce the circulation of ideas is the one whose benefits are most certain.

At the time of the Renaissance in the arts, scholars and even poets had adopted the habit of writing everything in the same language, Latin, so as to have no need of being translated to be understood. That might have been advantageous for the sciences, whose development has no need of the charms of style. But it nonetheless resulted in several Italian treasures of this type remaining unknown to the Italians themselves, because the majority of readers only understood the idiom of the region. Furthermore, when writing on science and philosophy in Latin, it is necessary to create words that did not exist in the works of ancient authors. Scholars thus used a language that was at once dead and artificial, while poets restricted themselves to strictly classical expressions; and Italy, where Latin still resounds on the banks of the Tiber, has had writers like Fracastoro, Politian, and Sannazaro, who are said to approach the style of Virgil and Horace. But if their reputation endures, their works are no longer read outside the circle of the learned; and it is a sad literary glory that must be grounded in imitation. Indeed it is so natural to prefer the language which recalls the emotions of your own life over that which you can only reconstruct through study that those medieval Latin poets have been translated into Italian in their own homeland!

I will allow that the best way to do without translations would be to know all the languages in which the works of great poets have been composed: Greek, Latin, Italian, French, English, Spanish, Portuguese, and German; but such an undertaking requires much time, much assistance, and one could never delude oneself that knowledge so difficult to acquire could be universal. Yet one must aim at the universal when one wishes to do men good. I will go further: even when one understands foreign languages well, one can still savour a more familiar and intimate pleasure from a skillful translation in one's own language. These naturalized beauties also endow the national style with new turns of phrase and more original expressions. Translations of foreign poets can, more effectively than any other means, safeguard a country's literature from those banal formulations that are the surest signs of its decay.

But to draw a real benefit from this work, one must not follow the French in giving one's own flavor to everything one translates; even when one would thereby unquestionably turn everything one touched into gold, one would not, for all that, find any nourishment there; it would produce no new food for thought, and we should always see the same face with scarcely different adornment. This reproach, justly deserved by the French, stems from the many shackles their language imposes on the art of writing in verse. The rarity of rhyme, the uniformity of verse forms, and the difficulty of inversion enclose the poet in a circle that necessarily returns, if not to the same thoughts, at least to similar hemistiches[1] and some form of monotony in poetic language, from which genius escapes when it rises to great heights, but from which it cannot free itself in transitions, developments, in short, in all that prepares and assembles great effects.

It would thus be difficult to find a good translation into verse in French literature, apart from that of the *Georgics* by the Abbé Delille. There are fine imitations, conquests forever being mistaken for national treasures; but you could not find an example of a work in verse that bore the foreign character in any form, and I doubt that such an attempt could ever be successful. If the *Georgics* by the Abbé Delille have been justly admired, it is because the French language can assimilate itself more easily to the Latin language than to any other; it derives from it, and it preserves its pomp and majesty; but modern languages have so many varieties that French poetry could never submit to them gracefully.

The English, whose language permits inversion and whose versification is subjected to much less strict rules than that of the French, could have enriched their literature with translations that were both faithful and natural; but their important authors have not undertaken this work; and Pope, the only one who did dedicate himself to it, did two fine poems from the *Iliad* and the *Odyssey*; but he did not preserve that ancient simplicity that makes us aware of the secret of Homer's superiority.

Indeed, it is not likely that one man's genius should have surpassed that of all other poets of the last three thousand years; but there is something primitive in the traditions, customs, opinions, and atmosphere of that era of which the charm is inexhaustible; and, when reading Homer, this beginning of the human race, this dawn of time renews in our soul an emotion like the one we experience in the memories of our own childhoods. This emotion, confused as it is with our dreams of the golden age, makes us give preference to the most ancient of poets over all his successors. If you remove the simplicity of the first few days of the world from his composition, its uniqueness disappears.

In Germany, several scholars have claimed that Homer's works were not composed by a single man and that the *Iliad* and even the *Odyssey* must be seen as a collection of heroic odes for the celebration in Greece of the conquest of Troy and return of the victors. It seems to me that it is easy to refute this opinion, and that the unity of the *Iliad* especially does not permit us to adopt it. Why should the work have confined itself to the account of Achilles' anger? The subsequent events and the taking of Troy that brings them to a close must naturally have been part of the collection of rhapsodies that are supposed to belong to several authors. Only a single man could have conceived the unity of an event such as the anger of Achilles. Without wishing, however, to discuss here a system which one must be armed with fearsome erudition to support or attack, we must at least admit that Homer's principal grandeur stems from his century, since we have believed the poets of that time, or at least a very large number of them, had worked on the *Iliad*. It is one more proof that this poem is the image of a human society at a given moment of civilization, and that the imprint it bears is even more of an era than of a single man.

The Germans have not contented themselves with

[1] Half-lines of verse, broken by a caesura. [Ed]

scholarly research on the existence of Homer; they have striven to restore him to life in German, and the translation by Voss is acknowledged as the most faithful in any language. He made use of the rhythm of the ancients, and it is asserted that his German hexameter follows the Greek hexameter almost word for word. Such a translation is an effective device for accurate familiarity with the ancient poem; but is it certain that the original's charm, for which neither rules nor studies are enough, is fully carried over into the German language? The syllabic quantities are preserved; but the harmony of sounds cannot be the same. German poetry loses some of its innate quality by following the tracks of the Greek step by step, without being able to acquire the beauty of the musical language that is sung on the lyre.

Italian is, of all the modern languages, the one that lends itself most to providing us with all the sensations produced by Homeric Greek. It does not have, it is true, the same rhythm as the original; hexameter can hardly be introduced into our modern idioms; the long and short syllables are not sufficiently marked for us to equal the ancients in this regard. But Italian words have a harmony that can do without the symmetry of dactyls and spondees, and grammatical construction in Italian lends itself to the perfect imitation of Greek inversion: the *versi sciolti*, being freed from rhyme, hamper thought no more than prose while preserving the grace and meter of the verse.

Monti's translation of Homer is surely, of all those that exist in Europe, the one that comes closest to the pleasure that the original itself can give. It has both pomp and simplicity; the most ordinary customs of life, the clothing, and the feasts are noted with natural expressive dignity; and the grandest occasions are put within our reach through the lifelikeness of the scenes and the fluency of the style. No one in Italy will henceforth translate the *Iliad*; Homer has forever assumed Monti's costume there, and it seems to me that, even in the other countries of Europe, whoever cannot rise to the reading of Homer in the original will have an idea of the pleasure he can give through the Italian translation. To translate a poet is not to take a pair of compasses and reproduce the edifice's dimensions; it is to animate a different instrument with the same breath of life. In order to obtain a similar delight, we ask for more than perfectly similar features.

It would be highly desirable, it seems to me, for the Italians to attend to the careful translation of various new poems by the English and Germans; they would thus introduce a new genre to their compatriots, who for the most part stick to images drawn from ancient mythology, when in fact these are beginning to run dry and paganism in poetry is seen less and less in the rest of Europe. It is important for the progress of thought in lovely Italy to look often beyond the Alps – not to borrow, but to become acquainted; not to imitate, but to free themselves from certain conventional forms that persist in literature very like official phrases in society, and that likewise deprive it of any natural lifelikeness.

If translations of poems enrich great literature, those of plays may exercise a yet greater influence; for theater is truly the executive power of literature. A. W. Schlegel did a translation of Shakespeare, which, combining exactness with inspiration, is completely national in Germany. English plays thus passed on are staged in the German theater, and Shakespeare and Schiller have become compatriots there. It would be possible to obtain the same sort of result in Italy; French dramatic authors are as close to the taste of Italians as is Shakespeare to that of the Germans, and perhaps [Racine's] *Athalie* could be performed with success at Milan's beautiful theater by providing the choirs with the accompaniment of wonderful Italian music. You can say as much as you please that people do not go to the theater in Italy to listen, but to talk, to get together in the boxes with their close friends. But it is still true that to listen every day for five hours, more or less, to what people call dialogue in Italian operas is, in the long run, a sure way of diminishing the intellectual faculties of a nation. When Casti did comic operas, when Metastasio adapted to music thoughts full of charm and loftiness, amusement lost nothing and reason acquired much. In the midst of this habitually frivolous society where each person seeks out other people so as not to confront himself, if you could penetrate all this amusement with some ideas and feelings, you could plant something serious in the mind that would ultimately give it real value.

Italian literature is now divided between scholars who refer again and again to the ashes of the past in order to discover therein more sparks of gold, and writers who trust to the euphony of their language so as to make lovely harmonies without ideas, to string exclamations, declamations, and invocations together where there is not a single word that either comes from the heart or touches it. Would it not then be possible to restore by degrees, through active emulation of the theater's successes, the originality of spirit and lifelikeness of style without which there can be no literature, or even any of the essential prerequisites for one?

A taste for sentimental drama has taken hold of the Italian stage, and, in place of that saucy gaiety that previously prevailed, in place of those comedy characters that are classics throughout Europe, we see performed, from the opening scenes of these dramas, the most insipid murders, if I may say so, from which a miserable spectacle might be crafted. Does it not constitute a poor education for a rather considerable number of people that such plays are so often repeated?

The taste of Italians in fine art is as simple as it is noble; but speech is also one of the fine arts, and it must be attributed the same character; it is attached more closely to all that constitutes man, and one would sooner do without paintings and monuments than without the feelings to which they must be devoted.

The Italians are very enthusiastic about their language; great men have shown it to best advantage, and intellectual honors have been the only pleasures for the Italian nation, and often its only consolation as well. In order that every man capable of thought might feel motivated to develop himself, all nations must have an active principle of importance – some military, others political. The Italians must make themselves noticed through literature and fine art; otherwise the country will fall into a form of apathy from which the sun itself could scarcely awaken it.

Percy Bysshe Shelley

Percy Bysshe Shelley (1792-1822), one of the great English romantic poets, was also an avid translator – from ancient Greek especially, but also from the German of Goethe, from the Spanish of Calderón, and from the Italian of Dante. It is one of the typical ironies of Western translation theory that such a devoted translator, when he pronounced on translation in his 'Defence of Poetry', should attack it as 'vain'.

Shelley was born to a wealthy nobleman, Timothy Shelley; he attended Eton and, in 1810, entered University College, Oxford, which he enjoyed immensely until, with his close friend Thomas Jefferson Hogg, he was expelled for the writing of a pamphlet on 'The Necessity of Atheism'. A few months later, in August, 1811, he married the 16-year-old Harriet Westbrook; when Hogg tried to seduce Harriet soon after the wedding, the Shelleys fled London to the Lake District, where Percy unsuccessfully attempted to meet the older poets Wordsworth and Coleridge. He did meet and befriend the philosopher William Godwin, whose works he had read with reverence for several years; and as Harriet grew increasingly disaffected from Percy and his friends, Percy grew fonder of Godwin's 16-year-old daughter Mary, who had been raised intellectual and unconventional by her father and her mother Mary Wollstonecroft, the well-known writer and women's rights activist. Harriet gave birth to their daughter, Ianthe, early in 1814 (and a son, Charles Bysshe, later that same year); a few months later Percy eloped with Mary Godwin to the Continent, where they travelled extensively until they ran out of money. So ruinous were their debts, in fact, that upon their return to London the Shelleys were forced to live in hiding to avoid arrest. Percy's grandfather died the following January, however, and his debts were paid and a £1000 annual allowance settled on him.

All this while Shelley had been writing poetry – *Queen Mab* had appeared in 1813, *Alastor* in 1816 – and when he and Mary and their infant son William moved to Lake Geneva, Switzerland, in the summer of 1816, they made fast friends with Lord Byron, who was living in the house above them. Later that year Harriet committed suicide by drowning; the grieving Percy was denied custody of the two children Harriet had borne him by the Lord Chancellor. He and Mary were married December 30, 1816; she later gave birth to a daughter, Clara, but both William and Clara died before the age of 3. In 1818, after the famous writing contest that inspired Mary to write *Frankenstein*, they moved to Italy, where Shelley wrote most of his greatest poetry, including *Prometheus Unbound* and *The Cenci*, and did most of his translating. In 1820 their third son, Percy Florence, was born in that city; he was the only child to survive. Shelley drowned in the Gulf of Spezia in 1822, at the age of 30, when a sudden squall capsized his yacht, the *Don Juan*.

Shelley wrote 'A Defence of Poetry' in 1821 – in Pisa, where he and Mary formed the nucleus of what came to be known as the 'Pisan Circle' – in response to his friend Thomas Love Peacock's witty satire on romantic poetry of the year before, 'The Four Ages of Poetry'. His remarks on translation were not new – Dante had made similar claims half a millennium earlier – but the phrase "it were as wise to cast a violet into a crucible" stuck, and imagistically brought ancient anxieties about translation into the Industrial Revolution.

The Violet and the Crucible
From *A Defence of Poetry* (1821; first published, 1840)

Sounds as well as thoughts have relation both between each other and towards that which they represent, and a perception of the order of those relations has always been found connected with a perception of the order of the relations of thoughts. Hence the language of poets has ever affected a certain uniform and harmonious recurrence of sound, without which it were not poetry, and which is scarcely less indispensable to the communication of its influence, than the words themselves, without reference to their particular order. Hence the vanity of translation; it were as wise to cast a violet into a crucible that you might discover the formal principle of its colour and odour, as seek to transfuse from one language into another the creations of a poet. The plant must spring again from its seed, or it will bear no flower – and this is the burthen of the curse of Babel.

Arthur Schopenhauer

Arthur Schopenhauer (1788-1860) was a major transitional figure in German philosophy: reacting strongly against Hegelian idealism and its foundations in romanticism, he also mediated German romanticism for the twentieth century, especially through his influence upon Friedrich Nietzsche (and thus existentialism) and Sigmund Freud (and thus psychoanalysis).

Schopenhauer was born in Danzig (nowadays Gdansk, Poland); his father Heinrich was a wealthy merchant, his mother Johanna a writer who later became well-known as a novelist, essayist, and travel writer. Danzig had been seized by Prussia 16 years before his birth, but it was not officially annexed into the Prussian empire until he was 5; at that point, in 1793, the Schopenhauer family moved to the free city of Hamburg, where Arthur received a gentleman's classical education. He also spent two years between 10 and 12 living with a business colleague of his father's in Le Havre, France, in order to learn that language well. His father was grooming him to be a businessman like himself, and he attended a private business school and reluctantly agreed, in 1805, to be apprenticed into a commercial concern.

Shortly thereafter, however, his father died, and his mother and younger sister moved to Weimar, where Johanna managed to insinuate herself into Goethe's circle. Arthur remained behind in Hamburg for another year of schooling, but shifted his emphasis from business to the arts and sciences. In 1807 he followed his family to Weimar, and in 1809 entered the University of Göttingen to study medicine; the next semester, however, he shifted to the humanities, where he immersed himself in Plato and Kant. In 1811 he transferred to the University of Berlin, where he studied under Fichte and Schleiermacher – without being favourably impressed. He was already developing the pessimistic and pugnacious mentality that would become his hallmark as a philosopher, and he was particularly disgusted with the vagueness of Fichte. Two years later, in 1813, he completed his dissertation and took his Ph.D. at the University of Jena.

Moving back to Weimar, he worked closely with Goethe, whom he admired immensely, and who was already working on Eastern poetry; Schopenhauer soon became enamoured of the Vedanta, and in later years proclaimed the *Upanishads*, along with Plato and Kant, the foundation of his philosophical system. With characteristic asperity, however, he declared he could not stomach what he considered his mother's frivolous lifestyle, and moved to Dresden, where he wrote a treatise on colour theory that supported Goethe against Newton. Goethe was not impressed. Then followed several years of work on his magnum opus, *The World as Will and Idea* (1819), often called the summit of Schopenhauer's thought – his later work is generally regarded as little more than exposition. The next year he engaged Hegel in public debate, and came away feeling victorious; but Hegelianism was sweeping Europe, and Schopenhauer's lectures at the University of Berlin, scheduled at the same hour as Hegel's, did not draw students. *The World as Will and Idea* was largely ignored, his lecture hall stood empty semester after semester, and Schopenhauer sank further and further into a black despair. Before he took up his post in Berlin he had toured Italy; now he took a year to tour it a second time, and then spent another year lying ill in Munich. When he returned to Berlin in 1825 and found nothing changed, he retired to Frankfurt and took up, among other things, translation. He was to live there the remaining 28 years of his life, austerely, ascetically, in imitation of his mentor Kant, walking his poodle, in old-fashioned black clothes.

He continued to publish during these years, despite the utter neglect of his contemporaries: *On the Will in Nature* (1836), *On the Freedom of the Will* (1839), *On the Basis of Morality* (1840), and a greatly expanded *World as Will and Idea* (1844). This second edition, which was to make his reputation in later years, was almost impossible to publish; it was rejected by three publishers before a Berlin bookseller agreed to print it without paying Schopenhauer royalties. In 1851 he published his *Parerga und Paralipomena*, the essay collection excerpted below; and within a very few years the tide began to turn. Prominent attacks on Hegelianism began to appear, often mentioning Schopenhauer as a leading alternative figure; lectures began to be offered on his philosophy; an Italian scholar wrote a dialogue comparing him with Giacomo Leopardi, the Italian pessimist. In 1854 Richard Wagner sent him a copy of *The Ring of the Nibelung*, with a grateful inscription. Nietzsche's early work was heavily influenced by Schopenhauer, and Freud read heavily in both men's works. The Swiss historian Jacob Burckhardt was strongly influenced by him as well. During the last decade of his life he was gratified by a rising swell of attention; after his painless death in 1860 the swell became a flood.

Schopenhauer's essay 'On Language and Words' from the *Parerga* stands in a long tradition dating back to Roger Bacon and beyond, attacking translation as an unconscionable distortion of great originals and calling for a return to serious study of the classical languages. It also shows his training and interest in the natural sciences, in the image of the crucible, which Schleiermacher and Shelley had used before him: "Even if one is a wizard with electric machinery or has isolated the radical of fluoridic acid in a crucible, without Latin one still belongs to the vulgar [*Volk*]".

On Language and Words
From *Parerga und Paralipomena* (1851)
Translated by Douglas Robinson

306

The animal voice serves only the expression of the will, in its motions and commotions; the human voice serves that also of knowledge. This is why the latter almost always makes an unpleasant impression on us, bird sounds never.

Without doubt human language originated from interjections, which were the expressions not of concepts but, very like animal sounds, of feelings, the motions of the will. The different sorts of interjection then immediately emerged, and out of their differences the transition to nouns, verbs, personal pronouns, etc.

307

It is well known that, grammatically speaking, the older the language the more perfect it is; languages degenerate gradually from the noble Sanskrit down to the gibberish of English, patched together as it is from this and that mismatched piece of thought-clothing. This gradual degradation is a powerful argument against the fond theories of our insipidly smiling optimists about "humanity's steady ameliorative progress", to which they would twist the deplorable history of the two-legged species; but even apart from that it is a problem that is not easy to solve. We cannot help but think that the first human generation to emerge from the bosom of nature must have been more utterly and childishly ignorant than us, and as a result more coarse and ungainly. How then can such a species have developed this highly elaborate linguistic structure, these complex and manifold grammatical forms? – assuming, of course, the previous gradual accumulation of lexical items. On the other hand, we everywhere see children clinging to the language of their parents and making only small and gradual changes in it. Still, experience teaches us that languages are not perfected over the succession of generations but, as mentioned earlier, precisely the opposite: they become simpler and more wretched.

Should we nevertheless assume that a language is like a plant, which, having sprung from a simple seed, an unprepossessing shoot, gradually grows until it reaches its fullest growth, after which it begins to droop as it ages – and that we know nothing of its earlier growth, only of its decay? A mere figurative and therefore arbitrary hypothesis – a metaphor, not an explanation! In our quest for the latter it seems to me most plausible to assume that humans discovered language *instinctually*: inasmuch as that instinct lay dormant in them from the beginning, they were able to create essential tools and instruments of reason, without reflection or conscious design. Once language existed, then, the instinct was no longer needed for these applied purposes, and atrophied. And just as all natural works created by pure instinct – beaver dams, bees' and wasps' nests, bird nests in all their manifold and yet functionally adequate forms, and so on – have their own characteristic perfection in being precisely and perfectly *what they are* and serving the function called for by their purpose, impressing us with the profound wisdom lodged therein, so too is it with the first primordial language: it possesses the perfection of all instinctual works. The task of grammar, that branch of study that emerged thousands of years after that which it studies, is to trace this perfection so as to bring it into the light of reflection and articulate consciousness.

308

The human word is the most durable material. The most evanescent sensation, fleshed out by a poet in the words that fit it best, will live on in and through them for millennia, and will come alive again in every receptive reader.

309

The learning of other languages is at once a direct and an indirect way of forming one's mind, profoundly efficacious and spiritual. Thus the axiom of Charles V: "The more languages you speak, the more human you are". (*Quot linguas quis callet, tot homines valet.*) This rests on the following.

It is not always possible to find an exact equivalent in one language for a word in another. Thus concepts signified by words in one language are likewise never exactly the same as those signified by words in another; and if for the most part they are very close, sometimes strikingly so, as with συλληψιφ and *conceptio*,[1] *Schneider* and *tailleur*,[2] still we frequently find similar and related concepts that are yet, by some modulation, significantly different. Let me make plain what I mean with the following examples:

---

[1] Both meaning conception, becoming pregnant. [Tr/Ed]
[2] Both meaning tailor. [Tr/Ed]

αϖιδευτος, rudis, roh.[3]
ορμη, impetus, Andrang.[4]
μηχανη, Mittel, medium.
seccatore, *Quälgeist*, *importun*.[5]
ingénieux, *sinnreich*, clever.
Geist, *esprit*, wit.
Missig, *facetus*, *plaisant*.[6]
Malice, *Bosheit*, wickedness.

to which innumerable others, and certainly more apposite ones, might be added. This might be represented graphically with roughly superimposed but not quite concentric circles, thus:

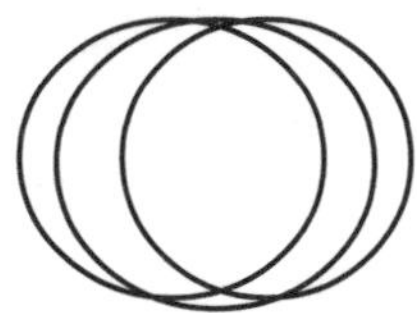

Sometimes the word for a concept is lacking in one language, while existing in most, maybe even all other languages; a most scandalous example is the absence in French of the verb 'to stand'. Conversely, some concepts can only be expressed in a single language, and the word for it is then borrowed into others: for example, the Latin 'affect', the French 'naive', the English 'comfortable', 'disappointment', 'gentleman', and many others. Sometimes a foreign language conveys a concept with a nuance that is missing in our own expression: then anyone concerned to express his or her thoughts precisely will use the foreign word and let the purists howl. Wherever a language does not use a specific word to signify the same concept as another, the dictionary will indicate as much with several related expressions that convey the concept's meaning, but not concentrically – rather, as in the above figure, in various directions around it, marking off the boundaries within which it signifies. Thus for example the Latin *honestum* is paraphrased with words like 'esteemed', 'honoured', 'honourable', 'respectable', 'virtuous'; likewise the Greek σωφρων.[7]

Hence the necessary inadequacy of all translations. It is almost never possible to transpose a sentence pregnant with meaning and character from one language into another so as to make precisely and perfectly the same impression on a speaker of the second. Even in bare prose the finest translation will at best stand in the same relation to its original as a piece of music does to its transposition into another key. Those who know music will know what this means. It is the reason why every translation must remain inert, its style stiff, forced, unnatural – or else free, which is to say it makes do with an *à peu près* ['pretty close'], and is thus false. A library full of translations is like an art gallery hung with copies. Translations of the ancients are surrogates for the originals, like chicory coffee for the real thing. *Poems* cannot be translated, only recast, and that is always a hit-or-miss affair.

In learning a language, therefore, the difficulty lies primarily in learning concepts for which the new language has words and our old language has none – at least no exactly corresponding ones. This is why learning a foreign language means mapping out in one's mind hitherto uncharted conceptual spheres. One does not merely learn words; one annexes concepts. This is especially true when learning the classical languages, for the ancients' expressive modes differ more markedly from ours than any modern language does from another. When translating into Latin, for example, one is forced to give the original text turns that are quite different from those of the original. Indeed one must usually 'render' the original ideas in the chemical sense of the word, melt them down and recast them – break them down into their smallest constituent parts and then rebuild the compound. And this is precisely where foreign language learning becomes so enormously beneficial for the mind. It is only when one has correctly grasped the concepts signified in the foreign language by individual words, and can directly and immediately *think* the concept corresponding to every word – *not* when one has learned first to translate a word into one's native language and then to think the concept through the mediation of this signification, which does not always correspond to the original – it is only then, I say, that one has grasped the *spirit* of the language to be learned. It is only then that one has taken a significant step toward an understanding of the nation that speaks the language: for as style is to the mind of the individual, so is language to that of the nation.[8] One has truly internalized a language when one can translate not books but oneself into it, and thus without losing one's individuality can communicate in it immediately, and be as pleasing abroad as one is at home.

[3] All meaning rough, raw, with varying connotations. [Tr/Ed]

[4] All meaning various kinds of rapid or violent impulse, such as an attack (*impetus*) or a rush (*Andrang*). [Tr/Ed]

[5] Italian, German, and French for a bore or irritating person. [Tr/Ed]

[6] German, Latin, and French for amusing, witty. [Tr/Ed]

[7] There is no adequate equivalent for the Greek σωφροσυνη in any other language. [Au] The adjective *sophron* is usually rendered 'sensible, discreet, prudent, wise', or 'temperate, moderate, chaste, sober'; the noun *sophrosune* 'soundness of mind, good sense, prudence, discretion, moderation'. [Tr/Ed]

[8] A true command of more of the newer languages, the ability to read in them with ease, is a key to overcoming the national narrow-mindedness that plagues us all. [Au]

People of below-average abilities will not pick up a foreign language easily. They'll learn the words themselves well enough, but will use them only in the sense of their rough equivalent in their native language, and will always cling to the turns and phrases typical of that language. They are incapable of appropriating the *spirit* of the foreign language, precisely because they think not with their own heads but, for the most part, with current turns and phrases borrowed from their native language. Even in their own language, therefore, they only use hackneyed phrases (*phrases banales*[9]), which they cobble together so ineptly as to underscore just how unconscious they are of what they're trying to say, just how restricted their thinking is to the words themselves. In fact their speech is little more than a parrot's prattle. Conversely, the originality and aptness with which a person turns a phrase are the infallible signs of a superior mind.

All of this makes clear that in the process of learning a foreign language:

– new concepts take shape in order to fill new signs with meaning;

– concepts take on new definition through the proliferation of words for them, where earlier the existence of a single word gave only a broad and indistinct impression of its meaning;

– one uncovers relationships of which one had not previously been aware, because the foreign language may express the concept with a unique trope or metaphor;

– one thus becomes conscious of an infinite number of nuances, similarities and differences, relationships between things, through the mediation of the language one is learning;

– and finally, through all this, one gains a multifaceted perspective on all things.

It follows that one thinks differently in every language, and that every new language we learn modifies and colors our thinking. Thus while polyglottism has many ancillary advantages, it is also immediately advantageous in forming the mind, for it corrects and matures our opinions through the increased multiplicity and fine-tuning of concepts, and at the same time enhances the agility of our thinking by gradually dissociating the concept from the word. This effect is disproportionately greater with the ancient than the modern languages, because their greater divergences from ours will not allow us to render them word for word, but demand rather that we melt them down and recast them in another form. Or, to extend that chemical metaphor, while translation from one modern language to another at most requires that the sentence to be translated be broken down into its immediate constituents and then reconstituted from these, translation into Latin frequently requires that it be broken down into its deepest and most basic constituents (pure thought content) and only then regenerated in totally different forms, so that, for example, what here is expressed with nouns must there be rendered with verbs, or vice versa. The same is true of translation from the ancient languages into the modern; and the process in either direction gives us some sense of how distant we remain from knowing the ancients by means of such translations.

The Greeks did without the advantage of language study, which did save them a good deal of time, but also led them to use that time far less economically, as is evident from their lounging around the αγορα [agora] all day every day – so reminiscent of the *lazzaroni*[10] and generally the way Italians hustle and bustle about their piazzas.

It's easy to see, finally, that the very best way to train oneself in the full and versatile expression of one's thoughts in one's native language is to imitate the style of the ancients in their own languages, so superior to ours in grammatical perfection. It is indispensable for one who would become a great writer – and the same is true of would-be sculptors and painters – to hold off on original composition until he or she has had sufficient practice at imitating ancient models. It is only by writing Latin that one learns diction as an art whose material is language, and which must thus be handled with the greatest care and circumspection. This sharpens the student's alertness to the meaning and value of words, to word order and grammatical forms; one learns to weigh these exactly and thus to handle the costly material designed to express and preserve worthwhile thoughts, to respect the language in which one writes, so that one doesn't play around with it whimsically, capriciously, reshaping it to fit one's every mood. Without this preparatory work, writing easily deteriorates into pure chatter.

People with no Latin are like those who travel through beautiful scenery in the fog: hemmed in by foreshortened vistas, they see clearly only what is in front of their nose; everything just a few steps away is lost in obscurity. The vista of Latinists, on the other hand, is wonderfully wide, taking in modernity, the Middle Ages, and classical antiquity. Needless to say Greek, let alone Sanskrit, widens their vista considerably more. Even if one is a wizard with electric machinery or has isolated the radical of fluoridic acid in a crucible, without Latin one still belongs to the vulgar.

Having learned Latin, you will soon care little more

[9] Schopenhauer gives both this French and the English ('hackney'd phrases') in the original languages. [Tr/Ed]

[10] A term used for the Neapolitan poor, who had remained monarchist in 1798 when the rich of Naples had proclaimed a republic. [Tr/Ed]

for your writers who have no Latin than you do for swaggering journeyman barbers. In fact, they're already well on their way to that moment, with their Gallicisms and their feigned lightness of style. Noble Germans, to vulgarity have ye turned, and mediocrity will ye find. For a true signboard of sloth and hothouse of know-nothingness, take a look at the German-annotated editions (how dare they face the light of day!) of Greek and even, *horribile dictu*, Latin authors! Yes, with notes in *German*! What infamy! How is a student even to learn Latin if he's constantly spoken to in Mrs Mother Tongue! That is what made *in schola nil nisi latine*[11] an excellent old rule. The humour of the thing[12] is that the teacher nowadays writes Latin no more easily than the student reads it – take that however you like. Sloth and its daughter know-nothingness are responsible, nothing else, and it's a disgrace. The one has learned nothing; the other wants to learn nothing. Cigar-smoking and tub-thumping these days have banished learning, just as picture books for grown-up children have replaced literary magazines.

In high school no Old German literature should be taught, no *Nibelungenlied*[13] and other medieval poems; important and well worth reading as these works undoubtedly are, they contribute nothing to the formation of taste and thus rob the student of the time required to learn the ancient, truly classical literature. You noble German patriots: if you displace the Greek and Roman classics with Old German doggerel, you will bring your children up to be no better than idlers. For to compare the *Nibelungenlied* with the *Iliad* is outright blasphemy, which the ears of our youth, most of all, should be spared.

Edward FitzGerald

Edward FitzGerald (1809-1883) is best known for his *Rubáiyát of Omar Khayyám* (1859), a free translation that has become a classic of English literature, the source of such famous phrases as "A jug of wine, a loaf of bread, and thou" and "The moving finger writes".

Educated at Trinity College, Cambridge, where he became (and remained throughout his life) friends with William Makepeace Thackeray, FitzGerald spent the 50-odd years of his life after graduation in semiretirement at his country estate in Woodbridge, where he was frequently visited by such friends as Alfred, Lord Tennyson and Thomas Carlyle. He also engaged in a voluminous correspondence with these and other notables of the day – a correspondence from which the excerpts below are taken.

FitzGerald is famous among readers of English literature for his free translations of Calderón, Omar Khayyám, and others; he is famous among students of translation for his pithy aphorisms in favour of free translation from the two letters below, "Better a live sparrow than a stuffed eagle" and "the live dog better than the dead lion".

Letter to E. B. Cowell (1859)

Geldestone Hall, Beccles. April 27

My Dear Cowell,

I sent you poor old Omar[1] who has *his* kind of consolation for all these things. I doubt you will regret you ever introduced him to me. And yet you would have me print the original, with many worse things than I have translated. The bird epic might be finished at once; but 'cui bono?' ['who profits?']. No one cares for such things; and there are doubtless so many better things to care about. I hardly know why I print any of these things, which nobody buys; and I scarce now see the few I give them to. But when one has done one's best, and is sure that that best is better than so many will take pains to do, though far from the best that *might be done*, one likes to make an end of the matter by print. I suppose very few people have ever taken such pains in translation as I have; though certainly not to be literal. But at all cost, a thing must *live*; with a transfusion of one's own worse life if one can't retain the original's better. Better a live sparrow than a stuffed eagle. I shall be very well pleased to see the new MS. of Omar. I shall *one day* (if I live) print the 'Birds', and a strange experiment on old Calderón's two great plays;[2] and then shut up shop in the poetic line. Adieu: Give my love to the Lady: and believe me yours very truly

E.F.G.

[11] "In school nothing unless in Latin". [Tr/Ed]

[12] Schopenhauer is alluding here to Shakespeare's *Henry V* 2.1.70. [Tr/Ed]

[13] 'Song of the Nibelungs', an epic poem written c. 1200 by an unknown Austrian, drawing on Old Norse legends (the Edda); its most famous artistic adaptation is Richard Wagner's opera cycle *The Ring of the Nibelungs*. [Tr/Ed]

[1] Omar Khayyám. FitzGerald had just published the *Rubaiyat* in English translation, in an anonymous pamphlet. He complains in the next lines about his readers' neglect; his success was not to come until the next year, 1860, when Dante Gabriel Rossetti and Algernon Swinburne discovered his 'Omar'. [Ed]

[2] FitzGerald had published his translation of *Six Dramas of Calderón* in 1853. [Ed]

Letter to J. R. Lowell (1878)

Woodbridge. Decr. 1878

My Dear Sir,

...

December 22.

I left off when my reader came to finish [Walter Scott's] *The Bride of Lammermoor*; as wonderful to me as ever. O, the Austens, Eliots, and even Thackerays, won't eclipse Sir Walter for long.

To come down rather a little from him, my Calderón, which you speak of – very many beside myself, with as much fair dramatic spirit, knowledge of good English and English verse, would do quite as well as you think I do, if they would not hamper themselves with forms of verse, and thought, irreconcilable with English language and English ways of thinking. I am persuaded that, to keep life in the work (as drama must) the translator (however inferior to his original) must re-cast that original into his own likeness, more or less; the less like his original, so much the worse; but still, the live dog better than the dead lion; in drama, I say. As to epic, is not Cary still the best Dante? Cowper and Pope were both men of genius, out of my sphere; but whose Homer still holds its own? The elaborately exact, or the 'teacup-time' parody?[3] Is not Fairfax' Tasso good? I never read Harington's Ariosto, English or Italian. Another shot have I made at *Faust* in Bayard Taylor's version; but I do not even get on with him as with Hayward, hampered as he (Taylor) is with his allegiance to original metres, etc. His notes I was interested in; but I shall die ungoethed, I doubt, so far as poetry goes; I always believe he was philosopher and critic.

Matthew Arnold

Matthew Arnold (1822-1888) was possibly the strongest and most influential voice of Victorian England. A poet and literary critic, he is best known to us today as a social critic, and specifically as an apostle of 'culture' in the high-romantic sense of the arts as secular religion.

Arnold's father was the famous headmaster of Rugby School, Thomas Arnold, and he himself attended Rugby as well before entering Balliol College at Oxford University, an institution for which he retained a lifelong passion. He held the chair in poetry there for a decade, from 1857 to 1867, during which period he delivered and subsequently published the famous lectures on translating Homer excerpted below; but for most of his adult life he travelled extensively as inspector of schools, and his influence on the British educational system, shaped by his love for the romantic pedagogies of Wordsworth and Coleridge, was large.

Arnold began to publish his poetry while at Oxford, winning a prize for his poem 'Cromwell' in 1843; around the time he stepped down from the Oxford chair, 1867, he seems to have stopped writing poetry almost entirely. In his preface to *Empedocles on Etna* (1852), he called for a new classicism, extolling formal unity and impersonal universality; and while his writing was always an attempt to mediate between the classical virtues and the romantic vision that struck a deep chord in his being, his poetry was always more romantic – sentimental, nostalgic, personal, even confessional – than classical.

Arnold's criticism, which rose from the dying embers of his poetry, was always driven by a deeply felt social vision. While in our century his critical principles – "to see the object as in itself it really is", "to try to know the best that is known and thought in the world" – have become watchwords of mystificatory conservatism, depoliticized formalism, his central concern was always with the effect of the creative and critical impulses on society, on the relative health or sickness of the body politic. In *On Translating Homer*, for example, Homer is not just a writer to him; he is a curative force in a sick world, a nexus of feeling whose plainness and nobility have the power to calm the frenetic, unify the divisive, deepen the superficial. He developed these ideas more fully in his most famous essay, 'The Function of Criticism at the Present Time' (1865), and his most famous book, *Culture and Anarchy* (1869).

The Translator's Tribunal
From *On Translating Homer* (1861)

... *Nunquamne reponam?*[1]

It has more than once been suggested to me that I should translate Homer. That is a task for which I have neither the time nor the courage; but the suggestion led me to regard yet more closely a poet whom I had already long studied, and for one or two years the works of Homer were seldom out of my hands. The study of classical literature is probably on the decline; but, whatever may be the fate of this study in general, it is certain that, as instruction spreads and the number of readers increases, attention will be more and more directed to the poetry of Homer, not indeed as part of

[3] Cowper's is the exact, Pope's the 'tea-cup time' parody that 'holds up'. [Ed]

[1] "Shall I never rest?" Juvenal 1.1. [Ed]

a classical course, but as the most important poetical monument existing. Even within the last ten years two fresh translations of the *Iliad* have appeared in England: one by a man of great ability and genuine learning, Professor Newman; the other by Mr Wright, the conscientious and painstaking translator of Dante. It may safely be asserted that neither of these works will take rank as the standard translation of Homer; that the task of rendering him will still be attempted by other translators. It may perhaps be possible to render to these some service, to save them some loss of labour, by pointing out rocks on which their predecessors have split, and the right objects on which a translator of Homer should fix his attention.

It is disputed what aim a translator should propose to himself in dealing with his original. Even this preliminary is not yet settled. On one side it is said that the translation ought to be such "that the reader should, if possible, forget that it is a translation at all, and be lulled into the illusion that he is reading an original work, – something original" (if the translation be in English), "from an English hand". The real original is in this case, it is said, "taken as a basis on which to rear a poem that shall affect our countrymen as the original may be conceived to have affected its natural hearers". On the other hand, Mr Newman, who states the foregoing doctrine only to condemn it, declares that he "aims at precisely the opposite: to retain every peculiarity of the original, so far as he is able, *with the greater care the more foreign it may happen to be*"; so that it may "never be forgotten that he is imitating, and imitating in a different material". The translator's "first duty", says Mr Newman, "is a historical one: to be *faithful*". Probably both sides would agree that the translator's "first duty is to be faithful"; but the question at issue between them is, in what faithfulness consists.

My one object is to give practical advice to a translator; and I shall not the least concern myself with theories of translation as such. But I advise the translator not to try "to rear on the basis of the *Iliad*, a poem that shall affect our countrymen as the original may be conceived to have affected its natural hearers"; and for this simple reason, that we cannot possibly tell *how* the *Iliad* "affected its natural hearers". It is probably meant merely that he should try to affect Englishmen powerfully, as Homer affected Greeks powerfully; but this direction is not enough, and can give no real guidance. For all great poets affect their hearers powerfully, but the effect of one poet is one thing, that of another poet another thing: it is our translator's business to reproduce the effect of Homer, and the most powerful emotion of the unlearned English reader can never assure him whether he has *re*produced this, or whether he has produced something else. So, again, he may follow Mr Newman's directions, he may try to be 'faithful', he may "retain every peculiarity of his original"; but who is to assure him, who is to assure Mr Newman himself, that, when he has done this, he has done that for which Mr Newman enjoins this to be done, "adhered closely to Homer's manner and habit of thought"? Evidently the translator needs some more practical directions than these. No one can tell him how Homer affected the Greeks; but there are those who can tell him how Homer affects *them*. These are scholars; who possess, at the same time with knowledge of Greek, adequate poetical taste and feeling. No translation will seem to them of much worth compared with the original; but they alone can say whether the translation produces more or less the same effect upon them as the original. They are the only competent tribunal in this matter: the Greeks are dead; the unlearned Englishman has not the data for judging; and no man can safely confide in his own single judgment of his own work. Let not the translator, then, trust to his notions of what the ancient Greeks would have thought of him; he will lose himself in the vague. Let him not trust to what the ordinary English reader thinks of him; he will be taking the blind for his guide. Let him not trust to his own judgment of his own work; he may be misled by individual caprices. Let him ask how his work affects those who both know Greek and can appreciate poetry; whether to read it gives the Provost of Eton,[2] or Professor Thompson at Cambridge, or Professor Jowett here in Oxford, at all the same feeling which to read the original gives them. I consider that when Bentley said of Pope's translation, "It was a pretty poem, but must not be called Homer", the work, in spite of all its power and attractiveness, was judged.

Ὡς ἄν ὁ φρόνιμος ὁρίσειεν,[3] – "as the judicious would determine", – that is a test to which everyone professes himself willing to submit his works. Unhappily, in most cases, no two persons agree as to who 'the judicious' are. In the present case, the ambiguity is removed: I suppose the translator at one with me as to the tribunal to which alone he should look for judgement; and he has thus obtained a practical test by which to estimate the real success of his work. How is he to proceed, in order that his work, tried by this test, may be found most successful?

First of all, there are certain negative counsels which I will give him. Homer has occupied men's minds so much, such a literature has arisen about him, that everyone who approaches him should resolve strictly to limit himself to that which may directly serve the object for which he approaches him. I advise the translator to have nothing to do with the questions, whether Homer ever existed; whether the poet of the

---

[2] Probably E. C. Hawtrey. [Ed]

[3] Aristotle, *Nicomachean Ethics* 1107a. [Ed]

Iliad be one or many; whether the *Iliad* be one poem or an *Achilleis* and an *Iliad* stuck together; whether the Christian doctrine of the Atonement is shadowed forth in the Homeric mythology; whether the Goddess Latona[4] in any way prefigures the Virgin Mary, and so on. These are questions which have been discussed with learning, with ingenuity, nay, with genius; but they have two inconveniences, – one general for all who approach them, one particular for the translator. The general inconvenience is that there really exist no data for determining them. The particular inconvenience is that their solution by the translator, even were it possible, could be of no benefit to his translation.

I advise him, again, not to trouble himself with constructing a special vocabulary for his use in translation; with excluding a certain class of English words, and with confining himself to another class, in obedience to any theory about the peculiar qualities of Homer's style. Mr Newman says that "the entire dialect of Homer being essentially archaic, that of a translator ought to be as much Saxo-Norman as possible, and owe as little as possible to the elements thrown into our language by classical learning". Mr Newman is unfortunate in the observance of his own theory; for I continually find in his translation words of Latin origin, which seem to me quite alien to the simplicity of Homer, – 'responsive', for instance, which is a favourite word of Mr Newman, to represent the Homeric ἀμειβόμενος:

> Great Hector of the motley helm thus
> spake to her *responsive*.
>
> But thus *responsively* to him spake god-
> like Alexander.

And the word 'celestial', again, in the grand address of Zeus to the horses of Achilles,

> You, who are born *celestial*, from Eld and
> Death exempted!

seems to me in that place exactly to jar upon the feeling as too bookish. But, apart from the question of Mr Newman's fidelity to his own theory, such a theory seems to me both dangerous for a translator and false in itself. Dangerous for a translator; because, wherever one finds such a theory announced (and one finds it pretty often), it is generally followed by an explosion of pedantry; and pedantry is of all things in the world the most un-Homeric. False in itself; because, in fact, we owe to the Latin element in our language most of that very rapidity and clear decisiveness by which it is contradistinguished from the German, and in sympathy with the languages of Greece and Rome: so that to limit an English translator of Homer to words of Saxon origin is to deprive him of one of his special advantages for translating Homer. In Voss's well-known translation of Homer, it is precisely the qualities of his German language itself, something heavy and trailing both in the structure of its sentences and in the words of which it is composed, which prevent his translation, in spite of the hexameters, in spite of the fidelity, from creating in us the impression created by the Greek. Mr Newman's prescription, if followed, would just strip the English translator of the advantage which he has over Voss.

The frame of mind in which we approach an author influences our correctness of appreciation of him; and Homer should be approached by a translator in the simplest frame of mind possible. Modern sentiment tries to make the ancient not less than the modern world its own; but against modern sentiment in its applications to Homer the translator, if he would feel Homer truly – and unless he feels him truly, how can he render him truly? – cannot be too much on his guard. For example: the writer of an interesting article on English translations of Homer, in the last number of the *National Review*, quotes, I see, with admiration, a criticism of Mr Ruskin on the use of the epithet φυσίζωος, 'life-giving', in that beautiful passage in the third book of the *Iliad*, which follows Helen's mention of her brothers Castor and Pollux as alive, though they were in truth dead:

> ὥς φατο τούς δ᾽ ἤδη κάτεχεν φυσίζωος γαῖα
> ἐν Λακεδαίμονι αὖθι, φίλῃ ἐν πατρίδι γαίῃ[5]

"The poet", says Mr Ruskin, "has to speak of the earth in sadness; but he will not let that sadness affect or change his thought of it. No; though Castor and Pollux be dead, yet the earth is our mother still, – fruitful, life-giving". This is a just specimen of that sort of application of modern sentiment to the ancients, against which a student, who wishes to feel the ancients truly, cannot too resolutely defend himself. It reminds one, as, alas! so much of Mr Ruskin's writing reminds one, of those words of the most delicate of living critics [Sainte-Beuve]: "Comme tout genre de composition a son écueil particulier, celui du genre romanesque, c'est le faux". The reader may feel moved as he reads it; but it is not the less an example of 'le faux' in criticism; it is false. It is not true, as to

[4] Latona (Greek Leto) was a Titan impregnated by Zeus who wandered about (in some versions, pursued by a jealous Hera) before finally giving birth to Apollo and Artemis on the island of Delos. [Ed]

[5] *Iliad,* iii. 243. [Au] "So said she; but them the life-giving earth held fast there in Lakedaimon, in their dear native land" (Andrew Lang, Walter Leaf, and Ernest Myers' translation). [Ed]

that particular passage, that Homer called the earth φυσίζοος because, "though he had to speak of the earth in sadness, he would not let that sadness change or affect his thought of it", but consoled himself by considering that "the earth is our mother still, – fruitful, life-giving". It is not true, as a matter of general criticism, that this kind of sentimentality, eminently modern, inspires Homer at all. "From Homer and Polygnotus I every day learn more clearly", says Goethe, "that in our life here above ground we have, properly speaking, to enact Hell:"[6] – if the student must absolutely have a keynote to the *Iliad*, let him take this of Goethe, and see what he can do with it; it will not, at any rate, like the tender pantheism of Mr Ruskin, falsify for him the whole strain of Homer.

These are negative counsels; I come to the positive. When I say, the translator of Homer should above all be penetrated by a sense of four qualities of his author: – that he is eminently rapid; that he is eminently plain and direct, both in the evolution of his thought and in the expression of it, that is, both in his syntax and in his words; that he is eminently plain and direct in the substance of his thought, that is, in his matter and ideas; and, finally that he is eminently noble; – I probably seem to be saying what is too general to be of much service to anybody. Yet it is strictly true that, for want of duly penetrating themselves with the first-named quality of Homer, his rapidity, Cowper and Mr Wright have failed in rendering him; that, for want of duly appreciating the second-named quality, his plainness and directness of style and diction, Pope and Mr Sotheby have failed in rendering him; that for want of appreciating the third, his plainness and directness of ideas, Chapman has failed in rendering him; while for want of appreciating the fourth, his nobleness, Mr Newman, who has clearly seen some of the faults of his predecessors, has yet failed more conspicuously than any of them.

Coleridge says, in his strange language, speaking of the union of the human soul with the divine essence, that this takes place

> Whene'er the mist, which stands 'twixt God and thee,
> Defecates to a pure transparency;[7]

and so, too, it may be said of that union of the translator with his original, which alone can produce a good translation, that it takes place when the mist which stands between them – the mist of alien modes of thinking, speaking, and feeling on the translator's part – "defecates to a pure transparency", and disappears. But between Cowper and Homer – (Mr Wright repeats in the main Cowper's manner, as Mr Sotheby repeats Pope's manner, and neither Mr Wright's translation nor Mr Sotheby's has, I must be forgiven for saying, any proper reason for existing) – between Cowper and Homer there is interposed the mist of Cowper's elaborate Miltonic manner, entirely alien to the flowing rapidity of Homer; between Pope and Homer there is interposed the mist of Pope's literary artificial manner, entirely alien to the plain naturalness of Homer's manner; between Chapman and Homer there is interposed the mist of the fancifulness of Homer's thought and feeling; while between Mr Newman and Homer is interposed a cloud of more than Egyptian thickness, – namely, a manner, in Mr Newman's version, eminently ignoble, while Homer's manner is eminently noble.

I do not despair of making all these propositions clear to a student who approaches Homer with a free mind. First, Homer is eminently rapid, and to this rapidity the elaborate movement of Miltonic blank verse is alien. The reputation of Cowper, that most interesting man and excellent poet, does not depend on his translation of Homer; and in his preface to the second edition, he himself tells us that he felt, – he had too much poetical taste not to feel, – on returning to his own version after six or seven years, "more dissatisfied with it himself than the most difficult to be pleased of all his judges". And he was dissatisfied with it for the right reason, – that "it seemed to him deficient *in the grace of ease*". Yet he seems to have originally misconceived the manner of Homer so much, that it is no wonder he rendered him amiss. "The similitude of Milton's manner to that of Homer is such", he says,

> that no person familiar with both can read either without being reminded of the other; and it is in those breaks and pauses to which the numbers of the English poet are so much indebted, both for their dignity and variety, that he chiefly copies the Grecian.

It would be more true to say:

> The unlikeness of Milton's manner to that of Homer is such, that no person familiar with both can read either without being struck with his difference from the other; and it is in his breaks and pauses that the English poet is most unlike the Grecian.

The inversion and pregnant conciseness of Milton or Dante are, doubtless, most impressive qualities of style; but they are the very opposites of the directness and flowingness of Homer, which he keeps alike in passages of the simplest narrative, and in those of the

6 *Briefwechsel zwischen Schiller und Goethe*, vi. 230. [Au] *The Correspondence Between Schiller and Goethe*. [Ed]

7 From an epigram on 'Reason', in Coleridge's *On the Constitution of the Church and State*. [Ed]

deepest emotion. Not only, for example, are these lines of Cowper un-Homeric:–

> So numerous seemed those fires the banks
> between
> Of Xanthus, blazing, and the fleet of Greece
> In prospect all of Troy;

where the position of the word 'blazing' gives an entirely un-Homeric movement to this simple passage, describing the fires of the Trojan camp outside of Troy; but the following lines, in that very highly-wrought passage where the horse of Achilles answers his master's reproaches for having left Patroclus on the field of battle, are equally un-Homeric:–

> For not through sloth or tardiness on us
> Aught chargeable, have Ilium's sons thine arms
> Stript from Patroclus' shoulders; but a God
> Matchless in battle, offspring of bright-haired
> Latona, him contending in the van
> Slew, for the glory of the chief of Troy.

Here even the first inversion, "have Ilium's sons thine arms Stript from Patroclus' shoulders", gives the reader a sense of a movement not Homeric; and the second inversion, "a God him contending in the van Slew", gives this sense ten times stronger. Instead of moving on without check, as in reading the original, the reader twice finds himself, in reading the translation, brought up and checked. Homer moves with the same simplicity and rapidity in the highly-wrought as in the simple passage ...

I must repeat what I said in beginning, that the translator of Homer ought steadily to keep in mind where lies the real test of the success of his translation, what judges he is to try to satisfy. He is to try to satisfy *scholars*, because scholars alone have the means of really judging him. A scholar may be a pedant, it is true, and then his judgment will be worthless; but a scholar may also have poetical feeling, and then he can judge him truly; whereas all the poetical feeling in the world will not enable a man who is not a scholar to judge him truly. For the translator is to reproduce Homer, and the scholar alone has the means of knowing that Homer who is to be reproduced. He knows him but imperfectly, for he is separated from him by time, race, and language; but he alone knows him at all. Yet people speak as if there were two real tribunals in this matter, – the scholar's tribunal, and that of the general public. They speak as if the scholar's judgment was one thing, and the general public's judgment another; both with their shortcomings, both with their liability to error; but both to be regarded by the translator. The translator who makes verbal literalness his chief care 'will', says a writer in the *National Review* whom I have already quoted,

> be appreciated by the scholar accustomed to test a translation rigidly by comparison with the original, to look perhaps with excessive care to finish in detail rather than boldness and general effect, and find pardon even for a version that seems bare and bald, so it be scholastic and faithful.

But, if the scholar in judging a translation looks to detail rather than to general effect, he judges it pedantically and ill. The appeal, however, lies not from the pedantic scholar to the general public, which can only like or dislike Chapman's version, or Pope's, or Mr Newman's, but cannot *judge* them; it lies from the pedantic scholar to the scholar who is not pedantic, who knows that Homer is Homer by his general effect, and not by his single words, and who demands but one thing in a translation, – that it shall, as nearly as possible, reproduce for him the *general* effect of Homer. This, then, remains the one proper aim of the translator: to reproduce on the intelligent scholar, as nearly as possible, the *general effect* of Homer. Except so far as he reproduces this, he loses his labour, even though he may make a spirited *Iliad* of his own, like Pope, or translate Homer's *Iliad* word for word, like Mr Newman. If his proper aim were to stimulate in any manner possible the general public, he might be right in following Pope's example; if his proper aim were to help schoolboys to construe Homer, he might be right in following Mr Newman's. But it is not: his proper aim is, I repeat it yet once more, to reproduce on the intelligent scholar, as nearly as he can, the general effect of Homer ...

I shall have to try your patience yet once more upon this subject, and then my task will be completed. I have shown what the four axioms respecting Homer which I have laid down, exclude, what they bid a translator not to do; I have still to show what they supply, what positive help they can give to the translator in his work. I will even, with their aid, myself try my fortune with some of those passages of Homer which I have already noticed; not indeed with any confidence that I more than others can succeed in adequately rendering Homer, but in the hope of satisfying competent judges, in the hope of making it clear to the future translator, that I at any rate follow a right method, and that, in coming short, I come short from weakness of execution, not from original vice of design. This is why I have so long occupied myself with Mr Newman's version; that, apart from all faults of execution, his original design was wrong, and that he has done us the good service of declaring that design in its naked wrongness. To bad practice he has prefixed the bad theory which made the practice bad; he has given us a false theory in his preface, and he has exemplified the bad effects of that false theory in his translation. It is because his starting-point is so bad that he runs so badly; and to save others from taking so false a starting-point, may be to save them from running so futile a course.

Mr Newman, indeed, says in his preface, that if any one dislikes his translation, "he has his easy remedy; to keep aloof from it". But Mr Newman is a writer of considerable and deserved reputation; he is also a Professor of the University of London, an institution which by its position and by its merits acquires every year greater importance. It would be a very grave thing if the authority of so eminent a Professor led his students to misconceive entirely the chief work of the Greek world; that work which, whatever the other works of classical antiquity have to give us, gives it more abundantly than they all. The eccentricity too, the arbitrariness, of which Mr Newman's conception of Homer offers so signal an example, are not a peculiar failing of Mr Newman's own; in varying degrees they are the great defect of English intellect, the great blemish of English literature. Our literature of the eighteenth century, the literature of the school of Dryden, Addison, Pope, Johnson, is a long reaction against this eccentricity, this arbitrariness; that reaction perished by its own faults, and its enemies are left once more masters of the field. It is much more likely that any new English version of Homer will have Mr Newman's faults than Pope's. Our present literature, which is very far, certainly, from having the spirit and power of Elizabethan genius, yet has in its own way these faults, eccentricity and arbitrariness, quite as much as the Elizabethan literature ever had.[8] They are the cause that, while upon none, perhaps, of the modern literatures has so great a sum of force been expended as upon the English literature, at the present hour this literature, regarded not as an object of mere literary interest but as a living intellectual instrument, ranks only third in European effect and importance among the literatures of Europe; it ranks after the literatures of France and Germany. Of these two literatures, as of the intellect of Europe in general, the main effort, for now many years, has been a *critical* effort; the endeavour, in all branches of knowledge, – theology, philosophy, history, art, science, – to see the object as in itself it really is.[9] But, owing to the presence in English literature of this eccentric and arbitrary spirit, owing to the strong tendency of English writers to bring to the consideration of their object some individual fancy, almost the last thing for which one would come to English literature is just that very thing which now Europe most desires – *criticism*. It is useful to notice any signal manifestation of those faults, which thus limit and impair the action of our literature. And therefore I have pointed out how widely, in translating Homer, a man even of real ability and learning may go astray, unless he brings to the study of this clearest of poets one quality in which our English authors, with all their great gifts, are apt to be somewhat wanting – simple lucidity of mind.

[8] Literature of the late sixteenth century, during the reign of Queen Elizabeth I. [Ed]

[9] One of Arnold's most famous phrases, first used here and defended at length in 'The Function of Criticism at the Present Time' (1865). [Ed]

Francis W. Newman

Francis William Newman (1805-1897), scholar, translator, and brother of Cardinal John Henry Newman, is best remembered today not for his translation of the *Iliad* (1861) but for the debate that translation sparked with Matthew Arnold.

Newman was born in London the third son of a banker and his wife, John and Jemima Newman, and was educated at the private school of the Rev. George Nicholas at Ealing and later at Worcester College, Oxford, where he lodged with his brother, the future cardinal. The boys' mother was a Huguenot, their father a deist of some sort, but John Henry converted to Catholicism while at Oxford; Francis resisted his older brother's influence then and for the rest of his life. In 1826 he took a double first in classics and mathematics and became a fellow of Balliol College – a position he would resign four years later, declining to take his M.A. Two of those four years he spent in Dublin, serving as tutor to the children of an Irish peer; it was here that he began attending nonconformist worship services.

After resigning his fellowship in 1830, he followed John Vesey Parnell to Baghdad, where he was impressed with Islam; but returned to England in 1833, where he became a classical tutor at Bristol College (a nonsectarian institution), and later, in 1840, professor of classical literature at Manchester New College (now Manchester College, Oxford); in 1846 he was appointed to the chair in Latin at University College, London. As a professor he was considered something of an innovator, introducing the Italian pronunciation of Latin and stressing student motivation over rote memorization; he lectured easily and enthusiastically, without notes. In the 1850s he published English translations of Horace's odes (1853) and Homer's *Iliad*; in later years he published Latin translations of Longfellow's *Hiawatha* (1862) and Defoe's *Robinson Crusoe*

(1884). He was an active polemicist in matter of religion and politics, in both of which he was a strong nonconformist; atheist and later unitarian in religion, politically he supported women's suffrage and strenuously opposed vaccination and vivisection. In the last decade of his life he also published a memoir of his brother the cardinal (1891).

Newman's *Iliad* was vociferously attacked by Matthew Arnold, in the Oxford lectures 'On Translating Homer' excerpted above, mainly for not appreciating Homer's 'nobleness' – Newman had translated the epic largely for ordinary people, and says so in no uncertain terms in the excerpt from his reply given below. The year after this exchange, in 1862, Arnold replied to Newman's reply in another lecture at Oxford, and published the entire debate in a book entitled *On Translating Homer.* Arnold's stature in the period and after has tended, in historical retrospect, to diminish the weight of Newman's remarks; but they remain forceful and interesting today, and in many ways anticipate the modernist attack on Victorian translation spearheaded by Ezra Pound.

The Unlearned Public is the Rightful Judge of Taste
From *Homeric Translation in Theory and Practice* (1861)

It is so difficult, amid the press of literature, for a mere versifier and translator to gain notice at all, that an assailant may even do one a service, if he so conduct his assault as to enable the reader to sit in intelligent judgment on the merits of the book assailed. But when the critic deals out to the readers only so much knowledge as may propagate his own contempt for the book, he has undoubtedly immense power to dissuade them from wishing to open it. Mr Arnold writes as openly aiming at this end. He begins by complimenting me, as "a man of great ability and genuine learning"; but on questions of learning, as well as of taste, he puts me down as bluntly, as if he had meant, "a man totally void both of learning and of sagacity". He again and again takes for granted that he has 'the scholar' on his side, 'the living scholar', the man who has learning and taste without pedantry. He bids me please 'the scholars" and go to 'the scholars' tribunal'; and does not know that I did this, to the extent of my opportunity, before committing myself to a laborious, expensive and perhaps thankless task. Of course he cannot guess, what is the fact, that scholars of fastidious refinement, but of a judgment which I think far more masculine than Mr Arnold's, have passed a most encouraging sentence on large specimens of my translation. I at this moment count eight such names, though of course I must not here adduce them: nor will I further allude to it, than to say that I have no such sense either of pride or of despondency as those are liable to who are consciously isolated in their taste.

Scholars are the tribunal of Erudition, but of Taste the educated but unlearned public is the only rightful judge; and to it I wish to appeal. Even scholars collectively have no right, and much less have single scholars, to pronounce a final sentence on questions of taste in their court. Where I differ in Taste from Mr Arnold, it is very difficult to find 'the scholars' tribunal', even if I acknowledged its absolute jurisdiction: but as regards Erudition, this difficulty does not occur, and I shall fully reply to the numerous dogmatisms by which he settles the case against me.

But I must first avow to the reader my own moderate pretensions. Mr Arnold begins by instilling two errors which he does not commit himself to assert. He says that my work will *not* take rank as *the* standard translation of Homer, but *other translations will be made*:– as if I thought otherwise! If I have set the example of the right direction in which translators ought to aim, of course those who follow me will improve upon me and supersede me. A man would be rash indeed to withhold his version of a poem of fifteen thousand lines until he had, to his best ability, imparted to them all their final perfection. He might spend the leisure of his life upon it. He would possibly be in his grave before it could see the light. If it then were published, and it was founded on any new principle, there would be no one to defend it from the attacks of ignorance and prejudice. In the nature of the case, his wisdom is to elaborate in the first instance all the high and noble parts *carefully*, and get through the inferior parts *somehow*; leaving of necessity very much to be done in successive editions, if possibly it please general taste sufficiently to reach them. A generous and intelligent critic will test such a work mainly or solely by the most noble parts, and as to the rest, will consider whether the metre and style adapts itself naturally to them also.

Next, Mr Arnold asks,

> Who is to assure Mr Newman that when he has tried to retain every peculiarity of his original, he has done that for which Mr Newman enjoins this to be done, – adhered closely to Homer's manner and habit of thought? Evidently the translator needs more practical directions than these.

The tendency of this is to suggest to the reader that I am not aware of the difficulty of rightly applying good principles; whereas I have in this very connexion said expressly, that even when a translator has got right principles, he is liable to go wrong in the detail of their application. This is as true of all the principles which Mr Arnold can possibly give as of those which I have given; nor do I for a moment assume that in writing fifteen thousand lines of verse I have not made hundreds of blots.

At the same time Mr Arnold has overlooked the point of my remark. Nearly every translator before me has *knowingly*, *purposely*, *habitually* shrunk from Homer's thoughts and Homer's manner. The reader will afterwards see whether Mr Arnold does not justify them in their course. It is not for those who are purposely unfaithful to taunt me with the difficulty of being truly faithful.

I have alleged, and, against Mr Arnold's flat denial, I deliberately repeat, that Homer rises and sinks with his subject, and is often homely or prosaic. I have professed as my principle, to follow my original in this matter. It is unfair to expect of me grandeur in trivial passages. If in any place where Homer is *confessedly* grand and noble, I have marred and ruined his greatness, let me be reproved. But I shall have occasion to protest that Stateliness is not Grandeur, Picturesqueness is not Stately, Wild Beauty is not to be confounded with Elegance; a Forest has its swamps and brushwood as well as its tall trees.

The duty of one who *publishes* his censures on me is to select noble, greatly admired passages, and confront me both with a prose translation of the original (for the public cannot go to the Greek) and also with that which he judges to be a more successful version than mine. Translation being matter of compromise, and being certain to fall below the original, when this is of the highest type of grandeur, the question is not, What translator is perfect? but, Who is least imperfect? Hence the only fair test is by comparison, when comparison is possible. But Mr Arnold has not put me to this test. He has quoted two very short passages, and various single lines, half lines and single words, from me; and chooses to *tell* his readers that I ruin Homer's nobleness, when (if his censure is just) he might make them *feel* it by quoting me upon the most admired pieces. Now with the warmest sincerity I say, – If any English reader, after perusing my version of four or five eminently noble passages of sufficient length, side by side with those of other translators, and (better still) with a prose version also, finds in them high qualities which I have destroyed, I am foremost to advise him to shut my book, or to consult it only (as Mr Arnold suggests) as a schoolboy's 'help to construe', if such it can be. My sole object is to bring Homer before the unlearned public: I seek no self-glorification: the sooner I am superseded by a really better translation, the greater will be my pleasure ...

If by happy combination any scholar could compose fifty *such* English hexameters as would convey a living likeness of the Virgilian metre, I should applaud it as valuable for initiating schoolboys into that metre: but there its utility would end. The method could not be profitably used for translating Homer or Virgil, plainly because it is impossible to say for whose service such a translation would be executed. Those who can read the original will never care to read *through* any translation; and the unlearned look on all, even the best hexameters, whether from Southey, Lockhart, or Longfellow, as odd and disagreeable prose. Mr Arnold deprecates appeal to popular taste: well he may! yet if the unlearned are to be our audience, we cannot defy them. I myself, before venturing to print, sought to ascertain how unlearned women and children would accept my verses. I could boast how children and half-educated women have extolled them; how greedily a working man has inquired for them, without knowing who was the translator; but I well know that this is quite insufficient to establish the merits of a translation. It is nevertheless *one* point. "Homer is popular", is one of the very few matters of fact in this controversy on which Mr Arnold and I are agreed. "English hexameters are not popular", is a truth so obvious that I do not yet believe he will deny it. Therefore, "Hexameters are not the metre for translating Homer". Q.E.D ...

Mr Arnold plays fallaciously on the words familiar and unfamiliar. Homer's words may have been *familiar* to the Athenians (i.e. often heard), even when they were *not* understood, but, at most, were guessed at; or when, being understood, they were still felt and known to be utterly foreign. Of course, when thus 'familiar', they could not 'surprise' the Athenians, as Mr Arnold complains that my renderings surprise the English. Let mine be heard as Pope or even Cowper has been heard, and no one will be 'surprised'.

Antiquated words are understood well by some, ill by others, not at all by a third class; hence it is difficult to decide the limits of a glossary. Mr Arnold speaks scornfully of me (he wonders *with whom Mr Newman can have lived*), that I use the words which I use, and explain those which I explain. He censures my little Glossary, for containing three words which he did not know, and some others, which, he says, are "familiar to all the world". It is clear, he will never want a stone to throw at me. I suppose I am guilty of keeping low company. I have found ladies – whom no one would guess to be so ill-educated – who yet do not distinctly know what *lusty* means, but have an uncomfortable feeling that it is very near to *lustful*; and understand *grisly* only in the sense of *grizzled, grey*. Great numbers mistake the sense of Buxom, Imp, Dapper, deplorably. I no more wrote my Glossary than my translation for persons so highly educated as Mr Arnold.

But I must proceed to remark: Homer might have been as unintelligible to Pericles as was the court poet of king Croesus, and yet it might be highly improper to translate him into an old English dialect; namely, if he had been the typical poet of a logical and refined age. *Here is the real question*; – is he absolutely antique, or only antiquated relatively, as Euripides is not antiquated? A modern Greek statesman, accomplished for every purpose of modern business, might find himself quite perplexed by the infinitives, the numerous participles, the optatives, the datives – by the particle αν – and by the whole syntax of Euripides, as also by many special words; but this would never justify us in translating Euripides into any but a most refined style. Was Homer of this class? I say that he *not only* was antiquated relatively to Pericles, but *is also* absolutely antique, being the poet of a barbarian age. Antiquity in poets is not (as Horace stupidly imagines in the argument of the horse's tail) a question of years, but of intrinsic qualities. Homer sang to a wholly unfastidious audience, very susceptible to the marvellous, very unalive to the ridiculous, capable of swallowing with reverence the most grotesque conceptions. Hence nothing is easier than to turn Homer to ridicule. The fun which Lucian made of his mythology, a rhetorical critic like Mr Arnold could make of his diction, if he understood it as he understands mine. He takes credit to himself for *not* ridiculing me; and is not aware that I could not be like Homer without being easy to ridicule. An intelligent child is the second-best reader of Homer. The best of all is a scholar of highly masculine taste; the worst of all is a fastidious and refined man, to whom everything quaint seems ignoble and contemptible.

Richard F. Burton

Sir Richard Burton (1821-1890) was one of the great English scholar-explorers of his day. Often described as able to pick up languages on the run, he learned two dozen major and minor languages and another dozen or so tribal languages in Europe, India, Africa, and South America, and wrote 43 volumes on his travels and nearly 30 volumes of translations, including the famous *Kama Sutra* and *The Book of One Thousand Nights and a Night* – which latter has daunted all competitors since.

The son of a retired army officer, Burton was raised all over the Continent, with only short stays in England; with his facility for languages he had learned not only Greek and Latin but French, Italian, and the Béarnais and Neapolitan dialects by the time he entered Trinity College, Oxford, in 1841. Apart from his early Arabic studies, he hated Oxford, and was glad to be expelled for attending a horse race in 1842. Over his father's protests he joined the 18th Regiment of the Bombay Native Infantry (a private army of the East India Company, which was then expanding its colonial holdings in India) and spent the next seven years in India, learning Arabic, Hindi, Persian, and numerous other languages and dialects so fluently that he could pass for a local, and frequently did – dividing his loyalties between the East India Company, for which he brought back intelligence reports, and his own quest for linguistic, ethnological, and religious knowledge. He mastered not only languages but religions, converting to several of them out of more or less passing interest – but more seriously, indeed devoutly, to Islamic Sufism.

Returning to Europe in 1850, he spent three years living with his mother and sister in Boulogne, France, where he met (but did not marry) his wife-to-be, Isabel Arundell, and published a brilliant work of ethnology, *Sindh* (1851). Two years later he made his famous pilgrimage to Mecca, entering the holy city disguised as an Afganistan Muslim; the book he later wrote on the expedition, *Pilgrimage to El-Medinah and Mecca* (1855-1856), was not only a huge popular success but is regarded by experts as the first accurate and insightful work to be written about Islam by a Westerner. The next year he became the first Westerner to enter another forbidden city without being executed, Harar in East Africa; this journey was described in *First Footsteps in East Africa* (1856). For the next few years he sought the source of the White Nile, without ever being sure whether he had succeeded or failed. He travelled to Salt Lake City in 1860 and wrote a sympathetic book on the Mormons (*City of the Saints*, 1861), dealing with their polygamy – scandalous to his contemporaries – with equanimity.

In 1861 he married Isabel Arundell, and accepted a consulship in Fernando Po, a Spanish island off the coast of West Africa. The many journeys he made into the African interior produced five books and again won him the acclaim of twentieth-century anthropologists; but, as in India, his propensity to 'go native' rendered him highly suspicious in the British Foreign Service's eyes. He managed to land a consulship in Brazil in 1864, and while he hated it there, he wrote a book on his experience (1869) and translated *Vikram and the Vampire* (1870), the preface to which is excerpted below. That same year he accepted a consulship in Damascus, in his beloved Middle East, but only lasted a year before local intrigues (fuelled by his Catholic wife's proselytizing) led to his dismissal. In 1872 he was appointed consul in Trieste, which, despite his early contempt for this European post, was to be his home for the rest of his life. It was here that he did his most famous translations, including the *Kama Sutra* (published anonymously in 1883, for fear of prosecution for obscenity) and the Arabian Nights (1885-1888). In 1886, four years before his death, he was knighted by Queen Victoria.

Burton did not adhere to a single method of translation, but varied his approach to suit his conception of the text at hand. His deepest instinct seems to have been to 'go native' in the sense of 'crossing over to the original author', as the German romantics would have said – assimilating English as far as possible to the source language – but he was also too forceful a personality to subsume himself entirely in the source text, and as a result built a powerfully personal vision into astonishingly faithful translations.

Clothing the Skeleton

From Preface to translation of *Vikram and the Vampire* (1870)

It is not pretended that the words of these Hindu tales are preserved to the letter. The question about the metamorphosis of cats into tigers, for instance, proceeded from a Gem of Learning in a university much nearer home than Gaur. Similarly the learned and still living Mgr. Gaume (*Traité du Saint-Esprit*, p. 81) joins Camerarius in the belief that serpents bite women rather than men. And he quotes (p. 192) Cornelius à Lapide, who informs us that the leopard is the produce of a lioness with a hyaena or a pard.

The merit of the old stories lies in their suggestiveness and their general applicability. I have ventured to remedy the conciseness of their language, and to clothe the skeleton with flesh and blood.

A Plain and Literal Translation

From Introduction to *The Book of The Thousand Nights and a Night* (1885)

Briefly, the object of this version is to show what *The Thousand Nights and a Night* really is. Not, however, for reasons to be more fully stated in the Terminal Essay, by straining *verbum reddere verbo*,[1] but by writing as the Arab would have written in English. On this point I am all with Saint Jerome (Pref. in Jobum) "Vel verbum e verbo, vel sensum e sensu, vel ex utroque commixtum, et medie temperatum genus translationis".[2] My work claims to be a faithful copy of the great Eastern Saga-book, by preserving intact, not only the spirit, but even the *mécanique*, the manner and the matter. Hence, however prosy and long-drawn out be the formula, it retains the scheme of The Nights because they are a prime feature in the original. The Ráwí or reciter, to whose wits the task of supplying details is left, well knows their value: the openings carefully repeat the names of the *dramatis personae* and thus fix them in the hearer's memory. Without the Nights no Arabian Nights! Moreover it is necessary to retain the whole apparatus: nothing more ill-advised than Dr. Jonathan Scott's strange device of garnishing The Nights with fancy head-pieces and tail-pieces or the splitting-up of Galland's narrative by merely prefixing 'Nuit',[3] etc., ending moreover, with the 234th Night: yet this has been done, apparently with the consent of the great Arabist Sylvestre de Sacy (Paris: Ernest Bourdin). Moreover, holding that the translator's glory is to add something to his native tongue, while avoiding the hideous hag-like nakedness of Torrens and the bald literalism of Lane, I have carefully Englished the picturesque turns and novel expressions of the original in all their outlandishness; for instance, when the dust-cloud raised by a tramping host is described as "walling the horizon". Hence peculiar attention has been paid to the tropes and figures which the Arabic language often packs into a single term; and I have never hesitated to coin a word when wanted, such as "she snorted and snarked", fully to represent the original. These, like many in Rabelais, are mere barbarisms unless generally adopted; in which case they become civilized and common currency.

Despite objections manifold and manifest, I have preserved the balance of sentences and the prose rhyme and rhythm which Easterns look upon as mere music. The 'Saj'a', or cadence of the cooing dove, has in Arabic its special duties. It adds a sparkle to description and a point to proverb, epigram and dialogue; it corresponds with our 'artful alliteration' (which in places I have substituted for it) and, generally, it defines the boundaries between the classical and the popular styles which jostle each other in The Nights. If at times it appear strained and forced, after the wont of rhymed prose, the scholar will observe that, despite the immense copiousness of assonants and consonants in Arabic, the strain is often put upon it intentionally, like the *Rims cars* of Dante and the Troubadours.[4] This rhymed prose may be 'un-English' and unpleasant, even irritating to the British ear; still I look upon it as a *sine qua* non for a complete reproduction of the original. In the Terminal Essay I shall revert to the subject.

[1] "To render word for word". A loose paraphrase of Horace; see above, 14-15. [Ed]

[2] "Either word for word, or sense for sense, or a type of translation made from a mixture of both extremes and the middle". From Jerome's *Preface to Job*. [Ed]

[3] French for 'night'. [Ed]

[4] The troubadours were lyric poets writing in southern France, northern Spain, and northern Italy from the late 11th to the late 13th century. [Ed]

On the other hand when treating the versical portion, which may represent a total of ten thousand lines, I have not always bound myself by the metrical bonds of the Arabic, which are artificial in the extreme, and which in English can be made bearable only by a *tour de force*. I allude especially to the monorhyme, *Rim continuat* or *tirade monorime*, whose monotonous simplicity was preferred by the Troubadours for threnodies. It may serve well for three or four couplets but, when it extends, as in the Ghazal-canon,[5] to eighteen, and in the Kasidah,[6] elegy or ode, to more, it must either display an ingenuity, a smell of the oil, which assuredly does not add to the reader's pleasure. It can perhaps be done and it should be done; but for me the task offers no attractions: I feel able to fence better in shoes than in sabots.

Robert Browning

Robert Browning (1812-1889), one of the great British poets in the Victorian era – some would say the greatest – also left a painfully literal translation of Aeschylus' *Agamemnon* that Ezra Pound and other modernists held up to ridicule as an example of clunky Victorian poetry. Part of the fame of Browning's literalism – as opposed, say, to that of Francis Newman's Homer, attacked by Matthew Arnold above – stems from the pithiness of Browning's defence of it in his preface: "literal at every cost save that of absolute violence to our language" and "as Greek a fashion as English will bear" have become English catchphrases for radical verbal fidelity.

Browning was born in London, the son of a clerk at the Bank of England, and lived with his parents until he was 34. His father taught him Greek and Latin, but he had little formal education; he dropped out of the University of London in the middle of his first session. In the thirteen years between his 21st birthday and his marriage to Elizabeth Barrett, he published ten volumes of poetry, including seven verse plays, all but one of them self-published at his family's expense.

He met Elizabeth Barrett, who had admired his own poetry in a collection of her own, in 1845, and the two soon fell in love. She was an invalid whom her jealous and possessive father thought incurable and confined to her bed; when her doctors recommended a trip to Italy and her father refused to let her go, the couple eloped and a week later left for Pisa. Elizabeth Barrett Browning's health was greatly improved by the warmer, drier climate, and the two, along with the son Robert they had in 1849, lived in Italy (mainly in Florence) until her death in 1861.

Browning wrote little while married, and for the period immediately after his wife's death devoted himself to the publication of her *Last Poems.* He began to attract attention with *Dramatis Personae* in 1864, and established his reputation as a major poet of the day with *The Ring and the Book* in 1868-1869. He continued to write critically acclaimed poetry until his death in 1889 – though unlike his wife's, his work was never really popular. His decision in the mid-seventies to translate an ancient Greek play reflects the dramatic bent of all his writing: most of his early work was for the theatre, while his later work explored the poetic resources of the dramatic monologue.

Literal At Every Cost
From Preface to Translation of Aeschylus' *Agamemnon* (1877)

May I be permitted to chat a little, by way of recreation, at the end of a somewhat toilsome and perhaps fruitless adventure?

If, because of the immense fame of the following tragedy, I wished to acquaint myself with it, and could only do so by the help of a translator, I should require him to be literal at every cost save that of absolute violence to our language. The use of certain allowable constructions which, happening to be out of daily favour, are all the more appropriate to archaic workmanship, is no violence; but I would be tolerant for once – in the case of so immensely famous an original – of even a clumsy attempt to furnish me with the very turn of each phrase in as Greek a fashion as English will bear; while, with respect fo amplifications and embellishments – anything rather than, with the good farmer, experience that most signal of mortifications, "to gape for Aeschylus and get Theognis". I should especially decline – what may appear to brighten up a passage – the employment of a new word for some old one – πόνος [labour/pain], or μέγας [big], or τέλος [end/purpose], with its congeners, recurring four times in three lines; for though such substitution may be in itself perfectly justifiable, yet this exercise of ingenuity ought to be within the competence of the unaided English reader if he likes to show himself ingenious. Learning Greek teaches Greek, and nothing else;

[5] The ghazal (or ghazel, or gasal) is a genre of lyric poetry that flourished in Islamic literature in the 7th and 8th centuries and was revitalized by Hafiz. [Ed]

[6] The kasidah was an Arabic poetic genre; Burton himself had published a pseudonymous collection of original poetry called *The Kasidah*, modelled on FitzGerald's *Rubáiyát of Omar Khayyam*, five years before this writing (1880). [Ed]

certainly not common sense, if that have failed to precede the teaching. Further – if I obtained a mere strict bald version of thing by thing, or at least word pregnant with thing, I should hardly look for an impossible transmission of the reputed magniloquence and sonority of the Greek; and this with the less regret, inasmuch as there is abundant musicality elsewhere, but nowhere else than in his poem the ideas of the poet. And lastly, when presented with these ideas, I should expect the result to prove very hard reading indeed if it were meant to resemble Aeschylus, ξυμβαλεῖν οὐ ῥάδιος, "not easy to understand", in the opinion of his stoutest advocate among the ancients; while, I suppose, even modern scholarship sympathizes with that early declaration of the redoubtable Salmasius, when, looking about for an example of the truly obscure for the benefit of those who found obscurity in the sacred books, he protested that this particular play leaves them all behind in this respect, with their "Hebraisms, Syriasms, Hellenisms, and the whole of such bag and baggage".[1] For, over and above the purposed ambiguity of the Chorus, the text is sadly corrupt, probably interpolated, and certainly mutilated; and no unlearned person enjoys the scholar's privilege of trying his fancy upon each obstacle whenever he comes to a stoppage, and effectually clearing the way by suppressing what seems to life in it.

All I can say for the present performance is, that I have done as I would be done by, if need were. Should anybody, without need, honor my translation by a comparison with the original, I beg him to observe that, following no editor exclusively, I keep to the earlier readings so long as sense can be made out of them, but disregard, I hope, little of importance in recent criticism so far as I have fallen in with it. Fortunately, the poorest translation, provided only it be faithful – though it reproduces all the artistic confusion of tenses, moods, and persons, with which the original teems – will not only suffice to display what an eloquent friend maintains to be the all-in-all of poetry – "the action of the piece" – but may help to illustrate his assurance that

> the Greeks are the highest models of expression, the unapproached masters of the grand style: their expression is so excellent because it is so admirably kept in its right degree of prominence, because it is so simple and so well subordinated, because it draws its force directly from the pregnancy of the matter which it conveys ... not a word wasted, not a sentiment capriciously thrown in, stroke on stroke![2]

So may it happen!

Friedrich Nietzsche

Friedrich Nietzsche (1844-1900) was one of the great modern philosophers, a powerful critic of civilized 'asceticism' who laid the groundwork for psychoanalysis, deconstruction, and post-structuralist Marxism.

Nietzsche was born in Prussian Saxony the son of a Lutheran minister who died before he turned five, and raised in a household of women: his mother, his sister, his grandmother, and two maiden aunts. An excellent student who thrived at Germany's finest Protestant boarding school, he matriculated at the University of Bonn in 1864 to study theology and classical theology, but left after only two semesters to follow his favourite professor, Friedrich Wilhelm Ritschl, to Leipzig. During the five years he spent there – excepting a year in the cavalry company of an artillery regiment, where he suffered a serious chest injury – he steeped himself in Schopenhauer's philosophy and met his idol Richard Wagner, to whose music he would dedicate ten sections of his first published book, *The Birth of Tragedy* (1872).

In 1869 Ritschl recommended Nietzsche for the vacant professorship of classical philology at the University of Basel – despite the fact that Nietzsche was then what we would now call A.B.D. (all but dissertation). Basel appointed him to the post, Leipzig awarded him the doctorate without examination or thesis, and he took up his professorial duties (and Swiss citizenship) at the age of 25. At the outbreak of the Franco-Prussian War, he took leave of absence to serve as a volunteer medical orderly, but within a month contracted dysentery and diphtheria and forever ruined his health, leading to frequent sick leaves and finally, in 1879, at the age of 35, retirement with a six-year disability pension.

The decade following his retirement was his most productive one, despite constant and excruciating physical pain and almost total neglect from his peers. All of his greatest books were written (and ignored) in this period: *The Gay Science* (1882), *Thus Spake Zarathustra* (1883-1885),

[1] "Quis Aeschylum possit affirmare Graece nunc scienti magis patere explicabilem quam Evangelia aut Epistolas Apostolicas? Unus ejus Agamemnon obscuritate superat quantum est librorum sacrorum cum suis Hebraismis et Syrasmis et tota Hellenisticae supellectii vel farragine". – Salmasius *de Hellenistica*, Epist. Dedic. [Au]

[2] 'Poems' by Matthew Arnold, Preface. [Au] Ellipsis Browning's. See also Arnold's similar remarks above, 250-55. [Ed]

Beyond Good and Evil (1886), *On the Genealogy of Morals* (1887), and, in 1888, his last year of sanity, *The Case of Wagner, Twilight of the Idols, The Antichrist, Nietzsche contra Wagner*, and *Ecce Homo*. In January, 1889, he suffered a nervous collapse in Turin, Italy, and spent the last eleven years of his life in asylums and the care of his mother and sister; since his death his symptomatology has been read as pointing to syphilis.

His sister Elizabeth had been married to a prominent German nationalist and antisemite who committed suicide in the year of Nietzsche's collapse, and during the years of his insanity she seized control of his literary estate, working to recreate her brother in her dead husband's image. In the interests of rescuing his work from his sister and her ideological kin the Nazis, Nietzsche's emotional health has sometimes been exaggerated; he does, for example, despite his overt opposition to antisemitism, lash out at Jews as the cause of much human suffering, and his misogyny was blatant. He was, however, no Nazi. He was a bitter critic of the ascetic mentality that would breed Nazis three decades after his death, and generally of the social malaise that ravages Western civilization, which he associated with Christianity as a religion of pity. His conception of the 'noble man', a kind of mystical aristocrat, as the healthy form of humanity was used by the Nazis to justify the blond Aryan beast; stripped of Nietzsche's class images, however, his portrait of human health is remarkably like that of the humanist psychologist Abraham Maslow in describing what he calls 'self-actualization'.

Nietzsche's passing remarks on translation from *The Gay Science* and *Beyond Good and Evil* are not particularly original, but hold interest as late-nineteenth-century examples of romanticism that point ahead to the hermeneutical translation theories of twentieth-century thinkers like Benjamin and Buber, Heidegger and Gadamer, Steiner and Derrida.

Translation as Conquest
From *Die fröhliche Wissenschaft* (*The Gay Science*, 1882)
Translated by Walter Kaufmann

Translations. – The degree of the historical sense of any age may be inferred from the manner in which this age makes *translations* and tries to absorb former ages and books. In the age of Corneille and even of the Revolution, the French took possession of Roman antiquity in a way for which we would no longer have courage enough – thanks to our more highly developed historical sense. And Roman antiquity itself: how forcibly and at the same time how naively it took hold of everything good and lofty of Greek antiquity, which was more ancient! How they translated things into the Roman present! How deliberately and recklessly they brushed the dust off the wings of the butterfly that is called moment! Thus Horace now and then translated Alcaeus or Archilochus; and Propertius did the same with Callimachus and Philetas (poets of the same rank as Theocritus, if we *may* judge). What was it to them that the real creator had experienced this and that and written the signs of it into his poem? As poets, they had no sympathy for the antiquarian inquisitiveness that precedes the historical sense; as poets, they had no time for all those very personal things and names and whatever might be considered the costume and mask of a city, a coast, or a century: quickly, they replaced it with what was contemporary and Roman. They seem to ask us: "Should we not make new for ourselves what is old and find ourselves in it? Should we not have the right to breathe our own soul into this dead body? For it is dead after all; how ugly is everything dead!" They did not know the delights of the historical sense; what was past and alien was an embarrassment for them; and being Romans, they saw it as an incentive for a Roman conquest. Indeed, translation was a form of conquest. Not only did one omit what was historical; one also added allusions to the present and, above all, struck out the name of the poet and replaced it with one's own – not with any sense of theft but with the very best conscience of the *imperium Romanum*.

Translating the Tempo of the Original
From *Beyond Good and Evil* (1886)
Translated by R. J. Hollingdale

That which translates worst from one language into another is the tempo of its style, which has its origin in the character of the race, or, expressed more physiologically, in the average tempo of its 'metabolism'. There are honestly meant translations which, as involuntary vulgarizations of the original, are almost falsifications simply because it was not possible to translate also its brave and happy tempo, which leaps over and puts behind it all that is perilous in things and words. The German is virtually incapable of *presto* in his language: thus, it may be fairly concluded, also of many of the most daring and delightful nuances of free, free-spirited thought. Just as the *buffo* and the satyr is strange to him, in his conscience, so Aristophanes and Petronius are untranslatable for him. Everything staid, sluggish, ponderously solemn, all long-winded and boring species of style have been developed in profuse multiplicity among the Germans – pardon me for the fact that even Goethe's prose is, in its blend of elegance and stiffness, no exception: it is a reflection of the 'good old days', to which it belongs, and an expression of the German taste of a time when there still was a 'German taste': it was rococo *in moribus et artibus* [in manner and art]. Lessing constitutes an exception, thanks to his histrionic nature, which was versed in and understood much: he, who was not for nothing the translator of Bayle and liked to flee to the neighbourhood of Diderot and Voltaire and even more to that of the Roman writers of comedy – in tempo too Lessing loved free-spiritedness, escape from Germany. But how could the German language, even in the prose of a Lessing, imitate the tempo of Machiavelli, who in his *Principe* lets us breathe the subtle dry air of Florence and cannot help presenting the most serious affairs in a boisterous *allegrissimo*: not perhaps without a malicious artist's sense of the contrast he is risking – thoughts protracted, difficult, hard, dangerous and the tempo of the gallop and the most wanton good humour. Who, finally, would venture a German translation of Petronius, who was, to a greater degree than any great musician has hitherto been, a master of *presto* in invention, ideas, words – what do all the swamps of the sick wicked world, even of the 'antique world', matter when one has, like him, the feet of a wind, the blast and breath, the liberating scorn of a wind that makes everything healthy by making everything *run*! And as for Aristophanes, that transfiguring, complementary spirit for whose sake one *excuses* all Greece for having existed, assuming one has grasped in all its profundity *what* there is to be excused and transfigured here – I know of nothing that has led me to reflect more on *Plato's* concealment and sphinx nature than that happily preserved *petit fait* [little fact] that under the pillow of his deathbed there was discovered no 'Bible', nothing Egyptian, Pythagorean, Platonic – but Aristophanes. How could even a Plato have endured life – a Greek life which he had denied – without an Aristophanes! –

Biographies of People Mentioned in the Text

Abelard, Peter (Pierre Abelard or Abailard, Petrus Abaelardus, 1079-1142), French theologian and philosopher whose famous love affair with and secret marriage to Heloise, the daughter of a clergyman, led to her flight into a convent and his castration.

Accius (or Attius), Lucius (b. 170-c. 86 B.C.E.), Roman tragic and historical dramatist.

Adrian VI (original name Adrian Florenszoon Boeyens, 1459-1523), Dutch pope (1522-1523) who was first professor at Louvain, where he was Erasmus' teacher.

Aelred of Rievaulx (or Aethelred, or Ethelred, 1110-1167), Northumbrian Cistercian abbot and historian who based his *De spirituali amicitia* ('On Spiritual Friendship') on Cicero's *De amicitia.*

Aeschines (390-c. 314 B.C.E.), Athenian orator.

Aeschylus (Aiskhylos, 525/24-456/55 B.C.E.), Greek tragic dramatist.

Aeserninus (fl. early 1st century C.E.), Roman orator under Tiberius.

Aesop (Aisopos, possibly 6th century B.C.E.), legendary figure to whom a collection of Greek fables were attributed.

Aethelred I (d. 716), king of Mercia.

Aethelweard (d. 998?), ealdorman (a royally appointed governor) of the western provinces of England (today's Devon, Somerset, and Dorset) and Latin chronicler; patron of Aelfric.

Aethelwold, bishop of Winchester 963-984.

Afranius, Lucius (early 1st century B.C.E.), Roman comic poet who borrowed heavily from Menander; only fragments survive.

Africanus: *see* Scipio.

Agrippa I, Marcus Julius (10 B.C.E.-44 C.E.), grandson of Herod the Great and mistakenly referred to as Herod in Acts 12; king of the tetrarchy of his uncle Philip and brother Herod.

Agrippa II, Marcus Julius (27/28-before 93/94 C.E., reigned 49/50-93/94), son of Agrippa I, king of Chalcis under Claudius and Nero.

Agrippina the Younger (15-59 C.E.), mother of the Roman emperor Nero.

Albertus Magnus, Saint (Albert der Grosse, c. 1200-1280), Dominican bishop and philosopher, teacher of St. Thomas Aquinas.

Albucius (or Albutius), T. (fl. 105 B.C.E.), Roman praetor in Sardinia.

Alcaeus (620-580 B.C.E.), Greek poet.

Alcibiades (c. 450-404 B.C.E.), Athenian politician and military strategist.

Alemán, Mateo (1547-1614), Spanish novelist, author of *Vida y hechos del picaro Guzmán de Alfarache, atalaya de la vida humana* (1599-1605), translated into English in 1622 as *The Spanish Rogue.*

Alexander the Great (356-323 B.C.E.), conqueror of the Persian empire, student of Aristotle, founder of Alexandria.

Alfred the Englishman (Aluredus Anglicus, early 13th century), Arabic-Latin translator in Toledo, Spain.

Algarotti, Francesco (1712-1764), Italian science popularizer who wrote a book on Newtonianism 'for the ladies' (1739), translated into English by Elizabeth Carter.

Allen, William (1532-1594), English cardinal and Bible scholar; supervised the English Catholic Douay-Rheims translation of the Bible.

Alphonsus de Castro (1495-1558), Renaissance Bible scholar.

Aluredus Anglicus: *see* Alfred the Englishman

Amasis (570-526 B.C.E.), king of Egypt who maintained close ties with Greece; Pythagoras and Solon are reputed to have visited him.

Ambrose (Ambrosius, 339-397), bishop of Milan and Church Father.

Ambrosius Theseus (1469-1540), Italian Orientalist.

Anacreon (c. 582-485 B.C.E.), Asian Greek lyric poet.

Anguillara, Giovanni de (known in English as John Anguillara, c. 1517-after 1564), Italian poet and translator of Ovid, part of the *Aeneid*, and (in a free adaptation) of *Oedipus Rex*.

Anne (1665-1714, reigned 1702-1714), queen of England.

Anselm of Havelberg (d. 1158), bishop of Freising.

Anthony of Egypt (c. 251-356), the most famous of the early Christian ascetics, largely due to the *Life of Anthony* written by Athanasius.

Antimachus of Colophon (fl. c. 410 B.C.E.), Greek poet and scholar.

Antipater of Sidon (fl. 140 B.C.E.), Greek Stoic philosopher; disciple and successor of Diogenes and teacher of Panaetius of Rhodes.

Antonius, Marcus (143-87 B.C.E.), Roman lawyer and politician who appears as one of the two speakers in Cicero's *De oratore* ('On the Orator'), the other being Crassus.

Apelles (fl. 4th century B.C.E.), Greek painter.

Aphthonius (fl. late 3rd century C.E.), one of Mani's twelve disciples, early Manichean leader.

Apollodorus of Athens (fl. 140 B.C.E.) wrote a *Chronicle* of Greek history that was often used by the comic dramatists.

Apollonius of Rhodes (born around 295 B.C.E.), Greek poet and grammarian.

Apuleius of Madaura, Lucius (c. 124-after 170 C.E.), North African Platonic philosopher and author best known for *The Golden Ass* (Latin *Metamorphoses*).

Aquila (Akilas, 2nd century C.E.), famous literal translator of the Hebrew Scriptures into Greek (c. 140 C.E.). His translation displaced the Septuagint among the Jews; Origen reprinted it in his *Hexapla*, a parallel edition of Greek and Latin translations.

Aquillius (fl. c. 175-154 B.C.E.), supposed author of the Latin comic drama *Boeotia*, which Varro attributed to Plautus.

Aratus (Aratos, fl. c. 315-c. 245 B.C.E.), Greek Stoic poet.

Arcadius (c. 377-408), joint Roman emperor in the East with his father Theodosius I from 383 to 395, and after that solely until 402.

Arcesilaus (316/15-c. 241 B.C.E.), Greek philosopher.

Archias, A. Licinius (b. c. 120 B.C.E.), Greek poet defended against the charge of illegally obtaining Roman citizenship by Cicero in *Pro Archia*.

Archilochus (seventh century B.C.E.), Greek poet.

Archimedes (c. 290/80-212/11 B.C.E.), Greek mathematician and inventor whose war machines protected Syracuse against Roman invasion.

Ariosto, Ludovico (1474-1533), Italian poet, author of *Orlando Furioso* (1516).

Aristides Quintilianus (fl. 2nd or 3rd century C.E.), Greek writer on music.

Aristophanes (c. 450-c. 388 B.C.E.), Greek comic dramatist.

Aristotle (Aristoteles, 384-322 B.C.E.), Greek philosopher and tutor of Alexander the Great.

Arius (c. 250-336), Alexandrian presbyter, founder of Arianism, a Christian sect declared heretical.

Arrian (Flavius Arrianus, c. 95-180 C.E.), pupil of Epictetus who wrote down and thus preserved the master's works: the *Discourses* and the *Encheiridion*.

Artemisia I (fl. first half of 5th century B.C.E.), queen of Halicarnassus.

Arthur (1486-1536), prince of England, son of Henry VII.

Arundel, Thomas (1353-1414), archbishop of Canterbury under Richard II and Henry IV; was known as a vigorous persecutor of the 'Lollards', followers of Wycliffe.

Asser (d. 909), Bishop of Sherborne (c. 892-909).

Atacinus: *see* Varro.

Athanasius (293-373), bishop of Alexandria and author of the *Life of Anthony*.

Atilius, Marcus: *see* Regulus.

Attius: *see* Accius.

Augustus, Caesar, called Octavian until 27 B.C.E. (born Gaius Octavius, adopted name Gaius Julius Caesar Octavianus, 63 B.C.E.-14 C.E.), Roman emperor.

Aurelius, Marcus (Marcus Annius Verus, 121-180 C.E., reigned as Caesar Marcus Aurelius Antoninus Augustus, 161-180), Roman emperor.

Aurogallus, Matthäus (or Goldhahn, 'gold hen'), professor of Hebrew at the University of Wittenberg.

Austen, Jane (1775-1817), English novelist.

Aventinus, Johannes (or Johannes Turmayr, 1477-1534) wrote the *Bavarian Chronicles* until 1519, first in Latin, later in German.

Avienus, Rufus Festus (late 4th century C.E.), Roman poet.

Bacon, Sir Francis, Viscount S. Albans (1561-1626), English philosopher, man of letters, and lord chancellor of England.

Bancroft, Richard (1544-1610), English divine who worked on the King James Version; later became Archbishop of Canterbury.

Barbarossa: *see* Frederick I.

Barclay, John (1582-1621), Scottish satirist and poet; author of the Latin *Euphormionis Lusinini Satyricon* (1603-1607) and *Argenis* (1621).

Bartas, Guillaume de Salluste, Seigneur de (1544-1590), French poet, author of *La Semaine* ('The Week'), translated into English by King James I.

Bartholomew the Englishman (Bartholomaeus Anglicus, fl. c. 1220-1240), Fransiscan encyclopaedist; author of *De proprietatibus rerum* ('On the Properties of Things').

Basil the Great (329-379), bishop of Caesarea and early Church Father, consolidated Church doctrine against the Arian heresy.

Battista Guarini, Giovanni (1538-1612), Italian playwright, author of *Il pastor fido* ('The Faithful Shepherd', 1590).

Bayle, Pierre (1647-1706), French philosopher, author of the *Dictionnaire historique et critique* (1697).

Beatus Rhenanus (Beatus Bild, 1485-1547), German humanist scholar.

Beckett, Samuel (1906-), Irish writer who first wrote several of his plays in French, then translated them into his native English – notably *En attendant Godot* (1952) and *Waiting for Godot* (1954).

Bede, The Venerable (Baeda, 672/673-735), Anglo-Saxon theologian, historian, and translator of parts of the Bible into Anglo-Saxon; best known for *The Ecclesiastical History of the English People* (731/32).

Benjamin, Walter (1892-1940), German critic, author of 'The Task of the Translator' (1923).

Bentley, Richard (1662-1742), British classicist and theologian and slightly older contemporary of Alexander Pope.

Bernadotte, Jean-Baptiste-Jules (1763-1844), French revolutionary general under Napoleon, marshall of France; elected crown prince of Sweden under the ageing and ailing (and childless) King Karl XIII in 1810, he later became regent and finally king of Sweden and Norway (1818-1844), under the name Karl XIV Johan.

Beroaldus, Mattheus (d. c. 1576), French theologian, mathematician, philosopher, and historian.

Beza, Theodore (Théodore de Béze, 1519-1605), French theologian and translator who assisted John Calvin and later succeeded him as the head of the Genevan Reformation. He edited the Greek New Testament and did a new translation of it into Latin.

Birger Jarl (Earl Birger, d. 1266), Swedish nobleman who became regent and the effective ruler of Sweden when his underage son Valdemar was crowned king in 1250; conquered Finland for Sweden in 1548.

Bitaubé, Paul (1732-1808), French novelist, critic, and translator who published popular French prose translations of the *Iliad* and the *Odyssey* in the 1760s. Late in life he also translated Goethe's *Hermann und Dorothea* (1804).

Blackwell, Thomas (1701-1757), English scholar, author of *Enquiry into the Life and Writings of Homer* (1735).

Boccaccio, Giovanni (1313-1375), Italian poet and scholar, author of the *Decamerone*.

Bochart, Samuel (1599-1667), French scholar, author of the *Geographie*.

Bodmer, Johann Jakob (1698-1783), Swiss historian, critic, and poet who translated Homer into hexametres.

Boétie, Étienne de la (1530-1563), French writer and close friend of Montaigne.

Boileau Despreaux, Nicolas (1636-1711), French critic who translated Longinus' *On the Sublime*.

Boleyn, Anne (1507?-1536), queen of England, second wife of Henry VIII, mother of Elizabeth I.

Bora, Katherina von (1499-1552), German nun who left her order to become Martin Luther's wife.

Bossuet, Jacques-Bénigne (1627-1704), French bishop and author of *Discours sur l'histoire universelle* (*A Discourse on Universal History*, 1681).

Boswell, James (1740-1795), Scottish friend and biographer of Samuel Johnson.

Boyle, Roger, first earl of Orrery (1621-1679), an Irish magnate who took the Parliamentary side during the Civil War but found favour as a poet and playwright in the court of Charles II upon the Restoration.

Broome, William (1689-1745) annotated Pope's *Iliad*, but (along with Elijah Fenton) played an active role in the translation of the *Odyssey*, translating books 2, 6, 8, 11, 16, 18, and 23.

Brutus, Marcus Junius (also called Quintus Caepio Brutus, 85-42 B.C.E.), Roman governor, praetor, and philosopher best remembered for his part in the assassination of Julius Caesar in March 44 B.C.E. None of his philosophical works survives; only two of the nine books of his correspondence with Cicero survive.

Buber, Martin (1878-1965), German religious philosopher and, with Franz Rosenzweig, translator of the Hebrew Bible into German.

Bucer (or Butzer), Martin (1491-1551) was a Protestant Reformer who tried to mediate between Catholics and Protestants and between Lutherans and Calvinists.

Buchanan, George (1506-1582), Scottish scholar and Latin poet who paraphrased the psalms in Latin between 1547 and 1552; his translation was long used to teach Scottish schoolchildren Latin.

Burckhardt, Jacob (1818-1897), Swiss historian.

Bürger, Gottfried August (1747-1794), German Romantic poet who translated Homer into German.

Burrus, Sextus Afranius (d. 62 C.E.), Roman praetorian prefect and co-advisor (with Seneca) of the emperor Nero.

Buxtorf[ius], John, the name of two sixteenth-century English scholars, father and son: the father (1564-1629) was a Calvinist divine and professor of Hebrew and Chaldaic languages at the University of Basel; the son (1599-1664), was a professor of Oriental language at the University of Basel. The father was the more famous scholar; both translated from the Hebrew.

Byron, George Gordon, 6th Baron (1788-1824), English romantic poet and satirist.

Cadmus, in Greek mythology, was the son of Phoenix or Agenor; according to legend he brought the alphabet to Greece.

Caecilius, Statius (c. 168 B.C.E.), Roman comic dramatist; a contemporary of Ennius, and the immediate predecessor of Terence.

Caedmon (mid-7th century), the first Anglo-Saxon Christian poet.

Caesar, Gaius Julius (100-44 B.C.E.), Roman general, dictator, and author of celebrated histories of the Gallic War (51 B.C.E.) and Civil War (45 B.C.E.).

Cajetan: *see* Tommaso.

Calderón de la Barca, Pedro (1600-1681), Spanish writer.

Caligula (Gaius Caesar Germanicus, 12-41 C.E.), Roman emperor.

Callimachus (305-240 B.C.E.), Greek poet and scholar.

Calvin, Jean (John Calvin, 1509-1564), Swiss Reformer.

Camerarius, Joachim (1534-1598), German natural philosopher.

Camus, Jean-Pierre (1584-1652), French religious writer.

Capella, Martianus Minneus Felix (fl. late 4th and early 5th century C.E.), Carthaginian author of *De nuptiis Philologiae et Mercurii* ('The Marriage of Philology and Mercury'), the first two books of an early-5th-century prose and verse book on the seven liberal arts.

Carbo, Gaius Papirius (d. 119 B.C.E.), Roman politician allied with Gracchus.

Cardano, Gerolamo (Jerome Cardan, 1501-1576), Italian physician, mathematician, and astrologer.

Carlyle, Thomas (1795-1881), English writer.

Cary, Henry Francis (1772-1844), translated Dante Alighieri's (1265-1321) *Divine Comedy* (1321) between 1805 and 1814.

Casaubon, Isaac (1559-1614), French classicist and theologian.

Cassius Longinus, Gaius (d. 42 B.C.E.), prime mover in Julius Caesar's assassination.

Castalio: *see* Castellio.

Castellio, Sebastianus (1515-1563), French humanistic theologian connected with Calvin, professor of Greek at Basel; translated the Bible into Latin and French.

Casti, Giovanni Battista (1724-1803), Italian poet, satirist, and librettist.

Catharine of Aragon (1485-1536), Spanish queen of England, first wife of Henry VIII.

Cato, Dionysius (12th century), reputed author of *Cato's Distichs*, an Old French didactic handbook.

Catullus, Gaius Valerius (c. 84-c. 54 B.C.E.), Roman lyric poet.

Celsus, Aulus Cornelius (1st century C.E.), Roman encyclopaedist, called the 'Hippocrates of the Romans'.

Chalcidius (fl. 4th century C.E.), translator of Plato.

Challoner, Richard (1691-1781), English Roman Catholic author who revised the Douay-Rheims Bible in 1749-1750, modernizing it and correcting its errors.

Chappuis, Gabriel (or Chappuys, 1546-1613), French historian and translator whose *Guzman* appeared posthumously, in 1625.

Charlemagne (Charles I le Grand, Carolus Magnus, c. 742-814), king of the Franks (768-814) and Lombards (774-814).

Charles the Bald (823-877), Frankish king, successor to Charlemagne.

Charles II (1630-1685, reigned 1660-1685), king of England who came to power with the Restoration after the parliamentary revolution (1648-1660).

Charles V the Wise (1338-1380, reigned 1364-1380), French king.

Charles V (1500-1558), Holy Roman Emperor (1519-56), who also reigned as King Charles I of Spain (1516-1556) and Archduke Charles I of Austria (1519-1521).

Charles VII (1403-1461, reigned 1422-1461), French king.

Charles IX (until 1560 Duc d'Orleans, 1550-1574, reigned 1560-1574), the emotionally disturbed child king of France who authorized the massacre of Protestants in 1572.

Chartier, Alain (1385-after 1430), French poet, official poet of Charles VII.

Chaucer, Geoffrey (1340/43-1366/67), English poet, courtier, diplomat, and civil servant; best known for the *Canterbury Tales*, translated the *Consolation of Philosophy* by Boethius in the 1380s.

Chilon (mid-6th century B.C.E.), Spartan ephor (magistrate) and purported utterer of the famous injunction, 'Know thyself'.

Chomsky, Noam (b. 1928), American linguist and political activist.

Chrétien de Troyes (fl. 1165-80), French poet.

Chromatius of Aquileia (d. 407), bishop who attempted to reconcile Jerome and Rufinus.

Chrysippus (c. 280-c. 206 B.C.E.), Greek philosopher who formalized Stoic philosophy, co-founder (with Zeno) of the academy at Athens Stoa.

Chrysostom, Ioannis (in English called John, c. 345-407), archbishop of Constantinople and early Church Father.

Claudian (Claudius Claudianus, c. 370-c. 404 C.E.), Roman poet, author of the epic poem *The Rape of Proserpine* (*Raptus Proserpinae*).

Claudius Caesar Augustus Germanicus, Tiberius (original name Tiberius Claudius Nero Germanicus, 10 B.C.E.-54 C.E., reigned 41-45 C.E.), Roman emperor.

Clayton, Thomas (c. 1673-c. 1725), English composer.

Clement of Alexandria (Titus Flavius Clemens, c. 150-211/15), theologian and teacher in the catechetical school of Alexandria; author of the *Stromateis* ('Streams' or 'Miscellanies').

Clement IV (original name Gui Foulques or Guido Fulcodi, late 12th century-1268, reigned 1265-1268), pope.

Clement VIII (original name Ippolito Aldobrandini, 1536-1605, reigned 1542-1605), Italian pope.

Coleridge, Samuel Taylor (1772-1834), English poet and critic.

Colet, John (1466/67-1519), English humanist theologian.

Cominius, Georgius Haloinus (fl. early 16th century), a contemporary of Erasmus.

Congreve, William (1670-1729), English playwright.

Conrad, Joseph (Jósef Teodor Konrad Korzeniowski, 1857-1924), Polish novelist who wrote in English.

Conrart, Valentin (1603-1675), French man of letters who was one of the prime movers in the founding of the French Academy (1634-1635) and its permanent secretary thereafter; in that capacity he inaugurated the regulatory role the Academy still plays to this day, becoming himself the overlord of correct French spelling, grammar, and word order.

Constant de Rebeque, Henri-Benjamin (1767-1830), Franco-Swiss novelist, author of *Adolphe* (1816); for twelve years the lover of Madame de Staël.

Corneille, Pierre (1606-1684), French dramatist, author of *La Mort de Pompée* (1643).

Cornelius Alexander Polyhistor, Lucius (d. c. 35 B.C.E.), Roman philosopher, historian, and geographer.

Cornelius à Lapide: *see* Lapide.

Cornelius Gallus, Gaius (c. 70-26 B.C.E.), Roman soldier and poet, translated Euphorion into Latin; best known for his four books of poetry to his mistress 'Lycoris' (an actress named Volumnia).

Cotterell, Charles (1612?-1702), master of ceremonies for the royal court and translator of 'The Temple of Death' by Phillipe Habert.

Cowper, William (1731-1800), worked on a translation of Homer toward the end of his life; the parts he completed were published posthumously in 1835-1837 in his 15-volume collected works edited by Robert Southey.

Crassus, Lucius Licinius (140-91 B.C.E.), Roman lawyer and politician who appears as one of the two speakers in Cicero's *De oratore* ('On the Orator'), the other being Antonius.

Crassus, Marcus Licinius (c. 115-53 B.C.E.), Roman politician who formed first triumvirate with Pompey and Caesar, died in Battle of Carrhae during ill-advised invasion of Parthia.

Croesus (d. 546 B.C.E.), last king of Lydia, renowed for his wealth.

Cromwell, Oliver (1599-1658), leader of the parliamentary forces during the English Civil War; from 1653 to 1658 the lord protector of England.

Cromwell, Thomas (c. 1485-1540), royal advisor to Henry VIII and principal architect of the English Reformation.

Crousaz, Jean-Pierre de (1663-1750), French philosopher, mathematician, logician, physicist, and educational theorist; he wrote a book on Pope's *Essay on Man* in 1737.

Ctesiphon (fl. 4th century B.C.E.), Athenian politician who proposed a bill in 336 to confer a golden crown on Demosthenes, provoking the famous oratorical clash between Demosthenes and Aeschines.

Cujas, Jacques (1522-1590), jurisconsult of Toulouse, Counsellor of the Parlement de Grenoble beginning in 1574, later professor of law at the University of Paris; Etienne Pasquier's law teacher in the late 1540s.

Curtius, Quintus: *see* Rufus.

Cyprian (Thascius Caecilius Cyprianus, 200-258 C.E.), bishop of Carthage.

Cyrus II ('the Great', 590/80-c. 529 B.C.E.), Persian general and conqueror.

D'Alembert, Jean Le Rond (1717-1783), French writer, philosopher and mathematician.

D'Andoins, Diane, countess of Gramont (1554-1620), wife of Philibert de Gramont, count of Guiche and mistress of King Henry IV from 1574-1591; popularly known as la Belle Corisande.

Dacier, André (1651-1722), French classical scholar, Anne Dacier's husband.

Damasus (c. 304-384), pope 366-384.

Dares Phrygius was a Trojan priest of Hephaestus (named in the *Iliad*) who reputedly wrote a pre-Homeric pro-Trojan eyewitness account of the Trojan War. A Latin work purporting to be a translation of this account (which does not survive, and may never have existed) appeared around the 5th century B.C.E. and was very influential in Europe until Homer's works were recovered in the Renaissance.

Defoe, Daniel (1660-1731), English novelist and journalist, author of *Robinson Crusoe.*

Delille, Abbé Jacques (1738-1813), French poet and classicist who translated Virgil's *Georgics* in 1770 and *Aeneid* in 1804, and Milton's *Paradise Lost* in 1805.

Demaratus of Sparta (c. 510-491 B.C.E.), Eurypontid king.

Demetrius of Phaleron (b. c. 350 B.C.E.), Athenian orator, statesman, and philosopher. He was governor of Athens when the old democracy was restored; he fled first to Thebes, then to Egypt, where he became a high official in Ptolemy's court.

Demophilus (fl. 4th/3rd century B.C.E.), Greek comic dramatist.

Demosthenes (384-322 B.C.E.), Athenian statesman and orator.

Denny (or Denys), Anthony (1501-1549), a favourite of Henry VIII.

Derrida, Jacques (b. 1930), French poststructuralist philosopher who has written on translation.

Descartes, René (Renatus Cartesius, 1596-1650), French philosopher, mathematician, and scientist.

Desfontaines, Abbé Pierre-Francois Guyot (1688-1745), French writer best remembered for his translation of Swift's *Gulliver's Travels* (1727).

Despreaux: *see* Boileau.

Dictys Cretensis was the supposed author of a pre-Homeric account of the Trojan War that was in fact probably written in Latin (probably by Lucius Septimius) in the 2nd or 3rd century C.E. According to legend, Dictys Cretensis followed Idomeneus from Knossos to Troy during the siege and wrote his eyewitness account in Phoenician; his work was found in the library at Alexandria and transliterated into Greek by order of Emperor Nero.

Diderot, Denis (1713-1784), French philosopher, scientist, novelist, playwright, and essayist, chief editor of the *Encyclopédie* (1745-1772).

Dilthey, Wilhelm (1833-1911), German philosopher.

Diocletian (Gaius Aurelius Valerius Diocletianus, original name Dioclus, 245-316, reigned 285-305), Roman emperor.

Diodorus Siculus (fl. 1st century B.C.E.), Greek historian.

Diogenes (fl. 2nd century B.C.E.), Greek Stoic philosopher.

Diogenes (d. c. 320 B.C.E.), Greek Cynic philosopher whose writings do not survive.

Dion Chrysostom, also called Dion Prusaeus (c. 40-c. 112 C.E.), Greek philosopher and rhetorician.

Dionysius of Halicarnassus (fl. c. 20 B.C.E.), Greek historian and rhetorician.

Diphilus (fl. late 4th century B.C.E.), Greek comic poet.

Dobneck, Johan (d. 1552), an enemy of Luther's who wrote a scurrilous biography of him.

Domitian (Caesar Domitianus Augustus, original name Titus Flavius Domitianus, 51-96 C.E., reigned 81-96), Roman emperor.

Donatus, Aelius (4th century C.E.), a famous teacher of grammar and rhetoric in Rome who taught Jerome.

Donne, John (1572-1631), English metaphysical poet.

Du Bellay, Jean (1492-1560), French cardinal; cousin of the poet Joachim du Bellay.

Ducaeus, Fronto (early 16th century), Renaissance scholar who translated John Chrysostom into Latin in the 1530s.

Durand de Villegaignon, Nicolas (1510-1571), French Huguenot explorer who led an expedition that landed in Brazil in 1555; the Ilha de Villagagnon or Villegagnon Island in southeastern Brazil is named after him.

Ebert, Johann Arnold (1723-1795), German translator in 1751 of Edward Young's *Night Thoughts* (1742-45).

Ebion was the semilegendary (perhaps apocryphal) founder of the Ebionites, an early Christian sect mentioned by Irenaeus in 185 C.E. The Hebrew word *evyonium* means 'poor men', and 'Ebion' may have been an etiological backformation from that. The Ebionites were intent upon removing interpolations from scripture.

Echius, or Eckius (1486-1543), Swabian professor and chancellor of the University of Ingolstad, best known for the popular *Manual of Controversy*.

Edward III (1312-1377, reigned 1327-1377), king of England.

Edward VI (1537-1553, reigned 1547-1553), king of England.

Eleazar, the name of many famous Jewish high priests and Talmud scholars.

Eliot, George (Marian Evans, 1819-1880), English novelist.

Eliot, T(homas) S(tearns) (1888-1965), American poet, playwright, and literary critic.

Emser, Hieronymus (d. 1527), who had critiqued Luther's translation in 1523, then, using his critique to get Duke Georg von Sachsen-Meißen to ban Luther's edition, published his own German version, heavily dependent on Luther's, in 1527.

Ennius, Quintus (239-169 B.C.E.), Latin epic poet, dramatist, and satirist, often called the founder of Roman literature.

Epicharmus (c. 530-c. 440 B.C.E.), Greek comic dramatist.

Epictetus (c. 55-c.155 C.E.), Phrygian philosopher associated with the Stoics.

Epicurus (341-270 B.C.E.), Greek philosopher who founded the philosophy of friendship and pleasure that bore his name.

Eriksson, Erik (1216-1250, reigned 1222-1229 and 1234-1249), king of Sweden, between 1229 and 1234 exiled to Denmark.

Eschenburg, Johann Joachim (1743-1820), German literary historian who translated Shakespeare's plays into prose in 1775-1782, revised edition 1798-1806.

Eugenius III (original name Bernardo de Pisa, d. 1153), pope 1145-1153.

Eunomius (c. 335-c. 394), Cappadocian religious leader who founded an extreme Arian sect known as the Eunomians.

Euphorion (b. c. 275 B.C.E.), Greek poet; byword of turgid, convoluted diction.

Euripides (c. 484-406 B.C.E.), Greek tragic dramatist.

Eusebius of Caesarea (early 4th century), bishop, theologian, and historian.

Eustochium (c. 370-419), friend of Jerome and Paula.

Evagrius (fl. 390), bishop of Antioch and Latin translator of Athanasius' *Life of Anthony*.

Fabianus (fl mid-3rd century C.E.), bishop of Rome.

Fabius: *see* Quintilian.

Fabius Valens (c. 328-378), Eastern Roman emperor.

Fabri, Johan (d. 1541), bishop of Vienna, one of Luther's most vociferous opponents.

Fabricius Luscinus, Gaius (3rd century B.C.E.), Roman general and statesman whose integrity was widely cited as a model of Roman virtue.

Fairfax, Edward (1575-1635), English poet who translated Tasso's *Gerusalemme Liberata* as *Godfrey of Bulloigne or the Recovery of Jerusalem* in 1600.

Fanshawe, Richard (1608-1666), English poet, translator, and diplomat; translator of Guarini's *Il pastor Fido* ('The Faithful Shepherd', 1647), parts of Virgil, Horace, and others.

Felix: *see* Minucius Felix.

Felix III (d. 492, reigned 483-92), pope.

Felltham, Owen (1602?-1668), English author of *Resolves Divine, Moral, Political* (1620, expanded editions in 1628, 1631, 1634, 1636, 1647, and 1661 during his lifetime).

Fénelon, Francois de Salignac de La Mothe (1651-1715), French theologian and Archbishop of Cambrai, author of *Les aventures de Télémaque* ('The Adventures of Telemachus', 1699).

Fenton, Elijah (1683-1730), English translator who helped Alexander Pope translate the *Odyssey*.

Ferdowsi, also spelled Firdausi, Firdusi, Firdousi, and Firdawsi, pseudonym of Abu Ol-Qasem Mansur (935-1020/26), Persian poet who 'wrote' (actually partly translated, partly adapted from a tenth-century prose chronicle) the Persian national epic *Shah-nameh* ('Book of Kings', 1010).

Fichte, Johann Gottlieb (1762-1814), German philosopher and nationalist.

Ficino, Marsilio (1433-1499), Italian theologian, philosopher, and linguist whose commentaries on and translations of Plato helped foment the Italian Renaissance.

Figueroa: *see* Suarez Figueroa.

Filelfo, Francesco (1398-1481), Italian humanist, poet, and translator.

Fillmore, Sir Edward (obscure), English court wit, translated one act of Corneille's *La morte du Pompee* ('The Death of Pompey', early 1660s).

Fischart, Johann (1546/47-1590), German author of the *Affentheuerliche und ungeheurliche Geschichtschrift* ('Farcical and Monstrous History', 1575, in later editions *Geschichtsklitterung*, 'Historical Daubing'). It was an expanded prose version of Rabelais' *Gargantua*, hence Fischart's nickname 'the German Rabelais'.

FitzJames, Richard (d. 1522), bishop of London.

Flaccus, Gaius Valerius (1st century C.E.), Roman author of an *Argonautica* that draws heavily on the *Argonautica* of Apollonius Rhodius of Alexandria and might be thought of as a translation of the earlier work.

Flacius Illyricus, Matthias (1520-1575), Luther's student in Wittenberg, later a professor of Hebrew.

Flaminius, Titus Quinctius (c. 227-174 B.C.E.), Roman general and consul under Philip V of Macedonia.

Flechier, Esprit (1632-1710), bishop of Nismes and classical scholar.

Fontenelle, Bernard Le Bovier de (1657-1757), French scholar and scientist.

Forster, Georg (1754-1794) translated Kalidasa's *Abhijnanasakuntala* from William Jones's English translation into German in 1791.

Foulis, Andrew (1712-1775) and Robert (1707-1776), English printers.

Fracastoro, Girolamo (Hieronymus Fracastorius, c. 1478-1553), Italian poet, physician, astronomer, and geologist.

François I (1494-1547, reigned 1515-1547), King of France.

Frederick I (byname Frederick Barbarossa, c. 1123-1190), German king and Holy Roman Emperor (1152-1190) and duke of Swabia (1147-1190).

Frederick II (byname the Great, 1712-1786, reigned 1740-1786), Prussian emperor.

Frederick II (1194-1250), king of Sicily (1197-1250), and Germany (1212-1250), duke of Swabia (as Frederick VI, 1228-1235), and Holy Roman Emperor (1220-1250).

Frederick III (byname the Wise, Friedrich der Weise, 1463-1525), elector of Saxony who protected Martin Luther while he was under imperial ban beginning in 1521.

Freud, Sigmund (1856-1939), Austrian neurologist and the founder of psychoanalysis.

Froissart, Jean (c. 1333-1400/1), European poet and court historian, author of the *Chronicles*.

Furetière, Antoine (1619-1688), French novelist, satirist, and lexicographer, author of the *Nouvelle allégorique* ('Allegorical Tale', 1658).

Gadamer, Hans-Georg (b. 1900), German philosopher whose *Wahrheit und Methode* (*Truth and Method*) contains a significant discussion of translation.

Galba: *see* Sulpicius.

Galen of Pergamum (Claudios Galenos, 129-c. 199 C.E.), Greek physician whose experimental physiology was extremely influential in the Renaissance.

Galileo (Galilei, 1564-1642), Italian mathematician, astronomer, and physicist.

Galland, Antoine (1646-1715), French Orientalist who adapted the Arabian Nights as *Mille et une nuits* in 1704-1717.

Galliard, John (c. 1687-1749), English composer whose opera *The Rape of Proserpine* was first produced in 1728.

Gallus: *see* Cornelius Gallus.

Gamaliel, the name of six Palestinian rabbis of the 1st, 2nd, and 3rd centuries C.E..

Gardiner, Stephen (c. 1482-1555), English bishop who supported Henry VIII's break with Rome but rejected Protestantism and, as a loyal Catholic supporter of Queen Mary I (reigned 1553-1558), became her Lord Chancellor and a strong advocate of persecuting Protestants.

Garrick, David (1717-1779), English actor, playwright, poet, producer, and co-manager of the Drury Lane Theatre.

Gaume, Jean Joseph (1802-1879), French abbé and polemicist.

Gay, John (1685-1732), English poet and dramatist.

Gaza, Theodore (c. 1400-1475), a Byzantine scholar who emigrated to Italy, was an early humanist who wrote several Latin translations of Aristotle (384-322 B.C.E.).

Georg von Sachsen-Meißen (1471-1539), German duke who banned Luther's translation of the Bible and promoted Emser's.

George I (Georg Ludwig, 1660-1727), elector of Hanover (1698-1727) and king of Great Britain (1714-1727).

Gerard of Cremona (Girardus Cremonensis, 1114-1187), a translator from Arabic to Latin in Toledo, Spain.

Germanicus Caesar (15 B.C.E.-19 C.E.), Roman consul, translator of Aratus' *Phaenomena* into Latin.

Gibbon, Edward (1737-1794), English historian, author of *The History of the Decline and Fall of the Roman Empire* (1776-1788).

Girardus: *see* Gerard of Cremona.

Godolphin, Sidney (obscure), English court wit, according to legend translated the 5th act of Corneille's *La morte du Pompee*.

Godwin Shelley, Mary (1797-1851), English author of *Frankenstein*, daughter of Mary Wollstonecraft and William Godwin, wife of Percy Shelley.

Godwin, William (1756-1836), English social philosopher and political journalist.

Gorionides, Josephus, aka Joseph ben Gorion ha-Kohen, Yosifon ben Goriyon, and Josephus Hebraicus, the supposed author of an anonymous Hebrew work called the *Josippon* (c. 953 C.E.), based loosely on two Latin translations of Flavius Josephus (Yosifon ben Mattathias), the *Jewish Antiquities* and *The Jewish War* (the *Hegesippus*). Joseph ben Gorion is mentioned in the latter as a general fighting the Romans; hence perhaps the confusion. An important medieval and early-modern source of information on the period of the later Old Testament books such as Esther and David, it was frequently quoted; even as late as the Renaissance it was often thought to have been written by Flavius Josephus.

Gower, John (1330?-1408), English poet, a contemporary of Chaucer.

Gracchus, Gaius Sempronius (160/153-121 B.C.E.), Roman tribune whose speeches were much imitated in Roman rhetorical schools.

Gratianus (late 11th century-before 1159), Benedictine monk who founded canon law by compiling nearly 3800 texts dealing with all areas of church discipline and regulation as the Concordia Disconcordantium Canonum (around 1140), often known as Gratian's Decretum.

Gregory II of Cyprus (birth name George of Cyprus, 1241-1290), Greek Orthodox patriarch of

Constantinople who wrote his autobiography (*Diagesis merike*) as a preface to a collection of his letters.

Gregory VII (original name Ildebrando, c. 1020-1085), pope.

Gregory XIII (original name Ugo Buoncompagni, 1502-1585, reigned 1572-1585), pope who promulgated the Gregorian calendar.

Gregory the Illuminator (240-332 C.E.), according to tradition the apostle of Christianity to Armenia

Gregory of Nazianzus (330-389 A.D.), Church Father.

Gregory of Nyssa (Gregorius Nyssenius, c. 335-c. 394 C.E.), mystic, philosopher, and theologian.

Gries, Johann Diederich (1775-1842) translated Ariosto's *Orlando Furioso* as *Der Rasender Roland* (1804-1808) and Tasso's *Gerusalemme Liberata* (1581) as *Befreiter Jerusalem* (1800-1803).

Grimm, Freidrich Melchior, Freiherr (Baron) von (1723-1807), German critic.

Grosseteste, Robert (1175-1253), English bishop of Lincoln and chancellor of Oxford University who translated numerous Greek and Arab works of philosophy and science (including Aristotle) into Latin.

Grotius, Hugo (Hugo/Huigh/Hugeianus de Groot, 1583-1645), Dutch jurist and scholar who wrote, in addition to his many Latin works, an introduction to the jurisprudence of Holland in Dutch (1631).

Guarini: *see* Battista Guarini.

Guillaume de Lorris (fl. 13th century), French author/translator of the first part (4058 lines) of the *Roman de la Rose* (c. 1230-1240).

Gustav I Vasa (original name Gustav Eriksson Vasa, 1496?-1560, reigned 1523-1560), king of Sweden.

Habert, Phillipe (1605-1637), French poet and academician, author of 'The Temple of Death'.

Hadrian (pope): *see* Adrian.

Hafiz (Mohammad Shams Od-Din Hafez, 1325/26-1389/90), Persian lyrical poet.

Hamann, Johann Georg (1730-1788), German philosopher.

Hammer-Purgstall, Joseph von (1774-1856), Viennese Orientalist, poet, and historian whose translation of Hafiz, *Hafischer Divan* (1812-1813) greatly influenced Goethe's *Divan.*

Harington, Anne (d. 1620), wife of Sir John Harington and mother of Lucy Russell; an active patroness of poetry, she and her daughter were John Florio's patrons in his translation of Montaigne.

Harington, Sir John (1561-1612), first lord Harington of Exton, husband of Anne Harington and father of Lucy Russell. He was given the task of translating Ariosto's *Orlando Furioso* (1516) by Queen Elizabeth as penance for translating a sexy story by Ariosto and circulating it among the court ladies. While translating *Orlando* he also invented the flush toilet and installed one for the Queen.

Har(r)iot, Thomas (1560-1621), English scientist.

Harris, James (1709-1780), English scholar, author of *Three Treatises Upon Art, Music, and Happiness* (1744), *Hermes, or A Philosophical Inquiry Concerning Language and Universal Grammar* (1751) and *Upon the Rise and Progress of Criticism* (1752).

Hawtrey, E. C. (d. 1861), Provost of Eton.

Hayward, Abraham (1801-1884), British essayist who translated Goethe's *Faust* in 1833.

Hecataeus of Miletus (fl. 6th-5th century B.C.E.) was a Greek historian and travel writer used by Herodotus.

Hegel, Georg Wilhelm Friedrich (1770-1831), German philosopher.

Heidegger, Martin (1889-1976), German philosopher who wrote briefly but importantly on translation.

Heinse, Wilhelm (1746-1803), German translator of Ariosto's *Orlando Furioso* as *Der Rasender Roland* (1781).

Heliodorus of Emesa (fl. 3rd century B.C.E.), Greek author of the *Aethiopica*, a long prose fiction.

Henry (d. 1156/60), English bishop of Uppsala, Sweden, who founded the Finnish Catholic Church while on a crusade to Finland with Erik Jedvarsson in 1155; was murdered by a peasant named Lalli.

Henry IV (byname Henri de Navarre, 1553-1610), king of France.

Henry VII (1457-1509), king of England.

Henry VIII (1491-1547, reigned 1509-1547), king of England who engineered the Protestant Reformation in England in order to divorce his first wife Catherine of Aragon and marry his second, Anne Boleyn.

Henry the Navigator (Henrique o Navegador, 1394-1460), Portuguese prince and patron of voyages of discovery.

Heracleides Ponticus (b. c. 380 B.C.E.), Greek philosopher, disciple of Plato and Aristotle.

Heraclitus (Herakleitos, c. 540-c. 480 B.C.E.), Greek philosopher, only fragments of whose works survive.

Hermann the German (Hermannus Alemannus, d. 1272), Arabic-Latin translator in Toledo, Spain.

Hermannus: *see* Hermann the German.

Héroët, Antoine (1492?-1568), French Renaissance court poet.

Hesiod (Hesiodos, around 700 B.C.E.), Greek poet.

Hess(us), Eobanus (1488-1540), German poet and scholar.

Hesychius (fl. 5th century C.E.), Greek lexicographer.

Hetzer (or Hatza, or Hätzer), Ludwig (c. 1500-1529), German Anabaptist.

Hieronymus ab Oleastro Lusitani (fl. mid-16th century), author of a commentary on the Pentateuch (1568).

Higden, Ralph (Ranulph(us) Higdon, c. 1280-1363/64), English Benedictine monk and chronicler, author of the *Polychronicon*, a universal history from creation to the mid-14th century.

Hilary of Poitiers (315-367), Gallo-Roman bishop and theologian.

Hippocrates (c. 460-c. 377 B.C.E.), Greek physician whose name has been associated since antiquity with the Hippocratic oath (not written by him).

Hippolytus of Rome (c. 170-c. 235 C.E.), Christian theologian and antipope.

Hobbes, Thomas (1588-1679), English philosopher and political theorist; translated the *Odyssey* in 1675 and the *Iliad* the year after.

Hody, Humphrey (1659-1707), English theologian and translator.

Hoffmann, E(rnst) T(heodor) A(madeus) (1776-1822), German romantic writer, composer, and painter, best remembered for his gothic tales.

Holliday, John (1730?-1801), English scholar who translated (but did not publish) the first eight books of Virgil's *Aeneid* into hexametres.

Homer (9th or 8th century B.C.E.?), Greek epic poet, presumed author of the *Odyssey* and the *Iliad*.

Honorius, Flavius (384-423), Roman emperor in the West from 393 to 423.

Hopkins, Gerard Manley (1844-1889), English poet and Jesuit priest.

Hortensius, Quintus (114-50 B.C.E.), Roman orator widely taken to represent the Asiatic school.

Hosius, Stanislas (1504-1579), Polish cardinal who opened the Council of Trent as legate from Pius IV.

Howard, Catherine (d. 1542), queen of England, fifth wife of Henry VIII.

Howard, Thomas, 1st earl of Suffolk (1561-1626), English commander and royal councillor.

Hugh of Saint-Cher (1200?-1263), French Dominican theologian, cardinal, and legate to Germany.

Hugo von Sitten (fl. 1015), bishop of Sitten, Switzerland (Fr. Sion).

Humboldt, Friedrich Wilhelm Heinrich Alexander, Freiherr (Baron) von (1769-1859), German explorer and geographer, author of *Kosmos* (1840s and 1850s); brother to Wilhelm von Humboldt.

Humphrey, Lawrence (1527?-1590), English divine, dean of Gloucester and Winchester; author of *Interpretatio linguarum.*

Hunne, Richard (d. 1514), English merchant arrested for refusing to pay the mortuary tax to bury his infant son, later found hanged by his own belt in prison. Dr. William Horsey, the chancellor of London, was accused of murdering him, but pardoned by King Henry VIII. After his death his house was searched for 'heretical writings,' and when an English Bible was found, his body was tried for heresy, found guilty and burned.

Hus, Jan (1372/73-1415), Czech religious reformer, burned at the stake for heresy.

Hyginus, Gaius Julius (fl. 1st century C.E.), Latin author and scholar, pupil of Cornelius Alexander.

Hyperides (390-322 B.C.E.), Greek orator thought to have been a student of Plato and Isocrates. Defended Phryne against the charge of blasphemy, a capital crime.

Illyricus: *see* Flacius Illyricus.

Innocent I (d. 417), pope who condemned Pelagianism.

Irenaeus (120/40-200/3 C.E.), bishop of Lugdunum (Lyon), was the premier 2nd-century Church Father and author of *Adversus haereses* ('Against Heresies', c. 180).

Isidore of Seville (c. 560-636), Spanish theologian, archbishop of Seville, and encyclopaedist.

Isocrates (436-338 B.C.E.), Greek orator, teacher, and founder of a school and tradition of rhetoric.

James (Jacopo, fl. 13th century), archbishop of Genoa; translated the Bible into Italian.

James I (1566-1625), king of Scotland (1567-1625) and England (1603-1625).

James II (1633-1701), last Roman Catholic king of Great Britain.

James of Venice (Jacobus de Venetiis, fl. 1128-1136), participant in the famous debate between the Eastern and Western churches in Constantinople, in 1136.

Jáuregui y Hurtado de la Sal, Juan Martínez de (1583-1641), Spanish scholar, critic, and religious poet who translated Martial, Horace, Lucan, and Tasso into Spanish.

Jean Paul (Johann Paul Friedrich Richter, 1763-1825), German novelist.

Jebb, Richard Claverhouse (1841-1905), English Greek scholar, translated *Oedipus the King* in 1905.

Jedvarsson, Erik (d. c. 1160), pretender to the Swedish throne who after his death was canonized as the patron saint of Finland.

Jerome of Prague (c. 1365-1416), Czech philosopher, theologian, and religious reformer, burned at the stake for heresy.

Joachim of Fiore (Gioacchinio da Fiore, c. 1130/35-1201/2), Italian mystic, theologian, and philosopher of history whose theory that history was divided into three ages, of the Father, the Son, and the Holy Ghost, formed the basis of Hitler's concept of the Third Reich.

John I (byname John the Great, João o Grande, 1357-1433), king of Portugal.

John of Damascus (Johannes Damascenus, c. 675-749), doctor of the Greek and Latin churches.

John of Jerusalem (356-417), theologian and bishop attacked by Epiphanius of Constantia for Origenism.

John of Seville (also known as John Hispalensis, d. 1157), Mozarabic Christian translator from Arabic into Latin of Al-Fargani, al-Battani, Maslama of Madrid, and al-Zarkali.

Jones, William (1746-1794), Welsh Orientalist, translator, and judge of the Supreme Court in Calcutta; wrote a *Grammar of the Persian Language* (1771) and translated digests of Hindu and Muslim law.

Jonson, Ben (1572-1637), English poet, dramatist, critic, and translator who translated Horace's *Ars poetica* twice (1604, 1616) and wrote a (subsequently lost) commentary on it. The translations are usually considered embarrassingly literal.

Josephus, Flavius (Yosifon ben Mattathias, Joseph ben Matthias, 37/38-c. 100 C.E.), Jewish priest, scholar, and historian.

Jovinian (fl. c. 400), Church Father best remembered for his denial of Mary's virginity at childbirth.

Jowett, Benjamin (1817-1893), British classicist; his translations of Plato remain definitive today.

Julian (380-c. 455), Pelagian bishop of Eclanum.

Julian Apostate (Flavius Claudius Julianus, 331/332-363), Roman emperor from 361 to 363 who converted the Roman Empire (which Constantine had converted to Christianity in 313) back to Mithraism.

Justin I (c. 450-527), Byzantine emperor.

Justinian I (Flavius Justinius, original name Petrus Sabbatius, 483-565, reigned 527-565), Byzantine emperor.

Justinus, Marcus Junianus (fl. 3rd century C.E.), Roman historian, author of an abridgement or *Epitome* of the *Historiae Philippicae et totius mundi origines et terrae situs* by Pompeius Trogus.

Juusten, Paavali (Paul Jausten, c. 1516-1576), bishop of Viipuri.

Juvenal (Decimus Junius Juvenalis, 55/60-127? C.E.), Roman satirical poet.

Kalchheim-Lohausen, Wilhelm von (also known as von Kalchum or Calchum, 1584-1640), German author who translated Sallust in 1629.

Kalidasa (fl. 5th century C.E.), Sanskrit poet and dramatist, author of the *Abhijnanasakuntala* and 'Meghadûta'.

Kant, Immanuel (1724-1804), German philosopher.

Keats, John (1795-1821), English romantic poet, author of 'Upon First Looking into Chapman's Homer'.

Khayyám, Omar (Abu Ol-Fath Omar Ebn Ebrahim Ol-Khayyami, 1048-1122), Persian poet, mathematician, and astronomer, author of quatrains (in Persian *roba'iyat*) famously translated into English by Edward FitzGerald as the *Rubaiyat.*

Killigrew, Thomas (1612-1683), English playwright and theatre owner/director.

Klopstock, Friedrich Gottlieb (1724-1803), German epic and lyric poet who anticipated the Romantics. His most famous work, *Der Messias* (1749-1773), inspired by Bodmer's Swiss translation of Milton's *Paradise Lost*, was written in unrhymed hexametres. Author of the *Dialogues on Grammar* (1794).

Kosegarten, Gottfried (1792-1860), German Orientalist who advised Goethe on the literary-historical background of the *West-Östlicher Divan.*

La Fontaine, Jean de (1621-1695), French poet, author of the *Fables.*

La Motte, Antoine Houdar de (1672-1731), French literary scholar and translator who translated Homer's *Iliad* in 1714.

Labienus, Quintus (d. 39 B.C.E.), Roman general who defected to the Parthian side.

Laelius Sapiens, Gaius, the Younger (fl. 2nd century B.C.E.), Roman soldier and politician who appears as a speaker in several of Cicero's books.

Lane, Edward William (1801-1876), British Arabic scholar who translated the *Thousand and One Nights* in 1838-1840.

Lapide, Cornelius Cornelii à (1567-1637), Jesuit Bible scholar.

Lee, Edward (c. 1482-1544), archbishop of York (1531-1544); a boyhood friend of Thomas More who conducted a long debate with Erasmus over the latter's Latin translation of the New Testament.

Lefèbvre, Tanneguy (1615-1672), French Hellenist scholar, father of Anne Dacier.

Lefèvre, Raoul (fl. 1460), author of *The Destruction of Troy*.

Lefèvre d'Étaples, Jacques (Johannes Faber Stapulensis, 1455-1536), French Bible scholar who translated the Psalms into Latin and the entire Bible into French from the Vulgate. Lefévre was accused of Protestantism and is often regarded as a Reformer on the eve of Reformation.

Leo X (originally named Giovanni de' Medici, 1475-1521, reigned 1513-1521), Italian pope. His harsh response to the Reformation (he excommunicated Luther in 1521) helped splinter the Western church; he also depleted the papal treasury while transforming the papacy into a political and cultural power.

Leopardi, Giacomo (1798-1837), Italian poet, scholar, philosopher, and translator.

Lessing, Gotthold Ephraim (1729-1781), German playwright, critic, and aesthetician.

Linck, Wenzeslaus (1483-1547), recipient of Luther's 'Circular Letter on Translation'.

Lindanus, William (b. 1525), Roman Catholic polemicist.

Livius, Titus (59/64 B.C.E.-17 C.E.), usually called Livy in English, was with Sallust and Tacitus one of the three greatest Roman historians.

Livius Andronicus, Lucius (c. 284-c.204 B.C.E.), Roman poet whose Latin *Odyssia* was probably a classroom crib for the original; only about 50 lines survive.

Lobo, Jeronimo (c. 1596-1678), Italian author, author of *A Voyage to Abyssinia.*

Locke, John (1632-1704), English philosopher.

Lockhart, John Gibson (1794-1854), Scottish writer.

Loisel, Antoine (1536-1612), French jurist.

Lombard, Pierre (1100-1160), bishop of Paris; his *Four Books of Sentences* was the standard medieval theological text.

Longfellow, Henry Wadsworth (1807-1882), American poet.

Longinus, also called Dionysius Longinus and Pseudo-Longinus (fl. early 1st century C.E.), reputed author of the Greek treatise *Peri Hypsous* ('On the Sublime').

Longus (fl. 2nd/3rd century C.E.), Greek author of the prose romance *Daphnis and Chloe.*

Lorenzo: *see* Valla.

Loschi, Antonio (d. 1441), Italian translator.

Louis IX (1214-1270, reigned 1226-1270, canonized 1297), French king.

Louis XIV (Louis le Grand, le Roi Soleil, 1638-1715, reigned 1643-1715), king of France.

Lucian (Lucianos, c. 120-after 180 C.E.), Greek satirist and rhetorician.

Lucilius, Gaius (c. 180-c. 103/2 B.C.E.), the inventor of poetic satire, and Gaius Laelius (d. after 160 B.C.E.), Roman general, both served in Spain under the Roman commander Scipio.

Lucius of Patrae, Greek author to whom Lucian of Samosata's *Lucius, or the Ass* was falsely attributed.

Lucretius Carus, Titus (fl. 1st century B.C.E.), Roman philosopher and poet best known for his long poem *De rerum natura* ('On the Nature of Things').

Lully, Jean-Baptiste (Giovanni Battista Lulli, 1632-1687), Italian-born French composer.

Lycurgus (fl. 7th century B.C.E.?), traditionally considered the lawgiver who created the institutions of ancient Sparta.

Lydgate, John (c. 1370-c. 1450), English devotional poet.

Lygdamus (b. 43 B.C.E.), Roman elegiac poet.

Lynceus of Samos (late 4th century B.C.E.), Greek historian, grammarian, and poet.

Lyndwood, William (1375?-1446), bishop of London, who collected and commented upon the synodal constitutions of the province of Canterbury from 1207 to the mid-15th century.

Lysias (c. 445-after 380 B.C.E.), Greek speechwriter known for the simplicity of his style.

Lysippus (fl. 4th century B.C.E.), Greek sculptor.

Macer, Aemilius (d. 16 B.C.E.), Roman poet.

Machiavelli, Niccolò (1469-1527), Florentine statesman and political theorist, author of *Il principe* (*The Prince* 1513).

Macrobius, Ambrosius Theodosius (fl. 400 C.E.), Roman philosopher and grammarian, author of the *Saturnalia.*

Maecenas, Gaius (c. 70-8 B.C.E.), Roman diplomat and wealthy patron of poets (Horace, Virgil).

Maffei, Raffaele (known in Latin as Raphael Volaterranus, 1451-1532), Italian Renaissance scholar who translated the *Odyssey* into Latin in 1524; a partial translation of the *Iliad* (books 1-2) also survives.

Maitre de Saci: *see* Saci.

Malherbe, François de (1555-1628), French poet and poetic theorist, precursor of classicism.

Malone, Edmond (1741-1812), one of several editors (including Samuel Johnson, George Steevens, and Isaac Reed) who brought out a 16-volume edition of Shakespeare between 1778 and 1790.

Malory, Sir Thomas (fl. c. 1470), English author of *Le Morte d'Arthur*.

Manasses, Constantine (d. 1187), Byzantine metropolitan of Naupactus who wrote a verse chronicle of world history from creation to 1081, a verse romance, and other poems and prose.

Mani (or Manes, or Manichaeus, 216-274? C.E.), the Iranian founder of Manicheanism, known as the 'Illuminator'. Augustine converted to Manicheanism, a dualistic Gnosticism that saw the soul as locked into mortal combat between powers of good and evil, in his twenties, on his way to becoming a Christian; he was later one of the most zealous (and effectual) fighters in the attempt to have it declared heretical and systematically eradicated.

Manuel I Comenus (c. 1122-1180, reigned 1143-1180), Byzantine emperor.

Marcian (396-457), Roman emperor in the East.

Marcion (2nd century C.E.), founder of the Marcionites, a Gnostic sect declared heretical in 144.

Margaret of Angoulême/Navarre (Marguerite d'Angoulême, de Navarre, 1492-1549), queen consort of Henri II de Navarre, author of *Miroir de l'âme pécheresse* (1531) and a work based on Boccaccio's *Decamerone*, the *Heptaméron* (1558-1559). A powerful patron and protector of humanist scholars, including Étienne Dolet, Clément Marot, and François Rabelais, she was in the end unable to save Dolet from his death sentence.

Marlowe, Christopher (1564-1593), English poet and playwright.

Maro: *see* Virgil.

Marot, Clément (1496?-1544), French poet who translated/edited the *Roman de la Rose* (1526), thirty of the psalms (1539-1542), and works by Catullus, Virgil, and Ovid. His translations of the psalms were condemned by the Sorbonne and he was forced to flee France to Geneva, where he was given sanctuary by John Calvin, who admired them.

Martial (Marcus Valerius Martialis, 38/41-c. 103 C.E.), Roman epigrammatic poet.

Marx, Karl (1818-1883), political theorist, sociologist, and economist.

Mary (byname Queen of Scots, 1542-1587), queen of Scotland (1542-1567) and queen consort of France (1559-1560).

Mary I (byname Bloody Mary, 1516-1558, reigned 1553-1558), first queen to rule England, known as Bloody Mary for her ruthless persecution of Protestants.

Mary II (1662-1694, reigned 1689-1694), queen of England, daughter of James II and wife of William III.

Matius Calvena, Gnaeus (fl. 1st century B.C.E.), Roman author, friend of Cicero; may have translated Homer into Latin.

Maximilian I (1459-1519), German emperor; commissioner, part-author, and hero of the verse works *Theuerdank* and *Weisskunig*.

Maximus the Confessor (c. 580-662), Byzantine theologian.

May, Thomas (1595-1650), English man of letters who translated Virgil, Martial, and Lucan.

Melancthon, Philipp (Greek for 'black earth', or Schwartzerd, his original surname; 1497-1560), German Reformer, professor of Greek at the University of Wittenberg, and close friend and defender of Luther's.

Menander (c. 342-c. 292 B.C.E.), Athenian comic dramatist.

Menippus (fl. 3rd century B.C.E.), Greek Cynic philosopher and satirist.

Messalla Corvinus, Marcus Valerius (64 B.C.-13 C.E.), Roman aristocrat, patron of literature, and orator.

Metastasio, Pietro (born Pietro Armando Dominico Trapassi, 1698-1782), Italian poet, librettist, and critic.

Methodius (c. 825-884), Macedonian theologian and linguist who together with his brother Cyril converted the Danubian Slavs to Christianity, invented the Cyrillic alphabet, and translated the Bible into Old Church Slavonic.

Michael Scot (1175?-1234?), Arabic-Latin translator in Toledo, Spain. Also famous as a magician, he was reserved a place in Dante's *Inferno* (Canto 20) for magic and appeared in a tale in Boccaccio's *Decamerone* (10th day, 5th tale); Sir Walter Scott also referred to him in *The Lay of the Last Minstrel.*

Michaelis, Dorothea Caroline Albertine (1763-1809), one of the most brilliant of the German romantics; married August von Schlegel in 1796, left him in 1803 for his younger colleague Friedrich W.J. Schelling.

Miller, John (1715-1790?), English translator.

Milo, Titus Annius (d. 48 B.C.E.), Roman politician whom Cicero defended against charges of murdering his political opponent Clodius; Cicero's defence, *Pro Milone*, survives.

Milo(n) of Croton (fl. late 6th century B.C.E.), famous Greek athlete, whose name was proverbial for superhuman strength.

Milton, John (1608-1674), English poet, author of *Paradise Lost* (1667).

Minucius Felix, Marcus (fl. 4th century) Christian apologist.

Mnesarchus (fl. 110 B.C.E.), Roman Stoic philosopher.

Molon of Rhodes (early 1st century B.C.E.), Roman teacher of rhetoric whose eclectic views influenced his student Cicero.

Monaeses (fl. 38-36 B.C.E.), Parthian general, Warden of the Western Marches, under King Phraates. Claiming to be afraid of his king's cruelty, he went to Antony, offering to sell out to the Romans; in return Antony promised him the Parthian kingdom. It is not clear whether Monaeses was really defecting or merely pretending to in order to glean intelligence, since soon after he returned to Parthia to reassume command.

Montagu, Elizabeth Robinson (1720-1800), one of the so-called Bluestockings; held an intellectual salon in her house.

Montalvo, Garci Rodriguez de (fl. 1500), Spanish author of *Amadis de Gaula*.

Monti, Vicenzo (1754-1828), Italian poet who translated the *Iliad* into blank verse in 1810.

Mucius: *see* Scaevola.

Münster, Sebastian (1489-1552), Hebrew scholar who edited the Hebrew Bible, with a literal Latin translation.

Musäus, Karl August (1735-1787), German author of *Folktales* (1782).

Naevius, Gnaius (c. 270-c. 200 B.C.E.), along with Ennius and Livius Andronicus one of the three most famous early Latin poets.

Nazianzen: see Gregory of Nazianzus.

Necos (Nechao, Neku, fl. early 7th century B.C.E.), king of Sais and Memphis, father of Psammeticus.

Nestorius (d. c. 451), bishop of Constantinople, founder of a Christian sect called the Nestorians.

Newman, John Henry (1801-1890), English Roman Catholic cardinal and man of letters, brother of Francis Newman.

Nezami, Elyas Yusof (b. c. 1141), Persian epic poet.

Nicander (fl. 3rd/2nd century B.C.E.), Greek poet.

Nicholas III (1210/20-1280, reigned 1277-1280), Italian pope.

Nicholas of Hereford (d. c. 1420), English theological scholar.

Nicholas of Lyra (1270-1349), Fransiscan theologian, wrote the first printed commentary on the Bible.

Nicias (fl. 4th century B.C.E.), Athenian painter known for painting some of Praxiteles' statues.

Nicomachus of Gerasa (or Gerasensis, fl. c. 100 C.E.), neo-Pythagorean philosopher and mathematician.

Ochino, Bernardino (1487-1564), Italian Protestant Reformer who lived in England in the late 1540s and early 1550s, fleeing the Protestant persecutions begun by Mary upon her ascension to the throne in 1553.

Octavian: *see* Augustus.

Ogilby, John (1600-1676), English poet and translator ridiculed by Dryden in *MacFlecknoe* and by Alexander Pope in the *Dunciad.*

Olof Skötkronung (Olaf the Tax King, d. 1022, reigned 994-1022), king of Sweden.

Opitz, Martin (1597-1639), German scholar; translated Seneca's *Troades* (1625), Sophocles' *Antigone* (1636), the Psalms (1637).

Oresme, Nicholas (Nicole d'Oresme, c. 1325-1382), French Aristotelian scholar, economist, and bishop, was asked (c. 1375) by King Charles V the Wise to translate Aristotle into French for him; he did versions of the *Ethics*, the *Politics*, and the *Economics*, and was rewarded with a bishopric in 1377.

Origen (Oregenes Adamantius, 185-254 C.E.), Alexandrian theologian and ascetic whose work powerfully shaped later Christian theology, but who was accused of many heresies in his own day and for many centuries after, largely for being more of a pagan philosopher than Christian theologian.

Ortunez de Calahorra, Diego (fl. 16th century), Spanish author of *Espeio de principes y cavalleros*, translated into English by Margaret Tyler as *The Mirrour of Princely Deedes and Knighthood* in 1578.

Osiander, Andreas (Andreas Hosemann, 1498-1552), a German Reformer whose position on the justification of sinners led to his being condemned by Lutherans.

Ovid (Publius Ovidius Naso, 43 B.C.E.-17 C.E.), Roman poet who wrote the *Art of Love* and *Metamorphoses*.

Ozell, John (d. 1743), English translator.

Pacorus I (Pakores, d. 38 B.C.E.), Parthian commander in the Battle of Carrhae, who later collaborated with Labienus to conquer all of Asia Minor, Syria, and Palestine; it was even feared that he would invade Italy.

Pacuvius, Marcus (220-c. 132 B.C.E.), a nephew of Ennius; his writing was confined almost entirely to tragedy.

Pagnini, Sante (Sanctes Pagninus or Pagnino, 1470-1536), Renaissance Bible scholar who did a literal Latin translation of the entire Bible (1528).

Palaemon, Quintus R(h)emmius (Fannius) (fl. 1st century B.C.E.), influential Roman grammarian known for his emphasis on the work of Virgil rather than the ancients.

Pamelius (fl. 13th century), author of the *Liturgicon.*

Pammachius (c. 340-409/10), Roman senator and son-in-law of Jerome's benefactor Paula, who upon the death of his wife gave up his political career and became a monk.

Panaetius of Rhodes (c. 180-109 B.C.E.), the founder of Roman Stoic philosophy; his *On the Appropriate* was the model (sometimes called the 'source text') for the first two books of Cicero's *De Officiis*.

Pancirollus, Guido (1523-1599), Italian Renaissance scholar.

Papinian (Aemilius Papinianus, c. 140-212), Roman jurist, considered by the Middle Ages the definitive authority on Roman law; author of the 37-volume *Quaestiones* and the 19-volume *Responsa*.

Papinius Statius, Publius (c. 45-96 C.E.), Roman epic and lyric poet.

Papitian (Aemilius Papixianus, c. 140-212), Roman jurist, for later Christian writers the supreme authority on Roman law.

Paracelsus (Philippus Aureolus Theophrastus Bombast von Hohenheim, 1493-1541), Swiss physician and alchemist, author of *Die grosse Wundartzney* ('Great Surgery Book', 1536).

Parthenius of Nicaea (or Nicenius, fl. 1st century B.C.E.), Greek poet and grammarian.

Paterculus, Velleius (c. 19 B.C.E.-after 30 C.E.), Roman soldier, politician, and historian.

Paul II (original name Pietro Barbo, 1417-1471, reigned 1464-1471), Italian pope.

Paulus Diaconus (Paul the Deacon, c. 772-c. 799), Lombard historian.

Pausanias (fl. 143-176 C.E.), Greek traveller and geographer.

Pavia: *see* Sauli.

Peacock, Thomas Love (1785-1866), English author of the parodic gothic novel *Nightmare Abbey* (1818); his satire on romantic poetry, *The Four Ages of Poetry* (1820), inspired his close friend Percy Shelley to write his 'Defence of Poetry'.

Peisander of Rhodes (mid 7th century B.C.E.), Greek poet.

Pelagius (c. 354-418), Christian theologian who deplored the passivity implied in Augustine's teaching that one must wait patiently for God's will to be done, and preached the importance of human effort in attaining salvation. In 418, largely due to Augustine's successful politicking, Pelagius and his group were declared heretical.

Pelagius II (d. 590, reigned 579-590), pope.

Pericles (c. 495-429 B.C.E.), Athenian statesman to whom is attributed the full flowering of Athenian democracy and the spread of the Athenian empire.

Perrault, Charles (1628-1703), French classical scholar.

Persius Flaccus, Aulus (34-62 C.E.), Latin Stoic satirical poet.

Petrarch (Francesco Petrarca, 1304-1374), Italian poet and humanist scholar.

Petronius Arbiter, Gaius (Titus Petronius Niger, d. 66 C.E.), Roman consul, reputed author of *The Satyricon*.

Pfinzig, Melchior (1481-1531), Austrian author who completed the allegorical poem *Der östereicher Theuerdank* ('The Austrian Theuerdank', 1517) begun by Maximilian I.

Pherecydes of Syros (fl. c. 550 B.C.E.), according to legend the teacher of Pythagoras, was a Greek mythographer credited with inventing the idea of metempsychosis.

Philemon (c. 368-c. 264 B.C.E.), Greek comic dramatist.

Philetas of Cos (c. 330-c. 270 B.C.E.), Greek poet and grammarian, reputed founder of the Hellenistic school of poetry.

Philip II (byname Philip of Macedon, 382-336 B.C.E.), Greek emperor, father of Alexander the Great.

Philip II (byname Philip Augustus, 1165-1223, reigned 1179-1223), French king.

Philip IV the Fair (Philippe le Bel, 1268-1314), reigned 1285-1314 as king of France and 1284-1305, jointly with his wife Joan I, as King Philip I of Navarre.

Philip V of Macedonia (238-179 B.C.E., reigned 221-179), Macedonian king defeated by the Romans.

Philoxenus the Leucadian (Philoxenos, late-5th/early-4th century B.C.E.), famous Athenian parasite, glutton, and debauchee satirized by Aristophanes and other comic poets.

Phryne (4th century), famous Greek courtesan.

Pighius, Albert (c. 1490-1542), Westphalian mathematician and controversialist.

Pilato, Leonzio (fl. 1360), Italian translator of Homer.

Pindar (Pindaros, 518/22-c. 438 B.C.E.), ancient Greek lyric poet. His *Epinikia* or odes consisted of the *Olympionikai* (Olympian odes), the *Pythionikai* (Pythian odes), the *Nemeonikai* (Nemean odes), and the *Isthmionikai* (Isthmian odes), all composed between 498 and 446 B.C.E..

Pius IV (original name Giovanni Angelo de' Medici, 1499-1565), Italian pope (1559-1565) who presided over the last segment of the Council of Trent.

Pius V (original name Antonio Ghislieri, known in Latin as Pius Quintus, 1504-1572), Italian pope (1566-1572) who spearheaded the Inquisition against Protestants, effectively squelching Protestantism in Italy.

Pius XI (original name Ambrogio Damiano Achille Ratti, 1857-1939, reigned 1922-1939), Italian pope who canonized Thomas More in 1935.

Plato (427-347 B.C.E.), Greek philosopher.

Plautus (c. 254-184 B.C.E.), Roman comic dramatist.

Plegmund of Canterbury (d. 914), archbishop 890-914.

Pliny the Elder (Gaius Plinius Secundus, 23-79 C.E.), uncle of Pliny the Younger, was the Roman author of the *Natural History.*

Plutarch (Plutarchos, c. 46-after 119 C.E.), Boeotian author and biographer.

Politian (Angelo Poliziano or Angelo Ambrogini, 1454-1494), Italian poet and humanist. Four books (2-5) of his Latin verse translation of the *Iliad* (which he began at age 16) survive.

Polybius (c. 200-c. 118 B.C.E.), Roman statesman and historian who wrote a history of Rome in 40 books (1-5 survive).

Polygnotus (c. 500-c. 440 B.C.E.), ancient Greek painter whose works do not survive, except in descriptions by Pausanias.

Pontano, Giovanni (1426-1503), Italian royal official and author of Latin poems and prose works.

Porphyry (original name Malchus, 234-305 C.E.), Neoplatonist Greek philosopher.

Posidonius (Poseidonius, c. 135-c. 51 B.C.E.), Greek Stoic philosopher.

Postel, Guillaume (1510-1581), French mathematician and linguist.

Potken, Johannes (early 16th century), printed the Psalter in a parallel edition in 1518, containing Hebrew, Greek, Chaldean, and Latin texts.

Pound, Ezra (1885-1972), American poet and critic.

Prior, Matthew (1664-1721), English poet, courtier, and statesman.

Priscian (Priscianus Caesariensis, fl. 500), Latin grammarian, author of the *Institutiones grammaticae*; did a verse translation of Dionysus' *Periegesis*.

Priscus, Helvidius (d. between 70 and 79 C.E.) and his son Helvidius Priscus the Younger were Roman senators known for their opposition to emperors, the father to Vespasian, who put him to death, the son to Domitian.

Probus, Valerius (20-105 A.D.), Roman scholar.

Propertius, Sextus (55/43-after 16 B.C.E.), Roman elegiac poet.

Prudentius, Aurelius Clemens (348-after 405 C.E.), Christian poet.

Psammetichus (reigned 652-598 B.C.E.), fourth Egyptian king in the Saitic dynasty, first king to open Egypt up to foreigners.

Pseudo-Dionysius the Areopagite (fl. 500 C.E.), Syrian monk whose writings sought to unite Neoplatonism with Christianity.

Pseudo-Hegesippus (fl. 300 B.C.E.), Greek comic poet.

Ptolemy II Philadelphus (308-246, reigned 285-246 B.C.E.), king of Egypt famous for his patronage of the arts and learning.

Purcell, Henry (c. 1659-1695), English composer.

Pyrrhus (319-272 B.C.E.), the Hellenic king whose costly victories over Macedonia and Rome were the first 'Pyrrhic' ones.

Pythagoras (c. 580-c. 500 B.C.E.), Greek philosopher.

Rabbula (c. 350-c. 435), theologian and reforming bishop of Edessa who translated the Gospels into Syrian (the Peshitta).

Rabelais, François (c. 1483-1553), bawdy French Renaissance writer, author of *Pantagruel* (1532) and *Gargantua* (1534).

Racine, Jean-Baptiste (1639-16990, French dramatic poet, author of *Britannicus* (1669), *Bérénice* (1670), *Bajazet* (1672), and *Phèdre* (1677).

Radulphus de Rivo, a late medieval scholar who translated part of the liturgy into Latin.

Radzewił, Mikołaj the Black (1515-1565), marshall of Lithuania and promoter of Calvinist Reformation in Poland and Lithuania.

Raleigh, Sir Walter (1554?-1618), English writer, adventurer, and New World colonizer.

Ramus, Petrus, or Pierre de la Ramée (1515-1572), taught an original blend of Ciceronian rhetoric and Aristotelian logic at the Collège de l'Ave Maria in France.

Raphael Volaterranus: *see* Maffei.

Regulus, Marcus Atilius (d. c. 250 B.C.E.), Roman comic poet who translated Sophocles' *Electra*.

Richard II (1367-1400, reigned 1377-1399), king of England.

Richilieu, Armand-Jean du Plessis, cardinal and duke of (1585-1642), chief minister to King Louis XIII of France.

Richter, Johann Paul Friedrich: *see* Jean Paul.

Ritchl, F(riedrich) W(ilhelm) (1806-1876), German classical scholar, teacher of Nietzsche.

Rollenhagen, Georg (1542-1609), German author of *Froschmäuseler* ('The Frog-Mouser', 1592).

Rossetti, Dante Gabriel (1828-1882), English Pre-Raphaelite poet and painter.

Rousseau, Jean-Jacques (1712-1778), French philosopher, political and educational theorist, and novelist.

Rufinus, Tyrannius (345-410/411), Roman priest, writer, and translator of Greek theological works.

Rufus, Quintus Curtius (1st/2nd century C.E.), Roman historian.

Ruistre, Nicholas, of Luxembourg (c. 1442-1509), chancellor of the University of Louvain beginning in 1487 and Bishop of Arras since 1501.

Ruskin, John (1819-1900), British critic and artist.

Russell, Lucy (d. 1627), daughter of John Harington and Anne Harington, married Edward Russell, third earl of Bedford, 1594; an active patroness of poetry, she and her mother were John Florio's patrons in his translation of Montaigne.

Rutilius Rufus, P. (fl. 111-95 B.C.E.), Roman statesman and orator.

Sabacon (or Sabacos, fl. early 7th century B.C.E.), Ethiopian king who dethroned the blind Egyptian king Anysis and drove him into the marshes.

Sachs, Hans (1494-1576), the popular German poet and songwriter eulogized in Richard Wagner's opera *Die Meistersinger von Nürnberg*.

Saci, Louis-Isaac Le Maitre de (1613-1684), French scholar and director of the Port-Royal community; he was also the primary translator in the group that produced a French Catholic New Testament based on the Vulgate, and he translated the Old Testament from the Vulgate while imprisoned in the Bastille for Jansenism (1666-1668).

Sackville, Charles, Lord Buckhurst (1638-1706), English court wit, translated the fourth act of Corneille's *La morte du Pompée*.

Sacy: *see* Silvestre de Sacy.

Sainte-Beuve, Charles-Auguste (1804-1869), French literary critic and historian.

Sallust (Gaius Sallustius Crispus, c. 86-53/34 B.C.E.), Roman historian.

Salluste: *see* Bartas.

Salmasius, Claudius (Claude de Saumaise, 1588-1653), French classical scholar.

Salvini, Antonio Maria (1654-1729), Italian Greek scholar, poet, and translator who is best remembered in that last capacity; he left behind literal translations of Homer's *Iliad* and *Odyssey*, Hesiod, Theocritus, Anacreon, Aristophanes, Horace, Ovid, and others into Tuscan.

Sandys, George (1578-1664), English poet, colonist, and foreign service officer who translated Ovid's *Metamorphoses* (1621-25), book one of Virgil's *Aeneid* (1632), and other ancient texts.

Sannazzarro, Jacopo (1456-1530), Italian poet, author of the *Arcadia* (1504).

Sappho (fl. c. 610-c. 580 B.C.E.), ancient Greek lyric poet.

Sardanapalus (7th century B.C.E.), legendary king of Assyria.

Sauli, Alessandro (1535-1591), bishop of Padova; a delegate at the Council of Trent.

Saussure, Ferdinand de (1857-1913), Swiss philologist, founder of modern linguistics.

Savage, Richard (d. 1743), English poet, playwright, and translator.

Scaevola, Publius Mucius (d. c. 115 B.C.E.), Roman tribune, praetor, consul, and Pontifex Maximus.

Scaliger, Julius Caesar (1484-1558), French poet, father of Joseph Scaliger.

Schelling, Friedrich Wilhelm Joseph von (1775-1854), German philosopher.

Schiller, (Johann Christoph) Friedrich (1759-1805), German romantic poet and playwright.

Schlegel, Friedrich von (1772-1829), German critic and philosopher and A. W. Schlegel's brother.

Schröder, Ludwig Friedrich (1744-1816), German actor and theatre manager.

Scipio Aemilianus Africanus Numantinus, Publius Cornelius (the Younger, 185/84-129 B.C.E.), Roman commander.

Scott, Jonathan (1754-1829), British essayist, translated the *Arabian Nights Entertainment* in 1811.

Scott, Walter (1771-1832), Scottish novelist, poet, and historian.

Scotus, John Duns (1266-1308), scholastic theologian.

Sebillet, Thomas (1512-1589), French writer and critic, author of *Art Poetique Francoys*.

Second, Jan Everaerts (1511-1536), French poet, author of the *Baisers* and Latin erotic verse.

Sedley, Sir Charles (1639-1701), English court wit, translated one act of Corneille's *La morte du Pompée*.

Segrais, Jean Regnauld de (1624-1701), French translator of Virgil's *Aeneid* (1668, 1681).

Sempronius: *see* Gracchus.

Serveto, Miguel (Michael Servetus, 1511?-1553), Spanish theologian condemned by both Protestants and Catholics and executed by Genevan Calvinists.

Shadwell, Thomas (c. 1642-1692), English playwright and poet laureate.

Shaftesbury, Anthony Ashley Cooper, first earl of (1621-1683), English politician.

Shakespeare, William (1564-1616), English dramatist.

Sherburne, Edward (1618-1702), English translator; best known for his translations of Seneca, he also translated Horace from the Latin, Coluthus and Pindar from the Greek, and Girolamo Preti and Giambattista Marino from the Italian and Marc Antoine Gerard, sieur de Saint-Amant from the French.

Sidney, Sir Philip (1554-1586), English poet, statesman, courtier, and soldier.

Sigeric (d. 994), archbishop of Canterbury.

Silvestre de Sacy, Antoine-Isaac (1758-1838), French Orientalist.

Simplicius of Cilicia (fl. 533 C.E.), Greek commentator on Aristotle and Epictetus.

Sixtus of Siena (Senesis, 1520-1569), Renaissance Bible scholar.

Sixtus V (original name Felice Peretti, known in Latin as Sixtus Quintus, 1520-1590), Italian pope (1585-1590).

Socrates (c. 470-399 B.C.E.), Athenian philosopher on whose conversations most of Plato's dialogues are based.

Skelton, John (c. 1460-1529), English poet and satirist.

Solon (c. 630-c. 560 B.C.E.), Athenian statesman and legal reformer.

Sophocles (c. 496-406 B.C.E.), Greek tragic dramatist.

Sotheby, William (1757-1833), English author who translated Wieland's *Oberon* (1798), Virgil's *Georgics* (1800), and Homer's *Iliad* (1830-1831) and *Odyssey* (1834).

Southey, Robert (1774-1843), English poet.

Sozomen (Salamanes Hermeios Sozomenos, c. 400-c. 450), Christian lawyer in Constantinople who wrote a famous church history.

Spenser, Edmund (c. 1552-1599), English poet.

Speroni, Sperone (1500-1588), Italian writer and critic, author of *Dialogo delle lingue* and *Dialogo delle rettorica.*

Spondanus: *see* Sponde.

Sponde, Jean de (Johannes Spondanus, 1557-1595), French humanist scholar, editor of the parallel Greek-Latin edition of Homer (1583) used by Chapman.

Standish, Henry (d. 1535), English bishop who attacked Erasmus' Latin translation of the New Testament.

Stapulensis: *see* Lefèvre d'Étaples.

Stapylton, Sir Robert (d. 1669), dramatic poet, translator, and gentleman in ordinary of the privy chambers to the Prince of Wales; translated Book 4 of the *Aeneid* in 1634, Pliny the Younger's

Panegyrics in 1644, Juvenal's *Satires* in 1644 and 1647, and Musaeus' *Loves of Hero and Leander* in 1647.

Staupitz, Johann von (1468/69-1524), vicar general of the German Augustinian Order during his one-time student Martin Luther's revolt against the Roman Catholic church.

Steele, Richard (1672-1729), English essayist, dramatist, journalist, and politician.

Steevens, George (1736-1800), one of several editors (including Samuel Johnson, Edmond Malone, and Isaac Reed) who brought out a 16-volume edition of Shakespeare between 1778 and 1790.

Stein, Charlotte von (née von Schardt, 1742-1827), German writer and Goethe's lover, the model for many of his female characters and the addressee of over 1500 of his love poems.

Stolberg-Stolberg, Friedrich Leopold, count of (1750-1819), German poet who translated the *Iliad* in 1778.

Strabo, Walafrid (c. 808-849), German Benedictine theologian and poet who wrote the *Liber de exordiis et incrementis quarundam in observationibus ecclesiasticis rerum* ('Book on the Origins and Development of Certain Matters in Church Practice', 841).

Stubenberg, Johann Wilhelm von (1619-1688), translated Francis Bacon from English and various works from Italian and French.

Stumpf, Johannes (1500-1578), Swiss historian.

Sturm(ius), Johannes (1507-1589), German educator and religious polemicist; took Zwingli's side against Luther.

Suarez Figueroa, Christoval de (c. 1571-1645), Spanish poet who translated Guarini's *Il pastor fido* into Spanish in 1609.

Suetonius Tranquillus, Gaius (c. 69-after 122 C.E.), Roman biographer and antiquarian.

Suidas (10th century C.E.), the name on a Greek lexicon that may have been the author's name or title or some other descriptive term.

Sulpicius Rufus, Publius (124-88 B.C.E.), Roman orator and politician whose orations do not survive.

Sulpicius Rufus, Servius (106-43 B.C.E.), Roman jurist who studied oratory with Cicero but (convinced he would never become as great a speaker as Cicero) gave up oratory for the law. He was successfully defended by Cicero on a bribery charge and became consul in 51 B.C.E..

Sulpicius Galba Maximus, Publius (fl. 200 B.C.E.), Philip V of Macedonia's commanding general in the 197 battle at Cynoscephalae, Thessaly, in which Philip was defeated by the Romans.

Swift, Jonathan (1667-1745), Irish-English writer.

Swinburne, Algernon (1837-1909), English Victorian poet and critic.

Sylvestre de Saci: *see* Silvestre de Saci.

Symeon Logotheta or Symeon Metaphrastes (fl. 9th/10th century C.E.?), Byzantine writer.

Symmachus (fl. 2nd century C.E.), Greek translator of the Hebrew Scriptures.

Tacitus, Gaius (or Publius) Cornelius (c. 56-c. 120 C.E.), Roman historian, orator, and public official.

Talon, Omer (Audomarus Talaeus, 1595-1652), taught an original blend of Ciceronian rhetoric and Aristotelian logic at the Collège de l'Ave Maria in France.

Tasso, Torquato (1544-1595), Italian poet, author of the pastoral drama *L'Aminta* (1573).

Taylor, James Bayard (1825-1878), American author whose translation of Goethe's *Faust* (1870-1871) is widely considered the best English version.

Tennyson, Alfred Lord (1809-1892), English poet.

Terence (Publius Terentius Afer, c. 190-159 B.C.E.), Roman comic dramatist.

Tertullian (Quintus Septimus Florens Tertullianus, c. 155/60-after 220), early Christian theologian, initiator of ecclesiastical Latin.

Thackeray, William Makepeace (1811-1863), English novelist.

Themistocles (c. 524-c. 460 B.C.E.), Athenian politician and naval strategist.

Theobald, Lewis (1688-1744), English librettist; wrote the libretto to Galliard's *The Rape of Proserpine* (1728), based on Claudian's epic poem.

Theocritus (310-250 B.C.E.), Greek poet.

Theodectes (c. 380-334 B.C.E.), Greek tragic poet and friend of Aristotle, who mentions him in the *Nicomachean Ethics*.

Theodore of Mopsuestia (Theodorus Mopsuestites, c. 350-428/29), Syrian theologian whose scientific exegeses of Biblical texts helped establish the historicity and canonicity of numerous scriptural works, and thus to found modern exegetics. Regarded as the main authority on doctrinal matters by the eastern Nestorian Church, which followed the School of Antioch (of which he was spiritual head), he was condemned by several later councils following the dominant School of Alexandria.

Theodoric I (d. 533/34), Merovingian king.

Theodosius I (the Great, 347-395), Christian Roman emperor sometimes blamed for the fall of Rome to the Goths; was indirectly responsible for the Nicene Creed. Father to Arcadius, with whom he reigned jointly in the East from 383 to 395 (and after that solely until 402), and Flavius Honorius, Roman emperor in the West from 393 to 423.

Theodotion (2nd century C.E.), Jewish scholar who 'translated' the Hebrew Scriptures into Greek around 180-190 C.E. - actually revised the Septuagint into a highly popular form.

Theognis (fl. late 6th/early 5th century B.C.E.), Greek elegiac poet.

Theophilus of Alexandria (fl. early 5th century), theologian and patriarch of Alexandria.

Theophrastus (c. 372-c. 287 B.C.E.), Greek Peripatetic philosopher, student of Aristotle.

Theopompus of Chios (b. c. 380 B.C.E.), Greek historian and rhetorician.

Theseus: *see* Ambrosius Theseus.

Thomas, Dylan (1914-1953), Welsh poet.

Thomas, Secker (1693-1768), bishop of Oxford.

Thompson, William Hepworth (1810-1886), master of Trinity College, Cambridge.

Thuanus, Jacob August (Jacque-Auguste Thou, 1553-1617), French statesman, bibliophile, and historiographer.

Thucydides (second half of 5th century B.C.E.), Greek historian, author of the *History of the Peloponnesian War*.

Tibullus, Albius (c. 55 -c. 19 B.C.E.), Roman elegiac poet.

Tickell, Thomas (1686-1740), English poet and translator who published the first book of his *Iliad* the same year as Pope did his, 1715; Addison called it "the best that ever was in any language", leading Pope to accuse Addison of being the translator or a collaborator himself.

Tieck, Johann Ludwig (1773-1853), German romantic author and translator (*The Tempest* in 1799, partial *Don Quixote* in 1799-1801).

Tommaso de Vio (Cajetan, or Gaietanus, of Gaeta, 1469-1534), Thomistic theologian and bishop of Gaeta who translated the Psalms into Latin from Hebrew (1527).

Torgils (or Tyrgils) Knutsson (d. 1306), Marsk or Marshall of Sweden who consolidated Sweden's control over Finland in the 'third crusade' in 1293; increasingly afraid of the Marsk's power, King Birger had him executed for treason in 1305.

Torrens, Henry Whitelock (1806-1852), English soldier who became a Bengali civilian, orientalist, and translator of the Arabian nights entertainment.

Tournebus (or Turnèbe), Odet de (1552-1581), lawyer in the Parlement de Paris.

Trajan (Marcus Ulpius Traianus, 53-117 C.E., reigned as Caesar Divi Nervae Filius Nerva Traianus Optimus Augustus, 98-117), Roman emperor.

Trithemius, Johannes (Johannes Tritheim, 1462-1516), Benedictine scholar and spiritual writer.

Tully: *see* Cicero.

Tunstall, Cuthbert (1474-1559), English prelate, bishop of London (1522-1530) and Durham (1530-1559).

Tyrtaeus (mid-seventh century B.C.E.), Greek elegaic poet who is thought to have written on military themes to inspire Spartan soldiers in the Second Messenian war.

Ulfilas (or Ulphilas, or Ulpilas, or Vulpilas), Arian bishop of the Goths, who translated the Bible into Gothic from the Septuagint c. 350 C.E.

Ulrich, Anton, duke of Brunswick (1633-1744), author of *Die durchleuchtigste Syrerin Aramena* ('The Luminous Syrian Aramena', 1669-1673) and *Octavia* (1677).

Urban IV (c. 1200-1264, reigned 1261-1264), French pope.

Valdus: *see* Waldo.

Valerius Flaccus, Gaius (1st century C.E.), Roman author of an *Argonautica* that draws heavily on the *Argonautica* of Apollonius Rhodius of Alexandria, and might be thought of as a translation of the earlier work.

Valla, Lorenzo (Laurentius Vallensis, 1407-1457), Italian humanist, philosopher, and literary critic.

Van Dale, Antonius (1638-1708), Dutch scholar who wrote *De oraculis veterum ethnicorum*; this Latin text was adapted into French by Fontenelle as *Histoire des oracles*, which became Aphra Behn's intertext for her 1688 translation *A History of Oracles, And the Cheats of the Pagan Priests*.

Varro, Marcus Terentius (116-27 B.C.E.), Roman satirist and scholar.

Varro of Atax (or Atacinus), P. Terentius (b. 82 B.C.E.), Roman poet who translated the *Argonautica* of Apollonius Rhodius of Alexandria.

Vega, Andreas de (1498-1549), Spanish Fransiscan theologian sent by Charles V to the Council of Trent.

Vegetius Renatus, Flavius (fl. 4th century C.E.), Roman military expert whose treatise *Rei militaris instituta* ('On Warfare') became the military Bible of European armies in and after the Renaissance.

Verres, Gaius (c. 115-43 B.C.E.), Roman magistrate successfully prosecuted for misconduct by Cicero.

Vespasian (Caesar Vespasianus Augustus, original name Titus Flavius Vespasianus, 9-79, reigned 69-79), Roman emperor.

Victorinus, Gaius Marius (d. 370), Roman patristic scholar who did a Latin translation of Aristotle, commented upon by Boethius.

Vida, Marco Girolamo, of Cremona (Marcus Hieronymus Vida Cremonensis, c. 1485-1566), Italian scholar and writer, author of the Latin *De arte poetica libri III.*

Vigenère, Blaise de (1523-1596), French translator of Plato, Cicero, Julius Caesar, Lucian, Tacitus, Philostratus, and others.

Vigilantius (fl. c. 400), Gallic Church Father who attacked the cult of relics; Jerome counterattacked in *Contra Vigilantium.*

Villegaignon: see Durand de Villegaignon.

Villey, Pierre (1879-1933), French scholar.

Virgil (Publius Vergilius Maro, 70-19 B.C.E.), Roman poet who wrote the *Georgics* and the *Aeneid.*

Volaterranus, Raphael: *see* Maffei.

Voltaire (Francois-Marie Arouet, 1694-1778), French philosopher, scientist, poet, novelist, and essayist.

Voss, Johann Heinrich (1751-1826), German poet and translator who translated Homer's *Odyssey* (1781) and *Iliad* (1793), *The Thousand and One Nights* (1781-85), Virgil (1789ff), Ovid (1798), Horace (1806), and, with his sons, Shakespeare's plays (1818-1829).

Vulpilas: *see* Ulfilas.

Waerferth (Wyrefrith), Bishop of Worcester 873-915.

Wagner, Richard (1813-1883), German composer.

Waldo, Peter (Pierre Valdés, d. 1179), French merchant and early Reformer who translated the four Gospels from Jerome's Latin into French; sometimes mistakenly thought to be the founder of the Waldenses.

Waller, Edmund (1606-1687), English court wit, translated the first act of Corneille's *La morte du Pompée* (1660?) and Virgil.

Warham, William (1456?-1532), archbishop of Canterbury beginning in 1503, later lord chancellor (1504-1515) and chancellor of Oxford University (1506-1532); one of Erasmus' most important patrons.

Webster, John (c. 1580-c. 1625), English playwright, author of *The Duchess of Malfi* and *The White Divel.*

Weigel, Erhard (1625-1699), math professor at the University of Jena.

Werder, Diederich von dem (1584-1657), translated Ariosto's *Orlando Furioso* as *Der Rasender Roland* (1626), and Tasso's *Gerusalemme Liberata* (1581) as *Befreiter Jerusalem* (1632-1636).

Wieland, Christoph Martin (1733-1813), German poet whose translations of 22 Shakespeare plays between 1762 and 1766 influenced Goethe's *Sturm und Drang* period.

William of Moerbeke (c. 1215-1286), Flemish archbishop, until Leonardo Bruni the most renowned Latin translator of Aristotle.

William III (William Henry, Prince of Orange, 1650-1702), Dutch ruler (stadholder of the United Provinces of the Netherlands 1672-1702) who by marrying Mary II became king of Great Britain (1689-1702).

Wilson, Horace H. (1786-1860), English Orientalist who translated the *Meghaduta* in 1813.

Wishart, William (d. 1753), principal of Edinburgh College.

Wollstonecraft, Mary (1759-1797), English feminist writer, author of *A Vindication of the Rights of Women* (1792); wife of William Godwin, mother of Mary Godwin Shelley.

Wolsey, Thomas (c. 1475-1530), English cardinal and statesman, stripped of his power and position in 1529 for failing to persuade Pope Clement VII to annul Henry VIII's marriage to Catharine of Aragon.

Wordsworth, William (1770-1850), English romantic poet.

Wotton, Edward (1548-1626), learned British diplomat.

Wright, Ichabod Charles (1795-1871), English translator who translated Dante's *Divine Comedy* (1833, 1837, and 1840) and Homer's *Iliad* (1859-1864).

Wycliffe, John (1329?-1384), probably did not actually write the English Bible translation usually attributed to him; his active sponsorship and perhaps direct guidance of the project did however link it closely to his name.

Xenophon (431-before 350 B.C.E.), Greek historian, author of the *Oeconomicus*, a Socratic dialogue on estate management.

Xerxes I (Khshayarsha, c. 519-465 B.C.E., reigned 486-465), Persian king.

Young, Edward (1683-1765), English poet, author of *Night Thoughts* (1742-45).

Zacharias (d. 752), pope 741-752 and Greek translator of St. Gregory the Great's *Dialogues*.

Zesen, Philipp von (1619-1689), German political publicist and novelist who translated Madeleine de Scudéry's (1607-1701) clef novels *Ibrahim ou l'illustre Bassa* ('Ibrahim or the Illustrious Bassa', 1642) in 1645 and *Sophonisbe* in 1647.

Zwingli, Huldrych or Ulrich (1484-1531), Swiss Protestant Reformer.

Further Reading

CLASSICAL ANTIQUITY

Bassnett-McGuire (43-45); Benjamin (on Plato, ch. 1, esp. 10-13, and ch. 5, esp. 151-57); Copeland (ch. 1); D'Alton (chs. 3 & 4); Williams (ch. 5)

Herodotus: Bernal (98-101)

Aristeas: Barnstone; Delisle & Woodsworth (163); Howard (41-44)

Cicero: Bassnett-McGuire (43-44); Cheyfitz (ch. 5, esp. 92 and 101, and ch. 6, esp. 112-19); Copeland (12-13, 26-27, 33-35, 46-48); Kelly *Interpreter* (36, 44-45, 80-81, 140-41); Robinson 'Classical' (256-59); Van Hoecke/Goyens; Vermeer 'Cicero'; Woll

Philo Judaeus: Delisle & Woodsworth (163); Partridge (9-10); Schwarz *Principles* (ch. 2, esp. 21-25)

Horace: Bassnett-McGuire (43-44); Copeland (28-29); Norton *Ideology* (Part 1, 57-110, is a useful discussion of the French Renaissance debate on lines 133-34 of Horace's *Ars*); Robinson 'Classical' (259-62)

Paul of Tarsus: Steiner *Babel* (239)

Seneca: Benjamin (39-59)

Pliny the Younger: Copeland (31-32); Rener (296-300, 304-6)

Quintilian: Bassnett-McGuire (51-52); Copeland (16-26); Kelly *Interpreter* (44-45); Rener (passim, see index, 362)

Aulus Gellius: Rener (309-10); Robinson 'Classical' (262-64)

Jerome: Arrowsmith; Bassnett-McGuire (46); Copeland (45-52); Delisle & Woodsworth (167-69); Kamesar (esp. ch. 2); Kelly *Interpreter* (9, 60, 70-71, 100-1, 112-13, 141); Kelly *Jerome*; Larbaud; Partridge (16-18); Rener (28-29, 97, 125-28, 188-89, and passim); Robinson *Taboo* (101-8); Sparks (110-15)

Augustine: Brown (esp. ch. 23); Burke (Part 2); Copeland (42-45); Delisle & Woodsworth (169); Kelly 'Linguistics'; Kelly *Interpreter* (8-10, 35, 112-14); Rener (17, 57-58); Robinson *Translator's* (38-58), *Taboo* (108-20, 137-43)

MIDDLE AGES

Amos (ch. 1, 3-46); Beaujolan; Beer; Brock; Copeland 'Fortunes'; Contamine; D'Alverny; Ellis 'Choices'; Ellis, ed., *Medieval Translator* 1, 2; Ellis and Evans, eds., *Medieval Translator* 3; Ellis and Tixier, eds., *Medieval Translator* 5; Haskins; Lindberg; Minnis; Minnis and Scott; Schwartz; Shull

Fortunatianus: Copeland (40-42)

Boethius: Copeland (52-55); Kelly *Interpreter* (71, 131, 222-24)

Gregory the Great: Kelly *Interpreter* (71)

Johannes Scotus Eriugena: Copeland (52-55, 91-92); Kelly *Interpreter* (36)

King Alfred: Amos (3-4); Bassnett-McGuire (50-51); Cassidy and Ringler (178-80; the original text of the letter to Waerferth is given on 180-83); Delisle & Woodsworth (27-29); Frakes; Frantzen (chs. 3-6 deal with King Alfred's translations of Gregory (3), Boethius (4), Augustine (5), and the Psalms (6); the preface to Gregory is discussed on p. 26-29); Partridge (20); Shull (4); Whitelock

Aelfric: Amos (4-5); Butterworth (25-26); Craigie (131-34); Delisle & Woodsworth (28-29); Hurt (ch. 2 on 'Catholic Homilies', ch. 4 on Bible translations; the prefatory remarks to 'Catholic Homilies' are quoted on p. 42, 121); Marsden; Minkiff; Partridge (20-21); Robinson *Taboo* (81-85); Shull (5-7); Wilcox

Notker the German: Braungart; Copeland (97-103); Delisle & Woodsworth (45); Frakes; Sonderegger; Zuff

Burgundio of Pisa: Backus; Haskins (206-212); Lindberg (71-72)

Thomas Aquinas: Kelly 'Medieval', *Interpreter* (71)

Roger Bacon: Bassnett-McGuire (52-53); Kelly 'Medieval', *Interpreter* (9, 113, 135, 206, 214); Linden; Rener (61, 315)

Jean de Meun: Buridant; Copeland (133-43); Cropp

Dante Alighieri: Bassnett-McGuire (52-53); Copeland (103-5); Kelly *Interpreter* (222-23)

Ovide moralisé: Copeland (107-26); Kelly *Interpreter* (57-58)

BIBLE TRANSLATION, 14TH TO 16TH CENTURIES

Baikie; Barnstone (135-216); Bassnett-McGuire (46-50); Bruce; Brulard; Butterworth; Conant; Deansley; Hammond; Hudson; Lawton (ch. 3, 52-86); MacGregor; Partridge; Robinson *The Bible*; Robinson *Taboo* (81-92); Westcott

Rolle: Allen; Lawton (58); Partridge (21)

John of Trevisa: Bassnett-McGuire (53); Edwards; Kelly *Interpreter* (189); Deansley (130-34, 142-43, 299-302); Greetham; Rener (101, 113, 230)

Salutati: Norton, 'Humanist', *Ideology* (36); Rener (212-15); Seigel (117)

Anonymous (John Purvey?): Baikie (113-45); Bassnett-McGuire (46-47); Bruce (12-23); Butterworth (39-47); Craigie (137-44); Deansley (chs. 10 and 11, 252-97); Kelly *Interpreter* (113-14); Lawton (60-61); Partridge (22-32); Rener (21, 97n, 120, 125, 138); Westcott (13-14)

THE RENAISSANCE

Bainton; Bassnett-McGuire (53-58); Hannay; Norton 'Fidus', *Ideology*, 'Translation'; Schwarz 'Fifteenth', 'Sixteenth'; Travitsky

Bruni: Delisle & Woodsworth (152); Kelly *Interpreter* (83, 122, 131, 222-23); Norton *Ideology* (39-43); Rener (123-24, 156, 164, 183-85, 198-99, 209-10, 274-76)

Duarte: Rener (262)

Caxton: Blake; Butterworth (51-55); Delisle & Woodsworth (30-32, 152)

Erasmus: Bassnett-McGuire (48); Delisle & Woodsworth (172); Jonge; Partridge (33-37); Rener (35-36, 143, 148); Schwarz *Principles* (ch. 5, 92-166); Summers

More: Anderson; Baikie (120-25); Bruce (22-23, 39-42); Chambers (Act IV, "The Lord Chamberlain," esp. 254, 256, 266, 281-82); Conant (175-260); Deansley (1-16); Kelly *Interpreter* (74); Lawton (52-53, 61); Partridge (41-46); Reynolds (203-13); Robinson *Taboo* (85-92)

Luther: Bainton; Bassnett-McGuire (49); Bluhm *Martin Luther* (esp. ch. 6, 125-66), 'Martin Luther'; Delisle & Woodsworth (46-50, 172-73); Garcia Yebra; Gardt; Hirst; Kelly *Interpreter* (176-77, 182); Rener (66-68, 128-32, 237-38, 245, 248, 250, 315-16); Robinson *Translator's* (69-81); Schwarz *Principles* (ch. 6, 167-212); Silzer; Zecher

Tyndale: Anderson; Baikie (157-69); Bruce (22-23, 25-52); Butterworth (56-64); Conant (124-74, 197-260, 288-306); Deansley (1-16); Delisle & Woodsworth (33-35, 174-75); Isaacs (149-67); Lawton (52-53, 61); MacGregor (114-25); Partridge (41-46); Reynolds (203-13); Westcott (25-54, 131-61)

Vives: Coseriu; Kress; Rener (184-86); Wayne

Dolet: Bassnett-McGuire (54-56); Christie; Delisle & Woodsworth (38, 141); Lloyd-Jones; Norton *Ideology* (203-17); Rener (261-62)

Elizabeth: Hughey 'Queen'; Prescott; Robinson 'Theorizing'; Salminen

Agricola: Delisle & Woodsworth (123)

Du Bellay: Delisle & Woodsworth (38, 142); Keating (ch. 2, 9-18); Lovian; Nais; Norton 'Renaissance' (esp. 35-37), *Ideology* (292-302); Rener (270-74); Wells

Cooke: Hughey 'Lady' (211); Lamb; Robinson 'Theorizing'

Peletier: Fink; Kelly *Interpreter* (84), Norton 'Fidus'

Ascham: Rener (303)

Pasquier: Kelly *Interpreter* (84); Norton *Ideology* (326-29); Rener (54, 69)

Tyler: Delisle & Woodsworth (150); Krontiris 'Breaking', *Oppositional* (44-49); Lamb (esp. 115); Robinson 'Theorizing'; Schleiner

Martin and Fulke: Kelly *Interpreter* (103-4); Partridge (95-103)

Montaigne: Black, Cheyfitz (142-57), Jean, Rendall, Zhang

Florio: Cheyfitz (72, 101, 142, 157); Conley; Matthiessen (ch. 4, 103-68); Murray

Chapman: Bassnett-McGuire (54-55); Blessington; Hermans; Kelly *Interpreter* (122); Sowerby; Snare; Spivack (51-57); Ure

Smith: Barnstone (211-16); Bois; Bruce; Deansley; Delisle & Woodsworth (175); Hammond

Chapelain: Rener (33n, 54, 84, 86-87, 93, 135, 138, 232)

Webbe: Kelly *Interpreter* (87-88)

Du Vegerre: Robinson 'Theorizing'

Denham: Bassnett-McGuire (59); Hermans; Rener (69); Venuti 'Destruction', *Invisibility* (44-63)

D'Ablancourt: Delisle & Woodsworth (143); Kelly *Interpreter* (88); Rener (33, 102, 143, 235, 255-56); Venuti *Invisibility* (48-50)

Cowley: Bassnett-McGuire (59-60); Kelly *Interpreter* (147); Martindale; Rener (203)

Huet: Bury; Kelly *Interpreter* (75-76)

Dryden: Bassnett-McGuire (60-61); Battigelli; Connelly; Fujimura; Hopkins; Kelly *Interpreter* (42); Kitagaki; Morsberger; Rener (6, 26, 68, 81n, 93, 103, 196, 199-200, 202, 203, 206, 291, 312); Shaddy; Venuti *Invisibility* (62-68)

Roscommon: Chamberlain (esp. 456); Kelly *Interpreter* (207, 220); Rener (201, 203, 240)

Leibniz: Rener (40-1, 51-2 on 'superfluity'; 57 on 'naturalization'; 70 on 'revival' of archaic words)

Dacier: Delisle & Woodsworth (150); Rener (205, 240)

Pope: Bassnett-McGuire (61-62); Connelly 'Ideology', 'Ut'; Crossley; Kelly *Interpreter* (114-15); Morsberger; Nash; Nuttall; Rener (234); Salmon; Thomas; Venuti *Invisibility* (65-67)

Batteux: Kelly *Interpreter* (19), 'L'Ordre'

Carter: Agorni

Johnson: Bassnett-McGuire (61); Rener (208)

Herder: Kelly *Interpreter* (26, 47-48); Lefevere *Translating* (30-34); Menze

Tytler: Bassnett-McGuire (63); Delisle & Woodsworth (152); Heygood; Kingscott; Rener (193-94, 254-55); Venuti *Invisibility* (68-76)

(PRE-) ROMANTICISM

Apel (ch. IV-V, 39-87, on the history of German translation theory since Luther); Berman; D'hulst; Huber; Huyssen; Lefevere 'German'; Sdun; Senger

Schlegel: Bassnett-McGuire (64-65); Gipper; Habicht; Lefevere *Translating* (46-57)

Novalis: Lefevere *Translating* (64-65)

Goethe: Bassnett-McGuire (62-63); Butzlaff; Lefevere *Translating* (35-39); Robinson *Translator's* (75-92); Solbrig (on Goethe's work with Hammer-Purgstall, ch. V.1.c., 124-49; on his work with Kosegarten, ch. V.2., 149ff)

Schleiermacher: Ammann; Bassnett-McGuire (67); Curran; Kelly *Interpreter* (28); Lefevere *Translating* (66-89); Lonkers; Pym; Robinson *Taboo* (176-81, 209-15); Venuti 'Genealogies', *Invisibility* (68-76)

Humboldt: Gipper; Kelly *Interpreter* (26-27); Lefevere *Translating* (40-45); Seppänen; Ulrich

Shelley: Bassnett-McGuire (66, 67); Webb (ch. 1, 14-50, is Webb's discussion of Shelley's theoretical pronouncements on translation; the rest of the book examines Shelley's own translations from Greek writers and from Goethe, Calderón, and Dante)

Schopenhauer: Lefevere *Translating* (98-101)

FitzGerald: Bassnett-McGuire (70-71); Prasad; Sareen

Arnold: Bassnett-McGuire (69-70); Kelly *Interpreter* (116-18, 196); Kitagaki 'Arnold'; Liu; Venuti *Invisibility* (129-41)

Newman: Venuti *Invisibility* (118-47)

Browning: Pound; Prins; Steiner *Babel* (312-15)

Nietzsche: Lefevere *Translating* (96)

References

A. Primary Sources

Adams, Hazard. *Critical Theory Since Plato*, New York: Harcourt Brace Jovanovich, 1971.

Addison, Joseph. 'National Accents'. In Vol. 1 of the *Spectator* (4 vols) no. 29 (1711) by Joseph Addison, Richard Steele & Others, edited by G. Gregory Smith, London: Dent, 1930.

Aelfric. 'Translating into Idiomatic English'. In *Biblical Quotations in Old English Prose*, edited by Albert S. Cook, London: Macmillan, lxx-lxxi, 1898.

------. 'Translating Into Our Ordinary Speech' and 'Pure and Plain Words'. In *The Homilies of the Anglo-Saxon Church. The First Part Containing the Sermones Catholici or Homilies of Aelfric* (2 vols), edited by Benjamin Thorpe, London: Aelfric Society, 1844-1846.

Agricola, Mikael. 'Alcupuhe se wden Testamentin päle' ('Preface to the New Testament'). In *Vanhan kirjasuomen lukemisto*, edited by Martti Rapola, Helsinki: Finnish Literature Society, 20-21, 1959. English translation previously unpublished.

Alfred (King). 'Translating Plainly and Clearly'. In *King Alfred's Anglo-Saxon Version of Boethius, De Consolatione Philosophiae: With a Literal English Translation, Notes, and Glossary*, translated by Samuel Fox, New York: AMS Press, ix., 1970.

------. 'Translating Books Which Are Most Necessary For All Men to Know' (Letter to Bishop Waerferth, in 'Preface to St. Gregory's *Pastoral Care*'). In *Anglo-Saxon Prose*, edited & translated by Michael Swanton, London: Dent, 30-32, 1975.

Anonymous. 'Another Meaning'. Excerpted from *Ovide moralisé*, translated & cited by Copeland (1991), 109-13.

Anonymous ('Aristeas'). 'The Work of the Seventy Two'. Excerpted from *Aristeas to Philocrates (Letter of Aristeas)*, edited & translated by Moses Hadas, New York: Ktav Publishing, 113-21 (ll. 35-51), 167-69 (ll. 172-75), 217-25 (ll. 301-160), 1973.

Anonymous (John Purvey?). 'On Translating the Bible'. In Pollard (1903), 193-99.

Anonymous. 'The Three Kinds of Translating'. Quoted in Charles S.F. Burnett, 'Translations and Translators, Western European', in *Dictionary of the Middle Ages*, edited by Joseph R. Strayer, New York: Scribner's, 12:139, 1989.

Aquinas, Thomas. 'Proem'. From 'Contra Errores Graecorum'. In *Sancti Thomae Aquinatis Doctoris Angelici Ordinis Praedicatoris Opera omnia*, Vol. 15, edited by Vernon J. Bourke, New York: Musurgia, 1950. English translation previously unpublished.

Arnold, Matthew. 'The Translator's Tribunal'. Excerpted from 'On Translating Homer'. In *On the Classical Tradition*, edited by R.H. Super, 97-216. Vol. 1 of *The Complete Works of Matthew Arnold*, 1960; reprinted Ann Arbor: University of Michigan Press, 1979.

Ascham, Roger. 'The Ready Way to the Latin Tongue'. Excerpted from *The Scholemaster*, edited by William Aldis Wright, 238-46, 1570; reprinted Cambridge: At the University Press, 1904.

Augustine (Aurelius Augustinus). 'The Use of Translations'. Excerpted from *On Christian Doctrine*, translated by D.W. Robertson, Jr., Indianapolis: Bobbs-Merrill, 34-50, 1958.

Bacon, Roger. 'On the Usefulness of Grammar'. 1268? In *Opus Majus*, 1.3.1. (2 vols), translated by Robert Belle Burke, New York: Russell & Russell, 1962.

Batteux, Charles. 'Principles of Translation'. In *A Course of the Belles Lettres, or the Principles of Literature*, translated by John Miller, London: Printed for B. Law & Co. T. Caslon, J. Coote, S. Hooper, G. Kearsly & A. Morley, 284-87/333-58, 1761.

Behn, Aphra. 'An Essay on Translated Prose', 1688. Reprinted in Vol. 2 of *Histories, Novels, and Translations Written by the Most Ingenious Mrs. Behn*, London: W. O. for Samual Briscoe, 1-20 (after 98 pages of *The Theory or System*, etc.), 1700.

------. 'The Preface to the History of Oracles', 1688. Reprinted in Vol. 2 of *Histories, Novels, and Translations Written by the Most Ingenious Mrs. Behn*, London: W. O. for Samual Briscoe, unpaginated (after 'An Essay on Translated Prose'), 1700.

Boethius, Anicius Manlius Severinus. 'Committing the Fault of the True Interpreter'. Excerpted from *In Isagogen Porphyrii commenta*, edited by George Schepss & Samual Brandt, Vol. 48 of *Corpus scriptorum ecclesiasticorum latinorum*, Vindobonae: Tempsky, p. 46, 1905. English translation in Charles S.F. Burnett 'Translations and Translators, Western European'. In *Dictionary of the Middle Ages*, Vol. 12, edited by Joseph R. Strayer, New York: Scribner's, p. 139, 1989.

Browning, Robert. 'Literal at Every Cost'. Preface to 'The Agamemnon of Aeschylus, 1877'. In Vol. 11 of *The Complete Works of Robert Browning* (12 vols), edited by Charlotte Porter & Helen A. Clarke, New York: Crowell, 1-4, 1898.

Bruni, Leonardo. 'On the Correct Way to Translate'. In *The Humanism of Leonardo Bruni: Selected Texts*, translated & edited by Gordon Griffiths, James Hankins & David Thompson, Binghamton, NY: Center for Medieval & Early Renaissance Studies, 216-29, 1987.

Burgundio of Pisa. 'Incipit prologus Burgundionis iudicis in commentatione Iohannis Crisostomi supra evangelium sancti Iohannis evangeliste'. In *Burgundio von Pisa: Richter - Gesandter - Übersetzer*, edited by Peter Classen, Heidelberg: Carl Winter-Universitätsverlag, 84-102, 1974. English translation previously unpublished.

Burton, Richard F. 'A Plain and Literal Translation'. Excerpted from 'Introduction', vi-viii. Richard F. Burton (translator) Vol. 1 of *The Book of The Thousand Nights and a Night: A Plain and Literal Translation of the Arabian Nights Entertainment* (6 vols.), i-xii, 1885; reprinted New York: Heritage Press, 1934.

------. 'Clothing the Skeleton'. Richard F. Burton (translator) *Vikman and the Vampire, or, Tales of Hindu Devilry*, London: Longman, Green, xviii-xix, 1870.

Carter, Elizabeth. Letters to and from Miss Talbot and the Bishop of Oxford. From Montague Pennington, *Memoirs of the Life of Mrs. Elizabeth Carter*, Boston: Greenleaf, 126-31, 133, 138, 140, 146, 150-51, 153, 162, 1809.

Cassidy, Frederic G. and Richard N. Ringler (eds.). *Bright's Old English Grammar and Reader*, New

York: Holt, Rinehart & Winston, 1971; 3rd edition.

Chapelain, Jean. 'Au Lecteur'. Preface to translation of *Le Gueux, ou la vie de Guzman D'Alfarache*. In *Opuscules Critiques*, Paris: Droz, 48-58, 1936. English translation previously unpublished.

Chapman, George. 'The Preface to the Reader'. In *The Iliad*, Vol. 1 of *Chapman's Homer*, edited by Allardyce Nicoll, New York: Pantheon, 14-18, 1956.

Cicero. 'Translating Greek Philosophy into Latin'. Excerpted from *De finibus bonorum et malorum*, translated by Harris Rackham, London: Heinemann, 5-13, 1931.

------. *De optimo genere oratorum/The Best Kind of Orator*, translated by H. M. Hubbell. In *De Inventione, De optimo genere oratorum, Topica*, Vol. 2 of *Cicero in Twenty-Eight Volumes*, 1949; reprinted London: Heinemann, 354-72, 1976.

------. 'Translating Greek Orations into Latin'. Excerpted from *De oratore/On the Orator*, translated by E.W. Sutton & H. Rackham, Book 1, Chapter 34 (154-55); 105-7. In Vol. 14 of *Cicero in Twenty-Eight Volumes*, London: Heinemann, 1976.

Cooke, Anna. *Fouretene sermons of Bernadine Ochyne ... Translated out of Italian in to oure natyve tounge by A. C.*, London: John Daye, 1550? Excerpted in Travitsky (1981), p. 143.

Copeland, Rita. *Rhetoric, Hermeneutics, and Translation in the Middle Ages: Academic Traditions and Vernacular Texts*, Cambridge: Cambridge University Press, 1991.

Cowley, Abraham. 'Preface to *Pindarique Odes*'. Excerpted in Steiner (1975), 66-67.

D'Ablancourt, Nicolas Perrot. *Dédicaces et Préfaces des Traductions*, edited by Robert Zuber, Paris: Didier, 1972. English translation previously unpublished.

Dacier, Anne. 'My Condemnation'. Excerpted from 'The Preface', xxviii-xxxvii, translated by John Ozell. In *The Iliad of Homer*, translated by Ozell, Broom, & Oldisworth, London: printed by H. Woodfall for Bernard Lintot, i-lx, 1734; 3rd edition.

Dante Alighieri. 'Translation Destroys the Sweetness of the Original'. Excerpted from *The Banquet of Dante Alighieri*, translated by Katherine Hillard, London: Kegan Paul, Trench, Chapter 7, 22-26, 1889.

Denham, John. 'Preface to *The Destruction of Troy*'. Excerpted in T.R. Steiner (1975), 64-65.

------. 'To Sir Richard Fanshaw Upon His Translation of Pastor Fido'. Excerpted in T.R. Steiner (1975), 63-64.

Dolet, Étienne. 'La maniere de bien traduire d'une langue en aultre'. In Dolet et al., *Quatres traités de grammaire*, Geneva: Slatkine Reprints, 11-16, 1972.

Dryden, John. 'Preface to *Ovid's Epistles*'. Excerpted in T.R. Steiner (1975), 68-72.

------. 'Dedication of the *Aeneis*'. Excerpted in T.R. Steiner (1975), 72-74.

du Bellay, Joachim. 'The Defense and Illustration of the French Language', translated by James Harry Smith & Edd Winfield Parks. In *The Great Critics: An Anthology of Literary Criticism*, edited by Smith & Parks, 165-77, 1932; revised edition, New York: Norton, 1967.

Duarte (King). 'A arte de traduzir latim'. In *Textos Portugueses Medievais,* edited by Antonio Correa de Oliveira & Luis Saavedra Machado, Coimbra: Coimbra Editora, 545-46, 1969. English translation previously unpublished.

Epiphanius. 'Producing an Unadulterated Translation'. In *Aristeas to Philocrates (Letter of Aristeas),* edited and translated by Moses Hadas, New York: Ktav Publishing, 1973.

Erasmus, Desiderius. *The Correspondence of Erasmus*, translated by R.A.B. Mynori & D.E.S. Thomson (8 vols.), Toronto: University of Toronto Press, 1974-1988. From Vol. 2, *Letters 142-297, 1501-1514* (1975): letters to Nicolas Ruistre, November 17, 1503 (#177), & William Warham, January, 24, 1506 (#188), & November 1507 (#208). Annotations by Wallace K. Ferguson. From Vol. 6, *Letters 842-992, 1518-1519* (1982): letter to Maarten Lips, May 7, 1518 (#843). Annotations by James K. McConica.

FitzGerald, Edward. *Letters of Edward FitzGerald* (2 vols), London: Macmillan, 1894. Letter to E.B. Cowell, 2:4-5. Letter to J.R. Lowell, 2:261-62.

Florio, John. 'The Epistle Dedicatorie' and 'To the curteous Reader'. In *The Essayes of Michael, Lord of Montaigne*, 1-4, 7-11, 1603; translated by Florio; reprinted New York: E.P. Dutton, 1928.

Fortunatianus. 'Translation as *Exercitatio*'. Excerpted from *Artes rhetoricae*, translated & cited in Copeland (1991), p. 40.

Fulke, William. 'That None Of These Five Abuses are Committed By Us'. Excerpted from *A Defence of the Sincere and True Translations of the Holy Scriptures into the English Tongue, Against the Cavils of Gregory Martin*, imprinted by Henne Bynneman for George Bishop, 1583; edited by Charles Henry Hartshorne, Cambridge: Cambridge University Press, 7-13, 46-60, 1843.

------. 'The Holy Scriptures Should Always Be in Our Mother Tongue'. Excerpted from *Confutation of the Rhemish Testament*, 13-15, 1589; reprinted New York: Leavitt, Lord, 1834.

Gellius, Aulus. 'On the Importance of Avoiding Strict Literalness'. Excerpted from Vol. 2 of *The Attic Nights* (3 vols.), Book 9, Chapter 9; translated by John C. Rolfe, London: Heinemann, 175-83, 1927.

Goethe, Johann Wolfgang von. 'On Carlyle's *German Romance*', translated by Ellen von Nardroff & Ernest H. von Nardroff. In *Essays on Art and Literature* (12 vols), Vol. 3 of *Goethe's Collected Works*, edited by John Gearey, New York: Suhrkamp, 206-8, 1986.

------. 'Prose Translations'. Excerpted from *Poetry and Truth*, translated by Robert R. Heitner. In *From My Life*, Vol. 4 of *Goethe's Collected Works* (12 vols.), edited by Thomas P. Saine & Jeffrey L. Sammons, New York: Suhrkamp, 365-66, 1987.

------. 'The Two Maxims'. Excerpted from 'Rede zum Andenken des edlen Dichters, Bruders und Freundes Wieland', 320-21. In *Annalen oder Tag- und Jahreshefte als Ergänzung meiner sonstigen Bekenntnisse von 1749 bis 1822*, Vol. 21 of *Goethes sammtliche Werke* (33 vols.), Stuttgart & Tübingen: Gotta'scher Verlag, 311-30, 1851. English translation previously unpublished.

------. 'The Translator as Matchmaker'. Excerpted from *Maximen und Reflexionen* #946, #947 (449). In *Schriften zur Kunst, Schriften zur Literatur, Maximen und Reflexionen*, Vol. 12 of *Goethes Werke* (14 vols.), edited by Herbert von Einem, Hans Joachim Schrimpf & Werner Weber, 365-547, 1953; reprinted Hamburg: Wegner, 1967. English translation previously unpublished.

------. 'Übersetzungen'. Excerpted from 'Noten und Abhandlungen zu Besserem Verständnis des West-Östlichen Divans', 255-58. In *Gedichte und Epen*, Vol. 2 of *Goethes Werke* (14 vols), edited by Erich Trunz, 126-270, 1949; reprinted Hamburg: Wegner, 1969. English translation previously unpublished.

Gregory the Great. 'Giving the Sense'. Excerpted from Letter to Aristobulus. In *Epistles of St. Gregory the Great*, translated by James Barmby. In *Leo the Great, Gregory the Great*, Vol. 12 of *A Select Library of Nicene and Post-Nicene Fathers of the Christian Church*, edited by Philip Schaff & Henry Wace, New York: The Christian Literature Company, 1895.

------. 'Mangling the Sense'. Excerpted from Letter to Narses. In *Epistles of St. Gregory the Great*, translated by James Barmby. In *Leo the Great, Gregory the Great*, Vol. 12 of *A Select Library of Nicene and Post-Nicene Fathers of the Christian Church*, edited by Philip Schaff & Henry Wace, New York: The Christian Literature Company, 1895.

Herder, Johann Gottfried. 'The Ideal Translator as Morning Star'. Excerpted from Section 1 of 'Von der Griechischen Litteratur in Deutschland', 273, 274, 288-91. Second collection of *Über die neuere Deutsche Litteratur. Eine Beilage zu den Briefen, die neueste Litteratur betreffend. Fragmente.* In Vol. 1 of *Herders Sämmtliche Werke* (33 vols), edited by Bernhard Suphan, 131-531, Berlin: Weidmannsche Buchhandlung, 1877 (1877-1913).

------. 'Language as Maiden'. Excerpted from revised first collection of *Über die neuere Deutsche Litteratur. Fragmente*, Part III, Section 14, 106. In Vol. 2 of *Herders Sämmtliche Werke* (33 vols), edited by Bernhard Suphan, Berlin: Weidmannsche Buchhandlung, 1877 (1877-1913).

Herodotus. 'The Twittering of Birds' and 'The Origins of the Class of Egyptian Interpreters'. Excerpted from *The Histories*, 150-52 & 190-92; translated by Aubrey de Selincourt; revised, with an introduction & notes, by A.R. Burns, 1954; revised edition Harmondsworth: Penguin Books, 1972.

Horace (Quintus Horatius Flaccus). 'The Art of Poetry', translated by E.C. Wickham. In Adams (1971), 68-75.

Huet, Pierre-Daniel. *De interpretatione libri duo*, 1666; reprinted Stade, Holweg, 1680. English translation previously unpublished.

Humboldt, Wilhelm von. 'The More Faithful, The More Divergent'. Excerpted from 'Einleitung', 15-21. In *Aeschylos Agamemnon metrisch übersetzt*, translated by Humboldt, 3-37, Leipzig: Gerhard Fleischer dem Jüngern, 1816; reprinted in Störig, 71-96 (80-84). English translation previously unpublished.

Jean de Meun. 'Translating for Lay People'. Excerpted from prologue to *Roman de la Rose*, translated & cited by Copeland (1991), p. 134.

------. 'Plainly Rendering the Sense'. Excerpted from dedication to translation of Boethius' *Livres de Confort de Philosophie*, translated & cited by Copeland (1991), 133-34.

Jerome (Eusebius Hieronymus). 'On the Best Kind of Translator' (Letter 57 to Pammachius), translated by Paul Carroll. In *The Satirical Letters of St. Jerome*, Chicago: Gateway, 132-51, 1958.

------. 'Who Was The First Lying Author?'. In *Aristeas to Philocrates (Letter of Aristeas)*, edited & translated by Moses Hadas, New York: Ktav Publishing, 1973.

Johannes Scotus Eriugena. 'Translator, Not Expositor'. Excerpted from prologue to translation of *De caelesti hierarchia* by Pseudo-Dionysius the Areopagite, translated & cited by Copeland (1991), p. 52.

John of Trevisa. 'Dialogue Between a Lord and a Clerk Upon Translation'. In Pollard (1903), 203-8.

Johnson, Samuel. 'The Art of Translation', *The Idler* 68/69, 1759. Excerpted in T.R. Steiner (1975), 117-21.

------. 'From *Life of Pope*'. Excerpted in T.R. Steiner (1975), 121-23.

Leibniz, Gottfried Wilhelm. 'Enriching the German Language'. Excerpted from *Unvorgreifliche Gedanken, betreffend die Ausübung und Verbesserung der deutschen Sprache*, edited by Uwe Pörksen, Stuttgart: Reclam, 26-32, 1983. English translation previously unpublished.

Luther, Martin. 'Sendbrief vom Dolmetschen'. In Störig (1963), 14-32. English translation previously unpublished.

Martin, Gregory. 'The Holy Scriptures Ought Not be Read Indifferently of All'. Excerpted from 'The Preface to the reader treating of these three points: of the translation of holy scriptures into the vulgar tongues, and namely into English: of the causes why this new Testament is translated according to the auncient vulgar Latin text: & of the maner of translating the same', np. In *The New Testament of Iesus Christ, translated faithfvlly into English, out of the authentical Latin, according to the best corrected copies of the same, diligently conferred with the Greeke and other editions in diuers languages: With ARGUMENTS of bookes and chapters, ANNOTATIONS, and other necessarie helpes, for the better vnderstanding of the test, and specially for the discouerie of the CORRUPTIONS of diuers late translations, and for cleering the CONTROVERSIES in religion, of these daies*, np., Rheims: John Fogny, 1582. Facsimile reprint, London: The Scolar Press, 1975.

------. 'Five Sundry Abuses or Corruptions of Holy Scripture'. Excerpted from *A Discoverie of the Manifold Corruptions of the Holy Scriptures by the Heretikes of our daies, specially the English Sectaries, and of their foule dealing herein, by partial & false translations to the aduantage of their heresies, in their English Bibles used and authorised since the time of Schisme*, Rheims: John Fogny, 1582. Excerpted passage intersticed paragraph by paragraph with Fulke's reply in Fulke (1583/1843), 7-13, 46-60.

Montaigne, Michel Eyquem de. 'On Cannibals', translated by J.M. Cohen. In *Essays*, Book One, Harmondsworth: Penguin, Chapter 31, 105-19, 1958.

More, Thomas. 'Whether the Clergy of This Realm Have Forbidden All the People to Have Any Scripture Translated into our Tongue'. Excerpted from *A Dialogue Concerning Heresies*. In Vol. 6 of *The Complete Works of St. Thomas More*, edited by Thomas M.C. Lawler, Germain Marc'hadour & Richard C. Marius, New Haven: Yale University Press, Book III, Chapters 14-16, 314-19, 330-41, 1981.

Newman, Francis W. Excerpted from *Homeric Translation in Theory and Practice*, London & Edinburgh, 1861. Reprinted in *Essays*, edited by Matthew Arnold, London: Oxford University Press, 313-76 (313-18, 321-22, 342-43), 1925.

Nietzsche, Friedrich. 'Translating the Tempo of the Original'. Excerpted from *Beyond Good and Evil: Prelude to a Philosophy of the Future*, translated by R.J. Hollingdale, Harmondsworth: Penguin, #28, 41-42, 1973.

------. 'Translation as Conquest'. Excerpted from *The Gay Science*, translated by Walter Kaufmann, New York: Vintage Books, #83, 136-38, 1974.

Notker the German. Letter to Bishop Hugo von Sitten, translated & cited by Copeland (1991), p. 98.

Novalis. 'Three Kinds of Translation'. Excerpted from *Blütenstaub*. In Vol. 1 of *Novalis Werke*, edited by Gerhard Schulz, Munich: Beck, p. 337, 1969. English translation previously unpublished.

------. '146. Novalis an August Wilhelm Schlegel in Jena' ('Letter to A. W. Schlegel'). In *Briefe und Tagebücher, Charakteristiken von Zeitgenossen*, Vol. 4 of *Novalis Schriften*, edited by Richard Samuel, 212-13, Leipzig: Bibligraphisches Institut, 1929. English translation previously unpublished.

Pasquier, Estienne. *Choix de lettres sur la littérature, la langue et la traduction*, Geneva: Droz, 124-39, letter to Jacques Cujas, 125-27, letter to Odet de Tournebus, 131-36, 1956. English translation previously unpublished.

Paul of Tarsus. 'Rather Five Words With the Mind Than Ten Thousand in a Tongue'. 1 Corinthians 14. *The New Covenant, Commonly Called the New Testament of Our Lord and Savior Jesus Christ*, Revised Standard Version, New York: Thomas Nelson, 1946.

Peletier du Mans, Jacques. 'Des Traductions' ('On Translations'). In *L'Art Poétique*, Geneva: Slatkine Reprints, 30-34, 1971. English translation previously unpublished.

Philips, Katherine. 'Translating *Pompey*'. Excerpted from *Letters from Orinda to Poliarchus*, Printed by W.B. for B. Lintott, 65-69, 178-81, 1705.

Philo Judaeus. 'The Creation of the Septuagint'. Excerpted from *De vita Mosis/Moses*, translated by F.H. Colson, 2.5.25-44, 461-71. In *On Abraham, On Joseph, Moses*, Vol. 6 of *Philo in Nine Volumes*, London: Heinemann, 273-595, 1935.

Pliny the Younger. 'Letter to Fuscus Salinator' (no. 9). In *The Letters of the Younger Pliny*, translated by Betty Radice, 190-92, 1963; reprinted Harmondsworth: Penguin, 1981.

Pollard, Alfred W. *Fifteenth Century Prose and Verse: An English Garner*, New York: Dutton, 1903.

Pope, Alexander. 'Preface to the *Iliad*'. Excerpted in T.R. Steiner (1975), 90-95.

Quintilian. 'On What We Should Employ Ourselves When We Write'. Excerpted from *Institutes of Oratory; or, Education of an Orator* (2 vols), translated by John Selvy Watson, London: George Bell, Book 10, Chapter 5, par. 1-8; 2:292-94, 1876.

Rolle, Richard. 'Following the Letter'. Excerpted from 'Prologue' to The English Psalter and Commentary, 68-69. In *Richard Rolle: The English Writings*, translated & edited by Rosamund S. Allen, New York: Paulist Press, 66-69, 1988.

Salutati, Coluccio. Letter to Antonio Loschi. In Vol. 2 of *Epistolario*, edited by F. Novati, Rome: Istituto Storico Italiano, p. 356, 1893. English translation previously unpublished.

Schlegel, August Wilhelm von. 'At Once Faithful and Poetic'. Excerpted from 'Etwas über Wilhelm Shakespeare bei Gelegenheit Wilhelm Meisters'. In *Sprach und Poetik*, Vol. 1 of Schlegel, *Kritische Schriften und Briefe*, edited by Edgar Lohner, 88-122, Stuttgart: Kohlhammer, 98-101, 1962. English translation previously unpublished.

------. 'Noble Rust'. Excerpted from 'Dante - Über die göttliche Komödie', 85-87. In *Sprach und Poetik*, Vol. 1 of Schlegel, *Kritische Schriften und Briefe*, edited by Edgar Lohner, Stuttgart: Kohlhammer, 67-87, 1962. English translation previously unpublished.

------. 'Poetic Translation an Imperfect Approximation'. Excerpted from 'Homers Werke von Johann Heinrich Voss', 115-22, 149-52. In *Vermischte und kritische Schriften*, Vol. 10 of Schlegel, *Sämmtliche Werke*, edited by Eduard Böcking, Leipzig: Weidmann'sche Buchhandlung, 115-94, 1846. Fascimile edition Hildesheim & New York: Georg Olms Verlag, 1971. English translation previously unpublished.

------. 'Projecting Oneself into Foreign Mentalities'. Excerpted from *Geschichte der klassischen Literatur*, Vol. 3 of Schlegel, *Kritische Schriften und Briefe*, edited by Edgar Lohner, Stuttgart: Kohlhammer, 16-18, 1964. English translation previously unpublished.

------. 'The Speaking Voice of the Civilized World'. Excerpted from *Geschichte der romantischen Literatur*, Vol. 4 of Schlegel, *Kritische Schriften und Briefe*, edited by Edgar Lohner, Stuttgart: Kohlhammer, 34-36, 1965. English translation previously unpublished.

Schleiermacher, Friedrich. 'On the Different Methods of Translating' ('Ueber die verschiedenen Methoden des Uebersezens'). Lecture 3 of *Abhandlungen gelesen in der Königlichen Akademie der Wissenschaften* (207-45). In Vol. 2 (1838) of Schleiermacher, *Zur Philosophie* (9 vols.; reprinted in 4 vols.: 1-2, 3-4, 5-6, 7-9), Berlin: G. Reimer, 149-495, 1835-1846. Part 3 of *Friedrich Schleiermacher's sämmtliche Werke*; reprinted in Störig (1963), 38-70. English translation previously unpublished.

Schopenhauer, Arthur. 'On Language and Words'. Excerpted from 'Über Sprache und Worte', #306-309, 599-607. In *Parerga und Paralipomena*, Vol. 6 of *Arthur Schopenhauer's sämmtliche Werke*, edited by Julius Frauenstädt, Leipzig: F. A. Brockhaus, 1923. #309 (601-607) reprinted in Störig (1963), 101-107. English translation previously unpublished.

Shelley, Percy Bysshe. 'The Violet and the Crucible'. Excerpted from 'A Defence of Poetry', p. 501. In Adams (1971), 499-513.

Staël-Holstein, Anne-Louise-Germaine Necker, baronne de. 'On the Spirit of Translations' ('De l'esprit des traductions'). In *Mélanges*, Vol. 17 of *Œuvres complètes de Mme. la Baronne de Staël*, Paris: Treuttel et Würtz, 387-99, 1821. English translation previously unpublished.

Steiner, T.R. (ed.). *English Translation Theory, 1650-1800*, Assen/Amsterdam: Van Gorcum, 1975.

Störig, Hans Joachim (ed.). *Das Problem des Übersetzens*, 1963; reprinted Darmstadt: Wissenschaftliche Buchgesellschaft, 1973.

Travitsky, Betty (ed.). *The Paradise of Women: Writings By Englishwomen of the Renaissance*, Westport, CT: Greenwood Press, 1981.

Tudor, Elizabeth. Letter to Catherine Parr. Preface to *The Mirror of the Sinful Soul*, edited by Percy Ames. Facsimile edition London, 1897. Excerpted in Travitsky (1981), 76-77.

------. *A godly Medytacyon of the christen Sowle*. Excerpted in Travitsky (1981), 142-43.

Tyler, Margaret. 'M.T. to the Reader'. Preface to Diego Ortunes de Calahorra *A mirrour of princely deedes and knighthood*, translated by Margaret Tyler, London: T. East, 1578. Excerpted in Travitsky (1981), 144-46.

Tyndale, William. 'How Happeneth That Ye Defenders Translate Not One Yourselves?'. Excerpted from *An Answer to Sir Thomas More's Dialogue*, 165-69, 1536. Facsimile edition New York: Johnson Reprint Corporation, 1968.

Tytler, Alexander Frazer. 'The Proper Task of a Translator'. Excerpted from *Essay on the Principles of Translation*, 13-18, 23, 28-29, 109-112, 117-19, 132-33, 208-13, 224-25, 1791. Facsimile edition Amsterdam: John Benjamins, 1978.

Vegerre, Suzanne du. 'The Authors Epistle to the READER'. Preface to du Vegerre, *Admirable Events, selected out of four bookes, written in French by John Peter Camus*, London: T. Harper for W. Brooks, 1639. Excerpted in Travitsky (1981), 159-62.

Vives, Juan Luis. 'Practice in Writing'. Excerpted from *Vives On Education (De Tradendis Disciplinis)*, edited & translated by Foster Watson, 1913; reprinted Totowa, NJ: Rowman & Littlefield, 1971.

------. 'Translation and Interpretation'. Excerpted from *De Ratione Dicendi*, translated by Mary Jean Thomas, 356-63. In Mary Jean Thomas, *The Rhetoric of Juan Luis Vives*, Ph.D. Thesis, Pennsylvania State University, 1967.

Webbe, Joseph. 'Perceiving the Custom of the Ancients'. Excerpted from *An Appeal to Truth, Concerning Art and Use*, London: Printed for George Latham, 1622.

Wentworth, Thomas, Earl of Roscommon. 'An Essay on Translated Verse'. In T.R. Steiner (1975), 75-85.

B. Secondary Sources

Agorni, Mirella. 'Women Manipulating Translation in the Eighteenth Century'. In *The Knowledges of the Translator: From Literary Interpretation to Machine Classicification*, edited by Malcolm Coulthard & Patricia Anne Odber de Baubeta, 135-43, Lewiston: Edwin Mellen Press, 1996.

Allen, Rosamund S. 'Introduction: Richard Rolle: c1300-1349'. In *Richard Rolle: The English Writings*, translated & edited by Rosamund S. Allen, 9-62, New York: Paulist Press, 1988.

Ammann, Margret. 'Von Schleiermacher bis Sartre: Translatologische Interpretationen'. In *Translation Studies: An Interdiscipline*, edited by Mary Snell-Hornby, Franz Pöchhacker & Klaus Kaindl, 37-44, Amsterdam: John Benjamins, 1994.

Amos, Flora. *Early Theories of Translation*, 1920; reprinted New York: Octagon Books, 1973.

Anderson, Marvin W. 'William Tyndale (d. 1536): A Martyr for All Seasons', *The Sixteenth Century Journal* 17.3 (Fall): 331-51, 1986.

Apel, Friedmar. *Literarische Übersetzung*, Stuttgart: J. B. Metzler, 1983.

Arrowsmith, William. 'Jerome on Translation: A Breviary', *Arion* 2: 358-67, 1975.

Backus, Irena. 'John of Damascus, De Fide Orthodoxa: Translations by Burgundio (1153/54), Grosseteste (1235/40), and Lefevre d'Étaples (1507)', *Journal of the Wartburg and Courtauld Institutes* 49: 211-17, 1986.

Baikie, James. *The English Bible and Its Story: Its Growth, Its Translators and Their Adventures*, Philadelphia: Lippincott, nd.

Bainton, Roland H. *Women of the Reformation* (3 vols.), Minneapolis: Augsburg, 1971, 1973, 1977.

------. 'Martin Luther's Principles of Bible Translation', *Notes on Translation* 4.3: 54-59, 1990.

Bassnett-McGuire, Susan. *Translation Studies*, 1980; revised edition New York: Routledge, 1991.

Battigelli, Anna. 'Nature, Time, and Translation: Dryden's 'To the Memory of Mr. Oldham' and the Poetic Tradition', *Restoration* 14.1 (Spring): 22-32, 1990.

Beaujolan, G. 'Medieval Science in the Christian West', translated by A. J. Pomerans. In *History of Science: Ancient and Medieval Science From the Beginnings to 1450*, edited by René Taton, 468-532, 1957; New York: Basic Books, 1963.

Beer, Jeannette (ed.). *Medieval Translators and Their Craft* (Studies in Medieval Culture 25), Kalamazoo, MI: Medieval Institute Publications, Western Michigan University, 1989.

Benjamin, Andrew. *Translation and the Nature of Philosophy: A New Theory of Words*, New York: Routledge, 1989.

Berman, Antoine. *The Experience of the Foreign: Culture and Translation in Romantic Germany*, translated by S. Heyvaert, 1984; Albany: SUNY Press, 1992.

Bernal, Martin. *The Fabrication of Ancient Greece 1785-1985*, Vol. 1 of *Black Athena: The Afroasiatic Roots of Classical Civilization* (2 vols. to date), 1987; reprinted New Brunswick, NJ: Rutgers University Press, 1991.

Black, Moishe. 'When Montaigne Conducts You on a Visit to His Cannibals, Take Care Not to Get

Eaten by the Guide', *Dalhousie French Studies* 16 (Spring-Summer): 15-36, 1989.

Blake, Norman. 'William Caxton'. In Edwards (1984), 389-412.

Blessington, Francis. 'Homer Transported: Chapman's Method', *Classical Bulletin* 63.2 (Spring): 1-6, 1987.

Bluhm, Heinz. *Martin Luther: Creative Translator*, St. Louis: Concordia, 1965.

------. 'Martin Luther and the English Bible: Tyndale and Coverdale', *Michigan Germanic Studies* 10.1-2 (Spring-Fall): 112-25, 1984.

Bois, John. *Translating for King James: Being a True Copy of the Notes Made By a Translator of King James' Bible, the Authorized Version, as the Final Committee of Review Revised the Translation of Romans Through Revelation at Stationer's Hall in London in 1610-1611*, 1611. Fascimile reprint, Nashville: Vanderbilt University Press, 1969.

Borchart, Rudolf. 'Translation as an Act of Restoration'. Excerpted in Lefevere (1977), 109.

Braungart, Georg. 'Notker der Deutsche als Bearbeiter eines lateinischen Schultextes: Boethius De Consolatione Philosophiae', *Zeitschrift für Deutsche Philologie* 106: 2-15, 1987.

Brock, Sebastian. 'Aspects of Translation Technique in Antiquity', *Greek, Roman, and Byzantine Studies* 20 (Spring): 69-87, 1979.

Brown, Peter. *Augustine of Hippo*, Berkeley: University of California Press, 1967.

Bruce, F.F. *The English Bible: A History of Translations*, New York: Oxford University Press, 1961; *The English Bible: A History of Translations from the Earliest English Versions to the New English Bible*, revised edition New York: Oxford University Press, 1970; *History of the Bible in English: From the Earliest Versions*, revised edition, New York: Oxford University Press, 1978.

Brulard, I. 'La Traduction comme miroir d'un changement dans l'approche du sens à la Renaissance', *Cahiers de l'Institut de Linguistique de Louvain* 16.1: 13-21, 1990.

Buridant, Claude. 'Jean de Meun et Jean de Vignay, traducteurs de l'Epitoma Rei Militaris de Vegece: Contribution à l'histoire de la traduction au Moyen Âge'. In *Études de langue et de littérature françaises offertes à André Lanly*, edited by Bernard Guidoux, 51-69, Nancy: University of Nancy, 1980.

Burke, Kenneth. *Rhetoric of Religion: Studies in Logology*, Berkeley: University of California Press, 1961.

Bury, Emmanuel. 'Bien écrire ou bien traduire: Pierre-Daniel Huet theoricien de la traduction'. In *La Traduction au XVIIe siècle*, edited by Suzanne Guellouz, 251-60, Paris: Klincksieck, 1991.

Butterworth, Charles C. *The Literary Lineage of the King James Bible, 1340-1611*, Philadelphia: University of Pennsylvania Press, 1941

Butzlaff, Wolfgang. 'Goethe als Übersetzer', *Jahrbuch des Wiener Goethe-Vereins* 92-93: 33-64, 1988-1989.

Chamberlain, Lori. 'Gender and the Metaphorics of Translation', *Signs* 13: 454-72, 1988. Reprinted in *Rethinking Translation: Discourse, Subjectivity, Ideology*, edited by Lawrence Venuti, 57-74, London & New York: Routledge, 1992.

Chambers, R.W. *Thomas More*, New York: Harcourt Brace, 1935.

Cheyfitz, Eric. *The Poetics of Imperialism: Translation and Colonization from 'The Tempest' to 'Tarzan'*, New York: Oxford University Press, 1991.

Christie, Richard C. *Etienne Dolet: The Martyr of the Renaissance (1508-1546)*, London: Macmillan, 1899.

Conant, H.C. *The English Bible: History of the Translation of the Holy Scriptures into the English Tongue; With Specimens of the Old English Versions*, New York: Sheldon, Blakeman, 1856.

Conley, Tom. 'Institutionalizing Translation: On Florio's Montaigne'. In *Demarcating the Disciplines: Philosophy, Literature, Art*, edited by Samuel Weber, 45-58, Minneapolis: University of Minnesota Press, 1986.

Connelly, Peter J. 'Pope's *Iliad*: Ut Pictura Translatio', *Studies in English Literature, 1500-1900* 21.3 (Summer): 439-55, 1981.

------. 'The Ideology of Pope's *Iliad*', *Comparative Literature* 40.4 (Fall): 358-83, 1988.

Contamine, Genevieve (ed.). *Traduction et traducteurs au Moyen Âge*, Paris: Éditions du Centre National de la Recherche Scientifique, Diffusion, Presses du CNRS, 1989.

Copeland, Rita. 'The Fortunes of *Non Verbum pro Verbo*: or, why Jerome is not a Ciceronian'. In Ellis (1989), 15-35.

------. *Rhetoric, Hermeneutics, and Translation in the Middle Ages: Academic Traditions and Vernacular Texts*, Cambridge: Cambridge University Press, 1991.

Coseriu, Eugenio. 'Das Problem des Übersetzens bei Juan Luis Vives'. In *Interlinguistica: Sprachvergleich und Übersetzung Festschrift zum 60. Geburtstag von Mario Wandruszka*, edited by Karl-Richard Bausch & Hans-Martin Gauger, 571-82, Tübingen: Niemeyer, 1971.

Craigie, William A. 'The English Versions (To Wycliffe)'. In Robinson (1940), 128-45.

Croce, Benedetto. *Aesthetic as Science of Expression and General Linguistic*, translated by Douglas Ainslie, 1903; reprinted Boston: Nonpareil Books, 1983.

Cropp, Glynnis M. 'Le Prologue de Jean de Meun et le Livre de Boece de Consolacion', *Romania* 103: 278-98, 1982.

Crossley, Robert. 'Pope's *Iliad*: The Commentary and the Translation', *Philological Quarterly* 56: 339-57, 1977.

Curran, T.H. 'Schleiermacher: True Interpreter'. In *The Interpretation of Belief: Coleridge, Schleiermacher and Romanticism*, edited by David Jasper, 97-103, London: Macmillan, 1986.

D'Alton, J.F. *Roman Literary Theory and Criticism*, 1931; reprinted New York: Russell & Russell, 1962.

D'Alverny, Marie-Thérèse. 'Translations and Translators'. In *Renaissance and Renewal in the Twelfth Century*, edited by Robert L. Benson & Giles Constable, 421-62, Cambridge: Harvard University Press, 1982.

D'hulst, Lieven. 'The Conflict of Translational Models in France (End of 18th - Beginning 19th Century)', *Dispositio* 7.19-20: 41-52, 1982.

Deansley, Margaret. *The Lollard Bible and Other Medieval Biblical Versions*, Cambridge: At the University Press, 1920.

Delisle, Jean & Judith Woodsworth (eds). *Translators Through History*, Amsterdam: John Benjamins, 1996.

Eckhardt, Caroline D. 'The Art of Translation in *The Romaunt of the Rose*', *Studies in the Age of Chaucer* 6: 41-63, 1984.

Edwards, Anthony S.G. 'John Trevisa'. In *Middle English Prose: A Critical Guide to Major Authors and Genres*, edited by Anthony S.G. Edwards, 133-46, New Brunswick: Rutgers University Press, 1984.

Ellis, Roger. 'The Choices of the Translator in the Late Medieval Period'. In *The Medieval Mystical Tradition in England*, edited by Marion Glasscoe, 19-46, Exeter: University of Exeter, 1982.

------ (ed.). *The Medieval Translator*, Cambridge: Brewer, 1989.

------ (ed.). *The Medieval Translator II* (Westfield Publications in Medieval Studies 5), London: Centre for Medieval Studies, Queen Mary & Westfield College, University of London, 1991.

------ and Ruth Evans (eds.). *The Medieval Translator 4* (Medieval and Renaissance Texts and Studies 123), Binghamton NY: SUNY Press, 1994.

------ and René Tixier (eds.). *The Medieval Translator 5*, Turnhout: Brepols, 1995.

Fink, Robert J. 'Une 'Deffence et illustration de la langue français' avant la lettre: La Traduction par Jacques Peletier du Mans de l'Art Poétique d'Horace (1541)', *Canadian Review of Comparative Literature* 8.2 (Spring): 342-63, 1981.

Frakes, Jerold C. *The Fate of Fortune in the Early Middle Ages: The Boethian Tradition*, New York: Brill, 1988.

Frantzen, Allen J. *King Alfred*, Boston: Twayne, 1986.

Fujimura, Thomas H. 'Dryden's Virgil: Translation as Autobiography', *Studies in Philology* 80.1 (Winter): 67-83, 1993.

García Yebra, Valentín. 'Lutero, traductor y teórico de la traducción', *Arbor* 339: 23-34, 1979.

Gee, John A. 'Margaret Roper's English Version of Erasmus' *Precatio Dominica* and the Apprenticeship behind Early Tudor Translation', *The Review of English Studies* 13: 257-71, 1937.

Gipper, Helmut. 'Understanding as a Process of Linguistic Approximation: The Discussion Between August Wilhelm von Schlegel, S.A. Langlois, Wilhelm von Humboldt and G.W.F. Hegel on the Translation of the Bhagavadgita and the Concept of *Yoga*'. In *Studies in the History of Western Linguistics*, edited by Theodora Bynon & Frank Robert Palmer, 109-28, Cambridge: Cambridge University Press, 1986.

Greetham, D.C. 'Models for the Textual Transmission of Translation: The Case of John Trevisa', *Studies in Bibliography* 37: 131-55, 1984.

Habicht, Werner. 'The Romanticism of the Schlegel-Tieck Shakespeare and the History of Nineteenth-Century German Shakespeare Translation'. In *European Shakespeares: Translating Shakespeare in the Romantic Age*, edited by Dirk Delabastita & Lieven D'hulst, 45-53, Amsterdam: John Benjamins, 1993.

Hammond, Gerald. *The Making of the English Bible*, New York: Philosophical Library, 1983.

Hannay, Margaret Patterson (ed.). *Silent But for the Word: Tudor Women as Patrons, Translators, and Writers of Religious Works*, Kent: Kent State University Press, 1985.

Haskins, Charles Homer. *Studies in the History of Medieval Science*, Cambridge: Harvard University Press, 1924.

Hermans, Theo. 'Literary Translation: The Birth of a Concept', *New Comparison* 1 (Summer): 28-42, 1986.

Heygood, J.R. 'Tytler: Voltaire and Shakespeare', *The Linguist* 28.6: 184, 1989.

Hirst, Ann E. 'Luther's *Sendbrief vom Dolmetschen*: His Theory and Practice', *The Linguist* 25.4 (Autumn): 205-8, 1986.

Hopkins, David. 'Dryden as Translator', *Translation and Literature* 2: 132-40, 1993.

Howard, W.F. 'The Greek Bible'. In Robinson (1940), 39-82.

Hudson, Anne. *Lollards and Their Books*, London: Hambledon, 1985.

------. *The Premature Reformation: Wycliffite Texts and Lollard History*, Oxford: Clarendon, 1988.

Hughey, Ruth. 'Lady Anne Bacon's Translations', *Review of English Studies* 10: 211, 1934.

------. 'Queen Elizabeth's *Godly Meditation*', *The Library* (4th ser.) 15: 237-40, 1935.

Hurt, James. *Aelfric*, New York: Twayne, 1972.

Hyrde, Richard. Dedicatory letter to Margaret More Roper, *A deuout treatise vpon the Pater noster/*

made fyrst in latyn by the moost famous doctour mayster Eramus Roterodamus/ and tourned into englishe by a yong vertuous and well lerned gentylwoman of .xix. yere of age, London: Thomas Berthelet, c. 1525; reprinted in *Erasmus of Rotterdam: A Quincentennial Symposium*, edited by Richard L. DeMolen, 97-104, New York: Twayne, 1971.

Isaacs, J. 'The Sixteenth-Century English Version'. In Robinson (1940), 146-95.

------. 'The Authorised Version and After'. In Robinson (1940), 196-234.

Jacobsen, Eric. *Translation: A Traditional Craft; An Introductory Sketch With a Study of Marlowe's Elegies*, Copenhagen: Gyldendal, 1958.

Jean, Raymond. 'Pourquoi des cannibales?', *Europe* 68.729-730 (Jan-Feb): 102-7, 1990.

Johnston, Otto W. *The Myth of a Nation: Literature and Politics in Prussia under Napoleon*, Columbia, SC: Camden House, 1989.

Jonge, Henk J. de. 'The Relationship of Erasmus' Translation of the New Testament to that of the Pauline Epistles by Lefevre d'Étaples', *Erasmus in English* 15.8: 2-7, 1987.

Kamesar, Adam. *Jerome, Greek Scholarship, and the Hebrew Bible*, Oxford: Clarendon Press, 1993.

Keating, L. Clark. *Joachim du Bellay*, New York: Twayne Publishers, 1971.

Kelly, J.N.D. *Jerome: His Life, Writings, and Controversies*, New York: Harper & Row, 1975.

Kelly, Louis G. 'Linguistics and Translation in Saint Augustine', *The Bible Translator* 24: 134-39, 1973.

------. *The True Interpreter: A History of Translation Theory and Practice in the West*, New York: St. Martin's, 1979.

------. 'Medieval Philosophers and Translation'. In Vol. 1 of *History and Historiography of Linguistics: Papers from the Fourth International Conference on the History of the Language Sciences, Trier, 24-28 August 1987* (2 vols.), edited by Hans-Joseph Niederehe & Konrad Koerner, 205-18, Amsterdam: John Benjamins, 1990.

------. 'L'Ordre Naturel and Charles Batteux: À bas les philosophes'. In *Diversions of Galway: Papers on the History of Linguistics*, edited by Anders Ahlqvist, Konrad Koerner, R.H. Robins & Irene Rosier, 135-44, Amsterdam: John Benjamins, 1992.

Kingscott, Geoffrey. 'Bicentenary of Tytler's *Principles of Translation*', *Language International* 3.1 (February): 13-16, 1991.

Kitagaki, Muneharu. *Principles and Problems of Translation in Seventeenth-Century England*, Kyoto: Yamaguchi, 1981.

------. 'Arnold to Newman no ronso'. In *Bungaku to kotoba*, edited by Toshio Kimura, Hisao Kanaseki & Isamu Saito, 207-18, Tokyo: Nan'un do, 1986.

Kress, Dorothy M. 'Juan Luis Vives: A Study in Renaissance Theories in Methodology in Foreign Language Instruction', *Modern Language Journal* 25.1 (October): 19-25, 1940.

Krontiris, Tina. 'Breaking Barriers of Genre and Gender: Margaret Tyler's Translation of *The Mirrour of Knighthood*', *English Literary Renaissance* 18.1 (Winter): 19-39, 1988.

------. *Oppositional Voices: Women as Writers and Translators of Literature in the English Renaissance*, London & New York: Routledge, 1992.

Lamb, Mary Ellen. 'The Cooke Sisters: Attitudes toward Learned Women in the Renaissance'. In Hannay (1985), 107-25.

Larbaud, Valery. 'Le Patron des Traducteurs'. In *Sous l'invocation de Saint Jérôme*, Paris: Galli-mard, 1946; translated by Jean-Paul de Chezet as *An Homage to Jerome*, Marlboro VT: Marlboro Press, 1984.

Lawton, David. *Faith, Text and History: The Bible in English*, Charlottesville: University Press of Virginia, 1990.

Lefevere, André. *Translating Literature: The German Tradition from Luther to Rosenzweig*, Assen/Amsterdam: Van Gorcum, 1977.

------. 'German Translation Theory: Legacy and Relevance', *Journal of European Studies* 11.1: 9-17, 1981.

------. *Translation/History/Culture: A Sourcebook*, New York: Routledge, 1992.

Levi, Peter. *The English Bible 1534-1859*, London: Constable, 1974.

Lindberg, David C. 'The Transmission of Greek and Arabic Learning to the West'. In *Science in the Middle Ages*, edited by David C. Lindberg, 52-90, Chicago: University of Chicago Press, 1978.

Linden, Stanton J. 'Roger Bacon in the Age of Francis: The Mirror of Alchimy and the Mirror of Nature', *Cauda Pavonis* 10.1 (Spring): 10-13, 1991.

Liu, Zhongde. 'Matthew Arnold on Translating Homer's Epic', *Waiguoyu* 4.32 (July): 45-49, 1984.

Lloyd-Jones, K. 'Humanist Debate and the 'Translative Dilemma' in Renaissance France'. In *Medieval Translators and Their Craft*, edited by Jeanette Beer, 347-71, Kalamazoo: Western Michigan University, 1989.

Lonkers, Fred. 'Der fremde Sinn: Überlegungen zu den Übersetzungskonzeptionen Schleiermachers und Benjamins'. In *Proceedings of the XIIst Congress of the International Comparative Literature Association, Munich 1988: Space and Boundaries in Literary Theory and Criticismm*, edited by Roger Bauer & Douwe Fokkema et al., 345-52, Munich: Iudicium, 1990.

Lovian, Alexandre. 'Du Bellay: Un Traducteur contre les traducteurs'. In *Du Bellay*, edited by Georges Cesbron, 477-84, Angers: Press de l'Universite d'Angers, 1990.

MacGregor, Geddes. *The Bible in the Making*, Philadelphia: Lippincott, 1959.

Marsden, Richard. 'Aelfric as Translator: The Old English Genesis', *Anglia* 109.3-4: 319-58, 1991.

Martindale, Charles. 'Unlocking the Word-Hoard: In Praise of Metaphrase', *Comparative Criticism* 6: 47-72, 1984.

Matthiessen, F.O. *Translation: An Elizabethan Art*, Cambridge: Harvard University Press, 1931.

Menze, Ernest A. 'On Herder as a Translator and On Translating Herder'. In *Johann Gottfried Herder: Language, History, and the Enlightenment*, edited by Wulf Koepke, 151-62, Columbia, SC: Camden House, 1990.

Minkoff, Harvey. 'Some Stylistic Consequences of Aelfric's Theory of Translation', *Studies in Philology* 73: 29-41, 1976.

Minnis, A.J. *Medieval Theory of Authorship: Scholastic Literary Attitudes in the Later Middle Ages*, London: Scolar Press, 1984.

------ and A. Brian. Scott (eds.). *Medieval Literary Theory and Criticism, c. 1100-c.1375*, Oxford: Clarendon Press at Oxford University Press, 1988.

Morsberger, Katharine M. 'Voices of Translation: Poet's Voice and Woman's Voice', *Pacific Coast Philology* 28.1 (September): 3-19, 1993.

Murray, Timothy. 'Translating Montaigne's Crypts: Melancholic Relations and the Sites of Altarbiography', *Bucknell Review* 35.2: 121-49, 1992.

Nais, Hélène. 'Traduction et imitation chez quelques poètes du XVIe siècle', *Revue des Sciences Humaines* 4.180: 33-49, 1980.

Nash, Richard. 'Translation, Editing and Poetic Invention in Pope's *Dunciad*', *Studies in Philology* 89.4 (Fall): 470-84, 1992.

Norton, Glyn P. '*Fidus interpres*: A Philological Contribution to the Philosophy of Translation in Renaissance France'. In *Neo-Latin and the Vernacular in Renaissance France*, edited by Grahame Castor & Terence Cave, 227-51, Oxford & New York: Clarendon Press, 1984.

------. 'Translation Theory in Renaissance France: The Poetic Controversy', *Renaissance and Reformation* 11.1: 30-44, 1975.

------. 'Humanist Foundations of Translation Theory (1400-1450): A Study in the Dynamics of Word', *Canadian Review of Comparative Literature* 8.2 (Spring): 173-203, 1981.

------. *The Ideology and Language of Translation in Renaissance France and Their Humanist Antecedents*, Geneva: Droz, 1984.

Nuttall, A.D. 'Moving Cities: Pope as Translator and Transposer'. In *The Enduring Legacy: Alexander Pope Tercentenary Essays*, edited by G.S. Rousseau & Pat Rogers, 151-70, Cambridge: Cambridge University Press, 1988.

Partridge, A.C. *English Bible Translation*, London: Andre Deutsch, 1973.

Picchio, Luciana Stegagno. 'The Portuguese, Montaigne, and the Cannibals of Brazil: The Problem of the 'Other'', *Portuguese Studies* 6: 71-84, 1990.

Pound, Ezra. 'Translators of Greek: Early Translators of Homer'. In *Literary Essays of Ezra Pound*, edited by T.S. Eliot, 249-75, New York: New Directions, 1954.

Prasad, Indira. 'Translation and Adaptation: Their Respective Roles', *International Journal of Translation* 2.1 (January-June): 37-45, 1990.

Prescott, Anne Lake. 'The Pearl of the Valois and Elizabeth I: Marguerite de Navarre's *Miroir* and Tudor England'. In Hannay (1985), 61-76.

Prins, Yopie. "Violence Bridling Speech': Browning's Translation of Aeschylus' *Agamemnon*', *Victorian Poetry* 27.3-4 (Autumn-Winter): 151-70, 1989.

Pym, Anthony. 'Schleiermacher and the Problem of *Blendlinge*', *Translation and Literature* 4.1: 5-30, 1995.

Rendall, Steven. 'Dialectical Structure and Tactics in Montaigne's *Of Cannibals*', *Pacific Coast Philology* 12: 56-63, 1977.

Rener, Frederick M. *Interpretatio: Language and Translation from Cicero to Tytler*, Amsterdam: Rodopi, 1989.

Reynolds, E.E. *Thomas More and Erasmus*, New York: Fordham University Press, 1965.

Robinson, Douglas. 'Classical Lessons for Modern Teachers: Cicero, Horace, Aulus Gellius, and the Training of the Translator'. In *Horizons: Proceedings of the 32nd Annual Conference of the American Translators Association, October 16-20, 1991, Salt Lake City, Utah*, edited by A. Leslie Willson, 255-65, Medford, NJ: Learned Information, 1991.

------. *The Translator's Turn*, Baltimore: Johns Hopkins University Press, 1991.

------. 'Theorizing Translation in a Woman's Voice: Subverting the Rhetoric of Patronage, Courtly Love and Morality', *The Translator* 1.2 (November): 153-75, 1995.

------. *Translation and Taboo*, DeKalb: Northern Illinois University Press, 1996.

Robinson, H. Wheeler (ed.). *The Bible in its Ancient and English Versions*, Oxford: At the Clarendon Press, 1940.

Salminen, Renja. *Marguerite de Navarre*, Helsinki: Annales Academiae Scientiarum Fennicae no. 22, 1979.

Salmon, F.E. 'Alexander Pope and Circe's Sacred Dome', *Review of English Studies* 42.168 (November): 523-31, 1991.

Sareen, S.K. 'The Factor of Intertextuality in Translation', *International Journal of Translation* 1.1 (January): 41-48, 1989.

Schleiner, Louise. 'Margaret Tyler, Translator and Waiting Woman', *English Language Notes* 29.3

(March): 1-8, 1992.

Schwartz, Werner. 'The Meaning of *Fidus Interpres* in Medieval Translation', *Journal of Theological Studies* 45: 73-78, 1944.

------. 'Translation into German in the Fifteenth Century', *Modern Language Review* 39: 368-73, 1944.

------. 'The Theory of Translation in Sixteenth-Century Germany', *Modern Language Review* 40: 289-99, 1945.

------. *Principles and Problems of Biblical Translation: Some Reformation Controversies and Their Background*, Cambridge: At the University Press, 1970.

Seigel, Jerrold E. *Rhetoric and Philosophy in Renaissance Humanism*, Princeton: Princeton University Press, 1968.

Seppänen, Lauri. 'Sprachliche und andere Relativitäten: Humboldt, Whorf und die Möglichkeit des Übersetzens'. In *Neuphilologica Fennica*, edited by Leena Kahlas-Tarkka, 489-95, Helsinki: Memoires de la Société Néophilologique de Helsinki no. 45, 1987.

Shaddy, Virginia M. 'John Dryden and D'Ablancourt's *Belles Infidèles*', *Seventeenth Century Review* 26.1 (Spring): 35-36, 38, 1984.

Sheehan, James J. *German History, 1770-1866*, Oxford: Oxford University Press, 1989.

Shull, Donald Marshall. *The Effect of the Theory of Translation Expressed in the Anonymous Romans of Partenay (T.C.C. MS R.3.17) Upon the Language of the Poem*, Ph.D. Thesis, University of North Carolina at Chapel Hill, 1984.

Silzer, Pete. 'Luther on Translation: The Primacy of Meaning', *Notes on Translation* 66: 38-40, 1977.

Snare, Gerald. *The Mystification of George Chapman*, Durham: Duke University Press, 1989.

Solbrig, Ingeborg Hildegard. *Hammer-Purgstall und Goethe: 'Dem Zaubermeister das Werkzeug'*, Bern: Herbert Lang, 1973.

Sonderegger, Stefan. 'Notkers des Deutschen Terminologie des Übersetzungsvorganges', *Zeitschrift für Deutsche Philologie* 106: 15-24, 1987.

Sowerby, Robin. 'Chapman's Discovery of Homer', *Translation and Literature* 1: 26-51, 1992.

Sparks, H.F.D. 'The Latin Bible'. In Robinson (1940), 100-27.

Spivack, Charlotte. *George Chapman*, New York: Twayne, 1967.

Steiner, George. *After Babel: Aspects of Language and Translation*, New York: Oxford University Press, 1975.

Summers, Kirk. 'Early Criticism of Erasmus' Latin Translation of the Bible', *Comitatus* 22: 70-86, 1991.

Thomas, Claudia. 'Pope's *Iliad* and the Contemporary Context of His 'Appeals to the Ladies'', *Eighteenth-Century Life* 14.2 (May): 1-17, 1990.

Ulrich, Miorita. 'Wilhelm von Humboldt und die heutige Übersetzungstheorie', *Acta Linguistica Hungarica* 40.3-4: 467-73, 1990-1991.

Ure, Peter. 'Chapman as Translator and Tragic Playwright'. In Vol. 2 of *The New Pelican Guide to English Literature*, edited by Boris Ford & Brian Vickers, 420-35, Harmondsworth: Penguin, 1982.

Van Hoecke, Willy and Michele Goyens. 'Translation as a Witness to Semantic Change', *Belgian Journal of Linguistics* 5: 109-31, 1990.

Venuti, Lawrence. 'Genealogies of Translation Theory: Schleiermacher', *TTR Traduction, Terminologie, Redaction: Études sur le texte et ses transformations* 4.2: 125-50, 1991.

------. 'The Destruction of Troy: Translation and Royalist Cultural Politics in the Interregnum', *Journal of Medieval and Renaissance Studies* 23.2 (Spring): 197-219, 1993.

------. *The Translator's Invisibility*, London & New York: Routledge, 1995.

Verbrugge, Rita. 'Margaret More Roper's Personal Expression in the *Devout Treatise Upon the Pater Noster*. In Hannay (1985), 30-42.

Vermeer, Hans J. 'From Cicero to Modern Times: Rhetorics and Translation'. In *Translationstheorie – Grundlagen und Standorte*, edited by Justa Holz-Mänttäri, 93-128, Tampere: Studia Translatologica A.1., 1988.

Wayne, Valerie. 'Some Sad Sentence: Vives' *Instruction of a Christian Woman*'. In Hannay (1985), 15-29.

Webb, Timothy. *The Violet in the Crucible: Shelley and Translation*, Oxford: At the Clarendon Press, 1976.

Wells, Margaret B. 'What Did Du Bellay Understand by 'Translation'?', *Forum for Modern Language Studies* 16: 175-85, 1980.

Westcott, Brooke Foss. *A General View of the History of the English Bible*, New York: Macmillan, 1927.

Whitelock, Dorothy. 'The Prose of King Alfred's Reign'. In *Continuations and Beginnings: Studies in Old English Literature*, edited by Eric Gerald Stanley, 67-103, London: Thomas Nelson, 1966.

Wilcox, Jonathan. 'A Reluctant Translator in Late Anglo-Saxon England: Aelfric and Maccabees'. In *Proceedings of the Medieval Association of the Midwest II*, edited by Mel Storm, 1-18, Emporia, KS: Emporia State University Press, 1993.

Williams, Gordon. *Tradition and Originality in Roman Poetry*, Oxford: At the Clarendon Press, 1968.

Woll, Dieter. 'Übersetzungstheorie bei Cicero?'. In Vol. 3 of *Energeia und Ergon: Sprachliche Variation – Sprachgeschichte – Sprachtypologie* (3 vols.), edited by Jens Ludtke, 341-50, Tübingen: Narr, 1988.

Zecher, Henry. 'The Bible Translation That Rocked the World', *Notes on Translation* 7.2: 12-15, 1993.

Zhang, Longxi. 'The Cannibals, the Ancients, and Cultural Critique: Reading Montaigne in Postmodern Perspective', *Human Studies* 16.1-2 (April): 51-68, 1993.

Zuff, Herta. 'Bedeutungsdifferenzierung durch Prafigierung in den Übersetzungen Notkers des Deutschen'. In *Litterae Medii Aevi*, edited by Michael Borgolte & Herrad Spilling, 93-108, Sigmaringen: Thorbecke, 1988.

Name Index

Subject Index

Title Index

Note: Due to significant variations in titles over the 23-century period covered here, each title is indexed separately. For example, the Greek oration of Demosthenes usually called *Pro corona* in Latin appears in English as *In Defence of Ctesiphon*, *The Oration on the Crown*, and *On the Crown*; Dante wrote a book that is called *The Banquet* in English, and is referred to as both *Il Convito* and *Il convivio* in Italian. Page references for each of these appear separately in the proper alphabetical location; nowhere are all the page references for the 'same' book gathered together in a single entry. Cross-references to other titles will help readers track down other page references. Exceptions have been made when all the variations are similar enough that they would appear consecutively (e.g. *Andria/Andrian Girl*); in these cases the entries have been integrated. Radical historical fluctuations in what constitutes a 'book' or an 'article' also make it difficult to decide what to italicize, what to place within inverted commas; all titles therefore appear in roman type.